DESTINATION: MOONBASE ALPHA

THE UNOFFICIAL AND UNAUTHORISED GUIDE TO *SPACE: 1999*

DESTINATION: MOONBASE ALPHA

THE UNOFFICIAL AND UNAUTHORISED GUIDE TO *SPACE: 1999*

Robert E Wood

First published in the United Kingdom in 2009 by
Telos Publishing Ltd
5a Church Road, Shortlands, Bromley, Kent, BR2 0HP, UK
www.telos.co.uk

Telos Publishing Ltd values feedback. Please e-mail us with any comments you may
have about this book to: feedback@telos.co.uk

This Revised and Updated Edition: 2015
Slight textual corrections: June 2019

ISBN: 978-1-84583-906-2

For Barry Morse (1918-2008) and Johnny Byrne (1935-2008).
The heart and soul of *Space: 1999*, both on-screen and behind the scenes.

'To everything that might have been …
To everything that was.'

CONTENTS

INTRODUCTION AND ACKNOWLEDGMENTS

In late 1973, a television production team came together to create what they intended to be the most spectacular space science fiction series ever. Following an unprecedented shooting schedule of over 15 months, *Space: 1999* premiered in 1975 with a spectacular opening episode, 'Breakaway'. The programme continued through a second season, for a total of 48 episodes of widely varied style, tone and content – concluding in 1977 with an episode called 'The Dorcons'. Despite *Space: 1999*'s relatively short run, the adventures of Moonbase Alpha would continue to capture the hearts and minds of viewers in all the years since.

Regardless of what happened with network schedules, rating shares and critics in the 1970s, it is clear that today – more than 30 years since the series ended – *Space: 1999* retains a loyal cult following around the world. Ultimately this is its vindication against whatever the harshest and most biased of critics could hurl at it. This book is presented in the desire to provide that conclusive reckoning owed to *Space: 1999* – the crown jewel in Gerry and Sylvia Anderson's television career and, indeed, the crowning achievement in the careers of many of those who worked on it.

Barry Morse once said to me, in relation to another topic, 'I don't know if the subject is thoroughly exhausted, but I certainly am!' Those words echo in my mind as I consider the effort and time involved in writing this book … but it's been an amazing pleasure.

A note on the number ratings I've assigned to the episodes in this book: I have endeavoured to compare each season on its own merits. Therefore, Year One episodes are judged against other Year One episodes, and the same for Year Two. This seemed the fairest way to rate the episodes, given the divergence between the seasons. Many of Year Two's episodes would have ranked significantly lower if I had judged them against the standards of the first series.

Many people have contributed to the creation of this volume and I am delighted to acknowledge them. First, I want to thank Martin Willey (webmaster of The Catacombs – www.space1999.net/catacombs) for his generous assistance in so many ways, including providing an invaluable edit of this tome. The contributors to The Catacombs whose work has also helped enrich this book must be thanked, including Marcus Lindroos and Shaqui le Vesconte. I am greatly appreciative of all the assistance, advice, permissions, information and encouragement provided to me by the following: Martin Bower (model-maker extraordinaire – visit him online at www.martinbowersmodelworld.co.uk), Kit Bevan, Anthony Wynn, Paul Stankevitch, Hayward Morse, Sandy Byrne, Sandra Sprecker, David Ross, Ken Scott, Terry S Bowers, Tim Mallett and Glenn Pearce (Kindred Productions), Fanderson, Lis Therkildsen and Steen Pederson, Jovan Evermann, Phil Merkel and Chris Bentley (author of *The Complete Gerry Anderson*). I'd also like to thank Telos Publishing Ltd, Stephen James Walker and David J Howe for inviting me to embark on this project, and for making the experience so enjoyable.

A special thank you to Prentis Hancock for being the ever-observant and supportive core of Main Mission – to this day. I am enormously grateful to Zienia Merton for her foreword, and all her valuable and caring encouragement. I am also deeply honoured to thank the late Barry Morse posthumously for his afterword, and his endless kindness.

Finally, my eternal thanks to all of the actors, writers and production team quoted within these pages – it is through your words that this book is able to deliver a truly comprehensive account of *Space: 1999*, Moonbase Alpha, and those who sailed on her …

Robert E Wood

FOREWORD
Zienia Merton

I remember that whilst having lunch at Pinewood during the first few months of Year One of *Space: 1999* an actor (I had worked with him previously) promptly proposed to me on learning of the length of my contract. Well, why not – I could have taken care of the rent for a good wee while. I was always aware that while most of my fellow actors rather envied the long term run of the job, they were rather disdainful of the subject matter – a 'sci-fi' series – oh, the poor soul. Much more kudos on your CV to be 'third attendant from the left' in an out-of-town production of *Much Ado About Nothing*. Well, they may have been right – I have no way of knowing.

However, *Space: 1999* has certainly reached a greater audience, and as a young actress, Year One was my university. Working on a daily basis with an incredibly professional, helpful and warm group of people enabled me to learn (and, as important, relax) my craft. Invaluable and a gift from the gods.

This book is a tribute to all who worked on and enjoyed the series, and Robert E Wood is to be praised for his dedication in the hours he spent editing and transcribing the myriad of tapes and interviews from the various conventions over the years. I know from speaking to a few folk that they have found it an invaluable record of the show from various aspects.

There has always been some discussion as to a preference for either Year One or Year Two. I am definitely a Year One kinda gal. (The departure of Sylvia Anderson made it a very simple choice for me!) Well, no doubt the debate will continue. What I do want to say is that from conversations with fans across the globe, I know that they did love the series, and because of that common ground, amazing and lasting friendships have been formed, traversing all boundaries, and I feel honored to have been part of a team that brought that about. If these friendships were Moonbase Alpha's legacy then we can all feel proud of it.

Zienia Merton

element of *UFO* was abandoned. The discussions took place at Elstree Studios about the ways in which we might launch a group of Earthly humans off on this odyssey through space. The notion of … the nuclear waste dumps on the surface of the Moon evolved, and the idea of the explosion pushing the Moon off onto its journey was the origin of the series. All of that took place at Elstree Studios. It was about three weeks later that we moved to Pinewood.'

Following days of rehearsal and screen tests, filming finally commenced at Pinewood Studios in Buckinghamshire, England, on Monday 3 December 1973. Special effects filming had already begun at Bray Studios on Tuesday 5 November 1973. Live-action filming was primarily conducted on the L and M stages of Pinewood Studios. L stage housed the regular standing sets (such as Main Mission in Year One, and Command Centre in Year Two), while M stage was utilised for episode-specific sets such as alien worlds or spacecraft. Other stages at Pinewood were also used as required for various episodes throughout the filming of the series.

Keith Wilson was responsible for the design and look of the interior of Moonbase Alpha, as well as all the aliens and environments encountered throughout the series. He recalled, 'I had two basic stages. I had one stage with all the Alphan sets on it. I had designed a modular system so I could – overnight – build a set very quickly, because every panel was exactly the same size as the next. So it was like a big Lego kit. I could put all of these pieces together. So if there was an episode that took place on the Moon, or Alpha, it was very easy. It would give me a chance then to plan ahead. But if it had a big new set – an interior of a spaceship, or a planet surface – then I would have to work very fast. But I would have the other stage to do that. They were identical size stages. So I had one for Moonbase Alpha, and the other for all those planet surfaces. I would have ten days to do anything that had to be done. It wasn't a problem: I was well organised and I just did it.'

Writer and story editor Johnny Byrne recalls joining the production: 'I was called down to Pinewood when they were still considering *Space: 1999* as a follow-on from *UFO*, and I heard nothing for some time. I met Chris [Penfold] there. Then some time later I was called in again when it was now *Space: 1999*, and I was asked to re-write a script that eventually became the second episode, "Matter of Life and Death". I found myself, shortly thereafter, in a private little part of Pinewood, away from all the madness of L & M Stages.'

Christopher Penfold said: 'I asked Johnny Byrne to come on to the show. When he joined we began to work very closely together. I commissioned him, first of all, to write a script. Then very quickly he became a part of the writing team and did a lot of absolutely wonderful work. I had admired Johnny's work, which was the reason I asked him on. We got on extremely well together, and we were doing pretty much what we wanted to do, within the parameters of the series. We were on a high, there's no doubt about that … I certainly loved what I was doing. I think that's the secret – passionate commitment.'

The production encountered problems from the beginning, as Gerry Anderson recollects: 'We had so many problems … When we first started filming *Space: 1999*, we had a horrendous situation in the financial sense. We shot six weeks of effects without getting one shot in the can. Every day when we went to screen the dailies the density of the image was in constant fluctuation. Under normal circumstances, this is a problem that can be tracked down quickly, but we just could not discover the cause of it. We changed cameras. We changed lenses. We called in experts from Eastman Kodak. We called in camera engineers. We had daily conferences trying to find out what the trouble was. We even used different film stocks. Then we shot in black and white instead of colour. Nothing worked. We lost everything. Finally, we found out it was a very simple fault. It was a brake on one of the film magazines, which was dragging. Every time it dragged it slowed down the transport mechanism, thus increasing the exposure. It was a minute problem but we lost thousands and thousands and thousands of pounds.'

Special effects for *Space: 1999* were nothing short of earth-shattering by television standards and were accomplished by a team under the leadership of Brian Johnson, who had previously worked on the visuals for *2001: A Space Odyssey*. The influence of Johnson's effects work on science fiction television and films to follow (notably *Star Wars*) is undeniable.

An early glimpse of *Space: 1999*'s spectacular special effects was seen on the 23 December 1974 edition of *Horizon*, a science program on the BBC. This particular episode was titled "How On Earth Do They Do That?" and focused on the special effects industry. The footage provides a fascinating look behind-the-scenes, and this *Horizon* segment has been included on DVD releases of *Space: 1999* as a bonus feature.

The budget for the first season of 24 episodes was £3.25 million, making *Space: 1999* the most expensive science fiction television series ever produced at that time. Those 1973 funds, adjusted for inflation, would now have the buying power of well over £27 million!

PERSONNEL

As viewers would soon discover, *Space: 1999* told the tale of 311 men and women living on the Moon. Christopher Penfold said: 'I didn't really know a lot about science fiction when Gerry Anderson approached me, but I very quickly [learned] … Although the subject has always interested me, this was the first time I had worked on a sci-fi series. And when you are tackling something new, you do your best to bring a brand new approach to it. Since most of the investment money actually came from the United States through ITC, the first thing that they wanted to have was an American story editor on board and to include a large number of scripts from American writers. Gerry and Sylvia went off to find an appropriate script editor in the States, and found George Bellak. Principally, George and I created the characters in conjunction with Gerry, and Sylvia had some input in the early stages. George left the series quite early on as he didn't get on very well with Gerry, so the ball was back in my court. It meant I had the responsibility for finding the writers, talking about ideas for individual episodes, commissioning them, and doing the normal script editing jobs, and eventually writing a fair number of the scripts myself.'

The lead roles of Commander John Koenig and Doctor Helena Russell went to husband and wife stars Martin Landau and Barbara Bain, while Barry Morse came aboard as Professor Victor Bergman. Sylvia Anderson has stated: 'Initially Martin was not my choice – I have to say that. I wanted Robert Culp, someone a bit more offbeat. I think Martin grew very well into the role … He's a very serious actor, and a fantastic character actor. I never thought that he was really a lead, but when he was given the lines in a serious scene, I think he played it very, very well. One of the problems in the show, really, was that Martin and Barbara wanted to be in every scene and make every decision. Now there was nothing unusual about that because they were the stars. Well, Nick Tate's a very good actor, and I cast him because he was a younger element and had great authority on the screen, but invariably if he had more lines than Martin there would be a problem. Nick Tate had to walk three paces behind Martin. So we did have that all the time, but I think given a good scene … Martin rose to the occasion. He's a very good actor, there's no doubt about it. I just think that … he and Barbara were a force to be reckoned with in terms of getting their own way. So that was a problem we had on the show. We had to cast Barbara and Martin, whom I freely admit I did not want. I battled very hard and stood up to Lew Grade and said, "I don't think they're right. They were okay in *Mission: Impossible*, but having seen them I don't think we're going to get what we should get." I'm not saying they were bad, I just think they could have been so much better.'

Sylvia has also shared her perspective on characterisation: 'I think unless you have strong characterisation, you don't have anything … I remember sitting with Martin Landau and Barbara Bain in the Beverly Hills Hotel talking about their characters in *Space: 1999*. And I didn't quite understand – I didn't appreciate at that time – back-story. They started talking very earnestly about how he came from the Mid-West and Barbara was talking about how they met, and I thought, "Where on Earth is this going?" But of course it was all back-story for their characters. So I always remember that – you never write a character without thinking, "How did they get there?"' So that was a very important lesson for me personally. And so, for me, characterisations are just as important, if not more, than all the bangs that are going on, and all the other wonderful things.'

Bain and Landau had experienced their greatest success on *Mission: Impossible*, while Morse had achieved his widest recognition chasing *The Fugitive*. Morse was also attractive to ITC because of his proven track record with them. He had been the second lead in *The Adventurer* and one of the four stars of the European-based ITC series *The Zoo Gang*. With this team of internationally known and award-winning performers, *Space: 1999* was clearly led by a strong and appealing triumvirate.

Barbara Bain explains: '*Space: 1999* was a project put together by English people. They came over to talk to us about it and we hired a story editor – an American story editor [George Bellak] – because it was going to be broadcast here [in the US]. They wanted a certain kind of mix with the English-based show. They were able to do the technology much cheaper there than here, all the effects, that sort of thing. Okay, so that was all exciting. But they wanted to prepare it for the American market as well as the world, which meant a certain kind of writing. With English television, there is a commercial network, but they're also kind of brought up on the BBC, which does not have commercial interruption. As a result, it's a very different dramatic form. We have – if you'll pardon me – six to eight "climaxes" an hour, dramatic moments where you have a commercial; cliff-hangers. The English don't, nor do they quite understand it. So we went over there with the American story editor. Then he left – about an hour after he touched ground in England!'

Bain also recalled, 'The first day I arrived in England I went into what was going to be my dressing room. I had asked them to please build me a bar … I walk in and there are a bunch of carpenters, and they're building me a *bar*! Like a bar for whisky and beer. What kind of actress asks for [that]? I meant a ballet bar! I said, "Look guys, all you need is a dowel and a couple of things to hang it up on." They were building me a bar … I don't drink! There were all kinds of moments like that, that were fun.'

19

The three lead characters were all carefully delineated in the original Writer's Guide, although certain details were altered or expanded upon as the series developed. Certain later details (such as the death of Koenig's wife in World War III, as posited in the Year Two episode "The Rules of Luton"), however, completely contradict the details established in the Writer's Guide. Only the three leads were examined in the Guide, and it did provide a reasonably detailed look into their personal character traits.

John Robert Koenig is said to be 'not only the American Commander of the Moonbase, but at 40 he is an astrophysicist of very high repute ... an interesting and somewhat complex man. He has two streaks in him: one, rather ruthless and efficient, the "mind-as-computer" aspect; and on the other hand, a moody and introspective strain. Born in 1959, he is *not* the total space child. He has had, along with science, more humanities education than some others of his generation.' The Writer's Guide goes on to explain that he had been 'married for five years to a woman who was a highly gifted artist.' However, they had separated more than six years prior to 1999 and 'John Koenig carries the scars with him and holds back at relating deeply to other women. As to men, Koenig demands a lot, but he demands a lot of himself too.' Koenig is summed up as being 'a man with one foot somewhat in the past and one foot somewhere in the future. The Commander's last name is symbolic of his position on the base, originating from the German word 'König', which means 'King'.

Of Dr Helena Russell, the Writer's Guide states: 'Her cool good looks belie her abilities and her responsibilities ... A woman in her early thirties (born, say, in 1965) whose father was a West Coast physician of great energy and drive.' Barbara Bain herself has explained that in her own envisioning of the character, she decided that Helena's father had been the one to discover the cure for cancer. There was thus a pressure on her to live up to the expectations put upon her by following her father's footsteps in the medical profession. The Writer's Guide also states: 'Helena drove through medical school, where she met and married a fellow student ... Telford Russell ... Telford became a medical mission man – going out into space. Helena, now in her late twenties, worked at NASA and delved into space disorientation and psychology ... Then a mission disappeared into space ... Telford was on that mission, and Helena to all intents and purposes was widowed. Helena grieved and then went on working and living her full and liberated life ... As we pick Dr Russell up, she has been on Alpha for 12 months, working and living, and to some extent retiring emotionally in that space womb environment.'

Barbara Bain's hairstyle for Year One was created by Michael Rassner, of famed London salon Michaeljohn. Rassner was quoted as saying at the time of the series: 'The Barbara Bain assignment was a difficult one. Her hair, as it is today, suits her so perfectly that I doubt if she will change it very much in the future – even in 1999! I had several things to bear in mind. One: Miss Bain is portraying a girl stranded on the Moon when it breaks out of orbit, and as she wouldn't have hairdressers around her she would need something simple that she could control herself. Two: it was necessary to keep to a style that would suit her own personality. Three: it would be her own hair and not a wig – and that she would therefore have to be seen outside the studios as well as on the screen with whatever style I chose ... It is basically classical. The colouring is very much Barbara Bain's own, but I have taken the silver of the Moon to symbolise the setting by introducing blonde highlights, which give a subtle lift for the hair. She is lucky. Her hair is fantastically lovely.'

Professor Victor Bergman is also detailed in the Writer's Guide, although his name had not at that point been determined. The Guide states, 'The Professor, born in the early '40s, is a brilliant teacher and theoretician. Rarely involved in worldly things, the Professor nonetheless achieved a reputation as a tremendous mind in force-field theory… John Koenig was one of the Professor's outstanding students years ago. Since then, a bond of affection has grown between them.' It goes on to say: 'The Professor looks upon his times with a somewhat rueful eye. He is more of a throwback – a 19th Century scientist-philosopher-humanist – and he is an intellectual counterbalance to the 21st Century we are about to enter.' The Guide goes on to explain that the Professor has an artificial heart.

Barry Morse explains how he joined the series: 'It came about, like so many things do in our lives, by a series of flukes and coincidences. There was a great, very prominent British producer (long gone now, but at the time probably the most prominent producer in the UK) called Lew Grade, for whom I had done two series (*The Adventurer* and *The Zoo Gang*). He had an option on my services and said to me, "Do you want to take up the option and come play in this whole new series we're going to film based on a science fiction scheme, called *Space: 1999*?" I asked where it was going to be shot and learned it was to be shot in London – well, Pinewood. By this time, my wife Sydney and I had been visiting and working a great deal in other countries all over Europe, so the idea of doing a series that was going to be shot entirely in London was very appealing. So I said, "Shall I look at some scripts?" He said, "Well, that's the trouble. We don't really have what you might call a completed script." I said, "Excuse me, Lew, I think there's something wrong with the phone. I thought I just heard you say that you're starting a series and you don't even have a single completed script." Indeed it was so. There's Lew Grade, Mr Lord High Everything in our profession, and he's apparently prepared to embark on this thing without a single polished script. So I thought, "He's got courage." When he told me that Martin and Barbara were going to be in it, I thought, "Well, they've got courage. And they're good pros and they know what they're doing." So I thought, "Why not?" and I signed up, as it were.'

The Writer's Guide character outlines were apparently never shown to the actors (although the details provided might still have seemed insufficient to the performers, even if they were aware of them). Barry Morse, for example, has stated, 'We started out with not even the bare bones of who our characters were. We had to put flesh on whatever skeleton was there for us, out of our own imaginations. It's not a question of adding something of one's self to the role, but something of what one perceives, or conceives, as the character that one is being called upon to play. I did write a biography of dear Victor Bergman, because going into the series there was virtually no indication of the nature of the characters at all, beyond the fact that Victor Bergman was the oldest inhabitant and a kind of "Space Uncle". Among other things, I remembered the sort of people in the world that are, or have been, or might become Victor Bergmans.

'I didn't want Bergman to be the typical, anonymous American, which was indicated in the initial script. I didn't think he was entirely British, either. I visualised he acquired a kind of orthodox English accent, more or less like my own, by virtue of having spent many of his more mature years as a professor at one of the older universities in the UK. I thought Victor should be a chap of a varied background and of mixed race – ultimately a great deal more eccentric and individual than he eventually became. I felt a chap who was the scientific expert on the crew of Moonbase Alpha could perhaps have a European origin. I visualized his having been brought as a child refugee out of Austria, before the War, because one of his parents was partly Jewish (which I took from his name). He then studied in various parts of the world, principally and more recently, in England. I worked out all the chronological details to bring him up to the age he was presumed to be.

'Of course, an obvious comparison was somebody like Einstein, who was a keen musician. I used to play the fiddle very badly, and I thought it might be fun if somewhere down the line, during some emergency, Victor was twiddling away a bit of Mozart. But we never did it. Once in a while, when I got the chance, I would whistle bits of one of the Brandenburg Concertos as a little thing to help him along when he was working something out. I hoped I was going to be able to make more than infrequent use of that device. I did think Victor was particularly interested in music, specifically that of Johann Sebastian Bach – it is the kind of music that would appeal to a man with a scientific mind as it is so marvellously organised. I saw Victor as someone who is so much concerned with abstruse scientific matters that he has very little knowledge of, or interest in, the day-to-day happenings of the world. I looked on him as being an absent-minded and other-worldly chap who might tend to put on odd socks, wear a cardigan with the elbows out, go about in tennis shoes without the laces, and be generally untidy and careless about his dress and appearance. He might have a rather unkempt beard and straggly hair, and be, in other words, kind of an absent-minded professor. I didn't fully succeed, of course.

'I tried as tactfully as I could to inject a bit of humanity, but starting a large scale series as we did with only one script, many people would say is an act of blatant insanity. It is as if Shakespeare had arranged for the first production of *Hamlet* after he had written the first line. Where is it going to go? So what we were able to do in clothing with flesh, you might say, the very sketchy characters that were laid out for us was mostly a matter of the inventive imagination of the actors involved. Inevitably as time went by certain characteristics were fastened on, certain interests were battened on, and so forth. But it wasn't by any means a completed work of art when we started.'

The character of Main Mission Controller Paul Morrow, portrayed by actor Prentis Hancock, was originally to have been a Russian called Vorkonen. Hancock explains how he joined the series: 'Out of my work on *The Protectors* ... I was just offered, *Space: 1999*. Most of my work during my life has been actually just offered ... [They said,] "Come and see [the director] Lee Katzin." I did, on a Saturday morning. Lee H Katzin talked about the series and I thought, "Wow, that sounds fantastic," but ... I was working for the BBC and I was thinking about which of the parts was the right one to do. Well, as the money was astronomically higher [for *Space: 1999*] than the BBC used to pay, there was no question in my mind what to do. I got back and I looked at [the script] and read it again, and I thought, "the part of Carter is the one to go for." On Monday my agent phoned, and I said, "I think Carter ..." and he said, "Well don't worry about it, we've already done the deal on Morrow." And that was it. He'd done the deal before I went to see Sylvia and Gerry, so there was no question of auditioning for it, or anything like that.

'They were saying [my character] Paul was the second in command. I was the fourth lead on the show. When I first went to work, there were four of us on it. The rest of the cast joined in the following week. And I had every reason to think this was going to go very, very big ... When it started shooting, it was the most expensive television series ever made. There was a two-page spread in *Variety* the day we started shooting at Pinewood Studios, advertising how expensive our new production was ... We all thought we would be Hollywood bound in five years.

'There were a number of first days. I joined in for costumes and getting to know people … Gerry and Sylvia were there all the time doing things. Barbara and Martin were moved in, and so was Barry. That was like the Monday, Tuesday, Wednesday, and I think I joined in about the Thursday. People joined all the time until we got everybody together and then there were about 300 of us who walked on to M stage, where this enormous set was. What was quite nice about the set, although it was enormous, it was not intimidating. You didn't walk onto it and think about the big arches and panels and what-have-you, and miles of space. The whole thing had an intimacy about it. I think it was the tables and chairs, so it was quite office-y, and that kept it human in scale, in spite of it being quite large, and large in terms of television. We filled more than half of M stage, which was one of the big stages at Pinewood.'

Dr Bob Mathias, played by actor Anton Phillips, was originally conceived as the Japanese Dr Fujita. Phillips states: 'I hadn't heard anything at all about *Space: 1999*. I didn't know it was happening. I was in a play at a very small theatre called the King's Head Pub … very small. This was a lunchtime play I was doing. It was very *avant-garde*. I didn't have any idea what it was about! Neither did anybody else in the play, or the director, or the writer! Michael Barnes, the casting director [for *Space: 1999*] came to see another actor in the play and invited me to come to Pinewood Studios the next day. I went in and they asked me to do one episode, and after they looked at the rushes, they invited me to be in all the remaining episodes. It was purely by accident and the rest is history, as they say.'

Phillips also said, 'My trip to Pinewood Studios to do the spot was my first time in a film studio. So coming in and having Barbara and Martin as examples of what to aspire to was great. I couldn't have had better role models in acting technique, in lessons, and everything else. I was very lucky. I worked mainly with Barbara; not so much with Martin, and it was wonderful … *Space: 1999*, when I got the part, was I think the third part I had had, out of drama school. No, it was more than that, but walking onto a movie set – that was the first time I had been into a studio. There's a kind of magic to walking on to work in Pinewood Studios. It was all really magical for me, and it was all a learning experience as well. That's where I met some realy terrific people; worked with some very helpful directors – Charlie Crichton, Ray Austin; and it was just great for me. Sylvia Anderson was really so nice to me. It was all just like a kid in a candy shop, really.'

Until the last minute, the producers were trying to find an actor to play the final uncast regular role – Italian Eagle pilot Alfonso Catani. Actor Nick Tate explains that he was offered two different series at the same time: 'One of them was *Space: 1999*. I had a very positive meeting with Sylvia Anderson and her casting director, but they told me the show was all cast and that the most they could do was bring me in as a guest star in the first episode (as a doomed astronaut). After the usual wait, both the productions suddenly rang and offered me work. I had to choose. I think I must have been clairvoyant. I decided to go with [the guest star part in] *Space: 1999*, because the whole concept of it appealed to me. I wasn't really a huge science fiction fan, but I'd read some Asimov and Arthur C Clarke, who I really thought was a wonderful man. Also, I was a pretty gung-ho kind of a young kid. I liked surfing a lot and riding horses, so I always wanted to get into a cowboy movie. The thought of playing an astronaut appealed to me in a similar vein.

'Gerry [Anderson] said to me [when I started on the show], "I have to tell you – I don't like actors." Great beginning! I was like, "Thanks a lot, Gerry, I feel really secure about that!" But he was okay. I got on very well with Gerry.

'Lee Katzin had taken a shine to me during the preparatory shooting and he came up to me and said, "I want you to come and audition for this [regular] role [of Alfonso]. Can you do an Italian accent?" As a young Australian actor, the only Italian I knew was from the Italian greengrocer in Australia, so my Italian accent was hysterical. My audition was quite a joke, and Gerry and Sylvia fell about laughing! At the end they said, "Thank you very much, Nick. We think we'll just leave you playing the character that you're playing." [Lee] suddenly said, "What are we doing? Australian astronauts are up there as well." Well, the Andersons were dead against that. They said there wouldn't be any Australians up there! Naturally, I got angry about it and said, "What do you mean there wouldn't be any Australians up there? Bloody English people trying to tell Australians they shouldn't be up in space!" I was getting a bit aggressive about it, but Lee thought it was hysterical. He said, "This guy's perfect – look at the aggression in him!" Then the Andersons said I would sound too much like a Cockney, and that really angered me, because for years Australian actors had always missed out on all the good roles to Cockney actors. I was adamant that an Australian didn't sound anything like a Cockney, and I demonstrated that very clearly. Finally, the Andersons relented. So I went in with my broad Australian and did this character, and they loved it. By the time I got home, my agent was ringing me saying, "They want you in the series playing not Alfonso Catani, but Alan Carter."

A similar transformation occurred with the character of Data Analyst Sandra Benes, as actress Zienia Merton explains: 'It was a very big series when they were starting to do it. Everybody I knew – all my actor friends – were going up for it. I said to my agent, "Look, why can't I go up for this part?" He said, "No, no. They don't want you". So that was three months before they started. Finally, I was doing a television show and my agent rang me up and said, "Can you get to Pinewood tomorrow?" This was a Friday. I said, "No, because I am doing this television show. I'm in the studio." If you're in the studio you can't leave, no matter what happens. So he said, "Well, forget it. It'll be gone by Monday." I said, "All right." Well, Monday he rang me up and said, "Can you get to Pinewood and see Gerry and Sylvia Anderson?" Well, that Monday I went to Pinewood. Tuesday I heard that I was starting the next day, which is very quick, even in our business. And that was it for the next 15 months.

'I was supposed to be Sandra Sabatini, but by that point they were so desperate that they let me do any accent I felt comfortable in. Well, I've got a sort of "Foreign Mark I" accent that covers a multitude of things. Eastern, western, middle Europe, anything where hopefully people won't listen too carefully and say, "That doesn't sound like so-and-so." And I do still remember my first line on Moonbase Alpha, "There is a steep rise in heat levels in Disposal Area One." And Sandra's punch line, "This is impossible." Boom! Next minute the Moon's gone, right? I actually had to walk while I was saying that, which frightened the life out of me. They did ask me if I could do Italian. I could, but the thing about Italian when you hear it is that it's a very romantic, musical kind of language. Sandra … was rather clipped. I think she was quite repressed, actually. The way I did it was kind of clipped and matter-of-fact. I thought, as an actress, if I said it with an Italian accent it would, as an ongoing character, actually hold back the dialogue. That's what I felt. Lee Katzin said to me, "That doesn't sound Italian." I said, "No, no, it's not." He said, "What do you think you are, then?" I said, "I don't know. What does it sound like to you?" Lee then said I couldn't be Sandra Sabatini, because I wasn't doing an Italian accent. So he said, "What do you want to be called?" I said, "Well, I don't know a lot of mid-Europeans, so I'm kind of lost. So can you tell me?" He said, "Hey, there's a great deli in Los Angeles called Benes' – you're Sandra Benes." And that's how I was born.'

Benjamin Ouma, played by Lon Satton, was the computer expert on Moonbase Alpha. However, Satton was unpopular with some of the other performers in the cast and was replaced by Clifton Jones as David Kano from episode two until the end of the first season. Nick Tate recalled, 'I don't really know why Lon Satton was dropped [after the first episode] – I know it was something between him and Martin. I don't know whether Martin said something to him, or whether Martin just felt that the mix wasn't right. Martin had a lot of power over the show. I don't think he had it written in his contract that he could make those kinds of decisions, but he was the driving force of the show.'

Production was co-financed by an Italian network, RAI. It would seem that Lew Grade was keen on these European tie-ups at the time. *Space: 1999* overlapped production with ITC's *Moses the Lawgiver*, which was also an RAI co-production and was partially shot in Italy. The agreement with RAI stipulated that a certain number of Italian actors receive guest roles throughout the series. They included Gianni Garko in 'Dragon's Domain', Giancarlo Prete in 'The Troubled Spirit', Carla Romanelli in 'Space Brain' and Orso Maria Guerrini in 'The Testament of Arkadia'. This caused frustrations for the production as the Italian actors experienced some difficulty with the English language. Voice-over artist Robert Rietty was brought in to re-dub the voice of actor Orso Maria Guerrini. On the positive side, the Italian presence helped solidify the cosmopolitan nature of the crew. Many of the other guest performers hired for various episodes were well known and highly regarded: Peter Cushing, Christopher Lee, Brian Blessed, Joan Collins, Margaret Leighton and Leo McKern, among others.

Rudi Gernreich, a world name in fashion, was hired to design the uniforms for Moonbase Alpha. These costumes featured colour-coded left sleeves, differentiating the sections of Alpha in which their wearers were stationed. Black was Command, White was Medical, Flame (red) was Main Mission, Purple was Security, Yellow was Data, Orange was Reconnaissance and Brown was Technical. Professor Bergman did not have a coloured sleeve, which meant he was officially a Visitor to Moonbase Alpha. The flared trousers/bellbottoms clearly date *Space: 1999* as being a product of the 1970s.

Barbara Bain recalls the origin of the costumes: 'When we spoke about who would design the clothes for the series, Sylvia Anderson said that the only American designer she would be interested in approaching was Rudi Gernreich, so I said that he was a very dear, close friend … He was as much a philosopher as a dress designer and his thinking was reflected in the first meetings we had with him. There we were in 1973 talking about what people would be wearing in 1999, and Rudi said that people would be wearing armour and face masks. He thought that the world would become such a hostile place that we would encase ourselves in metal and cover our vulnerable parts. We thought about that, but we couldn't do that for the show because we wouldn't have been able to move and we couldn't wrap our faces.'

Production designer Keith Wilson comments on the costumes: 'I was told that we were going to have this guy from America to design the clothes and his name was Rudi Gernreich. His [claim] to fame was that he had designed the topless dress. I thought, "What the hell has that got to do with us?" It's something I've always been very bitter about. Obviously, he got paid a huge amount of money to do one drawing, and all that credit … his name at the front, while I was still at the back. So I was very bitter about that … He came over with this one design that was universal. It had to fit everybody. Well, this is fine if you've got a beautiful body, but not all of our actors had beautiful bodies. I remember one particular occasion – we were shooting a particular sequence with an actor. He was very young, looked really good in costume, fresh young body … but he needed to wear something under it so it wouldn't be obscene. I said to Sylvia, "What do we do? He looks great in costume, but we do have a slight problem." And we had to go and tell him to go and put a jock strap on. Anyway, we had to put up with this costume, and I hated it from the word go. It hadn't been thought out. It was this one quick little drawing. It looked beautiful on paper, but you put it on people and of course it never worked. When we came to do the second series we very quickly designed bits to go with it. We still had to use the original costume, but we added jackets and badges, anything just to jazz it up.'

Barry Morse was frequently known to talk about the costumes: 'I felt there was far too much uniformity in the whole structure of the crew and the personnel, which was exemplified by that uniform we all wore. I suggested I *not* wear the same silly uniform we all eventually did wear – but, oh no, that idea didn't go at all well! Gerry and Sylvia were terribly keen on those dreadful uniforms. That uniformity seeped through, it seemed to me, to everybody in the crew. It was very difficult to distinguish who we all were. What did Nick Tate's character have about him that could distinguish him or mark him off from Prentis Hancock's character, or Zienia Merton's? Never mind me. I felt we were considerably lacking in individuality. I did, I remember, let my hair grow rather long, to indicate Victor had other things on his mind than getting his hair cut or taking care of his appearance. There had not been enough attention paid in the writing, or indeed in the production as a whole, to developing individual characters, which are ultimately the making of any successful dramatic series.'

Keith Wilson also commented on the distinctive orange space suits featured throughout the programme: 'So much of the action in the series takes place against the stark black-and-white of the Moon's surface that the suits have been designed to provide contrasting colour, also with the logical reason that those wearing them could be seen clearly.'

SETTING AND HARDWARE

Moonbase Alpha itself was a large and self-sustaining lunar colony constructed inside a crater. Built in the design of a wheel, with various sections radiating out from the central hub, the base is undoubtedly the single greatest defining element separating *Space: 1999* from other space-faring science fiction shows in which the protagonists fly around in such ships as the *USS Enterprise* or the *Battlestar Galactica*. The design of Moonbase Alpha is at least partially a tribute to *2001: A Space Odyssey*'s Moonbase Clavius. Buildings of essentially identical shapes make up both bases and, aside from Clavius appearing somewhat more complex and larger than Alpha, they could be the same place. Located in the central hub of the Alpha base was the command tower, and at its heart the vast Main Mission control room, which would be the most important set of Year One.

Brian Johnson discusses designing the exterior of the base: 'I just imagined a colony on the Moon and visualised a sort of modular construction for the things – but being modular they could be expanded to whatever you wanted; you could take license with them. For Moonbase Alpha I imagined the control centre (Main Mission) would be in the middle and everything else would radiate out from that. I originally envisaged the whole thing being underground, but Gerry Anderson persuaded me that it wouldn't be visually very exciting if we didn't show something on the surface. So I added a lot more than I was originally going to, and we made it much bigger than the original. However, this also allowed us to put new areas into the show without anybody realising they weren't there in the first place. If you have a small complex, people begin to orientate themselves around that, so when you suddenly come up with a new section they say, "Oh, they added that? Where did they get it from?" But our thing was so big, nobody knew where the hell they were anyway. It was like being in a city.'

Keith Wilson recalls his collaborative work with Brian Johnson on Moonbase Alpha: 'I've known Brian Johnson for a long time. He started for Gerry Anderson at the same time that I did. His first series was *Fireball XL5* too. He was [visual effects designer] Derek Meddings' assistant. I've known Brian as long as I've been in the business. I knew what he could do and he knew what I could do. We were able to work very well together … When we came to do Moonbase Alpha, I said, "I want to do this style of modular building that will alter the shape of your model". So, from that point of view, we worked very closely together. But he was at Bray Studios, and I was at Pinewood, so we saw very little of each other, in fact.'

Alpha's power was produced through a combination of nuclear generators and solar batteries. Food was produced partially through hydroponics, while water and air were recycled. Transport around Alpha was via the Travel Tube, a Moonbase version of a rapid mass-transit system, which received detailed explanation in the 1973 Writer's Guide.

Displaying more of *Space: 1999*'s inspiration from *2001: A Space Odyssey*, Alpha was equipped with the powerful, speaking X5 Computer, which became a virtual member of the cast. Known as Main Computer, it was often referred to by characters simply as 'Computer' – an entity rather than a piece of equipment. In the original drafts of scripts for early episodes such as 'Black Sun', Computer was substantially more interactive with other characters and involved in plotlines. Computer even watched the crew via cameras around the base. Looking at these scripts, one can clearly see how inspiration for Computer was derived from *2001*'s HAL-9000. The original Writer's Guide referred to it as 'Central Computer' and focused mostly on its technical aspects.

Moonbase Alpha was equipped with a fleet of Eagle spaceships, which were originally referred to in the Writer's Guide as the MTU (Multiple Transportation Unit), and described as 'a workhorse; thoroughly utilitarian spacecraft'. The Eagles are an all-purpose space shuttle/workhorse able to be equipped with a variety of six different service modules. These modules are:

- Passenger module (standard on most Eagles)
- Laboratory pod (seen in many episodes of both seasons, debuting in 'Guardian of Piri')
- VIP pod (seen only in the debut episode, 'Breakaway', and featuring orange sides)
- Cargo platform (seen in 'Breakaway', carrying waste canisters.)
- Winch pod (a Cargo pod, with the addition of a winch mechanism, seen in the episodes 'Breakaway' and 'Missing Link' with a magnetic grappler, and in 'Space Brain' with a physical grab)

- Rescue pod (seen in 'Earthbound', 'Missing Link', 'Space Brain' and 'Collision Course', and featuring distinctive red stripes).

The Eagles served as transport for the Alphans around the Moon, into space and to new alien worlds. The image of the Eagle spacecraft has always been one of the most identifiable and popular features of *Space: 1999*, and the ships appeared in all but six episodes of the series. The Eagle is nothing less than an icon of science fiction spacecraft design.

Transport on the lunar surface (and occasionally on alien worlds) was afforded by the yellow Moon Buggy. Capable of operating with equal ease in the void of space or in atmospheric conditions, the Moon Buggy was usually crewed by two astronauts, but that number was flexible, and it could even be operated by remote control. The Moon Buggy was realised on screen through the use of no fewer than four different-scaled models. The life-size version was a modified Amphicat – a real-life 6x6 amphibious all-terrain vehicle.

Props for the series were diverse and unique, the most famous being the Commlock and the Stun Gun, both created by Keith Wilson. The Commlock (referred to in the Writer's Guide by the temporary name 'IDX') is a dual communications and locking device worn on the belt by all personnel. It is equipped with a view screen for visual and audio two-way communications and (much like today's remote keyless locking systems) operates on the push of a button to open doors. The Stun Gun, with its distinctive wrap-around configuration, is an unmistakable design element of the series. The Writer's Guide introduces the gun as a TSLA, which stood for Tranquilliser, Stun, Laser, Atomic. It features different barrels from which various types of beams (such as stun or kill) would be produced, although this feature was not fully developed on screen in the episodes. Script consultant and writer Christopher Penfold has stated that he was against the concept of the Stun Gun: 'I recall, very early on, having an absolutely passionate debate – lasting about two hours – about whether or not we should have such a thing as a Stun Gun. I was absolutely opposed to the notion of a Stun Gun.' Among other props seen throughout the series was the laser rifle. Communications posts are also detailed in the Writer's Guide, and remain virtually the same on-screen; a ubiquitous fixture in every area of Alpha.

Frequent mention is made throughout the series of life support systems, airlocks, recycling plants, power drains, fuel consumption, radiation sickness, gravity generators and explosive decompression – all examples of the thin line between survival and extinction for those human beings living in the vacuum of space. The Alphans did not take their situation, or their survival, for granted. In *Space: 1999*, space travel was as perilous as it has proven to be in the real world, and the technology of Moonbase Alpha largely remains a highly believable extension of our present day capabilities.

MUSIC

For a series produced on the monumental scale that *Space: 1999* was, the musical score would prove to be of utmost importance. Long-time Gerry Anderson collaborator, classically-influenced composer Barry Gray, provided the majestic orchestral opening and closing themes, as well as scores for the specific episodes 'Breakaway', 'Matter of Life and Death', 'Black Sun' and 'Another Time, Another Place', which would go on being used throughout the remainder of Year One, re-arranged as required by music editor Alan Willis. Gray would also compose the primitive percussion tracks heard in 'The Full Circle'. Artist Jim Sullivan composed and is seen on screen playing the sitar performance in 'The Troubled Spirit', while Willis himself worked with Vic Elms to compose music for 'Ring around the Moon'. Elms (whose surname is actually spelt 'Elmes') had been a pop musician with the band Christie, who were well known for their number one hit 'Yellow River'. He was married to Sylvia Anderson's daughter Dee, which is how he became involved with *Space: 1999*. Elms performed the electric guitar solo on the title theme, as well as the guitar arrangment of the theme featured in 'Matter of Life and Death'. He was to have scored 'Ring around the Moon' on his own, but because he was unable to read music or conduct an orchestra, the session musicians refused to work with him. Alan Willis took over, and in the end they created the score for 'Ring around the Moon' together. However, Elms wasn't asked to perform or compose any further music for the series. Elms had also created the music for Gerry Anderson's unscreened 1972 pilot *The Investigator*.

Throughout Year One, Willis made extensive use of music originally composed by Gray for previous Anderson productions, as well as library tracks by composers Tomaso Albinoni, Gustav Holst, Jack Arel and Roger Roger, and more. While some were magnificent classical pieces (Albinoni's gorgeous *Adagio in G Minor*, heard in 'Dragon's Domain' in an arrangement by Allain Lombard), others included electronic cacophonies (such as *Experiments in Space – Dorado*, composed by Robert Farnon, featured in 'End of Eternity') or were as simple as a few heart-wrenching notes played on piano (*Dark Suspense No 1* by Beda Folten, as used in 'The Infernal Machine'.)

Barry Gray recalled: 'My involvement with each episode was very, very slight. Because of the [limited] music budget, they recorded only the minimum number of sessions for the series as were required by the musicians' union. So the music editor used to lay music for different episodes either from music that we'd done before for other episodes, or he was allowed to call on library music when he was short of music. This is how the other pieces of music came into the series.'

The combined impact of the musical scoring and selections for *Space: 1999* is inextricably connected to the success and emotional impact of the series. Unforgettable sequences – such as the journey of the Ultra Probe in 'Dragon's Domain', the passage through the 'Space Brain', the survival ship leaving Alpha in 'Black Sun', or the battle sequences of 'War Games' – owe an incalculable degree of their success to the featured music. Whether poignant or powerful, light-hearted or terrifying, the soundtrack stands as one of the grandest in terms of scope and execution ever composed and compiled for a science fiction television series, and never ceases to impress.

THE DIRECTORS

The first 24 episodes of *Space: 1999* were helmed by a roster of directors.

RAY AUSTIN, who directed six episodes, had formerly been a successful stuntman in both the UK and the US (where he worked on movies including *Spartacus, Operation Petticoat, Have Gun Will Travel* and *Johnny Staccato*.) As a director he oversaw episodes of *The Saint, Department S, Randall and Hopkirk (Deceased), Shirley's World* and *UFO* (of which he commented, '*UFO* never seemed real to me. It was theatrical as opposed to

Space: 1999, which seemed more realistic.') Austin had also directed such films as *Oh, What a Lovely Way to Go, The Virgin Witches, Fun and Games* and *The Zany Adventures of Robin Hood*.

CHARLES CRICHTON, who directed eight episodes, was a famed director of Ealing Studios films, including *Dead of Night* and *Hue and Cry*. He had also directed the celebrated Alec Guinness film *The Lavender Hill Mob*. In addition, he had experienced great success on television with such programmes as *Danger Man* (aka *Secret Agent* in the USA), *The Avengers, Man In a Suitcase, Strange Report, The Protectors* and *Black Beauty*. He directed more episodes of *Space: 1999* (Year Two as well as Year One) than any other director.

LEE H KATZIN, who directed just two episodes at the beginning of Year One, was an American noted for his work on such films as *The Salzburg Connection, Le Mans* and *What Ever Happened to Aunt Alice?* His television credits included episodes of *The Wild Wild West, Mission: Impossible, The Mod Squad* and *Mannix*.

DAVID TOMBLIN, who directed four episodes, had previously worked with the Andersons on *UFO* and *The Protectors*. He joined *Space: 1999* as the replacement for Lee H Katzin when Katzin was judged an unsuccessful match with the production. Tomblin had previously been writer, producer and director on *The Prisoner*, and had served as assistant director on such programmes as *Invisible Man, Danger Man* and *One Step Beyond*, and films including *Night Must Fall, Murder Most Foul, A Warm December* and *The Adventures of Sherlock Holmes' Smarter Brother*.

BOB KELLETT, who directed three episodes, was well known as a director of comedy movies including *Up Pompeii, Up The Chastity Belt, The Garnett Saga, Up The Front* and *Our Miss Fred*. Kellett also had extensive experience as a documentary producer and director. He joined *Space: 1999* as the replacement for David Tomblin while Tomblin was working with Stanley Kubrick on the film *Barry Lyndon*.

CONCEPTS

Space: 1999 began with the premise that modern scientific man is responsible for his own downfall. The blast that hurls the Moon out of Earth orbit is the fault of technology and our inability to control what we create. Throughout the series are examples of failed space missions from Earth that not only harm those aboard them ('Death's other Dominion'), but sometimes the alien civilisations they encounter ('Voyager's Return'). The original Writer's Guide recognised the rather unique viewpoint that the Alphans were effectively an invading presence in the galaxy, stating, 'The Moonbase will be left upon its own to survive, to seek a friendly planet to colonise, and to defend itself against other space-lives, for now they are invading aliens.' (This perspective had also been acknowledged when the production team had considered *Space Intruders* as a title for the series.)

The show went on to demonstrate frequently that the Alphans have much to learn about the universe they live in, and they aren't always welcomed by those beings they meet on their journey. Aliens encountered throughout *Space: 1999* are usually vastly advanced in terms of science and medicine. They might, for example, have mastery over anti-matter or have perfected immortality or suspended animation – frequently referred to as 'stasis'. Some aliens are malevolent ('End of Eternity'), while others are seeking the Alphans' help ('Mission of the Darians') or welcome their friendship ('Earthbound').

The Alphans themselves were an extension of present day thinking, rather than originating from a far-flung futuristic time. Thus the series and its characters found a large audience that identified with various aspects of the Alphan plight – who doesn't relate at times to the thought of being alone, lost or at odds with the universe around them? Issues confronted in various episodes include faith ('Collision Course'), vanity ('The Infernal Machine'), cannibalism ('Mission of the Darians'), and obsession ('Dragon's Domain') – sometimes on the part of the Alphans themselves, and other times on the part of the beings they encounter.

The episodes of *Space: 1999* would feature a variety of story settings ranging from alien planets to spacecraft, while some would be entirely Alpha-bound segments. Christopher Penfold has said: 'When we began, we were in very much the same situation as the characters. We had the basic premise of a colony stranded on a runaway Moon, without any means of controlling its movements. Obviously, there was a limit to the dramas that could take place on the Moon itself and it was only as the writing of the series developed that ever-widening potentialities presented themselves. Gerry Anderson's own description is that the Moon is a rogue planet wandering at random through space. But with the gravitational pull from other planets and stars, there is always the possibility of finding a new home … which could offer fresh life for the Moon's inhabitants. This is a theme that runs through the scenarios: the search for a new home away from the artificial environment of the Moon. But as fresh ideas were tossed around, we realised more and more that there are mysteries in outer space that are beyond man's understanding and that we could dramatise these. Time, as we know it, means nothing. Distance, as we know it, is incomprehensible. We assume that there is life on other planets, with civilisations and mental developments millions of years older than on Earth. The possibilities are as limitless as space itself.'

As part of efforts to ensure that the series would appeal to a United States audience, American writers Irving Gaynor Neiman and Art Wallace were commissioned to provide early scripts. Neiman's contribution, 'A Breath of Death', progressed as far as a second draft before it was deemed unsuitable and abandoned. Wallace's contribution, 'Siren Planet', was re-written and became the second episode filmed, 'Matter of Life and Death'.

One defining aspect of *Space: 1999*'s Year One has long been described as the 'Mysterious Unknown Force', though it is never identified as such on screen. This MUF is present throughout the first series to varying degrees, and at its core is the concept that the Alphan journey into space did not occur by accident: it was pre-destined since the dawn of time. The Alphans are following a destiny that will see them 'prosper and increase in new worlds, new galaxies,' where their 'odyssey shall know no end' (Arra, 'Collision Course'). The MUF may have had a hand in allowing the Moon to survive being ripped out of Earth orbit in 'Breakaway', something critics of the show love to point out as being scientifically impossible. Obviously if their journey has been pre-destined then the small matter of blowing a Moon out of planetary orbit is a minor event to plan in the metaphysical scheme of things. Consider also that the Moon survives the crushing forces of the 'Black Sun'. This must be thanks to the presence of the MUF, as Professor Bergman – and the other Alphans – clearly lack confidence that Bergman's own force field will protect them. Bergman asks Koenig if he ever wonders just how or why they have survived and proclaims that he is not exactly thinking about God, but a 'cosmic intelligence'. On this journey through a black hole, the Alphans talk with a mysterious voice – God? The Mysterious Unknown Force? It is left decidedly unclear, in true *Space: 1999* style, allowing the viewer to place together the pieces of the puzzle, just as the Alphans themselves are doing. In 'War Games', Commander Koenig professes his belief that God 'or someone or something' is looking after them, and that they will survive. He comments that there is no rational explanation as to why the Alphans have survived their perilous journey. Of course there isn't – the explanation is not rational: it is one of a mystical faith in an unknown entity.

Then, in the season's last episode, 'The Testament of Arkadia', the Moon is stopped cold in space by an unknown force, and Alpha's power levels start to drop. On the planet Arkadia, amazing discoveries are made that clearly show that mankind originated not on Earth, but on this seemingly alien world. The Arkadians themselves had spread the seeds of life into the galaxy, as their world was about to die. And there are mysterious forces at work that want the Alphans to complete the cycle and bring life back to the dead world of their ancient ancestors.

Regarding the MUF, Christopher Penfold said, 'My father was a clergyman in the Church of England. I have arguments with close friends about the position I adopt, which is one of agnosticism, as opposed to atheism. My argument is that atheism is itself a form of belief, and belief is the point at which you begin the abandonment of reason. Those are the sorts of themes I wanted to put forward. I recognize the huge power of the hunger for spirituality, and experience itself as strongly as anybody else. But as to the ways in which that can be channeled, I would like it to be much more sophisticated than doctrinal forms of religion … I think that was the area in which we boldly went. There was an element of feeling that we were children who had been given a whole lot of new toys to play with, and we could do something quite different in terms of television drama. The opportunity to do a drama, which was a drama of ideas, was something we very avidly espoused.'

At a time when the concept of long-term story arcs in science fiction television storytelling was still undreamt of, *Space: 1999*'s first 24 episodes incorporated a remarkable number of plot threads and character developments tying them together and defining their position in Year One. Some of these elements are subtle; to be discerned, they really require the episodes to be viewed in production order, which differed from transmission order. Throughout the cycle of this first season, the Alphans succeeded on their own merits as Earthmen in space, fulfilling numerous seemingly pre-destined encounters.

Amazingly, these first 24 episodes were fully produced prior to any broadcasting arrangements being made …

US SYNDICATION

The plan ITC and Lew Grade had with *Space: 1999* was to produce the series and sell it to an American network on the strength of the production values and on the appeal of popular American actors Martin Landau and Barbara Bain being cast in the lead roles. Indeed, Landau and Bain had been cast partly because a US network had made a verbal agreement to purchase the series if they were the stars. The series was to debut in September 1974, but the executives changed at the US network, and the prior verbal agreement was worthless.

The American market was vitally important financially as the huge investment made in the series could not hope to be recouped without it, and so ITC again tried to sell the series to the American networks for the 1975 fall season. The networks, however, turned the series down. As Abe Mandell said in October 1975: 'The networks just don't like to accept any project they don't have complete control over,' and *Space: 1999* was by that point a *fait accompli*. Besides, added Mandell, 'It's all shot in England, far out of reach, and they don't like that idea.'

ITC, not willing to concede failure, proceeded to embark on the first major syndication effort in television history, touring around the United States and selling the series directly to the individual broadcasters that would air it, including network-affiliated stations. Many of these stations eventually pre-empted programming from their own networks in favour of *Space: 1999*. In those days, that was quite a major departure, but these stations were eager to broadcast *Space: 1999* as the 1975 fall network schedule was largely being judged a colossal disappointment. The shows most frequently dropped in favour of *Space: 1999* were *The Invisible Man* (NBC), *Barbary Coast* (starring William Shatner, on ABC) and CBS's *The Montefuscos* and *Fay*. Other shows that were replaced by the adventures of Moonbase Alpha included: (on ABC) *Welcome Back Kotter*, *Happy Days* and *The Six Million Dollar Man*; (on CBS) *Rhoda* and *Phyllis* (both spin-offs from *The Mary Tyler Moore Show*), *Good Times* and *Cher*; (on NBC) *Ellery Queen* and *Sanford & Son*.

On 12 March 1975, ITC ran a four-page feature in *Variety* proclaiming *Space: 1999* to be 'The Ultimate Adventure Series,' and hyping the 'Simultaneous world-wide premiere in 101 countries in September 1975.' The ad consisted of quotes from station executives around the United States, as well as a letter from Abe Mandell in which he wrote: 'We wish to thank all our friends in broadcasting for the unprecedented way in which they have so enthusiastically welcomed our new space science fiction series, *Space: 1999*. It is completely overwhelming ... *Space: 1999* is a dramatic and unqualified sales success in every way that a new product can be judged a sales success, and in some new ways. Many local stations have bought the series to pre-empt prime time network entries starting in September '75 ... Everyone has told us that *Space: 1999* will be the big hit of the 1975-76 season.'

Among the vast amount of praise heaped upon the series by the 36 television executives quoted in the ad were the following:

'The special effects are really out of this world and Martin Landau and Barbara Bain are excellent. We are betting that New Yorkers will eat up *Space: 1999*, and I expect the rest of the country will as well.' – Hendrick Booraem, Jr., Vice President/Programs, WPIX, New York City.

'*Space: 1999* is the finest programme that I have seen in years and I cannot understand how the networks let this slip by.' – Robert M. Bennett, Vice President, General Manager Operations, WCVB-TV (ABC), Boston.

'*Space: 1999* meets the test of all family programming. Great production values! Great star quality! By far the most promising and exciting first-run series for the coming season.' – David E. Henderson, President Broadcast Division, WJAR-TV (NBC), Providence.

'I can't tell you how happy we are to own *Space: 1999*. It's a magnificent show – superb acting – and has splendid special effects.' – Ro Grignon, Vice President and General Manager, WDAF-TV (NBC), Kansas City.

This has got to be one of the best-looking hours of television I have seen … The effects approach those only seen previously in movies like *2001: A Space Odyssey*. Best of all the storyline and the scripts will support the fantastic job done in effects, sets, and attention to detail. Martin Landau and Barbara Bain once again look like real winners.' – Tay Voye, Director of Program Operations, WTVJ (CBS), Miami.

'I'm certain that the star power coupled with the outstanding special effects and cinematography will make the show a real winner.' – Art Glenn, Vice President and General Manager, KMGH-TV (CBS), Denver.

'It holds viewers glued to their seats. This programme tops them all. *Space: 1999* will set a new standard of programme excellence. Top talent, top production, top writers, equals top of the world.' – Robert J. Sinnett, Vice President and General Manager, WHBF-TV (CBS), Davenport/Rock Island/Moline.

'At last – a series that should provide edge of the chair excitement for the entire family. We can't wait to read the numbers in the fall.' – Charles Whitehurst, Vice President and General Manager, WFMY-TV (CBS), Greensboro/Winston-Salem/High Point.

'*Space: 1999* is without question one of the best-produced programmes I've seen. I am very surprised that one of the networks didn't make it part of their program schedule.' – Conrad L. Cagle, Director of Television Operations, WAVE-TV (NBC), Louisville.

'It's the best thing I've seen in many a moon. I look forward to the return of the Martin Landau-Barbara Bain magic.' – Doug Duperrault, Assistant to the President, Program Director, WFLA-TV (NBC), Tampa.

'The special effects are fantastic, the writing is excellent and the stars add the right dimension that makes me feel ITC and WCPO have a winner.' – Ben Havel, Assistant General Manager, WCPO-TV (CBS), Cincinnati.

'*Space: 1999* is San Antonio's kind of show! We know we'll own that time period next fall.' – James Schiavone, Vice President & General Manager, KSAT-TV (ABC), San Antonio.

'One of the most fantastically exciting and extremely well-produced series I have seen. Production qualities exceed anything I've seen.' – Frank

Chappell, President of Broadcast Division, KARD-TV (NBC), Wichita.

'An exciting concept, fine production and outstanding stars, should make it an excellent series.' – Everett H. Hughes, Program Manager, WDBO-TV (CBS), Orlando.

'This series has a great cast along with top quality production. We look to great success with *Space: 1999*.' – Tom Rose, Assistant General Manager, WLWI-TV (ABC), Indianapolis.

'We think *Space: 1999* is the best combination of stars, sets and special effects we have seen in one show.' – A. Phillip Corvo, Program Director, KGTV (NBC), San Diego.

'Television has needed a believable new sci-fi series since the advent of the seventies. *Space: 1999* fills the void with class. For fantasy, realism, quality and exciting entertainment, the search has ended with *Space: 1999*.' – Don E. Fuller, Vice President and General Manager, WSJV-TV (ABC), South Bend/Elkhart.

While *Space: 1999* was a British series, the UK market was not as large or as important to its financial success (or failure) as the US market was. Also, ironically, its country of origin was virtually the only other one apart from the US where it was not networked. Although it was transmitted on ITV, one of the two major channels, it suffered badly by being scheduled differently and in undesirable and constantly changing time slots – sometimes early Saturday morning, or late at night – in the different ITV regions, such as ATV (Midlands), LWT (London), Yorkshire (North East), Granada (North West), Anglia (South East) and HTV (Wales and West Country). In addition, the series did not receive as much media coverage in the UK as it did in the US, and much of what it did receive was negative.

RATINGS

Prior to *Space: 1999*'s American premiere, *Time* magazine posed the question, 'Can a $6.5 million show tailor-made for national TV survive rejection by all three networks and win success anyway? ... With confidence bordering on brashness, ITC predicts that it is giving the networks their biggest ever prime-time challenge and in the process producing the season's first big hit ... *Space: 1999* is a futuristic Arthurian fantasy ... *Space: 1999*'s success could not only bite deeply into the audience ratings for the network shows, but perhaps even sink a couple in the first critical weeks.'[1]

When it debuted in the US in September 1975, *Space: 1999* proved to be a success, as reporter Harry F Waters commented in a piece entitled *Spaced Out* in the 20 October 1975 edition of *Newsweek*: 'With what looks like a record crop of fall-

---

[1] *Time*: 'Spacing Out The Networks.' 1 September 1975.

season flops, the television networks have few programmes to cheer about. And the surprise hit, *Space: 1999*, isn't one of them. The British-made science fiction series is getting cosmic ratings … but it is not a network property.'

Specific details on the ratings for the series included the following: 'During the month of October (airing on Los Angeles station KHJ-TV), *Space: 1999* appears to have earned an average 9.4 rating in the local Nielsen survey … A respectable if not spectacular score for an independent station, especially in a market as crowded as this one. In November, *Space: 1999* averaged an 8.7 rating … WPIX in New York averaged a 9.5 over the past two months; the Cleveland UHF station which carries *Space: 1999* showed little fall-off from the amazing ratings it had been getting. The Chicago independent station was still racking up a 12 rating.'[2]

Further ratings details included: '(On Channel 7 in Washington, DC) up against two situation comedy reruns, two talk shows and a *Star Trek* rerun in its 7.00 to 8.00 pm Saturday time slot, *Space: 1999* finished first four times and second three times in the eight weeks rated so far this season locally by the A C Nielsen Co. Nationally, the record has been spotty. In markets like Seattle, Portland Ore, and San Francisco, viewers ate it up. In Philadelphia, against [the variety show hosted by] Lawrence Welk, it got an early cancellation and Welk – who appeals to older folks – is reportedly killing it elsewhere in competition. But with the younger crowd, *Space: 1999* is doing well in the so-called "demographics" – the "whos" rather than numbers in the all-important ratings. In Channel 7's book, for instance, the sci-fi hour was very successful with both men and women in the 18-49 age group – the people who buy things.'[3]

'In Chicago, *Space: 1999* recently took 35 percent of the television audience, outrunning *The Wonderful World of Disney*, pro football, and even the World Series. The show did equally well in New York and Los Angeles.'[4]

It was also reported: '*Space: 1999* … has been a consistent ratings winner throughout the country. One New York public relations agency reports that for the first five weeks since its premiere, the show won its time period in all leading markets except Los Angeles. The local Arbitron rating for its 13 September premiere in Cleveland was 15, or a 32% share of the audience.'[5]

To put those ratings into a more recent context, *Star Trek: Enterprise* premiered on 26 September 2001 with a 7.0 rating, but on several occasions in its first season it scored only a 3.0. By its fourth and last season, ratings were even lower – at their best scoring a meager 2.2 (for the final episode on 13 May 2005) and at worst an abysmal 1.4 (on 22 April 2005). Another modern comparitor would be the revived *Battlestar Galactica*. A brief sample of ratings for this space series includes one of its better performances at 2.6 on 14 January 2005 ranging down to an astonishingly low 1.1 on both 25 February and 4 March 2007. Certainly the television markets of the 21st Century are more fragmented than those of the 1970s, but it's clear that either of these series could only dream of securing the ratings that *Space: 1999* enjoyed.

---

[2] Adler, Dick. *Los Angeles Times*: 'Some Lame Rerunning.' 9 January 1976.

[3] Carmody, John. *The Washington Post*: '1999 Gets Humanised.' 2 January 1976.

[4] Bassi, Bob. *Triad* magazine, December 1975.

[5] *TV Showtime* (*The Cleveland Press*), 21 October 1975.

As Martin Landau stated, 'As we all could have predicted, when the series was sold to individual stations across the [US] it sold like hotcakes. The ratings showed it to be miles ahead of anything else in that time slot, including all the network programmes.'

The 155 US stations that screened the show (88 of which pre-empted network programmes in favour of it) represented 96% of American homes. Abe Mandell stated at the time: 'We've created our own network – the *Space: 1999* network.'

The ratings response to the series in the UK was far less successful than in the US. The poor showing of Year One ended up resulting in Year Two failing to secure the nation-wide screening that Year One received, as these quotes attest: 'The first series of *Space: 1999* was not a success in this region. In consequence, we did not screen … series two.'[6] 'Imaginative storytelling combined with visual excellence created in the first series of *Space: 1999* not only Anderson's crowning achievement, but also what has turned out to be the apogee of science fiction on the small screen. Regrettably, although it became a cult series overseas, as far as the ITV companies were concerned it was a ratings flop, so when the second series came along it was [considered] an item principally for export.'[7] Nonetheless, *Space: 1999* did find its niche in the science fiction void between the landmarks of *Star Trek* and *Star Wars*.

Airing in over 100 countries worldwide, *Space: 1999* went network virtually everywhere around the globe except the US and the UK. The series was broadcast in Italy under the title *Spazio: 1999*, France as *Cosmos: 1999*, Portugal and Brazil as *Espaço: 1999*, Germany as *Mondbasis Alpha 1*, Denmark as *Månebase Alpha*, Sweden as *Månbas Alpha 1999*, Finland as *Avaruusasema Alfa*, Poland as *Kosmos 1999*, Hungary as *Alfa holdbazis*, Poland as *Kosmos: 1999*, Mexico as *Odisea 1999*, in Spain, Argentina, Chile, Colombia and Venezuela as *Espacio: 1999*, and in South Africa as *Alpha 1999*. Around the world, viewers were entertained by the voyage of Moonbase Alpha.

RECKONING

Space: 1999 has often been a target for criticism over the years – much of it arguably unwarranted, and most of it sadly uninformed. In fact, the most damning criticisms have tended to be the least accurate, and have often been peppered with comments betraying the reviewer as cannibalising previous negative reviews rather than offering a fair-minded, first-hand opinion. Other commentators have simply failed either to appreciate or to comprehend what *Space: 1999* was attempting to present. Actually more than the sum of its parts, it is – as writer Johnny Byrne explains in the coming pages – an epic origin story of a remarkable tribe of humans. None of this is to say that *Space: 1999* should be exempt from criticism – certainly, all dramatic productions open themselves up to the potential praise or scorn of viewers. What *Space: 1999* does deserve is an honest reckoning, not just through the words of a critical analysis, but also through the retrospective wisdom of those

---

[6] Simmons, Robert (head of press and public relations, HTV West). *The Bristol Evening Post*, 18 July 1979.

[7] *The Television Year Book* (Virgin, 1985).

who worked on the show.

Some contemporary critics loved the series, as the following selection of comments attests:

'*Space: 1999* has demonstrated itself to be the finest SF television series ever produced, both in concept and in execution.'[8]

'*Space: 1999* is like *Star Trek* shot full of methedrine. It is the most flashy, gorgeous sci-fi trip ever to appear on TV.'[9]

'To put it simply, *Space: 1999* is the best science fiction show on television … The believability is heightened by handsome, authentic-looking sets and some good performances by Barbara Bain, Martin Landau and others.'[10]

'The second episode in the series ("Matter of Life and Death") gave several indications the series will offer that which science fiction fans have been clamoring for. Its story was an adult theme complete with moral; its production values stressed explosive special effects as well as impressionistic renderings; the direction by Charles Crichton was imaginative and the acting was unimpeachably above the average for television. It was material far better suited for the big screen than little.'[11]

'*Space: 1999* is a visually stunning, space-age morality play that chronicles the downfall of 20th Century technological man … That *Space: 1999* is a brilliant piece of 20th Century technological art, filmmaking, is readily evident at a glance. What is perhaps less obvious is that the producers are using technology and art to talk about other issues.'[12]

'*Space: 1999* is important because it fills a need. It satisfies a genuine hunger in the TV audience: a national longing for a good new science fiction series. The networks, economically flat and creatively stale, seem locked into a mind-set incapable of imagining anything but new cops and sitcom spin-offs. *Space: 1999* is a handsome rebuke to that kind of thinking.'[13]

---

[8] Denney, James D. *Art and Story No. 2*: '*The Metamorph* and the metamorphoses.' August 1976.

[9] Stein, Benjamin. *Wall Street Journal*: 'Sailing Along on a Moonbase Way.' 7 November 1975.

[10] O'Flaherty, Terence. *San Francisco Chronicle*: 'Fasten Your Seat Belts!' 5 September 1975.

[11] Stanley, John. *San Francisco Datebook*: 'Moonbase Gone Astray Two Years Before the Odyssey.' 7 September 1975.

[12] Emmett, Arielle. *Science Digest*: '*Space: 1999* – Adventures in Science "Faction".' November 1975.

[13] Winfrey, Lee. *Chicago Tribune*: '*Space: 1999* is a 1976 Smash for Landau, Bain.' 21 October 1975.

Other commentators, by contrast, hated the show:

'The plots and characterisation on *Space: 1999* have been primitive. All the events that take place are science fiction clichés.'[14]

'This series wasn't produced – it was committed, like a crime … The special effects are good, but the actors are awful, even Martin Landau and Barbara Bain. Miss Bain's part is the zombiest, which is some distinction, as the cast is huge.'[15]

'*Space: 1999* is also guilty of giving its actors lines pedestrian enough to qualify as instant camp.'[16]

'A disappointing collage of wooden characters, boring dialogue and incomprehensible plots.'[17]

'The main characters were all as cold as a Pluto moonrise, and the plots didn't make a lot of sense.'[18]

Some aspects of *Space: 1999*, such as the subtle performances of many cast members, play better now than they did decades ago. Today, viewers have adjusted to a more understated style of acting thanks to shows like *The X-Files*. Back in the mid-1970s, people who were expecting Martin Landau to emote like William Shatner on *Star Trek* would have been disappointed.

There are those who might infer that *Space: 1999* is limited by the date in its title and is now little more than a relic of the past. However, George Orwell's *1984* and Stanley Kubrick's *2001: A Space Odyssey* are shining examples of science fiction with virtues that carry on untarnished by the passage of dates on a calendar. *Space: 1999* presented stories of people like us, alone against the unknown and often in awe of the infinite complexities and mysteries of the universe. At times abstract, esoteric and metaphysical, *Space: 1999* was anything but a standard by-the-books televised adventure series.

In the words of Johnny Byrne, '*Space: 1999* was remarkable for many things, but one of the things that it was truly remarkable for … wasn't so much that it was multicultural – there was no talk of white or black, or Jew, or straight or gay, or men or women. What united [the characters] was the thing that unites all of us. I think it's summed up in "The Metamorph" with, "We're all aliens until we get to know each other." It is that humanity. Sometimes humanity does not march to the same beat as political expedience … The only divisions the Alphans had were the coloured costume sleeves that showed the areas in which they worked. There never seemed to be a problem.'

---

[14] Asimov, Isaac. *Cue*: 'An Expert's Verdict: *Trek* Wins.' 20 December 1975.

[15] Amory, Cleveland. *TV Guide*: '*Space: 1999*.' 28 February 1976.

[16] Waters, Harry F. *Newsweek*: 'Spaced Out.' 20 October 1975.

[17] Javna, John. *Best of SF TV*. 1987.

[18] Carmody, John. *The Washington Post*: '1999 Gets Humanised.' 2 January 1976.

In the following pages, the episodes will be explored in depth. Complementing this author's Reviews are the Commentary sections, featuring the words of the actors, writers, producers, and others who actually made *Space: 1999*. Finally, memorable dialogue quotes round out the review sections and help to provide a greater sense of the highs (or lows) of each episode.

As promotional material for *Space: 1999* would state, 'The Future is Fantastic!'

YEAR ONE
PRODUCTION CREDITS

CREDITED ON EPISODES

Executive Producer	Gerry Anderson
Producer	Sylvia Anderson
Story Consultant	Christopher Penfold (1.1, 1.2, 1.3, 1.4, 1.5, 1.6, 1.7, 1.8, 1.9, 1.10, 1.12, 1.13, 1.14, 1.15, 1.16)
Script Editors	Edward di Lorenzo (1.1, 1.2, 1.5, 1.6, 1.8), Johnny Byrne (1.3, 1.4, 1.7, 1.10, 1.11, 1.13, 1.14, 1.15, 1.17, 1.18, 1.20, 1.21, 1.23) * No Script Editor credit appears onscreen for episodes 1.9, 1.12, 1.16, 1.19, 1.22 or 1.24.
Moon City Costumes	Designed by Rudi Gernreich
Series	Created by Gerry and Sylvia Anderson
Music	by Barry Gray
Music Associate	Vic Elms
Special Effects	Brian Johnson
Production Designer	Keith Wilson
Production Manager	Ron Fry
Director of Photography	Frank Watts BSC
Casting Director	Michael Barnes
Supervising Editor	David Lane
Camera Operators	Tony White (1.1), Neil Binney (1.2, 1.3, 1.4, 1.5, 1.6, 1.7, 1.8, 1.9, 1.10, 1.11, 1.12, 1.13, 1.14, 1.15, 1.16, 1.17, 1.18, 1.19, 1.20, 1.21, 1.22, 1.23, 1.24)
Assistant Director	Ken Baker
Sound Recordist	David Bowen
Editors	Derek Hyde Chambers (1.2, 1.4, 1.6, 1.8, 1.10, 1.12, 1.14, 1.16, 1.18, 1.20, 1.22, 1.24), Alan Killick (1.9, 1.11, 1.13, 1.15, 1.17, 1.19, 1.21, 1.23), Mike Campbell (1.3, 1.5, 1.7) *No Editor credit appears on episode 1.1, although this is attributed to Supervising Editor David Lane.
Sound Editors	Peter Pennell (1.1, 1.3, 1.5, 1.7, 1.9, 1.11, 1.13, 1.15, 1.16, 1.17, 1.18, 1.22, 1.23, 1.24), Roy Lafbery (1.2, 1.4, 1.6, 1.8, 1.10, 1.12, 1.14, 1.19, 1.20, 1.21)
Music Editor	Alan Willis
Continuity	Gladys Goldsmith (1.1, 1.2, 1.3, 1.4, 1.5,

	1.6, 1.7, 1.9, 1.10, 1.11, 1.12, 1.13, 1.14, 1.15, 1.16, 1.17, 1.18, 1.19, 1.20, 1.21, 1.22, 1.23, 1.24), Phyllis Townsend (1.8)
Make-up	Ann Cotton (1.2, 1.3, 1.5, 1.7, 1.10, 1.11, 1.14, 1.15, 1.17, 1.20, 1.22, 1.24), Basil Newall (1.1, 1.3, 1.4, 1.6, 1.8, 1.9, 1.12, 1.13, 1.16, 1.18, 1.19, 1.21, 1.23)
Hair Designer	Helene Bevan
Wardrobe	Eileen Sullivan
Special Effects Director	Nick Allder
Lighting Cameraman	Harry Oakes
Camera Operator	Frank Drake
Electronics	Michael S E Downing

An ITC-RAI Co-Production
Produced by GROUP THREE for World-Wide Distribution
Made at Pinewood Studios, Buckinghamshire, England
Special Effects created at Bray Studios, England
Processed by Rank Film Laboratories

UNCREDITED ON EPISODES

Miniatures and Space Models	Brian Johnson, Martin Bower, Wag Evans, Terry Reed, Derek Freeborn, Brian Eke, Eric Backman and Mike Trim.
Matte paintings	Ray Caple (Zenno, Daria interiors, 'Last Enemy' surface)
Floor SFX	Les Bowie

The following additional production employees were listed on an August 1973 Group Three Productions 'unit list' for *Space: 1999*:

Executive –
Group Three Productions	Reg Hill
Second Assistant Director	Steve Lanning
Third Assistant Director	Roy Button
Production Secretary	Jane Oscroft
Gerry Anderson's Secretary	Kate Curry
Sylvia Anderson's Secretary	Linda Matthews
Follow Focus	Mike Tomlin
Clapper/loader	Paul Turtle
Boom Operator	Fred Tomlin
Sound Camera Operator	Maurice Smith
Sound Maintenance	Austin Partridge
Electronic Effects Operator	Geoff Grimmell
Electronics Engineer	Michael Faithful
Assistant Art Director	Michael Ford

Draughtsman	Dennis Bosher
Art Department Assistant	Richard Holland
Production Buyer	Sid Palmer
Construction Manager	Bill Waldron
Hairdresser	Maud Onslow
Wardrobe Assistants	Elvira Angelinetta and Betty Rogers
Script Secretary	Diana Healy
First Assistant Editors	Peter Gray and Colin Needs
Second Assistant Editor	Linda Pearce
Assistant Dubbing Editors	Phillip Sanderson and Edward Bond
Special Effects Technician	Alan Bryce
Casting Secretary	Rosemary Palmer
Production Accountant	Terry Connors
Assistant -	
Production Accountant	Ray Buckley
Accounts Assistant	Margaret Woods
Secretary to M Landau	
and B Bain	Gail Samuelson
Driver to M Landau	
and B Bain	Ray Atkins
Unit Drivers	Doug Lister and Brian Boreham
Electrical Supervisor	John May
Chargehand Electrician	Freddie Webster
Chargehand Props	Wally Hocking
Standby Props	John Gillies and K Wilks
Chargehand Dressing Props	Chick McCarthy
Standby Carpenter	K G Mears
Standby Stagehand	L Bailey
Standby Rigger	J Kelly
Standby Painter	G Honor
Grip	Michael Beauchamp
Unit Runner	Steven Homes
Special Effects Unit (Bray Studios)	
Special Effects Art Director	Cyril Forster
Design Draughtsman	Ron Burton
Special Effects Assistant	Alan Barnard
Focus Puller	David Litchfield
Clapper/loader	Terry Pearce
Secretary	Jill Larkin

1.1
BREAKAWAY

Screenplay by George Bellak and Christopher Penfold*
Directed by Lee H Katzin

*Christopher Penfold does not receive on-screen credit.

Selected Broadcast Dates:

UK	London Weekend Television (LWT):	
	Date: 6 Sept 1975.	Time: 5.50 pm
	Granada:	
	Date: 26 Sept 1975.	Time: 6.35 pm
US	WPIX (New York):	
	Date: 20 Sept 1975.	Time: 7.00 pm
	KRON (San Francisco):	
	Date: 5 Sept 1975.	Time: 10.00 pm
Australia	HSV7: *Space: 1999* World Premiere	
	Date: 23 July 1975.	Time: 7.30 pm

Credited Cast: Martin Landau (Commander John Koenig), **Barbara Bain** (Doctor Helena Russell), **Barry Morse** (Professor Victor Bergman), **Prentis Hancock** (Controller Paul Morrow), **Zienia Merton** (Data Analyst Sandra Benes), **Anton Phillips** (Doctor Bob Mathias), **Nick Tate** (Captain Alan Carter), **Philip Madoc** (Commander Anton Gorski), **Lon Satton** (Benjamin Ouma), **Eric Carte** (Astronaut Collins)

Guest Artist: Roy Dotrice (Commissioner Simmonds)

Uncredited Cast: Suzanne Roquette (Tanya Alexander), **Barbara Kelly** (Voice of Computer), **Don Fellows** (GTV Newsman), **Roy Scammell** (Jim Nordstrom), **Alf Joint** (Steiner), **Laurie Davis** (Eagle Stewardess), **David Rhys Anderson** (Frank Warren), **Shane Rimmer** (Voice of Eagle 2 Pilot), **Loftus Burton** (Operative Lee Oswald), **Chai Lee** (Operative Anna Wong), **Paul Weston** (Operative Lew), **Michael Zorba** (Operative Michael), **Christopher Matthews**, **Valerie Van Ost**, **Norma West**, **Maggie Wright** (Main Mission Operatives), **Alan Harris** (Alphan), **Tony Allyn** (Security Guard Tony Allan), **Quentin Pierre** (Security Guard Pierce Quinton), **John Clifford** (Security Guard)

Previously Titled: 'Zero G' (a 30 minute script by Gerry and Sylvia Anderson), 'The Void Ahead' (a 60 minute script by George Bellak) and 'Turning Point' (60 minute length, re-written by Christopher Penfold)

Plot: In the year 1999, mankind is using the Earth's Moon as a dumping ground for nuclear waste. Moonbase Alpha, with a population of 311 men and women, has been established in order to monitor the waste dumps and function as a large-scale scientific space research station. While Alpha prepares the launch of a probe to the newly discovered planet Meta, problems are mounting … An unexplained illness – the Meta Probe Astronaut Virus Infection – is killing astronauts, magnetic radiation of unprecedented violence has been detected and Nuclear Waste Disposal Area One burns itself out in a sub-surface firestorm. Then, on 13 September 1999, Nuclear Waste Disposal Area Two erupts in a massive explosion. The blast, acting like a gigantic rocket motor, hurls the Moon and Moonbase Alpha out of Earth orbit on an unknown trajectory into deep space …

Quotes:
- **Collins:** 'Move aside, Commander – I'm getting out of here.'
- **Koenig:** 'The giant leap for mankind. It's beginning to look like a stumble in the dark.'
- **Helena:** 'We're looking for answers, Commander. Not heroes.'
- **Koenig:** 'You were right, doctor. It was radiation – magnetic radiation. Now we're sitting on the biggest bomb man's ever made.'
- **Koenig:** 'I see men risking their lives to avert disaster – total disaster. Now wake up, Commissioner. If this goes wrong there won't be anybody to issue a communiqué. There will be no survivors!'
- **Paul:** 'Commander! It's going up!'
- **Computer:** 'Human decision required.'
- **Koenig:** 'Attention all sections Alpha. This is Commander John Koenig. As you know, our Moon has been blasted from orbit. We are completely cut off from planet Earth. As we are, we have power, environment and therefore the possibility of survival. If we should attempt to improvise a return to Earth without travel plots, without full resources, it is my belief that we would fail. Therefore, in my judgment, we do not try.'
- **Koenig:** [Final voice-over] 'September 13, 1999. Meta signals increasing – yes, maybe there …'

Significant Dates (Prior to Filming) from Barry Morse's Diaries:
- Monday 19 November 1973 (Wardrobe appointment at Pinewood Studios for actor Barry Morse.)
- Wednesday 21 November 1973 (Appointment at 'Bally' for fitting of *Space: 1999* boots for actor Barry Morse.)
- Friday 23 November 1973 (Wardrobe appointment at Pinewood Studios for actor Barry Morse.)
- Monday 26 November 1973 (First rehearsal for 'Breakaway'.)
- Wednesday 28 November 1973 (Second full day of rehearsal for 'Breakaway'.)
- Thursday 29 November 1973 (Film tests shot, and further rehearsal for 'Breakaway'.)
- Friday 30 November 1973 (Fourth day of rehearsal for Breakaway'.)

Filming Dates:
Monday 3 December – Friday 21 December 1973

Thursday 27 December – Friday 28 December 1973
Wednesday 2 January – Friday 11 January 1974
Friday 22 February – Tuesday 26 February 1974

Commentary:
Martin Landau: 'I never thought "Breakaway" was ready. I kept saying "Postpone it". They did postpone, but it was never there. I never thought it was a good script. It was filled with the wrong kinds of stuff … [They would say,] "Well, we have to establish the fact that the Moon…" I said, "But you see that! You don't talk about it!" We didn't have a lot to back it up. Then we started – in a sense – falling behind.

'There was one thing on that big set [of Main Mission] I contributed to – that giant globe of the Earth, which was a real globe with real colours. I made the suggestion that they paint it the same colour as the set, because I felt it looked out of place. So they painted the globe in various shades of that beige-gray, and that was done the day we started shooting "Breakaway", because I walked in and I saw that it still hadn't been done. I thought having that colourful globe in the middle of that big set, even though it was a reminder of Earth, just looked wrong. So they heeded my advice and it literally got done with quick-drying paint the day we started shooting the first episode.'

Barbara Bain: 'The actor [Eric Carte] who played the part in "Breakaway" [of the man] who flipped out and went bananas, was [not the first choice] … There was another actor cast originally. You see how show business is. The actor couldn't do his role because he was ill or something and they'd already made those "milk eyes" for him. And they were very expensive to make, so they re-cast the part on the basis of who [had the right shaped eyes to] fit those lenses! So, I don't know if it's a good thing for an actor to come into a part on the basis of the curvature of his eye. That's how that was cast!'

Barry Morse: 'We sometimes used to send the scripts up. Since our producers had primarily come to prominence as puppet producers, I suggested one day to Martin [while filming 'Breakaway'] that we should play our parts as if we *were* puppets. I said to Frank Watts, our cameraman, "Just keep rolling – whatever we do!" And so we started this scene. You can imagine my stiff and stilted movements, rather like an Anderson puppet, as I said, "But-there-are-men-dying-out-there-John," and he said, "Gee-I-know-and-it-feels-terrible-to-be-responsible," or whatever his line was. We persuaded them to print it, hoping Gerry and Sylvia might get a subtle hint from this as to what we thought of the depth and quality of the dialogue being written for our characters, but they obviously thought we were just being mischievous.'

Nick Tate: 'They got me to do the first episode, 'Breakaway', and then they said, "Right, we liked that; now we'd like to try you on the second one". It took me about five episodes before they actually took out the fountain pen and said, "Right, you're in for the run". I did all 24 episodes of the first season.'

Gerry Anderson: 'The New York office assured me that Lee Katzin was "the best pilot director in America". The schedule to shoot the first episode was ten days, but it overran and we were soon tens of thousands of pounds over budget. It ran for two hours and I thought it was awful. He went back to America and I sent a cutting copy of the episode to Abe Mandell. Abe phoned me in a fit of depression, saying, "Oh my

God, it's terrible – what are we going to do?" I wrote a lot of new scenes myself and these were filmed over three days. I'm pretty sure I directed them myself. I then totally re-cut the episode to 50 minutes, integrating the new footage.'

Christopher Penfold: 'George Bellak had written the first episode, which was eventually titled "Breakaway", but I actually re-wrote it after he had left, and most of it is my work … I think it was my idea to have this nuclear waste dump on the Moon go out of control.

'As far as the nuclear waste dump is concerned, I was already pretty worried about the politics of nuclear power at the time when I was starting work on *Space: 1999*. I think the fact of that issue being raised in the context of popular drama series has had something to do with the demise of that abhorrent technology. So I think *Space: 1999* might have been a start of that.

[Regarding Computer's statement, 'Human decision required.'] 'Koenig makes a relatively logical decision [not to attempt a return to Earth]. We are living in a binary age, in which we believe that there is either a Yes answer or a No answer to every question. I know computer scientists who believe that serious computer systems are not able to make that decision all the time; that we live believing that those systems govern us in a logical way but there are statistically unlikely – but possibly inevitable – occasions when that indecision could lead to catastrophic circumstances. So when we're talking about philosophical precepts, we do so in theory, but what happens here in the context of a decision about whether to attempt a return to Earth or stay with what [they had], the facts that [Koenig] was in possession of were actually terribly inadequate.'

Bloopers: Two bloopers are found in the opening sequence before the titles. The first comes in the form of the on-screen caption 'The Dark Side of the Moon'. There is no 'dark side' of the Moon, but there is a 'far side', which is always pointed away from the Earth. The second is that Nordstrom's spacesuit helmet pops open as he throws Steiner over the Moon Buggy. It happens quickly, and obviously the producers didn't expect the viewer to catch it. As well, Nordstrom's name is misspelt on his helmet as 'Nordstom'.

Another recurring error throughout the series has to do with matching up effects and live-action shots. Here, Koenig's Eagle docks on the Port side (left), but he exits on the Starboard side (right).

Koenig's spacesuit collar changes from a flat and smooth style to a corrugated one, repeatedly, during his Eagle flight to check Nuclear Waste Area Two. The same mysteriously transforming spacesuit collar also appears on Eagle Pilot Collins – watch for it!

Observations: It's unfortunate that the sub-plot of the planet Meta isn't pursued in the following episode. The build-up through the show culminates at the end with Koenig speculating that the Alphans' future may lie with Meta (which, presumably, they are heading towards after they break out of orbit), but this plot thread is promptly forgotten by episode two. However, as fans of the series will know, the real year 1999 would see the premiere of a new short film entitled *Message from Moonbase Alpha*, bringing the entire series full-circle while revealing the true origins of the Meta Signal. Knowing the resolution of *Message from Moonbase Alpha* gives new meaning to the line

Koenig speaks when looking at the mysterious signal, 'Maybe that's where our future lies'. This is indeed the case, but in a way none of them could even guess at. Full details appear later in this book.

It's entertaining to watch the opening title sequence for shots that ended up not appearing in the final cut of the episode, or which appear in slightly different versions – there are many, including a rockslide, and the spectacular effects sequences of purple lightning striking an Eagle (which, despite its brief on-screen appearance became an iconic *Space: 1999* image), and a nuclear waste canister (attached to an Eagle's magnetic grappler) exploding when it hits the laser barrier.

This is the only occasion where seat belts are featured in the Eagle passenger module. This is also the only occasion where the monitor in the Eagle cockpit features a colour screen – in all others the screens are black and white.

Review: Taking place between 9 and 13 September 1999, 'Breakaway' is a spectacular opening episode presenting life on Moonbase Alpha in as realistic and believable a vision of the future as possible. Some may complain about the scientific implausibility of the Moon being able to withstand the shockwaves of an explosion large enough to rip it out of Earth orbit, but once viewers accept that (and, after all, this is science *fiction* and suspension of disbelief is a prerequisite!) they are ushered into a truly realistic and highly detailed world.

This attention to detail is illustrated by the presence of video cameras in the Nuclear Waste Area, providing the video feeds watched by the crew in Main Mission, and used by Dr Russell and Professor Bergman when they're monitoring the astronauts Steiner and Nordstrom. As well, Commlocks are actively used to open doors and communicate with Computer (as in Medical Centre scenes with Dr Russell). This is a clear presentation of defined technology and creates a tangible element of believability to life on Moonbase Alpha. There is a general 'buzz' of background noise and activity throughout the show that lends an additional aura of reality to Moonbase Alpha – unfortunately, this element will be gradually left behind over subsequent episodes.

The special effects contained within 'Breakaway' are light years ahead of anything previously seen on television, and many of them hold up remarkably well all these years later. The laser barrier at the Nuclear Disposal Area is particularly effective, especially considering how few force fields will be visually depicted throughout the run of the series – and some of those that will appear in episodes from the second season will have a remarkable tendency to look like sheets of coloured Perspex. Special effects and models are highly detailed – notably Koenig's crashed Eagle and the Space Dock explosion. The model of the Space Dock will appear again, slightly altered, in the episode 'Dragon's Domain', when it will be referred to instead as the 'interplanetary space station'. The physical manifestations of the Meta Probe Astronaut Virus Infection include milky eyes and a progression to quite gruesome facial symptoms as the infected astronauts near death – made all the more chilling by them being bathed in the blue light of the Medical Centre isolation area.

The major plot-point of magnetic radiation causing brain damage (amongst other problems) is particularly interesting to modern viewers who have heard numerous news reports about the suspected dangers and cancer-causing potential of the electro-magnetic fields from high-voltage power lines and mobile cell phones.

To those special effects that haven't aged as well, and other aspects of the production tying it to the time of its creation (like the flares/bellbottoms of the crew's uniforms), there remains a certain charm. Strings appear holding up the Eagle spaceships in a couple of scenes but, ultimately, like any quality science fiction series that created a complete and distinct universe for itself (as in *The Prisoner*), the series is a piece of art, with colours and textures all its own.

The window view to the Eagle hanger bay is very impressive and adds to the scope of Moonbase Alpha – this is a big place! It's too bad this view is seen only here in 'Breakaway' – it could have been a very worthwhile recurring set. Lee H Katzin (who would return to helm the third episode, 'Black Sun') was an American director who had previously worked with Martin Landau and Barbara Bain on *Mission: Impossible*, and it has been reported that he was hired to helm these early *Space: 1999* episodes at the specific request of Bain. Helping to build tension throughout the proceedings is the masterful score by Barry Gray.

The cast are impressive as they find their way with the roles in this premiere segment. Victor Bergman, who proves to be an ongoing 'Space Uncle' figure throughout the series, is notable here for prompting the initial meeting of John Koenig and Helena Russell, which goes on to be the primary relationship at the heart of *Space: 1999*. This episode really belongs to Martin Landau's Commander Koenig. The structure of the entire story is based around him: from his arrival on the Moonbase, through to his post-breakaway decision that they will not attempt a return to Earth. Koenig is the motivational force, the instigator, the hard-edged and strong leader who will be chiefly responsible for the decisions affecting the future survival of Moonbase Alpha.

'Breakaway' includes many similarities in concepts, settings and situations to the film *2001: A Space Odyssey*. While the connections to *2001* with regard to the design of Moonbase Alpha, and the artificial intelligence of Computer, have already been mentioned, others are worthy of note. The first is Koenig's Eagle flight to the Moon, complete with stewardess. The Eagle itself is redolent of *2001*'s Moonbus, while the interior design of Moonbase Alpha recalls the minimalist interiors of the earlier film. Add to these the sub-plots of a virus infection, and a space mission to another planet following signs of alien life, and the result is a remarkable homage to a classic film.

'Breakaway' conveys with great success the downfall of modern mankind. Failures of technology abound, and will form one of the most distinctive continuing themes of the series (recurring in such future episodes as 'Another Time, Another Place', 'Mission of the Darians' and 'The Testament of Arkadia'.) The series opening portrays the very realistic challenges of space exploration, and the even more realistic organisational and funding difficulties involved. Internal politics abound on Alpha and, most significantly, within the Space Commission. Motivated by these, and by a desire to cover over any hint of failure and reach simple solutions as quickly as possible, the Commission (embodied by Commissioner Simmonds) behaves as most present-day Earthly political organisations behave – very slowly. The Commission is seemingly more occupied with treating the symptoms of their problems than the causes. Even the appointment of Commander Koenig, and therefore the corresponding demotion of Commander Gorski, is ratified only after Koenig is already in Command uniform and aboard an Eagle en-route to the Moon! A very telling exchange between Koenig and Carter (regarding the Meta Probe Astronaut Virus Infection) reveals the depths of politically motivated cover-up even amongst high-ranking members of the Moonbase crew – all instigated by the Space Commission:

> **Carter:** 'But, I was told …'
> **Koenig:** 'You were told lies. Earth Command wanted you to think it was a temporary setback.'

As viewers will discover in upcoming episodes, the Meta Probe is only the most recent in a long line of disastrous space missions from Earth. Taking this into retrospective account, the pressure that Commissioner Simmonds and Commander Gorski are under to launch the Meta Probe and combat (or cover up) the Virus Infection becomes all the more evident, and Gorski's seeming relief at being removed from his command of Alpha becomes that much more appreciable. Gorski was more a caretaker than a Commander and unable to resolve the challenging issues, as evidenced in the later flashback episode 'Dragon's Domain' by Professor Bergman's statement,'We can't leave it to Gorski'. Gorski is also quite sharply presented as being spineless. (Koenig: 'He's always been very flexible.') Quite simply, there is a lot of subtext behind this episode!

Interestingly, as the Alphans break away from Earth physically they also break away psychologically from these types of political entanglements and deceptions. It's a symbolic break from the corruption they're leaving behind.

At its core, 'Breakaway' has a dual theme. While it is a cautionary anti-technology tale it is also making powerful environmental statements. These aspects are numerous and hinge mostly on nuclear power and the waste produced by it. What are we to do with such waste? The answer of shipping it to the Moon is a logical one. The Moon being ripped out of Earth orbit leaves the planet in environmental chaos, with earthquakes and tidal waves being reported on the final broadcast the Alphans pick up from their former home.'Breakaway' succeeds in presenting a dynamic and interesting group of people with whom viewers are about to embark on an incredible odyssey, including the edgy Commander Koenig, cool Dr Russell and hotheaded Alan Carter. It sets the stage for many future episodes in which the Alphans will be literally hurled into dangerous situations for which they find themselves totally unprepared; and, if one is inclined to think of it in such terms, 'Breakaway' is an apt metaphor for life itself.

Although lacking in some of the richer thematic concepts of certain later episodes, this is an admirable and highly refined debut for the series, full of spectacular visuals and promising characters. 'Breakaway' sets a high standard to live up to.

Rating: 8/10

1.2
MATTER OF LIFE AND DEATH

Screenplay by Art Wallace and Johnny Byrne
Directed by Charles Crichton

Selected Broadcast Dates:

UK	LWT:	
	Date: 29 November 1975.	Time: 5.50 pm
	Granada	
	Date: 19 December 1975.	Time: 6.35 pm
US	KRON (San Francisco)	
	Date: 29 November 1975.	Time: 7.00 pm

Credited Cast: Martin Landau (John Koenig), **Barbara Bain** (Helena Russell), **Barry Morse** (Victor Bergman), **Prentis Hancock** (Paul Morrow), **Clifton Jones** (David Kano), **Zienia Merton** (Sandra Benes), **Anton Phillips** (Bob Mathias), **Nick Tate** (Alan Carter), **Stuart Damon** (Parks)

Guest Artist: Richard Johnson (Lee Russell)

Uncredited Cast: Suzanne Roquette (Tanya Alexander), **Barbara Kelly** (Voice of Computer), **John Oxley** (Bannion), **Shane Rimmer** (Voice of Eagle Pilot), **Loftus Burton** (Operative Lee Oswald), **Chai Lee** (Operative Anna Wong), **Jeremy Anthony**, **Andrew Dempsey**, **Christopher Matthews**, **Michael Stevens**, **Maggie Wright** (Main Mission Operatives), **Melita Clarke** (Main Mission Technician), **Tony Allyn** (Security Guard Tony Allan), **Quentin Pierre** (Security Guard Pierce Quinton), **Alan Harris** (Alphan), **Saad Ghazi** (Orderly), **Christopher Williams** (Orderly)

Previously Titled: 'Siren Planet'.

Plot: Trouble brews on the beautiful planet Terra Nova as a Reconnaissance Eagle encounters problems and returns to the base with an extra passenger – Helena Russell's husband Lee, who was presumed dead when his spacecraft the Astro 7 disappeared near Jupiter in 1994. Lee warns that if the Alphans land on the seemingly tranquil and hospitable world, their opposite will annihilate them.

Quotes:
- **Koenig:** 'In three days we'll be out of range of that planet. Every hour that passes lessens our chances of finding a decent home. There are 300 lives, Helena. Can you or I deny them that chance?'
- **Helena:** 'Lee, try to help us. Help us to understand.'
- **Lee:** 'You face power beyond your understanding. It will destroy you.'
- **Victor:** 'So we've always thought – on Earth. But we're a long way from home and we're going to have to start thinking differently if we're going to come to terms with

space.'
- **Helena:** 'The first time I lost Lee I thought I'd never survive it. Now that it's happened again, I'm just numb. I guess I never really had him back.'
- **Lee:** 'Nobody dies. Matter never dies, Helena. It changes its form. There are many forms of life in space and many forms of death, too. I'm the image in the mirror – the opposite of myself.'
- **Lee:** 'See what you want to see.'

Filming Dates: Monday 14 January – Wednesday 30 January 1974

Incidental Music: The first use of stock incidental music occurs in this episode, with the inclusion of a track composed by Barry Gray for the film *Thunderbirds Are Go*.

Commentary:
Zienia Merton: 'I loved Charlie Crichton, because he liked actors. He empathised with actors.

'They used to give us the script two days before we shot it. I went downstairs and said, "I have to see Sylvia." She said, "Right. Come in." I said, "Sylvia, I don't know how to say this ..." and she said, "Oh my God, you're not pregnant are you?" I said, "No, it's worse than that. It's the next script ['Matter of Life and Death']. It says here that Prentis and I are walking in the woods somewhere and something funny happens, and I look over, and there's a spider on his shoulder! I'm supposed to say, 'Oh look! Don't worry about it ...' [Zienia gestures as if to brush it off.] No way! I hate spiders. I absolutely loathe them. If that spider is in Pinewood, I'm not coming to Pinewood! If I break my contract, if you sack me, if you sue me – do it. But this place is not big enough for the spider and me. I'm not doing it!" And Sylvia very nicely said, "Oh darling, I know. I had a chaise longue in my house, and I found out there were mice in it. You know what I did? We moved house. We sold the house!" I thought, "Well, that's good." What happened was they decided that the events on the planet with the spider were too Earthly. It was too much of this Earth. So there was no spider.'

Johnny Byrne: 'They didn't have a second script. And so I found scripts that had been written before the series became a real series ... I had to write a script that was geared to the actual production, [and I] based [it] on Art Wallace's [pre-existing] script, but there wasn't really very much in it. I did that very quickly. And because I did it very quickly and because it was filmable, they asked me to stay on until the end. Basically I think they asked me to stay on so that I would write my own scripts instead of going off somewhere else.'We had great trouble with "Matter of Life and Death". I can't quite remember what Art Wallace's script was like. I was working under great pressure. Two weeks to get this thing ready and I was pitched in, as they say, into the deep end. So we came up with a story that concerned anti-matter. They had a very good actor for it, Richard Johnson. And it was me kind of edging my way into the kind of *Space: 1999* ethos ... the Alpha Moonbase ethos. I remember it being made very well, and it went over reasonably okay ... I was absolutely thrilled, of course, to find myself working with Charles Crichton, who's a legend. He and I always got on extremely well. He could rub people up the wrong way; drive them mad by his attention to detail on the floor and his absolutely picking away at a script. But I reckoned that a man of such experience – having virtually lived through the entire film industry – had a lot to teach people like me, relatively new to the actual job of making films, [although] not to writing. So, I learned all I could from Charles. I think, for me, [he was] the director who took my work and did the best possible job with it, the one who really excited me to work with creatively – ... but he never really had a good script together until we came to the second series. "Matter of Life and Death" had been written too hazily, and could've done with a lot more rethinking about it, but it had to be done. But I really started getting into my [stride] when I worked with [subsequent director] David Tomblin.'

Bloopers: The text on Computer's screen reads, 'Resources capable of sustaining human life,' but the spoken voice says, 'Resources to sustain human life unlimited.'

An early scene set in a travel tube features a unique camera angle shooting up through the metal structure of a hospital gurney from the floor. It looks great, but where is the mattress for the patient to lie on? Don't worry – by the time a patient is wheeled away, the mattress has magically appeared.

How does Koenig's Commlock manage to get an external view of Carter's Eagle while they're down on the planet?

And, lastly, viewers not interested in the plot can amuse themselves by playing 'spot the missing button' on Koenig's Commlock.

Observations: Main Mission is still in its initial design incarnation here, with stairs to the windows on the opposite side of the set from the Main Computer wall, and the desks arranged tightly together. The set will be revised in upcoming episodes, most notably in 'Earthbound'. The depiction of Moonbase Alpha itself has advanced in this episode compared to 'Breakaway' – in external shots, lights are now visible within the base: a nice special effects touch.

As with 'Breakaway', there are numerous scenes shown in the opening credits that do not appear in the episode itself, or are apparently from alternate takes, including a whip pan from a lunar landscape to an Eagle on a launch pad. Also, the shot of Parks being electrocuted lacks the lightning special effects shown in the episode itself, and was shot from a different angle.

Notable firsts include the rare occurrence of a Yellow Alert and the debut appearance of the Red Alert designation. The Year One practice of Command Conferences taking place amongst the main crew at the big round table in Koenig's office is also started here; it is intriguing to consider this as being inspired by Arthurian legend and the Knights of the Round Table.

This also marks the first use of the Commlock Locator Beam (the second will be in 'Death's other Dominion'.) ITC's original promotional material in the 1970s made the mistake of referring to this as a 'Camelot' Locator Beam – a term that has been repeated countless times since by critics cannibalising earlier reviews, or basing their reviews of the series on ITC's press releases, rather than actually watching the episodes themselves.

Also interesting is the statement that Operation Exodus – a total evacuation of Moonbase Alpha – would take 48 hours.

Review: This is a strong second episode that, while in terms of overall quality is slightly inferior to 'Breakaway', nevertheless proceeds to top that explosive premiere by completely blowing up the Moon and killing everybody except for Helena. It can't be said that *Space: 1999* didn't have nerve! The script for 'Matter of Life and Death' was singled out for high praise by one reviewer of the day with this comment: 'The script is by Art Wallace and Johnny Byrne – they deserve an Emmy nomination at least.'[19]Art Wallace had a wide-ranging experience in science fiction television, including scripting an episode for *The Invaders* and two episodes each for the original *Star Trek* and the *Planet of the Apes* series. His original draft for this episode was called 'Siren Planet'. It was considered to be unworkable and was subsequently rewritten by Johnny Byrne. Essentially, at least on the surface, this is a take on Milton's epic *Paradise Lost* – a Judeo-Christian story of the temptation of Adam and Eve and their expulsion from the Garden of Eden. Here John Koenig and Helena Russell even eat the fruit!

The exacting, technical approach to the procedures of the Alphans is continued from 'Breakaway', but here is placed in the unknown. The background activity and hum of life on Alpha is also carried over. Precise acting, production and direction (which comes to an exciting peak on the planet) also continue in the frequently note-perfect manner set by 'Breakaway'. The camera shots also feature a number of interesting and unusual angles, which contribute to the distinctive cinematic look of the series. The style and feel of the episode is distinctly that of the early Year One segments. The characterisation is quite subtly achieved, but it is present and displays great depth. There is a large amount of visible emotion ranging from jokes to tears. The interaction between the characters is fairly formal, as they are still (to a degree) getting to know each other and coming to terms with their journey. Character development is gradual, shifting and progressing from episode to episode. Vewers are given a welcome look into Helena's quarters, the décor of which suggests that she has an interest in Oriental artwork. (Her quarters will be seen again in the much later episode 'Dragon's Domain', but will be quite different from those shown here.) They are also treated with a view into Bergman's laboratory, filled with old books and scientific gadgetry.

Commander Koenig shows more of his personality, demonstrating that he has a tendency to ignore even the strongest advice of his closest advisors and friends – Victor Bergman and Helena Russell. His choice to go down to Terra Nova is a mistake, but also points to a prime factor about humans – we make mistakes, and Koenig is no exception.

Notably, 'Matter of Life and Death' makes it clear that some time has passed since 'Breakaway' and that the Alphans have had other adventures and encountered other planets in the interim. Two lines in the dialogue make this point; the first Eagle mission to Terra Nova relays the message, 'I think we made it this time,' and Koenig himself states, 'Many things have happened since we broke away from our solar system.' These lines were included to allow for the episode to be shown later in the run of the series if desired. Unfortunately, the structure of the procedures followed by the Alphans here would be out of place shown later in the season. This episode clearly belongs second after 'Breakaway' in running order. There are more subtle hints that a degree of time has passed since leaving Earth orbit, including the advancement in the relationship between Koenig and Russell – just note the transitioning terminology from 'Commander' and 'Doctor' to 'John' and 'Helena'.

There are strikingly produced electrical storms that hit Eagle One and then, later in the episode, Helena Russell – sending her (actually stuntwoman Deborah Ford) flying

---

[19] Alder, Dick. *Los Angeles Times*: 'Some Lame Rerunning.' 9 January 1976.

dramatically across Medical Centre. Anti-matter will return as the driving force behind the plot of Year Two's 'A Matter of Balance'. The outer space effects are beautiful and the set of Terra Nova is a most impressive first alien planet for the series, courtesy of production designer Keith Wilson. There are many elements – the red water and skies, the strange trees and fruit – that contribute to creating a thoroughly convincing alien world. The sequences of the storm ripping across the planet, killing everyone but Helena, are some of the most successfully filmed and dramatic of the series. Parrots also feature on Terra Nova, providing a splash of colour and life to the planet. Zienia Merton has related an incident that took place while filming on the Terra Nova set, in which the actors all stopped the scene when they heard director Charles Crichton's instruction, 'Cut!' However, it wasn't Crichton – it was one of the parrots, which had learned to mimic the distinctive voice of the director. The parrot was then removed from the set.

The supporting characters are used to significant effect in this episode, with all of them – Paul, Sandra, Mathias and Carter – being the focus of key scenes. David Kano's impact lies in this being his first episode, and from the beginning Johnny Byrne's script creates an interesting relationship between Kano and Computer.

Following the space missions presented in 'Breakaway' – the successful Spacefarer 9 and the unsuccessful Meta Probe – viewers from here on will learn of an unbroken string of failed interplanetary and interstellar expeditions. In this episode it is the Astro 7, lost beyond Jupiter, and its crew presumed dead, until the discovery of Lee Russell here on Terra Nova. In future episodes ('Death's other Dominion', 'Dragon's Domain', 'Voyager's Return', 'Brian the Brain' and, with references to the Venus Space Station and its crew being wiped out by 'Venusian plague', 'The Exiles' and 'The Lambda Factor') these doomed space explorations are given focus and, combined, paint a very negative image of Earth's space program. Indeed, they make one question man's ability to travel into space, as alluded to in a line later spoken in the episode 'War Games' when Koenig is informed on an alien world, 'You have no place in space at all.' Parallels, connections and threads of themes are woven intricately throughout the entire series, awaiting discovery.

There is a lot of sadness in this episode, as well as a degree of wish fulfilment. It is a very pure example of *Space: 1999*, and the entire thrust of the story is about bereavement – focused on the character of Helena Russell. While 'Breakaway' was John Koenig's episode, 'Matter of Life and Death' belongs to Helena. She must face the loss of her husband for the second time, and on top of that must cope with the violent destructive forces of the planet killing all of her companions, her new potential love (Koenig), and stripping away the beauty of the paradise around her. Left with desolation and death, all alone, Helena cries to herself. It is a sequence of emotional power rarely felt in science fiction and caps off the remarkably varied performance Barbara Bain gives through this episode. Indeed, for fans of Bain and her character, 'Matter of Life and Death' must rank highly. Some have criticised Bain's performance in this episode as being unexpressive, but it can be suggested that they are missing the point entirely. Helena is in a state of shock and numbness at encountering her lost husband. She's enveloped in a fog through which she doesn't even hear John Koenig asking her questions. Considering this, Helena is portrayed exactly as she should be – with restraint and subtlety, and looking beyond these 'shock' scenes, she is played with a wide range of emotion.

The theme of first impressions is given treatment here (as it will be again in future episodes). As Shakespeare wrote, 'All that glisters is not gold,' and what looks like a paradise turns out to be anything but. In other words, 'Look before you leap'. It's an eternal life message, well delivered. The lovely ending is one of the most effective in the series – featuring optimism for the future and profound sadness for their loss, as well as the aforementioned appealingly hopeful concept of wish fulfillment.

Despite all of these positives, there are some lapses in story logic that undoubtedly are the fault of the speed at which this script had to be prepared and ready to shoot. It certainly could have been better if Johnny Byrne had been given more time to write it (see 'Commentary'). The scene where Koenig selects the landing crew is very stilted, both in the writing and in Martin Landau's performance. There are other scenes with similar problems. The motivations of Lee Russell are unnecessarily murky. Why is he so evasive? Why doesn't he just cut to the point with a clear early warning to the Alphans? Perhaps he is now so far removed from the human being he once was that he finds communication in such terms difficult. Or perhaps he isn't really Lee Russell at all, but an alien projection culled from Helena Russell's mind. Whatever the answers are to these questions, the character isn't completely effective, and neither is the actor; Richard Johnson has had a long and successful career in the business, but his performance here is far too rigid. As a side note, Lee Russell's interrogation features unusual red lighting and plays as if he is being tortured – if not physically, then psychologically. While there are interrogation-type scenes in future episodes, none carry the impact and implications of this one. It is unique within the annals of *Space: 1999*.

'Matter of Life and Death', overall, is quite entertaining – but it falls short of being one of the best episodes of the season.

Rating: 7/10

1.3
BLACK SUN

Screenplay by David Weir
Directed by Lee H Katzin

Selected Broadcast Dates:

UK	LWT:	
	Date: 8 November 1975.	Time: 5.50 pm
	Granada:	
	Date: 28 November 1975.	Time: 6.35 pm
US	KRON (San Francisco):	
	Date: 8 November 1975.	Time: 7.00 pm

Credited Cast: Martin Landau (John Koenig), **Barbara Bain** (Helena Russell), **Barry Morse** (Victor Bergman), **Prentis Hancock** (Paul Morrow), **Clifton Jones** (David Kano), **Zienia Merton** (Sandra Benes), **Anton Phillips** (Bob Mathias), **Nick Tate** (Alan Carter), **Jon Laurimore** (Smitty)

Guest Artist: Paul Jones (Michael 'Mike' Ryan)

Uncredited Cast: Suzanne Roquette (Tanya Alexander), **Barbara Kelly** (Voice of Computer), **Jan Harvey** (Alpha News Service Girl), **Vincent Wong** (Toshiro Fujita), **Ronald Chenery** (George Osgood), **Loftus Burton** (Operative Lee Oswald), **Chai Lee** (Operative Anna Wong), **Andrew Dempsey**, **Michael Stevens**, **Marc Zuber** (Main Mission Operatives), **Tony Allyn** (Security Guard Tony Allan), **Quentin Pierre** (Security Guard Pierce Quinton), **Alan Harris** (Alphan), **Melita Clarke** (Main Mission Technician), **Maggie Henderson** (Alphan Medic), **Sandor Eles** (Eagle Technician)

Plot: Following a diverted collision course with an asteroid, the Alphans discover that the Moon is being drawn into a Black Sun. Professor Bergman devises a powerful force field in an attempt to protect the base, and a survival ship is launched. As the Moon passes through the Black Sun, Koenig and Bergman have an amazing encounter.

Quotes:
- **Paul:** 'Commander, it's impossible, but we're changing course.'
- **Alan:** 'I'll send you a postcard.'
- **Helena:** 'I remember when I was a little girl, I was afraid of the dark. Isn't that funny?'
- **Sandra:** 'And I was afraid of doctors.'
- **Victor:** 'I'm a scientist. I don't know anything about God.'
- **Victor:** 'Ultimately, I suppose we all believe what we want to believe. Perhaps that's what reality is. One thing, though – the line between science and mysticism is just a line. And sometimes it makes me feel quite old.'

- **Tanya:** 'Paul – mind if I share the music with you?'
- **Koenig:** 'So that everything is everything else.' … 'Everything is everything else, and the whole Universe is living thought.'
- **Mysterious Voice:** 'I think a thought, perhaps, in every thousand of your years. You are never there to hear it.'
- **Victor:** 'Are you God?'
- **Mysterious Voice:** 'It was good to have known you.'

Filming Dates: Thursday 31 January – Thursday 21 February 1974

Commentary:
Martin Landau: 'I liked "Black Sun" early on and hoped that the entire texture of the show would be in that vein. Certain people in New York (at ITC) did not like "Black Sun". They were nervous about it. We wanted to make a show of that kind of quality. When they saw "Black Sun", there was some panic. Then, in the first year, they started changing the texture of the scripts … I was hoping that the series would continue to have that quality. It never quite did. Sometimes it got close to it, but it was always a fight. Not so much that "Black Sun" itself was a great episode, but it was the kind of show I felt the series should be. Well, there were a lot of episodes I liked. A lot of them were difficult.

'We had relationships, humour, a bunch of us, and music … beautiful! Unfortunately you didn't see the version I liked. It was jazzed up because some people said it was too slow. That was a period of finding out. That was the direction Barbara and I wanted the show to go in. Gerry also. We watched "Black Sun" and said it was really marvellous and it was what *Space* needed. It was the direction the rest of the show should have.

'It was very intimate and character driven, and we had a female God, which doesn't happen everyday. There was something about that that was somewhat haunting. It had a sort of a mystical quality about it. Barry and I sitting there having that drink of brandy and waiting for doomsday, so to speak.'

Barbara Bain: '"Black Sun" was a beautiful one. That was a quality script. It was a direction the show was starting to take and I wish had taken more. That's what the hope and excitement of doing it was. They were concerned that it was a [bit too] intellectual, which is unfortunate. I loved that – a beautiful script. The scene between [Barry and Marty] is marvellous … [Regarding the cigar and brandy in the episode.] 'Barry. Yeah, that was his [idea]. I think he brought that in … We were always looking for those types of touches. We wanted a pet up there, but we didn't get a pet.'

Barry Morse: 'I do remember our third episode, "Black Sun". It asked the question, "What's it all about?" There was that famous scene between the two of us in which we drank brandy and talked about what we thought was our impending demise, expressing what we felt about the purpose of life. And that's the occasion where we spoke those lines, which many people (I'm touched to discover) remember, when Martin – drinking the brandy – said, "To everything that might have been." And I said, "To everything that was." It's one of the moments in *Space: 1999* that I'm most proud of. It had human values and no explosions, just two human beings. It's very gratifying to Martin and me, that on any list of the audience's preferences among the different episodes, "Black Sun" will almost always come out very near, if not on, the top. I like to think that it was because of the input that we, the actors, had on the script. Incidentally, I think I improvised the scarf that I wore in that sequence because it was an opportunity to hint a little bit that Bergman was not entirely conventional in his tastes.

'It was one of the episodes where we *did* get to grips with some more philosophical speculation, and I only wish we had done it more. It drew into question what we believe and how and why we believe it. That seems to have caught hold of the imaginations of our viewers in all the years since, perhaps more than any of the other episodes. If only the general production and the writing had had more of that sort of character about it. It certainly remains in my remembrance as one of the very best episodes, where Martin, Barbara and I were able to inject rather more in the way of human interest in the show. That, I always felt, was the sort of thing that might have been.

'When Martin and I were drinking the brandy, we were actually consuming burnt sugar and water, as it always is when it comes from the prop department! [Viewers] sometimes imagine – and it has happened of course – that [actors] do use real alcoholic drinks. In the matter of shooting a television series, when you may have as many as seven or eight different takes of one scene, you'd drink yourself into insensibility and be flat on the floor if you drank real brandy! There's always been a convention that the prop department would supply a liquid, which in this case looked satisfactorily like brandy. If you sip it and react in the manner that you probably would if you were drinking a good old brandy, well then the audience is convinced that you are indeed drinking a brandy.

'I think I'm at one with most followers and fans of *Space: 1999*, because the question of favourite episodes is quite often asked at conventions and meetings … It's very striking that a majority of people will tell you that their favourite episode is "Black Sun".'

Zienia Merton: '"Black Sun" is a really good episode. The whole first series was. We really got shortchanged – it actually was a lot better than we got credit for.'

[Regarding God in the episode.] 'I must admit when I heard it, the concept that He was a She was very advanced thinking. And the voice did sound like me, but it wasn't. That would really have been cheap to use me, and one thing they were not on that production, was cheap.

'[My character] had another boyfriend to begin with. I had Paul Jones and they kept saying, "You have a boyfriend in the next show," and I thought, "Great!" I never met him! Because he was on the screen and I was in Main Mission. It was the most remote controlled romance anyone has ever had.'

Prentis Hancock: 'The one I liked the best always was "Black Sun". I think, for me, it encapsulated the best of what the series was about in terms of exploration and human spirit, and conquering the odds and not losing hope. It had a lot of very, very nice qualities. That's the one I would take with me to the desert island if I had just one to take.

'I've often thought about why I particularly enjoyed the opening episodes of *Space: 1999* … I felt there was something really *happening*, which tended to dissipate a bit, I think. One always thought it was the money, the dreadful strikes, the three-day week, and all the stuff we had. Our whole industry was in a mess in the '70s. I sometimes thought we were dragging a '60s series into the '70s. Well, I [still] think there were elements of that, but I think there were also other wonderful things. It is the intrinsic, sort of organic, quality that I think attracts the fans to the series. There's something about the ideas in the centre of "Breakaway" and "Black Sun", which are fairly universal.'

'"Black Sun" I would think is the favorite episode because it showed us off-duty, facing up to reality and those things that human beings have to do in television series without the fun and games of another episode. We're just ourselves. I think one of the defining moments is before Koenig and Bergman have their scene together; they dismiss me with a line, "He's a good man, Paul." So there was a continuity about relationship with each other. Had I been a bigger character, had I been a star, they'd have kept me in that scene. But I was second rank, and that's fine – that's the way that series was. But I was also part of the command structure, so I never really went against what was going on because my loyalty was to the Commander. Not to Nick Tate, who would sometimes take him on, but he was an outsider flying a spaceship around the place. So my loyalty was to Koenig; if Koenig had gone down I took over. There was no question of me going against the grain.

'Lee Katzin was the director, who – along with George Bellack and [Christopher Penfold] – engendered for me the spirit of the first series, with "Black Sun", and then we lost Lee … he just vanished. But I think he deserves credit.'

Sylvia Anderson: 'Barry Morse was playing with Martin (in one of the most notable scenes in "Black Sun"), and I think they worked very well together. I think "Black Sun" was a very good episode. It was a very intense subject, thinking about it, so when we had a chance to do something really serious and thought provoking, I think that's when the show really worked for me. I think when it goes on to be a bit too pantomime, if you like, and weird creatures are showing up, then it lost it for me.'

Christopher Penfold: 'David Weir is a wonderfully talented and imaginative writer, and it was my decision to approach him to write a script for the series. I had long admired the work he had done on other films and television drama series in Britain. The notion of travelling through a black hole was something that engaged both of us. We discussed, in broad terms, the outline of a story to encompass that theme. David then went off and wrote an episode, and – I remember I was actually shocked by this, because he was so experienced – the first draft that he delivered was actually twice as long as it should have been. It was quite clear that the very notion that David was dealing with had just blown his mind. So I was confronted initially, even with the first draft, with the almost impossible task of trying to cut down to 50 minutes something that, had it been shot in that form, would have run for 120. So I went back to David for a second draft and we got closer. But the pressures of production began to mount up, and the need for that episode to be finished was pressing. What I would ideally have loved to do would have been to work with David and educate him in the ways of this particular series, so that he could have done the work. And had there been time, I'm sure that would have been possible. But there came a cut-off point at which I had to take the script home on a Friday night and come back on a Monday morning with it ready to go into pre-production. In that weekend I wrote "Black Sun". Johnny and I spent a Friday afternoon just kind of kicking around the idea, and I drove back from Pinewood to my house in London on Friday night and sat down in the shed at the bottom of my garden on Saturday morning and wrote "Black Sun" and took the script into the studio on Monday morning. It's rough in all kinds of ways, but I think it has that kind of naked creative intensity behind it, which can sometimes – not always – come out of crisis management, but occasionally it works well.

'I think philosophy is a science, and "Black Sun" has a lot of philosophy. I was much more interested in the philosophical implications of stretching time and increasing time.

'If scripts weren't working, I had both Johnny Byrne and Edward di Lorenzo with me as script editors, and quite a lot of the episodes they and I were credited with were rescue operations … It was a very technical business writing for *Space: 1999*, understanding the requirements of that strange mixture of studio and special effects, and quite a lot of writers didn't really get hold of it.

'"Black Sun" is pretty much as I wrote it, actually, and it's intentionally vague. I haven't had many conversations with God myself, so I had little to go on. It was more a question of engaging with the idea of there being a super-entity. And of how one might respond in the face of that kind of direct encounter.

[Regarding whether or not "Black Sun" was influenced by *2001: A Space Odyssey*.] 'Quite possibly. I think it's a great movie. Who knows the extent to which other experiences or other films, movies, or poems by John Keats [are inspirations]? It's very difficult to identify them as particular influences, but they very well could have been. I don't remember making that immediate connection, but my enthusiasm for *2001* is very great … But, [with] "Black Sun", having taken on David's idea, I hope he felt and feels that we did some kind of justice to it. I felt pretty pleased with the way that one came out, too.'

Johnny Byrne: '"Black Sun" was a very interesting experience. Again, there wasn't that much knowledge about black holes at the time. But I remember long sequences of Koenig and Bergman just sitting there, talking. It was amazing. Freddy [Freiberger – Year Two producer] would never have allowed that. Well, you see, the dictates of plot-plot-plot, relentless story-story-story deny you that.'

Bloopers: How does Alpha manage to see the side profile view of Ryan's ship as it flies toward the Black Sun?

In the scenes of the survival Eagle, compare the effects shots with the interior shots of the pilot's section. Specifically, watch for Carter's helmet visor – it's down for the effects shots and up for the interiors.

Observations: On the technology front, viewers are introduced to the watch-like vital sign monitors worn by everybody on Alpha. Their presence has previously been inferred in 'Breakaway', and the devices will appear again in future episodes.

Review: The rewards of this episode lie in the Alphan characters quietly biding their time – talking, playing guitar, sharing a drink and some philosophy. There are interesting parallels between the plight here of Moonbase Alpha and that of the *Titanic*. As the Moon is about to sink into the depths of the Black Sun, they even go so far as to launch a lifeboat in the form of the survival Eagle.

Some of the special effects in this episode are a bit unconvincing. There are several instances that stand out, including the shot of the laser beam firing into the Black Sun, as the two elements appear entirely out of proportion to each other – the Black Sun too small and the laser beam too large. As well, the superimposed explosion of the Eagle is entirely unconvincing. But these lapses are forgivable, especially in light of the overwhelming quality of the character drama; and other effects are absolutely stunning, including most of the views of the Black Sun itself.

This is an episode that allows the entire cast to shine brightly. 'Black Sun' is really a character piece. It focuses sharply on the people of Moonbase Alpha and stays there through most of the hour, and by doing so it provides the greatest wealth of subtle, rich characterisation to be found in the entire series. It is virtually unimaginable that the episode could have been more successful in portraying human warmth between the Alphans.

The relationships between the characters are continuing to develop. Paul spends what he believes to be his last moments playing guitar, and is joined by a lonely Tanya, trying to cover up her fear as she wraps herself in a jacket to keep warm. It's one of the most sexually charged scenes in the series. Oh yes, and Sandra gets to faint – something that actress Zienia Merton quite correctly felt was inappropriate for a supposedly highly trained professional on Moonbase Alpha.

The long discussion between Bergman and Koenig leading up to their encounter with the Black Sun is compelling, and their toast ('To everything that might have been' 'To everything that was') constitutes the single most memorable moment of *Space: 1999*. Not only that, but it's a wonderful way to look at life.

The actress who provided the voice of God in the Black Sun was un-credited and her identity has long been a mystery to fans of the series. While this is not a confirmed fact, it has been suggested that Joanna Dunham might have performed the voice-over. She was at Pinewood Studios filming her role in the upcoming episode 'Missing Link' while 'Black Sun' was in post-production. Did she provide the voice of God? Listen to her performance as Vana in that later episode and compare it against the voice in the Black Sun: there is a marked similarity. While 'Breakaway' was constructed around Koenig and 'Matter of Life and Death' focused on Helena, 'Black Sun' is primarily a character study of Professor Bergman. So much of his character is fleshed out here, as are his relationships with Koenig, Helena and Kano. It is obvious that the amiable Bergman is unimpressed with Alpha's Computer and considers the human mind superior. 'I ought to know better than to ask you,' he says to Computer before shutting it off and doing some calculations himself. He also grows impatient with Computer's slow calculations and says, 'One jump ahead of you, Computer.' Viewers are introduced to the fact that Bergman has an artificial heart – a plot device that will be used again in future episodes, although never to its full potential. Here Bergman is saved from electrocution by virtue of his mechanical heart. One of the most beautiful little scenes in the series features Bergman and Helena, just before her departure on the survival Eagle; he gives her a jacket, a kiss and a smile, and then they walk away, with neither of them having said a word. It's incredibly touching. Bergman's wisdom shines through the darkness of the Black Sun and shows him to be somewhat more of a metaphysical professor than a cold, hard scientist.

The science of 'Black Sun' has often been the subject of scorn from critics, but it is all quite convincing within the context of the episode itself. The descriptions of the Black Sun are in reference to what is commonly called a Black Hole. It can be surmised that the writers selected the term 'Sun' instead of 'Hole' for use in the *Space: 1999* universe as an artistic, almost poetic, choice. Call it what you will, it doesn't change what it is. This

'Black Sun' terminology will continue to be used in later episodes ('Dragon's Domain' and 'Seed of Destruction'), providing a very welcome element of continuity.

Director Lee H Katzin was not invited back to helm any additional episodes after this one due to the fact that his segments were taking too long to film. 'Breakaway' had taken 26 days, while 'Black Sun' took 15. The aim was to complete episodes in nine days each, according to accounts from actor Barry Morse, although other sources cite an intended 12-day principal photography shoot. No matter how long it took, Katzin did manage to create a classic episode of science fiction television. There are marvellous aspects to his direction, including making effective use of the scale of the sets to amplify feelings of fear on the part of the Alphans in confronting the Black Sun – they are very little when they come face to face with the forces of the universe.'Black Sun' is one of the most metaphysical shows (if not *the* most metaphysical) in the series. Like 'Breakaway' before it, it owes a lot to *2001: A Space Odyssey*. The Mysterious Unknown Force (discussed above in the opening article on Year One) not only aids Moonbase Alpha in surviving its journey through the Black Sun, but it also mysteriously returns the survival Eagle to the base, safely, across the universe. (One question, though – why did the MUF not intervene to save Mike Ryan?) Then there is the conversation that Koenig and Bergman have in the Black Sun with God (or the Mysterious Unknown Force). Although it is never explicitly identified as such, the characters acknowledge the mysticism with which they are faced and consider the possibility that there is a cosmic intelligence looking out for them. As Helena states at the end of the show, 'Something brought us home.' The complete picture of the purpose of the MUF in the lives of the Alphans is never completely clear, but the concept of predestination is introduced to their journey. The episode only really falters in its earliest scenes with the character Mike Ryan. The character is irresponsible, the dialogue is weak ('Sir, all it has is a lot of gravity') and Paul Jones gives an amateurish performance lacking necessary depth.'Black Sun' is about many things – it is obviously an examination of belief, spiritual and metaphysical concepts, as well as the differences (or similarities) between science and religion. There are also significant themes of home and belonging as the Alphans begin to accept their situation and their lives on the Moon; this is the first reference to Alpha as 'home'. All in all, 'Black Sun' is one of the most intriguing and important episodes of *Space: 1999*.

Rating: 9/10

1.4
RING AROUND THE MOON

Screenplay by Edward di Lorenzo
Directed by Ray Austin

Selected Broadcast Dates:

UK	LWT:	
	Date: 17 January 1976.	Time: 11.30 am
	Granada:	
	Date: 30 January 1976.	Time: 6.35 pm
US	KRON (San Francisco):	
	Date: 27 December 1975.	Time: 7.00 pm

Credited Cast: Martin Landau (John Koenig), **Barbara Bain** (Helena Russell), **Barry Morse** (Victor Bergman), **Prentis Hancock** (Paul Morrow), **Clifton Jones** (David Kano), **Zienia Merton** (Sandra Benes), **Anton Phillips** (Bob Mathias), **Nick Tate** (Alan Carter), **Max Faulkner** (Ted Clifford)

Uncredited Cast: Prentis Hancock (Voice of Triton Probe), **Suzanne Roquette** (Tanya Alexander), **Andrew Dempsey, Robert Phillips, Michael Stevens** (Main Mission Operatives), **Tony Allyn** (Security Guard Tony Allan), **Quentin Pierre** (Security Guard Pierce Quinton), **Alan Harris** (Alphan), **Christopher Williams** (Medican Orderly Williams)

Plot: Alpha finds itself enveloped in a ring of force projected by an alien probe that is using engineer Ted Clifford's mind as an organic computer relay, eventually resulting in his death. From the planet Triton, these aliens are on a mission to collect information, and the next Alphan they select to use as a tool is Helena Russell. The race is on to stop the Tritonian probe before Dr Russell's brain is burnt up like Ted Clifford's.

Quotes:
- **Victor:** 'I've got a nasty feeling we're being watched.'
- **Triton Beings:** 'Earthmen – do not resist. You are the captives of the planet Triton.'
- **Alan:** 'Me? No, I was in Never-Never Land.'
- **Triton Beings:** 'We are the eyes of the planet Triton. Everything that is, has been and will be is recorded by us.'
- **Triton Beings**: 'Time is an illusion, Commander Koenig.'
- **Mathias:** 'You have a lovely optic nerve, Doctor Russell.'
- **Victor:** 'Perhaps knowledge isn't the answer, after all.'
- **Koenig:** 'Then what is?'

Filming Dates: Wednesday 27 February – Thursday 14 March 1974

Observations: One type of Moonbase Alpha medical technology used quite frequently throughout the series is thermographic scans. From 'Breakaway' all the way through Year Two, these would provide a useful visual aid to explaining such medical conditions as the ever-problematic 'brain damage'.

The set of the Medical Care Unit is re-used from 'Matter of Life and Death'. This is unusual, because throughout Year One the Medical Centre sets were changed quite regularly. Rather than this showing a flagrant lack of continuity, it suggests the diversity of rooms or departments making up the medical section of Alpha – rather like a hospital on Earth.

Review: The opening teaser is tense and dramatic. It demonstrates the clear and distinctive style of an early 'pure' Year One episode and is marred only by the stiff performance of Max Faulkner as Ted Clifford. The musical score adds greatly to the drama, from eerie sound effects to the up-tempo track accompanying the lunar walk sequence – there's something oddly entertaining about disco sci-fi!

There are a number of visually dynamic stunts in the opening sequence alone, including the hurling of Kano across Main Mission, Paul leaping at Clifford and the shockwave from the Triton Probe's force field sending those in Main Mission tumbling. The cinematography in 'Ring Around the Moon' is unique among the episodes of *Space: 1999* and is almost abstract or psychedelic in some of its depictions. Iconic series imagery abounds. It's a very colourful episode, and the editing is sharp and distinctly adds to the proceedings.

A bothersome flaw in the episode is the expectation that Bergman or Computer should know something about the planet Triton – its location or other such information. This goes against the Year One emphasis on limited, imperfect and improvised technology and knowledge, and seems even to be out of place with much of this episode itself. This is knowledge the Alphans should not even consider having.

The interaction between Koenig and Alan Carter continues to develop. They are still tense and disagreeable, but even through the course of this one episode an astute viewer can sense the progression of their understanding towards each other, thanks to the writing of di Lorenzo and the performances of Martin Landau and Nick Tate. Landau is also outstanding during a scene (also featuring Bergman) set in the Medical Centre as Koenig is regaining consciousness. Aptly placed rapid-cut images of Helena intersect with Landau's disturbed, weak and disoriented portrayal of Koenig – a marked contrast to the solemn certainty displayed by Barry Morse. Also interesting in terms of characterisation is a possibly disturbing aspect of Kano's personality, touched on with his line, 'It's no use, sir.' This displays a rather fatalistic and pessimistic side to him that contrasts with the good humour he displays at other times. It is a fascinating trait to consider, and will appear again in the episode 'The Infernal Machine'. Clifton Jones effectively portrays these conflicting elements inherent in David Kano.

'Ring Around the Moon' has many appealing special effects, including the sequence showing an Eagle (deflected from the Triton Probe) tumbling back to the Moon. Another very unusual and impressive effect displays an Eagle traveling through the absolute blackness within the Triton Probe. The final destruction of the Probe is a spectacular display of *Space: 1999*'s fireworks-style explosions. Unfortunately, not all of the effects are of the same quality. Some of the energy beams from the Triton Probe, and the force field around the nose cone of the Eagle, are poorly done and rank among the worst effects of the first series.

It is interesting to note the similarity Bergman points out between the 'Eyes of

Heaven' in the Pyramid Texts of the Old Kingdom from Earth and the 'Eyes of Triton'. There's also the eye-like appearance of the probe, as well as that of the Tritonians themselves. It draws a fascinating comparison that could suggest that the Tritonians had been to Earth in ancient times, observing, and were recorded by the humans of those times as the 'Eyes of Heaven'. It's the first apparent inspiration from author Erich von Däniken (*Chariots of the Gods*) to appear in *Space: 1999*, and it won't be the last. As stated in the show, the only purpose of the Triton Probe is to collect and record information: 'We are the eyes of the planet Triton. Everything that is, has been and will be is recorded by us.' Unfortunately, we don't learn *why* they do this, and without that motivation they remain hollow ciphers.

Thematically, 'Ring Around the Moon' is about exploitation. The Triton Probe uses Ted Clifford and Helena Russell to its own advantage, with no regard to their wellbeing. To the Tritonian way of thinking, the end justifies the means. Their purpose is simply to possess knowledge, and that is also their flaw. What the Alphans are learning on their journey is clearly stated by Bergman (in his wisdom), 'Perhaps knowledge isn't the answer, after all.' To which Koenig replies, 'Then what is?' As they speed through the universe, encountering moral and ethical challenges along with the purely physical ones, the Alphans are on a quest to find the answer to that question. The answer, as they come to realise, is the wisdom to use the knowledge. Although not a fundamental flaw of the plot, another factor that mars 'Ring Around the Moon' is that the script exhibits some astonishingly bad astronomy, confusing the terms 'galaxy' and 'universe'. As well, there is an apparent lack of certainty from the writer as to what the point of the whole episode is. There is a strong degree of repetition in the back-and-forth Eagle flights (which accomplish nothing except to extend the running time of the episode), and a limited amount of story logic. In presenting the Voice of Triton, the decision was made to use Prentis Hancock projecting a forced whisper, when undoubtedly a better alternative could have been found that might have come across as somewhat more threatening.'Ring Around the Moon' is one of the poorest episodes of the first series, but still works on enough levels to be regarded as acceptable viewing. Even when Year One is bad, it's still reasonably good.

Rating: 6/10

1.5
EARTHBOUND

Screenplay by Anthony Terpiloff
Directed by Charles Crichton

Selected Broadcast Dates:

UK	LWT:	
	Date: 6 December 1975.	Time: 7.00 pm
	Granada:	
	Date: 26 December 1975[20]	
US	KRON (San Francisco):	
	Date: 14 February 1976.	Time: 7.00 pm

Credited Cast: Martin Landau (John Koenig), **Barbara Bain** (Helena Russell), **Barry Morse** (Victor Bergman), **Prentis Hancock** (Paul Morrow), **Clifton Jones** (David Kano), **Zienia Merton** (Sandra Benes), **Anton Phillips** (Bob Mathias), **Nick Tate** (Alan Carter)

Guest Artist: Roy Dotrice (Commissioner Simmonds)

Special Guest Star: Christopher Lee (Captain Zantor)

Uncredited Cast: Suzanne Roquette (Tanya Alexander), **Barbara Kelly** (Voice of Computer), **Sarah Bullen** (Operative Kate), **June Bolton** (Operative June), **Loftus Burton** (Operative Lee Oswald), **Andrew Dempsey, Joy Harrison, Robert Phillips, Maggie Wright** (Main Mission Operatives), **Tony Allyn** (Security Guard Tony Allan), **Quentin Pierre** (Security Guard Pierce Quinton), **Alan Harris** (Alphan), **Roy Everson** (Security Guard in corridor), **Maggie Henderson** (Alphan Medic in corridor), **Rhonda Parker** (Female Kaldorian), **Christine Hewett** (Female Kaldorian)

Plot: Bound for Earth, an alien ship from the planet Kaldor crashes on the Moon. As the Alphans befriend the Kaldorians, the offer is made for one human to travel with Captain Zantor and his people back to Earth. Commander Koenig institutes a review by Computer to select the most suitable person on Alpha to make the journey … but Commissioner Simmonds plots to be the one to return – at any cost!

Quotes:
- **Simmonds:** 'Impossible? The impossible takes just a little longer, that's all, Commander.'
- **Zantor:** 'The similarities between us are greater than the differences.'
- **Simmonds:** 'I've been a politician all my life. I don't believe in chance.'
- **Simmonds:** 'I got to be Commissioner by doing what was necessary, not what was

---

[20] In some instances the Granada broadcast dates recorded in this book do not include time of day as the information is unavailable.

right.'
- **Helena:** 'We can't encourage false hope.'
- **Simmonds:** 'Hope is the key to morale.'
- **Alan:** 'The relative position of Earth, sir …' [Pointing] 'It's that away.'
- **Zantor:** 'The Libra bird was our symbol of peace and freedom, but like everything else on our planet, it ultimately became sterile. When we left, there were only two surviving pairs, and their eggs – when filled with gold – were greatly prized as memorials to our fading life.'
- **Victor:** 'Maybe I've had enough of Earth and its so-called civilisation.'
- **Simmonds:** 'Hello, Earth. Hello, Earth. This is Commissioner Simmonds, returning home after 75 years.'

Filming Dates: Friday 15 March – Monday 1 April 1974

Commentary:
Martin Landau: '*Space: 1999* was a difficult show to do on a weekly basis because of the special effects, because of the logistics, because of the problems with miniatures and all the stuff that was done on the screens down at Bray Studios. There were questions one had to ask all the time: "What does the spaceship that we're frightened of look like? How big is it?" Take the Chris Lee show ["Earthbound"], which was early on, where we were reacting to this thing coming towards us. When I saw the thing in the rushes it looked like a flower! I couldn't believe it. I walked into Gerry's office and said, "You can't use that! Take those things off, because it looks benign. It looks harmless, sweet, like a panda." Anyway, he did. He changed it. But it still didn't look as precocious as it should. It didn't look as if it had enough history behind it.'

Barbara Bain: 'I liked doing "Earthbound". We had the most amazing moments in that. Christopher Lee was probably six foot five or eight inches tall. He was an enormous, tall, sweet, gentle man. His height was intrinsic to the story and I had some scenes with him. I'm not six foot six, but they wanted as much disparity as possible. They put him on a box. They used to do it, and still do it in the movies, to line up the height between the two principals. They call it an "apple box", or "half an apple". Christopher Lee never in his life had to stand on a box! They usually have to prop up everybody next to him. He couldn't believe it. So, they did prop him up on a box, which of course made the disparity between us even greater. He was stunned, but he enjoyed it. It was fun. That was the only time in his life he's ever been asked to be taller!'

Barry Morse: 'Roy Dotrice was one of our guest stars, appearing in our "Breakaway" and "Earthbound" episodes. I don't think I'd worked with him before, but he's a good pro and a good actor. Christopher Lee was a chum of ours, and I had worked with him before.
'The political structure of Moonbase Alpha wasn't discussed, but there again I have to revert to saying that there was precious little time for in-depth discussion of relationships or structures, because we were starting with less than one script and it was immensely important to get on with just shooting it. So, unfortunately, there was very little opportunity to discuss such things as the militaristic as opposed to socialistic structure of the community itself. These things emerged more by chance than by consideration. It may have been presented that the crew of Moonbase Alpha were a

more or less socialistic outfit. They needed to be, of course, having been cut off from Earth. It may be this sense of community gradually established among the Alpha crew was perhaps interpreted as being *too* socialistic by people in the United States who had control over the various networks. I don't know what Gerry's or Sylvia's personal political views might be – I never discussed it with them, and they didn't express any firm opinions about such things.'

Prentis Hancock: 'When you do something like *Space: 1999* you work in a vacuum, in a way. We see what we do, our work. Down the road at Bray Studios there were a whole bunch of other guys working on special effects. And Barry Gray was working elsewhere on music. The only time we saw them was when they melded together and we saw the whole finished show. I think one of the biggest and best compliments we ever heard was when Zienia and I were watching this thing and some of the boys from the special effects department – who had previously done a lot of puppets for Gerry – left the screening saying, "It's better with actors!"'

Zienia Merton: 'We had very bad arrangements at the stages. There were hardly any dressing rooms and we often had to double up. But I do remember one episode with Christopher Lee and the Kaldorians. The three Kaldorian girls shared my dressing room, which I didn't mind, except they were so big and I was so tiny. I felt like I was intruding. So I said, "Next time, I only want people my size". On the first series I always had my own dressing room. If I was away, someone else might use it, but I'd always come back to it. There was none of that on the second series. I was shunted around like no one's business. But I never felt on the first series that I was being hard done by in sharing my dressing room. After all, you have to muck in.

'On the first series, they didn't actually write [specifically] for us. They said they did, but we all struggled like mad to find something human, something plausible in all the characters. I remember on the second day, we did a sort of mock test, everybody coming along and introducing themselves, saying, "I'm Zienia Merton, playing the part of Sandra Benes, chief data operator." I could never say that. And I hated it so much that I was very coy about it. I hate being brash [anyway], although some people said very brashly, "Hi, I'm so and so and I'm terrific," and so on … I sort of crept forward and quietly mumbled my lines. The scriptwriters worked up on this, [so] in subsequent plots I would smile shyly at someone. But the point is that I wouldn't be that timid or reserved for the position I was holding in Main Mission. Actually, someone in America wrote and said, "Thank God you're in the series, because at least we get a signal about what the plot is saying. Because it seems anytime anything is about to happen, you fall down and faint, and we know when the action is over because you get up." I was a sort of emotional barometer.'

Christopher Lee: '[*Space: 1999*] was an interesting thing to do because, I think I'm right to say, it was almost the first British science fiction television [film] series. British in so far as it was made in Pinewood. And we, as I recall, were aliens who were in a state of suspended animation, lying inside these great big sarcophagi. You might say that this sort of series preceded a great many of the [later] science fiction films and television. The clothes were fascinating actually because we weren't like [aliens are portrayed] today – or have been for the last 10 or 15 or 20 years. We weren't creatures who were unrecognisable. We were to all intents and purposes more or less human beings. Of course, everyone was very, very tall, including the girls … They were very charming, too. It gives one a little bit of hope for the future if you can explore space and find girls like that.'

Keith Wilson: 'Christopher Lee is a very grand gentleman, very powerful. I designed the make-up for him, and it meant I had to fill in his nose [between his eyes]. It was an integral part of the make-up, and he said, "Do I have to have this here?" I said, "Well, if you wouldn't mind." He said, "Well, all right then." Anyway, we did the make-up and we came to the end of the day. The make-up people took this off and it took the skin off his nose! He looked at me and went, "Are you satisfied now?"'

Bloopers: When Christopher Lee lies down in Zantor's stasis chamber towards the end of the show, the white wig he is wearing falls off, revealing his own dark hair beneath. This same white wig will later appear on Peter Cushing in 'Missing Link', Margaret Leighton in 'Collision Course', Leo McKern in 'The Infernal Machine' and Joan Collins in 'Mission of the Darians'.

When Carter drops off the crew and passenger module at the alien ship, a special effects mistake has the departing Eagle already off the lunar surface before firing its booster engines.

Another blooper occurs in the scene where Alan Carter and his co-pilot watch the crash-landing of Captain Zantor's ship. Keep your eye on the co-pilot, because in one shot he disappears!

And, finally, while Simmonds is screaming in his casket at the end of the episode, one of the Kaldorians (wearing orange) sits up inside her stasis chamber, and another (in green) turns his head to look at Simmonds.

Observations: The Main Mission set is revamped here, removing the stairs that previously led to the windows on the opposite wall from the X5 Computer and balcony, and rearranging the desks with space between each.

A shot of Barry Morse as Bergman accompanies his credit in the opening titles of the series for the first time. Until now his credit had been displayed over a space effect background.

Review: Rebounding from the early low-point of 'Ring Around the Moon', 'Earthbound' is *Space: 1999's* first exploration into immortality and is set up with a degree of detail that lends believability to the scientific concepts and alien technology contained within. In common with the preceding episode, it involves an encounter with aliens on their way to Earth. Here, though, the Kaldorians are a wonderfully conceived and presented alien culture. They are peaceful, freedom loving, benevolent and soft-spoken. It's a nice touch that they are the first actual aliens embodied for the Alphans and that it is an encounter culminating in friendship, demonstrated clearly with the Kaldorian gift of their treasured golden eggs. This is an optimistic encounter that shows the Alphans can find a common bond with other travellers and races in the galaxy. The Kaldorian ship looks a bit like a surrealistic Easter egg, but the special effects are outstandingly produced. One oddity here is that two Rescue Eagles (identified by red stripes on their passenger modules) are sent out to intercept the alien ship at the start of the episode, when normally the standard Reconnaissance Eagles would be used. This is, notably, the first appearance of the Rescue Eagle. There are some wonderful Eagle effects throughout, including the Rescue ship leaving its passenger module behind at the Kaldorian craft, and the sequence of an Eagle flying low over the lunar terrain. Also impressive is the return visit to the Eagle hangers – previously seen in the background of 'Breakaway'.

The highpoint of cinematography in this episode comes when Koenig enters the Kaldorian ship for the first time, a distorted dark shape moving amongst the light. It's very alien-looking and very effective.

All of the performances are excellent, but guest stars Christopher Lee and Roy Dotrice excel, their characters sharply in contrast with each other – Zantor is tranquil and peaceful; Simmonds is angry and desperate.

Commissioner Simmonds returns in this episode, making it almost a sequel to 'Breakaway'. This also brings a return to some of the politics of Earth, as featured in 'Breakaway'. In a series that will later all too often abandon regular characters, or randomly create new ones, it's very much appreciated that the production team thought to bring back the Commissioner for a repeat performance. It's obvious that Simmonds is not only unsuited to Alpha and unhappy being there, but he is also greatly disliked and unwanted by his fellow crewmembers on the base. That he would be the one selected to return to Earth with the Kaldorians is obvious from the start. He knows he should go, but he is unwilling to leave the matter to chance or to a decision that is out of his own hands. His blackmailing of Alpha to get what he wants is successful, but at the ultimate price: there isn't time for Zantor properly to program Simmonds' matrix into the Kaldorians' computer for the suspended animation journey to be successful. Zantor's possible motivations here are left open to question. Simmonds awakens shortly after leaving the Moon – a prisoner in a stasis chamber that will be his casket. He's effectively buried alive. It is a chilling end to the episode and to the Commissioner. Simmonds represents the worst of humanity and is a character bound to the Earth. He symbolises what the Alphans have left behind and his place is not with them on their journey through space. As Zantor states, 'The Commissioner is diseased.' He simply had to go, and his comeuppance is richly deserved.

'Earthbound' has the dual concepts of betrayal and friendship as its central contrast. Simmonds betrays everyone on Alpha – his own race, even if he has nothing in common with them besides genetic history – for his own selfish purposes. And the first-contact friendship between the Alphans and Kaldorians is best personified by the relationship between Captain Zantor and Helena Russell, who manage a subtle flirtation and obvious connection in their scenes together.

It would have been very nice for the Alphans to communicate more with the aliens about what they could expect to discover when they reached Earth, but they were obviously busy, so this can be forgiven.

'Earthbound' is well conceived, written, performed, designed and directed. It isn't the most well paced, memorable, or profound segment, but it does deliver a powerful twist ending in the best tradition of *The Twilight Zone*, and is ultimately very effective.

Rating: 8/10

1.6
ANOTHER TIME, ANOTHER PLACE

Screenplay by Johnny Byrne
Directed by David Tomblin

Selected Broadcast Dates:

UK	LWT:	
	Date: 6 March 1976.	Time: 11.30 am
	Granada:	
	Date: 16 January 1976.	Time: 6.35 pm
US	KRON (San Francisco):	
	Date: 21 February 1976.	Time: 7.00 pm

Credited Cast: Martin Landau (John Koenig), **Barbara Bain** (Helena Russell), **Barry Morse** (Victor Bergman), **Prentis Hancock** (Paul Morrow), **Clifton Jones** (David Kano), **Zienia Merton** (Sandra Benes), **Anton Phillips** (Bob Mathias), **Nick Tate** (Alan Carter)

Guest Artist: Judy Geeson (Regina Kesslann (Carter))

Uncredited Cast: Suzanne Roquette (Tanya Alexander), **Barbara Kelly** (Voice of Computer), **June Bolton** (Operative June), **Loftus Burton** (Operative Lee Oswald), **Andrew Dempsey**, **Joy Harrison**, **Robert Phillips**, **Michael Stevens**, **Maggie Wright** (Main Mission Operatives), **Tony Allyn** (Security Guard Tony Allan), **Alan Harris** (Alphan), **Alan Roberto** (Alphan Child), **Claire McLellan** (Alphan Child)

Plot: The Moon hits a particle storm in space and is catapulted a vast distance across the galaxy, apparently returning to its original orbit around Earth. But problems mount … On Alpha, Regina has nightmare visions and believes she is living on Earth, in some future time. The Earth's axis has tilted and civilisation has been wiped out. Another Moon is discovered in a slightly faster orbit, and on it an abandoned duplicate Alpha. The two Moons will collide, and in an effort to survive, the Alphans select the valley of Santa Maria as the most promising settlement location. A Reconnaissance team fly down and discover a village populated by their alternate selves.

Quotes:
- **Victor:** 'I just know we're not where we ought to be.'
- **Koenig:** 'I know less and less about this universe, Victor. But that's got to be more than chance.'
- **Victor:** 'Yes, there's a logic to it somewhere, John. There is some frame of order. We may make all sorts of blunders, wander off the path now and then, but ultimately we belong where we belong – on Earth.'
- **Victor:** 'Somehow, we've caught up with ourselves.'

- **Sandra:** 'They are going home.'
- **Victor:** 'And heading back into future time. It's an interesting thought.'
- **Victor:** 'This is the Earth, but not the world we knew. It's an Earth where perhaps we never existed. Or perhaps we have yet to be born. But apart from us it's empty now. A civilisation once flourished here – another Atlantis, perhaps. There are signs of them everywhere.'
- **Victor:** 'Wait – all of you. Paul is right. You cannot live here, or anywhere else on this planet. If you were to come here there would be chaos and disaster. We know that Regina died when she confronted herself in her mind. Our Helena died when she confronted herself in the flesh. We are trapped in different times. But when those two Moons collide, time will correct itself. Normality will return. There will be one Moon, one community, one time. You must go back. If you are not back on your own Moon when time does correct itself, you will have nowhere to die.'

Filming Dates: Tuesday 2 April – Friday 19 April 1974
Tuesday 23 April – Thursday 25 April 1974 (Second Unit)

Commentary:
Barbara Bain: 'I liked the thinking and the interest in "Another Time, Another Place."'

Nick Tate: 'I liked "Another Time, Another Place" because it did some good things for my character and gave me some real development. I like the fact that there was a lot of emotion in that episode. I remember enjoying very much working with Judy Geeson. I liked that whole concept – it was a really good one for me to do … "Another Time, Another Place" gave me a chance to get my teeth into a really good storyline.'

'I don't think I'd ever worked with an actress that showed such incredible emotion [as Judy Geeson], and the tears were flowing … There was no acting on my part at all; I was just stunned that this incredible gorgeous creature in my arms could fall apart like that. It was just magnificent.'

Zienia Merton: 'The first series was surreal. For example, "Another Time, Another Place". Keith Wilson, the designer, did the most incredible thing of all those trees and then just painted a background behind them … But you'd never think so; it looked as though we were outside.

'I always found it strange that in one episode I would hardly talk to Paul – obviously we'd had a terrible row or something – and then the next episode we'd be all over each other. Sylvia was very good at marrying up people. I thought Prentis and I looked good together – it worked well. So when there was a need for a baby-manufacturing machine in "Another Time, Another Place", I was there with Paul.'

Judy Geeson: 'The thing that I see when I look back on [*Space: 1999*]; it was so beautiful. It was so high-tech, the way it was done. It was stunningly beautiful. For an actor to play somebody who is suffering in that way is always the best part. It always is. You see many actors get their Oscars, or whatever, for playing somebody who is in some way deranged, because it gives you a license to behave in a strange way … It was lovely to do. It was a very good character for an actress to play … I remember the joy of having two brains. Which of me is going to say this? It's a lovely thought. The thing is there has to be a divide [between actor and role], otherwise you'd go mad. You have to know that you're giving a performance. You have to try your hardest to be completely in the moment, and when you're working with good actors it's so much easier. You just live in that moment, but you have to be able to leave it. You have to be able to go home. It was such a good experience. As I say sometimes, the higher up the ladder you go the sweeter the people are – they don't have anything to prove. Both [Martin Landau and Barbara Bain] were so gracious. Both of them were so lovely.'

Johnny Byrne: '"Another Time, Another Place" was very exciting. It was the first script I did for *Space* on my own, in my position as story editor. There's no sort of set way of writing scripts. In "Another Time, Another Place" I thought – the way you're faced with a blank page of paper and you've got to get a script ready in three weeks, a very complicated script, sets would be built, a hundred thousand pounds or something would be spent – how do you start? Where do you start from? So the first [question] I came up with was: what is the worst thing I can possibly imagine happening to those people? Let's say they're hit by a mad cloud or particle storm in space. What would happen if a certain kind of ionised particle storm hits them? So I imagined their bodies separating, their images separating and [them] watching themselves moving away from themselves. Now, that's as far as I had thought. What are the implications of that? Okay, they all pass out; nobody knows who's who, because one lot has seen the other lot sort of passing away. That's the act ending – that's a fairly strong one – but that's only the hook. But we've got an hour's screen time to fill.

'I thought, "Can I sustain a story developing like this?" Okay, we've come back now after the credits and they find that they're not where they were. That's good. So where are they? They look up and, my God, they're travelling back to occupy the spot in space they occupied before they were blown out of orbit! All they can do is scratch their heads. They have got some kind of data on the kind of weird force that struck them, but no real idea …'[That] is one of the reasons I like *Space: 1999*. Their knowledge was fairly limited so you could endlessly speculate. I built a story purely empirically by building situation on top of situation. It all stemmed from the initial logic of the set-up. That was, I think, the easiest way to write that kind of story. It was not possible to do all the stories like that – very few of them you could do like that. That was the fun way. I really enjoyed putting myself in a corner and writing myself out of it. Problems came a good deal along the way, because you could actually [genuinely] put yourself in a corner and yet your efforts to get you out could [appear] fairly gratuitous, or not wholly believable, unless you could find a really stunning turnabout. I was fortunate [that] there with a nice little twist to give it ["Another Time, Another Place"] … Along the way, it dealt with notions of identity, reality and fantasy, and one or two other interesting things about the relationships as well on Moonbase … I like that episode very much, and I thought David Tomblin directed it very well.

'"Another Time Another Place" was not just about individual Alphans confronting their doppelgangers, but about experiencing a revealed vision of a possible future. It also highlighted the cyclic nature of human experience – the catastrophic failure of 20th Century techno man established in "Breakaway" and a new beginning of the process. A theme also echoed in "Troubled Spirit". But here I may be expressing retrospective wisdom. Most, if not all, my episodes were written from the inside out. By that I mean they were never planned as vehicles for issues big and small, and frequently the end result was just as surprising to me as to others. Clearly they were tapping into themes and concepts swirling around in my mind at the time. It perhaps explains why episodes of this type finished so multi-faceted – simple on the surface, very complicated within. I particularly remember the highly charged excitement I felt when writing "Another Time, Another Place". I wrote it at Pinewood, and oft times I'd simply down tools and rush along the corridor to blast Chris's ear with new and ever more fascinating conundrums arising as the script developed. I also remember knowing *exactly* what I meant by Bergman's weird but nonetheless clinching comment that if they didn't get back to Alpha before the Moons collided, they'd have no place to die. Today, if dwelt on, it raises more questions than it answers. So far as I know, I was on nothing more stimulating than the stodgy food served at the studio restaurant.

'It's a long time ago now, but thinking back about it, I remember it vividly. It had Judy Geeson in it, who I felt was very good, and I was very sad to see that she didn't develop her career. I had a very fond feeling for it, simply because it was the first one that I wrote entirely myself. And it was also directed by David Tomblin, whose work I admired enormously and with whom I had a very strong working relationship throughout the series.

'I'm sure the spark for the stories concerning time is rooted in my Irish background and the pervasive long-lived effects of Celtic myth and legend in Ireland. Their strong hold on the imagination of the ancient pagan Gaels was already firmly in place long before the island was formally Christianised in the early 5th Century. It survived virtually intact until the end of the 17th Century and thereafter externally in fragmented form, and internally in the minds of our people until the present time … As kids growing up, we knew endless places – churches, rocks, wells – where legend had it that walking around them anti-clockwise a certain number of times could result in meeting yourself, or even something nastier!

'I wanted the repercussions to affect the Alphans on the human and emotional level, rather than [through] in-your-face gothic horror. [The story] would also, I hoped, open up the relationship of Koenig and Helena in a way that was not normally possible. Carter I chose because I wanted to highlight the man of feeling behind the macho image. I thought he beautifully captured the poignancy of his relationship with the doomed Regina. On the planet, Morrow's aggressive response was rooted in fear for the community they were struggling to establish. It embodied elements of the rural idyll/Technological Man dilemma … Morrow and the others had decided to establish a community that, though less comfortable, was infinitely more predictable. Out were the vast uncertainties of the wandering Moonbase Alpha. At least here they knew what to expect and were prepared to make it work. The second Moon's arrival and Koenig's appearance on the scene revived all the uncertainties they had hoped to put behind them. Complicating that was the primitive, visceral fear of people mingling with their other selves. The same fear we see expressed today on the subject of human cloning – one of the big issues of our increasingly Brave New World.'

Bloopers: Watch the buttons on Martin Landau's Commlock – in some scenes they're all squished together.

Also note the two children on Earth – when they are seen facing the camera, the girl is considerably shorter than the boy; but when they are seen facing away from the camera, she's somehow taller!

Finally, there are continuity issues in the scene where the future Helena kisses Koenig: watch younger Helena in the background, because in close-up shots she's in an entirely different position than she is in the long shots.

Observations: The highly effective shot of the Alphans leaving the Eagle will re-appear in the last Year One episode, 'The Testament of Arkadia'. The production team did not construct a full-size version of the Eagle – this effect was achieved by using a two-dimensional cutout that convincingly simulated the life-size ship. Victor mentions that 24 hours are required for total evacuation of Moonbase Alpha (Operation Exodus). This is down significantly from the 48 hours quoted in 'Matter of Life and Death' – they've obviously been working to speed up the process in case they encounter a habitable planet.

Watch the opening 'This Episode' sequence for a view of another Alphan settlement on Earth, absent from the episode itself.

Review: While the first five episodes bear evidence of a series trying to find its footing and path, 'Another Time, Another Place' represents the crystallisation of a firm direction that the rest of Year One would follow to a very large extent. The teaming of writer Johnny Byrne and director David Tomblin (making his debut on the series) results in the only first season episode to deal with time travel, with the Alphans encountering their future selves. There is also the appealing, romantic notion of returning to a time when life was less complex.

Filled with impressive imagery and effectively subdued and atmospheric lighting, the episode is visually superb. One of the only things that could be fairly criticised is the make-up depicting Regina's sunburn, which is somewhat unconvincing. 'Another Time, Another Place' has (as Zienia Merton points out in the commentary below) some very surrealistic elements to it. The spatial special effects are stunning, including the Eagle flight sequences between the two Moons, and the Eagle flight over Earth. Regina's painting of the Santa Maria settlement (actually the work of designer Keith Wilson, and similar in appearance to his original production design paintings for Santa Maria) is a nice touch, showing Alpha has art materials available for use as a leisure pursuit. The settlement itself is a thoroughly realistic vision of the kind of colony the Alphans would establish if they were to colonise a planet. John and Alan still have the tense, argumentative relationship they've demonstrated since 'Breakaway', although they are now appearing to become more adjusted to each other. They're less aggressive and are obviously forging the connections of the deep friendship they will soon have. Alan is his gung-ho self, wanting to get down to the planet as soon as possible. Koenig, in a subtle pointer toward the agrarian lifestyle their alternate future selves follow, displays a lack of reliance on Computer. He states, 'Computer … Computer can't even tell us why Earth doesn't answer our signals.' It is very easy to see how the alternate Koenig came to the decision to move his people down to Santa Maria, favoring a natural environment over a technological one.

The Alphans' decision to establish a number of settlements throughout the area is a very sensible one, serving to separate each village from potential calamities that might happen to befall others. Examples could be crop failure, natural disasters or sickness.

The relationship between Alan and Regina is very well presented, with Nick Tate's effective mix of disbelief and compassion as the former and Judy Geeson's moving portrayal of the latter's conflicted nature. Regina's two brains parallel the two Moons – dichotomies abound throughout this episode. It could have been more effective to portray Regina as having two brainwave patterns, rather than two actual brains, which is a physical impossibility. That said, this has no negative impact on the story itself, and is an element easily forgiven.

Barbara Bain, Barry Morse and Nick Tate give some of their strongest performances in the series. The rest of the main cast – Martin Landau, Zienia Merton, Prentis Hancock, Clifton Jones and Anton Phillips – are all in their usual top form, with the added bonus of most of them being able to present their characters as themselves, and also as their counterparts years into the future. The time spent with the other Alphans on Earth offers additional character points (Paul with a beard, Paul and Sandra's children, Victor's gardening, David's greying hair, and more). Barry Morse provides an effective piece of linking characterisation by whistling as both versions of Victor, and Barbara Bain excels depicting the subtle changes in Helena Russell between her optimistic and wide-eyed present and resigned older selves. Helena's conversation with her future self is both touching and eerie, and a seamlessly filmed example of split-screen effects. The scene is spoken in whispers and, indeed, a lot of Year One features such subdued dialogue – effectively contrasting the intimacy and closeness of such quiet communication against the cold vastness of deep space. It is very moving to see the 'future' Helena encounter and kiss her long-lost love, John Koenig. It is the last moment of her life, and she is completely at peace.

A fascinating scene shows Helena in Medical with the dead bodies of the alternate John and Alan. She can't bring herself to raise a sheet over the dead Koenig's head, even though she has just done the same thing, with no difficulty, to Carter. It is obvious the relationship between her and John is advancing. Another gentle, delicate scene shows Carter placing flowers on Regina's grave.

The line, 'If you were to come here there would be chaos and disaster,' points to interesting parallels with 'Matter of Life and Death'. The colliding of the two Moons here is also similar to the plotline in the later 'Collision Course' involving the giant planet Atheria – the use of colliding planets as a plot point resonates with some of the most mystical and metaphysical elements of the first series. The possibilities are thought-provoking: what could happen in a situation like this? What would happen if we were to meet ourselves?

Elements of horror are common in Year One stories; here it is the spine-chilling scene where Koenig and Carter discover their own dead bodies in the crashed Eagle, followed by Koenig seeing himself on the autopsy table in Medical. Additionally, the visit to the empty, lifeless alternate Alpha is a remarkably haunting sequence. All are unnerving.

The main themes from 'Breakaway' recur, notably the dual focus on environmental and anti-technological aspects, encapsulated here by the contradiction between Technological Man and Biological Man – the more we progress toward science the less connected we are to nature. Additional themes are introduced that will reappear in numerous upcoming Johnny Byrne episodes, including the aforementioned nostalgia for a simpler, more natural way of life (which features again most notably in 'The Testament of Arkadia'), violent or mysterious events (as in 'The Troubled Spirit', 'End of Eternity' and 'The Immunity Syndrome'), and gloomy locales (again, 'The Testament of Arkadia'), but always with the potential for a brighter future. More than anything,

'Another Time, Another Place' is about belonging (with whom, and in what place and time), and the fact is that the Alphans are not yet ready for the life they see their alternate selves living. The loss of this alternate Earth, as melancholy as the experience is, makes the glimmer of hope for a new world more rewarding.

Gothic and philosophical in nature, this is a superior example of the series and genre. In the beginning, the space storm caused the Alphans to separate from themselves. In the resolution, the two Moons collide and time corrects itself – 'Normality will return. There will be one Moon, one community, one time,' says the prophetic Bergman. The agrarian and technological Alphans are reunited and are whole, pointing out that our best hope lies not in a complete focus on either extreme, but in embracing both the past and the future.

There is a haunting power to the line, 'If you are not back on your own Moon when time does correct itself, you will have nowhere to die.' This opens up the possibility that the Alphans could be trapped in some form of limbo or purgatory, and makes the rush to return to Alpha all the more urgent. The delivery of this line, and the entire preceding speech, constitutes some of Barry Morse's most inspired acting, and is one of the stand-out moments in *Space: 1999*, reconfirming Professor Bergman as not just a scientist, but also a philosopher.

In all regards, this episode shows a series that has found itself. It knows what it wants to express and what it wants to leave more vaguely to the imagination of the viewer. 'Another Time, Another Place' is an atmospheric masterpiece that achieves the combination of style and substance, of tone and pace, and of science and mysticism with which most of the best of *Space: 1999* would remain forever associated.

Rating: 9.5/10

1.7
MISSING LINK

Screenplay by Edward di Lorenzo
Directed by Ray Austin

Selected Broadcast Dates:

UK	LWT:	
	Date: 24 January 1976.	Time: 11.30 am
	Granada:	
	Date: 6 February 1976.	Time: 6.35 pm
US	KRON (San Francisco):	
	Date: 17 January 1976.	Time: 7.00 pm

Credited Cast: Martin Landau (John Koenig), **Barbara Bain** (Helena Russell), **Barry Morse** (Victor Bergman), **Prentis Hancock** (Paul Morrow), **Clifton Jones** (David Kano), **Zienia Merton** (Sandra Benes), **Anton Phillips** (Bob Mathias), **Nick Tate** (Alan Carter)

Guest Artist: Joanna Dunham (Vana)

Special Guest Star: Peter Cushing (Raan)

Uncredited Cast: Patrick Brock (Zennite), **Suzanne Roquette** (Tanya Alexander), **June Bolton** (Operative June), **Andrew Dempsey**, **Christine Donna**, **Robert Phillips**, **Alan Harris** (Main Mission Operatives), **Tony Allyn** (Security Guard Tony Allan)

Plot: Koenig's Eagle crash-lands on the lunar surface, leaving the Commander near death. While Helena struggles to save him, the society of Moonbase Alpha begins to crumble without his leadership. Koenig, meanwhile, finds himself in a fabulous city on the planet Zenno, where he meets the alien anthropologist Raan and his daughter Vana, and learns that the Alphans are the Zennites' missing link.

Quotes:
- **Raan:** 'This is my home. It is made of light. Outside is our city, one of many. … A city of light. Light is alive. Colour is alive. Magnificent. Ah – at last you are impressed.'
- **Koenig:** 'Every scientist makes that claim. The end justifies the means.'
- **Koenig:** 'Without feeling hate, one cannot feel the joy of love.'
- **Duplicate Victor:** 'Oh, don't philosophise, John! Not with me. I'm not talking about Sandra – I'm talking about everything! When are we going to stop kidding ourselves? We're never going to get off this rock. This is our tomb! We walk about here breathing, but we're not living, we're existing! I tell you, I've just about had enough of it. I want to live like a human being again.'
- **Duplicate Victor:** 'How does it feel to play God every day?'
- **Alan:** 'Tanya, you have the most beautiful voice in the world.'

- **Raan:** 'As a scientist I owe it to humanity to learn all I can. It is the only way to help man; to bring him closer to his true destiny.'
- **Helena:** 'It may simply be John's time to die.'
- **Vana:** 'A world without fear.'
- **Raan:** 'Until tomorrow, John Koenig. Until tomorrow ...'

Filming Dates: Monday 22 April – Thursday 9 May 1974
Monday 22 July 1974 (Second Unit)

Incidental Music: From the *Stingray* episode 'Ghost of the Sea', composed by Barry Gray. Utilised here for the Zennite city, it is later used as 'Kara's Theme' in the episode 'Mission of the Darians'.
'Vana's Theme', consisting of electronic organ music, was composed for 'Breakaway' by Barry Gray, with the intent that it would be used as a general establishing theme for views of Moonbase Alpha. This never happened, and the theme features only in this one episode, projected from Vana's mind.

Commentary:
Zienia Merton: 'One of the funniest incidents I can remember ... They built a huge tent [for "Missing Link"] and they pumped it full of dry ice to get a misty effect. The cameramen were given directions, and they got lost! We couldn't see anybody in that mist. It was Ray Austin who directed. I said, "Listen Ray, how far is this mist coming up?" and he said, "To Martin's chin." You know how little I am, so I said, "Well, if it's coming up to Martin's chin, I can throw my lines in. I needn't appear. All Martin has to do is hold a black mop for the top of my head." He said, "Yes, I see what you mean." We had marks to walk forward to, but there was no point because we couldn't see anything. It was absolutely fogged up. Poor Gladys, the continuity lady – who always sits on a stool – we never saw poor Gladys the whole time we were doing that.
'It was a marvellous show, but you get very wet as well in the dry ice, and it's an awful feeling. And of course I had these pajamas on – I won't tell you what it felt like. Between each take, of course, they'd pump in more dry ice as well, because it evaporates so quickly. It's a wonderful effect, and it was terribly funny as well. Because, as you know, Peter [Cushing] brings me back, and the running gag was that because I was so small, every time I had to do a shot they'd stand me on something or else everybody else had to take their boots off. I remember turning around, and there was this great trestle table suspended six feet off the ground and I said, "Hey, I'm not that short!" But the effect they wanted was to make it look as if we were floating in the air, and it was a marvellous effect. "Missing Link" was good, and it was nice my knowing that something was wrong ... because of course in the Eagle crash both Martin and I had head injuries, and that's why we could go to Zenno.
'Poor Joanna was in a costume that she couldn't even sit down in, so they gave her this thing that made her look like a Mummy ... a sort of thing with armrests, and that's where she rested. She couldn't sit down. Peter could sit down. And that gold paint as well – that wasn't pleasant and took hours to apply.'

Nick Tate: 'Peter Cushing was a charming man, and an extraordinary actor.'

Anton Phillips: 'Peter Cushing in "Missing Link" was terrific. I really liked him. He was such a charming, charming person. And he was always impeccably polite to you, and complimentary. He really was nice. Of all our guest stars, he was the one that made the most impact on me, because he was such a nice person. And then there was Christopher Lee [in "Earthbound"], who was not like Peter Cushing. He was very, very grand.'

[Regarding a fight scene in 'Missing Link' between Alan Carter and Bob Mathias:] '[Nick Tate] knocked me. He didn't knock me out. He made a mistake. We'd rehearsed the fight all morning, and all I had to do was hold him (with both arms on his shoulders), and he had to break free, step back and throw a punch past my chin. So he broke free but instead of stepping back he stepped forward, and it took me across the chin. That was my involvement with the scene. After that, my stunt man, Paul Weston, came in. The rest of it was him fighting. I think Nick was really very shocked when that happened. Because he thought he would hurt me, and he didn't. He was surprised that I didn't go down!'

Martin Landau: [Regarding Nick Tate accidentally hitting Anton Phillips during the filming of 'Missing Link'] 'Yes, I remember that. I don't believe in that. When you actually hit someone, it doesn't look as good. Most of the time, you cry. I hate to see a grown man cry.'

Johnny Byrne: 'Ed [di Lorenzo] wrote "Missing Link" and "Ring Around the Moon", but they were heavily re-written by Chris [Penfold]. Wonderful man though he was, and a writer with a delicate touch and philosophical feel, Ed had problems with the type of story needed for *Space: 1999* at the time. His great love was the book he was writing. I think it was called *White Light*, and like his script work, it was poetic, delicate, a sort of post-hippy *Jonathan Livingstone Seagull* (Chris's description). According to Chris, Ed left because he was fed up with the rewrite demands, and anyhow, his book was his first priority. I was very sad and disappointed when he left, because I felt he would have grown into the series and thus made it all the more special.'

Bloopers: When the Eagle crashes at the start of the episode, to the left of the ship one of the small special effects explosions detonates and launches a puff of dust where it shouldn't be. A second error marks an obvious continuity flaw. Or does it? The name Koenig is misspelled 'Keonig' on the duplicate Alpha's medical monitor. In an adjacent scene, the spelling is shown correctly. Was this a mistake, or was it a sign to Koenig that something was wrong? Was it meant to demonstrate a degree of fallibility on Raan's part?

One definite mistake occurs as the nose cone of the crashed Eagle is lifted away from the body of the ship – interior shots show the Stewardess Section of the ship being moved, which is clearly not the case when you see the exterior angle. The same error will be seen again in 'Dragon's Domain'.

Observations: The Main Mission set receives a revamp with this episode, as Kano's revolving desk appears for the first time.

One entertaining story that is sometimes told in relation to this episode concerns Barry Morse's hair. Morse believed that Victor Bergman would have matters of greater importance on his mind than his appearance, so the actor didn't have his hair cut throughout the filming of the entire series. If you watch, you'll see it getting longer as the episodes continue.

This wasn't the first time modern film science fiction retold Shakespeare's *The Tempest* (see the classic movie *Forbidden Planet*) and it wouldn't be the last (see *Space: 1999*'s upcoming Year Two opener 'The Metamorph' and *Doctor Who*'s 'Planet of Evil'.)

Of interest to *Space: 1999* trivia fans – in real life, there is an impact crater on the Moon called Zeno in honor of the philosopher.

Review: This episode is the second teaming of writer Edward di Lorenzo and director Ray Austin (the other being the abstract 'Ring Around the Moon'), and is di Lorenzo's final script for the series. 'Missing Link' is filled with tension, character drama and emotion on both Alpha and Zenno. The special effects, cinematography and direction beautifully combine with a perfectly fitting musical score (mysterious and lovely) during Koenig's journey from the crash site to Zenno. The tumbling Eagle and the crash itself are certainly some of the finest Eagle effect sequences in the series. The story excels once the magical world of Zenno is shown; it's no wonder Koenig believed it to be all a dream. The planet is wonderfully presented through the use of a convincing matte painting, given life by an overlay of moving lights.

'Missing Link' is a fairly straightforward re-telling of Shakespeare's *The Tempest*, in which Prospero possesses magical powers and lives on an island with his daughter Miranda. (Here we have Raan and daughter Vana on the planet Zenno.) The play opens with Prospero discovering that his brother Antonio is passing nearby on a ship. Prospero summons the tempest to cause the ship to wreck on the shores of his island. Also in the boat is Ferdinand, whom Prospero encourages into a relationship with his daughter. The two fall in love quickly, though Prospero worries about the strength of the relationship. In the end, Prospero uses magic to return everyone to Italy, as Raan does to return Koenig to Moonbase Alpha. *The Tempest* is essentially a romance, as is 'Missing Link', featuring a tale set far from ordinary life, in an exotic locale. Koenig serves as a composite of both Antonio and Ferdinand – flying nearby Zenno in his Eagle, crashing, and then falling in love with Vana. Koenig is also symbolic of Prospero's brother, as he is a 'missing link' between the Zennites and their ancient ancestors – essentially a distant part of Raan's 'family'. Raan does say, 'His blood is our blood,' though Koenig is also the missing link between a purely emotional state and an entirely logical one. Common romance themes include loss and retrieval, and exile and reunion – in 'Missing Link', Alpha loses and then regains its commander, and Koenig is trapped on Zenno and then later reunited with Helena.

There are several other themes apparent in 'Missing Link', including the now tried-and-true one of the failures and limitations of technology (which has been repeating to varying degrees since 'Breakaway', here represented by Eagle malfunctions and the subsequent crash, as well as the inability of Alpha's medical technology to save John). It all comes down to Mind versus Machine (or Mind versus Body/Heart) – Koenig's soul exists in a world of thought, while his body lies on the brink of death, kept alive by technology in Moonbase Alpha. The Zennites have no need for machinery, because they control the powers of the mind. As Raan says, 'The mind is master of all things.' Koenig, rather clumsily, encapsulates the Heart versus Mind theme with his line, 'I still believe it is more important to feel than to think.' Raan responds with what might be considered the episode's raison d'etre, 'It is the perfect balance between the two that must be achieved.' Koenig has already demonstrated his basic tenet of following his heart, rather than any degree of amassed evidence before him, in previous episodes

('Matter of Life and Death' is an obvious one), and will do so again (the upcoming 'Collision Course' being possibly the strongest example). This episode does provide an answer to the conflict of Mind versus Heart when Vana states, 'Love is the bridge between all worlds.' Koenig himself says, 'Cross the bridge between your world and mine. As long as you think of me, feel for me, I'll be with you.'

There is also an attempt to examine the true nature of human life and consciousness – is it spiritually or organically based? It's intriguing to note that the medical monitors don't register Koenig's life-signs because his soul is no longer with his body. That provides – at least – Edward di Lorenzo's answer to the question.

While on the subject of the multiple themes explored in 'Missing Link', one can't ignore the obvious statement against animal testing. The inhumanity of the physical or mental exploitation of other creatures is clearly stated, and personified by Raan's experiments on Koenig.

Nick Tate delivers an excellent performance, showing the amazing devotion Alan now has for Koenig – a clear testament to the character development that has been progressing through these first seven episodes of the series. During the earliest episodes Alan Carter was often in obvious and unrestrained disagreement with his Commander. By this point, they are friends with respect for each other. This episode also features a frightening depiction of what could happen on Moonbase Alpha if not for the strong leadership of John Koenig. The power struggle and explosions of temper that develop show the Alphans as human beings – with all their faults and fears. The faults and fears of the Alphans will also become a major plot point in 'War Games', and both episodes boldly feature a 'world without fear' – an interesting parallel.

This is one of Barbara Bain's most powerful episodes. The emotional range she conveys as Helena is clear, and the breakdown of her cool shield of composure (as she turns off Koenig's life-support systems) is one of the most heartfelt moments of the series.

Zienia Merton meanwhile delivers a notably restrained performance, conveying Sandra's emotions with subtlety. Merton's performance is another element serving the comparison of this episode to a dream – she ends up peacefully lying back down in bed, with a contented look on her face.

Peter Cushing and Joanna Dunham are both wonderful. Cushing's gentle and subtle performance (with an underlying sinister tone) is in sharp contrast to Martin Landau's rugged emotional range. Landau is portraying the emotional Earthman, while Cushing is portraying the dispassionate thinker. Joanna Dunham's Vana is doe-eyed and innocent. Like Maya in Year Two's 'The Metamorph', she is naïve and doesn't know her father's true methods and purpose – she says, 'We are not capable of deception,' when Raan clearly is.

The concept of the Earthman being the missing link to an advanced and otherwise alien race is interesting and well executed. The analysis of how the Zennites are different from contemporary humans is also very interesting. The scene with the duplicate Bergman and the horrifying one thereafter (where Koenig is assaulted by terrifying aliens), are connected and constitute some of the finest moments of the episode. No less frightening is when Koenig finds himself strapped to a chair, covered in cobwebs, screaming for help from a vision of his friend Victor – who is running, arm outstretched in aid, but never getting any closer. These images, and those of the evil alternate Bergman and the monstrous nightmare beings, stay with the viewer and provoke questions. Are they from Koenig's subconscious? Are they Koenig's own fears or demons? Or is Raan manipulating him with purely conjured visions? In keeping with the overall mood and atmosphere of a dream throughout 'Missing Link', these sequences depict a descent into nightmare.

The viewer is treated in this episode to another vision of a deserted Moonbase Alpha, which holds a certain visual and thematic appeal. A deserted Alpha was previously depicted in 'Another Time, Another Place' and another will appear in the second season's 'One Moment of Humanity'. The Zennites themselves make for another visual highlight – beautifully costumed in colourful robes, and with skin of silver and gold.

The name Zenno is derived from Zeno of Citium – the Greek philosopher and founder of Stoicism, the philosophy of the Stoics. Born c 334 BC, he lived for 72 years. His main belief was that 'tranquility can best be reached through indifference to pleasure or pain,' or 'Man conquers the world by conquering himself.' This idea of repressed feeling was also the model for Mr Spock and the Vulcan race in *Star Trek*.

What doesn't work in 'Missing Link' is the love story between Koenig and Vana. Confined by the limits of the episodic format, Koenig far too quickly gives up on his command, his fellow Alphans, and his emergent love for Helena. At the same time, he falls for Vana so rapidly that even romantics would have a hard time believing it. To make matters worse, the chemistry between Martin Landau and Joanna Dunham is negligible, at best. *Space: 1999* fans that dislike this episode usually cite these as the reasons, and valid ones they are. It could also be said that the 'love story' episodes of *Space: 1999* tended not to resonate with viewers – Helena had hers with 'Matter of Life and Death' and now Koenig has his with 'Missing Link', both episodes with many merits that ultimately fail to rank amongst the best of the series.

In the end, Koenig is waking from a nightmare – whether it was fantasy or reality is a matter of interpretation. And so this dreamlike *Space: 1999* version of *The Tempest* comes to a satisfying end. By the finale, John has taught Vana and the Zennites the emotion of love, and the ending is very touching. Ultimately, the Zennites aren't that different from the Alphans – an evolutionary premise the series will revisit more blatantly in 'The Full Circle'.

'Missing Link' is quite slow-paced and might be unappealing to the casual viewer, but it is certainly a beautiful entry in the series.

Rating: 8/10

1.8
GUARDIAN OF PIRI

Screenplay by Christopher Penfold*
Directed by Charles Crichton

*Christopher Penfold does not receive on-screen credit.

Selected Broadcast Dates:

UK	LWT:	
	Date: 15 November 1975.	Time: 5.50 pm
	Granada:	
	Date: 5 December 1975.	Time: 6.35 pm
US	KRON (San Francisco):	
	Date: 18 October 1975.	Time: 7.00 pm
	WPIX (New York):	
	Date: 1 November 1975.	Time: 7.00 pm

Credited Cast: Martin Landau (John Koenig), **Barbara Bain** (Helena Russell), **Barry Morse** (Victor Bergman), **Prentis Hancock** (Paul Morrow), **Clifton Jones** (David Kano), **Zienia Merton** (Sandra Benes), **Anton Phillips** (Bob Mathias), **Nick Tate** (Alan Carter), **Michael Culver** (Pete Irving)

Guest Artist: Catherine Schell (Servant of the Guardian)

Uncredited Cast: Suzanne Roquette (Tanya Alexander), **Barbara Kelly** (Voice of Computer), **John Gleeson** (Ed Davis), **James Fagan** (Ken Johnson), **Anne Hanson** (Sarah Graham), **June Bolton** (Operative June), **Loftus Burton** (Operative Lee Oswald), **Andrew Dempsey**, **Christine Donna**, **Raymond Harris** (Main Mission Operatives), **John Clifford** (Security Guard), **Trevor Ainsley** (Technical Head), **Tony Allyn** (Security Guard Tony Allan), **Quentin Pierre** (Security Guard Pierce Quinton), **Roy Everson** (Security Guard at party), **Gareth Hunt** (Eagle Pilot Irving), **John Lee-Barber** (Eagle Co-Pilot Davis), **Juliet King, Jodi Sherwood, Willow** (Nurses), **Alan Harris, Mike Stevens** (Alphans)

Previously Titled: 'Nobody's Perfect'

Plot: Alpha encounters the planet Piri, which seems to be a perfect world to colonise, but Eagle crews go missing, Computer malfunctions, and Commander Koenig encounters a beautiful woman – the Servant of the Guardian – and learns that no life exists on the world. Koenig escapes and finds the Alphans have succumbed to the Guardian's spell and are planning to colonise Piri. Koenig must break the Guardian's spell, or face the death of all his people.

Quotes:
- **Victor:** 'Computer's unusually reticent.'
- **Alan:** 'No place like home.'
- **Servant:** 'We have brought you here to relieve you of your human pain.'
- **Servant:** 'Millennia ago this planet was peopled by Pirians of great technical skill. They built machines to run the necessities of life so they could enjoy their pleasure. Then they created the Guardian to control the machines and save them from decision. Their life was perfect, and the Guardian was ordered to maintain it.'
- **Servant:** 'Absolute perfection lasts forever, and so the Guardian has suspended time.'
- **Sandra:** 'There are many forms of life, but this is beautiful.'
- **Koenig:** 'We've brought a dead planet back to life. Maybe we should have stayed.'

Filming Dates: Friday 10 May – Tuesday 28 May 1974

Incidental Music: The musical score is supplemented with Chuck Cassey's track, *Undersea*, sourced from the Chappell Recorded Music Library. It features here as the 'theme' for planet Piri.

Commentary:
Martin Landau: 'On "Guardian of Piri" we were looking at Piri on the screen. When we came to that scene I said, "Does anyone have an art rendering of that thing?" When we finally got it I said, "Why do we have to ask for these? It doesn't make any sense! Everyone here who is [acting] looking at this thing in awe should see what the hell they are looking at! Why should we be the last to see it?" Literally. So, we ran into that. If you didn't speak up, then that would happen. Next time, the pictures were there. We were looking at a big piece of black velvet and reacting to it, and we didn't know what the hell we were [really supposed to be] looking at – it was crazy! There was no excuse for that. I also knew there had to be drawings, because they were building the sets on the next stage. We only shot the Main Mission, or later Command Centre, stuff the first or the second day – first and/or second day for most episodes. Sometimes, we were there longer. This meant we did the beginning of the show, the middle, and the tag – all at once. That meant we knew everything that happened! … All I was asking for was to see what it looked like, because I was supposed to spend a lot of time there. And what about all these other people who were mesmerised? I mean *everyone* on the show winds up on Piri!'

Anton Phillips: 'I think "Guardian of Piri" was my favourite. I liked that one. I thought the set was terrific. Maybe it's the fact that [all the characters] lighten up in it, because they're all under the influence of … prescribed substances, or whatever. But I thought it had a really nice feel about it.'

Zienia Merton: 'Martin was a very physical actor. On "Guardian of Piri" we were all sitting there in a trance, and I was sitting there. Martin's rushing around trying to get everybody going again, and he literally grabbed my neck as he said, "Sandra!" I thought I was going to be in traction. When you watch it, see that moment – it's unbelievable. It really hurt. So months pass, and we do "Full Circle". This time I'm meant to hit Martin, as the caveman, with a rock. But it was a polystyrene rock. You had to pretend it was heavy. Barbara came and took me aside and she said, "Zienia, when you come to hit Martin – be gentle with him." I thought that was sweet.'

Catherine Schell: 'Keith [Wilson] was the one who designed the dress. When I was offered the part we had a meeting and he said, "I have to design this thing that will make you look spectacular." I told him all of my bad parts. I said, "I've got hips, and I haven't got [large] boobs, and I don't really like the tops of my arms very much." I said, "My neck is pretty good, so perhaps you could do something with that." Well, you know, necks are not glamorous. I said another thing. I said, "I tend to have a kind of straight figure. I don't have a bottle-glass figure. So if you could do something where you don't see that the waistline is not 22 inches, and the hips are 36, or whatever … It tends to be 22-22-22 all the way down." So when he actually put me into the costume I couldn't believe that he had [emphasised] all my bad points … The waistline was on show, the hips were, the small boobs were, and this thing covered the neck …

'The way I saw it, robots – even in the future – wouldn't be emotional. So it was a very flat performance – very nice, very smiley, but there was no depth to it in a way. I had a feeling that the director thought, "She can't bloody act!" But I hope in the end when you realise it was a robot … I never saw [the episode] myself, so I don't know whether it worked or not. I've seen clips of it, but I've never seen the whole episode.

'I'd never seen something so bizarre in all of my life. I have to say my mouth was agape. It was just so strange – all the balls [on the planet surface]. I remember there were balls absolutely everywhere, and I just didn't know if that would convey onto the screen. But I'm told it conveyed *beautifully*. I mean, it's Keith's work – he has the imagination. He knows where the camera angles are going to be, and actors don't always have that same kind of imagination – we do something else. But I thought, "Either this is going to be the biggest disaster, or it's going to be mind-blowing".'

Christopher Penfold: '"Guardian of Piri" is an odd one. [In 1992] I met a group of ex-Central [School of St. Martin's] fashion design students who now make extremely expensive gear, mostly for American pop stars, using *Space: 1999* as their inspiration. So these guys turned up at my house and we spent a very long Sunday afternoon in my garden in west London, with them asking questions about "Guardian of Piri". They were pretty sure that there was some hallucinogenic element in the bloodstream when I was writing it, which was not the case. There was a lot of adrenaline, but nothing else. As far as the sets are concerned, it was one of those … events where as a writer you sit down and write stage directions describing a physical environment that nobody in the world has ever seen – it exists only inside your own head – and it comes out on the printed page. This goes out to the art department and Keith is sitting there looking at it, thinking, "What on Earth am I going to do with this?" And then the art direction comes back and my initial reaction was, "This is nothing like what I wrote!" But, of course, it was fine. It was what was achievable. Keith was absolutely brilliant throughout the series, in responding to quite extraordinary requests from the scripts, in producing a physical environment in which actors could act and on which cameras could photograph, and which would make sense of the lunacy that was going on inside the writer's mind, and with peanuts at his disposal, really.

'With "Guardian of Piri", for one example, we were exploring what it means to be human. Perfection is not an attainable reality, but one for which we constantly strive. That line, "Leave me with my pain," follows Koenig committing – for him – an extremely irrational act. Immortality might be attainable. What are the consequences of obtaining that immortality? The process of getting there is more important than the arrival.'

Keith Wilson: '[Catherine Schell and I] worked together on "Guardian of Piri", which is for me one of the most extraordinary episodes. It's one of my favorite episodes. I enjoyed dressing this beautiful creature in that extraordinary dress. When we were shooting the sequence… she had white straps on the shoes that went up to the knees. I couldn't use ordinary string, or whatever, because it would just fall down. So I used sticky tape. Very delicate, but it would stick to her legs. I used to go in the dressing room every morning and sit on the floor, in between her legs, putting this white tape all the way up her legs… And my hands have a slight tremble. I've always had this tremble – just a slight one. And I was sitting between her legs one day and I looked up and she was standing there looking down at me with a huge smile on her face and she said, "Why are your hands trembling?" …

'The most expensive [*Space: 1999*] set, I think, was [the planet for] "Guardian of Piri". I was really trying to be different. and because of that I had to make a lot of things that didn't exist.'

Bloopers: As Carter and Koenig land on Piri for the first time, various Eagles are already visible on the surface. This is obviously a shot belonging later in the episode, after the exodus to Piri, which somehow got put in the wrong place.

Viewpoints are shown on the big screen in Main Mission which are impossible, including the opening shots of the Eagle flying over the surface of Piri, and then the image of Koenig speaking into his Commlock – how are the cameras picking up these shots?

Watch the Eagles for passenger modules that suddenly change configuration between their standard shape and the extended Laboratory pods (which appear here for the first time).

Observations: The design of Piri as a landscape of 'ball' trees was paid homage in the animated science fiction film *Titan A. E.*, which featured key scenes in a remarkably similar setting.

The original story concept was called 'Nobody's Perfect' and was written by David Weir, who was also responsible for 'Black Sun'.

The chain-reaction destruction of the Guardian is similar to the chain-reaction destruction of the alien planet in the later episode 'War Games' – perhaps not unsurprising as both scripts are by Christopher Penfold.

Watch for the 'Piri' graffiti scrawled on a lighting panel in Medical Centre.

A special effects shot of the surface of Piri was reused in the 1979 *Doctor Who* story 'Nightmare of Eden'.

Review: 'Guardian of Piri' is a visually astonishing episode featuring a powerful anti-conformist theme. The script by Christopher Penfold and direction by Charles Crichton are virtually faultless. Crichton's particularly effective in contrasting the vibrant psychedelic set of Piri against the dimly lit sequences featuring Koenig isolated on Alpha.

Utmost praise must be given to realisation of the planet Piri itself, and of the expansive mesa that is home to the Guardian – depicted via a dazzling, surrealistic, utterly otherworldly set. It is a beautiful design by Keith Wilson, unparalleled not only within the episodes of *Space: 1999*, but perhaps within all filmed science fiction.

Catherine Schell is brilliant in her portrayal of the robot servant of the Guardian, conveying outward warmth combined with an underlying coldness. The literary connections to Greek mythology and Homer's *The Odyssey* are apparent with Shell's lovely Servant fulfilling the role of *The Odyssey*'s Sirens, leading the wayward travellers (whether seafarers or spacefarers) to their deaths. As everyone who has more than a passing acquaintance with *Space: 1999* knows, Schell would return as the regular character Maya in the show's second season. It should also be noted that 'Guardian of Piri' is not the only episode in which she plays a robot in *Space: 1999* – in Year Two's 'The Taybor', a robot duplicate of Maya is constructed, and meets a fate uncannily similar to that of the Servant of the Guardian!

Martin Landau, Barbara Bain and Barry Morse are all in excellent form, as are the entire supporting cast. The background on David Kano is well played by Clifton Jones and is greatly welcome – here viewers learn that he was part of an experiment to implant computer connections in the human brain in order to link the abilities of the mind with those of a computer. This provides a fascinating insight into the advancements of human science in *Space: 1999*. It is significant that both he and Bergman (with his artificial heart) are among the first to succumb to the spell of the Guardian.

The party scene is highly enjoyable, depicting the Alphans inebriated under the Guardian's spell. Among other delights, watch for Helena and Victor playing peek-a-boo around a communications post, and Sandra dancing. Another comedic scene in this episode is set in Koenig's office, featuring Helena and Victor discussing the Commander and whether or not they'd like to take him to Piri. It's delightfully funny and shows Barbara Bain's deft handling of humorous material.

There is beautiful attention to detail in this production, as evidenced by such seemingly minor aspects as bubbles floating in the air and a butterfly fluttering around the robot body of the Servant in the epilogue. There is iconic series imagery here, including the flight of Eagles leaving Alpha, and while there are several small moments that don't quite succeed, including some of the miniature work with the Eagles on the surface of Piri, these criticisms are negligible.

The anti-conformist stance of Penfold's script is confirmed via the directive from the Servant of the Guardian, 'You must accept, Commander ... You must conform.' While the Alphans are taken in by the spell of the Guardian, they are under the impression that they are fully realising their potential as 'thinking human beings' (in Professor Bergman's words), while being granted immortality through the abilities of the Guardian to stop time. However, Koenig states the truth: 'Life is stopping for them.' The Alphans are indoctrinated into a world held in a state of static death, with no progress or future, visually symbolised by the Eagle suspended in mid-air and the near-motionless poses of the Alphans on Piri. Everything comes to a full stop on Piri – including life, as Koenig says.

Once the Guardian is destroyed and time is restored, the sterile environment of Piri returns to life and regains the promise of a future, as do the Alphans on their own voyage. As the Alphans realise, they brought a dead world back to life, which is an ongoing theme throughout their journey. Ironically, in the end, Piri could have been perfect for them.

'Guardian of Piri' is also concerned with the Man versus Machine conflict – here it is Koenig versus the Guardian. Man being overpowered by machines will return as a theme for future episodes, notably 'The Infernal Machine' and 'One Moment of Humanity'.

Another moral to the story is in the nature of man – Koenig states, 'Leave me with my pain. It reminds me I'm human.' This is in contrast to the unthinking existence of Piri, representing the escapism of the drug culture – note the glazed attitude of those under the spell of the Guardian! They're blissful, but they're under a spell that leads nowhere. It's a strong condemnation of drugs and extreme escapism. One also cannot blithely follow idealistic promises without thinking about them, and their potential ramifications. That is how the entire Pirian society perished, and the same fate nearly befalls the Alphans, as well. The Servant of the Guardian shows Koenig an image of Helena and tells him: 'Her nerves are relaxed, her appetite assuaged. The struggle is over. And you can join her in paradise.' Here, the ultimate lesson of the episode is being pointed out to Koenig: that, in reality, there is no ultimate paradise. The reality of life is inextricably bound to struggle, in one form or another. The idea that computers could take over all of society's work, leaving the people as unthinking hollow shells of themselves, remains thought provoking: does mankind run the risk of creating a Guardian here on Earth through its ever-increasingly technological world?

Visually stunning, and with much to say on the essence of being human, 'Guardian of Piri' is a classic episode of *Space: 1999* and a fine example of the potential of the science fiction television genre.

Rating: 9/10

1.9
FORCE OF LIFE

Screenplay by Johnny Byrne
Directed by David Tomblin

Selected Broadcast Dates:

UK	LWT:	
	Date: 13 September 1975.	Time: 5.50 pm
	Granada:	
	Date: 3 October 1975.	Time: 6.35 pm
US	KRON (San Francisco):	
	Date: 4 October 1975.	Time: 7.00 pm
	WPIX (New York):	
	Date: 18 October 1975.	Time: 7.00 pm

Credited Cast: Martin Landau (John Koenig), **Barbara Bain** (Helena Russell), **Barry Morse** (Victor Bergman), **Prentis Hancock** (Paul Morrow), **Clifton Jones** (David Kano), **Zienia Merton** (Sandra Benes), **Anton Phillips** (Bob Mathias), **Nick Tate** (Alan Carter), **John Hamill** (Mark Dominix), **Eva Rueber-Staier** (Jane – Solarium Girl)

Guest Star: Ian McShane (Anton Zoref)

Guest Artist: Gay Hamilton (Eva Zoref)

Uncredited Cast: Suzanne Roquette (Tanya Alexander), **Barbara Kelly** (Voice of Computer), **Lea Dregorn** (Hilary Preston), **June Bolton** (Operative June), **Sarah Bullen** (Operative Kate), **Loftus Burton** (Operative Lee Oswald), **John** Clifford, Andrew **Dempsey**, **Raymond Harris**, **Robert Phillips**, **Maggie Wright**(Main Mission Operatives), **Tony Allyn** (Security Guard Tony Allan), **Quentin Pierre** (Security Guard Pierce Quinton), **Vincent Wong** (Medic), **Maureen Tan** (Nurse), **Michael Stevens** (Alphan in corridor), **Alan Harris** (Alphan)

Previously Titled: 'Force of Evil'

Plot: An alien life force is drawn to Alpha and possesses technician Anton Zoref, who develops an uncontrollable need to absorb heat. While horrified by his plight, Zoref succumbs, and makes his way towards the ultimate source of heat and energy on the Moon – Alpha's nuclear generators.

Quotes:
- **Victor:** 'And this alien force is here – right now – somewhere on Alpha.'
- **Koenig:** 'Well, Victor, we can speculate forever – but that's not our problem. What we've got to do is destroy that force while it's still relatively weak.'
- **Helena:** 'Don't worry. He can't get out of there, and I'm certainly not going in.'

- **Victor:** 'Some sort of creative evolution. A stage in its development; perhaps the beginnings … A birth.'

Filming Dates: Wednesday 29 May – Friday 7 June 1974
Monday 1 July – Friday 5 July 1974

Incidental Music: Swings from bizarre, chilling and disorientating electronic cacophony ('Cosmic Sounds No. 1' and 'Cosmic Sounds No. 3' by Georges Teperino and 'Videotronics No. 3' by Cecil Leuter) to lounge music ('The Latest Fashion' by Giampiero Boneschi, heard during the Solarium sequence). All of these tracks were from the Chappell Recorded Music Library.

Commentary:
Zienia Merton: 'Everyone was always seen in Main Mission … Some of us should have been seen eating. One of the only times in series one they showed a bedroom [in "Force of Life"], we all had hysterics. We thought, "What? A bedroom! People actually sharing a bed … Husband and wife they might be … but is this possible on Moonbase Alpha?"'

Nick Tate: 'Another actor I liked very much was Ian McShane. He's a clever actor, and a good guy – a real man's man.'

Johnny Byrne: '"Force of Life" was previously [entitled] "Force of Evil". I was going to make it a much more malevolent force but, in fact, I reconsidered and then in talks with Gerry … I decided it was much better that this creature had no sort of actual human malevolence, that its actions should be [dictated by] what it was; without good, without evil, simply doing its thing.

'I wanted to get away from the notion of good and evil. You know, the nasty, mad alien and the cowering Earthlings. That's a valid form of story, and we'd seen it *ad nauseam* on *Star Trek*, and I think too much of it came in later on into *Space: 1999*. In "Force of Life", [we had the idea that] to many forms of life out in space, intelligent Earth life means bugger-all. It means as much as a wisp of gas up in space. And here I had the kind of mindless evolutionary imperative at work. We picked up a random force going through a kind of chrysalis stage in space. Its decision to latch itself onto Zoref was purely arbitrary. He happened to be in the right place at the right time and, of course, there was something about him that attracted the creature. But it hadn't any kind of intelligence in the sense we understand intelligence. It had an imperative, a kind of instinctive thing driving it. Of course, these things have to be visualised in terms of science fiction for the screen, so the way I found [the means] was to turn him into a heat junkie. He was just like an addict. The thing inside him would need a fix every so often, and we had him going through these spasms where he'd draw heat out of any object including coffee, including people, including anything finally – again I applied to the tail end the technique of the first story, where you look at the situation and see what's the inescapable logic and try to build on it. This force had been ripping its way as part of its evolutionary imperative through the base, and the effects it has on human rituals are very simple.

'Now, at the end of the day, our people ask what the hell has happened. They can work out a pattern to the thing and can make a guess at what it might be, but they don't really know. Someone, I think, forced me to put in the notion that it was a star in the making. I think that this was a foolish notion, because it was better to say that we simply didn't know what it was. If you want to draw a comparison, it's the caterpillar and the butterfly, but in some impossibly difficult and imponderable circumstances. It was one of those situations where not knowing the answer was where the drama lay. Knowing would have killed the drama.

'I think David [Tomblin] [directed] it very well … I worked very closely with David and he made a tremendous contribution to the scripts. Not so much to "Another Time, Another Place", but more so to this … We didn't sit down and say, "Let us make this a thriller." We had essentially a story, and we wanted to keep the story fairly simple. We wanted to make it different in the sense that it didn't have a kind of [standard] "heavy". It had a force effecting people. The force had its own reasons for doing what it did, and they were perfectly understandable in terms of itself. But it had a kind of unthinking, devastating effect on people. I thought the use of camera angles, pace and effects were quite stunning … David Tomblin got a tremendous sense of pace with Ian McShane striding through those corridors, which are usually the most boring of shots, but somehow David could invest them with tremendous energy and drama. David could communicate that sense of urgency – you would actually get off from watching somebody walking down the corridor.

'Given the nature of the relentless need for story in these things, it was often very difficult to develop aspects of character. There were a huge number of balancing acts and trade-offs that one had to incorporate into these stories: anything that walks in from outer space or outside Moonbase Alpha has to be explained whereas, in contemporary drama, anything that walks in off the street doesn't need any explanation; the story needs to be kept moving very fast because people are assumed to have the attention span of a gnat and [be unable] really to comprehend anything in the way of difficulty in terms of drama and ideas; and also [the need to achieve a] distribution of roles between the leading actors and those brought in for the episode. These things didn't always work, but I think that this [episode] perhaps worked better than most in terms of the directorial flare that David brought to it. I was very pleased with "Force of Life".

'I think "Force of Life" embodied the notion that here were people in an environment that could be hostile, indeed that was invariably hostile, encountering things about which they had not the faintest idea. Here, they encountered an emblem of the life that they had left behind: chrysalides that turn into caterpillars and caterpillars that turn into butterflies – these are part of the natural rhythms of our lives. Well, it seemed to me to be perfectly reasonable to suppose that this process was universal and that it could happen in the most extraordinary, interesting and completely mind-boggling way without understanding what made it work. And that's what "Force of Life" was about.

'What I particularly like about "Force of Life" myself, as someone watching it, is it concerned a villain, if you like, that was not present, was never seen … and that we never understood. I think it's the quintessence of *Space: 1999* – these ordinary people, these Earth people, were dealing with situations and responding to situations that they didn't understand. It was their responses that were important, more than the incident that had caused them. I think that story exemplified it very, very well.'

Bloopers: Not a blooper so much as a mistake in the writing – Mathias shouldn't have been fixing the burned out monitor in Medical himself – Technical should have been called to do it. One of Alpha's finest medical minds has better things to do than change light bulbs or power cells.

Observations: Sequences featuring the horribly disfigured, mutated Zoref with his glowing white eyes were edited from broadcasts in Germany, marking the first time *Space: 1999* was subjected to censorship. These same sequences caused complaints when they were shown in Denmark. The series would encounter similar problems with further graphic content in upcoming episodes.

Interestingly, the door to the Observation Room in Medical Centre opens conventionally, with a handle and manual push-button locking system, in contrast to the usual Commlock-operated sliding doors.

Review: *Space: 1999* excelled at depicting glowing balls of light, and 'Force of Life' provides the ultimate – an alien presence in the form of a ball of blue light that doesn't register on any sensors but proceeds to invade technician Anton Zoref, transforming him into an energy consuming monster. Visually, and artistically, the use of the colour blue for the alien life force signifies that it is cold, and is a subtle indicator that the entity is being drawn toward Alpha seeking warmth. Appropriately, as the alien absorbs energy, its glow shifts towards the warmer range of the colour spectrum and becomes purple.

Not a favourite of Eagle fans, this entirely Alpha-bound episode marks the introduction of another impressive and huge Keith Wilson set, Nuclear Generating Area Three. 'Force of Life' also features visually dynamic direction by David Tomblin, which adds to the style of the episode and heightens the inherent claustrophobia, tension and fear within the base. A prime example is the presentation of the death of medical orderly Hillary Preston, including dramatic slow motion and subordinated sound, coupled with a strange cacophonous score. It is a treatment that helps turn this episode into a horror classic, arguably unique amongst outer space science fiction television programmes. This pioneering horror-science fiction combination would later be used with great success in films including *Alien*. Without doubt, 'Force of Life' is a horror story, progressing to more and more frightening events as Zoref becomes less and less human.

'Force of Life' was the second episode to be helmed by Tomblin – the first was 'Another Time, Another Place' – and he was paired in both cases with screenwriter Johnny Byrne. Tomblin is likely the most cinematic of the *Space: 1999* directors. Here his remarkable visuals, dynamic lighting, jump cuts, askew camera angles and use of slow motion combine to utmost effect with the diverse score to effectively magnify the terror of the episode. Tomblin's flair for artistic visuals is in no greater evidence than during the opening sequence and the symbolic shot that rotates Zoref (and his life, as well as the lives of everyone on Alpha) upside down.

Ian McShane delivers a thoroughly convincing and engrossing performance as Zoref. The character is horrified at what is happening to him, while at the same time succumbing to his progressive, almost addictive, need to consume heat. The use of an eerie purple glow as Zoref consumes energy is successful in conveying the power of the alien force within him. And, considering that Zoref consumes heat and freezes everything he touches, it's appropriate that his name is an anagram of 'froze'.

The viewer's understanding of the scope of Moonbase Alpha, and the pattern of daily life on the base, is increased greatly by this episode. Alphans are depicted at home, at work, and relaxing off-duty in the Solarium. Anton and Eva Zoref are also the first married couple depicted on the base.

When the power is cut off within Alpha in an effort to drive Zoref towards a confrontation, the visual stage is set for the final horrific climax. In the dark, shadowed corridors of the base, Zoref becomes totally alien. Charred and burned to a blackened crisp by a Stun Gun blast, he nevertheless survives – animated by the alien force inside him, his eyes glowing white. He has become a grotesque monster that can't be stopped. It is a tribute to the make-up artists on the series that the Zoref monster, and the freezing effect he has on others, look as effective today as on original broadcast.

There is a scare with Bergman's artificial heart as he is running in the corridors while the oxygen levels in Alpha are dropping – it's nice to see Johnny Byrne utilising this established aspect of Bergman's character.

The explosion of Nuclear Generating Area Three is a showcase of excellent special effects and also highlights the actors' abilities to tumble across the sets in unison to the explosive shockwaves. Some of these shots are re-used from 'Breakaway'.

Then the alien force leaves, allowing Alpha to survive. As Bergman says, in reference to their nuclear generators, 'Just one was enough for its purpose.' The alien force has made a progression along the path of evolution, and Alpha was a catalyst that unwillingly helped in that growth. As Johnny Byrne states in the commentary section below, the idea is analogous to that of the metamorphosis of a caterpillar into a butterfly. Where will it go? What will happen to it? Will it continue growing, and what will it consume next? But apart from these speculations, 'Force of Life' contains more immediate and human impacts: on a large scale, Alpha itself is nearly destroyed, while on a human scale, the family of Anton and Eva Zoref is ripped apart.

This is an encounter with the absolutely unknown – a purely evolutionary instinct functioning in a completely alien life form. Alpha's vulnerabilities to the mysterious forces of space are encapsulated in this episode. If Alpha – home – is vulnerable to alien invasion, what psychological impact does this have on the people who live there? Byrne's script is completely successful in presenting the drama and horror of the segment, in constructing a constantly engaging show set entirely within the confines of the Moonbase, and in challenging the viewer to consider (along with the Alphans) what the evolutionary journey of this life force might be. Byrne eschews easy answers – as with real life, there aren't any. In the face of the utterly unknown and often frightening universe confronting them, Helena sums up the humanity of Year One when she says, while comforting Eva, 'We're living in deep space – there are so many things we don't understand. We don't know what that alien force was, why it came here, or why it selected Anton. But we've got to try to help each other to understand ...' With all their technology, they still don't have the answers, and finding comfort and support with each other, and believing in their future, is the greatest strength the Alphans possess.

'Force of Life' is a superbly suspenseful science fiction horror story.

Rating: 9/10

1.10
ALPHA CHILD

Screenplay by Christopher Penfold
Directed by Ray Austin

Selected Broadcast Dates:

UK	LWT:	
	Date: 18 October 1975.	Time: 5.50 pm
	Granada:	
	Date: 7 November 1975.	Time: 6.35 pm
US	KRON (San Francisco):	
	Date: 11 October 1975.	Time: 7.00 pm
	WPIX (New York):	
	Date: 25 October 1975.	Time: 7.00 pm

Credited Cast: Martin Landau (John Koenig), **Barbara Bain** (Helena Russell), **Barry Morse** (Victor Bergman), **Prentis Hancock** (Paul Morrow), **Clifton Jones** (David Kano), **Zienia Merton** (Sandra Benes), **Anton Phillips** (Bob Mathias), **Nick Tate** (Alan Carter), **Wayne Brooks** (Jackie Crawford)

Guest Artistes: Julian Glover (Jarak), **Cyd Hayman** (Cynthia 'Sue' Crawford / Rena)

Uncredited Cast: Suzanne Roquette (Tanya Alexander), **Sarah Bullen** (Operative Kate), **Loftus Burton** (Operative Lee Oswald), **Andrew Dempsey**, **Raymond Harris**, **Robert Phillips**, **Michael Stevens**, **Maureen Tan**, **Maggie Wright** (Main Mission Operatives), **Rula Lenska** (Joan Conway), **Tony Allyn** (Security Guard Tony Allan), **Quentin Pierre** (Security Guard Pierce Quinton), **Gerry Crampton** (Security Guard), **James Fagan** (Eagle Co-Pilot), **Vincent Wong** (Medic)

Plot: Jackie Crawford is born on Alpha, but the baby shocks the base by transforming into a five-year old. As alien spaceships take up orbit over the base, Jackie transforms again, into Jarak, an adult alien whose people are capable of concealing themselves by inhabiting the bodies of other life forms, but only during birth or death. To escape their pursuers, these body snatchers intend to kill the Alphans and occupy their bodies.

Quotes:
- **Helena:** 'Heaven knows I looked forward to this first child born here.'
- **Victor:** 'He senses you're not as willing to be charmed as the rest of us are.'
- **Helena:** 'I saw him smile. It sent a shiver up my spine. Almost as if he was mocking his mother's death.'
- **Koenig:** 'Ignorance is no reason to start shooting. After all, we're all afraid of the unknown.'

- **Jarak:** 'I like the intuitive quality of your human mind, Commander. I like the unpredictability of your human emotions. I like the difference between your people. But on our planet we faced extermination because we were different. Yes, we are running away … from genetic conformity, rigorously imposed. We are so happy to have found Alpha.'
- **Jarak:** 'The designated will die.'

Filming Dates: Monday 8 July – Monday 22 July 1974

Incidental Music: Barry Gray's score is supplemented by one of his own earlier compositions, from the 'Last Train To Bufflers Halt' episode of *The Secret Service*. It is heard here in a number of scenes, including the sequence where young Jackie is given a tour of Alpha.

Commentary:
Barbara Bain: 'I liked the idea of "Alpha Child". There was something marvellous in the potential of that whole idea.'

Julian Glover: '"Alpha Child" was totally ridiculous, but it was good fun to do. I mean, how many times do you get to run around in a silver skirt?'

Zienia Merton: 'The guest artists were smashing and one always tried to make them feel at home. We were the regulars, but they were down just for that one episode, and they found that they had to be crying, or making love to someone, two minutes after eating a sausage roll, or something … Frightening. So I used to say, "Would you like to come to lunch?" It's just hospitality. I remember meeting Cyd Hayman in the corridor [during the making of "Alpha Child"] and saying, "Hello, I'm Zienia Merton, would you like to come to lunch?" It was just to make people feel at home. They don't think, "Oh, I'm a guest star." Very few did that.

Christopher Penfold: 'The genesis of "Alpha Child" is quite difficult to recall. I'm pretty sure that the idea of a child being born on Alpha, and the kind of celebration of that event, being then undermined by the anxiety of the pace of development, was one that came from Gerry. I have pretty clear recollections of sitting in Gerry's office at Pinewood and us talking about that as an idea. I think that a lot of the actual plot of "Alpha Child" was probably straight from Gerry. Certainly, I think, the idea that it should turn out pretty nicely at the end.'

Martin Bower: 'Brian Johnson liked my work and gave me my first real break [in special effects], for which I shall always be grateful. He sent me a script from the episode "Alpha Child" and asked to see what I could come up with …'

Observations: This episode marks the first appearance of the highly impressive bomber-style spacecraft built by Martin Bower and inspired by the Discovery from *2001: A Space Odyssey*.

The lighting panels on the walls in Main Mission had, until this episode, been a stark white. They are now green, and will remain so until the episode 'End of Eternity'.

It's appealing to see the Nuclear Generating Area set reappear here, following its debut last episode.

Review: 'Alpha Child' began as a story idea by Gerry Anderson in conjunction with Christopher Penfold (see the commentary section for this episode), was developed into a script by Edward di Lorenzo (while he was still involved with the early days of *Space: 1999*) and was then subsequently completely re-written by Penfold, who receives sole on-screen credit for the episode. The results of this convoluted history are uneven, to say the least.

The direction by Ray Austin (his third instalment for the show) and lighting are outstanding, atmospheric and unusual. Austin has a meandering style with the camera, not always focusing on the conventional element, such as the person speaking in a particular scene. This helps to set his episodes apart from those of the other directors on the series.

From its astonishing beginning, this episode is filled with subtle details, minor character interactions, and a wealth of characterisation. Helena Russell displays the widest range of emotions (giving the lie to those critics who habitually slam Barbara Bain as being 'wooden'). Her ecstatic joy turns to shocked and horrified disbelief at the sight of the five-year-old child squeezed into the incubator where previously there had been a newborn baby, then to compassionate warmth as she spends time with the boy.

Amongst many noteworthy scenes is one showing Alan, Sandra, Paul, Tanya and Kano discussing whether Jackie's inhuman growth means they'll never be able to have normal children, or whether this is just a specific abnormality with a distinct cause.

The supporting cast members are all provided rich parts to play. The young Wayne Brooks is an excellent actor who hits the perfect expression in every scene. He was obviously both talented and well directed. He plays significant scenes with Martin Landau, Barbara Bain, Barry Morse and Nick Tate (who turns in some of his finest series acting in this episode). Note how differently the various characters relate to the young child: Bergman is a grandfather figure, Carter is a fun-loving uncle type, Helena is maternal, and so on. As the young Jackie spends more time with the Alphans, he displays a subtle learning process far beyond his years. It is a haunting and eerie scenario. The mysterious aspects of the boy accumulate, and for the first half of the episode, this is an outstanding show.

With the arrival of an alien ship, which is shrouded in as much mystery as young Jackie, the show is totally satisfying. The effectiveness comes from the mystery. As Koenig says, 'We're all afraid of the unknown.' And in that line, Koenig points to a possible moral of the story: that, although frightened by Jackie Crawford because they don't understand him, the Alphans nevertheless attempt to accept him and welcome him into their lives. It's a moral for life whenever anyone encounters someone different than themselves. Later, Helena sees Jackie smile in the presence of his suffering mother and then tells Koenig, 'I saw him smile. It sent a shiver up my spine. So knowing … almost as if he were mocking his mother's death.' Like John Wyndham's classic novel *The Midwich Cuckoos* (adapted for the screen as *Village of the Damned*), this is bone chilling and suspenseful material. There are also similarities to *The Omen*, filmed at Pinewood Studios at the same time as *Space: 1999*. It is the unknown-and-frightening horror approach that is a winner, until the unknown is revealed.

Upon the arrival of three more alien ships, young Jackie transforms into the grown form of Julian Glover as alien Jarak, and the episode itself transforms from excellent to inferior. Glover wears a little silver costume (which he gets from where? – a problem that will recur in Year Two with Alpha's new shape-shifter, Maya) and a disappointing, vaguely Roman hairstyle. From here on in lies the worst material of any Year One episode. It appears that the creative team behind this episode didn't know what to do with the superior premise already established and resorted to this ridiculous take on alien body snatchers. They should have stuck with the mysterious child.

Jarak kills his mother, who then transforms into his lover Rena (also mysteriously developing a shiny silver costume!) It's somewhat incestuous and disturbing, and their subsequent attempts to be menacing just aren't good enough, despite several effective scenes, including the alarming near-murder of everyone on Alpha. Ultimately, all this nonsense is ended by the arrival of another alien ship. The bomber blows up the first four ships, and some of the effects are very nice, while others now appear dated.

The pursuers take Jarak and Rena from Alpha and return Sue Crawford and her newborn baby to their proper selves, unaffected by their previous deaths and/or transformations. It is a bit disappointing that Jackie Crawford was never seen again in the series; it could have been a nice piece of continuity to have the baby make an appearance at some point in a future episode, adding to the sense of community on the base.

'Alpha Child' really doesn't have a lot to say, actually. It does begin to consider the population problems Alpha faces, but it's lacking in the sort of philosophical or metaphysical elements that mark the finest episodes of the series.

'Alpha Child' is replete with unfulfilled promise.

Rating: 5/10

1.11
THE LAST SUNSET

Screenplay by Christopher Penfold
Directed by Charles Crichton

Selected Broadcast Dates:

UK	LWT:	
	Date: 31 January 1976.	Time: 11.30 am
	Granada:	
	Date: 13 February 1976.	Time: 6.35 pm
US	KRON (San Francisco):	
	Date: 24 January 1976.	Time: 7.00 pm

Credited Cast: Martin Landau (John Koenig), **Barbara Bain** (Helena Russell), **Barry Morse** (Victor Bergman), **Prentis Hancock** (Paul Morrow), **Clifton Jones** (David Kano), **Zienia Merton** (Sandra Benes), **Anton Phillips** (Bob Mathias), **Nick Tate** (Alan Carter)

Uncredited Cast: Suzanne Roquette (Tanya Alexander), **Sarah Bullen** (Operative Kate), **James Fagan** (Eagle Co-Pilot Ken Johnson), **Loftus Burton** (Operative Lee Oswald), **Andrew Dempsey, Robert Phillips, Maureen Tan, Maggie Wright** (Main Mission Operatives), **Quentin Pierre** (Security Guard Pierce Quinton), **Alan Harris** (Alphan), **Janet Allen** (First Alphan), **Linzy Scott, Michael Stevens, Lynda Westover** (Alphans on Lunar Surface), **Rommo Gorrara** (Technician / Stunts), **Alf Joint** (Technician / Stunts), **Guy Francis Groen, Richard Adams, Jack McKenzie, Anita West** (Technicians)

Plot: The inhabitants of the planet Ariel supply the Moon with its own atmosphere, transforming the lunar surface into a potential paradise. But an exploratory party led by Helena crash-lands in a distant valley during a blinding sandstorm, and when the Moon doesn't go into orbit around Ariel's sun, Alpha must race to rescue the team before the atmosphere crystallises and buries the Moon's surface under a blanket of ice.

Quotes:
- **Victor:** 'If we go into orbit, I shan't care about symmetry.'
- **Sandra:** 'Do you know which Earthly sound I miss most in the silence of space?'
- **Paul:** 'Birdsong?'
- **Helena:** 'Computer's telling us nice stories today.'
- **Kano:** 'Computer never tells stories.'
- **Koenig:** 'Those circular lakes will look wonderful. But Alpha is built in a crater. And if it rains as hard as you hope it will, right at the bottom of one of those lakes will be Moonbase Alpha.'
- **Sandra:** 'Airsick! That's why I opted for the space program!'
- **Kano:** 'An atmosphere is a mixed blessing.'
- **Koenig:** 'Not much of a new world, is it? Not much of a place to be lost in.'

- **Paul:** 'That was sacred bread, Alan. That was sent to us in our time of need.'
- **Victor:** 'What we have here is a food substance amazingly rich in second class protein and many of the essential vitamins. We can grow almost limitless crops – once we've removed all the hallucinatory elements.'
- **Paul:** 'It wasn't a bad trip ... except for the ending.'
- **Ariel Voice:** 'Human nature is such that we could not afford to take the risk.'
- **Koenig:** 'Somehow, I don't think I'd like the people.'

Filming Dates: Tuesday 23 July – 6 August 1974
21 August 1974

Incidental Music: Older Barry Gray compositions are borrowed from the *Joe 90* episode 'King for a Day' (first heard when Helena learns Paul has left the shelter of the Eagle, and then while Paul is disturbed and irrational), *The Secret Service* episode 'A Case For The Bishop' (heard here while Paul Morrow performs a remote-contol landing of the Eagle with the alien object attached), the *Stingray* episode 'Raptures of the Deep' (heard while Sandra and Paul discuss Earthly sounds and kiss), an incidental library track from *Supercar* (used here while Sandra and Paul test the air on the surface, and when the Alphans are outside sunbathing and enjoying their new world), and the film *Thunderbird 6* (heard during the fight sequence, and while Paul is strangling Helena).

Commentary:
Prentis Hancock: 'I liked the mushrooms in "Last Sunset"!'

Zienia Merton: 'When I put my spacesuit on the crew said, "Here's Mrs Michelin!" It was very, very hot. It was actually one of the worst things. I must have lost five pounds that morning filming "Last Sunset", because of all the undergarments as well. Then it's all locked in. There's no air coming in at all. You're in your own mini-sauna ... You should have one at home. Prentis and I had to do our scene over and over and over ... I just thought I'd die ...

'In "The Last Sunset" I thought Sandra was actually a bit of a pain, like in old movies where the woman is always the one holding things up. But it was nice, and it was a good episode for Prentis. The other reason I liked "The Last Sunset" was that, because Paul and I, who were kind of the mainstay in Main Mission, had to go off, suddenly Kano took over and Tanya came in, and ... it gelled. "Okay, you guys have gone off, but we've got a backup and they're just as good." It was lovely to see Kano giving orders, and that was the kind of everyday vision of life on Alpha, so that people could go off and there was always a back-up team that came in and did it just as well.

'Series one didn't take off over here [in England] because it wasn't screened [as originally planned] ... We were going to be shown earlier, the whole point being that we'd get a [simultaneous transmission across the whole ITV] network, and we didn't ... *Space: 1999* was terribly well made and it could have gone out at 7.00 pm. I mean, if we can watch *The Six Million Dollar Man* being boring, I don't know why *Space: 1999* didn't get the airing. But they were anxious to sell it in America, and that's why they didn't bother about this country. Which is silly, because it was a very competent series, as good as anything the Americans can do.'

Christopher Penfold: 'One of the features of an open-ended journey was always the notion of an eventual return home. Seeing as we were never actually going to do that, "The Last Sunset" was an attempt to play with that idea and what that possibility might do to those people who had accepted that there would never be a homecoming.

'Charles Crichton was a brilliant director, very good for Johnny and me to be working with on the series. He had a lot to teach us. We were – Gerry was – extremely lucky that Charles's film career had been in the doldrums for some time and that he was available to work with us on *Space: 1999*. "The Last Sunset" has, I think, an epic idea – the idea of the human Diaspora that is Moonbase Alpha actually finding a home. A homecoming. That's a pretty powerful notion. That really was the motivating central idea. The possibility that presented to them. The possibility of finding a place in which all of those things that had been left behind on Earth would be rediscovered, was something that engaged me … And so, something of the idea that Moonbase Alpha finds this new environment where that which was left behind can be rediscovered, and the whole of western civilisation could then begin to be recreated – the whole sense of being given a second chance – was really the epic idea behind it.'

Bloopers: This is more of a flaw in the script, but why don't the Moonbase sensors detect the approach of the Ariel satellites before Tanya sees them outside the Main Mission windows?

Apart from the obvious plot requirements, why do Alan and Paul (upon leaving their crashed Eagle and seeing a search Eagle flying overhead) simply yell and wave their arms in the air to attract the attention of the pilots high above? At least one of them might have considered using his Commlock … Of course, that would have meant a much faster end to the episode.

Watch for missing buttons on Koenig's Commlock – Martin Landau must have been really rough with his props!

Koenig's desk has been pulled too far forward – it's actually in Main Mission, rather than his office.

Strings are visible on the Eagles in several shots, and on the alien probe as it attaches itself to the Eagle command module.

Observations: The Technical Section manual-closing door is shown, which marks another rare occurrence of these non-sliding doors on Alpha. This same Technical Section door is also blasted open by the escaping gas from the satellite.

The sequences that take place outside Alpha around an airlock when the Alphans run out to feel the rain were the first in the series to be filmed outdoors. They were shot in the parking lot of Pinewood Studios, and the artificial rain was very cold – as were the performers!

Review: 'The Last Sunset' opens with a gorgeous effects shot (one of the best in the series) of the Moon by the planet Ariel with a sun in the background, followed by a nicely chatty conversation between Koenig and Bergman. It successfully sets up the basis for the episode, and the teaser then ends with a good sense of suspense as Carter's Eagle is 'attacked' by the first Ariel satellite.

The shots of the escaping gas (before it is identified as air) are all wonderful. The sequence of the Alphans running through gas-filled corridors are similar to some in the later episode 'Space Brain', where Alpha's hallways fill with foam. It is always dramatic to see Alpha being 'invaded' by strange alien influences, whatever form they take. Also worthy of special note are the visual effects of the gas filling the Eagle hanger bay and the empty travel tube corridor.

The lovely first sunrise effect over the lunar surface signals the arrival of a new hope for the Alphans – that the Moon itself could be the new world they have longed for. It's a great premise. A stand out moment comes when Paul and Sandra go out onto the surface and breathe their new atmosphere for the first time. Their attempts to kiss in the spacesuit helmets are charming. There is a tremendous atmosphere of light-heartedness and joy throughout much of the first part of the show, until the Eagle commanded by Helena encounters problems and crashes. A genuine warmth and likeability radiates amongst the regular characters.

It has often provoked criticism that the windows in Victor's lab conveniently feature handles and are able to open, allowing in the breeze from the Moon's new atmosphere. This was addressed in the original script, and obviously it would have been nice if it had been explained in the episode itself, but an imaginative viewer can simply infer that the Moonbase technicians were overzealous in adapting the base to the new situation, and that the opening windows would have been changed back as soon as it became apparent the Moon wasn't going into orbit around Ariel's sun.

The intensifying drama of the episode is gripping. Helena, Alan and Paul struggle to survive in the harsh environment, while Sandra suffers massive concussion, and the Eagle fleet succumbs to the corrosive combination of Moon dust and an unknown element in the atmosphere. The Alphans fear for the safety of their friends in the crashed Eagle and worry about whether the Moon will go into orbit or drift back into deep space. Will Alpha, built in a crater, end up at the bottom of a rain-filled lake, or under the crushing weight of the frozen atmosphere? Christopher Penfold constructed layer upon layer of challenges, intrigue and possibilities in a script that truly challenges the Alphans. The discussions around the analysis of the alien object are also a believable portrait of the Alphans attempting to analyse the latest mystery confronting them.

After eating the mushrooms he finds growing on the Moon's surface, Paul experiences an hallucinogenic 'trip' that provides Prentis Hancock with the opportunity to deliver his strongest performance in the series, and the largest role in this episode. The whole supporting cast play vital parts throughout the episode in one of the best ensemble scripts of *Space: 1999*.

Helena Russell is not only a doctor, but also a leader and the real hero of this episode. She's strong, decisive, and yet caring at the same time. Her act of blowing up the Eagle to attract the attention of the passing search ship is one of quick thinking desperation and leadership strength. The sight of her holding the laser rifle and being blasted backward by the shockwave is particularly effective, since she so rarely even fires a Stun Gun in the series.

The direction by Charles Crichton is strong, if not as flashy as that of others such as David Tomblin and Ray Austin. *Space: 1999* would frequently pair the same screenwriter and director, so Penfold and Crichton would go on from here to create several more episodes together, including the classics 'War Games' and 'Dragon's Domain'.

The episode ends with the thought that human nature itself is what led the inhabitants of Ariel to keep the Alphans off of their world, despite their belief in the good intentions of the Alphans. It is an interesting concept, to be judged on the past history of the Earth, rather than on one's own merits. As in Penfold's 'Guardian of Piri', religious fanaticism is also explored here, with Paul consuming 'sacred bread' – manna from heaven – and taking on the role of a messiah. He also refers to a 'second coming'.

The word 'Ariel' is the name of an airy spirit in Shakespeare's play *The Tempest*, which had already proved a notable inspiration for 'Missing Link'. Amongst other similarities, including the crash of a ship, it is only appropriate for the mysterious and unseen inhabitants of the planet Ariel (almost spirit-like) to supply the Moon with an atmosphere.

It is an effectively melancholic atmosphere in Main Mission as the Alphans gather to watch the final sunset over the lunar surface before the Ariel satellites leave with the last of the air. There are many poignant moments throughout Year One, but watching the sun go down here is one of the most profound. Lost hopes abound in *Space: 1999* (including in previous episodes 'Guardian of Piri' and 'Matter of Life and Death' – another episode that shares elements with this one, including part of its *Paradise Lost* theme – as well as upcoming ones such as 'War Games') and, again, that's where much of the emotional reality of the series comes from: the Alphans may encounter failures and their dream may be just out of reach, but that's the way life can sometimes be.

Most memorable amongst the points made here is that the Alphans already have a home, right beneath their feet. Although occasionally a bit slow, 'The Last Sunset' is a memorably fine episode.

Rating: 7.5/10

1.12
VOYAGER'S RETURN

Screenplay by Johnny Byrne
Directed by Bob Kellett

Selected Broadcast Dates:

UK	LWT:	
	Date: 11 October 1975.	Time: 5.50 pm
	Granada:	
	Date: 31 October 1975.	Time: 6.35 pm
US	KRON (San Francisco):	
	Date: 22 November 1975.	Time: 7.00 pm

Credited Cast: Martin Landau (John Koenig), **Barbara Bain** (Helena Russell), **Barry Morse** (Victor Bergman), **Prentis Hancock** (Paul Morrow), **Clifton Jones** (David Kano), **Zienia Merton** (Sandra Benes), **Anton Phillips** (Bob Mathias), **Nick Tate** (Alan Carter), **Alex Scott** (Aarchon), **Lawrence Trimble** (Steve Abrams)

Guest Star: Jeremy Kemp (Dr Ernst Linden / Queller)

Guest Artist: Barry Stokes (Jim Haines)

Uncredited Cast: Suzanne Roquette (Tanya Alexander), **Sarah Bullen** (Operative Kate), **Loftus Burton** (Operative Lee Oswald), **Andrew Dempsey**, **Robert Phillips**, **Michael Stevens** (Main Mission Operatives), **Tony Allyn** (Security Guard Tony Allan), **Quentin Pierre** (Security Guard Pierce Quinton), **John Clifford** (Astronaut in corridor), **Alan Harris** (Alphan), **Laurie Davis**, **Al Flemyng**, **Anita West** (Technicians)

Plot: Alpha encounters the Earth space probe Voyager One, which contains vast amounts of information amassed on its journey. But powered by a Queller Drive – a fast neutron propulsion system that generates dangerous radiation – Voyager is capable of destroying the base. While the Alphans discuss the risk they face to gather the data from the ship, a new threat emerges: aliens whose worlds were destroyed by the Queller Drive are following Voyager and are intent on exacting revenge.

Quotes:
- **Linden/Queller:** 'I have been guilty of pride and arrogance.'
- **Helena:** 'They say the road to Hell …'
- **Linden/Queller:** 'Is paved with good intentions. And the road to Heaven too, apparently.'
- **Aarchon:** 'You came proclaiming peace, and you wrought destruction.'
- **Koenig:** 'His sacrifice gave us a future. His knowledge, hope. And now someone has to carry on his work.'
- **Linden/Queller:** 'Your people have suffered greatly. Therefore, punish me. Do not

condemn an entire world for the mistake of one man. My purpose was to unite a divided world; to reach out in the name of science and humanity; to illuminate the mysteries of space. To seek out other worlds, and offer the hand of friendship.'

Filming Dates: Wednesday 7 August – Monday 26 August 1974

Incidental Music: Includes music from the film *Thunderbird 6* previously heard in 'The Last Sunset'.

Commentary:
Prentis Hancock: 'As Paul Morrow, I was always there in a scene, but it was a bit thin on the ground on him actually getting involved. They came to me one day and said, "We've got a real character episode for you this week, Prentis," and I thought, "Great!" But it turned out to be one line in a conference in which a space voyage was mentioned in which my father had died!'

Zienia Merton: 'Actually, I got told off by Jeremy Kemp – nicely, of course. I was in awe of him and thought he was smashing. I thought he might just think I was pushy or a dreary little extra trying to chat him up, as I didn't have many scenes with him. So I kept out of the way. Then we had a party, and he said, "You're very naughty, you know … You should make people feel at home. After all, this is kind of your home." So I explained why I hadn't approached him, and I said I knew what he meant, and that of course it is an unwritten thing that you do welcome people.'

Johnny Byrne: '"Voyager's Return" began its existence in an idea from a friend of mine called Joe Gammon, who was a sort of young writer and also a film editor. He came up with a rough idea as a story, which he submitted because he knew I was story editor. It was way off target in terms of what was possible for us to do. It was a very complicated thing. The basic idea was that a ship had come back. And it's quite impressive in a way, because the Voyager probes were out there at that time. The ship would land on the Moon and would con them into providing systems of life support, and it was actually turning itself into a creature, rather like Frankenstein on a rack. Joe couldn't write the script at that time. There was a host of reasons why Joe couldn't be commissioned. But I asked him if I could do the story, and he was quite willing – he got paid for the idea of just the Voyager coming back. I was struck by the idea that something we carelessly sent out into space – in a sort of altruism – could possibly have unfortunate consequences for the things it comes into contact with. Basing it on that I built in a story of Ernst Queller, rather like … Wernher von Braun. He had been responsible for a nasty accident. His concept was so wonderful, but it was also very dangerous, and it sacrificed a lot of people.

'For dramatic purposes, we simply had him surfacing on the Moonbase, because this thing is coming back, and as it comes into contact it's got this drive that will switch on, which will annihilate them. They don't know how to stop it, but then Queller reveals who he is and he helps them do it. And then [we see] the full consequences of what he has done – again, building on the existing situation. When we think the story over, it's only really beginning, because [Voyager] is being trailed back to its home planet by people whose worlds have been absolutely destroyed and are intent on exacting a horrific revenge.

'So there was a kind of social message in that, a *slight* one, and one tried to make it as interesting and agreeable and as tense a situation as possible ... It was more a nuts and bolts story, that – a pure sort of nuts and bolts science fiction *Space: 1999* story. I particularly liked the interior of the Earth ship, the Queller ship. The alien ones looked a bit too stick-cricket-like. They didn't strike me as menacing enough. They were meant to be – and I laid this on very heavily in the script – extremely menacing. You could sense power but not see it, and you had the feeling that things were going to start poking out and start firing at you at any moment ...

'Here was a man who believed he had a great gift to give to space, people, other nations and other races if he brought contact between those two worlds. He *did* bring contact, but not in the way he expected. And I think there's a message there that – even today, when we're littering space with all kinds of hideous junk – we don't really give a thought to the consequences and the things we send out. Just as if something came from outside and landed here, with the thought of contamination – it's a grisly thought – we should have the same regard for what might be out there. That's not to say we shouldn't explore. We should be very responsible and treat space as much like our home backyard as we can. It's a curious thing, that. As we become more aware of how precious the Earth is, and how to look after it, the less we seem to care about space. Obviously, when we've sorted out our back garden and sorted out the Earth, then *perhaps* we'll sort out space. And by that time, let's hope that it hasn't gone too far ...

'I enjoyed it ... and I think the scientist was well played by Jeremy Kemp. I liked the story because it was simple, it was immediately comprehensible, it was relevant to people's lives, because it was directly linked to what was actually happening in terms of our rather misty-eyed notions about mankind sending [out] universal messages of love, hope and peace. Well, we know where that kind of thing ends up, don't we? It usually ends up with someone getting their arse kicked. It's self-deluding to believe that by sending things out into space you are actually helping to extend mankind's mission to civilise. We know what happened in Earthly terms when this kind of thing was tried: you had missionaries arriving in [places] like Africa, and when they arrived they had the Book and the Africans had the land – by the time they left, the missionaries had the land and the Africans had the Book. This is, I should imagine, the kind of fate that will befall those aliens unfortunate enough to encounter us. If they are of a lower level of competence and technology, their fate won't be a nice one.

'So it's about the assumptions that we bring to our understanding of what constitutes life and the arrogance that we have about our own form of existence and our own way of living. We see it played out on the small scale of the planet Earth. Played out on a vast scale up in the stars, it's just too horrendous to contemplate. I think that all of those aliens who ever said, "Stay where you are and leave us alone," have got it right and probably will have for at least the next five million years!

'I wanted to give Queller a Germanic type of façade. I never saw him as a "nasty" – I didn't see him as a Nazi. I had in mind those haunted individuals who had avoided being taken by the Russians at the end of the Second World War and found their way, sort of bribed, into service by [the] American and British [governments], serving in the Cold War. These were people who were intelligent enough to know that the end product of their science and their genius was the destruction of people and it was in the service of a despotic master. They, by their own reckoning, were not evil men – they were perhaps scientists; they were idealists; they were all sorts of things. But if we talk about the downfall of 20th Century Man, this is the classic symptom of that malady.

They took their poison chalice, they took their shilling, and they lived with the guilt. This man [Queller] perhaps exemplified it that bit more severely, because what he had done was to actually kill people in the service of trying to improve humanity's lot. He carried the guilt; he found a way to bury himself, lick his wounds, and hopefully everybody would forget him. That was his situation. He was too brilliant to be wasted, and the powers that be knew about him and they had him there doing something very important out of sight and out of mind. We *all* deserve a second chance, and [Queller] exemplifies the larger condition of the Alphans being people who were set on a course of redemption for humanity as a whole. Don't forget the almost biblical destruction of the Earth. And these people were given the opportunity, one could say, of redeeming whatever caused the fall: man's second chance.'

Bloopers: Watch the shots of Voyager One flying – liquid Freon can be seen dripping from the bell rockets and dropping to the bottom of the screen (which it wouldn't do in zero gravity in outer space).

Review: 'Voyager's Return' features an effectively chilling opening, with the Voyager probe destroying an Eagle and killing Alpha pilot Abrams, as well as damaging Eagle One and injuring Carter, before relaying the message, 'This is the voice of Voyager One. Greetings from the people of the planet Earth.' The death of pilot Abrams is one of the most visually accomplished in the series – he is literally sucked out of the Eagle's shattered view-port. It is a short sequence, but certainly on a par with similar later shots of explosive decompression in the "War Games" episode.

The destructive force of the Queller Drive is best stated by Paul Morrow when he says, 'You'd survive better standing smack in the middle of a nuclear explosion.' The knowledge that the Queller Drive killed Paul's father provides both intriguing character background and enlarges the strong supporting role for Prentis Hancock.

The episode plunges the viewer effectively and immediately into discussions on what to do with Voyager: Helena wants it stopped before it can do any more harm, while Victor wants the scientific information it contains. As Bergman states, 'For 15 years Voyager has been photographing other planets, analysing atmospheres, detailing all forms of life, recording gravities, temperatures … It would take 100 years to learn what Voyager already knows.' Koenig finds himself in a position of balancing the various opinions around him and seeking an acceptable middle ground. The Alphans are quite divided on what to do with Voyager, making this an intriguing examination of the way the command of Alpha is often open for discussion.

This episode provides a highly refined portrait of Ernst Linden/Queller as he tries to atone for his longstanding private guilt over the deaths for which his creation has been responsible. The presence of the Sidon aliens (and their marvellously insect-inspired ships) shows that Voyager has destroyed other alien civilisations as well, making the scientist's grief that much greater. He is perfectly portrayed by Jeremy Kemp – alternately powerful, sympathetic, heroic, or simply a tired old scientist who has been worn down by years of accumulated guilt. It's a richly written and performed role, and Kemp joins the roster of talented guest artists who have appeared in the series to date. Faced with the destruction of Alpha by the superior technology of the Sidons, Queller attempts to reason with the aliens, making an impassioned plea of good intentions. When the aliens fail to listen to reason, Queller uses his Drive as a weapon, destroying the Sidons and then activating self-destruct mechanisms within Voyager and killing himself, but saving Alpha in the process.

One rather strong political statement is made with Victor's line, 'We believe that revenge, sanctioned by authority, is also a sign of a debased culture.' To put it another way, justice is not accomplished through revenge. Thus, for example, a civilised culture could never permit the use of the death penalty.

Barbara Bain performs a wonderful arc of character development through this episode, as Helena progresses from a cold distrust of Queller to an obvious warmth and compassion towards him. Helena also serves her frequent role as the voice of caution – appropriate for Alpha's top doctor.

Johnny Byrne's script clearly draws parallels between Ernst Queller and Wernher von Braun – the real-life German scientist who was responsible for the design and creation of the V-2 combat rocket during World War II and then entered the United States at the end of the War and became the primary designer of the Saturn V super-booster that propelled Americans to the Moon. With such rich inspirational material for the script, it's unfortunate that the episode didn't turn out better. This is the directorial debut of Bob Kellett on the series, and unfortunately his work comes across as unremarkable when compared with that of David Tomblin (whom he was temporarily replacing while Tomblin served as assistant director on the film *Barry Lyndon*), Ray Austin or Charles Crichton.

Disappointingly, the information from the Voyager One memory banks will never be mentioned again in the series, although it will be made use of in the tie-in novel *Android Planet*. Voyager One and Voyager Two are further failed Earth space missions (following the Meta Probe and the Astro 7) – part of the unfolding negative image of mankind's exploration of space. This theme, which could be regarded as depressing in its almost unrelenting string of failure, also constitutes a cautionary tale. As these failed missions continue to pile up over future episodes, the question will arise whether they were all initiated by the same space agency or whether some funding came from other organisations, countries or private corporations.

It is the disturbing irony of the episode that Earth's peacefully-intended efforts to explore space via the unmanned Voyager ship should end up being so horribly destructive to the alien life it discovers. As Linden/Queller says, 'The responsibility for what Voyager did to the Sidons I must bear alone. Two worlds made lifeless. Millions of people dead … I had no wish to harm them; to harm anyone.'

'Voyager's Return' is an exploration of redemption, guilt, hubris, repentance and forgiveness. But although it is a solid science fiction story, it ends up being somewhat too conventional in execution, and falls short of being one of the best episodes of the series.

Rating: 7.5/10

1.13
COLLISION COURSE

Screenplay by Anthony Terpiloff
Directed by Ray Austin

Selected Broadcast Dates:

UK	LWT:	
	Date: 20 September 1975.	Time: 5.50 pm
	Granada:	
	Date: 10 October 1975.	Time: 6.35 pm
US	KRON (San Francisco):	
	Date: 27 September 1975.	Time: 7.00 pm
	WPIX (New York):	
	Date: 11 October 1975.	Time: 7.00 pm

Credited Cast: Martin Landau (John Koenig), **Barbara Bain** (Helena Russell), **Barry Morse** (Victor Bergman), **Prentis Hancock** (Paul Morrow), **Clifton Jones** (David Kano), **Zienia Merton** (Sandra Benes), **Anton Phillips** (Bob Mathias), **Nick Tate** (Alan Carter)

Special Guest Star: Margaret Leighton (Arra)

Uncredited Cast: Suzanne Roquette (Tanya Alexander), **Sarah Bullen** (Operative Kate), **Loftus Burton** (Operative Lee Oswald), **Annie Lambert** (Operative Julie), **Vic Armstrong, Andrew Dempsey, Michael Stevens** (Main Mission Operatives), **Tony Allyn** (Security Guard Tony Allan), **Quentin Pierre** (Security Guard Pierce Quinton), **Alan Harris** (Alphan), **Alf Joint** (Balcony Alphan), **Glenda Allen** (Nurse)

Plot: The Moon is on a collision course with the giant planet Atheria. While the Alphans enact a plan to save themselves, Koenig's Eagle is captured by a spaceship belonging to the alien queen Arra, who tells Koenig that the Alphans are on a pre-destined voyage, and that the collision with Atheria will not result in destruction, but in the evolution of her people.

Quotes:
- **Alan:** 'Take me to your people!'
- **Koenig:** 'Don't worry – I'll wear my galoshes.'
- **Arra:** 'Oh, poor John Koenig. How you belittle yourself in the scheme of things. And yet how small you are, to be so great.'
- **Koenig:** 'I trust her. I believe her.'
- **Arra:** 'The gene, of which I and my people are a part, shall mutate. We shall take on another form, unrecognisable, spiritual if you like. But once changed we shall become immutable, for time inconceivable.'
- **Kano:** 'It defies logic.'
- **Victor:** 'Yes, it's a thing called faith.'

- **Arra:** 'We have met with purpose. We must not fail our destiny.'
- **Arra:** 'I go to shape the future of eternity. And I need your help.'

Filming Dates: Tuesday 27 August – Tuesday 10 September 1974

Incidental Music: This episode features Barry Gray compositions from the *Joe 90* episodes 'Arctic Adventure' and 'Operation McClaine', which here are combined to form one track heard in a number of scenes featuring Arra, such as when Carter regains consciousness and when Koenig receives the orbital reference. In addition, music from the film *Thunderbird 6* (previously used in 'The Last Sunset' and 'Voyager's Return') is heard again.

Bloopers: Watch Helena's Commlock for missing buttons.

Observations: The planet name Atheria was misspelled as 'Aestheria' in some original ITC promotional material. This error has often been repeated to this day, as has the also-incorrect variant 'Astheria'.

The impressive-looking throne on which Arra sits will later appear in the episodes 'The Infernal Machine' (as Companion's bed) and 'The Dorcons' (as Archon's throne).

Special effects footage of Koenig's Eagle being swallowed by Arra's ship was used in a 1979 episode of *The Tomorrow People* titled 'War of the Empires'.

Review: Beginning with an intense opening teaser as Eagles work to plant nuclear charges on the approaching asteroid threatening to destroy them, 'Collision Course' is a largely successful episode.

Viewers are immediately struck by Martin Landau's emotionally charged performance, which is one of his finest in the series. The entire cast receive solid treatment from this script. Prentis Hancock, in particular, gets one of his rare opportunities to leave the Main Mission set, and excels in the role. Here his character is on the Rescue Eagle mission to save Alan Carter from the deadly radiation cloud, following the asteroid explosion. Nick Tate also stands out as the bewildered Carter. There are many small moments of simple and subtle human warmth.

The special effects of the radiation cloud hovering like a fog over Alpha are highly effective. As well, the landing of the two docked Eagles onto a single launch pad is a unique and impressive visual.

'Collision Course' was filmed in late August and early September 1975. Guest star Margaret Leighton was suffering the effects of multiple sclerosis, and passed away only a few months later, in January 1976. She relied upon a great deal of direction in order to help her through the complicated dialogue, as related by Keith Wilson: 'She was wonderful, but she didn't understand a word she was saying … She was really quite worried about it.' Leighton also knew she didn't have long to live and told director Ray Austin, 'You'd better get this shot, because I'm not going to last long.' Despite all of this, her performance stands out as one of the most powerful and dignified guest appearances seen in the series. She captures and conveys the ageless wisdom, as well as the contrast of fragility with great strength, intrinsic to the character of Arra. Arra is presented as a mysterious figure of great knowledge and influence. Her nearly mystical presence is suggested not only through Leighton's performance, but also through Austin's direction.

An exceptional scene begins as Arra visits Alan in Medical: as he lifts her veil, he is really lifting his hands into Helena's hair. Alan is sedated and then John and Helena have a tense confrontation rivalling their later arguments in 'Dragon's Domain' (in which they will fight over the mental state of astronaut Tony Cellini, as here they are engaged about the mental and physical health of astronaut Alan Carter). Ray Austin again displays his use of unusual camera angles, taking a shot of Koenig and Russell through a shelving unit. He later uses this same striking approach in Koenig's quarters.

Faith shows itself as a prevalent theme in Anthony Terpiloff's writing – here, Koenig's faith in Carter is demonstrated, Koenig's faith in Arra is tested, and the faith of the Alphans in their Commander is strained. Arra herself says, 'I have faith in you, John Koenig.' Koenig responds, 'And I have faith in you. But what is faith against the fact of imminent collision?' Religion itself is drawn into question – in an allusory fashion – as the Alphans are asked to believe Koenig and have faith in a being/race/power that is mysterious, invisible and greater than themselves. This theme will appear again in later Terpiloff scripts. It's interesting that an episode titled 'Collision Course' would make the physical collision itself of secondary importance behind the thematic collision of faith and trust versus logic.

Koenig's meeting with Arra inside her cobweb-filled and darkly dramatic ship is a gorgeous example of all the elements of this production working together in harmony – the performances, script, direction, musical score and lighting, as well as the lovely and eerie monochromatic set.

The underlying distrust in science shown by *Space: 1999* must have had a degree of negative impact on the portion of North American viewers and critics (so conditioned to the rose-tinted future of *Star Trek*) who didn't respond well to the series. Another example of this distrust in science appears here, as, despite everyone's faith in the Professor, Bergman's Operation Shockwave doesn't hold the answers to their survival. They must follow the advice of Arra and allow their two planets to collide, going against all scientific knowledge and logical thinking, putting trust in Arra and the Mysterious Unknown Force. Koenig is convinced that Arra is right, but he also knows that his scientifically-minded friends won't believe him. He says, 'What you tell me sounds magnificent here in this chamber, and from your lips. But how will it sound in the cold light of Moonbase Alpha? They'll never believe me ...'

The idea that Alpha's journey was predestined is of significant importance. Arra states, 'We have expected you for many millions of years. You see, your destiny has always been our destiny.' She also asks Koenig, 'Are you unfit to play the part for which you have been destined since the beginning of time?' The alien Queen also offers a prophecy for the Alphans' future: 'You shall continue on. Your odyssey shall know no end. You will prosper and increase in new worlds, new galaxies. You will populate the deepest reaches of space.'

Intriguingly, there is a parallel in dialogue between this episode and 'Black Sun'. In that earlier episode, Victor asks the mysterious voice in the Black Sun, 'Who are you?' The answer is, 'A friend.' Here, in 'Collision Course', Alan asks Arra, 'Who are you?' and receives the same reply, 'A friend.' Could there be a connection between the voice in the Black Sun and Arra, or is this purely coincidence?

The culminating scene in Main Mission as Koenig and Carter take over (in their pajamas!) and force the end of Operation Shockwave is an absolutely riveting sequence. The duo can be viewed as religious zealots – madmen leading their people to death through the lunacy of their beliefs … and yet, they are right. As Koenig says in the epilogue, 'How could anyone possibly know that a planet on a collision course would not collide, but simply touch?'

Of course, the science in this episode leaves much to be desired: Operation Shockwave could never work because shockwaves don't travel in the vacuum of space, let alone be strong enough to force apart the Moon and Atheria. Apart from that, 'Collision Course' successfully presents the kind of mature, philosophical, metaphysical thinking that sets *Space: 1999* apart from other television science fiction programmes.

Rating: 9/10

1.14
DEATH'S OTHER DOMINION

Screenplay by Anthony Terpiloff and Elizabeth Barrows
Directed by Charles Crichton

Selected Broadcast Dates:

UK	LWT:	
	Date: 4 October 1975.	Time: 5.50 pm
	Granada:	
	Date: 24 October 1975.	Time: 6.35 pm
US	KRON (San Francisco):	
	Date: 20 September 1975.	Time: 7.00 pm
	WPIX (New York):	
	Date: 4 October 1975.	Time: 7.00 pm

Credited Cast: Martin Landau (John Koenig), **Barbara Bain** (Helena Russell), **Barry Morse** (Victor Bergman), **Prentis Hancock** (Paul Morrow), **Clifton Jones** (David Kano), **Zienia Merton** (Sandra Benes), **Anton Phillips** (Bob Mathias), **Nick Tate** (Alan Carter), **Mary Miller** (Frieda)

Guest Star: Brian Blessed (Dr Cabot Rowland)

Guest Artist: John Shrapnel (Colonel Jack Tanner)

Uncredited Cast: Suzanne Roquette (Tanya Alexander), **Sarah Bullen** (Operative Kate), **Loftus Burton** (Operative Lee Oswald), **Annie Lambert** (Operative Julie), **Andrew Dempsey** (Main Mission Operative), **Robert Phillips** (Main Mission Operative), **David Ellison** (Ted Foster), **Valerie Leon** (Thulian Girl), **Jack Shepherd, Laurie Davis, Eddy Nedari, Tony Houghton, John Lee-Barber, Suzette St Clair, Barbara Bermel, Jenny Devenish, Carolyn Hudson, Glenda Allen, David Murphy, Michael Ryan, Anette Linden** (Thulians), **Adrienne Burgess, Lesley Collet, Robert Driscoll, Margaret Lawley, Terry Rendle, Ian Ruskin, Ellen Sheehan** (Revered Ones)

Plot: On the ice planet Ultima Thule the Alphans encounter the survivors of the Uranus Probe of 1986, who have carved out a home within underground caverns. But not everyone sees Thule as a paradise, and it is revealed that life here is immortal – these Earthmen are frozen in time and have lived for 880 years! Attempting to persuade his fellow humans to relocate on Thule, Dr Rowland accompanies the Alphans for a flight to the Moon, but as they leave the icy atmosphere the extent of Thule's influence becomes clear.

Quotes:
* **Jack:** 'I am the dog that bays the Moon who sets her cats amongst your pigeons,

doctor.'

- **Jack:** 'Good doctor, revel while you can. The hour is late. Our end is near. The road to paradise has seized up.'
- **Alan:** 'Come on, you beautiful bird. Lift off. Lift off!'
- **Helena:** 'But Alpha isn't home. It's a barracks, on a barren rock, flying endlessly through space! We want a real home. A place to live … to raise children.'
- **Jack:** 'A death on Thule would be a marvellous thing.'
- **Rowland:** 'The blight of human life has been death. The most brilliant minds cut off. Progress held back. We have lived on Thule for 800 years. We have immortality.'
- **Jack:** 'Oh yes, wonderful. Science in the belly and salad on the brain.'
- **Koenig:** 'Come on, Jack. There's more in that mind of yours than meets the ears.'
- **Jack:** 'The ultimate welfare – where want is dead.'
- **Jack:** 'By all dishevelled, wandering stars, I tell you – death has dominion!'
- **Koenig:** 'Is it death that gives meaning to life, in the end?'
- **Jack:** 'If there is an end.'

Filming Dates: Wednesday 11 September – Monday 23 September 1974

Incidental Music: Includes a track by Barry Gray from the *Joe 90* episode 'Big Fish', heard at the start of the episode while Jack and Dr Rowland discuss the Moon, and as Rowland calls Alpha.

Commentary:

Barry Morse: 'In "Death's other Dominion" I was obliged to spend the day struggling through a studio blizzard. I evidently managed to get through it all right. It was very comical, that snow storm, and gave rise to a lot of giggles, especially from Brian Blessed. Dear Brian and I had some testing moments playing together, because you'd only have to give the slightest twinkle of your eye and Brian would be off giggling. We had a wonderful time. I also remember John Shrapnel playing his character rather like The Fool from *King Lear*. The entire episode had a rather Shakespearean tone to it.'

Christopher Penfold: 'The episode "Death's other Dominion" was written by Anthony Terpiloff. I got Anthony Terpiloff involved because he had written an absolutely brilliant television play about Dylan Thomas, in New York, which is about as far removed from a science fiction subject as you could possibly get, but I just thought he was a great writer. So the reason for bringing him on to the show was not because he was a science fiction expert or that he had a great background in science fiction writing, but because he was actually just a great writer. The science fiction expert on the team was Johnny Byrne, and it was a team.'

Sylvia Anderson: 'When we were preparing for the show there were a lot of strikes going on, so we only had so many days a week that we could work, [and] we brought our own generators into Pinewood Studios. One day I walked in and they were building this fantastic futuristic set [of the ice caves for "Death's other Dominion"]. And I said, "My God, no-one can work in this." They were using embalming fluid to build the set! I said, "We can't do this." Everyone said, "Don't say anything. Wait for the actors to come on." Anyway, Martin Landau and Barbara Bain came on and within seconds they were absolutely falling about and came over to me saying, "What's happening, what's happening?" So we had to do something about that.'

Keith Wilson: 'The cheapest set I did was [for] the ice one with Brian Blessed, "Death's other Dominion" … It was the Ice Palace, the interior. I built it out of rubbish. Literally. We walked around the lot and we picked up rubbish and we constructed … I would say, "A bit more here … An archway there …" and once it was built – out of literally rubbish – we sprayed it all with this foam. It went crispy, but it left (I think) formaldehyde, and it gave a smell. For a few minutes it would make your eyes water. On Friday, the set was being finished and Martin and Barbara just wandered [in] to see what they were going to be shooting on Monday. Martin went, "What's that smell?" and somebody said, "Oh, it's formaldehyde. It'll give you cancer, that will." We're shooting the bloody thing on Monday! Martin went wild. He left the stage, he went to Gerry, and he said, "This set will give me cancer!" We had to get scientists in to take tests [and confirm it was safe], and it went on all over the weekend. I had finished the set, but I had to work all weekend because if we couldn't shoot in it, we had nothing to shoot on Monday. During this period when we had scientists there taking tests, there were a couple of riggers sitting there having their lunch on the set. They were eating shrimp sandwiches, or something, and the scientists said to them, "Does this smell worry you?" They said, "What smell?" They'd been working in it and they'd got used to it. But it was a great worry. It was one of the biggest worries on the series, because I thought, "What the hell are we going to do?"'

Bloopers: In the command module, Carter brings up an image of the Eagle being buried in snow – but where does this image come from? It is an impossible viewpoint.

Observations: One interesting 'behind the scenes' anecdote – the soap that was used to simulate blowing snow during the blizzard sequences was apparently quite abrasive and took the skin off of Martin Landau's face.

'Death's other Dominion' features the largest cast of any *Space: 1999* episode.

Review: 'Death's other Dominion', first and foremost, presents a tale of immortals living on an ice planet – what more appropriate setting could there be? Everything freezes in this giant icebox and essentially lasts forever – including the people.

Perhaps the most staggering individual guest appearance in the entire series comes from John Shrapnel as Jack Tanner. He gives himself to the role entirely, and is flanked in all directions by outstanding performances from his fellow Thulians (including the charming Mary Miller as Frieda) and the Alphans. Brian Blessed makes his first of two *Space: 1999* appearances here – the other will come as Mentor in 'The Metamorph' – and the parallels between them are quite striking. In both, he rules in underground cavern-worlds symbolic of Hell. His characters both have immense magnetism, charisma and power (all of which are admittedly hard to avoid when you cast Blessed in the role!) The scene here where his laboratory is destroyed is initiated by Koenig, as will be the equivalent scene in 'The Metamorph', and in both instances the hubris of Blessed's character is his downfall. Both Rowland and Mentor have crossed the ethical boundaries of their scientific profession – it's a fascinating comparison. Rowland's end is the most gruesome scene in the series. The depiction of his corpse is horrifying: the culmination of the many nightmarish aspects of the episode.

Ultima Thule is a believable frozen world (despite the strangely foamy snow), and the caverns are a model of art direction, design and construction. Thulian life is detailed, with attention to their clothing (fur and skins from a species of Ox mentioned by Foster) and food (at once nauseating, but adaptable). Also deserving of note are the Alphan snowsuits and sweaters, a striking combination of blue, white and red. They are seen only in this one episode. Martin Bower's model of the *Phoenix* (the ship the Thulians are constructing in order to leave their ice world) is an impressively detailed miniature, inspired by the unfinished rocket in the film *When Worlds Collide*. It would have been lovely if the *Phoenix* had received more screen time.

Characterisation is mixed, unfortunately. Martin Landau gives one of his strongest performances as Koenig, showing a leader at odds against an adversary he doesn't fully understand, and at the same time lacking the support of his closest comrades. Koenig, above all, is sensible. On the other hand, both Helena and Victor are inconsistent and come across as naïve – simplistically falling under Rowland's charismatic spell. Bergman's customary wisdom and Helena's usual caution are completely absent, and there really is no basis for their gullibility, other than the convenience of the script. Viewers are left with two of the three series leads acting well out of character, with no reasonable explanation being provided.

The sequences back on the Moonbase show the starkly contrasting environments of life on Alpha and in the Ice Palace on Thule. Charles Crichton's direction excels as he follows the twists, turns and revelations of the plot, and tells this tale of the dangers of immortality. Crichton previously directed the storm sequences in 'Matter of Life and Death' and, although the blizzard here isn't as dynamically shot, it is still highly memorable.

This episode tests the faith of characters – Helena's and Victor's misplaced faith in Rowland; Rowland's faith in mankind's ambitions; and the crisis of faith shown to Koenig. Faith is always a theme in Terpiloff's scripts (see the previous episode 'Collision Course' and, notably, Year Two's 'Catacombs of the Moon'). As with 'The Infernal Machine', Terpiloff's work here is heightened by the contribution of his wife and co-writer Elizabeth Barrows. Koenig desires humanity, which Russell and Bergman have overlooked in their quest for scientific perfection. Jack Tanner fills the Shakespearean role of the 'Fool' of Thule, around to ridicule and debase authority figures. Many of Jack's lines have a decidedly Shakespearean flavour to them. The role reversals between Rowland and Jack are notable. When the Uranus Probe left Earth, Jack was in command. On Thule, Rowland takes over until his death, when Jack attains the leadership position again. Also of interest, the name 'Jack' is a diminutive for 'John', so when the Alphans leave Ultima Thule, they have left behind another Commander John. It is also worthy of note that while Jack Tanner seems to have Shakespearean inspirations, his name is the same as that of the central figure in a masterpiece by another literary genius – George Bernard Shaw's *Man and Superman*.

Alan, alluding to future events, sings of 'Lucifer' – the Devil. (The song he's singing, 'Pack Up Your Troubles in Your Old Kit Bag and Smile, Smile, Smile', was a popular marching song during the First World War and the 'Lucifer' in question is actually a brand name of matches.) Jack leads Koenig to the Cave of the Revered Ones, the place of (what passes for) death on Thule. The Cave of the Revered Ones is equated to Hell by red lighting and their descent into it.

Amongst many other historical meanings, some sources denote 'Ultima Thule' as the Latin name for Greenland when the designation 'Thule' is used for Iceland. Also, in medieval times, 'Ultima Thule' was the designation given to any place situated beyond the 'borders of the known world'. Obviously, the name 'Ultima Thule' is highly appropriate for this frozen world, located an unknown distance from Earth.

The Uranus Probe joins the list of Earth's failed space missions, along with the Ultra Probe, Astro 7 and Voyager One. The recurrent *Space: 1999* distrust in science also appears here, with Rowland's experiments being the cause of the mindless state of the Revered Ones. Once again, mystical or mysterious events in *Space: 1999* do not require scientific explanation, and this is acknowledged when Frieda says, 'We have the secret to eternal life. Must we also seek to understand it?'

Thematically, the value of life is explored through the eternally intriguing topic of immortality; the statement being that the true value of life can be measured only against a fear of death. Immortality is undesirable, and is a trap the Thulians fell into. As so often happens with *Space: 1999* episodes, viewers are left with any number of questions. Here these questions are mostly centred on the Thulians. Will they manage to restore the Revered Ones? Will they discover the source of their immortality, or ever find a way to be free of it? And, if immortality becomes unbearable, would they eventually use the *Phoenix* spaceship as a way to end their eternal existence? It's a chilling thought, adding layers of meaning to Koenig's statement that the Thulians' future 'will haunt us till the end.'

The Shakespearean tone of the episode is not its only link to literature: in basic plot, 'Death's other Dominion' is a re-telling of *Lost Horizon*, the 1933 novel by English writer James Hilton. *Lost Horizon* follows a group of people who end up in utopian Shangri-La after their plane crashes. As they settle into their new home their aging slows; but if they leave the valley they will age quickly and die. Cabot Rowland is much like the novel's character Conway, who believes that his party's plane has 'progressed far beyond the western range of the Himalayas towards the less known heights of Kuen-Lun.' This statement is paralleled in Rowland's account, 'We travelled at unbelievable speed to the farthest limit of the then known universe – and beyond.' In the end, Conway agrees to leave the valley and meets his demise, as Rowland unwittingly does upon leaving Ultima Thule. There is also apparent reference to Milton's *Paradise Lost* when Rowland calls to the Alphans, 'Thule is a lost paradise,' while Jack Tanner adds, 'Lost, and with no final end.'

The combination of Shakespearean-styled scripting with the futuristic atmosphere of *Space: 1999* is a marvel, but unfortunately, due mostly to the weakness in characterisation, 'Death's other Dominion' falls short of being a masterpiece.

Rating: 8.5/10

1.15
THE FULL CIRCLE

Screenplay by Jesse Lasky Jnr and Pat Silver
Directed by Bob Kellett

Selected Broadcast Dates:

UK	LWT:	
	Date: 13 December 1975.	Time: 6.25 pm
	Granada:	
	Date: 12 March 1976.	Time: 6.35 pm
US	KRON (San Francisco):	
	Date: 6 December 1975.	Time: 7.00 pm

Credited Cast: Martin Landau (John Koenig), **Barbara Bain** (Helena Russell), **Barry Morse** (Victor Bergman), **Prentis Hancock** (Paul Morrow), **Clifton Jones** (David Kano), **Zienia Merton** (Sandra Benes), **Anton Phillips** (Bob Mathias), **Nick Tate** (Alan Carter), **Oliver Cotton** (Spearman)

Uncredited Cast: Sarah Bullen (Operative Kate / Cavewoman), **Suzanne Roquette** (Tanya Alexander), **Annie Lambert** (Operative Julie), **Andrew Dempsey** (Main Mission Operative / Caveman), **Lynda Westover** (Main Mission Operative / Cavewoman), **Robert Phillips** (Main Mission Operative), **Michael Stevens** (Main Mission Operative), **Tony Allyn** (Security Guard Tony Allan / Caveman), **Christopher Williams** (Orderly / Caveman), **Alan Meacham** (Sandos), **Colin Rix** (Co-Pilot / Caveman), **Chai Lee** (Alphan Nurse), **Glenda Allen** (Nurse / Cavewoman), **Kathy Mallory** (Nurse / Cavewoman)

Plot: An Eagle sent to the planet Retha is brought back to Alpha with a dead caveman aboard. Koenig and Russell's rescue team follows the first reconnaissance party and disappears into a strange mist. Carter is attacked by cavemen and Sandra is taken captive, which leads her to make the shocking discovery that there are no native Rethans – the only people are the Alphans themselves, transformed into their Cro Magnon counterparts by the mists of Retha.

Quotes:
- **Alan:** 'It looks like the jungle in Brazil.'
- **Paul:** 'Where the nuts come from?'
- **Victor [To Koenig]:** 'Lucky for you, you have a thick skull.'
- **Victor:** 'No sign of them at all. Just markers going into the mist.'
- **Sandra:** 'Oh God, what has happened?'
- **Sandra:** 'We got frightened, angry, jealous … vengeful.'

Filming Dates: Tuesday 24 September – Tuesday 8 October 1974

Commentary:

Barbara Bain: 'Dirt on the face; blackened teeth. That was fun, actually. I, as an actress, knew that was not a usual role. I didn't have a lot of experience playing such a creature. So, it was fun to think about, to do. I had a moment in there when I discover Koenig dead, when I scream. I thought a nice, polite scream wasn't going to do. I have screamed on occasion in a role. I thought, "What am I going to do?" It's got to be more than that. It has to be something very primitive and guttural. We broke for lunch, and the scream was coming up after lunch. I went upstairs into my dressing room and I wondered if I could just march out there and *hope* some great scream would come out, or what. Am I going to try it up here? And I did! I made this *ungodly* noise at Pinewood. I don't know if people were worried about what was going on in there! That was good. At least I heard it, and I thought, "Okay, that'll do it."

'[In this episode] Zienia was carried on a [pole]! Zienia's terrific! A very special person. She was *game* … among other things. I wouldn't have liked that part; headed toward the fire. It was fun to do that, actually. It was interesting, too. The movement of it was interesting to me. I always had a big interest in dance, and movement, and the physicality of it.

'The funny part of it was that my oldest daughter, Susan, was coming home from school with her first boyfriend, and I came home not quite rid of the (cavewoman) makeup. When you're in high school and your mom shows up like that, it can't be too terrific. So we tried to make peace over it, but I know I embarrassed her. It's interesting, because when you [think of favourite filming memories] … there's always some moment that's kind of part of your life, and part of the actual shooting, that stays interwoven, so it has a double level.'

Barry Morse: '"The Full Circle" was looked forward to with great glee among a lot of us, for the opportunity of shooting outside. But unfortunately, at the time we shot that episode, we had a succession of the most appallingly bad weather days England had seen for many months. So the only chance we got to be out of doors was in swamping rain and perishing cold. Some of our colleagues were a bit upset about the prospect of working in this weather. The general feeling was – here we were, hoping and praying to get an episode we could film outside, and when we finally get one, it's drenching down with rain all the time! I can't say the episode was particularly impressive or successful, or even one of the happiest times we spent filming, but I for one certainly did enjoy the change. It was funny to me because I always get a certain amount of amusement from how members of the human race respond to given situations, and in or out of favourable conditions.'

Zienia Merton: 'It was filmed at what we call Black Park, which is behind Pinewood Studios. It was the end of November, so the weather was not all that pleasant. My bits [of the filming] were outside. All I had [to wear] was this little leopard skin. The director said to me, "I'm not going to have you like Raquel Welch," – which I'm not – "in a fur-lined maiden form bra." He said, "This has got to look real. This is your leopard skin. Go to wardrobe and make a costume out of it. That's all you're getting; nothing else." So I went to wardrobe and we put the bits and pieces all around and pinned them, so it looked as if it was a costume made on the spot. And we went out to film. I had to be running through the forest – running, running, running – and finally I would collapse by a tree, exhausted. And it started to rain; but just a drizzle, not much.

So they said, "Well, we'll wait a bit. The caravan is too far away. It's too long to take you there. So we'll stay here." But, they gave me a huge plastic bag, which I got in to wait for the rain to stop … They didn't want the fur to get wet! *Fur* harder to dry than *actress*!

'I was lying there in my plastic bag and I suddenly thought, "God, my leg!" About 60 insects had bitten me; they'd all homed in on my leg. I was shivering because I had nothing else on – just the leopard skin and a small pair of trousers, and that was it. So our production manager – who's usually very strict, because he is responsible for making the budget work – came to me and said, "Zienia, darling, I think you need this." And it was a little teacup. I thought, "Ah, tea!" But it was brandy. It was neat brandy. I thought, "Oh, this is nice." So I started [taking sips] in my little plastic tent, and before lunch I must have had half a bottle of brandy; I was completely blotto. But I didn't mind, because I had no words, so all I had to do was run in a fairly straight line, and maybe no-one would notice.

'So, while I was filming by the tree, I was lying down and I got up … Always while you're filming, the continuity lady is right by the camera making sure that every word you say is the same, or if you use your right hand one time, that the next time you don't use your left – continuity. So she was sitting there. She's a wonderful woman, Gladys; a very nice, comfy mother figure. So I'm lying there and I'm getting up and she goes [making faces as if to subtly point out something wrong], and I looked, and I had fallen out of my costume! The rest of the crew said, "Aw, Gladys, you spoil sport!"

'I know that a lot of the criticisms of Year One of *Space: 1999* were [to the effect] that we were wooden or one-dimensional, or whatever people wanted to say. But looking at "The Full Circle", there were a lot of good funny bits there that I think were really valid, and should have been promoted. That was the kind of joking that I would have liked – you know, the inter-relationship between people and how they reacted. I mean, Kano had a wonderful line. He had never said anything funny before, but he actually said, "God, I hate back seat drivers," and I just think it's great. It's something we can all identify with. And also he said terribly chauvinist things like, "I hope she's getting lunch ready." There were silly things in it, and that is the key to humanising a show – it doesn't always have to be traumatic. There was an awful lot of that in "The Full Circle".

'I thought it was a super episode. It was lovely, we had a kind of flirtatious little thing, and Nick built this up. When we went down together in the Eagle, Prentis called to say, "Give my love to Sandra," and Nick said, "Not if I can help it," and then we built it up. I started panicking and worrying, and … before [Nick] fell in [the pit] he said something like, "Going on like this, you'll get Paul jealous." It was smashing. It was human emotion and [was] natural. But because we were sweet on each other, they thought we should be hugging each other every time we were alone together, and I said, "Don't be silly. We'd be hugging when we weren't in Main Mission." Away from prying eyes, so to speak. People don't suddenly clinch because the moment is right … But it was nice to get out. It was the first time we'd been out on location, and I know the crew thought it was [a novelty], because it was the first time they saw my legs! They said, "Oh, she's actually got legs." You know, I used to sit behind my desk, and I could have been crippled for all you saw of my movements.'

Nick Tate: 'I liked "The Full Circle", where we had to get out and fight the cavemen. That was the first time we went outside. They dug a great big pit outside Pinewood Studios and I went down in the pit and I fought this guy down there…'

Bloopers: When the third Eagle lands on Retha, the far one is an obvious cardboard cut-out.

Observations: The cave set is re-used from 'Death's other Dominion', where it was the Ice Palace. Here, re-painted and re-decorated, it's virtually unrecognisable to the casual viewer.

This is the first time the Stun/Kill sliding setting is seen on the Stun Guns.

Review: 'The Full Circle' takes the old saying about 'the mists of time' to its ultimate extent. And what a contrast this lush green world of Retha is after the frozen wasteland of Ultima Thule in the previous episode. This is a fascinating script, with Retha as a Bermuda Triangle of planets – resulting in repeated unaccountable disappearances of both reconnaissance teams and individual Alphans.

Bob Kellett's direction is at its best in his depiction of Sandra's run through the woods and her near death at the hands of the cave-woman Russell, and overall is his finest of the three episodes he helmed. Kellett has stated that he re-wrote much of the script himself.

Art direction is of special note within the caves, with the walls adorned by primitive Stone Age paintings. Note as well the massive mammoth tusk in the cavern. The special effects throughout are generally excellent, and the planet looks marvellously authentic in the views from outer space. The procedure of reconnaissance landings is somewhat different than normal, as this is one of the few times that the initial excursion team is not made up of series regulars. The use of markers to show the path the scouting party took into the forest is welcome and logical. It would have been worthwhile to utilise this system again in future episodes. It's also interesting to note the tracking device used to follow the previous teams into the forest – a piece of Alphan technology used only in this episode.

The effectively primitive drum music (Barry Gray's final recording for the series) heightens suspense and the prehistoric slant of the story, while providing another level of contrast to the futuristic science fiction trappings and outer space effects. There are well-incorporated signs of animal life on Retha, notably the giant dinosaur footprint and the rustling trees. And, compellingly, 'Retha' is an anagram of 'Earth'.

Director Bob Kellett reportedly encouraged the production to move outdoors, and 'The Full Circle' was the result. The episode was filmed near Pinewood Studios in Black Park, and is the only segment of Year One to feature extensive outdoor filming. The location shoot for this episode provides an absolutely beautiful setting to represent Retha, complete with authentic atmospheric mists.

Zienia Merton's performance is very strong and demonstrates that she can excel in a large leading role. If only she had received the opportunity more frequently. The flirtatious interplay between Sandra and Paul is greatly enjoyable, and especially so when contrasted against Paul's obvious jealousy. Along with Merton, Prentis Hancock, Nick Tate and Clifton Jones are all given an opportunity to shine, and all exude a likeable warmth of characterisation. Barbara Bain's performance as the howling cave-woman is outstanding, while Martin Landau impresses as a primitive version of himself. The primitive counterparts of Russell and Koenig still retain their strongest traits – he is the leader of his tribe and is quick to temper, while she is a compassionate and caring healer.

In a truly unusual example of an Eagle crew, Professor Bergman and David Kano serve as co-pilot and pilot on a launch down to Retha. The scene presenting the genial Bergman, Kano and Carter camping during the night on Retha, gathered around a blazing campfire and eating a hot meal, is appealing not only for the visual incongruity of these futuristic space travellers camping in the woods, but also for the simple fact that is shows them eating – something rarely done in *Space: 1999*. Although the sequence does have the stated appeal, logic is absent: enjoying the fresh air is one thing, but what possesses otherwise reasonable-minded people like Bergman and Kano to camp outside when they have no fewer than three perfectly safe Eagles to sleep in? Especially when other exploratory teams have gone missing, and strange cave-people and the occasional dinosaur-like creature are roaming about.

But lapses in logic aren't confined to the campers – Carter goes wandering off on his own to explore, without so much as leaving a note to tell Sandra what he is doing. Once he finds himself stuck in the pit, Carter should try using his Commlock to call Sandra, but instead he ignores it and actually leaves it behind. Sandra Benes suffers here, also. Having previously stated, 'Wild horses wouldn't drag me out of here,' she nonetheless proceeds to open the Eagle door without so much as a Stun Gun in her hand. A more natural action for her character would be to wait until Bergman and Kano arrive – it is only going to take them ten minutes to reach her. Once the door is opening and she can see the caveman standing outside, she should shut the door instead of remaining frozen. But the script did have to contrive some way of her getting captured, and at least she puts up a brave fight. With all these complaints about lack of character sensibility, it should be mentioned that there are many genuinely appealing interactions and warm moments in this episode, including smiles, laughter, jokes, flirtations, fears and hugs.

An arguable dialogue disaster occurs with Bergman's line about Carter being down on the planet with 'a ray gun'. The 'ray gun' term was long outdated even when this episode was made; but then again, Professor Bergman is a bit of an old-fashioned guy in some senses, so the reference might be said to be simply in character, rather than a script flaw.

One more complaint: why should the search radius that Koenig establishes be 100 miles? The missing party couldn't possibly have covered that much territory on foot, and there is no indication of any other method of transport. Given the time period and the densely forested terrain, a search radius of 10 or even 20 miles would have been far more than enough. It's a plot mistake that shouldn't have happened.

The enjoyable contrast at the heart of the entire episode is between the clean, futuristic and artificial environment of Alpha, and the primitive caverns, cave-people and natural forests of Retha. This does contain echoes, however faint, of Johnny Byrne's theme of the Technological Man versus Biological Man at the heart of 'Another Time, Another Place'.

Questions are raised. How does the mist regress people to their primitive counterparts? More pointedly, how are their uniforms transformed into primitive fur garments, and then back again? These are leaps of faith that some viewers can't manage, but then the series couldn't very well have had Barbara Bain and her comrades walk out of the mist stark naked. Of course, viewers have seen clothing transformations previously in 'Alpha Child', and they will become a regular occurrence with Maya in Year Two.

Rather like the opening 'Dawn of Man' sequence of *2001: A Space Odyssey*, 'The Full Circle' is commenting on mankind being closer to our ancient ancestors than we would like to believe. The core premise behind both productions, *2001: A Space Odyssey* and 'The Full Circle', is the evolution of man. The moral that mankind continues to battle its (possibly inherent) violent tendencies is evident in the dialogue:

> **Helena:** 'Under the skin, do you think we've changed all that much in forty thousand years?'
> **Victor:** 'Do you think we ever will?'

Whether Victor's line implies a cynicism that mankind is unable to progress beyond its primitive instincts, or whether it alludes to a more hopeful belief that mankind is able to change, is open to debate. Beyond that, there aren't very many thought-provoking issues arising from this rather lightweight episode. At least viewers are provided a change of pace from the frequently philosophical tone of Year One, and while 'The Full Circle' isn't among the best episodes of the series, it is certainly unique and amusing to watch.

Rating: 6.5/10

1.16
END OF ETERNITY

Screenplay by Johnny Byrne
Directed by Ray Austin

Selected Broadcast Dates:

UK	LWT:	
	Date: 22 November 1975.	Time: 5.50 pm
	Granada:	
	Date: 12 December 1975.	Time: 6.35 pm
US	KRON (San Francisco):	
	Date: 15 November 1975.	Time: 7.00 pm

Credited Cast: Martin Landau (John Koenig), **Barbara Bain** (Helena Russell), **Barry Morse** (Victor Bergman), **Prentis Hancock** (Paul Morrow), **Clifton Jones** (David Kano), **Zienia Merton** (Sandra Benes), **Anton Phillips** (Bob Mathias), **Nick Tate** (Alan Carter), **Jim Smilie** (Mike Baxter)

Guest Artist: Peter Bowles (Balor)

Uncredited Cast: Suzanne Roquette (Tanya Alexander), **Sarah Bullen** (Operative Kate), **Binu Balini, Laurie Davis, Andrew Dempsey, Raymond Harris, Jan Rennison** (Main Mission Operatives), **Tony Allyn** (Security Guard Tony Allan), **Quentin Pierre** (Security Guard Pierce Quinton), **Martin Grace, Colin Skeaping, Eddie Stacey, Paul Weston** (Security Guards / Stunts), **Anthony Scott** (Astronaut 6 (Hayes)), **Uffe Neumann** (Astronaut 8), **Vincent Wong** (Toshiro Fujita), **Paul Kirby** (Medical Orderly), **Christopher Williams** (Medical Orderly), **Judith Hepburn** (Nurse), **Kathy Mallory** (Nurse), **Robert Atiko** (Alphan), **Michael Stevens** (Alphan), **Laraine Humphreys** (Information Girl (Karen)), **Alan Harris** (Patient), **Glenda Allen** (Nurse)

Plot: The Alphans blast into a hollow chamber in an asteroid and discover a man on the verge of death. They transport him to Alpha. He dies, but before an autopsy can be performed, his body regenerates itself. Balor, of the planet Progron, is immortal and has been waiting a thousand years to be set free. Now he intends to exploit the Alphans in his sadistic experiments of torture and pain.

Quotes:
- **Victor:** 'Well, John, as far as I can see there's nothing else here. It's a one-room world.'
- **Balor:** 'How can you value life if you do not fear death?'
- **Balor:** 'A thousand years of reflection have convinced me I was right, and now I have the golden opportunity to prove it, with you.'
- **Koenig:** 'You're evil, Balor. And what you offer is evil. We will resist you and what you stand for.'

- **Balor:** 'I'm going to make you suffer, Koenig.'
- **Helena:** 'We must learn to leave some things alone.'

Filming Dates: Wednesday 9 October – Wednesday 23 October 1974

Incidental Music: The score, as with that of 'Force of Life', is greatly enhanced by electronic library music. Featured here are 'Videotronics No. 3' by Cecil Leuter and 'Cosmic Sounds No. 1' by Georges Teperino (both previously heard in 'Force of Life'), 'Experiments In Space – Malus' (heard while the Alphans set up the explosives on Balor's asteroid) and 'Experiments In Space – Dorado' (heard while Balor fights Alphan guards outside Medical Centre) by Robert Farnon, and 'Stratosphere' (heard throughout the episode in scenes featuring Balor, such as when the alien heals Koenig's wounds, and when he confronts Helena in Medical Centre) by David Snell. All of these tracks were from the Chappell Recorded Music Library.

Commentary:

Johnny Byrne: '"End of Eternity" is not one of my favourite stories. It started off with a very good idea. First the discovery of finding a creature entombed in a rock, then discovering that the guy has powers of regeneration, which means that he's immortal. Then discovering that he's a psychopath. How do you kill an immortal killer? That was what really got me going on it. In the playing of it, in the confines of Main Mission and the other places, it should have been a story in many ways that required opening out onto another landscape. I felt it was too claustrophobic and too confined.

'It was a tense story. The idea of the confrontation between it and Koenig – it's like Jack & The Beanstalk and the Giant – you know, trying to outwit the giant. It all worked, I think it all hung together very well. But for some reason it's not one of the ones that I like. I felt that I'd just turned out a decent story for that slot... I didn't feel inspired writing it, I just felt it was a writing job, and I tackled it the best way I could. I think it had to do with the nature of Balor: he was very one-dimensional. He was a psychopath, and the moment you say that to yourself you make people very single-minded. All they want to do is destroy. He never had any real reasons to do so. That, to me, is *not* good drama... It had all the potential for action, for movement, for pace and things like that. But on reflection, if I had looked and tried to work harder at that I think I could have made him a much more interesting and *subtle* destroyer, and at the end of the day, a more effective and permanent one. When he turned nasty there seemed to be a fairly arbitrary decision and there was no real build-up, I think, to his unmasking. And he should have had another purpose, a higher purpose, than simply the urge to indulge in mindless killing. *That*, I think, was the weakness of it. Other than that it worked as a sort of action-adventure story because of the way it was shot, the acting, the production values and the dramatic elements in the story.

'I felt that the character had not been fully exploited. He was a character who had some very interesting qualities about him. And I'll tell you how I was going to bring him back. In the third series, we would be scooping up some mineral rich particles somewhere in space. They would be brought back to Moonbase to be used in some way. And once back in a living environment Balor would re-form out of these particles, because he had been atomized, and essentially he is immortal – spontaneous regeneration – so he would only ever be in a form of stasis. He wouldn't be dead. And we would have had Balor back, and we would have had a much more interesting examination of what type of person, and what type of psychology motivated him. He was a very favorite character of mine, but I felt disappointed because I think he was worth more on screen. And Peter Bowles, I thought, gave a wonderful portrayal. He was genuinely frightening, I thought.

'My reservations at the time about "End of Eternity" had to do with my own perhaps overly ambitious hopes for the story. I felt constrained by the episode length when writing it. However, since it had to play within 50 minutes, I concentrated much more closely on how scenes played than was usual. Instead of unraveling the historical and cultural reasons why Balor behaved as he did, the emphasis hinged more on the psychological. The circumstances of his discovery suggested the outcast; an outsider consumed with a lust to dominate for its own sake – in essence a power freak. He was less interested in the exercise of that power than a total abasing acceptance of it by those he'd left behind, and even more so the Alphans, given their relative powerlessness. Everything he did on Alpha after his release was motivated by that psychopathic compulsion.

'It's arguable that nobility of spirit is universal, not purely human. That being said, this seemed an opportunity to put an alien beyond reach of anything remotely human in his interior make-up. In the event, I went for an irredeemable form of personalized evil, but one that had an impact on humans.

'That's why I called him Balor, after a vengeful Celtic god of darkness, also Baal, the related Phoenician god. Human sacrifice was offered up to Baal, especially first-born children who were burnt alive while encased within his statue. The Phoenicians were a cultured and very powerful nation, yet this most primitive form of superstitious evil flourished among them. If there is a weakness in Balor's portrayal, it's that I failed to adequately clarify the nature of the civilization that produced him. On screen this showed up as fudged motivation for his apparently motiveless need to kill.

'Balor is on a par with the being which infiltrates Alpha in "Force of Life". Both were meant to portray an observable, but incomprehensible alien imperative at work. In "Force of Life" it was sensed rather than seen and generally speaking it worked. In "End of Eternity" the imperative was seen but not sensed strongly enough. I think Balor needed a stronger cultural context for his actions. I smiled when I later saw how Sigourney disposed of the alien in *Alien* …'

Bloopers: Just before the door to Balor's asteroid prison explodes, Martin Landau walks past the character Mike Baxter and says, 'Excuse me, Jim.' Jim, of course, is the actor's rather than the character's name.

Balor heals Koenig's wounds after Mike Baxter's attack, but how does he get the blood out of the Commander's uniform?

Observations: Some scenes were edited out of this episode before it was televised. These featured Commander Koenig covered in gruesome blood after being beaten nearly to death by Mike Baxter. They were deemed too graphic for mid-1970s television. The scene as it stands in the episode is still very disturbing. Dried blood remains briefly visible on the floor, which is highly effective on its own. It is often the case with horror, that the most terrifying aspects are the ones imagined by the viewer, not the ones displayed with visual gore.

This is the only episode that features yellow lighting panels in Main Mission. They have previously been white or green, and following this episode they will become orange (or red in the case of the emergency lighting in 'War Games').

The lighting panels in Commander Koenig's office also change in this episode from white (as they have been since 'Breakaway') to yellow.

Balor's exit from Alpha – being sucked out of an airlock – could have been an inspiration for a similar scene in Ridley Scott's *Alien*.

Review: 'End of Eternity' opens with a dynamic prologue. The blast explosion that opens up the asteroid is very impressive on screen, with the chunks of rock floating up instead of down. Balor's terrifying paintings were by production designer Keith Wilson: these chilling, nightmarish visions of torture, pain and destruction are brilliantly executed.

The stylishness of the direction is undeniable; some of the most effective sequences play out with the natural sounds and dialogue completely subordinated to music, as when Helena dramatically calls, 'John!' into her Commlock, shockingly breaking the silence. Director Ray Austin utilises striking visual techniques throughout the episode, including numerous examples of first-person camerawork (such as when Balor is roving through the base, and when Baxter is beating Koenig with a model plane and the camera takes on the viewpoint of the aircraft). This approach, combined with the outstanding cacophonous score, creates tension, suspense, and more than a little terror. 'End of Eternity' fits in perfectly with such other horror-styled episodes as 'The Troubled Spirit', 'Dragon's Domain', 'Force of Life' and 'Alpha Child'. Most similar to 'End of Eternity' would be 'Force of Life'. Both are Johnny Byrne scripts featuring one man (whether alien or possessed by an alien force) on a rampage through the base, causing death and destruction. Both feature similar menacing walks down the corridors of Alpha and effectively serve to probe Alpha's vulnerabilities and weaknesses. 'Force of Life', though, is the superior of the two segments.

Peter Bowles is dramatic and inspired as Balor, conveying the depths of his psychosis. Balor is undoubtedly one of the most effective and frighteningly memorable alien adversaries that Alpha encounters. He is made all the more menacing through the manner in which he is filmed – camera angles amplify his height, with size equating visually to power. Assisting the perception of power and menace are Balor's black costume and Peter Bowles' expressive features. Balor's false history of his planet Progron is compelling, and does raise enough questions to provide motivation for Koenig to doubt him. Balor's own motivation comes from the depths of his disturbed mind and his lustful pleasure at inflicting pain and suffering. This is summed up when Balor urges Koenig, 'Accept the challenge, Koenig. Surrender to the exquisite forces of pain and suffering, and you will transcend your limitations.' His confrontations with both Koenig and Russell are spine chilling.

The flaw of the episode relates to Balor himself: the driving influences that caused him to become evil are never stated. He is, purely, evil. As Johnny Byrne has said, being a psychopath isn't necessarily enough to drive a successful story, and Byrne himself would have liked to have made Balor a much more 'subtle destroyer'.

There is some nice series continuity as Helena says, 'We know immortality is possible,' recalling the Alphans' experiences in 'Death's other Dominion'. And, as in that earlier episode, immortality is again shown to be a trap – or a form of imprisonment – with Balor literally imprisoned in his asteroid cell. 'End of Eternity' is largely a display case for the showdown between Koenig and Balor, and their final confrontation features a decidedly Western motif – almost as if they were the stereotypical sheriff and outlaw dueling on a dusty street. While the focus is clearly on Koenig and Balor, Helena does have a very strong role and makes an indelible impression on the episode. The remainder of the cast are largely underutilised.

Mike Baxter's quarters are well decorated with models of aeroplanes and pictures of early space missions. These are the keys to the dreams and aspirations of the character, and they tie in very well with his fate: being grounded due to a damaged optic nerve. And since Baxter's love is flying, when he attacks Koenig it is symbolically appropriate that he uses a model plane as the weapon.

Unlike with many other successful episodes, few questions remain unanswered at the end of the show (although one might wonder what the point was of blowing up Balor's asteroid – so it would regenerate around him, perhaps?) Not a profoundly philosophical episode, or a very thought-provoking one, 'End of Eternity' is fairly straightforward. Nevertheless, this is a fearsome script, complemented most notably by the direction, soundtrack and the menacing characterisation provided by Peter Bowles. If Johnny Byrne were to have had the opportunity to bring Balor back for another episode, he undoubtedly could have added layers of depth and subtlety, but as it stands, 'End of Eternity' is a darkly distinctive entry of *Space: 1999*.

Rating: 8/10

1.17
WAR GAMES

Screenplay by Christopher Penfold
Directed by Charles Crichton

Selected Broadcast Dates:

UK   LWT:
            Date: 27 September 1975.   Time: 7.00 pm
            Granada:
            Date: 17 October 1975.   Time: 6.35 pm
US   KRON (San Francisco):
            Date: 25 October 1975.   Time: 7.00 pm

Credited Cast: Martin Landau (John Koenig), **Barbara Bain** (Helena Russell), **Barry Morse** (Victor Bergman), **Prentis Hancock** (Paul Morrow), **Clifton Jones** (David Kano), **Zienia Merton** (Sandra Benes), **Anton Phillips** (Bob Mathias), **Nick Tate** (Alan Carter)

Guest Star: Anthony Valentine (Male Alien)

Guest Artist: Isla Blair (Female Alien)

Uncredited Cast: Suzanne Roquette (Tanya Alexander), **Sarah Bullen** (Operative Kate), **Loftus Burton** (Operative Lee Oswald), **Binu Balini**, **Andrew Dempsey**, **Raymond Harris, Maggie Wright** (Main Mission Operatives), **Uffe Neumann** (Main Mission Pilot), **James Fagan** (Eagle Co-Pilot Pete Johnson), **Roy Everson** (Security Guard in corridor), **Judith Hepburn** (Nurse), **Kathy Mallory** (Nurse), **Robert Atiko** (Alphan), **Alan Harris** (Alphan), **Paul Weston** (Alphan sucked into space), **Colin Skeaping** (Alphan sucked into space), **John Clifford** (Injured Alphan)

Plot: As the Moon nears a planet it is attacked by a fleet of Mark IX Hawk warships. The battle rages and Moonbase Alpha is devastated. Facing an impossible situation and with 128 Alphans dead, John and Helena travel to the alien world to seek asylum for the survivors, but they are unprepared for their alien encounter – Koenig is killed and Helena is indoctrinated into the alien world; a world in which she shares the power to save Koenig and possibly even free herself.

Quotes:
- **Paul:** 'We ask for mercy to be shown to the survivors of this base.'
- **Koenig:** 'Ever since we were blasted away from Earth we've been fighting for survival. We have survived. Now how, I don't know. There's no rational explanation, but what I do have is an absolute faith in the strength of the human spirit, and the belief that someone or something is looking after us – God, if you like – and we will survive!'

- **Victor:** 'We are mankind. We came from planet Earth and we built this base called Alpha to learn more about space. But human error blasted this Moon out of the Earth's orbit, and so we have travelled the universe looking for a place to live. Now, we can no longer live here, and we go to face an uncertain future on the planet that has nearly destroyed us. You, whoever you are, who find this empty vessel of Alpha … come and seek us out – if we still exist. Come and teach us all you know. Because, we have learned many things … But most of all, we have learned that we still have much to learn … Goodbye, Alpha.'
- **Male Alien:** 'You have no future. You carry with you the seeds of your own destruction. You are a contaminating organism, a fatal virus, a plague of fear.'
- **Male Alien:** 'In our world there can be no fear.'
- **Koenig:** '97 minutes of life and then no oxygen; hallucination; a slow and peaceful drift from dream to real eternity … or just nothing. The ultimate negative – poison and pain and yet more pain, until nothing. This body a piece perhaps for some future archaeologist to fit into an historical puzzle. John Koenig from planet Earth – ninth and last Commander of Moonbase Alpha.'
- **Helena:** 'I remember: a world without fear. It was very strange – beautiful … We've lost it.'

Filming Dates: Thursday 24 October – Thursday 7 November 1974

Incidental Music: The score is augmented by the astounding Mike Hankinson library track 'The Astronauts' (heard during the opening attack on Alpha), undoubtedly one of the finest pieces of accompanying music in the series. This track was from the Chappell Recorded Music Library.

Commentary:
Martin Landau: 'There were a couple [episodes] that reverberate … "War Games" was one. It was amazing the sets were still standing after that one. I can't say that was my favorite, but it was one that does reverberate a bit.'

Barbara Bain: [On her favourite episodes] 'I don't know that. It's really hard. It's always the one you're doing at the moment. It just *has* to be. One I liked was "War Games"; that was kind of interesting. There always has to be a combination of [the] premise [and my] role in it. That comes to mind.'

Barry Morse: 'The "War Games" episode concerned the fears that lead us to destroy each other in wars, and how we can conquer our fears. It's like George Bernard Shaw said: mankind's worst destructiveness comes either through anger or from fear. And in most cases the anger and the fear are without foundation. The human race does get itself into terrible states of anger and fear, and thereby into terrible programmes of destruction.'

Zienia Merton: 'I thought "War Games" was magnificent. I thought it was stunning, and incredibly well put together. We had a theory that Charles Crichton, who directed "War Games", and was a brilliant and wonderful man, had shares in the Fuller's Earth company. Fuller's Earth was the brand name for the dust they would drop onto the set, and Charlie loved it. They had platforms suspended in various places in the Main

Mission set, and when you came to a big disaster shot, like in "War Games", they would drop the Fuller's Earth. I remember a funny story. We were preparing to film in Main Mission, and I saw all this Fuller's Earth coming in and I thought, "Oh, it's going to be dirty!" I thought, "What do I do?" Charlie said, "Would you all be natural. Do what you would do if a plane was coming to crash into Main Mission. Do whatever you have to do." When it came to the shot, they called "Action" – and I went under a desk! I thought, "This is a good place." What was funny was that I found [Barry] down there as well! And he gave me a thumbs up and a wink! I looked up and saw Prentis, standing at his Main Mission station hitting all these little knobs *covered*, absolutely. He looked as if he'd fallen into a bag of flour. Actually, there were three cowards – [Clifton] was down there, too. We were all down there pointing and laughing at the idiots up there getting covered in Fuller's Earth. We were the smartest ones on the Moonbase.

'It was nice that, for example in "War Games", when the red alert sounded you had people tumbling out of bed and arriving in Main Mission in their pajamas. It would of course have been nice if one of us had come into an episode halfway through and said, "Hi, I'm back on duty." Say Prentis and Clifton were on duty. Just the two of them could have been used much more fully than when we were all present in Main Mission all the time. And again in "Troubled Spirit", we could have been in a corner saying, "Do you think so-and-so's gone off his head and has put us in jeopardy?" And at the beginning of that episode at the concert scene, some of us could have said, "God, I can't stand that music. Let's go and do something else." But they came up with the idea of a concert and threw everybody into it. I mean, who was in Main Mission that day? I think only Prentis was absent. He can't run the shop on his own. Everybody could have been used much more fully. Gladys, the continuity lady, was marvellous – but of course she doesn't write the scripts.

'But I adored the beginning of "War Games". What I loved about "War Games" was that as a group we were in jeopardy, and we all pulled together. I loved Isla Blair – I've worked with her about three times and she's a gorgeous lady, although I didn't work with her in "War Games". She is really one of the nicest women you could work with. But in the first ten minutes of "War Games" I felt there was a great cohesion with the characters. And we had Charlie Crichton directing, who was amazingly imaginative.'

Anton Phillips: [On things that stood out for him in the making of *Space: 1999*] 'Getting blown through that window [in "War Games"] stands out [in my mind].'

Julian Glover: 'My wife, Isla Blair, did one where she had a most extraordinary makeup that was ridiculous. She and Anthony Valentine both had these appliances on. They couldn't look at themselves without laughing, which is why they did all of their scenes facing away from each other. That's the glamour of the theatre for you!'

Christopher Penfold: [Regarding the alien perception of the Alphans as a contaminating virus] 'It was something that I personally was very horrified about: What were we doing? We were at that time just launching out beyond the envelope of the Earth's atmosphere. We were doing so in the form of rockets, which were themselves pretty heavily polluting machines. In much of the science fiction, and in the way that the possibility of alternative life forms in space was discussed, I think that the overwhelming response to that possibility was really one of fear and ignorance. It engendered fear. So I was really quite anxious to point out, in the context of an adventure story, that as a species exploring into territories we hadn't been in before, we carried with us the same kind of responsibilities as the Spaniards brought to the New World when they spread German measles and Smallpox. That there are dangers involved; there are dangers in genetic engineering. It was that kind of feeling that I wanted to introduce into the story.

'Charles would probably not have thought of himself as a science fiction director until Gerry asked him to do the show. His experience and his devotion to detail and determination to get the scripts right put me on a vertical learning curve, and it was a wonderful working relationship that I look back on with a great deal of affection. Charles Crichton had an enormous influence on the success of the episodes he directed.

'Charles was actually able to demand the kind of respect from the production department that the script demanded. The kind of producer decisions that have to be taken on a multi-episode series like this one are that, when a story comes up that of its very nature is going to make bigger budgetary demands (like "War Games"), then you do rob Peter to pay Paul.

'One of my favorite guiding quotations in life has been the philosopher Santayana, 'Those who do not remember the past are condemned to repeat it.' And when human beings go to war my heart sinks; I just think it's so damn stupid … I was very much affected by and reading a lot of the French philosopher Teilhard de Chardin at the time … He had this notion of the noosphere to which all the intelligence of people who have lived on earth and subsequently died is somehow collected in this noosphere. And it was that philosophical idea that I wanted to try to get into the form of popular drama. And I think the reason that ["War Games"] actually worked as well as it did was very much down to Charlie Crichton and the way in which he chose to direct Anthony Valentine and Isla Blair, and then also the way in which it was so successfully inter-cut. ["War Games"] probably is my favorite episode, actually … Again, if you don't remember the past you're condemned to repeat it. And I just think that as a species we swing back and forth and I think the pendulum has swung in a fairly disastrous direction in the last few years. I'm hoping that it might actually have reached its nadir and start swinging back again. I think all you can do as writers and creative people and communicators is to try and persuade other people of that.

[Regarding Bergman's line, 'We have learned many things … But most of all, we have learned that we still have much to learn.'] 'The more we know, the more we realize we don't know. Prior to the Renaissance it was achievable for a person to know all there was to know. We know a little more now, but there's a hell of a lot more we don't know.

'I think the one episode that gave me the most satisfaction as being something that I conceived from the beginning myself and followed through in the way I wanted to follow through, was probably "War Games".'

Bloopers: Watch for the cardboard cutout Eagle exploding on the launch pad during the Hawk attack.

Observations: In the initial wave of attacks, Main Mission is hit by severe structural damage. Beams fall from the ceiling and wires drop down. If you watch this in slow motion you will see Bergman, Sandra and Kano all duck for cover underneath desks in Main Mission – as Zienia Merton relates below, in her commentary on this episode.

The alien planet is notable as the only instance in *Space: 1999* of a world orbiting a double-star system. It's a nice, subtle detail that goes unmentioned in the dialogue, but is shown during the effects sequences of the planet.

The shot of the arrival of the massive alien bomber overhead is mirrored in *Star Wars*, with the underbelly debut of the Star Destroyer.

Review: 'War Games' is an immensely complex episode and is considered to be the closest the series ever came to representing literary science fiction on the screen. Some go so far as to say that Christopher Penfold's script works better on the page than on film. Through astute viewing, the complexities of 'War Games' explain themselves. So, here is 'War Games', in detail …

Moonbase Alpha is approaching a planet, and the intent of the episode is to show the fears of the Alphans being tested. In a situation like this, what would they fear most? Answer: an unprovoked attack.

'War Games' jumps directly into the action with a sudden (apparent) alien attack. However, while the alien ships are approaching in a threatening manner, the Alphans – out of fear of being attacked – actually fire first. The Alphans' own thoughts and fears lead to each subsequent escalation of the war. After the initial three Hawks are destroyed, Carter expresses his opinion, 'It was too easy.' This belief that there must be more to the alien threat leads to the next contact – another wave of Hawks.

The fan-favourite Mark IX Hawks are Earth ships similar in some ways to the Eagle, but designed as fighters. They are sleek and visually dynamic, and it would have been very interesting if Moonbase Alpha had been equipped with a small Hawk fleet for defensive purposes. As it is, they appear within the alien-induced dream that constitutes this episode, drawn from the fears and memories of the Alphans themselves. As the aliens eventually state, 'Our only defense was to make your fears appear real.'

The shots of Alphans being sucked out into space through heavily damaged corridors by explosive decompression are incredibly effective. The vast destruction of Moonbase Alpha is, certainly by this point in science fiction television history, an unparalleled defeat for the heroes of a show. As a pre-*Star Wars* example of a production presenting extensive spaceship battles and model work, 'War Games' is a visual champion, featuring the most spectacular collection of effects in all 48 episodes of *Space: 1999*.

The death of series regular Bob Mathias is dramatic and heroic. If this were to have been the end of his character, it certainly would have been noble. However, as fans of sci-fi know, there are very few deaths that can't be reversed.

At the Command Conference following the Alphans' defeat, Helena states the grim fact that there are 128 dead. Kano reports that they are running off solar batteries, and that on minimum requirements they'll be exhausted in eight days. The least badly damaged Nuclear Generating Area will take a minimum of four weeks to repair. Many anti-gravity units are smashed beyond repair. Sandra states that the food production and recycling plants are very badly damaged; the water is heavily contaminated. It will take nine weeks minimum to fix the food production problems, and another two more months before crops can be harvested.

At this point, in short, Alpha is virtually dead, and her people know their situation can get no worse, so the attack stops. Again, this development is tied in with their minds and their perception of the situation. When they think there is no point in the attack continuing, it stops. As they are virtually destroyed, the only course of action they can take is to go down to the planet. John and Helena encounter the Male and Female Aliens in their tactile, translucent surroundings. There are many wonderful science fiction concepts addressed throughout their encounter, one of which arises from Helena's line, 'The lights, the colours ... maybe they're part of their language.' It's an intriguing idea.

The aliens themselves are cold and emotionless, with domed bald heads. On one view this is a sci-fi cliché, but on another these are among the most purely alien humanoid species Alpha encounters. Their world is deeply enriched by the script. It is made up of a series of 'brains', which control and perfect their society. This is along the lines of the macro-brain concept Christopher Penfold also worked at exploring in 'Space Brain'. These aliens are understandable and three-dimensional, despite their emotionless demeanor, and consider the Alphans to be a 'plague of fear,' no more than a virus waiting to contaminate their world. This raises questions worth considering. Do humans belong out in space? Can we comprehend the implications our being out there might have for the life forms we encounter?

Koenig's use of minor physical violence on the planet (striking out at some fragile-looking equipment) leads to his and Helena's fear of retaliation – which, of course, causes the aliens to appear with laser guns and kill the Commander. Helena, left alone, fears many things, and the result is her indoctrination into the alien brain, an experience that ends in her coming close to understanding their world. With her fears gone, Helena is able to share in the alien powers, allowing her to bring John back to life. Having conquered her fear, Helena is at peace, takes on alien traits, and achieves greater understanding. Koenig, however, immediately returns to the war-like ways inherent in much of humanity. He plans to take the planet by force. It shows that the Alphans are still Earth people, still flawed and imperfect. And in those flaws, oddly enough, lies a certain kind of beauty; as Helena says, 'We are what we are.'

Victor Bergman's goodbye speech to the Alphans' Moon home provides Barry Morse with the opportunity and material to deliver one of his finest, most emotional and subtle performances in the series. His speech encapsulates the essence of *Space: 1999*; that, although mankind has learned many things we still have much to learn. As the remaining command crew exit Main Mission for what they believe to be the last time, comforting each other, viewers are shown a society of comrades and friends, not just the co-workers introduced in 'Breakaway'.

Koenig and Carter head towards the planet, intent on attacking, and are met with an opposite force – a defence field. Of course they encounter defences from the planet – they expect them! By expecting them, and being afraid of them, John and Alan actually bring these defences into being. If they had no fear, there would have been no force field. As they plow through it in their Eagle, Carter is clearly afraid. He says, 'We can't do it. She'll break up.' And that is exactly what happens. Carter's death is, like that of Mathias, a clue that there is more to this plot than first meets the eye.

Helena begins to learn the truth of what is happening to them in the following dialogue exchange:

Helena: 'And you defend them with bombers and Hawks like those of the planet Earth.'
Female Alien: 'We have no fighting machines of our own. Why should we? We have no fear.'

Helena: 'You do. You used them to destroy Alpha. Didn't you?'
Male Alien: 'Mankind is full of fear.'

But then, as she is beginning to understand fully, Helena thinks of John and becomes aware that he is in danger of dying, adrift in space, with only his limited spacesuit oxygen supply keeping him alive. (Consider Koenig's freefall through space is a tribute by Christopher Penfold to *2001: A Space Odyssey*. In that movie, the character Frank Poole drifts slowly through the void, his breathing symbolic of man in space being a 'fish out of water'.) Koenig's plight awakens Helena's human emotions. Her fear of death wells up and breaks the indoctrinating influences of the aliens, and she returns to her normal self:

Helena: 'John. Come back.'
Female Alien: 'He has faced death. He has conquered his fear.'
Helena: 'I want him back – as he was. I want him here. I am afraid of death. I don't want your world.'
Male Alien: 'If you bring him back he will have to face the agony of his own fear.'
Helena: 'I want him as he was, with all his faults and fears.'
Female Alien: 'He would destroy us all.'
Helena: 'We are what we are!'

That segment displays some of Barbara Bain's finest acting in the series. Her performance is absolutely gripping as she portrays Helena acknowledging her fears and essentially pleading for John Koenig to live. This scene also shows that the Alphans are unable to sustain themselves for long in the alien world without their emotions and fears rising up again. It's notable that Helena saves Koenig here, as she does in 'Matter of Life and Death', by wishing it.

But note what the Male Alien stated: 'If you bring him back he will have to face the agony of his own fear.' What does John Koenig fear? He fears losing Helena, and he fears that there could be no future for his people…

Koenig's arrival on the planet is quickly followed by his use of a Stun Gun. He aims at the Male Alien (who sits with an expression of almost solemn sadness at the act he knows is about to take place), and fires. This kind of intense violence – the firing of a gun with the intent to kill – is the result of fear. Fear for what the aliens may do to Helena. Fear for all their futures. And such an intense unleashing of violence (which has not happened on the planet before – remember, the aliens have no weapons and therefore never actually fired upon or killed Koenig) results in a massive chain reaction, almost destroying the entire world. His grief is the fear of Helena being killed, and she nearly is. As the Male Alien foretold, if Helena brought Koenig back he would have to confront the agony of his own fear. Together they sit out the monstrous destruction they have caused. The final culmination of destruction on the alien planet is portrayed through the use of stock footage of a real nuclear explosion. The use of this stock footage serves to strike at a conscious or unconscious fear instilled in people since the 1950s, essentially restating (even if unintentionally) Christopher Penfold's dislike of nuclear technology and continues the anti-nuclear undertones present in the series since 'Breakaway'.

Now, with no hope for life on Alpha or on the planet, Koenig orders the evacuating

Eagles back to their base, where his people will all die. It is Koenig's ultimate fear come true. And this is the point at which the story returns to its beginning moments, in Main Mission, shortly before Koenig orders the destruction of the first flight of Hawks. This time, he orders his Eagles to hold their fire. Koenig and Helena remember portions of the collective dream they have just experienced, and know that they are not threatened by this alien world. They have no fear, and the alien threat vanishes.

The aliens had no weapons or ships of their own, and now they trust that the Alphans will stay away, and pass by their world without interference – interference that could mean the death of them all. This has been a shared dream in the minds of the Alphans, taking place in a single moment of time, with all of their fears influencing the course of their demise. Fear is the root of failure. Fear is the cause of war and destruction. And their own fear is what defeated the Alphans.

'War Games' is an immensely detailed episode and touches on a wealth of complex concepts. The Mysterious Unknown Force is referenced when Koenig expresses to the aliens his belief that someone or something is looking after them, and they will survive. The direction from Charles Crichton is possibly his finest work in the series, and 'War Games' is the culmination of his collaborations with Christopher Penfold. The sets of the alien world are beautiful. The performances are captivating and deliver an intense depth of emotion, while some of the characterisations advance notably, such as with the background revelation that Koenig is Alpha's ninth Commander. As well, the relationship between Koenig and Helena is fleshed out further, and Sandra shows she is a significant and dependable part of the command staff – no fainting here!

If this successful combination of dynamic action-adventure with philosophical underpinnings and strong characterisation were to have been carried over into additional episodes (possibly replacing some of the weaker segments, such as the upcoming 'The Last Enemy'), there would certainly have been no reason for the production team to make substantial changes for Year Two.

'War Games' is Christopher Penfold's magnum opus. It is a potent anti-war statement and a consummately structured, profoundly interesting and ultimately demanding experience for the Alphans, and the viewer.

Rating: 9.5/10

1.18
THE LAST ENEMY

Screenplay by Bob Kellett
Directed by Bob Kellett

Selected Broadcast Dates:
UK   LWT:
            Date: 28 February 1976.   Time: 11.30 am
            Granada:
            Date: 19 March 1976.   Time: 6.35 pm
US   KRON (San Francisco):
            Date: 10 January 1976.   Time: 7.00 pm

Credited Cast: Martin Landau (John Koenig), **Barbara Bain** (Helena Russell), **Barry Morse** (Victor Bergman), **Prentis Hancock** (Paul Morrow), **Clifton Jones** (David Kano), **Zienia Merton** (Sandra Benes), **Nick Tate** (Alan Carter), **Maxine Audley** (Theia), **Kevin Stoney** (Talos), **Carolyn Courage** (First Girl)

Guest Artist: Caroline Mortimer (Dione)

Uncredited Cast: Suzanne Roquette (Tanya Alexander), **Sarah Bullen** (Operative Kate), **Loftus Burton** (Operative Lee), **John Lee-Barber** (Eagle 5 Pilot), **Shane Rimmer** (Voice of Eagle 2 Pilot), **Laurie Davis, Andrew Dempsey, Claire Lutter, Andrew Sutcliffe, Maggie Wright** (Main Mission Operatives), **Tony Allyn** (Security Guard Tony Allan), **Quentin Pierre** (Security Guard Pierce Quinton), **Robert Case** (Security Guard), **Uffe Neumann** (Astronaut in corridor), **Linda Hooks** (Second Girl), **Tara Faraday** (Third Girl), **Alan Bennion** (Male Alien – cut from final print)

Previously Titled: 'The Second Sex' and 'The Other Enemy'.

Plot: Moonbase Alpha drifts into the middle of an ancient and ongoing battle between two worlds, Betha and Delta, which circle their sun in opposite orbits. Both alien worlds see the arrival of the Moon as an opportunity to set up missile platforms to attack each other, and the Alphans find themselves attempting to mediate – and survive – an alien war.

Quotes:
- **Koenig:** 'I would love to remain neutral. But my idea of neutrality is not being a sitting duck and being shot at by both sides.'
- **Koenig:** 'Protect Alpha? What do you care about Alpha? You send up reinforcements, they send up reinforcements. You fire at their reinforcements, and they fire at your reinforcements. And where the hell are we? We're the little guy in the middle. No thank you, lady – it's not our war.'
- **Victor:** 'What a waste – total waste. Still, perhaps some good will come of it. Maybe

now they'll learn to live together.'

- **Koenig:** 'Yeah, too late. They've got their war, and we have all of space in which to find a home … somewhere.'

Filming Dates: Friday 8 November – Tuesday 19 November 1974
Tuesday 25 February – Thursday 27 February 1975

Incidental Music: Includes 'Cosmic Sounds No. 3' by Georges Teperino (previously heard in 'Force of Life'), from the Chappell Recorded Music Library.

Commentary:
Martin Landau: 'I've always loved the genre … I've always felt that science fiction allows the most interesting writing to come through, because it can draw parallels to things that are happening today, but in interesting ways. And at the same time, it can entertain people while revealing things to them and informing them. I always felt a show like *Space: 1999* or *Star Trek* allowed you to do that. I remember one of the episodes of *Space: 1999* where our Moon is hurtling through space and becomes caught virtually between two warring planets ['The Last Enemy']. At the same time, Henry Kissinger as Secretary of State was in the throes of doing the very same things. On *Space: 1999* we were able to take that and turn it into something that we hoped would make people aware of [the current events], and hopefully entertain and inform them. It's easier to do timely and topical and philosophical and psychological drama as point of view in a science fiction format. I've always liked that. Isaac Asimov was somebody who fascinated me, as did the older writers, like Jules Verne and H G Wells. I was fascinated when I was a kid by artists' renditions of what the future would look like. They used to have, from time to time, true glimpses into the future, and I'd see things that were obviously fanciful, but that allowed my imagination to travel.'

Johnny Byrne: 'A lot of money [was] spent on some episodes that were unacceptable [as originally shot], making them acceptable for the screen. I remember one ghastly occasion – it was on "The Last Enemy" – where Caroline Mortimer strides about as a dominatrix and she's trying to get her steel barbs into Koenig. I remember being with David Lane, post-production, with two editing machines, looking at everybody's position in those scenes to write things that would link them up and make sense out of something that had not happened. That should not have happened. And a lot of money was spent trying to make something that I think had always been an unacceptably low-grade episode into an acceptable one. Whereas the money should have been spent on making good stories better. There were lessons to be learned from that.'

Bloopers: Moonbase Alpha is being bombarded, buildings are being blown up and Helena clearly makes a statement that casualties are mounting … Somehow by the end of the episode there have been no casualties and Helena announces that there are only five cases of middle ear damage on the base.

Observations: The sequence of *Satazius* flying over Moonbase Alpha would later appear in an episode of *Wonder Woman* titled 'Time Bomb'. The borrowed effects footage was given the added caption, 'Planet Earth: November 10, 2155.' (Also borrowed for that episode of the Lynda Carter series were shots of the domed cities of future Earth from Year Two's 'Journey to Where'.)

In the opening credits, one can see the Moonbase Alpha surface tanks that will feature in the later episode 'The Infernal Machine'. However, they do not appear within the episode itself.

Additional scenes were scripted by Johnny Byrne and filmed at the end of the season (following 'The Testament of Arkadia'), because the episode ran short. As Byrne recalled, 'One major post-production event was the re-shooting of parts of the story starring Caroline Mortimer. Editing machines had to be set up and complex moments rewritten and shot to fit in with the existing material. David Lane directed these re-shoots.' The additional scenes included the ending, and account for a lot of the episode's visual inconsistencies.

Review: Following the triumph of 'War Games', the disappointment of 'The Last Enemy' was almost inevitable. It is a very simplistic action script containing none of the metaphysical or philosophical aspects of the series. It is an obvious attempt to showcase the battle of the sexes: the Bethans shown are all women and the only Deltan shown is a man. But it's a muddled battle lacking detail.

The views of Dione's spaceship *Satazius*, and of Betha as the ship launches, are stunning. The name *Satazius* is rather appropriately derived from Sabazios, who was the God of the sky for the ancient Phrygians and Thracians. *Satazius* is one of the most spectacular spacecraft featured in the series, having some interesting similarities to the design of the original *Battlestar Galactica*.

The surface of Betha is depicted by an impressive matte painting – notable as this technique was used only rarely on *Space: 1999*. The Deltan battleship is the bomber from 'War Games', which has been painted yellow for this episode. Special effects are frequent, but they are also a bit repetitive and sometimes less than convincing, such as the paltry flames trailing the alien missiles. However, there is a truly classic visual sequence as a remote-controlled Moon Buggy (with an empty spacesuit simulating Koenig) heads toward *Satazius*, which is parked on the lunar surface. As the buggy nears the ship, the spacesuit helmet falls off and lands in the lunar dust. It is a very effective and highly memorable scene.

An early flaw in the script is the volatile Koenig ordering Eagles up with an intention to attack. This is too aggressive an action for his character, especially after the lesson learned in 'War Games'. This episode also features the worst over-use of sound in space; the missiles flying over Alpha cause deafening sound and vibration inside the base.

Caroline Mortimer is capable in her large role as the arrogant Dione, although she is not among the best of the guest actors featured in *Space: 1999*. The less said about her motorbike outfit and helmet, the better; this costume is not one of Keith Wilson's finer efforts. Thankfully the regular supporting cast – Hancock, Tate and Merton – all have interesting, if minor, parts to play. During the course of the show, Dione seeks asylum on Moonbase Alpha and Commander Koenig has her share Sandra's living quarters. Of course, Koenig probably felt it was safer for Alpha to have someone keep an eye on Dione. During the filming, Zienia Merton wrote a joking note to Martin Landau that said, 'When I volunteered for this job it was on the understanding I would have private quarters, and I'm not sharing with a ruddy alien.'

The script is plodding and repetitive, holding the episode back from achieving the potential that might have been contained within the basic concept. As it is, it has nothing substantial or insightful to say about the gender war. It has been widely reported that 'The Last Enemy' was based on an idea conceived by Barbara Bain, and that she prompted Bob Kellett in the writing of it. He, as the story goes, never quite grasped what she was trying to achieve. Perhaps if he had, 'The Last Enemy' might have been a successful episode. This was Bob Kellett's final turn directing for the series (following 'Voyager's Return' and 'The Full Circle') and the nadir of his efforts. His previous segments were more successful, particularly 'Voyager's Return', which thanks to the script by Johnny Byrne feels united to the general tone of the series and contains levels of depth and substantial allegorical thought. Unlike fellow directors David Tomblin, Charles Crichton and Ray Austin, Bob Kellett left little memorable impact on the series.

This is an uncharacteristic episode that largely fails to fit within the realm of Year One. Beyond some of the special effects and the weakly stated lesson on the futility of war, there remains little to praise about 'The Last Enemy'.

Rating: 5/10

1.19
THE TROUBLED SPIRIT

Screenplay by Johnny Byrne
Directed by Ray Austin

Selected Broadcast Dates:

UK	LWT:	
	Date: 14 February 1976.	Time: 11.30 am
	Granada:	
	Date: 27 February 1976.	Time: 6.35 pm
US	KRON (San Francisco):	
	Date: 7 February 1976.	Time: 7.00 pm

Credited Cast: Martin Landau (John Koenig), **Barbara Bain** (Helena Russell), **Barry Morse** (Victor Bergman), **Prentis Hancock** (Paul Morrow), **Clifton Jones** (David Kano), **Zienia Merton** (Sandra Benes), **Anton Phillips** (Bob Mathias), **Nick Tate** (Alan Carter)

Guest Artists: Giancarlo Prete (Dan Mateo), **Hilary Dwyer** (Laura Adams), **Anthony Nicholls** (Dr James Warren)

Uncredited Cast: Jim Sullivan (Musician), **Val Musetti** (Spirit Mateo), **Suzanne Roquette** (Tanya Alexander), **Sarah Bullen** (Operative Kate), **Loftus Burton** (Operative Lee Oswald), **Binu Balini**, **Andrew Dempsey**, **Jan Rennison**, **Andy Sutcliffe**, **Maggie Wright** (Main Mission Operatives), **Tony Allyn** (Security Guard Pierce Quinton), **Quentin Pierre** (Security Guard Pierce Quinton), **John Clifford** (Security Guard in concert), **Xanthi Gardner** (Botanist), **Vernon Morris** (Botanist), **Christopher Williams** (Medical Orderly), **Jeannie Galston**, **Judith Hepburn** (Nurses), **Robert Atiko**, **Eddy Nedari**, **Richard Shore** (Alphans)

Plot: Dan Mateo conducts a scientific seance to establish contact between human minds and plants, but this results in the awakening of a spirit on Alpha. This horribly disfigured apparition has come from the future to avenge its own death, which hasn't happened yet! No matter what efforts the Alphans make to save Mateo, the Alphan is inextricably drawn towards his predestined demise.

Quotes:
* **Helena:** 'You're probing into areas of the mind we know very little about. Of course, that's what makes it so fascinating.'
* **Victor:** 'Whether we believe in the occult or not, there is a tradition in our culture of ghosts, spirits; some force that continues to work after death, coming back in search of revenge or justice or whatever. But this thing that Mateo has summoned up is coming back to avenge a terrible death – its own death, which has not happened yet.'
* **Mateo:** 'We are living out here in space, living on borrowed time. If only one of our

essential support systems fails, maybe we'll survive. But if our food chain goes, we are finished. My work is important because I know it can increase the margin of survival.'

- **Sandra:** 'Does it matter what it is or where it came from? The important thing is that it is here, amongst us.'
- **Helena:** 'Life and death. Still the big questions … the greatest mysteries.'

Filming Dates: Wednesday 20 November – Wednesday 4 December 1974

Commentary:
Johnny Byrne: 'I wanted to do something completely different. I wanted to do the first science fiction ghost story, and it would have all the classic elements of a ghost story, but inextricably bound up with the high technology of science fiction.

'So it had a beautiful symmetry, and I tried to get the best value out of it. I was very pleased with the shape of that story. There are certain things that please a writer. Like an artist who has a particular idea about a painting, a writer has an idea about the shape of a story. The shape of this story was rather interesting: something unspeakable happens to somebody and everybody realises what it is. They realise that some force is coming back to avenge a horrible death and this death hasn't happened yet. And everything they do to avert that death – that awful thing – from happening, is pushing the thing toward the conclusion it came back to sort out in the first place. So it had a symmetry that was fun to do at the time.

'What you had to be left with in the epilogue was [a sense of] how much [the Alphans] didn't know and how flexible are the barriers between what we consider life and death. It's all tied in with time. When you mix all these equations up, your thoughts and feelings and beliefs simply don't make any sense and you have to be *infinitely* flexible. One of the good things about the Alphan situation was that, since they were moving out, moving all the time – exposed to these extraordinary situations – their flexibility, not necessarily their knowledge, but their ability to adapt to the mysterious and to the unknown, was expanding as the distance between Earth and them lengthened. It would have been wrong to put pat answers on some of these thoughts we had.

'From day one, apart from some creative input [from Sylvia] into "The Troubled Spirit" – she liked it at script stage – all my contact was with Gerry. He worked very closely on all my scripts. But I think that's how it was meant to be – Sylvia mainly concerned herself with other aspects of the production, as did Reg Hill – the third partner in the production company … "The Troubled Spirit" was a story idea that Sylvia liked very much. She was interested in developing it with me, to the extent that she oversaw it in the way that Gerry normally oversaw the other tales that I was writing. In other words, when I was having story discussions it was usually with Gerry, but in this instance it was with Sylvia.

'I was interested in [the story] for a number of reasons. I am interested in things of the heart and the spirit as well as of the mind, and there was also a bit of a challenge in trying to construct a story that would effectively be a ghost story in space. As in all of the stories that I wrote, I tried to find a point of departure that the people who would watch it could lock onto. In that context, there was a lot of stuff being written at the time about how plants could communicate with people. There were also a number of scientific theories being mooted to the effect that the human brain only engaged about

35 percent of its capacity. The rest of it was one great question mark, and no-one really could understand its potential. Taking all of those things and putting them into a technological context, it seemed reasonable to me that the Alphans could have a device that would boost signals that came from those uncharted areas of the brain. They could also log them and connect them up with plants, which were emitting signals of a matching kind. So we had, in effect, a form of electronic, technological séance happening on Moonbase Alpha.

'It was to do with plants and how plants were the essence of the Alphans' continued survival on the Moon. The development of how they could feed themselves was obviously something that had to be continuous – without it they would simply perish. Anything that would enhance research and development into the production of food was essential, so on that basis it was a valid story. It was also valid on the basis of what was happening on Earth at that time in terms of the philosophical and scientific investigations into the nature of plant and human communications. So we took that as a starting point … "The Troubled Spirit" was interesting and I think as a story it had a very interesting construction, if you look at it purely in the abstract. As a ghost story, I think it worked within the context as well.

'Bergman combined something of the scientist, philosopher, mystic, a steady presence and essential counterweight to the more visceral, upfront Koenig. In time, I think this aspect of his presence on Alpha might have taken on greater significance. He could have proved to be the human personification of the Mysterious Unkown Force, driving the Alphans' spiritual odyssey.'

Alan Willis: [Regarding the sitar concert performance] 'That piece was written and played by the artist you see on the screen [Jim Sullivan], rather than being written by Barry [Gray] or anyone else. He would play sections of the tune as we were filming different angles and then at the end of the day we took him into a quiet studio where he played the whole piece through once again. At the editing stage, this meant that I could chuck out the original sound and overlay the complete version onto the images.'

Bloopers: When Mateo's ghost appears in front of the group of Alphans performing the séance, his yellow sleeve is on his right arm (instead of his left) and his horrible facial scars are on the left … In the next scene, the sleeve and scarring are correct. This was due to the use of a half-silvered mirror to superimpose the ghost into the scene, which reversed the image.

Later, when Mateo dies after fighting his ghost, his left side is forced into the lethal force field, but the scarring is on his right.

Review: 'The Troubled Spirit' is another episode, like 'Force of Life', that takes place entirely within the confines of Alpha. It begins with a great glimpse into Alpha's leisure activities, portraying a large audience appreciating a music concert (by Jim Sullivan, who wrote the original sitar score, and is also seen performing it onscreen); they even have programmes for the evening's *Alpha Music Recital*. The event is broadcast throughout the base for all to enjoy, showing the Alphans as a community of real people who appreciate and enjoy entertainment – not just a group of sci-fi adventurers. This opening teaser is one of the most successful in the series, consisting of long uncut tracking shots, without a single word of dialogue. Everything is conveyed through pictures, facial expressions and the stirring music. As the opening culminates, a dramatic wind sweeps through the base, combined with a drop in temperature and lowered lighting levels. It's eerily effective to see a wind, drawn up by supernatural forces, inside Alpha's enclosed environment.

Giancarlo Prete was the first of the Italian guest stars featured in the series as a result of the Italian RAI network's investment. He is powerful and convincing in the role; a very good actor with a strong screen presence. Italian-born stuntman Val Musetti meanwhile portrays the scarred spirit of Mateo. The presence of Italians on Alpha helped to build on the perception of the base being a truly international endeavour; it was something that didn't need to be blatantly stated – Alpha simply comprised an inclusive and varied population. Due to the believable and horrific make-up used on the spirit of Mateo, this episode was another that encountered difficulty with censors, and in order to make it less frightening to a young audience, portions were cut.

Anthony Nicholls is another very talented guest actor and makes a wonderful impression as Dr Warren. It's nice to see the wisdom of another older scientist on Alpha, and the mentor-pupil relationship between Dr Warren and Mateo recalls the earlier pairing of Ernst Queller and Jim Haines in 'Voyager's Return'. The difference here is that Mateo can't stand Warren, and Warren is an old fool who looks down on Mateo for ignoring his authority and warnings.

The Hydroponics section is presented, consisting of a complex set filled with greenery and technology, with the notable addition of a large section of geodesic glass panels exposing the area to natural starlight, in addition to the ample artificial light. Notice the green floor – very appropriate for the Hydroponics section. It's a great set, with extraordinary atmospheric potential as a setting for such a spooky episode.

'The Troubled Spirit' is the chilling ghost story of *Space: 1999*, told in shadowed nighttime Alphan settings. It is an episode that only gets better and better upon repeated viewings. Johnny Byrne's script is highly impressive and successful on many levels: his Irish Catholic background is surely an influence on the exorcism sequence, and he revisits the concept of characters foreseeing the manner of their own death, which he had previously explored in 'Another Time, Another Place', and invites the viewer to ponder the psychological implications of such encounters. Byrne's usage of psychic connections with plants is another fascinating element of the script. Although it is an aspect that some people might dismiss as ridiculous, it works perfectly well within the parameters of the series and story. The plant seance does raise the frequent Johnny Byrne concern about the relationship between Technological Man and Biological Man – it is inherent in the contrast of scientists on a Moonbase attempting to connect on a mental level with plants. Byrne is pointing out that the direction we're heading in with our technology and science is possibly the wrong course; there may be things to learn from our connection with the natural ecosystem. It's more subtly suggested here than it is in 'Another Time, Another Place', where the alternate Alphans have abandoned their futuristic environs for a back-to-the-Earth agrarian lifestyle, but it still provides interesting ideas for consideration.

The scene where Helena encounters the horribly scarred spectre in the dark Medical Centre is genuinely frightening. This is a very fine episode for Helena Russell, and also for Victor Bergman – as usual, he's at his best when bridging gaps between science and mysticism. The big seance sequence (including John, Helena, Victor, Sandra, Paul, Alan Kano and Mateo) is probably one of the most memorable of the entire series. All of the characters are well utilised and Sandra not only gets to act in her customary role as an emotional barometer for Moonbase Alpha but also shows strength and common sense.

Ray Austin has delivered here one of the most striking directorial efforts of the first series: his work is atmospheric, moody and scary, essentially transforming Moonbase Alpha into a haunted house. In classic horror form, the most is made of unusual camera angles, dramatic shadows and lighting, as well as subtle moments like when a door momentarily jams, indicating that there is something strange going on – prime illustrations that special effects aren't required to generate a haunting atmosphere. As an example of the quality of Austin's marvellous direction, watch the command conference sequence carefully – it is one long uninterrupted shot, passing from person to person.

The interactions between the regular characters add charm and warmth, as when Barry Morse plays a significant scene as Bergman leaning the whole time on Kano's shoulder – demonstrating a clear closeness and friendship between them. These are real people, and this is an episode in which they are absolutely terrified: it's one to watch in a darkened room.

There are very few external effects shots, but there is one stunning visual of the spinning Moon moving on towards a nebula – a shot that is able to stand against any effects produced today. It's quite short, but completely amazing.

One line that Paul Morrow says just before the Command Conference ends must be pointed out. He states, 'It's a totally esoteric supposition,' which is not the type of dialogue found in most science fiction television shows. But as this episode attests, *Space: 1999* is not like most science fiction shows. This tale is played to adults: a man haunted by his own ghost, which has come back to avenge its death, which hasn't happened yet. It's a brilliantly nightmarish concept.

'The Troubled Spirit' is atmospheric, appealingly stylish, captivating and very spooky.

Rating: 9/10

1.20
SPACE BRAIN

Screenplay by Christopher Penfold
Directed by Charles Crichton

Selected Broadcast Dates:

UK	LWT:	
	Date: 7 February 1976.	Time: 5.50 pm
	Granada:	
	Date: 20 February 1976.	Time: 6.35 pm
US	KRON (San Francisco):	
	Date: 31 January 1976.	Time: 7.00 pm

Credited Cast: Martin Landau (John Koenig), **Barbara Bain** (Helena Russell), **Barry Morse** (Victor Bergman), **Prentis Hancock** (Paul Morrow), **Clifton Jones** (David Kano), **Zienia Merton** (Sandra Benes), **Anton Phillips** (Bob Mathias), **Nick Tate** (Alan Carter), **Derek Anders** (Wayland)

Guest Artists: Shane Rimmer (Kelly), **Carla Romanelli** (Melita)

Uncredited Cast: Suzanne Roquette (Tanya Alexander), **James Snell** (Cousteau), **Sarah Bullen** (Operative Kate), **Ann Maj-Britt** (Operative Ann), **Loftus Burton** (Operative Lee Oswald), **Laurie Davis**, **Jacqueline Delhaye**, **Andrew Dempsey**, **Michael Stevens**, **Maggie Wright** (Main Mission Operatives), **Tony Allyn** (Security Guard Tony Allan), **Quentin Pierre** (Security Guard Pierce Quinton), **Alan Harris** (Alphan), **Judith Hepburn**, **Diana Reeves**, **Erica Svenson** (Nurses), **Robert Atiko** (Technician), **Michael Sirett** (Technician), **Carol Dee** (Patient), **Marc Boyle**, **Joe Dunne**, **Dorothy Ford**, **Eddie Stacey** (Stunts)

Plot: Alien hieroglyphics flood Alpha's screens and an investigating Eagle is crushed beyond recognition and hurled back to the Moon. Carter and co-pilot Kelly search for the first ship, and on a spacewalk Kelly is taken over by a massive alien space 'brain' – the centre of life for the galaxy. The brain attempts to help the Alphans change the course of the Moon to avoid a collision, but the attempts are unsuccessful and the Moon plunges into the nebula-like entity.

Quotes:
- **Paul:** 'Time we had a new world.'
- **Victor:** 'It's either a practical joke or something very interesting.'
- **Victor:** 'This foam, as you call it, could crush anything.'
- **Koenig:** 'It's a living organism, like a brain, pulsating with life and light. It's the centre of a whole galaxy … maybe even hundreds of galaxies. Planets, stars, strange life forms – and in the middle of it all is this brain.'

- **Victor:** 'It's a miracle we're alive, John … Complex as the human brain; and just as vulnerable.'

Filming Dates: Thursday 5 December – Thursday 19 December 1974
Thursday 27 February – Friday 28 February 1975

Incidental Music: The use of Gustav Holst's orchestral classic 'Mars – The Bringer of War' adds dramatically to Alpha's journey through the space brain. This arrangement, by Malcolm Sargent, was published by EMI Music for Pleasure.

Commentary:
Martin Landau: 'The director [Charles Crichton] wasn't getting what he wanted and he asked them to stop the foam. But the crew couldn't hear him and the foam kept coming. Soon it was up to our ears and Charlie waded right into it, all the while yelling, "Stop the foam! Stop the bloody foam!"'

Barry Morse: '"Space Brain" concerned some alien force that flooded the whole of Moonbase Alpha with soap bubbles. It had to be shot with all these bubbles and foam, which had to be pumped into the set. We did the first take and this foam gradually spread out onto the set and filled it up. The director, Charles Crichton, cut and said, "All right now, take two," and everybody looked very blank because no-one had thought how to get all these soapsuds out of the set! It took hours and hours; the result being that by the time we came to take two we realised we could not stop for anything. Whatever happened, we had to keep going. Take two began and they started pumping in all the soapsuds. Unfortunately, when the young boy who did the clapper board came in front of the camera and did his clapper, he slipped on this foam and fell to the floor! Well, being the good technician he was, he stayed put, because he knew if he got up he would spoil the take. So we went on playing this wretched scene, whilst he was being smothered by foam – scarcely able to breath. Thankfully, he did survive and we all had a good laugh about it afterwards.'

Nick Tate: 'There was one episode, "Space Brain", where the whole of Moonbase Alpha was engulfed in foam. They rented these huge machines that pumped soap bubbles everywhere. The machines worked fabulously and filled the entire sound stage with foam, making it look very peculiar and eerie. Unfortunately, nobody stopped to think that we had slippery floors, and the soap bubbles made them more slippery. People would just vanish inside these bubbles and we would find them slithering around on the floor. It was all very amusing, but at the same time very dangerous. After one scene, director Charlie Crichton raced in to call "Cut," and because he was moving so fast, he hit the soap bubbles and vanished from sight with the most terrible thud. There was this awful silence for a few seconds and then we heard Charlie call out, "Don't panic – I'm all right!" He came crawling out of the foam covered in soap bubbles and looking like a Yeti.'

Zienia Merton: '"Space Brain" was just so funny because there was just so much of that foam stuff and the joke was that we didn't have enough space packs to go around. Prentis and I could never appear in the same shots – if there were eight main characters, there were only six packs. So what happened was that he was "6" and I was "9" and we used the same pack but turned it around.

'I remember [in Space Brain]. Prentis and I in Main Mission doing late night duty, or something, and to soften it and make it more normal and real they gave me a tapestry to stitch, thinking poor old Sandra would be doing that. It was Helene Bevan – our hairdresser lady – it was hers, and I made such a mess of it I felt so bad for her. I was stitching away and it was all rubbish, but never mind.'

Shane Rimmer: 'Working with Gerry Anderson was a lot like being in a repertory company. If you saw somebody show up in one series he eventually turned up in another, which was good for everybody, because you got to learn how Gerry worked. You got used to the kind of interplay that he really liked to use in his plays … Gerry had a creative organisational flair and he had an amazing facility to be just a little ahead of the game, and he could predict a lot of times very successfully what was going to happen and what was going to be in vogue.

'When I got the script for "Space Brain", I think it talked about low-level suds, just above the floor. But those suds were ten feet high! I was strapped to an operating table; everybody else left the studio … I've sort of recovered. It was very much enjoyed. I remember the line, "You must not touch my brain!" The soapsuds – honestly, there was so much soap in that studio you could have washed the place down four times over and still had enough for a year's laundry. It was everywhere. I think it looked all right. But the big problem was trying to remain comatose and not sneeze or cough or whatever, while all this stuff was building up.

'There has to be a very strong explorative theme in these things and sometimes they forget to consult the people who are going through these things. Everything is tremendously orientated toward the special effects and toward the wonder and mystery of space, which is fine. But if you're not really too concerned about the people who are going through these things, it starts to dwindle a little bit. The one thing I was always very impressed with was the way [*Space: 1999*] made you actually get quite concerned about whether they were going to get through it or not. You knew it wasn't going to be a succession of special effects – somehow they were going to get through it themselves. I think this is the way the series developed. They went into new situations in space not having a clue how to deal with them.

'What was striking about that leading bunch – Martin Landau, Barbara Bain and Barry Morse – was their conviction: they could sell refrigerators to Eskimos. They had enough good talent on that show that they could parlay that cast into all sorts of situations. So although the soapsuds situation isn't one of my happiest experiences, it was thrilling to be in *Space: 1999*. They used what they knew they had and there was a great realism and naturalism in that series that I thought was terrific. I think all the casting and the script set up was well done.

'Sylvia was terrific working with actors. There were no limitations, or obvious ones, placed upon anybody. Nick Tate was terrific – he could grab a part, with that Australian moxie, just increase it and amplify the part, still staying true to what was conceived. A lot of good actors do that.

'I still maintain that the longevity of *Space: 1999* is because of the honesty and the interplay between the main characters who were there. Somewhere in that main five, in that amalgamated effort, there was a solution. Everybody had a go at it, and I think the most interesting things in our lives are when you have a cumulative effort like that. *Space: 1999* had a kind of conviction about it that I don't see very often in these types of space series.'

Christopher Penfold: 'The idea springs to mind of space as being a macro brain. We also toyed with the idea of doing a micro story. The idea of the heavenly bodies as being macro brain cells is one that appealed to me, and still does. What was achieved on the set with foam wasn't quite in line with that!

'That fire-fighting foam may have been where the production answers to the problems posed by the script came from, but I can certainly say that detergents weren't seriously engaging my mind as a writer. Microbiology was the idea of "Space Brain": the notion that microbiologists spend their time looking at smaller and smaller particles. We spend billions of dollars building particle accelerators and looking at, and looking for, smaller and smaller particles. It seemed to me that it might be quite interesting to turn that around and head off in the other direction. To think of the entire planet Earth as a very small particle; and that it was itself a particle within a very large entity – which might be the universe – and that we might think of the universe as a brain.'

Johnny Byrne: 'I have one image ingrained on my mind … In the making of "Space Brain", Main Mission was filled by these big machines that pumped out thousands of cubic tons of foam. Certain sequences of "Space Brain" were in fact the last to be filmed for the series, and I remember there was only one sequence to be done: it was where Main Mission is invaded by brain cells; in other words, tons of foam. Everybody was pissed off because they wanted to get over to the party, have the end-of-shoot party and get drunk and things. Also it was a question whether or not Charles would finish it on time, I think. But I have this image of Charles Crichton standing there in great big waders shouting, "More foam!" and the foam machines kept coming in and they went absolutely mad. "More foam!" until there was so much foam he was swallowed up and disappeared under it all. It was a wonderful image!'

Bloopers: Two Eagles are moving in to dock with each other but due to the double-exposure of the sequence and the positioning of the models, they are seen to briefly merge together.

Observations: Additional scenes for this episode were the last filmed for Year One, following completion of 'The Testament of Arkadia'.

Lasting for over seven minutes, the opening pre-credits sequence is the longest of the series.

Christopher Penfold reportedly departed the series shortly after 'Space Brain' began filming. His final script for Year One, 'Dragon's Domain', had already been written and would later be produced as episode 23. Of his departure, Penfold recalled, 'As the series developed, the increasing concerns of ITC for a kind of science fiction which I felt very alien to me began to have the effect of undermining the scripts that were being written. We had very good scripts that had to go back to the drawing board to meet a requirement, which had come from Abe Mandell, who didn't appear to have any understanding that if you take one strand out of a script, it affects everything else in the script. So a lot of rewriting – needless rewriting – went on and this had the effect of bringing the scripts further and further behind schedule. The difficulties came to a head and Gerry asked me to leave the series. I don't remember having any severe falling out with him, but I realised the way the wind was blowing as far as story content was concerned and I was, at that point, utterly exhausted anyway … I think sorrow had set in before, so the moment of actually leaving was one of some relief. I would have liked, of course, for it to have continued the way we set out.'

Review: 'Space Brain', another pairing of writer Christopher Penfold and director Charles Crichton, is dramatic, enjoyable and one of the most visually memorable episodes of *Space: 1999*. However, it ends up being several notches below other episodes such as 'Black Sun', 'Another Time, Another Place' or 'War Games'. What is most appealing is the concept of a space entity that could be considered the brain of an entire galaxy – it's a vast concept, but one fraught with difficulty in terms of realisation.

Martin Landau conveys a desperate hope and urgency: the tension in Main Mission is palpable when communications are lost with the Eagle investigating the space brain and as Koenig says, 'Boost to interstellar strength.' It is greatly to the credit of Martin Landau, Barry Morse and Barbara Bain that this episode is successful. As Moonbase Alpha is threatened and flooded with foam, all of the actors treat it as a serious danger. This apparently unflinching belief in the threatening situation is what gives 'Space Brain' its drama. It certainly isn't the use of large quantities of fire-fighting foam. There was a minor trend in science fiction shows of that era to have episodes featuring terribly dangerous foam. (Others were the 'Fury from the Deep' story of *Doctor Who* and the 'Doomsday is Tomorrow' episode of *The Bionic Woman*.) It's a rather dubious sub-genre.

While the main cast are as sturdy as ever, the guest casting somehow fails to work. Shane Rimmer, a familiar face and voice from Gerry Anderson productions over the years and a very capable and likeable actor, comes across as rather stilted and cold here, while Carla Romanelli (another Italian performer brought aboard due to the financing from RAI) is a hollow shell – she emotes at her husband's plight, but isn't believable. As a couple on Moonbase Alpha, Kelly and Melita are not nearly as developed or interesting as Anton and Eva were in 'Force of Life'. Who is Kelly? What are his characteristics and how do they change once he is taken over by the space brain? He remains undefined and appears just as stiff before as he is after the alien presence controls his mind.

In a low-point for dialogue in the series, 'Space Brain' manages to deliver two of the worst lines voiced in Year One. First, Kelly utters the cringe-worthy line, 'You must not touch my brain!' It's a laughable moment that completely undermines any sense of drama in the proceedings. Secondly, Koenig says, 'It is neither a sun, a star or a planet.' But is it a senseless line? Yes, because suns *are* stars and one look at the space brain could tell you it isn't a planet. The line is useless filler and should have been eliminated.

There are, though, a number of appealing elements of characterisation in this episode. Most notable is Koenig's remorse regarding the attack on the space brain. It's also nice to see Paul relaxed with his feet up, reading a book in Main Mission. In an interesting depiction of off-duty activity, a number of Alphans, including John and Helena, are shown piecing together jigsaw puzzles. This adds a bit of an amusing angle to Victor's comment that the meteorite that crashes near to Alpha early in the episode 'puzzles' him. Puzzles seem to be an Alphan craze.

Writer Penfold was evidently intrigued by the possibilities of linking the human brain with computers; the theme is prominent here as Koenig is linked via computer to Kelly's brain, and was also notably displayed in 'Guardian of Piri'. While Penfold raises the potential, and acknowledges possible dangers, he seems to refrain from making any judgment about the practice – unlike his obvious distaste for nuclear technology, here he seems simply to be questioning the outcome of human minds being linked to computers.

Also on Penfold's mind was the thought of mankind being nothing more than a virus in the universe; a concept he so eloquently explored in 'War Games'. Here the Alphans are again a contaminating organism, as they enter and destroy the space brain. The fact that the destruction isn't intentional is part of the point – it's a statement that people don't give enough consideration to the ecosystem around them (whether on Earth or in space) and their potentially damaging impact on it. This perspective resonates today, with civilisation's impact on global climate change making headlines around the world.

Thematically, communication being the route to avoiding misunderstanding and disaster is explored. Remorse is a prominent emotion throughout – Helena's remorse at leaving Kelly to die in the foam and Koenig's remorse at the death of the space brain and the impact this may have on the worlds that were dependent on it. But 'Space Brain' is ultimately a visual episode and as such it is a dynamo to be enjoyed for the sincere performances and for the sheer spectacle – a good example of which is one of the most spectacular Eagle crashes to be featured in the series, including the separated nosecone tumbling along the lunar surface. While Christopher Penfold had some undeniably fascinating concepts in mind while writing 'Space Brain', they ultimately fail to translate effectively to the screen.

Rating: 6.5/10

1.21
THE INFERNAL MACHINE

Screenplay by Anthony Terpiloff and Elizabeth Barrows
Directed by David Tomblin

Selected Broadcast Dates:

UK	LWT:	
	Date: 10 January 1976.	Time: 11.30 am
	Granada:	
	Date: 23 January 1976.	Time: 6.35 pm
US	KRON (San Francisco):	
	Date: 28 February 1976.	Time: 7.00 pm

Credited Cast: Martin Landau (John Koenig), **Barbara Bain** (Helena Russell), **Barry Morse** (Victor Bergman), **Clifton Jones** (David Kano), **Zienia Merton** (Sandra Benes), **Nick Tate** (Alan Carter), **Gary Waldhorn** (Winters)

Guest Star: Leo McKern (Companion / Voice of Gwent)

Uncredited Cast: Sarah Bullen (Operative Kate), **Loftus Burton** (Operative Lee Oswald), **Andrew Dempsey**, **Michael Stevens**, **Andrew Sutcliffe**, **Maggie Wright** (Main Mission Operatives), **Tony Allyn** (Security Guard Tony Allan), **Quentin Pierre** (Security Guard Pierce Quinton), **Alan Harris** (Alphan)

Plot: A bizarre sentient spaceship called Gwent asks for Alpha's help. Aboard is one man, Companion, an ancient traveller who knows the true reason why Gwent wants Commander Koenig, Dr Russell and Professor Bergman to come aboard. Once inside the ship, the trio discover they are not free to leave.

Quotes:
- **Computer:** 'I have nothing to say on that subject ...' 'My information is privileged ...' 'I am otherwise occupied.'
- **Alan:** 'Survival first, brotherhood after.'
- **Gwent:** 'A wise man knows when to be afraid.'
- **Companion:** 'Companions die, but Gwent goes on – forever.'
- **Gwent:** 'You're only good for killing each other.'
- **Gwent:** 'When will you learn to obey?'
- **Gwent:** 'I am Delmer Powys Plebus Gwent of the planet Zemo – a man of considerable importance on that planet, perhaps not fully recognised as the scientific genius I am. I created this entity: an extension of myself. My entire personality is here, and combined with it is the superior ability of a computer's brain and all the might and power known to our planet. I am impervious to destruction and powerful enough to destroy an entire universe. That is who I am – Delmer Powys Plebus Gwent!'

- **Victor:** 'Oh, my dear Gwent. You were wrong from the beginning. To attempt to preserve one's personality is the ultimate vanity.'
- **Gwent:** 'It is vanity. The first and last of all sins.'
- **Koenig:** 'A lonely, blind creature … looking for his death.'

Filming Dates: Friday 20 December – Tuesday 24 December 1974
Monday 30 December – Tuesday 31 December 1974
Thursday 2 January – Thursday 9 January 1975

Incidental Music: The musical score is lovely and conveys a profound sadness as the episode draws to an end – this is 'Dark Suspense No. 1' composed by Beda Folten, heard while Koenig, Russell and Bergman remain trapped inside Gwent after the ship has shut itself off. Other library tracks include 'Outer Space' by Robert Farnon (heard while Gwent approaches Alpha), 'Lunar Landscape' by Roger Roger (heard as the Alphan trio enter Gwent), 'Mission Control' by Harry Sosnik (heard at the beginning of the show as Koenig gives an update on Morrow's injury), 'Subterranean' by Joe Venuto and 'The Monsters' by Ivo Vyhnalek. All of these tracks were sourced from the Chappell Recorded Music Library. Additionally, Barry Gray music is borrowed from the 'Terror in New York City' episode of *Thunderbirds*, and is used here during the attack on Gwent.

Commentary:
Barry Morse: 'I admire and like Leo McKern so much. Leo is a wonderful actor; one of the greatest actors of our time, and he is always remarkable in everything he does. He played so beautifully a character called Companion in this episode, as well as the "Infernal Machine" itself. I'm proud to say I was partly responsible for suggesting that he should play both the guest roles in this episode. It occurred to me that with this script, if you had an actor of the huge range and versatility that Leo has, you would be doing the script a great favour if you had him playing both the parts.'

Nick Tate: 'I loved working with Leo McKern who, incidentally, is Australian. He is a wonderful actor and a true star.'

Prentis Hancock: 'I got into makeup early one morning at 6.30. The makeup chairs are like dentist chairs, and I leaned back in the chair and the makeup artist said to me, "You've got a lump in your throat." And I had. That weekend I went to hospital to have it removed, and [in "The Infernal Machine"] they got somebody else to cover for me. They sent me the most amazing card, signed by every member of the cast and crew, with a drawing by Keith Wilson of Main Mission with an arrow to my chair, saying, "We miss you." In the end, the result of my test was that [the lump] was benign – but nobody told me. I had to phone the hospital to find out! Gerry and Sylvia were just terrific. I got a huge bowl of fruit from them and they said, "No problem – we'll cover for you. You get the best treatment you can." And I did and I was back in the saddle the following episode.'

Johnny Byrne: 'There wasn't a great deal of humour. There could have been a bit more, but the problem was what the Americans call humour and what the English call humour are two different things. In America it's sort of cracking jokes, one-line throwaways, and it always seemed gratuitous to me. Humour to me essentially comes from character, the strange things that people go through and their response to situations. But there was a more profound reason why you wouldn't really get in proper humour. You wouldn't build it into the plots because that would have detracted from the seriousness of the plots. The nearest we came to that was probably in "The Infernal Machine", where it was a situation that had humour in it, comic tragedy. The rest of the time you could try to have people make "in" kind of jokes about Moonbase Alpha and not succeeding, really. You'd get a required grin out of the character at the other end of the remark. But he's on screen and told to laugh because it says to in the script. But there's very little spontaneous humour in those situations. Humour is not an essential ingredient in that sense, but it is essential that you have the kind of eccentricity of character.'

Review: The title of this episode comes from the 1934 play by Jean Cocteau, *The Infernal Machine*, based on the ancient Greek tragedy by Sophocles, *Oedipus Rex*, which was first performed circa 429 BC. Here Gwent takes on many of the traits of Cocteau's character: Oedipus is pompous, possessing extreme pride and an arrogant nature; arrogance being a trait that ultimately has destructive capacity. Cocteau's Oedipus feels guilt and, as a self-inflicted punishment, blinds himself; while in this episode the blind Gwent – with arrogance and pride replaced by guilt and self-pity – commits suicide. Oedipus is even told by the old priest Tiresias, 'You are seeking classic glory,' which sounds very much like Alpha's wise old Bergman telling Gwent, 'To attempt to preserve one's personality is the ultimate vanity.' Basically, as Cocteau did with the original *Oedipus Rex* by Sophocles, this episode transforms a Greek myth into a modern (and in this case futuristic) tragedy.

The background of life on Alpha is shown quite effectively at the start of the episode, as an obviously tired Koenig leaves duty in Main Mission to retire to his quarters and encounters a couple of people to whom he wishes, 'Goodnight,' leading one of the Alphans to reply, 'Good morning, Commander,' a subtle and effective indicator that Koenig is working a little too hard.

The absence of Paul Morrow and the introduction of his temporary replacement, Winters, are handled satisfactorily despite the comparative blandness of actor Gary Waldhorn's performance. There is an interesting depth to Kano that is hinted at through his line, 'Destruction of Alpha imminent.' He has a dark side – a fatalistic or pessimistic streak, which would have been quite a unique personality trait to explore in greater depth.

It is fascinating to follow the episode as Gwent learns more about the Alphans, while they learn more about him: in particular, the facts that he needs to conserve energy and is blind. The script is rich in humanity and a great depth of characterisation. The pace and plotting are ideally matched with the demanding emotional qualities of the show – the Alphans are in danger: Koenig, Russell and Bergman may never get away; Gwent tortures them and those on Alpha, kills the pilots of several Eagles and of the ground tanks (although, arguably, the latter could have been under remote control). Despite this, the lead characters must be able to understand and sympathise with Gwent and ultimately express sadness for his demise. This is very challenging for the actors to perform, and it is also challenging for the audience to appreciate. But 'The Infernal Machine' is very much worth the effort and, as in the earlier episode 'Guardian of Piri', the computer character of Gwent is a formidable enemy, much like HAL 9000 in

2001: A Space Odyssey; all are powerful machines that have evolved beyond their expected limitations and are out of control.

In terms of on-screen realisation, Gwent is another marvel of *Space: 1999*. It is purely alien on the outside and impressively massive inside. As an internal alien spaceship set, Gwent is arguably the finest in the series. Again, *Space: 1999* is the champion of television science fiction set design, thanks to the talents of Keith Wilson. David Tomblin, with his dynamic and cinematic direction, makes the most of the scope of the set. The special effects and models of 'The Infernal Machine' are also some of the finest in the series, including the depiction of Moonbase Alpha's impressive laser tanks and of Gwent itself.

Leo McKern, yet another stellar guest in an increasingly impressive list, delivers a compassionate, memorable performance as both Companion and the voice of Gwent. It is a great irony that Gwent – a machine – is the most sympathetic alien character in the first season. This episode also showcases the stars of the series. Martin Landau, Barbara Bain and Barry Morse are all excellent in their multi-faceted roles, each playing a wide range of emotional notes and working in harmony with each other. Credit goes to writers Anthony Terpiloff and Elizabeth Barrows, along with the performers. Gwent is untrusting, suspicious, cynical and perhaps paranoid. Gwent needs company and becomes lonely in isolation. He has a personality, is blind and feels grief and sadness. To give these qualities to a spaceship/computer and to follow through to the point where the computer commits suicide because it can't take the loneliness, grief and remorse it feels, is a challenge well met by this script. As a team, Terpiloff and Barrows contribute another script (the first being 'Death's other Dominion') with ties to classic literature – it's worth comparing this with Terpiloff's solo scripts, which seem to lack these inspirations and focus almost solely on the theme of faith. The contribution of Elizabeth Barrows, apparently, was the source of the ties to ancient Greek tragedy here and Shakespearean tragedy in 'Death's other Dominion'.

On the surface this is an obvious 'man versus Machine' story similar to others before, notably 'Guardian of Piri', not least because in both cases the central machine is not alone – the Guardian has its Servant, while Gwent has Companion. While one of the peripheral subjects explored here is vanity, 'The Infernal Machine' makes a statement about its central theme of isolation as Gwent says, 'None of us exists except in relation to others. Alone we cease to have personalities; isolation … Do you understand?' Isolation and loneliness are also exemplified by the vast empty spaces within Gwent and are personified by Companion – alone in deep space with only a machine version of himself as company. Isolation here is shown to be a danger of immortality – Companion programmed his entire personality into the ageless body of Gwent, only to discover that the immortal and sentient Gwent requires companionship and cannot live alone. Ultimately, this version of immortality is unsustainable and ends in suicide. Once more (as in 'Guardian of Piri', 'Death's other Dominion', 'End of Eternity' and the upcoming 'Mission of the Darians') the writers raise a doubt regarding the value of the pursuit of eternal life. Suspenseful to the end and visually beautiful, 'The Infernal Machine' is undoubtedly the most emotional, touching and gently endearing segment of the series.

Rating: 9/10

1.22
MISSION OF THE DARIANS

Screenplay by Johnny Byrne
Directed by Ray Austin

Selected Broadcast Dates:
UK   LWT:
            Date: 1 November 1975.   Time: 5.50 pm
            Granada:
            Date: 21 November 1975.   Time: 6.35 pm
US   KRON (San Francisco):
            Date: 1 November 1975.   Time: 7.00 pm

Credited Cast: Martin Landau (John Koenig), **Barbara Bain** (Helena Russell), **Barry Morse** (Victor Bergman), **Prentis Hancock** (Paul Morrow), **Clifton Jones** (David Kano), **Zienia Merton** (Sandra Benes), **Nick Tate** (Alan Carter), **Paul Antrim** (Bill Lowry), **Robert Russell** (Hadin), **Gerald Stadden** (Male Mute), **Jackie Horton** (Female Mute)

Guest Star: Joan Collins (Kara)

Guest Artists: Dennis Burgess (Neman), **Aubrey Morris** (High Priest)

Uncredited Cast: Sarah Bullen (Operative Kate), **Loftus Burton** (Operative Lee Oswald), **Ann Maj-Britt** (Operative Ann), **Binu Balini, Andrew Dempsey, Michael Stevens** (Main Mission Operatives), **Ron Tarr** (Darian Guard), **Linda Hooks** (Blonde Female Darian), **Jenny Cresswell** (Female Darian)

Previously Titled: 'Mission of the Daria'

Plot: Moonbase Alpha encounters the massive space ark *SS Daria* – devastated 900 years previously by a nuclear explosion. A message cries out for assistance and the Alphans journey to the *Daria*, where they split up and encounter a race of highly advanced Darians on a mission to a new world, and a primitive tribe that has degenerated into savagery; hunting mutants born of the radioactive devastation and sacrificing perfect bodies to their God, Neman.

Quotes:
- **High Priest:** 'Here in this sacred shrine of knowledge, we dedicate this perfect body. We pledge her in the spirit of true science; we pledge her in the light of clear knowledge and maintain that she is free of the Mutant, whom we abhor in all its manifestations. This we pledge on the sacred book of Neman, maker of Man, father of Spirits. To you, Neman, we the survivors of Level 7, offer this body.'
- **Victor:** 'That's it, John – living human bodies.'
- **High Priest:** 'Defiler of truth … Killer of spirit … Enemy of Neman.'

- **Alan:** 'Spirit? This is no spirit. Look, they have deceived you. He's a man; a man like you; a man like me.'
- **Hadin:** 'Neman – you are not a God.'
- **Koenig:** 'These people are your future now. Prepare them to survive in space. We'll help you, but the rest is up to you.'

Filming Dates: Friday 10 January – Friday 24 January 1975

Incidental Music: Includes the introduction from 'The White Mountain' by Frank Cordell (heard in several scenes including when Koenig meets Kara, and when the Eagle returns to Alpha), and 'Experiments in Space – Vega' by Robert Farnon (heard during the opening sequences with the discovery of the colossal spaceship). These two tracks were from the Chappell Recorded Music Library. Additional Barry Gray compositions are included from the *Joe 90* episode 'King for a Day' and the *Stingray* episode 'Ghost of the Sea' (heard here as Kara's theme, and utilised previously as the beautiful dream-like music on Zenno in 'Missing Link'.)

Commentary:
Barry Morse: '"Mission of the Darians" was an attempt to engage in a certain amount of philosophical argument regarding racial purity. Even the name "Darian" equates with "Aryan". So it was admirable in that respect.'

Nick Tate: 'I found Joan Collins to be very friendly. We had lunch at the studio a few times while she was guest-starring.'

Johnny Byrne: 'I think "Mission of the Darians" is probably the one I like best. It is perhaps the most serious of all the stories I wrote. It has the cruel, inescapable things that life sometimes forces upon us. If you remember, there was a crash in the Andes and the people, in order to survive, had to eat their fellow passengers. I don't think that book had been published when I wrote this story.' [The book and subsequent film were called *Alive*. Another account, *Miracle in the Andes*, was published in 2006.]

'First of all, I was excited by the thought of a 50 mile long spaceship. Secondly, my mind harked back to a wonderful story that I had read by Brian Aldiss many, many years ago. It was called *Non-Stop*. That always set up an echo in my mind and, while not plagiarising Brian, I couldn't help dealing with a theme of people cut off and sort of drifting, and the mystery about them. So here they are in this wonderful spaceship. They discover that thousands of years ago the original people who owned this ship, who had taken the ship and who were on their way to a new world, had a huge accident, and now there is a small group of the original aliens plus the atomic survivors – the mutants of their own people. It's not a co-incidence that they are called Darians, it was meant to equate with Aryans, the life theme of the Aryan race, the sort of proto-Nazi thing – not fascism and not Nazism, but the kind of primal racial instinct. [They were meant to be] kind of superior beings, knowing that they've got to keep [the mutants] alive so that they can survive; and once there on a new world, they would be disposed of. But here in the gene bank is all they require to remanufacture the race again.

'The thing was – and I thought it was well worked out – that a kind of religion was built around a sort of disfigurement and the things that would obviously weigh large in people's minds in a post-atomic situation. Lots of stillbirths and horrific mutants and things like that would appear. The structure of social groups would be incredibly rigid and they would try to eliminate the mutants, in the way the Spartans would dispose of daughters or deformed children to keep the purity going. And of course they would feed these into the food chain. That was what was keeping the "good" Darians alive. The name of the game is survival, and that's what they were doing. Essentially we are talking about cannibalism, no matter how science fiction it was.

'At the end of the day, the resolution was a very humane one, where the idea was that the gene bank is now destroyed. It should've been destroyed in the first place – *these* are the people who own the future. The two groups have got to be connected so that by the time they land they *will* have their own people. Not the same, but they will have people. So they basically needed each other. Again, there were no heroes and villains, but *things* that people had to do.

'All of the stories were full of contrived incidents. At the rate we were getting through Alpha Moonbase personnel, I'm amazed that any remained at the end of the first season! But it was important to show, I think, this whole obsession [the Darians] had with mutants. It was important to have one Alphan character [Bill Lowry] there who could be disposed of to show how deeply rooted this tradition was; basically how ignorant, how clueless [the Darians] had become about the real world. And how they were simply acting on a kind of ritual memory rather than common sense. We did actually have two dwarfs in it, which I thought added immensely to the value. And there were some magnificent glass shots in it. There was a view when you came in through a door and you saw the entire huge bay of the spaceship. We didn't do many glass shots, but that was one, and it really added immensely. The sight of that massive ship moving through the frame in the first shots was excellent. Ray Austin did a marvellous job of directing this … We had a brilliant model maker – absolutely brilliant. He gave it that distinctive kind of Lego style. It really looked mind-bending on a big screen, which I used to see it on in rushes.

'Names that I keep using are Neman and Hadin. Hadin comes from the *Sagas of Icelanders*, which have been the great source of my inspiration, and Hadin comes from one of the most famous, *Njal's Saga*. One of the sons of Njal was Skarp-Hedin, the ferocious man, and I was so impressed by that character that whenever possible I try to use his name, because it gives me a sort of fix on the character. Both these names, Hadin and Neman, are in "Mission of the Darians". It was originally called "Mission of the Daria"; this envisaged the Darians as more sort of genetically Nazi-like, where they were going to turn out endless warriors and they were in a big ship full of tanked sperm, or something. But it was completely different to what turned out ultimately.

'It was a very fundamental human problem: what do people do when they're in a situation and they have no food? They eat each other – they always have done. And it was a re-statement of the principle that the desire to survive and live is very strong; and for me to find a way in which I could a) express that idea, and b) do so in such a way that it wouldn't be banned from popular television – after all, it was about cannibalism – was well worth the effort … So, it worked on many, many different levels. It had, I suppose, the most fundamental question of all at the heart of it: what will people do, and is there any limit to what people will do, in order to survive? And the answer's basically, "No, there isn't."

'It probably helped that we had Joan Collins, the perfect example of the imperishable survivor. Sometimes I think that she probably fed on too many spare parts in that particular episode, because she seems to be surviving, unchanged, 20-odd years later! I think, in that sense, Joan Collins was the perfect choice for this Darian super goddess. I quite enjoyed working with her and being there when they were shooting it.'

Sylvia Anderson: 'Generally speaking [Martin and Barbara] were okay, but of course the problem is that whenever you have Hollywood actors over to England their attitude is that, "We're big time. We're big Hollywood people and we've done a big series." So they had to have the Rolls Royce to transport them from the shooting studio, which was about 50 yards away, to the restaurant everyday. So there were a lot of things like that. I will say this – when Joan Collins came on in a guest spot [in "Mission of the Darians"], Barbara stuck very, very closely to Martin. And, incidentally, Barbara's expression *did* change. Normally she was very expressionless.'

Review: 'Mission of the Darians' is a perfectly realised epic about survival, both thrilling and horrifying, which incorporates a number of classic science fiction concepts including immortality and the multi-generation space ark. The generation ship idea has been utilised to great success in novels before, but on television the idea has tended to fall flat – see the early 1970s Canadian science fiction series *The Starlost*, for example.

The plotline follows three separate story threads that ultimately pull back together in the climax, creating one of the most complexly plotted segments of the series. The procedure the Alphans follow is totally believable, as is the holocaust portrayed. The theme is that of the downfall of an advanced race due to failures of technology, and it demonstrates that the future lies ultimately with the people themselves – not with their carefully cultivated technological achievements. As such, this episode embodies what is perhaps the greatest overarching concept of the series.

The mutant characters add immensely to the portrayal of distinct and separate societies existing in isolation from each other in the immense *Daria*. The *Daria* itself is remarkably similar to the freighter *Nostromo* in the later film *Alien*. The detailing of this miniature is outstanding for a television production and the massive scope of the ship is demonstrated when the tiny Eagle approaches. Interiors of the *Daria* are enriched through the use of several matte paintings conveying the craft's immense scale.

The experiences on Level 7, within the *Daria*, are terrifying. The scene leading Helena, Lowry and the Female Mute to be judged as mutants is genuinely frightening, aided by eerie sound effects and subordinated natural sounds and voices – a hallmark technique of director Ray Austin, which he had utilised to great effect in previous episodes, notably 'End of Eternity'.

This is very much an ensemble episode. Barbara Bain is remarkable, conveying Helena's terror for herself and her horror at what happens to those around her. The entire cast of regulars and guests are on top form, notably Prentis Hancock, relishing the opportunity for Paul Morrow to get out of Alpha and into the action; he and Nick Tate made a very effective team. Barry Morse is also noteworthy as Bergman, with several memorable scenes demonstrating him as vital to the progress of the storyline. Martin Landau's Koenig is at his edgiest, confronted with an alien vision of what he must consider to be a potential outcome for his own people, should any of the links in their food chain break.

Joan Collins, who leads the guest cast, is very good throughout, and is delightful at the end as her character Kara looks at Hadin, obviously considering what their future together might entail.

Of interest is the portrayal of security guard Bill Lowry. Far too regularly (not just in *Space: 1999*, but in science fiction television in general) the security guard is present as a glorified extra who can be discarded at any moment with no lingering effect. Here, Lowry is not only integral to his portion of the story, but an actual three-dimensional human being, and his loss is profoundly felt by both the viewers and the characters onscreen – exemplified by Helena in the Eagle at the episode's end, the empty seat and the remembered tune hummed by Lowry. It's a poignant moment.

The sets are inspiring and the use of matte paintings and attention to detail within the interiors of the *Daria* combine to provide a significant and convincing degree of reality. Matte paintings were also utilised in prior episodes 'Missing Link' and 'The Last Enemy', but the ones here are possibly the best and are certainly the most effectively integrated into the episode.

As a final teaming of writer Johnny Byrne and director Ray Austin (following their pairing in 'End of Eternity' and 'The Troubled Spirit'), 'Mission of the Darians' marks the culmination of their efforts together. Byrne's script again raises the memory of World War II and the Nazis, as in 'Voyager's Return'. The word 'Darian' equates with 'Aryan' – the idea of a superior, master race whose genetic purity and perfection was to be preserved to thrive at any cost. In the same manner, 'Neman' can be interpreted as 'New Man' – all the more important a connection as Neman has led the advanced Darians in the genocide of the mutants. The concept of an advanced race being forced to resort to cannibalism in order to survive is presented in a believable manner, and it leads one to wonder what the Alphans themselves would do if confronted with a similar situation. The theme of the episode can be summed up with a single word: survival. Indeed, the dialogue of this script features no less than 23 references to 'survival', 'survive', 'survived' or 'survivors.' The resultant moral question being: to what lengths would we go to ensure our own survival?

In typical *Space: 1999* style, the questions raised have no simple answers, but latent implications that continue to reverberate to this day: what would mankind do to preserve itself? Would the Alphans have done anything differently than the Darians? What is the price of our survival? And as our own planet Earth becomes more crowded and we face mounting environmental concerns, could there be a nightmare outcome like this awaiting the whole world? This last question dovetails into another message inherent in the episode – that the races of Earth must come together; our future is with each other, just like that of the Darians (and, indeed, the Alphans). Each society has strengths to benefit the union: it would be difficult to imagine Kara and her people surviving on a new world without the practical grounding of the other survivors to help them, but in such a colonisation attempt the more advanced Darian technology would also be of great use. Essentially, they are stronger together than they are apart.

With the Darian ship's nuclear catastrophe, 'Mission of the Darians' also provides an echo of the original nuclear disaster that plunged the Alphans into deep space in 'Breakaway'. The complete episode, with its disturbing aspects contrasted against the hopeful ones (rather like life itself), is simply outstanding!

Rating: 9/10

1.23
DRAGON'S DOMAIN

Screenplay by Christopher Penfold
Directed by Charles Crichton

Selected Broadcast Dates:

UK	LWT:	
	Date: 25 October 1975.	Time: 5.50 pm
	Granada:	
	Date: 14 November 1975.	Time: 6.35 pm
US	KRON (San Francisco):	
	Date: 13 September 1975.	Time: 7.00 pm
	WPIX (New York):	
	Date: 27 September 1975.	Time: 7.00 pm

Credited Cast: Martin Landau (John Koenig), **Barbara Bain** (Helena Russell), **Barry Morse** (Victor Bergman), **Prentis Hancock** (Paul Morrow), **Clifton Jones** (David Kano), **Zienia Merton** (Sandra Benes), **Anton Phillips** (Bob Mathias), **Nick Tate** (Alan Carter), **Barbara Kellermann** (Dr Monique Bouchere), **Michael Sheard** (Dr Darwin King), **Susan Jameson** (Professor Juliet Mackie)

Guest Stars: Gianni Garko (Tony Cellini), **Douglas Wilmer** (Commissioner Dixon)

Uncredited Cast: Suzanne Roquette (Tanya Alexander), **Bob Sherman** (Space News Newsreader), **Sarah Bullen** (Operative Kate), **Loftus Burton** (Operative Lee Oswald), **Ann Maj-Britt** (Operative Ann), **Andrew Dempsey, Michael Stevens, Andrew Sutcliffe, Maggie Wright** (Main Mission Operatives), **Tony Allyn** (Security Guard Tony Allan), **Quentin Pierre** (Security Guard Pierce Quinton), **James Fagan** (Eagle 2 Pilot Pete Johnson), **Laraine Humphrys** (Nurse Anne), **Alan Harris** (Alphan), **Gwen Taylor** (Earth Nurse)

Previously Titled: 'Web'

Plot: Launched in 1996, the Ultra Probe was piloted by Tony Cellini on a mission to investigate Ultra, a tenth planet in Earth's solar system. The Ultra Probe encountered a spaceship graveyard populated by a monster, and Cellini was the only survivor. Now, on Alpha, Cellini believes he is nearing another encounter with this terrifying enemy. His foreboding is met with scepticism, until a spaceship graveyard is discovered near the Moon and the Ultra Probe is located within it.

Quotes:
- **Helena:** 'It was the eight hundred and seventy-seventh day since our Moon left Earth orbit. We were between galaxies, drifting through empty space, when Tony Cellini began to believe that he was closing for a second time with his mortal

162

enemy.'

- **Kano:** 'Computer's probably angry because you insulted her.'
- **Koenig:** 'If we think we know everything that goes on out there, we're making a terrible mistake.'
- **Victor:** 'They do look somewhat like flies, caught in a spider's web.'
- **Koenig:** 'Which brings us back to monsters.'
- **Koenig:** 'Just because we haven't experienced something doesn't mean it doesn't exist.'
- **Helena**: 'Where do you think he was trying to get to out there in his pyjamas?' … 'He didn't even take his toothbrush.'
- **Helena:** 'The monster was more than any of us could believe. According to our criteria it was never alive, so how could we be sure that it was dead? As we hurried back to Alpha, before our Moon drifted beyond reach, we could only wonder about the astronauts of those other fabulous ships. All we know about them is their terrible fate: the fate of Tony Cellini.'

On-screen Date: 877 days since leaving Earth orbit.

Filming Dates: Monday 27 January – Monday 10 February 1975

Incidental Music: The Ultra Probe's voyage is scored by the beautiful and haunting neo-baroque piece 'Adagio in G Minor'. This composition is now recognised as being an original composition by Remo Giazotto (published in 1958), although Giazotto had fabricated a story that it was based upon a fragment of music by Tomaso Albinoni (and the piece is frequently referred to as 'Albinoni's Adagio'.) This arrangement is by Allain Lombard and was published by Delyse [Envoy] Recording Co.

Commentary:

Nick Tate: 'In the first series the show was devised very much around the concept of Martin Landau and Barbara Bain having been big stars in America. They wanted to shoot the show very much all about them, and the rest of us were very peripheral. They intended bringing on guest actors who would have nice, meaty roles and then go away again, because the nature of the beast was that they were an alien who would go away, or they were a character who would be brought up from the bowels of *Space: 1999* and they would die in space somewhere and never be seen again. That's how they handled actors who had larger roles.

'For the most part they didn't want us other [regular] actors – Prentis and Zienia and Clifton, Anton and me – to have big parts. I just got lucky that Alan's character grew. But I did have an awkward time in "Dragon's Domain". I had seen an early draft of that script and my character was the character that saved the day and killed the dragon. The writer, Chris Penfold, had in fact originally written the episode for me. It was a great break for me and I was very excited about it. I was not supposed to see any of the early drafts, but I did see it, because I'd gone to Johnny Byrne's house and he'd told me about it and I'd seen the draft. I liked that early script the best; I took it home and learned a lot of it … When the shooting script came down six weeks later, my character is in the first three pages and then gets knocked on the head and spends the rest of the episode in the infirmary. They brought in an Italian actor to play a new character, Cellini, and of course the Dragon kills him and Martin then kills the Dragon and saves the day.

'I couldn't understand the great change in that script. I went in to Sylvia to ask her why, and she closed the door and said, "There are things that go on in a series that you should understand. This is not something that I can change for you." I said, "But you told me how much you liked me, and how much you wanted things to improve for me. This was going to be my big break." She said, "Yes, it was, but there are other people here that have more power than I do." It turned out that Martin didn't want it to be. He'd read the draft and said, "Nick is not to play that role. That's not his position here." I've kept that pretty much under my hat for a long time, but that's the reason why most of us were not given ongoing relationships within the show, because Martin and Barbara didn't want it. That's the truth. And it was the downfall of the show, really, if you want to know the truth of it.

'When the show aired in America, one of the main complaints about it was that there wasn't a great deal of interrelationships and things going on with the people, and the viewers wanted to know why there wasn't a lot of human stuff happening with them. The reason was because – stupidly – it was decided that all those relationships should be contained within the two lead actors, or guest actors who would come on and be killed or fired; and it was a big mistake. Sylvia loved all the actors she had on the show and she was a great supporter of me and Prentis and Zienia, and she wanted us to do more. But we weren't allowed to do more.

'They brought in Gianni to play the role [of Cellini] ... I remember the first day that he worked I had to do a scene with him, and the irony was that his English was really very poor. He was a very good Italian actor who could speak broken English, but to do all that dialogue, it just wasn't there for him. So he came to me – I don't think he realised the role was originally written for me, otherwise he probably never would have had the gall to ask me this – but he said, "Would you help me learn the role?" I said, "Sure, of course," because I liked him. He came to my dressing room and we read the lines over and over. I tape-recorded every one of his lines for him in English and he went away and learned them – parrot fashion – from me. He was such a nice guy, and he deserved to do it well.'

Johnny Byrne: 'I thought "Dragon's Domain" was awfully good. Again, it was different, because we had a voice-over, but it worked awfully well in it. That was a really spooky dragon they had, and I saw the poor thing mouldering away outside in the back-lot for the remainder of the series. And, poor little thing, I used to take my dogs up to the studios and we would go chasing rabbits around the back-lot and they would always end up somehow having a pee on the old octopus, or whatever it was!'

Christopher Penfold: '"Dragon's Domain" was an attempt to take on the whole issue of monsters in what I hoped was a fairly creative and constructive way. I saw that episode for the first time [around 1993] and I felt quite pleased with it. It treats monsters in quite a philosophical way. The special effects in view of what we have seen in *Alien* and *Star Wars* now look laughable, but in a way it didn't matter.

'I think that in "Dragon's Domain" what I was taking on was the notion of how we deal with the idea of monstrosity. We live in a world that insurance companies attempt to persuade us is insurable in every respect. Security is something that we strive for, and yet all of us know, either at the back of our minds or indeed around the corner, there can always be arbitrary and unexpected horrors. The whole horror genre is built on that. In "Dragon's Domain" I really wanted to take that on and to tell a story in which the belief in the monster would turn out to be real, in the sense that it was an aspect of the unknown universe with which an individual suddenly becomes confronted; in the face of no experience, other than the kind of accumulation of mythological stories that have dealt with this notion. That was the only equipment that they, the Alphans, had to deal with the Dragon.'

Bloopers: Watch the effects shot immediately before Cellini says, 'There's got to be someone around.' In this (and the following) shot of the spaceship graveyard the Ultra Probe is clearly shown already docked to the Dragon's ship and already missing its pilot's section … In story terms, of course, the Probe hasn't even docked yet! Another case of special effects shots being inserted in the wrong order into an episode.

The Dragon is shocking enough for any horror film – just ignore the strings manipulating its tentacles as Cellini becomes entangled in its grip.

The Space News broadcast gives the current date (leading up to the launch of the Ultra Probe) as 3 September 1996; but Helena later chronicles the launch date of the Ultra Probe as 6 June 1996. The problem was simple: the script had the date written in the European order of day, month, year (as '9-3-96' – 9 March 1996), however actor Bob Sherman read the date in the American order of month, day, year, as 3 September 1996.

Observations: Helena Russell's personal quarters are shown again, for the first time since 'Matter of Life and Death'. Apparently she's either moved or renovated, because they're different than they were before.

The special effects team experimented with including the TARDIS from *Doctor Who* and a model of *Star Trek*'s *USS Enterprise* in the spaceship graveyard, before ultimately abandoning the idea.

'Dragon's Domain' is another episode that tested the boundaries of what could be considered 'family viewing' due to the graphic nature of the Dragon swallowing its prey and spitting them back out again as grotesque smouldering corpses.

Strikingly, 'Dragon's Domain' is the fifth episode in a row that takes place purely in outer space and doesn't feature a planet at all, which makes one of the criticisms the series frequently faced – that the Moon was improbably encountering a different planet each week – difficult to comprehend and goes a long way to demonstrating that the critics making such statements never actually watched the programme.

Actress Barbara Kellermann's name is more commonly spelt 'Kellerman', but she does occasionally get credited either way in various productions.

Review: The final association of writer Christopher Penfold and director Charles Crichton, 'Dragon's Domain' is an unforgettable science fiction landmark. Penfold takes his first inspiration from the ancient tale of Saint George and the Dragon and projects a childhood fear onto the Alphans – what monster lies waiting for us in the dark of space?

'Dragon's Domain' begins 877 days after the Moon left Earth orbit, placing a timeline to the journeys of Moonbase Alpha. It's interesting to see that the events of the first series to date have occurred not within one year, but well over two years of Alphan time. Sadly, this timeline would be ignored by the second series, which would begin its premiere episode 'The Metamorph' at 342 days after leaving Earth orbit.

Tony Cellini's quarters are likely the most personal presented in the series, decorated with a variety of ancient weapons and artwork. Kano is again seen playing chess, a hobby of his – either playing against other people or against Computer. Here he gets to beat Commander Koenig as the two lounge on the steps in Main Mission for their match. There is a wealth of character conflict and drama, especially between Koenig and Dr Russell, who are at odds over Cellini. Koenig respects his old friend, while Helena thinks Cellini is unstable and a threat to the safety of Alpha.

The back-story is wonderfully detailed. Viewers learn that Professor Bergman discovered and named Ultra in 1994, and there is a flashback to events on Moonbase Alpha in 1996 as preparations build for the Ultra Probe mission. Koenig appears here in an orange-sleeved Reconnaissance uniform, contrasting against his usual Command black. Colourful jackets are also on display, as well as name badges – both would become regular features in Year Two. While 'Another Time, Another Place' showed a possible future life for the Alphans, 'Dragon's Domain' shows their past. Barbara Bain, Barry Morse and Martin Landau all shine portraying slightly younger versions of their characters. Gianni Garko is also memorably effective as the obsessed Cellini.

During the flashback sequences, the *Space: 1999* term 'black sun' is used again in reference to black holes. The term would also be used in the Year Two episode 'Seed of Destruction'. The flashback and narration itself effectively set the tone and maintain the mood of the episode.

The journey of the Ultra Probe is also shown through flashback, with a voice-over by Helena. These sequences feature the use of silent space, both scientifically accurate and extremely rare for a filmed science fiction production. (Indeed, with the depiction of silent space and use of a classical orchestral score, the voyage of the Ultra Probe bears a resemblance to that of the Discovery in *2001: A Space Odyssey*.). The Ultra Probe joins the growing list of Earth's disastrous space exploration missions in *Space: 1999*, including the Meta Probe, the Astro 7, Voyager One (and Voyager Two), and the Uranus Probe.

The Ultra Probe is a stunningly designed and completely believable miniature, coupled with perfectly matched and impressive interior sets. The model work by Martin Bower in this instalment – specifically for the Ultra Probe and the spaceship graveyard – is without doubt the best in the series. While watching the spaceship graveyard scenes, viewers can see Arra's craft from 'Collision Course' and the bomber most famous from 'War Games', among other familiar ships.

Keith Wilson designed the incredible Dragon, which is the most convincing and thoroughly 'alien' creature to appear in *Space: 1999*. It is horrifying, and so utterly otherworldly that it failed to register as a life form on the Ultra Probe's Black Box, or on the scans from Alpha or the Eagle. With the arguable exception of the mutated Anton Zoref in 'Force of Life', this is the only alien monster to appear throughout the 24 episodes of Year One.

Barry Morse always wanted to do unique and different things to add to the characterisation of Victor Bergman, and this desire shows itself during the flashback scene in Commissioner Dixon's office. As the men take their seats, Bergman sits on the arm of his chair, crosses his legs and slouches comfortably sideways while drinking a cup of coffee. It's a subtly sharp contrast to the bearing of the other actors (Martin Landau and Gianni Garko), who simply sit down in their chairs in the conventional manner.

Also of interest in this scene, for those viewers who like to take note of set details, are some good views of a Keith Wilson painting hanging to the side of Dixon's desk. It's quite futuristic looking, with a predominance of red and yellow, and several figures.

Nick Tate gets to act a lighter moment in this tense episode ('What's that guy got against me?'), as do Landau and Bain as he gives her a flower and they share a tender exchange. These are effective counterpoints to the horrifying aspects of the story. Another enjoyable comment comes from Helena, when she remarks somewhat pointedly about Cellini, 'He didn't even take his toothbrush.' This all adds greatly to the warmth of the characters in general and the developing relationship between Koenig and Russell especially. As usual, Helena is the sensible one throughout this adventure, while Koenig is hot-headed – a perfect match for each other.

Koenig delivers a memorable speech: 'Now Commissioner, we just can't scrap the Ultra Probe and ignore those ships out there. We've had a lot of successes so far. We've learned a great deal about our solar system. We know what dangers to expect out there from black suns, neutron storms, radiation and the like, but if we think we know everything that goes on out there, we're making a terrible mistake!' The final sentence defines much of the prevailing moral of the first series and has been stated before, notably in 'War Games', another tour de force by Christopher Penfold.

'Dragon's Domain' is about obsession – specifically Tony Cellini's obsession with the monster. It is a tragic episode chronicling his absolution and almost inevitable demise. As *Space: 1999* has repeatedly shown, some events are beyond our understanding; here it is the re-appearance of the spaceship graveyard, somehow aligning Cellini for another encounter with his Dragon, through which he is vindicated. His fate was sealed in much the same way as was Mateo's in 'The Troubled Spirit'. The very essence of this concept – that the fates have something to do with the outcome of our lives – is of central import to the stories of Year One. By contrast, in the premiere second season episode, 'The Metamorph', Koenig will state, 'We'll determine our own destiny.' That one line might be the single most important statement defining the difference between the Alphans who appear in Year Two and those of Year One. Meanwhile, the superior quality of Christopher Penfold's 'Dragon's Domain' and the thoroughly outstanding production values create a truly timeless *Space: 1999* segment.

Rating: 9/10

1.24
THE TESTAMENT OF ARKADIA

Screenplay by Johnny Byrne
Directed by David Tomblin

Selected Broadcast Dates:
UK   LWT:
            Date: 21 February 1976.   Time: 11.30 am
            Granada:
            Date: 5 March 1976.   Time: 6.35 pm
US   KRON (San Francisco):
            Date: 3 January 1976.   Time: 7.00 pm

Credited Cast: Martin Landau (John Koenig), **Barbara Bain** (Helena Russell), **Barry Morse** (Victor Bergman), **Prentis Hancock** (Paul Morrow), **Clifton Jones** (David Kano), **Zienia Merton** (Sandra Benes), **Anton Phillips** (Bob Mathias), **Nick Tate** (Alan Carter)

Guest Stars: Orso Maria Guerrini (Luke Ferro), **Lisa Harrow** (Anna Davis)

Uncredited Cast: Suzanne Roquette (Tanya Alexander), **Sarah Bullen** (Operative Kate), **Loftus Burton** (Operative Lee Oswald), **Ann Maj-Britt** (Operative Ann), **Andrew Dempsey**, **Michael Stevens**, **Andrew Sutcliffe**, **Maggie Wright** (Main Mission Operatives), **Tony Allyn** (Security Guard Tony Allan / Irwin), **Quentin Pierre** (Security Guard Pierce Quinton / N'Dole), **Shane Rimmer** (Operative voice), **Robert Reitty** (Luke Ferro voice dubbing)

Plot: The Moon is stopped dead in space by an unknown force near the planet Arkadia. As power levels begin dropping, the Alphans are forced to consider evacuating to the planet, and a reconnaissance mission is launched. Once there, they learn the true origin of humankind. The Arkadian influence remains, and leads two Alphans to stay on Arkadia to sow the seeds of life on the world from which their ancient ancestors originated.

Quotes:
- **Koenig:** 'Our struggle to survive in a hostile universe had long erased the memory of the cataclysmic disaster that first hurled our Moon out of Earth's orbit. The recent events that occurred on the planet Arkadia have revived that painful memory and forced us to reconsider our purpose in space.'
- **Kano:** 'Computer's not a crystal ball, Commander. She can only predict on specific data.'
- **Koenig:** '… A force, an indefinable intelligence, did exist on the planet …'
- **Alan:** 'When the ship's sinking, the rats are the first to leave.'
- **Luke:** 'If it is Alpha's fate to be the sacrificial lamb, so be it. Don't you understand? It was no accident that brought us to that planet. Our destiny is clear. Preordained

from the moment the Arkadians set foot on Earth.'
- **Luke:** 'Be warned. Any attempt to stop us will fail and bring down upon you the terrible forces of chaos and destruction.'
- **Helena:** 'You're going to a living Hell.'
- **Luke:** 'No, Doctor. We are going home.'
- **Koenig:** 'We must keep faith and believe that for us – for all of mankind – there is a purpose.'

The Testament of Arkadia: 'I, the guardian, salute you. We are an accused people. We who caused our own destruction have paid the price of ignorance and greed. To you who seek us out in the ages to come, we salute you. The desolation you find grieves we few who will soon die. Our civilisation gone, our world Arkadia poisoned, dying. We who caused our own destruction. No need now to tell of the final holocaust then our world flamed in the inferno of a thousand exploding suns. Arkadia is finished. But she, Arkadia, lives on in the bodies, hearts and minds of those few who left before the end, taking the seeds of a new beginning, to seek out and begin again in the distant regions of space. Heed now, the Testament of Arkadia. Neither past nor future; you who are guided here, make us fertile. Help us live again.'

Filming Dates: Tuesday 11 February – Tuesday 25 February 1975

Incidental Music: The musical score is one of the most effective in the series and incorporates library pieces 'Picture of Autumn' by Jack Arel and Pierre Dutour (heard during Luke's and Anna's experience in the cave), and 'Suite Appassionata – Andante' by Paul Bonneau and Serge Lancen (featured throughout the episode, including as the Eagle journeys to Arkadia, and as the Alphans explore the planet, as well as during Koenig's opening and closing entries to his journal). Both pieces were from the Chappell Recorded Music Library.

Commentary:
Barry Morse: 'Following completion of "The Testament of Arkadia", we returned to shoot extra scenes for some previous episodes, "The Last Enemy" and "Space Brain" among them, and finally we finished shooting the first series on 28 February, 1975. But my final day of work on *Space: 1999* was Friday 11 April 1975, when I was called upon to return to Pinewood Studios to do some post-synching.

'"The Testament of Arkadia" featured a world destroyed by its people's technology and nuclear war. Well, there's another philosophical subject I think might have been explored a bit more thoughtfully…'

Zienia Merton: 'You found if an extra person went down with you to a planet, then he would be killed off or left behind, as in "Testament of Arkadia". I know this was because of [the dictates of the] writing, but I do think they could have thought a little more about it.

'I think I was on three sets on that last day filming, because we were finishing the last episode, I was dubbing a previous episode, and I was picking up shots on another episode. And I just said to whoever it was, "For God's sake, wheel me in and tell me what I'm doing, honey, because I don't know where I am!" Because what you have to remember is that we were also having to dub episodes as we went along, so there was always a backlog. Yes, I think I am right. On the last day I was on three shows – dubbing one, filming one, and picking up on another, which was the one I did with Caroline Mortimer, "The Last Enemy".'

Johnny Byrne: '"The Testament of Arkadia" had a strange genesis. There was a requirement to do a script, and David Tomblin started talking over ideas, and in essence much of what finally came out stemmed from the kind of story David wanted to do. I then had always considered that life did not begin on Earth, but was brought to Earth. It's not the kind of story I would normally write. Somehow the logic of the situation plus my close collaboration with David pushed me that way, and I found myself doing a story that had this kind of connotation, and once I had launched on it, it had to be pursued to the very end.

'It has a strange kind of eerie quality about it. It looks out of place in the welter of all the *Space: 1999* stories. It has, I think, a serious message. It was bedevilled, like many of the stories at that time, by the fact that we had to use Italian leading men because of the money connections with Italy. And many of them couldn't speak English very well, and it was a big problem. They brought in a wonderful man who would dub these voices, Bob Rietti. He can simply stand there and speak in their voice and correct it and re-dub it. A lot of Luke's stuff was re-dubbed. They would take sometimes only a word in a sentence and this guy would pick it up perfectly.

'The idea that we may have been influenced by a superior intelligence in our distant past is a very valid one and a very profound one. It's certainly not beyond the bounds of possibility to assume that something strange has happened to the people of this planet. About 15,000 years ago, it seems that there was a sudden burst of knowledge and creative activity that, after millions and millions of years, accelerated the pace of evolution and pitched humankind into being the dominant species on this planet. Now, archaeologists may give you all sorts of explanations as to how this came about, but any other reason is just as valid. You could say the human gene-bank was, in some way, seeded with knowledge by visitors from outer space, totally transforming the thinking on this planet. Less than 100 years ago, the Wright brothers were flying something with a bit of string. Now we're flying to the Moon. That development has taken place in only 100 years. If you take that pace of development, or if you take how fast that development can happen, you see that something quite remarkable did happen in that very short time all those years ago, in terms of human understanding, social organisation, technology and all the rest of it.

'I think "The Testament of Arkadia" showed the effects of under-budgeting. For one reason or another it had less money available for it and so, in terms of production values, it didn't *quite* measure up to some of the others … That's my feeling about it. But I thought it was quite well directed and it was quite eerie and spooky in a strange way. Well, it's not one of my favourites. But I feel it's quite a special one, quite outside the stream. I always felt very uneasy about it because its statement was so direct. And it had too much of it related to a purely spiritual impulse in terms of the characters. So much had to be taken for granted. Luke being taken over by this force was a kind of religious obsession, but it was never adequately explained how … Well, we knew that the motivation was because at the end what we're saying is, "We left Adam and Eve", and it's an Adam and Eve story. It's starting again … The Adam and Eve story is a very primal type of story in our consciousness. It's difficult to say whether it's purely biblical, some form of inspiration, or whether it maybe matches up to some sort of race memory that we have of a time when we all did live in some kind of land of plenty, a veritable Eden. There's a symbolism in the Adam and Eve story that is good for all time and, I think, whether you're religious or not, it has a kind of sense to it – a philosophical sense.

'It didn't really examine that process of spiritual possession, which I'd like to have done. I think that's where it sort of falls down for me. But again, writers are never, *never* satisfied. It's one of those stories I can look at now and feel very nervous about when it's coming on, but feel okay about at the end. I thought the performances were well done and that the scenes in the cave where they discover that it's Sanskrit, and all of that, were very spooky and effective … When it came to it, I enjoyed constructing the story: the idea of arriving on a planet, discovering something peculiar in a cave, and discovering words written in Sanskrit. This latter part interested me enormously, because I'm deeply versed in the history of the ancient Celtic civilisations of Ireland – the pre-history of my own country. The Gaelic language is one of the most ancient of all the Proto-European languages. It's immensely old – in its most primitive form, its alphabet is only 16 letters, which makes it more primitive than any other. It has very strong links with so many of the other most ancient languages like Cheldeic, Sanskrit and Syriac. I found connections with all of this in the story. We were talking about Sanskrit, the primal Indo-European language, and the fact that it was here and that it was saying something important invested the story with a certain profundity that you either addressed or you chose to ignore. I believe that if you're going to do this kind of story, you have to go for it on the nose, so the fear that I had about writing it was matched up with the demands of such an important and profound theme, which you couldn't avoid even if you wanted to. That was one of the great things about the first season of *Space: 1999* – you had to take things to their logical conclusion, otherwise they lacked all credibility.

'It seemed to me to be too "on the nose": making a very direct form of statement about who we were, and the way in which the story was being driven, to the point where we were imposing a very definite form of religious context into it. Now, although I'm not a practicing Catholic, I am an Irish Catholic, which is like saying that I have Catholicism "genetically coded" in my system. I was a very devout Catholic growing up, as most people of my generation were, and that spiritual exercise is what develops your spirituality. If you practice Catholicism or not, that expanded presence inside you is there and it finds an outlet in all sorts of other different ways: in humanism, in philosophy, in understanding, and in a speculative consciousness – that is, the capability to not dismiss things because they're not provable. The most important thing is to accept that there are mysteries to life and that if things are not provable, it doesn't necessarily mean that they don't exist. This, to me, is a fundamental part of my development as a writer: that I don't need to prove things to know that they are real.

'If you look at many of my stories, they do have this *slightly* spiritual quality about them. Philosophical implications of meeting yourself; the problems of the inanimate force taking you over – the one you can't communicate with, it's simply using you and disposing of you, in a way. Man proposes and God disposes. The story of the Darians. Again, there's a spiritual element in it: people desiring to stay alive at any cost, and the effect it has on their spirits – they all have this element of … moral uncertainty or spiritual uncertainty.

'To my knowledge the MUF element was never discussed or consciously developed in the sense that we've now come to understand it … The operative word above is "consciously". As the stories began to explore the implications of what had happened to the Alphans, and the truly awesome nature of their plight, we the writers started to follow where it took us; one of the advantages of a format not unchallengeably carved in stone ... "The Testament of Arkadia" was written completely blind to the knowledge that it was closing this kind of loop. All the more remarkable when you consider that it was never planned to be anything other than a stand-alone episode. It raises the interesting thought of how *Space: 1999* might have developed if this element had been pre-planned. Speaking personally, I'm glad it wasn't. The fact that it revealed itself the way it did says far more about the series and its potential than a possibly mechanistic application of pre-digested MUFfery. In time, I'm sure it would have come together in a way understandable to the Alphans, but that's another story.

'You could see that, by the end of the first 24 episodes, we were learning to deal with things in a slightly more efficient way. We were getting slightly less surprised, but with that was coming a greater understanding, and in that sense it was a series about hope. We concentrated this kind of extraordinary process, which will take a much longer period of time, obviously, in real life, and projected ideas about what would happen if this occurred and how we would respond. So, yes, there were stories that simply dealt with the nuts and bolts of science fiction, that looked back, but many of them dealt with situations that looked forward – to encounters and the confronting of certain kinds of problems. I would like to have seen more of it in the context of action-adventure, but whenever it happened, I thought it worked well.

'It could have been one of those stories that would have fitted more comfortably into a longer time-frame. I'd like to have done it as a longer story, but it simply wasn't possible. I am told that people like it very much. It does express a certain spiritual aspect of my own upbringing and background, and I'd like to feel that the element I brought to it was reverence where reverence was due – not a backhanded attempt at it. And if that came through, then I would feel that I had succeeded even in that small way.'

Observations: This episode was constrained by being produced at the end of the season, after most of the money had already been spent. However, there is no obvious visual evidence of a lack of budget, or of a production limited in any way.

Alpha's silver jackets are seen again, having previously appeared in 'Black Sun', which was the other occasion when Alpha became cold enough to scrape frost off the Main Mission windows.

Review: 'The Testament of Arkadia' utilises flashbacks and narration for the second time in the series: the first being in the immediately preceding 'Dragon's Domain'. Here it is Koenig who provides the narration, adding tremendously to the atmosphere of the episode as he reflects in his journal on these events, and indirectly on many other significant elements from earlier in the season. From the Kendo match between John Koenig and Luke Ferro in the opening moments of the episode, the viewer is faced with a unique instalment to the series.

The script is one of Johnny Byrne's best, paired again with David Tomblin's direction. There is a lot here in common with their earlier pairing, 'Another Time, Another Place', including similarities in overall style and tone and of course in the visual depictions of future Earth and Arkadia. Additionally, the shot of the Alphans walking out of the Eagle onto the planet surface was re-used from that earlier episode. Sections of Byrne's dialogue contain an atmospheric poetry, as when Koenig says in his voice-over: 'Overpowering impressions crowded in on us as we stepped out onto the alien planet: a sense of timeless solitude, the silent touch of an empty world, the total absence of life. Death had visited this world – so our data told us – and as we moved on we could feel it closing in around us like a shroud.' This story advances an array of underlying themes and concepts of the series and creates new ones.

The special effects are all competent, and the shot of the Eagle flying towards Arkadia at sunrise is absolutely beautiful. The Arkadia planet surface is a superb set, with dead trees and a rocky landscape featuring mountains in the background and gentle winds. It is an atmospheric locale that matches in perfect harmony the tone of the script and spirit of the direction.

As in the early episodes of Year One, there is a logical, believable, systematic survey of an alien world, and the discoveries here are astonishing. It is rewarding to see the Alphans going about their morning routine as the Reconnaissance Eagle nears Arkadia and paying attention to plant and soil analysis – all lending authenticity to their exploration of an alien world.

The cast perform with clear emotions and subtlety. More than almost any other episode, this one has an undeniable soul. There is a history, an epic feeling to the Alphan journey and a richness to the characters and their interactions with each other. The range within the characterisations and performances is wonderful. Watching the original team of Martin Landau, Barbara Bain, Barry Morse, Prentis Hancock, Nick Tate and Zienia Merton in their final episode together shows how successful a union they were. All their performances are award-worthy. Clifton Jones and Anton Phillips also give performances that rank amongst their finest in the series, although their parts here are smaller. Hancock has the second largest part in this episode and gives an impressive performance in one of Morrow's strongest showings as Main Mission Controller. One small example of the degree of subtlety between the characters comes when John and Helena are seen sharing a cup of coffee on their Eagle flight to Arkadia – they aren't flagrantly advertising their relationship, but through this simple act it is clear they are intimate.

Guest stars Orso Maria Guerrini and Lisa Harrow (who is incorrectly credited onscreen as Liza Harrow) are both effective in their roles and believably convey the absolute determination of their characters to live on Arkadia. It is, as Koenig put it, their 'fanatical obsession.'

It is also interesting to hear David Kano say, 'Don't worry – it can only get worse.' This marks another occurrence of his previously noted pessimistic side (though this is worded as a joke). It remains an intriguing aspect of his personality, albeit one that is only briefly hinted at throughout the series (as in 'The Infernal Machine').

This chapter in the Alphan journey has been predestined, as have others in their past, such as the events of 'Collision Course'. The Mysterious Unknown Force asserts itself to ensure that not only do Luke and Anna colonise Arkadia, but also the rest of the Alphans continue on their journey into unknown space. At least part of the mystery of the Mysterious Unknown Force is solved with the discovery of Arkadia, bringing to a resolution mysteries that have lingered since the start of the series. The discovery that Earth life originated on Arkadia and that the Arkadians came to Earth as space travellers is the kind of thinking being propounded at the time by author Erich von Däniken in books such as *Chariots of the Gods* and *Gods from Outer Space*. Going back to the earlier episode 'Missing Link', Raan stated to Koenig, 'I am as human as you are,' which implies (with the retrospective knowledge gained on Arkadia) that the

Arkadians colonised both Zenno and Earth – although the different worlds have obviously followed divergent evolutionary paths. This leads one to wonder if any of the other humanoid aliens Moonbase Alpha encountered – including the Kaldorians, Atherians, Bethans, Deltans and the Darians, to name a few – were also seeded by the Arkadians.

In 'The Testament of Arcadia' the purpose of Alpha's journey into space is revealed (at least partially) – they were meant to bring life back to its place of origin. The theme of purpose is woven through the script, including in this dialogue:

> **Anna:** 'Try to understand. Think of all we've had to suffer since the Moon was cast out to roam the wilderness of space. Inexplicably to stop here? Think, Doctor. It gives meaning to all this.'
> **Luke:** 'Believe us. There is a purpose.'
> **Helena:** 'A purpose? And you believe this purpose of yours justifies destroying Alpha?'
> **Luke:** 'Doctor, when the lines of destiny meet, the tools it uses are no longer necessary. Isn't that so?'

Most pointedly, the theme of purpose arises in Koenig's opening narration, 'Our struggle to survive in a hostile universe had long erased the memory of the cataclysmic disaster that first hurled our Moon out of Earth's orbit. The recent events that occurred on the planet Arcadia have revived that painful memory, and forced us to reconsider our purpose in space.' Purpose is raised again by Koenig's final entry into his journal where he writes, '… The creation myth of the first man and woman has a new significance. Our immediate struggle is over. For Luke Ferro and Anna Davis, it has just begun. They have found their beginnings. We still wander the emptiness of space seeking ours. We must keep faith and believe that for us, for all mankind, there is a purpose.' Entwined through this episode (as it is through our lives) the search for one's purpose is an eternal quest.

The chill in the air on Alpha and the blowing leaves in the final glimpses of Luke and Anna on Arcadia provide an autumnal feel, appropriate for the end of the season. The last view of Luke and Anna – as the camera rises up and away from them – is also effective in amplifying how alone they are: the only two people on an entire world. The future of Luke and Anna remains a mystery for viewers of the series, but the assumption is that they will survive. One more example of the series coming full circle is Alan Carter being out in space in an Eagle as the Moon starts to move again – just as he was when it originally blasted out of Earth orbit; it's an appealing symmetry.

The ending, with Koenig laying down his pen on the closed book, is both poetic and symbolic. The future is left open – anything can happen, but what has occurred up to this point is now a closed book.

'The Testament of Arcadia' strikes a feeling of awe and spirituality or mysticism throughout its story of the origin of humanity and the cycle of life. Touchingly, it demonstrates that following each ending is a new beginning. This is a wonderfully crafted episode bringing the first season to a satisfying and rewarding close, fulfilling prophecies and destinies and adding to the mythology and magnificence of *Space: 1999*.

Rating: 9/10

YEAR ONE: OVERVIEW

With hindsight, what did those involved in the production of *Space: 1999* Year One think about the show, and the experience of making it?

Barbara Bain notes: 'Science fiction was new turf for me. I'd read quite a bit of it, but I certainly wasn't a buff. The thing I loved about the concept was that we [as the characters] were not there because we wanted to be. The accident that thrust us out into space was unexpected, and whatever we encountered we had no way to cope with. We were ultimately homeless, looking for a place that would accommodate us, and there was something quite romantic about that. The best scripts were the ones that kept to that.'

Sylvia Anderson recalls the show's origins: 'My role [in the production of *Space: 1999*], as with most of the shows that we did, was mainly to work on the initial idea with Gerry, and choose the initial script. This idea – *Space: 1999* – came out of some other ideas that we [worked on] that didn't happen. So as we went along with all our various space ideas, *Space: 1999* evolved. It's something that we did for quite a while. So my main thing was casting the characters, and [devising] the look. That was really the main thing. Obviously I was involved in the scripting, and how we worked it during the first series was that Gerry and I would work on alternate scripts. We would have script discussions on every other episode, if you like. Martin Landau and Barbara Bain were very hands-on people. They wanted to know every line, so we worked very hard with them. And as far as the concept goes, it actually didn't enter our heads that people wouldn't suspend disbelief on this. I think that's because we ourselves were thinking ahead and arrived at *Space: 1999* being evolved from all the other previous series that we'd done. This time, obviously, with actors [rather than puppets]. So I think we really believed in it so much ourselves that we, really arrogantly, couldn't quite conceive of someone else not believing in it.'

Johnny Byrne was one of those people who initially had difficulty believing in the show's format: 'I had problems right from the beginning. My main problem was having come to science fiction television through the respectable route – not the route of SF films or series, but through SF … literature. And there's a distinct difference. Science fiction writers don't know how to write scripts, and scriptwriters invariably know little about science fiction. It's not just a question of writing another script. There's a whole sort of history and it has its own kind of universe, universal values in terms of writing SF. That's why [literary] SF writers are rarely satisfied with what they see on the screen. But anyway, I found it difficult to accept that the Moon could travel through space at … whatever velocity they gave it, and week after week, considering the immense distances that the Moon would have to cover … There was a basic element that was unbelievable, and SF has to have a basis in truth, or experience or psychology, or something you can latch on to. The fundamental element is the Moon travelling through the universe and week after week coming into the range of another planet and then another planet, and God knows how many light years we are away … That I found very difficult to take. It took me a good three or four weeks. Obviously I didn't press it, because it was something that you had to put aside and to see how in fact it affected the writing of stories, as far as I was concerned. And as I got into my stories, I found that it didn't really affect my stories and my concept of how the stories should be. It offered the kind of scope, and if you could suspend judgment to the extent that the Moon was *here*, *that* thing was *there*, and *these* situations were occurring, *then* it was possible. But there was that necessary suspension of disbelief as to how it got there. Here, what have we got? We have a credible existence on a Moon where people can be seen to be leading a fairly believable existence, reasonably expected around that period. Thinking of it in those terms, it's quite exciting. It didn't move them out into the impossible future, but kept them in a fairly discernible future. Having established that, the philosophical part of it, it was quite easy.

'Chris [Penfold] and I lived in some state in the central unit of Pinewood, the central country house, and there we did our dirty deeds. I remember we did more talking, perhaps, than writing. We seemed to exist in a state of perpetual excitement ... [Maybe] that was to avoid the dreadful food we had to eat downstairs ... anything to avoid eating. It was high-octane living.'

Barry Morse recalled some early difficulties: 'In the earliest days, Martin and Barbara and I would meet in various five-handed meetings with Gerry and Sylvia Anderson. Gerry and Sylvia were full of excitement at how wonderful the explosions were going to be. Then Martin or Barbara or I – usually me because I'm always the troublemaker – would say, "Yes, thank you. Very interesting. Hmmm ... But what about the people?" Gerry and Sylvia would then say, "Well, the boots are going to be ..." And so it was ... And apropos of the uniforms – I'm glad to hear that Keith [Wilson] thought them as dreadful as I did. My first response to the idea of this uniform was that a fellow as individual and absent-minded, in the true sense of those words, as Victor Bergman, wouldn't for a moment submit himself to wearing this dreary uniform.'

Some of the actors were less critical of the Moonbase Alpha uniforms. Prentis Hancock commented: 'The fashion of Rudi Gernreich ... I mean, we might complain about the fact we couldn't roll our sleeves up or relax, because they made you tend to sit a bit stiffly. That doesn't matter – he was trying to make us interesting, different sort of clothes.' Gerry Anderson, meanwhile, said of Gernreich: 'He created the basic designs – at a huge cost – and we completed the rest of the look. The end result was hardly spectacular, but we did get his name on the screen!'

Barbara Bain had her own challenge with the uniforms: 'One of my struggles was in the morning at Pinewood. The heat hadn't been turned on yet. It's very cold in England and they turn the heat on later. I'd been up in my dressing room at six o'clock in the morning. Rudi Gernreich had done those costumes with those wonderful industrial zippers – cold beyond belief! All made up with my hair done, I'd slip into that thing with the cold, inch-thick, metallic zipper. Okay, as it got colder and they did put the heat on, I got the brilliant idea of putting it on the radiator to warm it up. But then I had to be very careful or it would be too hot; you could burn yourself with it. But those are some of the slings and arrows you suffer. But, the teakettles were all plugged in. The English are totally dependant on having teakettles plugged in. Everyone had a teakettle – even when the National Grid went out, which was good to see.'

Also on the subject of teakettles, Bain recalled, 'We happened to be there during a major strike. We were declared an essential industry, so Pinewood kept shooting ... However there were certain things not available, like hot water. So we managed to heat the teakettle – the ubiquitous English teakettle – to wash my hair in the morning. In other words, the English are the best at making do; making something work no matter what. So that's what we did: we washed my hair with the teakettle. You could never not plug in the teakettle. We had that, but no running hot water.'

Keith Wilson recalls his involvement in designing for Anderson productions: 'I worked very closely with Sylvia, and it was because of her ... She said, "I think you should design this." And then I went ahead, and that's exactly what I did. I worked with Sylvia for 14 years and we were very good friends. She was the person up front; she was the one that did all the shows, went to the press. She was the showman. So, the two of us were very, very good friends and she relied on me totally. She couldn't draw, she had no idea of visuals: that was my job. On *UFO*, although she gets the credit, I designed all the costumes and the wigs. We may have discussed it and she may have said, "Wouldn't it be nice if all the girls had purple wigs?" Fine, so I designed the costume and gave the girls purple wigs, [but] I didn't get the credit – she did. They formed a company, a design company; it was for Sylvia. Though my name was not mentioned, I did all the designing. She didn't design anything. We talked about it, obviously, and she would approve it – or not – as the case may be. This even went to Ed Bishop's wig in *UFO* – it was my idea to give him blond hair, because he's actually a very plain-looking man. All of a sudden, when you put the wig on him, he looks amazing. That was my idea. So all of the creative side, from every single angle – anything that was visual – was mine.

'I wanted this clinical science fiction look, and I had to be able to reconstruct sets very, very quickly. We virtually had an alien planet or an alien spaceship every two weeks. So I couldn't spend a lot of time on the Moonbase sets. I designed the modular system so that, within hours, I could build another set or another room, or I could just open the whole thing up and make it into a series of corridors very quickly, because everything fitted together like a big jigsaw. I spent a lot of time and a lot of money at the beginning of the series designing the system, knowing that once it was built, I could virtually forget about it and I could concentrate all my efforts on the alien planets. It was the only way to do it.

'Doing *Space: 1999* was a problem, because I had created a clinical atmosphere. Therefore, expressing personality was very difficult. This room that we're sitting in [for this interview] has little touches of me because I live here, and have lived here for a while. It has accumulated its personality from my personality. But to put a group of people on the Moon in a clinical atmosphere, and give that atmosphere a personality, is very, very difficult.

'Let me tell you about the Commlock. When it came to do this, I had to do a design for it. We had found the smallest television in the world at this time, but it had all this stuff coming out of the back, so you could only ever see it from one angle. You couldn't do anything with it. So, then you would cut out and use a dummy one without the screen in it. And also, of course, we didn't have colour television in those days. That's why all the monitors were in black and white – we didn't have colour in England.[21] That's the only reason they weren't in colour – it was too expensive. It was the size of the tube that determined the design of the actual Commlock. I was given the tube and I just designed something to go around it. Of course it was meant to have other uses – opening doors, all that sort of stuff. But the principle was actually just based around the

---

[21] In fact, colour television was introduced in the late 1960s in the UK, but sets were still very expensive at the start of the 1970s and most families still watched in black and white.

size of the tube. It's part of a period. It's a period piece, the black and white screens ... Everything about it is of the period.'

Gerry Anderson commented on the design of the Eagles: 'It was very much Brian Johnson's design, in as much as I had imagined an encased fuselage. He came up with this non-aerodynamic design on the basis that if it was to fly in a vacuum, what the hell would it matter – which, of course, was perfectly correct.'

Barbara Bain said, at the time of filming the show: 'There has never been this kind of production on a television series. And outside of *2001*, there have never been special effects like ours. As a matter of fact, Brian Johnson, who did them, is the same man who did the special effects for Kubrick in *2001*. And we are pleased that it is not just an adventure series. We feel there is real depth and meaning in many of the segments. There is something to be learned in looking at your own civilisation through a fictionalised one.'

Keith Wilson commented on the stairs in Main Mission below the windows, which disappeared after the first few episodes: 'I'd actually forgotten that those stairs were there. I sort of remember what happened. The set was built as a four-sided one, and although the walls were very easy to take out, the stairs weren't, because they were so big. After the first couple of episodes, it was realised by the directors and cameramen that this was a slight problem ... So it was decided that we would still have a four-sided set, but we would take those stairs out [permanently]. So it would [then] be very easy [to reconfigure the set] – in a few minutes we could take the walls out and move a camera in and they could carry on shooting. That's the only reason the stairs went; it was just economic to take them out. You never really knew if they were there or not, and it actually didn't make any difference to the action or the look of the set. It wouldn't spoil the look of the set. So it was decided we would take them out to make life easier for the directors and cameramen.'

Regarding lighting the Main Mission set, Wilson stated: 'Well, actually, it was very easy to light. The set was designed so that the lights were permanently in position. When the cameraman walked on to the set, all he had to do was flick one switch and all the lights came on. It was as simple as that. The set was designed to be lit from the outside. So the ceilings, wall panels, they were all lit. The lights were already permanently there. One switch lit the set. There's a story, which Barbara Bain tells, that it took a very long time. Lovely set, she said, but it took so long to light. If the truth was known, Barbara's make-up took a long time.'

Barbara Bain recalls additional difficulties the production encountered: 'Gerry Anderson absolutely wanted to photograph a television screen without [a dark] bar flopping [on the picture], which is impossible to do. He wanted a clean shot: he did not want the bar on it, because ... that would have been primitive filming. So, at least the first ten days of shooting, all our concern was to try and get this bar not to flop around! So all those intercom scenes when one of us was standing next to the screen chatting to whomever, we were at the mercy of trying to get that bar out. We would do some of those scenes 103 times to get it, and just at the last moment, the bar would show up! Then, when we went onto the generators later, as opposed to the National Grid, the connections were very delicate and it came back to haunt us. We were, again, stopped down endlessly trying to get that shot. So, it was funny that with all this extraordinary technology, we were still at the mercy of that bloody bar going around!

'We went through the shut-down of the country, which had all kinds of interesting ramifications. There was the miner's strike that took place in 1974, which caused the general blackout [of] the entire country. They went on a three-day work week, a sort of critical time in English economic history. All of the shops and streets were without light. They unplugged the National Grid. If you think about it, there is one electrical source in England, called the National Grid, and they pulled the plug! So there were a lot of kerosene lamps in all the shops, the street lights were down and businesses were functioning three days a week. *We* were declared an essential industry. Plus, Sir Lew Grade – later *Lord* Lew Grade – had influence in the government, and because he was employing so many people, it made a case for allowing us to shoot on a five-day week. That sounded great. We had our own generators in the studio and weren't dependent on the National Grid. But, the labs were down to their three-day week. So we could produce, but we couldn't get our stuff back. We had these interesting kinds of problems. At least a year went by that first week; it *seemed* like a year.'

On the same subject, Prentis Hancock recalled, 'The series was given a lack of structure in the first weeks because of the three-day working week in the United Kingdom. At one time I had the right to get petrol coupons because oil was rationed at the pumps and I could get two gallons a day to get to Pinewood and back, and I would give Zienia a lift. That affected the first episode. That was imposed upon us. All the pre-recorded video that was on the [computer screens] was pre-done on the national grid, the electricity system. But it wasn't the same speed as the 5-day system we had from ATV television, which was Lew Grade's way of allowing us to work for five days. So we worked for five days, while the industry was working for three … Lee Katzin, I loved him; I thought he really was the director who had the vision, and the right vision, for the series. But he shot so much film through the camera that he would waste footage like it was going out of fashion. But in spite of all that we got it made, and we had 15 months of fun and games.'

Martin Landau had issues in dealing with picture elements being added in post-production: 'We'd always have to ask whether something [on the Main Mission screen] was going left to right, or right to left. Very important, because if the looks were wrong and [we were] looking at nothing, [it wouldn't work]! You couldn't flip [the picture], because most of those things had numbers on them. Very often in things you can "Turn a horse around." The director makes a mistake, let's say in a Western, and the horse is going that way and the people are looking this way, you just flip the film. You couldn't do that here.'

Barbara Bain was also troubled by the big screen in Main Mission: 'A big blank! And the problem was that, because they were working at Bray – the studio down the road about 20 miles – on all the special effects, we didn't even know what they had conjured. So [the script] might say it was a wild-looking blah-blah-blah, and that's what we were looking at. When they finally matted it in, either it was, or it wasn't! That was difficult. It was a big, blank, black screen, which was matted in.

'That studio [at Bray] was incredible! We were seldom able to get over there, but Brian Johnson was a brilliant genius, photographing glass fibres and all kinds of incredible things, and having the best time. We never saw what they were working on simultaneously. They weren't on the set with us, so we didn't know what they were producing until we saw a rough cut.'

Martin Landau recalled having to re-dub numerous lines of dialogue : 'Very often in speeches I had to get all the numbers right. They had to match up. "Eagle One landing at Pad Three, and ready for lift-off." All those numbers had to be right, always. The words usually were crippling, and much of the time I would have to say those things on the move, very quickly. Much of the time, because of problems, I would have to go to the dubbing room and post-sync. If I had a speech and talked in about this rhythm [he speeds up] I tended to run my words together, and we couldn't make loops. Most of the time, we had to do one line at a time. I used to have to basically lip-sync to an entire speech on one of those. I think in one of the early episodes I'm walking by a computer bank. That one is dubbed. It was miraculous that I could do it because I don't think I said the lines exactly as written. I added a word or two, but I had to say it walking up the steps, and I was walking down the bank of computers. I had to finish this long, black speech. In that *Space: 1999*, which Charlie Crichton was directing, he wanted me to move off camera just as the last word ended. I had to get it in there, so I had to talk fast.'

Difficulties were not confined just to technical areas of the production, as Christopher Penfold recalled: 'The problems were more with the American writers working with us. It was actually a silly idea to try to conduct script conferences over the telephone with people living and working in the United States, and after a while it became unworkable and we stopped. The only American input that we continued to have was through an American writer living in England at the time, Edward di Lorenzo. He became another script editor on the series, and wrote a couple of episodes himself.

'When the series was set up, there was a very short lead time, which is a problem of television production. Once the money becomes available, you have a certain space of time in which the money has to see a return. So we didn't really have enough time to prepare the scripts before the series went into production, [and] we were always running to catch up. As I see it, there is little distinction between story consultant and story editor, or the term I promote now, which is script editor. In the context of a multi-episode drama series, the script editor would be responsible for choosing the writers who are going to contribute to the series; for providing a kind of overview for those writers of what the series ... is going to do. Each individual writer is primarily, if not solely, concerned with his or her own episode, but they have to be educated into the wider, larger context of where their episode is going to fit. That's the function of the script editor, and the function I would have expected to be performing on *Space: 1999*. The [fact] that the lines of demarcation became blurred was entirely due to the pressures of actual production. I found myself in a position of commissioning writers too late to provide that kind of overview for them. So the scripts, when they came in, really often weren't fitting with the overview of the series, as it was constantly developing. By that time, it was already in production, so even when writers were commissioned, it wasn't possible to give them a Bible for the series, which would have contained, for instance, Barry Morse's biography of Victor Bergman (the character I was most interested in). Those things were constantly changing. So it was a difficult role. I would normally expect the script editor not actually to be writing or re-writing the episodes for which other writers are credited. It was a set of circumstances that brought that about. Sometimes it was something I regretted, but some of the episodes that as a story editor I effectively *completely* rewrote, for which I didn't get a writing credit, I feel pretty good about – "Black Sun", particularly.'

Johnny Byrne also commented on the difficult production schedule: 'Every script I wrote came completely from myself. There wasn't time for other people to come to me with ideas, because we had ten days or three weeks to make a new [episode]. To have it designed and to have it ready for the actors, prepared to be shot. It was an impossible situation … Not one story idea was dropped, because there wasn't time. There wasn't time to look at all the scripts and say, "This is a good one – that's a bad one." We needed every single one we did.

'There was a very short turnaround on all the scripts we had to do. There wasn't time to stop and stare. We had to really push on. There was certainly no idea about what the overall story arc was. We didn't [use] words like that. We probably didn't know about words like that. We were just concerned with creating episodes one by one as they came along, and being excited about the stuff that we would learn, at least in my case, episode by episode. I distinctly remember rushing into Chris's office saying, "What about this? This has happened. I've written this and suddenly all these implications are obvious." And he would say, "Get the script done. Press on." And so it went on, right to the very end, pretty much. It never let up. It was a wonderful master class for a writer like me, because we were making a film. I had daily contact with people like Keith Wilson and Brian Johnson. It was a wonderful thing for a writer. You could see; you could focus and get everything in perspective. Although it seemed to go at a very fast pace, in effect it was a wonderful thing for me.'

Martin Landau recalled some of his difficulties with the series: 'Another problem was, of course, when you're dealing with English writers, scripts are written [as if] for the BBC, and they don't have commercials. That leads to 12-and-a-half-minute acts, and some white knuckles. If you have a good script, you could have a 22 minute first act.' [Examples are in the episodes 'The Infernal Machine', 'The Taybor' and 'All That Glisters'.] 'It's terrific, but you've got to break it. I'd say, "You've got to break it here." And they'd say, "You can't break it there." I'd say, "It's a natural break!" Well, there was a lot of that. Charlie Crichton would sit there drinking scotch with Chris Penfold, Barbara, me, Barry and sometimes Gerry until one o'clock in the morning. I would say, "I don't understand this script! It doesn't make any sense. It's cryptic. I need a Rosetta stone! I don't know what the hell it means. What's going on here? What is this scene telling me?" In the script, [I'd have to] say, "Okay, let's go! Let's get out of here!" We don't have to talk about it! If you walk out the door, we know you're going! When I say we were there until one o'clock in the morning, I mean the only thing we doctored at that point was the stuff we were shooting the next morning. We had to regroup the next night and work on the other stuff. Hopefully, those guys would get some of that stuff done during the day. If not, that meant one o'clock in the morning again. And I had to be back at seven. I had to *learn* some of that stuff, too! Sometime in there I had to catch a little sleep. You know, at the beginning of *Space: 1999*, I must have been sleeping maybe three or four hours a night. I worked in practically every shot all day. So you've got to have an enormous kind of energy, and to keep involved it takes a particular kind of thrust. The English take a longer time to shoot. They don't work as fast as an American crew. At least, we were used to that.'

Barbara Bain recalled a similar difficulty with the scripts: 'We had a lot of lovely, talented young writers who just came out of Cambridge. They were very bright, very gifted and very imaginative – but the form was elusive in that they were used to writing very slow-built material, finally to a climax. They wanted to take their time in telling their stories and things like that. We had a lot of trouble getting them to understand that they had six minutes …' [Barbara claps in tempo.] 'And *bam*! What is going to happen, and get it going again? It was a struggle that was never really properly resolved. Therefore when we did go on to the set – they call it the floor – we weren't as prepared as we were on *Mission: Impossible*. We were struggling all the time to write as we went along – even though, in many instances, we achieved some wonderful kinds of stuff. It could have been *more* such, if it had been a tighter production. It was very hard to get that right, to get that idea that we were in jeopardy every six to eight minutes.'

Martin Landau continued: 'A lot of the critics used to say there wasn't a lot of humour on the show. There wasn't a lot of humour written *into* the show! I used to yell for humour. When you're in trouble, that's what you need. You can't get blood out of a stone, and there was very little fun! On the whole, no-one paid attention to that. They said they were going to do it – humanise the scripts – but they didn't. Now, the bottom line with this was that there was nothing frivolous about going through space and not being in control of your own destiny. Not having control over your trajectory, and basically being 20-some years into the future. So – technologically, emotionally – the people on Alpha were not ready for deep space. Whereas in *Star Trek* they were moving around on their own and were much further in the future. So, basically, the conditions were that of a pressure cooker. But it needed humour. I said, "These guys are people. They need battleground humour, or death-row humour." There were a lot of inconsistencies in the writing. It's very easy to act well-written material. Shakespeare is easy to act. It's not hard. Well, it's hard for some actors, but only because they can't hold their breath that long! The bottom line is – bad writing is hard to act. You could do some of your best work and would still not like it. You compensate a lot for it. Sometimes you succumb to it. But good writing is a piece of cake. A lot of the writing on *Space: 1999* was very bumpy ... I said, "I would never say this." A man walks into a room and says, "Hello, everybody! I'm embarrassed!" You don't do that! You do everything in the world not to do that. Lots of times, we had that [kind of thing]. I was a pain in the neck, part of the time, because I'd say, "What the hell is this? I'm wearing everything on my tongue here. I'm saying everything when we don't have time"!'

On this subject, Christopher Penfold has said: 'Barry Morse was reminding us that we, the writers, had very little opportunity to engage with the cast, and that's true. I actually very much like getting feedback from the cast. It is they who realise the characters. That's a cross-fertilisation process that there ought to be more time for. In the case of a theatre production, the play will be in rehearsal for several weeks before it's actually opened. The writer will be there working with the cast in the early stage – of course there has to be a time when the script is the script – but there isn't, in television, the opportunity for that kind of engagement. [Having said that,] we did have very useful engagement, or at least I did, with Martin and Barbara. I spent long hours into the night at their house talking about scripts, which I think was useful. It would have been very nice to have had more time to be able to do that with Zienia, Prentis and Barry.'

Regarding the writers, and the writing, Johnny Byrne stated: 'You had first of all Chris Penfold, who is the son of a vicar and who had a strong moral and social conscience and believed passionately in good. He also was an experienced writer, but these were his personal characteristics ... Chris Penfold was also sort of a liberal socialist. He would consider himself a liberal ideologue. He would see himself as someone who would be willing to sacrifice in order to salve his conscience. He was born with guilt. People of that type are born with guilt ... The Irish are different. There's a larger degree of mysticism in our background, and the mystical and the spiritual are very closely connected ... I had come from a very Irish sort of Catholic family, with an ingrained sensitivity to spiritual matters ... You only have to look at the episodes to see the consistency of our points of view. There's a running thing through my episodes that never really alters very much. It has many different faces, but essentially we were looking at the equivalent of mystery and miracles – the reassertion of, and the reenactment of, certain basic universal elements, so to speak. These *Space: 1999* episodes were a reflection of that, of two very different things.

'And there was Eddie di Lorenzo, who was also very interested in mental attitudes. He was a very sensitive writer, a very good one in my estimation. The three of us together almost chemically sparked off the kind of feeling that washed over all the episodes, even those we didn't write. There was a feeling, a concern … to carry the feeling of the humanity of the people on Moonbase Alpha out there, not necessarily as a spoken dialogue, but something in terms of the situations and [the characters'] responses, and their utter bewilderment. These were our people, our younger brothers and children, who were out there. And they should have echoed our concerns, our feelings of … human beings in a tremendous state of transition and change, with all their weaknesses and limitations. So that feeling carried over and was reflected in some of the stories that might have qualified as soft; certainly they were thoughtful, certainly they were exciting – but it was a good mix. We just went for stories that attracted us. And while some of the stories I wrote Chris didn't approve of – and some of the ones he wrote I didn't approve of, and the same with Eddie – that was the way it was. "The Last Sunset", "The Last Enemy", "Space Brain" – [those] and I think … one other one [were the ones] I didn't particularly like …

'Among the ones I didn't write I like particularly "Black Sun". I [also] love "War Games". I love what everybody else loves about this. You can't ignore the [ones] Anthony Terpiloff wrote, which are wonderful as well. I love the richness and the variety of the first season. The sense that something greater than the sum of the events we were recording seems to have taken hold of us early on. It showed itself most clearly in those episodes where the Mysterious Unkown Force, or MUF, is presumed to be present; and looking back, it was also there in many others. But it was never the result of any form of preplanning. It seems to have been working itself out below the level of conscious intent.'

Barry Morse stated: 'We must always go back to the guys who really engendered all of this, Chris [Penfold] and Johnny [Byrne] and George [Bellak]. They're the fellows who made it all happen. But they were confronted, as we were, with an almost impossible situation … I must eternally remind you that the real engenderers of any dramatic piece are the fellows who put the words together'

Would Christopher Penfold have done anything differently, if he had the opportunity? 'Adequate time in which to prepare scripts before going into production would be pretty much top of the list. Adequate time also in which to find and talk to and fully engage writers – I mean, I really don't like, as a script editor, simply having to reach the point where I have to take somebody else's material over because I haven't the time to educate them fully into the ways of the series. I would like writers to be responsible for their own development within a series. And the fact that finding the right writers is actually a very difficult thing to do. Every script editor worth his or her salt has a whole stock of knowledge about who writes well in which genre, and who might be appropriate for each particular story. This is what script editors do … Every writer has, like fingerprints, an individual tone of voice. The role of the script editor is to facilitate the expression of that voice. I would say what I would have liked would be to have continued in the same philosophical direction that we embarked on in series one, but to give us the time and resources to find the right people, because in the end it's the writers who give you what makes the series. The more they speak in their own voice, the more you get a quality of difference in each episode; so that the audience is almost subconsciously engaging with a different intelligence. Of course, there are overall series rules that have to be obeyed, but the real quality comes from the contributions of individual writers.'

ALPHANS AND OTHERS

What did the actors feel about their characters, or their fellow performers? Nick Tate begins: 'I was very lucky with [my character] Alan Carter. I think basically what happened with all of us in the series was that we felt rather like all the people that were on the Moon. We were out at Pinewood Studios, which is a long way from anything else – it's out in a farm district. The rest of the English acting fraternity didn't really dig what we were doing. They didn't understand it. They thought it was some strange American implant. And it was, in a way. We were a tight-knit little group ... As Alan Carter, I was allowed to do a lot of things that came naturally to me. The writers would meet with me and talk about the ideas I had. I actually wrote the history of my character – my own ideas. That was more important in the second series when the new people came in. When Freddy [Freiberger] came in, I had to let him know who my character really was. I would not have done anything differently [as Alan Carter], other than that I would have liked a little more to do. But when you work in a television series like that, there are a lot of people to serve, and everybody wanted more to do. I was very, very lucky.'

Barry Morse stated: 'I've generally felt that *Space: 1999* dealt much too much in hardware and special effects and not enough in thoughts, philosophies and feelings. As to [the frequent criticism of] the characters being one-dimensional and wooden, I understand Martin and Barbara have had some good things to say about the development of the characters, but my recollection is, I'm afraid, rather different. It is my firm opinion that the characters *were* one-dimensional and wooden. Martin and Barbara should be congratulated just as much as I should be that we managed to squeeze out something approaching an individual character for ourselves, because we had very little to go on in the way of writing.'

Prentis Hancock related: 'I asked for more definition of character, to know more about his background. I kept being told, "You'll be told. This will happen." I would have liked Paul to get out and about more. Go to more planet surfaces. You have to balance things. Carter was a character who went bouncing around in spaceships, and it would have been great fun to go out with him, and to go out with Koenig. But actually I was supposed to be in control of Main Mission. I wasn't the action man, in that sense ... I tried to play Paul terribly English in a sense, because everybody else in the series was kind of playing American, or mid-Atlantic. I was, in a way, the only Brit. I tried to make it the centre of Paul Morrow's character – [to indicate] that he was the Main Mission Controller [and] the calm at the centre of the storm. The trouble with that is it isn't terribly dramatic. You can be calm for hours and everybody goes to sleep. So we had to strike a balance. We had a lot of leading characters, and three stars. I sort of led the second eleven, and that's an awful lot of people to spread the camera around and give them screen time. Plus guest stars ... What I'm saying is there wasn't a lot to work with, because I was sitting in the same place week after week, doing the same sort of things. So I just tried to make him the centre of the storm, really, so when he blew, it was really quite interesting.

'One week Paul Morrow was taking Sandra out, and then the next week he didn't speak to her. Then he was taking Tanya out, which is fine, but … There is a skill now that has developed in long-running series called storylining. Take any series, there will be people who decide, "This line of stories on this family will go in this direction for the next couple of years and they'll end up over here. This other family will go this way and end up over there. Then in two years time we'll have some reason why this family gets it together with that family and they reconnect." Through that, writers are commissioned to write different stories. There might be six or seven different threads or storylines going out in different directions. I don't think we had *one* line in *Space: 1999* – apart from the fact that we keep going away from the Earth. I suspect that's why you get these sort of inconsistencies. And you just have to do it. Okay, I'm not talking to Sandra this week. Or, we're going out onto the Moon to have a kiss, or whatever we do. And you just have to accept that and do the best you can with it.

'But you know when we started I don't think they had more than one script idea, or one script written. Taking six and a half weeks to do the first episode, "Breakaway", allowed them time to write episode two. They've never denied it. It's very nice to think of the writers being with you, but they were in a room over there – they used to come in once in a blue moon to see us. I wish there had been more interaction, but I think they were fairly overloaded with what they had to do.

Anton Phillips reflected on his place in the cast: 'I suspect the reason Clifton and I were in it, and perhaps to some extent Zienia, was the American audience. I don't think they could have shown a major television series in America with an all-white cast. So certainly I think it was convenient for them to have Clifton and me in it. And, at the end of the day, I think they satisfied the minimum requirement [for ethnic actors], in as much as neither Clifton nor I really ever featured in any of the major storylines. Prentis did. Zienia did. Nick did. Barry, obviously … But I don't think I ever featured in the main storyline.'

Regarding character background, Phillips stated: 'I was given nothing at all, like most everybody else. This was my fourth job after studying acting in drama school and I think my very first, or second, television job. I had certainly no experience in a film studio. So I was really making it up as I went along. I had no idea what was going on. I was a stage actor; I was trained for the stage, and this was all really new to me. As we went along, I learned the profession of being a film actor and at the same time trying to put something together for the character. It sort of came together by accident, I guess … There were some nice moments when you actually got a chance to do something. All the people you see are really quite fine actors and have proven themselves time and time again on all sorts of things on stage, screen and television. So when we actually got an opportunity to *do* something, the danger was that we would overdo it. "Hey, finally a little bit of acting!" And we'd leap on there and beat it to death, when we really needed a light touch. So those moments were nice when they did come along.'

Zienia Merton recalled: 'Sandra fainted a lot. It was Ray Austin who said, "Hang on a minute … She can't keep falling down. If she keeps falling down, what's she doing on this base? Surely she must have done all these tests, gravity things and whatever, … and this woman's loopy! Consistently falling down." And so, luckily, some other poor girl had to fall down on that episode, and I obviously carried on. It would be quite strange that suddenly I would become *extremely* responsible. When they wanted everybody to be in Medical Centre helping out, Sandra's at the helm. She's running Main Mission. That was in "War Games". And I liked all that. But I had very little contribution toward the scripts. Trying to get those scripts out, we just didn't have the luxury to have little chats … So Sandra came and went depending on what was needed of her.

'Back in the '70s it was all hair and teeth … Girls were little dolls then. The ladies on *Space: 1999* did actually work hard for their money. They did go out and do things. I know a lot of people are not very happy with the Andersons – one way or the other – but in *UFO*, too, they did actually use women not as pretty set pieces but as creative working people.'

Johnny Byrne observed: 'Martin Landau is a very visceral actor, and [with Koenig] an emotional response was always jumping in ahead of the logical response. It was always a question of which would jump first. What determined it was the nature of the question. It didn't matter who it was coming from, whether it was one of his own, an alien, an official, a superior – whatever it was, if it hit off any of those buttons that Commander Koenig held sacred … you could almost feel the fear in the man. He defended [his principles] so fiercely. So he was a man who was obviously not secure in that position, but he defended them with tremendous fierceness, even when they were not necessarily under attack. So anything of that nature would be no surprise for Martin to respond in this way as John Koenig. Koenig was a man very, very much aware of his own mortality.

'Koenig was never put to the test, was he? They asked this question at the end of "Mission of the Darians". He was never put to the test, and in fact all the evidence points to Koenig being someone who would defend the individual interests rather than the general interests. He would defend one life and hold it more sacred than the overall security and sanctity of the mission. But it never came to the test. In his responses that we witnessed throughout the series, it was always in defence of one or two. The big question was, would he respond in that way when put to the ultimate test? There's a difference between morality and leadership. I think leadership changes depending on the threat and where the threat is coming from. I don't think we have a fixed position. We are moral people, but the nature of our morality will change.'

Christopher Penfold continued: 'Johnny is certainly right when he points out Koenig's preference for fighting in the individual's corner. But actually there are instances where collective security is his prime concern, and I think of Koenig as being somebody who is essentially human and who confronts each of those situations on its merits.'

Martin Landau noted of the cast: 'Overall, I would say it was a happy family. The cast was terrific. Every single one of those people was very volatile, talented, crazy … It was a challenge to get that large a group together and have a harmonious, pleasant existence. Everyone was good and very willing to help each other out. A lot of the people were terrific and everyone was nice. So it was a very pleasant, hard, difficult time. There was nothing easy about the show … While we were there Nick was doing some theatre there, too, and he was wonderful in the play that Barbara and I saw. [He] was the central character and carried that play, and brilliantly. These actors [the supporting cast] were underused actually; they had much more to give than they were given. But there was never any temper tantrums or temperament … we treated our guests who came in as fellows. It was a happy set overall. We had actors like Richard

Johnson come right into the swing of things and I'd heard he was difficult, after we worked with him. He was not difficult on our set ... To work a couple of years together and never really have an altercation. I mean we had individual problems here and there, but as a bunch of actors tossed together who never knew each other before this experience, it was amazing. There weren't any flurries of temperament or anger or petulance. We actually got along and respected each other, and we needed each other, and we knew it. It was like a family. And we were in a foreign country – Barbara and I, and so was Nick, actually ... Zienia was a delightful girl. She was always there, and there for you and professional, and delightful. All of the above. She was very sensitive to everybody ... She and Prentis were a great pair; they complimented each other in a wonderful way ... I miss Barry. To think what he did with himself, coming from where he came [his Cockney background], it was majestic. Barry was a very special guy ... He was just a delight. I thought that Professor Bergman was a terrific sounding board for Koenig; to have that kind of guy who doesn't necessarily agree with the choices he makes. That could have gone further ...'

Also on the theme of camaraderie amongst the cast, Barry Morse said: 'I recall all of my fellows with great pleasure and happiness. Martin and Barbara are both immensely skilled and experienced in our profession. They certainly were a joy to work with. No hint of any kind of grandeur, such as sometimes comes with such people. Much better *fellows*, in the real true theatrical sense, than many others I can think of. Martin's and Barbara's adaptability, professionalism, and above all their kindly and good-natured attitude towards their fellow artists and the members of our crew, were quite admirable. Then there was Nick Tate, an Australian chap. And dear, lovely Zienia Merton. All of them – Nick, Zienia, Prentis, Clifton and Anton – were relatively inexperienced and were being thrown into the deep end with Martin, Barbara and me. We were all insufficiently prepared, as I shall go on saying till my dying day. They had to hammer their way through it and stay afloat as best they could. And they – to do them all equal credit – dealt with it all with admirable patience and good nature, and good humour. I remember them all fondly. They were all very gifted and keen.'

Zienia Merton said: 'Considering the amount of time that we spent with each other, which was more than I spent with my own folk, I think it's incredible that there were no lawsuits, there were no divorces, and I know it's in retrospect, but I think we all just got on terribly well ... Prentis, Nick, Clifton, Anton, Suzanne and I had a table at the restaurant at Pinewood Studios and the staff used to be absolutely amazed. We used to walk in there day after day to have our lunch and they used to say, "God, you're still together? You're still eating together? You're still talking? God!" Fifteen months we did that – I think that's a pretty good record.

'You couldn't afford not to get along. I mean, we're all adults, so you can't have great feuds. We also used to have lunches with the Italians brought over for the series – if Nick, Prentis, Clifton or any of the others were free. I'd say, "Come round to lunch," and get whoever it was to come round. Nick would fetch them if they didn't have transport and they'd come round to dinner or lunch. I know what it's like filming in a foreign country, when everybody else has gone off to their wife and kids or friends and you're left alone. It's happened to me. And I thought it would be nice, if they had nothing to do.

'I'm immensely grateful for everything that I learned while I was working on *Space: 1999*. To spend 15 months or so – and here I'm talking about the first year, because that's where I learned it all – having that support of real good folk and everybody working together – the focus puller, the cameraman, the lighting cameraman … Learning where to stand and where to move to make it work for them – it was just an amazing university of filmmaking, which you couldn't pay money for, and I'm eternally grateful for that. So, in terms of my career, it was invaluable. You can't learn that – no drama school is going to teach you that. It was just incredible.'

Nick Tate recalled: 'Generally speaking, it was a very happy time on the series. Martin and I became close friends. I liked Barbara as well; she's a bright and friendly woman. I had great rapport with the rest of the cast, including Prentis, Clifton and Zienia. We all got on very well and spent quite a bit of social time together away from the set. It was a very fulfilling time for us as young actors. Perhaps a little more so for me as the writers tended to give my character a bit more to do … I had a marvellous time during the first season. The atmosphere on the set was extraordinarily positive. The cast got on terribly well. We all thought we were on a winner and enjoyed working on the show. I don't think there was ever a harsh word said on the set. Sometimes we were under time constraints and the pressure got on, but we all had a lot of laughs.'

Discussing Martin Landau and Barbara Bain, Tate also said, 'Barbara is the consummate actress. She and Martin were the royalty of our show; they would arrive every day in a Rolls Royce. I was awestruck. It was just wonderful to have two people at the head of your show that had such dignity and class and really were consummate professionals who knew their job and came from a long history of American production and great shows. It gave us a great goal to strive for, and I think we all eventually hit our marks. It was wonderful. And she was very friendly to us all. She and Martin were gracious. There was none of that Them & Us. It was all very friendly … Barbara was a very strong force. But Barbara was a very quiet person. Barbara's not demonstrative; she's very, very bright. I'm sure when she went into [Gerry & Sylvia's] offices and talked with them they towed the line and went with what she wanted, or at least listened to what she had to say. But she never demonstrated that out on the set. She was always immaculate and calm and I would sometimes see something in a scene that was happening that, if she didn't like it, she wouldn't say "I don't want to do it like this," or raise any negatives. She would just quietly go to the bathroom or something and she'd be gone for a little while, and things would change … Martin is very funny off camera. We used to joke around a lot together. He's very funny on camera, too, but in that show it didn't call for him being all that funny.'

Tate also praises Barry Morse, who passed away in 2008: 'Dear Barry. When I came on the show he was established as a star actor. He had been playing in *The Fugitive*. I'd seen him in other things. He was a man of wonderful poise, of intellect. Barry had much that he could have offered the show, and really wasn't given the sort of opportunities that he might have been given on it. He was a very private man. He was an intellectual human being who loved fine things, adored his wife … a family man. In many ways he was rather like Professor Bergman; he was interested in so many things. One could always go to him with questions about the script, and he would say to me, "You know, Nick, it isn't Shakespeare. We just have to try to make the best of it." I so wanted things to be right, and he knew what it was like to work in fast television, having done American series. He was a joy to work with, a real professional. He gave me, and others on the show, a sense of worth and value, because we valued his opinion and he told us that we were doing a great job. He would work with us when a script problem – or something else – arose; you could go and talk with Barry about it.'

Barbara Bain also fondly recalled Barry Morse, 'Everything about Barry was so dear. When I first met him he was trying to explain the Brits to me, so he brought in a [newspaper] headline from when he was a kid, and it said, "Storm in the Channel; Continent isolated." That sums it up; it was very helpful.'

Regarding the reception he and Barbara Bain received in the UK, Martin Landau has said: 'American actors in England had a reputation for being troublemakers then. And Barbara and I having left *Mission: Impossible* when we did, the studio had released a bunch of erroneous information about us that made us look like the bad guys. We dealt with the legacy of that and of a lot of the other American television stars that had been in England prior to our coming over. We quickly dismantled the rumour, because once they realised we were hardworking, serious, co-operative and certainly not troublemakers, the whole atmosphere of working on *Space: 1999* changed. I mean, all the snobbery broke down. Charles Crichton, who for one period of time directed almost every other show, had also directed *The Lavender Hill Mob* with Alec Guinness and went on to do *A Fish Called Wanda*, which he co-wrote with John Cleese. He realised Barbara and I were the most co-operative actors you could find, and in the end we got along wonderfully with everyone, by and large, on the set.'

Barry Morse agreed: 'The fact that Martin and Barbara had been successful Hollywood actors in *Mission: Impossible* was impressive in itself, but they are – as anybody who knows them would readily tell you – a couple of wonderfully relaxed professionals, with charming personalities, who don't have (as so many so-called Hollywood stars do) an inflated sense of their own importance or self-worth. They settled themselves down very readily amongst what was an almost entirely British cast and worked with marvellous equanimity with everybody in the unit. Of course, they were both of them experienced enough through their time with *Mission: Impossible* to know of the immense stresses that there always are in shooting a weekly television series. They were and are, both Martin Landau and Barbara Bain, first class real pros, as we say in the trade.'

Christopher Penfold recalled of Landau and Bain: 'They had a very serious interest in the scripts – not unnaturally, being the stars of the show – and they were at pains to ensure that the large roles were written for them. Beyond that, they had a very intelligent input into the kinds of stories that we were writing, and into the way individual scripts went. I enjoyed story meetings with them. There was the requirement for screen time for Martin Landau, but it was entirely appropriate that it should be through him that the philosophical side of the series should be expressed.

'It was incredibly valuable to have the experience and skill that both Barbara and Martin brought to the process of screenwriting. It was a huge learning experience for me. After we finished at the studios quite often we would go back to their house in Little Venice and work on the script for the next day until four in the morning. It was an extremely valuable experience for me, and for the show as well. It's not that often you get that level of commitment and involvement, with an overall determination to get the script right, and to be involved in the process with the two leads of the show as well was absolutely wonderful, and I think it shows … They were very keen about what their characters would do and what they wouldn't do … I learned more about script writing and script editing from Martin and Barbara in that house than I've ever learned since. It was a huge contribution that was made [by Martin and Barbara] to the show, not only in front of the screen, but in the scripts as well.

'If you're writing popular drama series you take constraints on. I mean, Martin is out there at the front of the show. He is being paid a lot of money to do it. He is there because the audience want to see him. That is part of the process of writing for television drama series, where audience identification and loyalty build up episode by episode, and is an important consideration. Of course, once you've cast Martin Landau in the lead, you want to make the most of it. My approach to storytelling when I first start talking to other writers who are going to contribute episodes to a series like this, is to say to them, "First of all, tell your story." Once you know as a writer what you want to write, once you've got the essence of it … and it may be more irritating for some people than it is for others, but you don't really engage in this business without accepting certain parameters. Once you've got the story, in essence, it's actually then relatively easy to crowbar and elbow the story around those kinds of production requirements. It's not often that the real guts of a story get compromised.'

Johnny Byrne recalled: 'Barbara was very different off camera – witty, great sense of fun, incredibly kind and caring … Martin and Barbara were highly intelligent, invariably courteous to all and generous to a fault. They were a joy to work with.'

Gerry Anderson simply stated: 'Both Martin Landau and Barbara Bain were very easy to work with. They were always on time, knew their lines and didn't bump into the furniture.'

Barbara Bain noted: 'We were behind the project from the start. The idea enthralled us. We knew the show could make it in prime time – *Star Trek* had proven that. We dug in and got acquainted with every aspect of the production – script conferences, casting calls, business meetings … The entire project was like a new baby to us … One reason we took the series in London was that it let us go home to the kids. We'd actually be home for dinner every night. That's unheard of over here. I loved being around the kids, and I wouldn't have done any TV at that time if I wasn't able to do that … I had it both ways, working on something that I cared about while keeping in touch with my family.'

What did the cast feel about some of the guest performers who appeared in the show? Barry Morse stated: 'Some of our guest stars were very good, [but] some were better actors than others …. My dear old friend Peter Cushing appeared as a guest in "Missing Link", and it was a joy to see him turn up on our show. He and his wife were deeply loving friends of Sydney (my wife) and me. And then there were other people like Joan Collins, she was a big name and was very disciplined and well behaved. I can't remember, truthfully, any of them that were in any way difficult or objectionable. They all fitted in pretty well … Another guest was Catherine Schell, and she had played a regular role in that other series I had done for Lew Grade called *The Adventurer*. So I did know her and had worked with her before.'

Johnny Byrne recalled: 'If it was an Alphan guest star, invariably he or she was going to die. At the rate we were killing people on Moonbase Alpha, they didn't have to find a new world, because nobody was going to survive!'

Zienia Merton also noted: 'I thought [the Alphans] kept losing people so often that there must have been an awful lot of empty bedrooms! And wasn't it nice to see a bedroom in "The Last Enemy"… although originally that scene wasn't in the show. They'd under-run an awful lot on that episode, so they put it in. I really loved things like that, though. Like on "Missing Link", when Wardrobe said, "You're going to be in pajamas." I thought, "Great – I'll get out of that uniform." Someone just sent me a first season paperback, and it's not one of the TV episodes, but it starts where we are going to have a play on Alpha and I'm afraid of heights – great! It's nice when people have failings, because you can identify with it.'

Sylvia Anderson also reflected on the subject of casting the guest roles: 'At that time, Lew Grade was trying to break away from constantly having to deal with the Americans, and he quite rightly looked to Europe for commercial input. But the Italians were very slow at putting in the money. We'd actually shot six or seven episodes before there was any Italian finance. We hosted a luncheon here at Pinewood [during filming of "Guardian of Piri"] for the people from RAI, and after that some money appeared. Then Lew Grade rang me up and said he wanted me on the first plane to Rome with the casting director to get some Italian influence in the cast. So I rushed off to Rome and found some marvellous actors. But then I had a run-in with Martin Landau, because he'd been holding the fort until then. Eventually, I got my way and cast people like Giancarlo Prete, who treated it all with great humour, but they always knew they had to walk three paces behind Martin Landau.'

What of Gerry and Sylvia Anderson themselves? Johnny Byrne begins: 'I did a lot of work with Gerry. He was excellent for a writer, because he had a strong sense of story and trusted his instincts enormously. He was highly creative and could make those leaps of imagination, which is very rare in a producer. Gerry's hard and fast, in the sense that his brilliance is on the technical side, but when you come to story terms, Gerry has very simple ideas, and all the better they are for it. If one was to qualify this effect: Gerry could make a good script infinitely better and make a bad script very much worse.'

Christopher Penfold agreed: 'Gerry had an incredible capacity for storytelling. He loved telling stories, but the problem with Gerry's storytelling was that as Executive Producer, once he'd hit upon a story and convinced himself it was going to work, there was very little opportunity for those with him to convince him that maybe it wouldn't work. A lot of the delays we ran into were really delays caused by Gerry's inflexibility over what was often a brilliant story idea. He very often had a mindset that made it impossible for him to accept that in principle something was a good idea but there might be some other way around it. That was often a source of conflict. Equally, Gerry was very good when we had those kinds of difficulties in [other writers'] storytelling. He had an ability to cut through a story that had become muddled and inject it with a new sense of purpose. Creatively, he was very strong like that. There was an upside and a downside of Gerry's effect on the storytelling.

'I remember Sylvia's input as being largely to do with the way things looked; the style of the series. She did have good contributions to make in story terms but she was never as good as Gerry in that department. She was very good at enthusing people and encouraging them when difficulties loomed. In actual storytelling terms, I don't remember Sylvia's contributions as being terribly significant.'

Barry Morse was always blunt in his appraisal of the Andersons: 'You have to be concerned about the people, not just the special effects. My character was a kind of space uncle and I was forever being called upon to stand by dreadful diagrams and maps and say, "We are now pointing towards planet Pluto," or some such boring rubbish, which would lead into special effects. I remember writing a memo one night that said, "Dear Gerry and Sylvia – please remember that geography is about maps; drama is about chaps." I thought it ought to have been embroidered and set above Gerry and Sylvia Anderson's beds! I'm sorry if this is hurtful to Gerry and Sylvia – but they are not the best producers I've ever come across!'

Zienia Merton, by contrast, has said: 'I thought Sylvia Anderson was terrific. She was a people person. She made her office totally accessible to everybody. She was terribly good. She's just a born communicator, in terms of making people feel good. She had that capacity to make people feel that they were important, which I think in a series is just invaluable.'

Martin Landau agreed: 'Sylvia was a charming and gregarious person, always ready for a good laugh, but very bright and serious when necessary. When it came time to do production on the second season, Sylvia's absence was strongly felt by me, as I liked dealing with her openness and her sensibilities … Gerry was happier with the puppets than he was with the actors. But Sylvia was there, and unfortunately their relationship changed and she suffered more, and we got Fred Freiberger.'

Nick Tate said, 'Sylvia got a bum deal not getting the second series. She was such a driving force. She was the creative one, the one that loved the actors. Gerry said to me very early on, "I don't like actors." And I don't think he ever changed his mind. But Sylvia said "I love you all," and she really did.'

The cast enjoyed a positive interaction with the studio crew, as Barbara Bain recalled: 'It was fun. It was a great set. Our whole relationship to everyone was fantastic. The crew was full of cute, funny people. And we had no trouble communicating, except when you got a guy who spoke with a Cockney accent …'

Martin Landau continued: 'We had a Cockney first director. He'd say something and I'd go, "Huh?" It didn't even sound like English. I thought I was in Bulgaria.'

Landau also commented: 'Our camera operator was a terrific guy, because there was a lot of movement in the show …. The light sometimes is very dim, which means you have to really be good on your marks. When the camera is out there, the focus point really has to be good. …When you're acting each scene on a different mark, it's tricky stuff. It wasn't an easy show to do, is what I'm saying. But we had a good crew. It's nice for an actor to know he can depend on his camera, and those guys are very important …'

Recalling some of the show's action sequences, Landau has also said: 'You can't have an explosion without gunpowder, and anytime you use gunpowder, that's dangerous. We blew up a lot of sets.' Barbara Bain added: 'One day a piece of fire fell on one of the stunt people. The director ran into the scene and snuffed out the person's clothes. The man with the suit ignited was actually seen on screen – the director just cut out the part where he put out the fire.'

Of the show's production executive, Anton Phillips recalled: 'Reg Hill was a very, very supportive kind of person, in his own quiet way. He helped a lot of people in all sorts of different ways. He's one of the unsung heroes, I think, of *Space: 1999*. A good man; a very nice guy.'

Phillips also said: 'I had a stunt double on the show called Paul Weston, who's one of the top stunt men in England. In normal life he looks nothing at all like me. I mean, he's *white* for a start! He's 6'3". Muscles. He's a big man. By the time Basil got through with him in the makeup department, with an afro wig and dark brownish skin and the same costume and everything else … I remember the first time I saw him he was walking on the set towards me and I thought I was walking towards a mirror. Just for that moment … My wife was in a couple of the episodes of *Space: 1999,* and on one occasion when she was on the set I said to him, "Go over there and give her a kiss." And he went up behind her and pecked her on the cheek and she said, "Oh, hi darling," and turned and did a double-take before she sort of screamed.'

Phillips has also praised the work of Barry Gray and Keith Wilson: 'The first time I heard the theme music was probably the first time I saw the first episode. I thought,

'This is terrific!' Keith Wilson is really a good person to talk to because he was working long before any of us did. And he designed the set so it could be broken down and [reassembled] in any configuration ... so you could suddenly create the hydroponics unit, or Medical, or whatever. All the bits were interchangeable. That was really smart. That was really thinking ahead, because they would work indefinitely.'

Sylvia Anderson also remembered Year One's musical composer: 'Barry Gray was a fantastic person. He was very unassuming, and if you met him and talked to him you wouldn't think he had the genius in him that he had. But he lived and breathed music. He lived in a little house with his mother – his marriage had broken up – and the house was full of musical instruments. He was just a fantastic person and a very, very talented musician. We owe a lot to him. I think he knew how we valued him – hopefully he did.'

Regarding stunts, Nick Tate recalled: 'I insisted that I do all my own stunts. I was very physical and fit and I was humiliated that they would bring in stuntmen. In the very early episodes they did, but they'd always bring in somebody who didn't look *anything* like me. The guy was always bald, or he had black hair or a big belly. [A stuntman doesn't have to have a face like mine], but he has got to have the same silhouette. In the end they said, "You've got to have a stuntman," so Timmy Condrun became my stuntman. I said, "Okay. We'll 'hold hands', we'll discuss what I'll do – but I'm going to do it." So they kind of agreed, and in the end it was okay. We would choreograph the whole thing so that it was completely worked out. I always wanted to work, incidentally, with other stuntmen. I didn't like fighting with Martin because he wasn't very [physically] articulate. So I would fight the stuntman and it would be shot from behind his shoulder and you couldn't see that it wasn't Martin, and then when they came around to the other angle over my shoulder, it would be Martin. There were those couple of times I had to fight Martin because I went crazy, or he went crazy.'

Cast members have frequently praised the show's directors. Barry Morse, for instance, noted: 'Our directors on *Space: 1999* varied in their different ways. Most of us knew Charlie Crichton and his fine reputation as a director of some of the famous Ealing comedy films. Charlie passed away in September 1999. Ray Austin had been originally a stuntman in our profession and has directed a great deal of television in the United States. Lee Katzin was notable for the fact he directed the initial episode, "Breakaway", which took twice as long as almost any other, running absurdly over schedule. I think there may have been good reasons on Gerry's and Sylvia's part that he didn't figure as a director on more than one episode after that first one. He shouldn't be entirely blamed for [the overrun], though, because he was confronting material put together with all too little preparation. David Tomblin I remember quite well. He was a good, sympathetic director of actors. Bob Kellett was a pleasant chap as well. They were all very good, workmanlike directors.'

Martin Landau said: 'Charles Crichton, who directed every third episode of our show, was a great comedy director. The only work he could get in the '70s was on our show. We were thrilled to have him. You're talking about a *great* director who wound up doing a science fiction television series ... In the beginning when I first got there – Barbara and I were the colonists. We were outsiders. Charlie Crichton was a bit standoffish at first. I'm pretty tactile; I like to shake hands and touch and stuff, so I would say hello and shake his hand, and at night before I left I'd shake his hand, until one day he exploded, "What is all this? You're not going to India, for God's sakes. I'll see you tomorrow morning." But about 6 months after the series he would come and put his arm around me and stick his hand out. So, I Americanized him. We had good directors…. But he was wonderful. He was awesome. I liked him; I wound up being really very fond of him … I loved working on that show. We had a great time. I sort of instigated that.'

Nick Tate said, 'Charlie Crichton was a really good director and a nice man. A very idiosyncratic, funny man … He used to have a Volvo that he would drive. And Charlie would get absolutely tanked every night after the show, and then drive this Volvo home. He was so drunk he couldn't stand up. I don't know how in God's name he got home in that car.'

Landau also remembered Crichton's drinking, 'You gotta know, too, that his license was taken away twice during our show. He was without a license two times because of DUIs, as we call them here. Driving under the influence … [Charlie Crichton] was a funny guy. I once saw Charlie at a party at Pinewood, on the second floor, and I saw him in the doorway, teetering, and falling, and I ran … there was a marble staircase there in that big building. Charlie had fallen down the staircase and had landed on his feet, and was waddling away. If he hadn't have been drunk he would have been dead.'

Zienia Merton recalls an amusing story regarding one director: 'There was one episode Ray Austin was directing, and in one scene we went into God knows how many takes, because I giggled. I got terrible giggles. I had to be standing there, looking terribly serious, and I kept laughing. Ray, instead of telling me to stop, set me up! He got a piece of paper and attached it to his head, saying "Don't laugh!" I was trying so hard. I wasn't looking until the last minute, until he said, "Action." Then I saw this "Don't laugh!" thing. They also put things on my desk – pictures of naked men and things like that – just to try and make me laugh. We had to do 15 or 20 takes on that one. In the rushes the next day there was Take One, when I started to giggle, and they said, "Cut." The next take was like Take 18 – and it looked as if I'd been laughing for 18 takes. But it wasn't my fault; it was Ray Austin's and the camera crew's!'

Nick Tate recalled Lee Katzin fondly: 'I loved him. He cast me in the show… He seemed to personify the attitude – at least for me, having come from another country – of an American director. He just epitomized that to me. He had authority, panache, knowledge, inventiveness; he was courageous; he was friendly, and just everything about him was awe-inspiring.'

Nick Tate shared another anecdote: 'Martin [Landau] worked only in left profile – you never saw Martin's right profile unless it was just moving quickly through the frame. If he had to come and stand here on my right side and turn and talk to me so that his right profile was showing, he'd walk in and around me – always. And I had this hang-up about my right profile, so initially I felt, "What am I going to do? I've got to work with him all the time." It completely cured me of my hang-up about my right profile, because I was in right profile throughout the entirety of *Space: 1999*! … It proved in the end to be great for me because it stopped that stupidity. It's really ridiculous. Ray Austin, the director, used to get furious with Martin, because he'd set up a scene and he wanted it to work in a particular way and Martin would always walk around [to a left-profile vantage point] and Ray would say, "No – I want you over here!" Ray would get so angry with him, but Martin wouldn't give in. In many ways, Martin was a real pussycat. I understand these foibles that he had; in many ways, it was rather sweet and childish. He just couldn't help himself – these were things he wanted and things he had to have, and it was his show. He said to me, "Nick, I had to put up with all that when I was in *Mission: Impossible*. I wasn't the lead of that show – I was one of the guys. This is my show, and I'm going to have it my way. When it's your show you can have it your way." But you know, even if it was my show, I swear to God I wouldn't do those things. Because it's detrimental to yourself: in the end, you just have to let go. There are other great people around you that support you.'

Johnny Byrne stated: 'As we see watching *Space: 1999*, when [the episodes] were good they could be *very* good. The directors brought so much to the scripts that we wrote as writers. And the actors, the artists, brought so much to the words and the characterisation.'

ITC AND COMPARISONS

Regarding ITC, Christopher Penfold has stated: 'Every time an episode was completed in script form it would be shipped off to ITC and they would make their comments. Unfortunately Gerry was very much in thrall to ITC when he felt his relationship with them was threatened. This was where a lot of disputes rose. Often what happened was that we'd finally get a script we were all pleased with; Gerry was pleased with it, Martin was pleased with it and Charles was pleased with it. Off it went to ITC and back it came with comments that just tore at the fundamental structure of the thing. Gerry would say, "Back to the drawing board ..."

'It was very demoralising to have to respond to that. We all felt that sufficient homage had been paid to the requirements of the American market in the way the whole thing had been set up in the first place. We also all felt that the way to succeed in the American market was actually to inject the quality of difference and the originality that we all had to bring to it ... I found I was publishing scripts that I didn't myself believe in one hundred percent. It became more and more impossible for me to stay there, and Gerry and Sylvia realised that.'

The cast and crew also had certain difficulties in dealing with ITC, as Zienia Merton recalls: 'We used to get this a lot in the first year. If they thought one of us might be getting out of line, they would say, "Somebody in America [at ITC] doesn't like you." And you were meant to be very, very frightened and just keep quiet. It used to be used as a threat now and again, like a big stick. Someone in America – they never told you who it was. It was, "This faceless person, who could actually kill you, doesn't like you, in America." It was brought out every now and again.'

Christopher Penfold added: 'I think that, as a person responsible for the making of a television drama series, you have an expression of faith in the product that you are putting your life into. The best of what we see on television are the successful expressions of those acts of faith. They're often original ideas and they almost invariably originate from the creative writer, not from a television executive. I think, as Johnny has said, that we actually snuck one in under the wire on the first series. The eye of the network, the eye of ITC, was not immediately upon us. So I think we evolved – in a fairly short space of time – a fairly coherent and quite ambitious idea of what we could achieve in this new [show]. And it was something to which we were passionately committed.

'I remember feelings of great dread when I saw a big car draw up outside the studios at Pinewood and the boot open and the film cans of the first episode went into this car, which was driven by a man who was at the time a lackey for Abe Mandell at ITC. This car took the first episode (or perhaps the first two episodes) off to be screened in front of what I think would now be called a focus group. My feeling about focus groups is that they are entirely [opposed to] the creative vision of the original writer. People who watch television without creating it – their yardsticks are what they last saw on television, or what they're accustomed to seeing on television. If what they are looking at is a piece of original work, which is surprising to them, initially their response is probably going to be negative. But I think the great television successes have been those programmes that have had the tenacity to hold on to that original vision in the face of some initial audience opposition. Gradually the audience comes around to it, warms to it and realises what that original vision was. Then they get behind it.

'What happened in the case of the first series of *Space: 1999* was that quite creative vision was constantly being eviscerated by negative responses from focus groups in Los Angeles or wherever they were. It was, I think, quite discouraging for us to receive the results of those. I mean, we would have received the results of the focus groups without too much trepidation, but when they came also with direct orders to change direction … then we felt pretty sad about that … It was very dispiriting to feel that time and again when our work was assessed the criteria being used were existing shows of a similar kind. We felt the secret of success was to make it that much different.'

Zienia Merton agreed that *Space: 1999* was unfairly compared to *Star Trek*: 'It's a different thing. Okay, they're both about space … But it was a totally different mentality in *Trek* to *Space*. The way we think to the way the Americans think.'

Nick Tate has said: 'I hadn't been a fan of *Star Trek*. When I was asked to do *Space: 1999*, I don't think I'd seen more than one episode of *Star Trek*, and I thought it was kind of like a pantomime in space. (I hated it when Fred Freiberger later tried to do that to *Space: 1999* …) So I didn't know much about *Star Trek*, but I did love cowboy movies and adventure stories. So when I was asked to audition for *Space: 1999*, the whole macho concept of being an astronaut was something that I found exciting. I never thought of the parallels between what *Space: 1999* was and what I'd known *Star Trek* to be. No-one ever mentioned it. We weren't trying to parallel it in any way. *Space: 1999* was intended to be a story of fact. Whilst it was science fiction, they tried very hard to make us believe that what we were dealing with was all real science. Everything we tried to do in the beginnings of *Space: 1999* was very possible and just how it would be. But we had to spice it up with some drama.'

Barry Morse commented: 'The roles of women – both stars and guest stars – were larger in *Space: 1999* than in other science fiction series before or since, including *Star Trek*. I have no idea if this had anything to do with Sylvia Anderson being credited as producer. I hope this was one forward-looking idea of our series. Even when we were shooting it, women's roles in society generally were not as substantial or as powerful as they are now – although they were beginning to be.'

Martin Landau stated: 'Science fiction is a literary form. A good writer can create a world in three paragraphs, and then the reader's mind can do anything with it. The danger is to disappoint in the visualisation. But we've created a world different from anything seen before on TV. Like *Star Trek*, we [present] contact with mind-bending, incredible things, but that show was [set] two thousand years into the future with everyone running around in a ship that could do all kinds of things. We're victims, something like pioneers, more identifiable as people … The important asset of *Space: 1999* is that it's set in 1999, not 200 years in the future. My guy was born in the 1950s. He grew up with the likes of John Glenn. *Space: 1999* is rooted in the present. We have taken a bunch of contemporary people and sent them flying, out of control, through space. We can't say, "Hey, let's go there, because that looks nice." *Star Trek* was kind of macho in a way. They had this big ship with big weapons that could destroy planets. We're at the mercy of everyone we encounter.'

Sylvia Anderson welcomed *Space: 1999* being compared to another famous science fiction production: 'Someone said that *Space: 1999* was Stanley Kubrick's *2001* every week. I thought that was the best – the most flattering – thing they could say about us.'

Regarding *Space: 1999*'s influences, Christopher Penfold observed: 'Actually, [Isaac Asimov's] *Foundation* I think is pretty seminal to a lot of what we were trying to do in *Space: 1999*; I think it's an absolute masterpiece. The notion of *Foundation* in relation to our world is a pretty powerful one and a pretty challenging one, even now. The kinds of things that Asimov was engaging with there – and seeing the success that he achieved in attempting to engage with those ideas – certainly encouraged us. We were of course aware of *Star Trek*. Science fiction is certainly an evolving genre. Isn't there a continual enquiry amongst us about where we will be in the future? I think that the great satirists of the 18th Century were writing science fiction in a way. Extrapolation from the contemporary into the future in order to look back at the way we live now and to ask questions about it, is something we will always be doing.'

Barry Morse also shared his thoughts on science fiction: 'It's not too difficult to direct or act William Shakespeare because if you ensure that the words are adequately heard, he'll take care of you. He is simply the greatest, most staggering entertainer that mankind has ever produced. It may interest science fiction buffs to contemplate what sort of scripts Shakespeare might have written for *Space: 1999*, because although it isn't often realised, he did write science fiction. What is *The Tempest*? It's about a mystical island with a magical proprietor and the even more extraordinary, basic and savage slave. What about *A Midsummer Night's Dream*, in which the impossible happens every five minutes? Science fiction has existed almost as long as the human race. What is science fiction, after all? It is something constructed to carry your imagination beyond the realms of what you know to be currently possible. Take the law of gravity, for example. Suppose I drop a piece of paper and suddenly I am in a world where, instead of it falling down and hitting the floor, it goes upwards and flies around the room. There have been wonderful, wonderful writers of science fiction long before our brave lads on *Space: 1999*. Many of the earliest mystery plays – as they were called – in Christianity, which examined human frailties and human emotions, were in essence science fiction plays. Shakespeare, as I indicated, wrote some of the best science fiction plays ever. Then we come to people like Lewis Carroll – a good example in my view of a wonderful science fiction writer – who takes us to Wonderland, where the Duchess in one sequence of dialogue announces that she sets herself to believe three impossible things before breakfast every day. Well, that's science fiction for you, isn't it?

'Another example is the plays written in the last century about reversals of time. British writer J B Priestley wrote a whole succession of stage plays in which he examined what the nature of time was and [presented] the theory that [history], instead of being a [linear] thread, is all going on at the same time; that the past, the present and the future could all be taking place at once. We recognise this with the phrase déjà vu – how many of us have had first-hand experiences where we suddenly stumble onto an [event] that somehow seems to chime with something that happened perhaps before we were born? And that's why I think the realm, the whole genre, of science fiction is so challenging and, if it's halfway decently done, so rewarding.'

CRUCIAL ELEMENTS

Johnny Byrne explained: 'The writers, like the Alphans themselves, were voyaging into the unknown. This was reflected in the progression of the first series. The further the Alphans receded from Earth, with all its apparent certainties, the more uncertain and challenging their lot became. They were confronting problems – moral, ethical, human, scientific – they didn't really understand. Or, if they did, their understanding was never more than superficial. This was a crucial element in the first series – the sense that often there are no set and definite answers. To [find an answer] meant first understanding the question, and often the Alphans didn't. Frequently they were dealing with matters the nature of which was beyond their Earthly limitations. Wisdom, when it did surface, was an acknowledgement of what they didn't know, rather than what they did.'

Christopher Penfold recalled the epic qualities in his episodes, such as 'The Last Sunset': 'I guess those epic qualities came from Aristotle and Socrates. I had a classical education and was pretty seriously impressed by the Greeks. It seemed to me that in dealing with what was not a very real circumstance – the idea of a group of human beings being cast adrift without any means of directing their future, beyond survival, in response to the circumstances that they encountered – that that in itself has a mythic quality about it. It really seemed to offer the opportunity of introducing into the context of what was always intended to be a popular drama series, those big questions that people sometimes are possibly a little bit frightened to ask themselves. That was really why a lot of the episodes I wrote had that decidedly mythic quality – it's something I try to encourage. I do a lot of script editing now, and quite a lot of teaching, and it's a quality that I try to encourage writers to find in almost all the work that they do. I think there is a mythic dimension even to a private eye series, or a detective story.'

Johnny Byrne again: 'The humanity [of *Space: 1999*] came in … putting the Alphans into situations wherein, to a large degree, it was their humanity that was being tested. It might have been [that] the heat levels were falling, or the food was running out, or something was about to hit [them]. Essentially in their contact with each other, and in their conflict with aliens and things like this, the Alphans' humanity was being tested; it was always a question of humanity, rather than straightforward "We take you – you can't stop us." So it was moral values more than anything that were being tested … If you look at the episodes in the order in which they were made, you will see that the progression of people who are fairly frightened and fairly clueless reflected the screenwriters' frightened, clueless attitude as to stepping out into the unknown, too. *We were out there at the same time.* When we became more familiar, our touches became more adept, responses more certain, weariness more pronounced, the further we went out. By episode 48, there wasn't a situation out there that we couldn't deal with! But on the way out, we didn't know where the hell we were or what the hell was happening to us, and that was reflected in the stories. After a few physical disasters, we felt we could cope. There was a huge sigh of relief at the end of the first series. And there was a great regret as well, because we knew that we had done something really special, but we knew that it wasn't perfect. Not at all.'

Christopher Penfold concurred: 'We made it up as we went along. I think there was a kind of philosophy behind series one – it evolved – that tended to focus the stories on quite challenging ideas, philosophical ideas, and questions. Who are we? Why are we here? Where are we going? What's the future of our universe? All that kind of thing. And during the course of series one, I think there was a gradual building of pressure to shift the focus of the show more in the direction of action-adventure entertainment; monsters-in-space. So I think that the collision of those two philosophies really resulted in the division between series one and series two … At some point, had the series been able to develop, generational change would have been something that we would have taken on board. I suppose that in the context of the first series, we thought that having cast the Moonbase adrift with them looking for or hoping to find some eventual sanctuary, that actual continuation of the species was something that they weren't particularly concerned about. If series two had continued in the vein of series one, I'm pretty sure that would have been something that we would have made good story material out of.'

In Byrne's view, 'The moral of the series often was found in the divergence of man as Technological Man and man as Biological Man. Biological Man is [very] undeveloped in terms of Technological Man, and the conflict and the antagonistic nature of Biological Man are always going to confound the successes and the productions of Technological Man. I think Chris caught that in "War Games" and even in "Black Sun". The application of metaphysics to science; Technological Man and Biological Man, and the difficulty of reconciling them.

'It was very important, this whole question of Technological Man and his responsibility for science; scientists and their responsibility for the wonders they produce. Chris had actually formulated this, and he had written another series called *The Brack Report*, which dealt with precisely this theme. We were very concerned about these things.'

Penfold mused: 'The series philosophy is that we are proud to be a pretty interesting, complex species. That we are cognisant of the possibility that there are much more interesting and complex species out there – of which we may even be a part – but to encounters with which and with whom the adventurous amongst us look forward with great excitement.'

SPACE: 1999 AS ORIGIN STORY

In an otherwise quite bizarre critical piece on *Space: 1999* in a 1975 issue of *Cinefantastique* magazine, the reviewer managed to identify a very central theme: '… Isn't there inherent poetry in the fantastic premise of the moon finally released, spinning through the void, taking a tribe of humans with it? I think so. If this had really happened centuries ago, even minus its human cargo, it would today be a legend of epic proportions. Like Gilgamesh and the Great Flood. It would have variants in all cultures.'[22]

What that reviewer hit upon is that *Space: 1999* is indeed an origin story of epic

---

[22] Stewart, Brian. *Cinefantastique* magazine: 'It's really disco, lost out there!' 1975.

proportions. As Johnny Byrne has mentioned over the years, origin stories take on mythical qualities and often incorporate elements that are unexplainable, with mystical, magical or religious undertones. The journey of the Alphans is not necessarily bound by the laws of reality or science, and incredible, unexplainable events happen with surprising frequency. Does this not go far to sum up *Space: 1999*, at least in its first season? Byrne stated: 'I think you come to a time when questions of identity and purpose are more in tune now than they were then. Indeed, much of the conflict in the world is related to these questions: who are we, and what do we want, and can we allow ourselves to be assimilated? A sense of identity, and a sense of purpose. And we seem to be losing, I think in purely Earth terms, a sense of belonging to the place. There's a sense of fragmentation. And I always saw *Space: 1999* as a unifying thing; something that would celebrate humanity no matter how strange and threatening, no matter how absurd and outlandish the places it took us to. That we would always hold on to those things and not simply relinquish them – certainly not easily. But also, something that is very important is the concept of an origin story: an origin theme ... [The Alphans] were people in the process of writing the history of their origins, their time and their place, their values. The Celts did it, the Jews did it; many other races have done this. We were in the process of seeing this, in the beginning, at the modern stage. I think part of the epic quality of *Space: 1999* was tied up in that concept. It was something larger than the sum of its parts, and that was [the idea of] people searching for a place.'

It's no wonder that critics, expecting – or hoping – to see another series in the familiar science fiction mold of *Star Trek* were (and some remain to this day) mystified and frustrated by *Space: 1999*, which took its format from the origin stories of human history – such as that of a people like the Hebrews, cast out to roam the desert on a random journey looking for a new home. *Space: 1999* was its own entity, and in that uniqueness lies its strength.

Another review that went far in understanding the series appeared in *Art and Story* in 1976 and stated: 'While not without its flaws, *Space: 1999* has demonstrated itself to be the finest SF television series ever produced, both in concept and in execution. Oddly, the show was quickly dismissed by the critics, most of whom seemed to miss the point of the programme. *Space: 1999* did not set out to become another *Star Trek*. Rather, the show's creators used the runaway moon concept as a vantage for observing human behavior in a situation of total disaster, total uncertainty, total helplessness in the face of incomprehensible dangers. Moonbase Alpha is a microcosm of human society on Planet Earth, and the errant moon is in many ways a scale model of our own world – out of control, embattled and wracked by disaster, its inhabitants mercilessly buffeted by forces beyond their comprehension. Some critics complained that the stories were too esoteric, too abstract. But if many episodes seemed to conclude without answers for the questions they raised, if they often seemed to indicate that science is incapable of providing solutions to the overwhelming problems that threaten human existence, if stories were often resolved metaphysically rather than technologically, with the intervention of Something very much like God – perhaps it's because such conclusions are closer analogues to our real-life (and real-death) situation on

Spaceship Earth than the merely technological or heroic solutions proffered by less cerebral, less cogitative programmes such as *Star Trek*."[23]

IMPACT AND ASSESSMENT

Nick Tate recalled: 'Towards the end of the first series I was invited to the US to a science fiction convention in Pittsburgh. I was the only person from the series invited. [Year Two producer] Fred Freiberger wasn't involved at this time, but once Gerry and Sylvia Anderson and Abe Mandell (head of ITC New York) learned what was going on ... they suddenly realised there was a lot of mileage to be made from this. They wanted general recognition for the series in the sci-fi world and here was one of the lead actors being invited to a sci-fi con. ITC said I had to stop in New York first and meet the press. So I went to New York first to have what was called Breakfast with the Press. It was like being Paul McCartney for the day. They put me in a beautiful hotel; I turned up at 8.00 in the morning for breakfast and there were ten people sitting around a table, all with notepads and cameras flashing. The New York press were there and they were telling me that I was getting 5,000 fan letters a week, that I was the most popular character in the series, and asking what it was like working with Martin and Barbara. I was getting a lot of fan mail and it was coming in bags, but it wasn't 5,000 a week, I can assure you. Nonetheless, ITC ran with this idea and said that I was the most popular character in the series. You can understand how I felt strange later on when ITC didn't know that they should naturally have me back for the second series!'

The impact of the series in the UK was dulled by its scheduling, as Johnny Byrne remembered: 'We were unlucky in the scheduling. I never saw an episode. In England, they were on at half past ten, half past 11, six o'clock, five o'clock, and nine o'clock ... I thought for a while that it was actually what they called a loss-leader: that they had found a way of laundering some very dodgy money by transforming it into a television programme and putting it out in a way that least disturbed the existing order of things. I would tune in for it at half past ten and not find it, and then when I was going out at half past 12, I'd see it coming on. I think it was some kind of financial deal there – some money was being laundered!'

Barry Morse said: '*Space: 1999* has many fans around the world and I think with younger people – people who in some instances weren't even born when we were actually doing the series – it has a strong impact, because it reminds them of where we've been and where we may be going as we reach another millennium. More and more people, especially younger people, are beginning to ruminate and speculate about the future of the human race. It'll only take the wrong hand on the wrong button at the wrong time for the human species to be completely wiped out, perhaps to leave the care of our planet to such superior species as the lice and the beetles. It's a sobering thought, an alarming thought, but a very realistic thought. I think that is what has impressed so many people. Those ingredients I think are part of the serious subtext of *Space: 1999*. Those are the sorts of speculative, soul-searching questionings that could and should have played a larger part in the dramatisation, but at least we touched on

---

[23] Denney, James D. *Art and Story*: 'The Metamorph and the Metamorphoses.' August 1976, No 2.

them some of the time. It's all too easy with hindsight, which is always infallible, to put your finger on where things went wrong. Well, ultimately, we can't say that they did go wrong. The series has maintained a very loyal cult following ever since those days more than 35 years ago when it all began. The support the series has maintained has been in many ways, to me, quite amazing.

'Over the years since *Space: 1999*, I have been to a number of conventions celebrating the series. I often think how very touching it is that this group of young people are so kind and devoted to each other. The initial subject of their coming together – the old series, and their attachment to us actors – is not really that important after all. They've become very much involved with each other and regard themselves as virtually members of the same family. I regard those young people as my honorary grandchildren.

'It is an extraordinary thing to me that just one more television show should have compelled such a nice group of people to have remembered it for such a long time. The conventions are very gentle and peaceful and loving occasions for a whole lot of people of different kinds, statuses and backgrounds being brought and held together by a common interest, but also by a sense of concern and affection for each other. It shows how different members of the human race can come together and wish nothing but good to each other and to the rest of the world. I'm terribly pleased and touched by that. There are many conglomerations of people who come together for much less honourable purposes.'

Johnny Byrne assessed the series: 'There was a lot of praise, of course, for the technical side of it, which was fully justified. There was a very mixed reaction to the stories themselves. The fans were hooked from day one – I'm talking about the audience as a broad mass. There were certain irritating things about it that made our lives difficult ... The problem had to do with the format. Barbara, I think, under the circumstances ... did awfully well, and as it went on. It was fully justified, because she came more out of Medical Centre, and was to stay out. They were finding their way and so were we. But sometimes the size of Koenig's office, that big office that opened out into Main Mission, and the low-pitched conversations, everybody being slightly too nice and respectful ... There were certain things that put people off. It was science fiction ... I didn't particularly like the costumes, either. So there were all sorts of reasons why people didn't accept it for what it was, which I thought was an absolutely astounding television production. It couldn't be done again and it will never be done again. In no way can that be matched. In retrospect, people are now beginning to see how good it was. If they saw [the episodes] now, many of the issues, the feelings and thoughts that permeate the stories, I think they would find to be more interesting to them now. I don't know why that is. I think they would find more for their minds to hold onto now than they did then, because they had been conditioned to *Star Trek*.'

Martin Landau said: '*Space: 1999* was an interesting show in that it touched on the Moon being used as a garbage dump for nuclear waste. It was only 25 years into the future when we did it. [The human race is], in fact, technologically and emotionally ill equipped to do what we were thrust into on the series. If we wanted to, we couldn't go into deep space with 300 people. Again, it was only a few years into the future. We were also asking what happens to Earth without the Moon. The last contact we have with the Earth is that there are tidal waves and earthquakes – an interesting concept.'

Sylvia Anderson summarised her thoughts on the series by saying: 'I think we had a marvellous opportunity. It looked good, but I think you underrate the audience's intelligence when you have a Commander who's always right.'

Prentis Hancock reflected: 'Every time I've been involved in anything that is a little more than just entertainment and actually looks into or goes beneath the surface of a subject, it seems to be not just reflecting – as art always does – what is going on in the real world, but almost ahead of it. I don't believe that art is ahead of [real life]; I just think it's at the leading edge all the time of what is really happening. And very often public opinion won't catch up in five or 50 years. In the case of our stories in *Space: 1999* … I think space exploration, in concert with the exploding of the atom bomb and the distribution of the pill, has been the third element that really has made the world be able to see itself as a global village. Of course, the Americans were responsible for that. From the time mankind – we – got off our own planet and were able to look back and actually take it in as being one single entity on which we all must co-exist in harmony or die eventually, perhaps, that has been possibly the most powerful, important element of the 20th Century. "Black Sun" always stays with me … "Black Sun" and "Breakaway", as the two episodes that sort of summed up that idea. Always, when you're involved with something that matters … you pick up a newspaper and there's a headline about it and you think, "Where did that come from?" You're open to what's going on.'

Nick Tate said: 'The risk came in the fact that they shot all 24 episodes before showing it to the public. The only people who knew what was going on with the series at the time were Gerry and Sylvia Anderson and the ITC bosses and, of course, the actors who were involved. They took a very big gamble … They didn't make a pilot episode and test it and show it to millions of people and ask them to write and tell them what was right or wrong about the series. They had great faith in the series. It was a project that they felt would go, and they didn't want to be influenced by outsiders telling them to do this or that … I thought *Space: 1999* would have been even bigger than it was. We were shooting every episode like a major film. It had a lot of technical excellence and it needed all of that shiny, pristine quality that it had.

'If you go back to the days of *Space: 1999*, people like Prentis and Zienia and I, we were paid £187 an episode. Well, that's what I got. Sometimes it wasn't a week's pay – often the episodes took two weeks to make. So you can do the math and find out how much we got. We also all had written into our contracts, residuals that they said were based on network sales. Of course, *Space: 1999* was claimed to be the most widely syndicated series in the history of television at the time of its original screening. So that meant that anybody who had a contract that said they got residuals on network sales didn't get any money, because the show was syndicated. There are no residuals on syndication unless you have syndicated residuals written into your contract. I've made a very good living out of this industry; I've been very lucky and I've had a lot of work and I've enjoyed myself immensely. But I haven't made the sort of money that actors make now.'

Johnny Byrne commented: 'It's strange looking back; by rights, if we'd had any sense, we would have committed suicide … But we were travelling on hope and optimism. And we didn't simply realise how difficult our situation was. We lived on optimism. Whereas the cast could go home at five o'clock, we often would keep working, sometimes in Gerry's house. I would wake up with a *Thunderbirds* puppet staring at me. Gerry would have me picked up and delivered and I would spend a day and a night at his house rewriting or writing a script. I think the quickest I ever delivered a first draft was in three days. Yet, it's important to note that there was no sense of pressure among the writers: we seemed to have an easy life …

'Chris and I occupied a block away from the main production unit, called the Punishment Block … The only casualty was the secretary in between our two offices – Chris Penfold's and mine. She went crazy dealing with rewrites, and from five storeys up she threw the typewriter through the window, and had to be taken away. We never saw the poor woman again. There were no computers in those days; every rewritten page had to be retyped, if there was only one line changed. So it was like the problems of today a hundred times over. And we loved every minute of it.'

SUMMARY

Barry Morse gave a perceptive summation of his thoughts on *Space: 1999*: 'I enjoyed working on the series, as I usually do. In a career that now has lasted more than 70 years, I've only very rarely had experiences where I wasn't comfortable and happy with the set-up in which I was working. In this instance we were working with a charmingly professional bunch of actors, most of them much younger than me, and the general atmosphere within the shooting period was really very friendly.

'One of the most pleasurable aspects of *Space: 1999* was that it recruited an army of fans from all over the world, whom I've met in the succeeding years. It's rather touching to find that there are whole groups of people from all sorts of different countries who are brought together and bound together by a mutual admiration for this series. So, indeed, it had a value from my own personal point of view, in that way, in that I've been able in the 30 years since we shot that series to meet the "customers" – the audience – in all sorts of different parts of the world. In normal circumstances, if you do a single television show, you're not likely to meet the audience in the same way and with the same friendship as I've been able to with fans of *Space: 1999*.

'From my point of view, I had spent well over a year – 16 months – virtually imprisoned in the studio. I felt I wasn't making the best use of whatever gifts I may have, in playing this rather dull role. I felt I hadn't created a particularly vivid character for Victor Bergman. It had boiled down to me – as Barry Morse – drifting through and saying whatever was set down for me. The problems that had been built in and created from day one were never successfully solved, in my view. Thus it was, that what could and should have been a most wonderfully imaginative and visionary work of science fiction, never fully lived up to the expectations and hopes I had for it. I thought the whole series was a good opportunity, largely wasted.

'If – in some future revival of the series – one were to try and explain what happened to Victor Berman and why he was no longer around, one would have to go one of several routes. One would be that he simply died [of old age], because presumably he was the oldest inhabitant of the crew. Another explanation might be that his artificial heart failed and he died. But a more imaginative explanation might be that they touched down somewhere on some or other outer planet and he, Victor Bergman, became deeply fascinated by the lifestyle of these people who lived on this other planet, XYZ. He then decided that the rest of the crew must go on in their explorations and he would remain with the XYZ population. He would study the way they lived, because he felt that it was rather superior to how the normal human race lived! That would have been an interesting development, wouldn't it? There are all kinds of other ways that his disappearance could be explained, but such a thing was never done in the original series. So it remains a mystery. Whatever happened to Victor Bergman?'

Keith Wilson recalled: 'What I would have to do, to control the whole series – or the budget of the whole series – was to have script control. I am one of the few designers who has ever had script approval. [I wouldn't] comment on the script, but I would see it before the actors, before anyone else, to say whether or not I could do it in the time. We had ten days to do each episode. I would look at the script and I would say, "I can't possibly do this in ten days," or "This is going to be so expensive." I would spend money on a particular episode and go over-budget on that episode, but I wouldn't spend any money on the next one, so it would balance itself out. They had to come up with scripts where I wouldn't have much to do, every now and again, so I could catch up. Almost every script had one huge new set, every ten days.

'I used to have lunch every day with the scriptwriters. Because of the nature of the series, I had to have a lot of say. Gerry obviously gave me the say, because he had to. It was no good scriptwriters writing some incredible thing, because I would get a copy of the scripts and I'd walk into Gerry's office and say, "This is impossible. I can't do it. I've got ten days, I'm already in the middle of a film that's very difficult and you expect me to do this?" So he used to say, "Well, what can you do? How can we alter it to make it work?" So I would spend a lot of time with the scriptwriters, and two in particular – Chris Penfold and Johnny Byrne. We used to talk every lunchtime. So a lot of ideas for the scriptwriters, particularly with those two scriptwriters, would spring from our conversations. I was always very keen on doing monsters and that sort of thing, because I felt that was what the public wanted. Whether I was right or wrong is another thing … We did things on *Space: 1999* that other people would hesitate to do even in a big feature film. With the budget that we had, I think we did very well.

'I loved the series. I loved doing the show, because I had so much freedom. There was nobody to tell me what to do. Not even Gerry Anderson. Nobody. I had total freedom with the look, costumes, hair, make-up … absolutely everything. So, for me, *Space: 1999* was a high. It's one of my favourite productions I've ever worked on.'

Sylvia Anderson said: 'I can only comment on the shows that I was involved in, and my battle, or my side, was always to develop the characters. I considered that however brilliant your effects are, if you don't care about the characters you don't have anything. And that's what happened years ago – you couldn't get a highly regarded actor to appear in a science fiction movie because usually people concentrated on effects and forgot about the characters … For that reason I'm not a great science fiction fan, I have to say, unless it's something really stunning. As I was saying, years ago you couldn't get good actors – they didn't want to appear as competing with the effects. But gradually we're getting rid of that idea and trying to build the characters to match the effects … After the first series, as everybody knows, Gerry and I went our separate ways and I wanted to do something completely different. And so I wrote my first novel, which was called *Love and Hisses*. It was quite successful and I was quite proud of that, because writing has always been the thing that I've enjoyed the best.'

Anton Phillips recalled: 'Having seen the first series I thought, "If I have this to do again, I'd really like to just loosen up a little." Mathias looked very serious and uptight, didn't he? He should have had a drink problem, really. He needed to loosen up a little, smile and have a bit more fun. Pinch Helena's bottom – that sort of thing.'

Christopher Penfold said: 'I think we were interested in asking questions that could not necessarily be answered. I think that was something that many of the stories gave us an opportunity to do. Not affecting closure, I think, is what it's about. A fine teacher explained to me that most of the action in a picture goes on outside the frame. I think that what you actually see on the screen sets off reverberations that are going to continue in the audience's minds at least beyond the next ad break. What we tried to do was to write stories that would excite that kind of curiosity, to stimulate the spirit of enquiry, to promote philosophical speculation. That's a reason why so many of the stories have that "What's next?" kind of ending.

'I think curiosity – God, this is *so* essential. I remember being told by a very fine teacher in my school days, "You have to ask questions. The minute you stop asking questions, you're dead." I still believe that, and it's certainly what we believed in *Space: 1999*. We *wanted* to leave [the Alphans'] big questions unanswered, because there are no answers – yet.'

THE METAMORPHOSIS OF *SPACE: 1999*

Final post-synching work on Year One was completed in April 1975: actor Barry Morse recorded the specific date in his diary as Friday 11 April. In the intervening period between completion of Year One and the start of filming on Year Two in January 1976, various cast and crew members scattered around the world and worked on different projects.

A NEW BEGINNING

Due to the departure of Sylvia Anderson and the fact that the first series of *Space: 1999* had received a mixed critical reaction (complaints focusing on the low-key characterisation and the more mystical plot aspects), changes were made to the show for its second season. The ratings for Year One had opened spectacularly and, judging from media reports, had largely stayed that way. However, also significant in the eyes of ITC New York was the failure of the first series to secure a spot on American network television.

Asked about the potential for the second series to have continued on in the vein of the first, Christopher Penfold responds: 'I'm pretty sure the first season format could have been successfully extended to a second season, yes. It was a creative powerhouse, and most of the stories were evolved in response to crisis of one kind or another. I suppose it's a somewhat arrogant statement to make, but I feel that those responses would have been there. We would have been able to find and continue the variety of that. I think that the possibilities of that format were – like the universe itself – infinite … The whole point of science fiction is that you extrapolate from the known into the unknown, in order to better understand the known. Capital punishment we could have taken on. Genetic engineering we could have taken on. Any issue that confronts us in our everyday lives has within it the germ of an idea, which within the contexts of science fiction can generate a story … We were interested in asking questions that could not necessarily be answered. That was something that many of the stories gave us the opportunity to do. Not effecting closure, I think, is what it's all about. What we tried to do was to write stories that would excite curiosity, stimulate the spirit of enquiry and promote philosophical speculation.'

Gerry Anderson had Johnny Byrne write a detailed analysis of Year One, considering the strengths and weaknesses of the programme, and looking for the most promising direction forward. Byrne recalls this period: 'Chris left just before the end of series one and I was somehow still there … There was a great deal of uncertainty at the end of the first series as to what the future was going to be. I stayed on at Pinewood during the long hiatus that followed. During that time I wrote *The Day After Tomorrow – Into Infinity*, an after-school special for NBC. We shot it around some rescued sets from series one. Main cast included Nick Tate, Brian Blessed, Joanna Dunham, two kids and – in one shot – my dog, Bones, which the space-voyaging family in the story were leaving behind.

'I was asked by Gerry to write a critical commentary on Year One, probably as a way of keeping me around and out of mischief. They were trying to get the second series going. So I wrote a very detailed thing. It was very critical, including of stuff I'd written myself. I was taking a very hard look at everything and trying to find the point of departure to move what we had – the considerable achievement I felt we had managed – forward, on the same path, but correcting obvious anomalies … We had been finding our way. Now it was time to really go for it.

'I was very hard on everyone. I was particularly hard on myself – I was feeling very sorry for myself. But I looked at some of the difficulties or the disadvantages of the system that we had evolved – Chris and I particularly. There were lessons to be learned about what Chris and I and the other writers had left in our wake – we had not been aware of the larger implications of what we were doing. But there is a good deal of truth in the notion that, as the Alphans were struggling to come to terms with that dangerous and threatening and different universe out there, they were echoing the state of mind and the state of being of the writers. So out of it had emerged what we now call a story arc, as such. And I think in the commentary I wrote I did pick up on this and said, "There is a very large theme here, that we can project forward. We can ask ourselves, 'What is *Space: 1999*? What is the basic nature of its appeal in the largest universal sense?'" And the idea was that it was an epic story. It was humanity condensed to a small number of individuals, with all their hopes and expectations, going out there. And for me particularly, with my background in Celtic history, it was an origin story – a great epic story of a people in search of a destiny, trying to fulfill a destiny, and a home. All of those things could have picked up from the point we left it at episode 24.'

Nick Tate recalls the period following Year One: 'Most times when you're [making] shows, they're already on the air and you're getting a lot of feedback, so you know what the audience wants. When we were making *Space: 1999*, we were nearly finished the first series before one episode was shown anywhere, which is an extraordinary thing to do. We were very slow in making them, [and in cases like that] producers have to be very careful about when they start airing. We didn't know how audiences were going to like the show, what characters were going to be popular and if we were going in the right direction. It turned out in the end that I think ultimately the first series concepts were the right ones and they should have stuck with them. Maybe they could have Americanised it more … It did tend to be very English, and I think that stood, to a certain extent, to its disservice. When we finished the first series, there was a lot of talk about us going straight into the second series. We finished in March 1975, but nobody knew when we might begin again. Most of us thought that the series would go on. We were thinking maybe August. Everybody was kissing each other, saying, "We'll see you in August." Then we didn't hear anything. Everybody said, "It's canned. It's not going to happen."

'They told us it was the largest syndicated show in the world, and indeed it was. It was groundbreaking. But, because it didn't get to be seen until September 1975, ITC was not prepared to go ahead with a second series. So we were all let go. We all went to various parts of the world. I went to Australia to do a film called *The Devil's Playground*, which was a very beautiful film. Then I came back and did another thing for Gerry Anderson: *Into Infinity* or *The Day After Tomorrow* – I don't think anybody could make up their mind what it was gong to be called, so they called it both those names. It was something Gerry did between *Space: 1999* seasons, because I don't think he knew if ITC was going ahead with another series of *Space: 1999*. Nobody knew.

'So now we're talking about September or October. I had actually turned down other work in Australia that I was offered. I had said, "No, I'm going back to England to do the second series of *Space: 1999*," which didn't happen [at that time]. Normally the hiatus is three or four months. So round about October or November, I was convinced that it wasn't going to happen... I did a lot of other things – got some work in the theatre, met my wife – and then I started to hear that *Space: 1999* was happening...'

In late October 1975, ITC New York finally indicated to Anderson that they would supply financing for a second season, provided an American head writer be brought in to redesign the show for the American market, with the hope a network deal might result. Anderson flew to Los Angeles to interview candidates for the position, continually reporting his progress to Abe Mandell in New York. Anderson selected Fred Freiberger, whose past series work had included *The Wild, Wild West* and, most significantly in this instance, *Star Trek*. An impressed Anderson hired Freiberger despite Mandell's concerns as to why he was available and not currently employed.

Freiberger later recalled how he came to join the series: 'Gerry Anderson came to Los Angeles, I guess around the end of 1975, and he was interviewing people for the story editor position on the show. I got the job as story editor. When I got to London, I didn't know if it was going to be a guaranteed year there – [or, more so,] if there was any [certainty] that there would be a continuation of the show. After three weeks, we got word that the show was cancelled. Lew Grade told us. So after about our third week there, we started to pack to go home. Now, I don't know if it was Gerry or I – the situation is a little hazy [in my recollection] – but either Gerry suggested to me, or I suggested to him, to do a critique of the show. To do something to see if we couldn't change Lew Grade's mind. I did a critique. One of Gerry's points in bringing me over, in bringing an American over, was kind of to create something that would appeal to American audiences, because that's where the money actually is in the business. So I did a critique. In my critique, I said that the show needed more youth. It needed work in order for *Space: 1999* to be picked up. And it needed more than just band-aids on what was there ...

'I came up with this new character called Maya. We sent that on to Lew Grade, and I'm convinced it was the character of Maya that made the second year possible. One of the reasons I was able to come up with Maya was part of my science fiction background. I'd worked for three years with Hanna-Barbera on their Saturday morning shows. Working in kids' television sparks your imagination; you can do some wild things. Nobody was thinking "token" anything [with Maya]. *Star Trek* did a lot of morality plays – that wasn't my concern here. I was [aiming] to get a show back on the air again that would get ratings and would be entertaining in the American sense.

'Once the show was picked up, Gerry asked if I would produce it. I had told my wife we'd go to London, I'd work as story editor, I'd work with writers, it would be easy and we would have all the great things England had to offer. When I told my wife I had accepted Gerry's idea for me to be producer – at no increase in salary – she said, "What about the great time we were going to have?" I said, "Well, I have a great rapport with Gerry and I think he needs me. And that's why I did it." She said, "No other reason?" I said, "Maybe I like the challenge, too." So that's the way I got mixed up into it.'

Fred Freiberger was tasked with drastically revising the series format. He flew to England in early November 1975 for four weeks. To prepare Freiberger for his new job, a screening was arranged for him of eight episodes from Year One. While only viewing eight episodes as a basis to judge and transform an entire series was undoubtedly insufficient, time was short. Freiberger came, saw, and – with the apparent blessing of Gerry Anderson – proceeded to change …

FRED FREIBERGER'S ANALYSIS

Excerpts from Fred Freiberger's analysis include:

As per your request, I have viewed eight episodes of *1999* and hereby is my assessment.

The production values are superb … But after your production values … what? Everything goes downhill. The format people are one-dimensional … They motivate nothing in terms of the action. They stand around talking instead of 'doing'. Therefore, the episodes are mild instead of dynamic, driving, searing. The relationships are plastic and meaningless … We, the viewers, have got to care about our format people. We don't give a damn about people we don't know, and we certainly don't know anybody on Moonbase Alpha.

The series fails on the story level in a number of areas. The basic science fiction concepts are usually valid, but the dramatisations of those concepts are poorly executed…

I feel the series has smash potential … but it needs massive shots of adrenaline.

1. Against the backdrop of those marvellous production values we must tell stories of people – thinking, feeling people – about whom we care … So that's our first task. To put meat and bones on our format characters. Give them dimensions, know who they are, learn to love them.

2. We're going to put flavour and charm and above all, humour, into the scripts.

3. We are going to introduce a new character to give the series a charged-up science fiction overlay. This character will be an outer-space alien … She will become the science officer on Moonbase Alpha.

When we inject the above elements into *Space: 1999* … a series with unsurpassed production values, we will have a show that in my opinion should go right through the roof.

So, having viewed eight episodes, Freiberger provided those opinions to both Gerry Anderson and Abe Mandell. Freiberger wanted a more emotional relationship between the Martin Landau and Barbara Bain characters. He wanted human-interest stories with more overt action-adventure, humour and character conflict. In Freiberger's own words, 'I think the show needed more pacing. Gerry had said he wanted something more American with this. I said to Gerry, "I'm only one American. Every American would have a different idea. But these are the things I think are necessary."'

Johnny Byrne was less than pleased with these ideas, as he later explained: 'ITC didn't understand what they had; what they were doing. It seemed to me that if they wanted to make an American series, why didn't they go to America and make it? And not expect us to try to be American – we were not American. We were what we were, and they were getting a hell of a lot more, very cheaply. And yet they still insisted on having all the advantages of working with Americans and paying the kind of wages that you pay a slave. We were doing it because we loved it, not because we were being paid. We were paid peanuts, and we were treated dreadfully. Every script I wrote was turned into a book, and nobody put my name on any of those stories. I certainly didn't get any money. So we had an awful lot to complain about.

'However, had they trusted us to do what we did best, instead of trying to be somewhere in the middle of the Atlantic, where we were going to end up pleasing no-one, I think we would have ended up pleasing a lot more Americans, at the end of the day. I feel a little bit seriously annoyed by the people who were forever being dreadful about the stories, who couldn't make the connection between pace and story [or understand] the trade-offs you have to make. Science fiction is very complicated: you have to explain pretty much everything you see. In a normal contemporary drama you see things and you understand them. In science fiction, you don't. If you're not very careful, you can spend 50 years simply explaining everything, and in the end you have nothing. If they'd trusted us – the best team that was possible in Britain – to turn out a series, they would have had a wonderful series. But who was going to listen to us? And, even, who was going to listen to Gerry Anderson? Gerry was very much on our side.

'In terms of story content, [the show] was still finding its way, but it did express our philosophy that the further we went out into space the more our understanding grew of ourselves and the environment. Freddy arrived and he was a very personable man – I got on very well with him – but it was clear that we were living in two completely different universes as far as stories and the understanding of drama were concerned. To me, it was going to lose that sense of wonder, of people in an expanding universe whose knowledge was only consistent with their Earthly origins – not people who've been out there mucking in and toughing it out with one lot of aliens after another, which usually means galloping around being very sweaty and completely over the top; and, of course, is just deathly boring. It wasn't so much that he was a bringer of wonder as that he was a bringer of the kiss of death to series. The notion of implanting the worst kind of sub-grade American humour into these things was one of Freddy's more disastrous ideas. To introduce crass one-liners of the type that you'd find in the lowest grade of sitcom humour in America wasn't what we were about, but it was what Freddy wanted to impose on the series. Freddy's notions of humour were quite unfunny. In fact, the funniest thing about Freddy Freiberger was the notion that he had of what constituted funny lines and drama: they were so utterly appalling that they were hilariously funny. Unfortunately, that couldn't be communicated to him, because he took it all very seriously.

'Freddy made some real contributions to the second series. There was more pace, there was more sense of immediacy, there was more believability about some of the characterisations, and so on. Because they were written (in the main) by good writers, even though many of the scripts were re-written by Freddy, the stories did come out as acceptable and up to the mark. He was a lovable, warm, generous man. But he should have been kept a million miles away from *Space: 1999*.

'We had been constantly under pressure from responses coming back from America. We would raise the hemlines, drop the necklines, speed the shows up, slow them down, add more characterisation; but if there's more characterisation, there's less pace, and so on. We tried to accommodate these things and still keep on an even keel. But Freddy felt that the whole sort of feeling about it should be changed. My own feeling was that the Main Mission set was too depersonalising, that the costumes were fairly depersonalising and there wasn't enough mix among the actual people we would see on the screen. They all tended to be too youthful, too pretty and too neutral. They needed sort of real flesh and blood. Freddy quite correctly picked up on this, and so some of the major characters left, like Bergman ... and one or two characters were brought in. Morrow left. And Main Mission was demolished and turned into Command Centre, which was meant to make it more claustrophobic ... This was meant to give it more immediacy and, you know, [a feeling of] real people under stress and all of that. Fair enough. It changed the look of it. It turned it, I thought, into more of a kind of *Star Trek* type series. And in the treatment of it, not the best of *Star Trek* – some of the later – because Freddy did do the third season [of that show], and it had many qualities that put it more in the mainstream of science fiction on television. But to me, despite all the faults that I knew about and that Freddy had partially corrected, [*Space: 1999*] had lost something quite important. It had lost its metaphorical way. It had become just another group of people involved in the nuts and bolts of survival, less in the state of their minds and the state of their feelings and their soul, if you like.

'To me, these were people on a kind of odyssey, not only physical progression, but also spiritual progression, and the inner world of *Space: 1999* seemed to have gone by the wayside. The problems became more immediate, more containable. They had more blacks and whites – I mean that dramatically – in characterisation, and issues were solved in an hour ... In many of the [Year One] *Space: 1999* episodes ..., as in life, situations were not always resolved. Certain things we don't understand. Do we need to understand certain things? Is it best to leave them not understood? And it lost that kind of slight feeling, that nice feeling of people more like us, with our kind of weaknesses and limitations, moving out into the great unknown. Now they were Spacemen as opposed to Earthmen. That was something that couldn't be helped, given the situation. It was Freddy's job to change it, to give the Americans what they wanted.

'I had tried to evolve a system whereby I could bring good science fiction book writers, story writers, into the process. When Freddy came, of course, the whole thing went wrong from that point of view. Freddy had a new job to do. It was his job to make it look as different from the first series as possible. You can't blame him for that. It was his job to be answerable to the Americans, and he knew the scene. He had worked on science fiction before, and he'd worked on *Star Trek*. And, while in the early days of *Space: 1999* we would always consciously try to steer this different path from *Star Trek* ... I think some of our best were equal, if not better than, the best of *Star Trek*, in terms of their stories, and we had the beating of it in technical production. And now the stories went into the stuff that was required for the new situation, and my interest simply dropped back to being a scriptwriter.'

Prior to Fred Freiberger's arrival, and without a firm commitment for a second series from ITC, Gerry Anderson had asked writers Johnny Byrne and Donald James to begin work on initial scripts. In September 1975, Byrne wrote one called 'The Biological Soul', which would later be transformed into the transmitted episode 'The Metamorph'. He also wrote one called 'Children of the Gods', of which he was very proud. The latter script no longer exists, but Byrne tells the story of what happened to it:

'When Freddy came in, he read all the old scripts that might have been used. Of course, he had to junk them, because he was starting his new reign, and such were the dictates of that kind of responsibility. And this one, called "Children of the Gods" … Gerry said to me it was the finest story that he'd ever read. I don't know where the script is; I haven't got a rough draft; I haven't got it in first draft. It got caught up in all the shunting about the studios, and that was in the days before word processors, so I don't know where it went. It was written; I think Freddy didn't like it.

'All I have is a very strong remembrance of what it was – everything is clear in my mind. I saw it as the end of a particular season of *Space: 1999*, possibly as the end of the entire series. It's about Moonbase Alpha, bit by bit, starting to disappear off the surface of the Moon. By the end of the hook, it's gone from the Moon. Now when we come back after the titles, we discover that Alpha is on some sort of planet. [We hear the] voices of children: "We are the children," sounds over the intercoms. Then [the Alphans are] in some kind of structure and there are two children. They've got these jewels in their foreheads, and they're incredibly evil. The kids are very indulged. There's an alien with the children, called Mentor, and he appears to indulge everything they do, to even desperate extents, where they start killing people. And these children have the Alphans in their power. They have complete mastery of time and space, and they put Moonbase Alpha personnel through weird time trips. Like Carter comes back, his mind completely cleaned, and believes he's a sort of gladiator from ancient Rome. There's a fight in it between Koenig and Carter …

'We discover later on that they – these children and this alien – have come from a future time, back to where they encounter the Alphans. We discover that these two children are Earth children who've been kidnapped from some future generation. And we discover that the alien, his people and the Earth people are about to make contact. We discover that the people they are about to make contact with in the far future are the descendants of Moonbase Alpha. And that they are testing the essential humanity of the Alphans by allowing these children to grow in a total moral vacuum, with tremendous power at their disposal, to see whether the Alphans can be trusted as people they could live with. The assessment that this alien makes of them will determine whether this meeting of the two species will ever happen or whether the aliens will simply zap the expanding Earth civilisation out of existence. That's the crux of it.

'The judgment is very much against. The children have demonstrated an innate ability to destroy and to really be unworthy of survival … It's an interesting idea that would have suggested that John Koenig's people would find a home, they would succeed, they would expand out – and now their existence right back to the very beginning depends on the actions of these children, because the alien is going to simply annihilate Moonbase Alpha and prevent the whole thing.

'I felt it was a wonderful thing. Mentor has decided that he wants to show Koenig why he has to be destroyed. You say, "But we're not destructive," then look at your offspring. Their essential natures have been allowed to develop with the power to indulge and they are turned naturally to evil. It was a wonderful story … And that, I think, would have been a fitting kind of finale for the season and for the series to go out on, because it would have illustrated their survival. They would have survived, they would have proven their worth through all the trials and tribulations that, as a small community of people, they had somehow managed to survive – not with Captain Kirk's endless resources, but simply on account of their humanity. It is an interesting speculative thought to imagine what became of Moonbase Alpha. "Children of the

Gods" would have pointed to one particular solution, and it was an intriguing one. It was one in keeping with what we had established, I think, and if I have any resentment against Freddy, it is that he didn't allow that story to get made.'

By 24 October 1975, Byrne had completed his third new script, 'The Face of Eden', which would later be filmed as 'The Immunity Syndrome'. As he recalled, '"The Face of Eden" was hacked about unmercifully to make it conform to Freddy's notion – "Above all it's got to have drama – above all it's got to have humour," and all of that kind of rubbish. It eventually appeared as "The Immunity Syndrome" and managed to maintain some of the stuff that I had put in and the kind of story I wanted to tell: one that would link very, very strongly with what we had been doing in the first series – which was probably why Freddy didn't like it. But it took a hell of a lot of arguing, so that's really when I disengaged myself from *Space: 1999*. I got married and came to live up here in Norfolk.'

THE DISAPPEARANCE OF PROFESSOR BERGMAN

The disappearance of Barry Morse's Professor Victor Bergman following Year One of *Space: 1999* has always been a matter of some mystery and dispute amongst fans. Through my long-standing friendship and working relationship with Barry, and in my capacity as co-author of his theatrical memoir, *Remember with Advantages*, I was allowed access to his personal diaries. Located within his diary for 1975, I discovered notes that do – finally – explain his departure. Barry came very close to telling the complete story himself, but there were always a couple of details he altered – as the very title of his autobiography suggests – with the benefit of hindsight.

So, what has been said about this in the past? Gerry Anderson, in his biography, stated that he felt a great loss to *Space: 1999* with 'actor Barry Morse being dropped from the second series.' Incoming series producer Fred Freiberger told the tale like this: 'Barry Morse's agent came in demanding a big raise. Gerry made him a counter-offer. Morse's agent made a bad tactical error, which was sheer insanity for an agent. He said, "No, if it's not going to be that amount, we're finished – we're out." So immediately Gerry said, "Okay, you're out." What an agent should say is, "He's out – except – I have to check with him."'

Barry Morse himself said, 'It was virtually by mutual consent that I dropped out of *Space: 1999* … There were endless discussions – mostly not involving me, but my agent – about whether or not I should return for a second series. One of the things my agent was very resistant about – naturally – was that they proposed for the second series I should be paid rather less than I had been paid for the first series! The outcome was, I didn't go into the second series. I finally went to Gerry and wickedly said, "Look, my dear, I've had a lovely time. I do wish you every kind of luck, but I shall be glad to go away and play with the grown-ups for a while."' Barry also commented on Year Two's new producer by saying, 'I had known Freddy in Hollywood in past times, and he's an admirable fellow. I'm sure he's kind to animals and writes regularly to his mother. But I didn't feel that he was likely to improve the quality of the scripts.'

Barry Morse's assertion that his pay was going to be cut for the second series is corroborated by numerous others involved in the production. Fred Freiberger himself made statements about the limited budget of the second series, noting: 'When we got the go-ahead, Gerry promised Lew Grade that we'd watch the budget and keep the budget down.' Freiberger also said, 'We, at the time, were talking about cutting back somewhere to stay within the budget. There was a big question of the budget. We made several trans-Atlantic calls to Martin Landau and Barbara Bain – would they take a salary cut? They wouldn't take a cut. People assume when you're making an offer that you're lying and that they're in the driver's seat. This show was on the edge for weeks – it looked like we were finished … The budget was always a problem.'

What about the other cast members? Zienia Merton explains, 'Year One I was hired and they thought enough about what my contribution might be that they gave me a contract, which meant that obviously on some episodes I had very little to do and on others I had more. My make-up call was always at 7.30 am, and I remember that one day Clifton and I were back on the motorway going home by 8.55 am. We'd done our bit for that episode; we had just one scene in Main Mission and we'd done it. Fine, this is the way it goes – I'm not a spoiled child and someone's taken away my ball. You can live with that. But I always felt that I was part of a team. There were bigger members, stronger members ... it didn't matter. We all pulled together. Second year came and there had been lots of stories in between. That's the business, that's the world, and there are always rumours.

'When you do a series, successful or not, when they go into a second run, you usually get more money. Mine was cut by half! I wasn't put under contract again; I was hired piecemeal. They said, "If we want you, we'll call you." They would ring the day before and ask if they could have me for half a day, or a day. And that was all the notice I got. Now the awful thing about this was that, because I'd done the first series, within the industry people thought I was still under contract for series two, so I wasn't even considered for other parts. But my problem was not to do with money, it's the respect people have for you .... That is why I walked, because if I'm not under contract, I'm not breaking anything. Eventually I said, "Look, I'm sorry, but if I'm not under contract then you don't want me. You've told me what you think of me – that I'm not worth a contract. So I'm not doing any more." They said, "You can't do that." I said, "Why? I'm not under contract, so why can't I? You treat me as casual labour – I am casual labour – and casual labour's going home!"'

Anton Phillips faced the same problem. 'The money they offered me for series two was actually less than the money they were paying me for series one. I thought, "Hang on. Inflation, and this, and ... they're paying me less? I don't think so."'

Clearly the budget cuts were affecting the entire production – not just negotiations with Barry Morse. But the finances were only a piece of the puzzle – what was happening creatively with Year Two? Johnny Byrne recalled, 'I was going to stay around, and series two was going to be a continuation of everything we had done: an improved continuation, hopefully. Then suddenly Gerry started to talk of an American producer coming over. Then I heard a tape of Freddy where he viewed some things and made some devastating comments about them.' Byrne also stated, 'Freddy was coming in on the basis that the first series hadn't worked, in the sense that it hadn't got the coveted network deal in America – and in England, too. This probably had more to do with politics at a high level in the television industry than anything else. Fred Freiberger, it must be said, was a man who was charged to either make this series shape up or ship out.'

So what did Fred Freiberger think about the series? 'My feeling about Year One was that having elderly gentlemen in the big set that looked like a living room was not very dramatic. I had talked to Gerry about that. My idea was to re-do it in a more dynamic setting. In terms of character, our Professor should have been 23 years old with a beard ...' Freiberger also stated, 'In my critique, I said that the show needed more youth.' Freiberger held also a universally negative view of the first season characters: 'There was nobody you cared about in the show – nobody at all. The people themselves didn't care about each other.'

Charged with revolutionising the series, Freiberger was granted considerable power under his title of Producer. Nick Tate explains, 'Fred Freiberger was the new partner and he was insistent that everything was going to be done his way; that Gerry didn't understand and should stick with the technicalities of the show – the models and the technical science fiction side of it. Freddy would control the actors and work with that aspect ... Freddy really did have a huge amount of control. Gerry seemed to have no control at all once Freddy came on. It was like his hands were tied. I don't know if he could have been stronger and stood up and said, "You're taking this in a direction that we never intended going ..." Both Gerry and Sylvia Anderson had conceived the show's original concept; when they broke up, it really destroyed much of what had been established during the first series. It seemed as if Gerry was prepared to allow somebody else to come in and totally change the humanity Sylvia had brought to the programme ... We weren't able to spend either money or time on the original concepts.' Actor Tony Anholt, a new arrival to the series with the second season, agreed: 'We all kept saying things and, indeed, we would try to change dialogue or add bits or subtract bits, provided we didn't overstep the mark. Ultimately Freddy Freiberger, more than Gerry, seemed to be the one who said "Yea" or "Nay" ... Gerry tended to be more background – he took a backseat, or appeared to take a backseat.' Zienia Merton had the same perception: 'Gerry was there, but Freddy was very much in charge.'

While Freiberger was completely responsible for the erasing of their characters from the series, he denied accountability for the actors not being hired again: 'In terms of when the show was picked up, all the actors and directors ... well, it's not my area of expertise. I don't make the deals. I had an idea of what Marty and Barbara got [under their contracts].'

What happened to those Year One actors who didn't appear in Year Two? Prentis Hancock explains, 'I wasn't informed that I wasn't going to be involved in the second series. Why should I be informed? You hire a plumber, he does a job; next time you hire a different plumber, do you inform the first plumber he's not going to come back?' Quite simply – they weren't informed that they were fired; they just weren't re-hired.

When Nick Tate returned for the second year, he was shocked by the missing characters: 'How can you make a series with all these characters in it and you come back for the next year and they've all vanished? They didn't even want to say where they'd all gone. I was introduced to Fred Freiberger and I said, "Can you explain to me where all these characters have gone?" He said to me, "Oh, there's a lot of people on the base. They've just gone; they're there somewhere." Fred Freiberger did not have any respect for audience knowledge, for audience memory. He said, "They'll forget." I said, "But they were characters that were loved." He said, "I didn't see any." He didn't ask me who – he was clever. He just said, "I've seen the show. Those characters are all expendable. We've got to get young, vibrant, meaningful characters."'

Among the actors who did return for the second series, certain perceptions are common. Zienia Merton has said, 'Freddy really didn't want me: I know for a fact he wanted someone younger and prettier – I'm not a classical beauty – and he just treated me appallingly. I have to say, I wasn't victimised – it wasn't victimisation of any sort. Freddy was a businessman and he went through and said, "Like her, don't like her, like him, don't like this ..." He did his sums. Practically half the cast had gone – it was a shock. Who would have thought that Barry would not be there? It was devastating.' Nick Tate had a similar feeling: 'I know that Fred didn't like me. He couldn't have liked me; if he'd liked me, he'd have brought me in from the beginning [of series two]. He didn't want me there.'

The facts continue to add up: Fred Freiberger didn't like the Year One cast of characters, and with the exception of Martin Landau and Barbara Bain didn't want any of them to return for the second season, and he specifically felt that Barry Morse's Professor Victor Bergman was too old for an action-adventure science fiction series. Those who did return for Year Two had a clear perception that they weren't wanted.

And what about Barry Morse – were any of his co-stars aware he wouldn't be returning? Martin Landau has stated, 'Gerry and Sylvia Anderson split up towards the end of the first season. That led the way for Freddy Freiberger. New York felt we needed a more Americanised show, which I felt was absolutely wrong! I was also not in favour of [the introduction of] an alien – I was in favour of Barry coming back, and right to the end I was fighting … I was still lobbying for Barry … I fought like a tiger.'

What was Gerry Anderson's involvement? While it is widely acknowledged that he made a significant contribution in script development during Year One, his other input remains more elusive, as Anton Phillips explains: 'I can't actually remember speaking to Gerry in the 16 months working on the series. I'm sure I must have, but I can't remember ever speaking to [him]. Sylvia I spoke to an awful lot, because she was always there and she was always open. She welcomed people. I think she genuinely liked the people that were there and enjoyed their company. So perhaps it was just easier to speak to Sylvia, and when you would pass by her office, just pop in and say, "Hi, how are you today?" and just chat about anything. Whereas Gerry, I think, was always a little bit more aloof in that respect. My dealings with Gerry were on no level whatsoever.' Long-time collaborator on numerous Anderson productions, production designer Keith Wilson, said: 'It was actually Sylvia. Sylvia was the driving force creatively. Gerry wasn't. I mean, he had ideas, but he didn't create literally. Sylvia did … She had the most creative vision of the two. Gerry was very good with the ideas, but that's where it stopped.' In addition, Barry Morse himself said: 'We were all working so hard and we had learned that we weren't going to get much of what you might call "creative inspiration" from dear Gerry Anderson. But I didn't have all that much to do with him. We weren't in any sense the closest of friends.'

With these facts established, it is time to state – once and for all – what really happened, as documented by Barry Morse in his diary. First, a couple of notes: Barry wrote his diaries in point-form, and often used abbreviations. Thus, in referring to himself, he would note 'B.M.', and in a similar manner, Gerry Anderson is referred to as 'G.A.', and Barry's then-agent, Michael Whitehall, is referred to as 'M.W.' Lesley de Pettitt, mentioned in the diary, was the casting director for *Space: 1999* Year Two. Capitalisation, punctuation, spacing etc of the entries, are as Barry wrote them.

Thursday 4 December 1975:
Lesley Pettitt makes offer re B.M. Space: 1999 to Michael Whitehall.
-Derisory
(Equivalent of 33% plus <u>CUT</u> – AND No Transport!)

Friday 5 December 1975:
M. Whitehall presents counter proposal to L. Pettitt

Wednesday 10 December 1975:
Lesley Pettitt to M. Whitehall –
Won't improve 'Space' offer.
– Stalemate – 4 pm.

Thursday 11 December 1975:
11:30 am.
B.M. called G. Anderson.

G.A. to 'call B.M. back.'

Friday 12 December 1975:
No call from Gerry Anderson.

Monday 15 December 1975:
11:30 am.
45 min phone talk with Lesley Pettitt.
'G.A. will call B.M. back.'

Tuesday 16 December 1975:
No call from Gerry Anderson.

Wednesday 17 December 1975:
4:30 pm.
M.W. calls G.A. to accept original offer.
'Other plans made.'
<u>Space: 1999 all over!</u>

So there it is – in indisputable notes that Barry Morse wrote in his diary. The offer he received for Year Two was equivalent to more than a 33% cut to his pay, and in addition he was not being offered any transport to or from Pinewood Studios, as he had received during Year One. In his own words, this offer was derisory. Morse's agent made a counter-proposal the following day, but then waited five days for the reply that the offer would not be improved upon. Barry then took it upon himself to try to contact Gerry Anderson and was twice promised that Anderson would call him back … but Anderson didn't, as is so poignantly noted in the diaries. With all dealings going through Lesley de Pettitt, and no contact from Anderson, Barry made a decision and on 17 December instructed his agent to call Anderson to accept the original offer – pay decrease and all. Sadly, the response was that Barry's services were no longer required: other plans had been made.

What it comes down to is that Barry Morse *did* want to return to the series, despite whatever reservations he had about the quality of the scripts in the first year. He even went so far as to accept, eventually, the huge pay decrease being offered him – but it was in vain. Clearly, his participation was not desired, as has been acknowledged by Fred Freiberger: 'We had big discussions about how to explain the disappearance of Professor Bergman, that he had a disease or something … Barry Morse is an excellent actor, but I felt his part was all wrong … I have great respect for Marty and Barbara, but I think science fiction should have young faces.' It can be easily concluded that Freiberger never really intended for Barry Morse to return to the series. Was the original offer of the pay decrease a ploy to string him along long enough for them to come up with the statement, 'Other plans made'? Anderson certainly shrank from his ample opportunities to speak with Morse personally. Additionally, it must be noted that production on Year Two did not begin until 26 January 1976 – well over a month after Morse attempted to accept the original offer presented to him. If there had been any desire on the part of the producers to return Morse to the cast, there was plenty of time to do it in, and to add his character into whatever scripts were being formulated. But it didn't happen.

So, Professor Bergman's presence was lost, and his character was never mentioned again in the series. Fred Freiberger proclaimed: 'Gerry was in charge of physical production. He was Executive Producer on the show. Nothing could go by unless it was okayed by him. But if people thought there was an error … that we didn't explain the characters, that's my fault. Like with the Tony Anholt character, or Barry Morse … I just felt that it wasn't necessary at the time to explain the changes … It's best if you don't start explaining things. Generally in a show you don't want to explain – it seems heavy-handed.'

What Freiberger misjudged the most was the popularity of Morse and his character: in all the years since the series was produced, Bergman has proven to be *the* single most popular character in either year of the programme. The loss of Morse was widely felt by viewers and by those who had worked with him. Martin Landau has said: '[Barry] was wonderful … He was always prepared, completely professional and always very good. He was a joy to work with. Barry was always there for you when you needed a friend, and I value the time we spent together … I was very sad when Barry didn't return to the series in its second, and final, season. Barbara and I fought to get Barry back on the show to no avail … The series was never as good without his character, Victor Bergman. He lent a large chunk of class to the series, and we missed his presence on the set immensely, not to mention on the screen.' Zienia Merton has said: 'Barry Morse was smashing and I thought it was a pity he wasn't with us for the second season, because he was a very good balance for us.' Johnny Byrne commented about Morse, and about the tone of Year One in general: 'The particular cleverness of Barry Morse's portrayal of Bergman was that when he said, "I don't know," what he was really saying was, "I might know, but I'm not telling you" … I could watch Prentis and Barry Morse and Martin Landau talking forever while they're waiting for the black hole to swallow them up. It doesn't matter that it's slow and people are not running around and bashing each other on the head. It's important that they're in that situation, they're sharing something warm and human, and they're also discussing interesting philosophical thoughts, as they occur.'

It can now be easily suggested that a degree of Morse's subsequent criticism of *Space: 1999* resulted from the disrespectful way he was treated by the show's producers, which coloured his recollections of the show. In later years, he reflected: 'I have been delighted to learn that Martin fought "like a tiger" for me to come back to the show. I wasn't aware of that at the time, but I can imagine it was the kind of friendly thing he would have done, and I'm very grateful to hear it. It's always amused me that I disappeared without any trace. People used to ask me, and still do sometimes, "Whatever happened to Victor Bergman? Why did he suddenly disappear?" and I'd say, "Well, I guess he fell off the back of the Moon."'

It was a joke that Morse enjoyed repeating, but there was an edge of truth to it, and it would be more accurate now to say that Professor Bergman was *pushed* off the back of the Moon – by Gerry Anderson and Fred Freiberger.

YEAR TWO

THE *SPACE: 1999* NETWORK

Movie industry news source *Screen International* reported on 22 November 1975 that Year One of *Space: 1999* was an international success. This was followed on 15 December 1975 by a press report from ITC that stated, 'Sir Lew Grade announced that due to the extraordinary success of *Space: 1999* in the United States and the rest of the world, we have decided to make another series of 24 one-hour episodes. The production will commence at Pinewood Studios in the middle of January 1976.'

ITC advertised in *Variety* on 28 January 1976: 'Within 24 hours after the announcement of second year production, stations representing 42% of US TV homes renewed ... Within the same 24 hour period, 69 countries renewed, including Canada's CBC network.'

Abe Mandell stated, 'The world-wide acclaim and popularity that characterised the first year of *Space: 1999* provides an inspiring platform for the second year. We will build on the success of *Space: 1999* ... Fast action will be the keynote, human emotion the propelling force and life-or-death suspense the theme in our sci-fi hours ... In 27 years in the entertainment business, I have never been as enthusiastic as I am about the second year of *Space: 1999* ... We are riding the crest of a huge wave of popularity throughout the world of science fiction ... We are on top of this crest with the only *new* science fiction series ... The world is going wild for sci-fi.'

ITC's self-branded '*Space: 1999* Network' issued its own 'Network News' publication, serving to promote the series to its affiliate stations in the US. Indeed, the second issue began with the statement, 'Welcome to new affiliates of the *Space: 1999* Network! The *Space: 1999* Network has been formed by ITC to better service those stations telecasting the only new sci-fi series. The Newsletter will keep you abreast of advertising, promotion and publicity plans by ITC and stations across the [US] telecasting the spectacular sci-fi series of the 1970s.'

One story of note, excerpted from the *Space: 1999* 'Network News', Issue 2: 'The Bicentennial Time Capsule in Kauai, Hawaii was spotlighted by ITC's contribution of the video cassette recording of the first episode of *Space: 1999* ... In his letter to the people of Kauai, to be opened in the Tri-centennial year of 2076, Abe Mandell, president of ITC, said, "Our objective was to entertain television audiences throughout the world with exciting adventures in space. Based on the widespread acceptance of the series, we feel we accomplished that and, as an added benefit, hope that we helped stimulate interest in space exploration, an exciting endeavour we trust has continued and pray will continue for many, many years."'

PERSONNEL

Changes to the regular cast were radical. Freiberger felt no connection to the characters he saw in the first season episodes and intended to replace all of them – apart from those of stars Martin Landau and Barbara Bain. He later recalled his impressions of Bain and Landau: 'When I had spoken on the phone to Barbara [Bain], whom I had never met, she was charming and delightful. I tried to give her more to do. I tried to give her character some sense of humour, because she's a natural in social situations. She's sharp; she knows story and character very well. Marty Landau was a delight, an excellent actor and fun on the set ... He tells beautiful stories.'

Gone were Prentis Hancock, Clifton Jones, Suzanne Roquette and, most significantly, Barry Morse, whose negotiations to return to the series had come to an unfortunate end on 17 December. Morse later noted: 'I've seen only odd snippets of shows done in the second series. I'm not a devoted TV watcher in any event, but I certainly didn't want to be taking up a lot of time watching what they were doing after I left. From what I've seen from the few glimpses I have had, the storylines got even more extravagant and wild. Whether the fans are merely being polite to me or not, the impression I get is that quite substantially the first series is regarded as being better than the second series. Well, as you know, I had my reservations about the first series, so I don't know what that says about the second! I do know that Martin and Barbara and I – having formed a very close and loving professional association during the shooting of the first series – were all rather regretful I was not going to be with them for the second series.'

Prentis Hancock also reflects on his departure from the series: 'Ultimately, I think, I was disappointed. At the time, no: I was quite surprised. It would have been nice to be informed. But, he who pays the piper calls the tune. The producers hired me, and I did the series. I was then free and at liberty to do anything else I liked, and I did. I learned that the series was going again, but it was a very strange season, and it had problems. I think a few years down the line I looked back and I was rather disappointed. It had meant more to me than I realised ... For me to weave a fantasy about how life might have been if I had done series two is nonsense ... It's a shame, I think. There was probably more to be made with that series. In some ways it was a '60s series, in the '70s. The world had changed ... But you cannot control things. Many series go down the drain that you think would have been lovely, and others, well ... and they seem to be successful. I don't think we can control anything in life.

'I was disappointed with the way series two went. I knew all about the budgetary stuff, and what have you. I wasn't asked to join series two, so I got on with my life as an actor. But I heard funny stories, and I got the odd message saying, "You're probably better off where you are." So that was quite rewarding for me in one sense, but I kept an eye out on the people who were involved...

'Paul Morrow wouldn't have fit into series two, and from what I hear Zienia tell me, I wouldn't have fit into series two, because I wouldn't have been there on those terms. In the first series, everybody made me very welcome. We were joined by Nick, Zienia, Clifton and Anton, and we did form a team. There were the stars up there on the top shelf, and then there was us. We gave the whole thing backbone and we were there all the time ... Paul Morrow [must have been] killed, or atomised, or whatever happened ... Actually, I think he went on holiday. He went with Victor Bergman and took up guitar playing, or chess manoeuvres. Perhaps he thought he'd join *The Hitchhiker's Guide* and see how it went. I think Paul wouldn't have coped with series two and would have had a nervous breakdown.'

By 22 December 1975, Johnny Byrne's script 'The Biological Soul' (originally written for the Year One format and cast) had been revised as 'The Biological Computer' and introduced for the first time the character of Maya, who – as portrayed by Catherine

Schell – eventually became one of the most memorable and defining aspects of *Space: 1999*. An emotional alien from the planet Psychon, capable of molecular transformation, she could become any living thing at will: monster, person, plant or animal. Freiberger created the character and envisioned her as Moonbase Alpha's science officer. The usage of 'Maya' as a moniker for a metamorph has been interpreted by fans in many ways over the years; one of the most significant meanings is that 'Maya' is the Sanskrit word for 'illusion'.

Fred Freiberger stated: 'We went after Teresa Graves for Maya. We wanted her but we heard she was deep into religion and had gone into retreat somewhere – had left acting. The original Maya was to have been a black girl. We did test a lot of black girls in England. Abe Mandell recommended Catherine Schell; we looked at the *Return of the Pink Panther* film she was in and were quite impressed. The character of Maya was a tough concept to sell to the British writers, but for some reason, easier to sell to the Americans. I knew that science fiction fans would accept this character if we did it right.'

Catherine Schell said: 'I know they had a tremendous problem casting Maya. It was all very strange. I was visiting some friends and I had lunch at their house that day. I hadn't worked for some time and I was a little bit desperate, and the friend's husband told me, "Don't worry about it Catherine. When you get home there will be a telephone call and you will get a wonderful job." I said to him, "But Gerald, it's Sunday. Agents don't work on Sunday." When I got home, the phone rang. It was Gerry Anderson. He said, "Excuse me for ringing you up personally, but we have a huge problem. We're desperate to cast this part in *Space: 1999* as a regular, and I'd love to see you and talk about it. Can I send my chauffer-driven Rolls Royce to come and pick you up?" I said, "But of course." I drove out and we had a long chat at his house, and he offered me the part. That's when Gerry actually said, "We are doing another series. We are introducing another character, and we would be very interested if you would play that character, and it's the character of an alien." The only alien that I'd seen up until then was Mr Spock, with the long ears. I said, "No ears!" It just sort of developed from there.' Schell also recalled actor Barry Morse from their time working together on *The Adventurer*: 'We got on very well. He's a nice man, and it was sad he wasn't in Year Two.'

Schell has also stated: 'Barbara was very much against my taking the part [of Maya], because we are very similar. Obviously, I'm younger than she is, but as types, we are similar. She was looking for an Asian girl or an African girl, someone who could really never be confused with her, so that these two women were completely alien to each other. But the production side wanted me to do this and so, obviously, I was going to have to look incredibly different.'

When it came to designing the look for Maya, Schell says: 'I did a sketch [of Maya]. The finished version of the make-up still has a lot of the ideas that were in that original sketch – the colouring was very much the same, the peak on my forehead, and the bit around my cheeks. The sketch was actually more pronounced. I was also willing to wear a white curly wig. The whole thing was sort of raccoon-like, with a mixture of dark and light. If you look at my first episode, "The Metamorph", you can see that my ears are brown. However, when they saw the finished episode they decided to drop that idea, because the Americans said that it looked as though my ears were dirty. They gave me the dark hair, which was to make me look more human, I suppose. It was the designer's idea to give me those octopus-type eyebrows, which he actually wanted to put all over my face. We did one screen test with these – we called them octopods – in various patterns on my cheeks and on my forehead. I said, "Well, if you want to make acne popular, we can begin here." It was really the most ridiculous idea ever. So we compromised and only the eyebrows were done.

'In the picture I drew, I had very short hair – like fuzz that I would have on my head. It was a thing of doing animals – different animals, different pigmentations and looking almost like a badger or a panda. That was in my mind, to do something like that. In the drawing, I even did a little whisker, and my neck was completely dark. Oh, very important – stars in my eyes. The pupils were stars, and I lived through a whole month of trying to piggyback contact lenses: soft lenses and hard lenses on top, with the stars. My eyes could never take it. The moment light would shine in, my eyes would water. So that's why that particular thing didn't happen. Then we did tests with Keith, and Keith had me as peacocks, multi-coloured, and all sorts of other things.'

Keith Wilson also recalled this period: 'Catherine was brought in to do the second series, and we spent a period of time working together. We built a little stage within the stage, had a video camera set up, and lights, and we would – just the two of us – just play, basically. I would come up with new ideas, Catherine would have an idea, and we'd get the make-up people in. And we just played for about two weeks. We had to send the videos to America, for Abe Mandell and the people at ITC to approve before the actual character was sort of agreed upon. It took about two weeks. Catherine would have an idea and she'd go off and I'd do something else for an hour or two, and she'd come back and have different make-up on. We'd film it and then she'd go off and do another thing. One particular time she stood there and said, "Are you ready?" I said, "Yes." I turned the camera on, she smiled, and she had blackened out her front teeth!'

Anton Phillips would return for the first two episodes of Year Two, until he would also choose to depart Moonbase Alpha. Zienia Merton would appear in more Year Two episodes, though she was also replaced by two different substitutes. Merton stated: 'I was told quite some time before that I would be in series two. But when I got to series two, the first thing Freddy [Freiberger] did was change my character's name to Sahn. He called me into his office – like I was a child – and he said, "I'm changing your name to Sahn." I said, "Why? Sandra isn't a difficult name." I think, in retrospect, it was Freddy trying to prove his power.

'Freddy had bottles of champagne waiting for us when we arrived, so I wasn't made to sit in a dungeon. I was given a dressing room, now and again. I'm not joking. Then they put me into a short skirt. Well, I do trousers or long skirts. I have friends who have never seen my legs. But they put me into this skirt and I didn't like it.'

Nick Tate managed to return and eventually appeared in 18 second season episodes – despite early efforts to remove his character as well, until ITC and Fred Freiberger realised the great popularity of the Australian Eagle pilot amongst fans. He was to have been dropped and replaced initially by a character called Gary Wolusky, who then went through a name change to become Mark Macinlock, before Nick Tate was invited back at the end of the first week of January 1976, to reprise the familiar role of Alan Carter. The Year One cast members who did return did so at the last minute, after Freiberger apparently realised the benefit of a couple more familiar faces being around on Moonbase Alpha, or learned of a character's popularity (as in the case of Tate specifically). As Tate recalled: 'I called my agent and said, "People are asking me if I'm going back into the series?" I was told that they were casting it again. How could this be? So I called Prentis, I called Zienia and I called Clifton – none of us had heard a word. Then some people started hearing that it was happening, but we weren't going back. Barry wasn't around, so I couldn't ask him. Martin and Barbara weren't around – they were back in the States – so I couldn't ask them. I didn't know whether it was real or not. I asked my agent to contact Gerry Anderson at Pinewood Studios and learned that they were indeed doing another series, but sorry – they didn't want to have anything to do with the actors from the first series. This was now going to be very controlled by America and they were bringing in a new Producer, called Fred Freiberger, and he had his own ideas about what he was going to do with the series. And so we all just had to eat it. Freddy didn't have a very high opinion of the first series at all and wanted to change everything. He decided to get rid of everyone on the show, apart from Martin and Barbara. So they recast the show and brought in a stack of new people.

'Early in January, I think it was 6 January, Gerry Anderson called my agent and said he wanted to meet with me. I couldn't work out why – I knew by this stage he must have had the thing cast. So I went down and met him. All the crew were there – I knew all the crew. I walked in and saw all the sets being built and changes being made. I saw Catherine Schell walking around – I didn't know her, but I could see that people were getting ready for tests and stuff. Gerry brought me into his office and said, "As you can see, we're getting ready for the new series." He said, "I've got some good news for you. They would like you to be back in the series." I said, "How is this possible, Gerry?" I looked at a script he showed me, and I could see my character wasn't in it, Prentis's wasn't there, Barry's wasn't there, and I couldn't believe that this was going ahead.

'The things that Fred said were logical and real and intelligent. We were dealing with a guy who really understood how to make television. But he didn't understand the show that we had. That was my argument about it – and a lot of other people felt about the same way – that the kind of show that we had and the direction that Sylvia Anderson had intended to go in [was not suited to what he wanted to do] … [Sylvia] might have been able to pull it off. He was clever and maybe would have been able to help her pull it off, but when he came onto the show, Gerry and Sylvia Anderson had been through an unfortunate break-up of their marriage and she was out. Sylvia was a wonderful woman and a wonderful producer. She was great fun and a rather clever actress. She understood the process greatly, and I think her instincts were very good. Her absence didn't help the show at all.'

'I was lucky to have even been invited back to the series and I was in a very tenuous situation, but he made certain promises to me about what would happen. I could tell straight off that I was dealing with somebody who was a manipulator. I therefore didn't sign a contract. I said, "I'll just come in and see what happens. You've got nine scripts written – seven done and two others [already] in production – and I'm not in any of them. You're just going to have me walk in and say, "Hi guys, I'm here."' I felt certain that they just wanted me back as window dressing. They had invited Zienia back, as well. I think there were also a couple of other very peripheral characters that had been around in the background before – one of them was [played by] Sarah Bullen. Freddy had to understand that if you had these people who were constantly in Moonbase Alpha in Command Centre, then you had to have some of the original people back, just to make it look like the same show. Even if you didn't like them. And I'm sure that was the situation with my hiring. Fred told me something very strange. He said, "You know the reason I'm asking you back in the show?" I said, "No, Fred, what's the reason you're asking me back?" He said, "My kids love you. My kids love the show and I went to them and asked who I should have back. They said I've got to have Nick Tate." What an extraordinary thing for him to say! Didn't he speak to his kids in all the weeks leading up to when we were going to start, or did he only have that conversation with them the day before? He was a very strange piece of work.'

The virtual slaughter of the Year One characters took place in the background and was not addressed in any regard in the episodes of Year Two. It was as if Victor, Paul, Kano and Tanya had never existed. And then, as Mathias vanished, Sandra was replaced on occasion and Nick Tate didn't appear in six of the new episodes, the programme ran the serious risk of alienating past viewers who might tune in and recognise no-one beyond Martin Landau and Barbara Bain. Landau recalled: 'We were testing black actresses like crazy. I was still lobbying for Barry. Right up until about three days before, there was a black actress going to play the part [of Maya]. She was terrible! She couldn't say three words in a row and chew gum at the same time – it was unbelievable! But I loved Catherine! In fact, when we did "Guardian of Piri", Catherine and I had enjoyed our time together. She's a delight. But I thought it was "Spock", you know? We had a magic person suddenly, and that wasn't what the show was. It was basically … again, you win some and you lose some. We lost some, but I've got to say, she was reality. Once you accepted the fact, there was never any reluctance. Nick wasn't receptive with the addition of Tony, and Nick got short-changed in the second season. Prentis certainly got short-changed. Clifton went by the wayside. But I think the first season was a superior season. Some people don't. I've talked to some people and they like the second season better …'

The loss of Professor Bergman was mentioned in Johnny Byrne's script 'The Metamorph', and Zienia Merton recalls filming the sequence, although the scene never made it to the final edit of the episode. The dialogue in question was to have come in Scene 146:

> **Simon** [later Tony Verdeschi]: 'I wish Bergman was here.'
> **Sandra** [nods]: 'But he isn't.'
> **Simon**: 'One lousy space suit with a faulty helmet and Victor had to be in it.'
> **Sandra** [gently]: 'We can't bring him back, Simon.'

A new crop of faces appeared. Apart from Catherine Schell, Tony Anholt joined the cast as Tony Verdeschi (originally called Simon Hays), a hot-blooded Italian in charge of Moonbase security. Anholt said: 'I got a phone call at home out of the blue from Gerry Anderson who said, "Have you seen *Space: 1999*?" I think I had seen one episode of it and, to be perfectly honest, had thought, "What a load of rubbish." I said, "No, I don't think I have. Why?" He said, "Well, we did a year of it and it was sort of shelved, and now we think we're going again with the second year. Freddy Freiberger is coming over to give it a slightly new feel and Abe Mandell," who is ITC New York, "wants you in it. Lew Grade wants you in it. I would be very happy to have you in it. Would you be interested?" The deal was set up and it all seemed favourable, so to the end of the following January I found myself in one of those outfits, as what I think was billed as "The Most Dynamic Explorer in the Universe" or something!'

John Hug took on the semi-regular role of Eagle pilot Bill Fraser. Fraser had a wife, Annette, who was introduced as a new supporting character in 'The Metamorph', portrayed by Anouska Hempel –,but she was promptly dropped and never heard from again! Jeffrey Kissoon played Dr Ben Vincent, replacing Dr Mathias … that is, until Dr Vincent vanished and was himself replaced by Dr Ed Spencer, played by Sam Dastor.

And then there was 'The Mark of Archanon', in which Dr Vincent is missing, replaced by Raul Newney as Dr Raul Nunez, who appears in only this one episode. Sandra's replacements would be Yasuko Nagazumi as Yasko Nugami and Alibe Parsons as Alibe. Also featured in several episodes was the character Petrov (originally called Jameson), stationed in Weapons Section, portrayed by Peter Porteous (husband of costume designer Emma Porteous). Confused? The producers didn't think the audience would notice.

Fred Freiberger made the following comments regarding the cast changes: 'We thought if we were going to drop a main character, we would drop Nick Tate, and then I reconsidered. I thought, "No, this guy's brilliant. He's a real asset to the show." So every time you want to cut something you can find it's an asset ... But we started the second season and we had Tony Anholt there ... We didn't have to explain Tony Anholt. He was just there – the characterisation, if it's done well, will explain in the action what's going on. When I first got to the show I got a call from Barbara, and she had a wonderful sense of humour. I wanted to give her character more of that. We may have discussed putting in explanations as to what happened, but I don't know. I don't remember if we did.'

SETTING

Major set alterations and relocations were implemented. Most significant of all, the vast Main Mission was replaced by the tighter confines of Command Centre. (While prominent signage utilised the American spelling of 'Center' – obviously tailoring the series to the American market as much as possible – smaller labelling also visible on-screen featured the British spelling, as does this book). In general, sets were smaller and more compact, and in an interesting twist, the producers decided to move most of the active areas of Moonbase Alpha into the underground sections of the base. This meant the elimination of the prominently featured windows from the first season. While no explanation was provided for any of these changes, the assumption and common behind-the-scenes explanation is that it was a choice made for the safety of the Alphans – they would be more sheltered from radiation, alien attack and other hazards in underground locations than in surface installations. It was also a stylistic choice prompted by Fred Freiberger, who felt the larger Year One sets were depersonalising and that the smaller scale would assist in his desire to achieve a sense of excitement and urgency. The Eagles shrank as well – in the second season, the Stewardess Section between the command and passenger modules is missing (which is, of course, incongruent with the external model design, which didn't change). Even the travel tubes became smaller and now included only four seats instead of six.

Keith Wilson discusses the design changes: 'I think the biggest mistake in the second series was concentrating everything – concentrating the scale of the sets, particularly. We'd achieved a scale on the first series that was big. On the second series – why, I don't know – they decided it was too big. I wasn't allowed to make the sets as big as I had on the first series. I think we lost a lot by doing that. Everything was concentrated, and I think it was a mistake, because I think it made the show "small".

'It was too claustrophobic. It was like they were living underground, and I didn't like the confinement. The fact of living on the Moon – I felt you could make the buildings as big as you liked. There were no restrictions. But Freddy Freiberger, and the powers that be, didn't feel that was correct. [On the base, however,] that main set was really the only one that suffered. Everything else was pretty much the same – the Eagle, the Travel Tube.

'I loved the scale of the first series. I loved the first shot when we see Main Mission and Koenig swings around in his chair and the wall separates and beyond you have this whole huge set. That's one of my favourite shots in the whole series. I thought we needed that scale; I thought it gave the series size. *Star Trek* didn't have that sort of scale. I can't think of anything else that had that scale. That's why I went for that sort of scale – I wanted it to be spectacular, and in my opinion it was ...

'It got much smaller in the second series ... I was just told to make it smaller. I would do a drawing and say, "This small?" Freddy would say, "Make it smaller," or "That's fine." So he had the last say. On the clothes as well – I hated the uniform for the first series, but I couldn't touch it because it was in Rudi Gernreich's contract that he had to have front credit. All he designed, in fact, was the uniform on the first series. I designed the alien costumes, alien make-up, everything alien. But by the second series his contract had ended, so I was able to do something with the costumes. I didn't want to change them too much, because everyone knew the uniform: it's part of the look of the show. But we gave them jackets and pockets, so they could do things with their hands. Otherwise, they'd just be standing there. It was dreadful. So we put badges on; anything just to get away from that dreadful uniform.'

Fred Freiberger recalled: 'One of the things we were talking about was to lower costs. Gerry mentioned to me to take out the little television screens from the Commlocks, and I said, "Gerry, I wish you wouldn't do that. I think that's such an asset to the show," and so he kept it in.'

MUSIC

The sound of the series was dramatically different as well, due to Year One composer Barry Gray being replaced by Derek Wadsworth, who had provided music for Anderson's pilot *The Day After Tomorrow (Into Infinity)*. While Gray was inclined towards grand orchestral scores, Wadsworth delivered a more action-orientated sound with up-tempo modern beats. While Gray's sound worked superbly within Year One, Wadsworth's distinctive jazz/pop contributions were ideally suited to the style of the second season, and his opening theme remains a favourite of many fans.

Wadsworth created individual scores for five episodes, with the resulting compositions totalling a little more than two hours. His first three scores were for the episodes 'The Metamorph', 'The Exiles' and 'One Moment of Humanity' – quite naturally, as these were the first three episodes filmed for the second season. Subsequent episodes that Wadsworth wrote scores for were 'The Taybor' and 'Space Warp'. The former called for a more light-hearted series of compositions, while the latter required a driving action score. These five episodic scores were re-mixed and re-used by music editor Alan Willis for the remaining 19 episodes of

Year Two. Due to the post-production schedule, the 'Space Warp' score was also used on the preceding episode, 'The Beta Cloud', to which it was also ideally suited.

THE DIRECTORS

As on Year One, directors on Year Two operated on a rotating basis. However, this time they tended to be a bit more transitory, with eight different individuals helming various episodes. They were:

CHARLES CRICHTON, who returned from the first season to helm an additional six episodes, including the Year Two premiere 'The Metamorph', making him the most prolific director of the second season (as he had been for Year One).

RAY AUSTIN, who also returned from Year One and took on directorial duties for an additional two episodes.

BOB BROOKS, who directed two episodes. Brooks had previously been a director of commercials. *Space: 1999* represented his first directorial work on a dramatic production.

TOM CLEGG, who took on five episodes, was a relatively new director at the time, having helmed episodes of *Marked Personal*, *Special Branch* and *Armchair Cinema*.

KEVIN CONNOR, who directed two episodes, had notable experience directing the fantasy films *The Land That Time Forgot* and *At the Earth's Core*, as well as *From Beyond the Grave*.

VAL GUEST, who directed three episodes, had extensive experience as a producer, writer and director of films and television. His film directorial credits included *The Quatermass Xperiment*, *Quatermass 2*, *The Day the Earth Caught Fire*, *The Abominable Snowman* and *When Dinosaurs Rules the Earth*. On television he had directed episodes of *The Persuaders!* and *The Adventurer*.

ROBERT LYNN, who directed two episodes, had extensive experience directing for television, including for such programmes as *Ghost Squad*, *The Saint* and *Captain Scarlet and the Mysterons*. His films had included *Dr Crippen* and *Mozambique*. He also served as assistant director on an additional ten episodes of Year Two.

PETER MEDAK, who directed two episodes, was notable for his credits on *The Strange Report* and *The Persuaders!*, as well as on films such as *The Ruling Class* and *A Day in the Death of Joe Egg*.

CONCEPTS

Episodes in Year Two normally began with a voice-over Status Report by Helena

Russell, introducing the viewer to the happenings on Alpha. This feature, while obviously inspired by the Captain's Log from *Star Trek*, was an addition that worked successfully and appealed to the audience. More significantly, Fred Freiberger completely changed the style and direction of the stories themselves. He was unimpressed by the metaphysical and mysterious aspects of the first season; in their place he wanted clearly explained stories grounded in science fiction and featuring lots of action. He increased the humour quotient in the scripts and altered the philosophy of the series in order to provide what he believed the American market wanted – namely, outwardly warmer (and younger) Alphans who more readily joked with each other. Indeed, the characters did become a more easily likeable group than in the first year. Gone, however, was the vision of the universe as a huge, mysterious place of great grandeur in which the Alphans were a lost and wandering tribe at the mercy of whatever they encountered. Gone too was the Mysterious Unknown Force that had seemed subtly to guide or direct the journey of Alpha in ways and for purposes often left to the imagination. Instead, the stories, characters and motivations became clearer (or occasionally, some would say, transparently shallow).

Keith Wilson offers his thoughts on the thematic side of the series: 'Freddy Freiberger was like a troubleshooter. It was his task to come in and change the show to make it more acceptable for an American audience. The first series, it was unusual that a science fiction show would be so intense. We were dealing with really quite important subjects – disguised subjects, but nevertheless. The second series it became like a comic strip. It lost that wonderful quality.'

The new series was truly tailored to be action-adventure sci-fi, which was Fred Freiberger's conception of what the show should be. In his own words, 'We cut down the whole vast control centre [Main Mission] ... cut down the loss of Eagles. I felt if we were going to use violence of that sort, use it meaningfully. The English, when they did these shows, desperately wanted to reach the American market, since that's where all the money is. And they would interpret "action" literally as action – shooting down a million Eagles ... and doing wild physical things ... instead of dramatic action, conflict. These are tough concepts for them to be able to understand and accept.' Freiberger also shared his thoughts on what he liked in Year One, 'I'd prefer to say the characters, but it was the special effects – they were just amazing. I admired the standard of the work these guys did. My main concern going into Year Two was getting stories. We had a situation with a preparation of ten days and a shoot of ten days. And it was meeting people: I didn't know any of the directors, so Gerry hired the directors; I didn't know any of the writers, so Gerry brought in the writers. I found everybody very eager, very professional and easy to work with.'

Perhaps if Freiberger had viewed more than eight episodes of Year One he would have felt differently about it. However, the responsibility for the changes made in the second series cannot be placed completely on his shoulders ...

THE PRODUCERS

Where was the co-creator of the series, the man credited as Executive Producer – Gerry Anderson? *Space: 1999* was his greatest success – it would be logical to assume that he would have had a great vested interest in controlling as much as possible the direction of the series that so prominently carried his name. For Anderson to have allowed outside influences to revamp drastically a 'Gerry Anderson Production', sitting seemingly quietly in the background even though he himself apparently did not think highly of the changes and scripts being produced (as interviews with him have since clearly shown), seems more than slightly strange. Even accepting that ITC New York was demanding changes be made in order to secure their financial backing, Anderson should surely have been triumphing the strengths of the first season and making sure that they were not overlooked while changes were implemented. He should have ensured that continuity between the two seasons was as strong as possible, and that inconsistencies of a significant nature were explained to viewers.

In recent years, Anderson seems to have had a revisionist view of history, to the point of ignoring any mention of his ex-wife and creative partner, Sylvia. He has also repeatedly claimed credit for aspects of *Space: 1999* in which he appears to have had little direct involvement, and – as shown in the commentary section for 'Breakaway' in this book – has gone so far as to portray himself as being single-handedly responsible for 'rescuing' the pilot episode. While Anderson blames Fred Freiberger and ITC for the ultimately unpopular changes made for Year Two, he has never acknowledged in interviews that he could have done more to stand up for his co-creation. But beyond the responsibilities of any one man (Anderson or Freiberger), ultimately the greatest blame lies with ITC for not having faith in the team producing the series, for not sticking with the original vision, and for ordering the implementation of changes. Anderson himself has said, 'When it came to the next series, they introduced the new member of the cast. They had this bloody silly idea of Maya turning into different creatures. I mean, if we could have done it with morphing, fine, but that wasn't possible at the time. The scripts became very juvenile. For me – I mean, I've met people who prefer the second series – but for me, the first series was infinitely better, and the second series was downgraded and almost "comic-cuts".'

Fred Freiberger was simply a producer hired to do a job. He was a hired gun. He did his job, made decisions he felt were for the best of the series, and is substantially to credit for the fact that there was a Year Two at all. Fans are free to criticise the changes he made, and it is often felt that many of them were misconceived. But he did undeniably do some things well, and to this day many fans love the second season.

Johnny Byrne's reflections on the development of Year Two included: 'It's hard to separate retrospective wisdom now from how I felt *Space: 1999* should develop then. But I always believed that Year One was a testing of the waters for the overall concept, with a result that demonstrated it could intrigue, mystify and entertain. A direct follow on Year Two would have been based on the enhanced awareness of the Alphans to their situation, leading to a greater ability to cope with it, not least philosophically, metaphysically and spiritually. It would also have shown in part a coming to terms with the knowledge that something greater than the random forces of space and time – the MUF, if you like – was an active player in their destiny. If one accepted the epic, mythic potential of the series, which I always did, then the Alphans were in the process of not just surviving and questing for a new home, but also creating their own origin legend. That being said, in some ways Fred returned the show to the basic mechanistic format concept of the Moon blown out of orbit. It was the writers of Year One, initially Chris and I, then others, who read into it the metaphysical and philosophical implications for the Alphans; an Earth in miniature, suddenly and catastrophically plunged down the snake to square one. I'm not sure Fred grasped this aspect of *Space: 1999* and its potential to lend enduring context to stories that would otherwise feature as "what you see is what you get" … The second season had, of course, a basic appeal, because it was more like *Star Trek*, and on that level, it made for easier viewing to a certain extent – but not more pleasurable viewing.

'Whatever the series was that Freddy was destined to enhance, it was not this one, but I pay him the greatest personal tribute, as he was personally very kind to both me and my wife, Sandy, when our first child was born, and we stayed with him and his wife, Shirley. But I have to be honest and say that *Space: 1999* was on a hiding to nothing with Freddy, that the value that he brought to the show was completely offset by the unconscious damage that he was doing to something that had its own universe and had its own journey to travel. It was as if you were to set off in a Concorde and end up in a train somewhere in the back of Outer Mongolia – you just didn't know where the hell you were and where the hell it was going.'

Sylvia Anderson also commented on the second season: 'By the time the second season happened, Gerry and I had separated, and they brought in this American, Fred Freiberger. Personally, trying not to be sour grapes about this, I just thought it became very silly. I looked at it and thought, "Do I really want my name on this?"'

THE PRODUCT

In 1976 Fred Freiberger stated: 'I firmly believe our new concept is far superior to anything other science fiction series have ever had to offer. We are not competing with *Star Trek* or any others, but are setting out with the premise that we must be creative in every respect. One aspect of our new stories is greater depth in the relationships between the characters. We want audiences to live the situations with them. It is important that they are likeable, believable people.' He later recalled: 'If Year One had been picked up [by a network], there would have been no need to make changes. The only reason to do something was to try to rescue the show. If the show was going on, why look for trouble? What was important was to get a second year out of the show. If with the second year, for some reason, we had been wrong and the powers that be had said, "Hey, we'll give you a third year, but go back to Year One style" – fine. Everybody wants to work on a hit show. It's pride that goes with it. One of the comments that has been made to me was that I came over to work on the show to sabotage it: an astounding misperception.

'As regards the direction of the show, when I first became Story Editor I was talking with Gerry about it, mostly in terms of the pacing, and in terms of the design of Moonbase Alpha. All I was thinking as a story editor and as a producer was to do good science fiction stories. You like to have everything: good character, good plot and good original stuff … So that's what I was trying to do. Bring in the character of Maya; give it a fresh kind of a jibe with this very interesting character, which makes it nice. We can get into the most impossible situation in the world, and we can get out. So, basically, I thought the Maya character was a big plus. She was the thing that got us picked up. And she was a lot of fun, that character. I thought Gerry had a great and brilliant idea when he zoomed the camera into her eyeball, where we would see an image to foreshadow what she was about to become.'

While Year One has a unique brilliance, Year Two also has a style, a feel and a look specific to itself. It is an enjoyable product, clearly made under less than ideal circumstances: the show's budget was drastically cut (despite publicity announcements at the time claiming that it was being raised) from the Year One figure of $6,500,000 (or $270,000 per episode). Fred Freiberger stated: 'We brought [the Year Two episodes] in for $185,000 [each], which got them fantastic production values. That $300,000 figure [quoted in the press] was probably just for publicity. No way can you get a show in America for $200,000.' Based on this assertion by Freiberger, the Year Two budget would have been $4,440,000. There are those who dispute Freiberger's statement on this and believe the official ITC numbers, which proclaimed a per-episode budget of $300,000 and a total Year Two budget of $7,200,000. However, even if those higher figures were correct, the inflation rate of 12% to 23% that prevailed over that time period, along with the declining value of the UK pound versus the US dollar, would mean that the trumpeted 11% increase in budget was still actually a decrease in real terms.

While the first season had taken a full 15 months to film, the second season would have a strict schedule imposed by ITC New York of 48 weeks and would end up filming from late January until just before Christmas 1976. In order to maintain the tight schedule, Fred Freiberger implemented a system of what were known as 'double-up' episodes. As the term suggests, this involved the cast and crew filming two episodes simultaneously in just slightly more time than it would take to complete a single show. Cast and crew were literally split in half, and while one show might feature Martin Landau and Catherine Schell and film on location, the other might star Barbara Bain and Nick Tate and film on the studio sets. Double-up filming is not uncommon in film and television production, but it usually involves a first unit and a second unit, rather than two first units. This dubious process of filming two episodes simultaneously with two first units was implemented simply to meet the shorter production time allotted. Because ITC had delayed in renewing the programme, the production was behind schedule from the beginning. The double-up script pairings were as follows:

'The Rules of Luton'/'The Mark of Archanon'
'The AB Chrysalis'/'Catacombs of the Moon'
'Space Warp'/'A Matter of Balance'
'Dorzak'/'Devil's Planet'

Year Two was to open with a voice-over by Commander Koenig. The original wording was to have been as follows:

> September thirteenth, 1999.
> A massive nuclear explosion … Cause – human error.
> The Moon is torn out of Earth orbit and hurled into outer space.
> Doomed to travel forever through hostile galaxies.
> And for the beings on Moonbase Alpha
> One overriding purpose. Survival.

This was reworded in a subsequent draft: 'September thirteenth' was changed to '*Space: 1999*, Moonbase Alpha'; 'galaxies' became 'environments' and the last sentence was removed. Finally, due apparently to difficulties laying Martin Landau's voice-over onto Derek Wadsworth's score, the wording was changed to the on-screen version used throughout the second series:

Moonbase Alpha …
Massive Nuclear Explosion …
Moon torn out of Earth orbit …
Hurled into outer space …
Space: 1999

US SYNDICATION

In the same manner that they had trumpeted complimentary reviews of Year One by station executives from the United States, ITC included a collection of 27 similarly enthusiastic reviews of Year Two in a promotional brochure distributed to American stations in 1976. While obviously ITC wanted to be as positive as possible about the new season, it is surprising and disconcerting to note how many of these reviews featured implicit or explicit criticism of Year One, often from the same stations that had previously raved about it. One thing these reviews serve to re-confirm, though, is that the ratings for Year One were very strong in the US. The comments included:

'*Space: 1999* Year Two is one of the finest productions I've ever seen. Barbara Bain is terrific in her new interpretation of Helena. I think the show now moves twice as fast. Every scene is packed with action.' – Lionel Schaen, VP and General Manager, KHJ-TV Los Angeles

'The new characters work well. Much better than the first season. A lot of care and a lot of dollars have been put into the second season. *Space: 1999* will be with us for a long time.' – Gordon Bussey, Sales Manager, KVAL-TV Eugene Oregon.

'There is much more action and better pacing in Year Two. Catherine Schell and Tony Anholt are tremendous assets. You have a new "wonder woman" of sci-fi in Catherine Schell.' – Jack Jacobson, VP Manager Programming, WGH-TV Chicago

'The improvements you promised for Year Two have been delivered. It is a much, much better programme. The weaknesses in scripting and characterisations have been completely corrected. We were very successful with Year One. Based on the improvements, the second year should be more successful.' – Irwin Stam, Program Manager, WMAL-TV Washington, DC

'The first season performed well in Providence, and was very strong among viewers 18-49. Now it's extremely improved. It's super!' – Gary Drevioul, Program Director, WJAR-TV Providence, RI

'Superb production values, fast-paced storylines and strong new characters, will make a very exciting and successful second year.' – Tom Rose, Program Director, WTHR Indianapolis

'Actors show much more emotion. It will definitely appeal to much broader audiences.' – Don Hoss, Program Manager, WDSU-TV New Orleans

'Our faith in the series has been justified by second year production. *Space: 1999* Year Two is much greater than the first year.' – Mark Booraem, Program Director, WPIX New York

'New elements added to a stunning production make *Space: 1999* Year Two an audience grabber. I am sure it will be a huge success.' – Jack Pedrick, VP and General Manager, KDNL-TV St Louis

'Martin Landau projects a stronger characterisation. The love relationship now clearly developed between him and Barbara Bain will make viewers really care. I loved it so much I'm moving it from fringe time to prime access.' – William Schuyer, President and General Manager, KMST-TV, Salinas, Monterey

'You now have all the elements needed for a successful sci-fi series. Meaningful improvements innovated by the new producer Fred Freiberger are evident.' – Al Holtz, General Manager, WPGH-TV Pittsburgh

'It did very well for us the first year. *Space: 1999* Year Two has even more production values and contains much more action.' – Jack Morris, General Manager, WUAB-TV Cleveland

'You have succeeded in getting away from the robot-like quality of the characters and made them more human. Greater action. Better pacing. Addition of Catherine Schell is a big plus.' – Tom Shelbourne, President, WNEP-TV Wilkes-Barre

'New cast, new music, outrageous aliens and better stories, make *Space: 1999* Year Two come off as the best sci-fi series ever! The changes in Year Two are just right.' – Art Dortner, President, WDHO-TV Toledo

'The new producer, Fred Freiberger, the casting changes, and the humanisation of the characters, deliver a winner.' – Jack Schaefler, Program Director, KGTV San Diego

'*Space: 1999* worked very well in our market, especially in the important 18-49 demographics. The second year is very much better as a result of all the dramatic changes made.' – Jack Decker, President and General Manager, WHEC-TV Rochester NY

'I'm very impressed with the improved action and youthful look of Year Two. The characters are far more vibrant and alive. The new music hits the right pace. Catherine Schell adds a fantastic new dimension.' – Charles (Chuck) Alvery, Program Manager, WUHO-TV Battle Creek

'Very impressed with Catherine Schell. The scripting is much stronger. The characters are more human.' – Tay Voye, Program Director, WTVJ Miami

The changes in *Space: 1999* Year Two are unbelievably great! It's a different, much improved show!' – Pep Cooney, General Manager, KRON-TV San Francisco

'Once I saw it, I renewed. You have performed miracles! It's breathtaking. Everyone will love it!' – Clark Davis, Vice President, WTVQ-TV Lexington KY

What is most curious about so many of the preceding reviews is how closely they parrot the publicity statements of ITC itself, and the negative comments about Year One made by Fred Freiberger. Cynical readers may wonder whether the comments were indeed written by the station executives in question, or by someone at ITC itself as a publicity ploy.

Of interest, some of the channels broadcasting *Space: 1999* in the US chose to telecast the second season premiere, 'The Metamorph', earlier than others as counter-programming during the Republican convention in mid-August 1976, with the hope that it would result in a huge audience not interested in Republican politics. To be fair politically, at least one station – WVTV (Milwaukee, Wisconsin) – led off the special parade of previews of Year Two by airing 'The Metamorph' in 14 July 1976, as counter-programming to telecasts of the Democratic National Convention.

UK BROADCASTS

As already noted, the UK ratings for *Space: 1999*'s first season were not impressive and led to the second season being considered primarily an export. As reported at the time: 'One great mystery mars the jollifications over ITV's much-publicised twenty-first birthday this autumn. What happened to one of the most expensive projects of this year or any other … *Space: 1999*? Most of the 15 independent programme companies have chosen to ignore ATV's new 24-part series. And the only major company that has bought it, London Weekend (LWT), is showing it on Saturday mornings during a children's session … Why has Britain rejected the new series? That's the mystery. Gerry Anderson … says sadly, "I am baffled … I think a British product should be given some kind of chance in its home country …" Financed by ATV, the series is, of course, shown in their Midlands area at prime time on Saturday evenings and is increasing its audience by the week. "I try to figure out what the companies have against it," says Anderson, "… No matter how I look at it I can't find the answer. It is quite heartbreaking. We have a marvellous team working on the show at Pinewood and it makes us despondent, but we will not allow that mood to find its way on to the screen. We still have a highly successful product to sell abroad"…'

Whereas Year One had been broadcast across the whole of the UK by the regional ITV broadcasters, Year Two's reception was poor, with only LWT and ATV picking up the series for its September 1976 debut. Its arrival in other regions would be delayed until 1977 in some cases, if at all. HTV, for example, didn't broadcast Year Two until 1983-1984, and even then failed to air the full series. Year Two began its LWT airings on Saturday mornings and the first 16 episodes were bumped around in various time slots (11.30, 11.00, 10.20, 10.55) from Saturday 4 September 1976 through to Saturday 18 December 1976, while the remaining episodes were in production. The final eight episodes were screened in similar Saturday morning time slots between 10 September 1977 and 12 November 1977.

Although the pick-ups for the second series were not as strong as they were for the first, the show nonetheless succeeded in making an indelible impression on science fiction audiences around the world. Now, here are the adventures of the second season of this classic British science fiction extravaganza. Travel with Moonbase Alpha and – as promotional material for Year Two stated – 'Escape Into Worlds Beyond Belief!'

Note: Year Two episodes will be listed in their widely-recognised order of production, although they were frequently dated in a different order by Helena Russell's on-screen Status Reports.

YEAR TWO
PRODUCTION CREDITS

CREDITED ON EPISODES

Space: 1999	- a Gerry Anderson Production
Production Executive	Reg Hill
Associate Producer	F (Frank) Sherwin Green
Technical Director	David Lane
Lighting Cameraman	Frank Watts BSC (2.1, 2.2, 2.3, 2.4, 2.5, 2.6, 2.7, 2.9, 2.10, 2.11, 2.13, 2.14, 2.15, 2.17, 2.18, 2.19, 2.20, 2.22, 2.23, 2.24), Brendan Stafford (2.8, 2.12, 2.16, 2.21)
Production Designer	Keith Wilson
Special Effects	Designed and Directed by Brian Johnson
Producer & Script Editor	Fred Freiberger
Music	by Derek Wadsworth
Production Manager	Donald Toms
Casting Director	Lesley de Pettitt
Editors	Mike Campbell GBFE (2.1, 2.3, 2.5, 2.7, 2.10, 2.13, 2.15, 2.19, 2.20, 2.23), Alan Killick (2.2, 2.4, 2.6, 2.9, 2.12, 2.14, 2.17, 2.18, 2.22, 2.24), Roy Lovejoy (2.21), Alan Patillo (2.8), Bill Blunden (2.11), Archie Ludski (2.16)
Sound Supervisor	Roy Baker
Sound Editors	Peter Pennell (2.1, 2.2, 2.3, 2.4, 2.5, 2.6, 2.8, 2.9, 2.10, 2.12, 2.13, 2.14, 2.15, 2.16, 2.17, 2.18, 2.19, 2.20, 2.21, 2.22, 2.23, 2.24), Jack T Knight GBFE (2.1, 2.3, 2.4, 2.5, 2.6, 2.8, 2.9, 2.10, 2.11, 2.12, 2.13, 2.14, 2.15, 2.16, 2.17, 2.18, 2.19, 2.20, 2.21, 2.22, 2.23, 2.24), Charles Crafford (2.7), Ted Bond (2.11)
Music Editor	Alan Willis
Financial Director	Terence Connors
Sound Recordists	Claude Hitchcock (2.1, 2.2, 2.3, 2.4, 2.5, 2.6, 2.7, 2.9, 2.10, 2.11), Brian Marshall (2.13, 2.14, 2.15, 2.17, 2.18, 2.19, 2.20, 2.22, 2.23, 2.24), John Brommage (2.8, 2.12, 2.21), Peter Sutton (2.16)
Camera Operators	Neil Binney (2.1, 2.2, 2.3, 2.4, 2.5, 2.6, 2.7, 2.9, 2.10, 2.11, 2.13, 2.14, 2.15, 2.17, 2.18, 2.19, 2.20, 2.22, 2.23, 2.24), Tony White (2.8, 2.12, 2.16, 2.21)
Costume Designer	Emma Porteous
Assistant Directors	Ken Baker (2.1, 2.3, 2.5, 2.7, 2.10, 2.12, 2.13, 2.15, 2.20, 2.21, 2.23), Dominic Fulford (2.14, 2.16), Robert Lynn (2.2, 2.4, 2.6, 2.8, 2.9, 2.17, 2.18, 2.19, 2.22, 2.24), Jack Causey (2.11)

Continuity	Gladys Goldsmith (2.1, 2.2, 2.3, 2.4, 2.5, 2.6), Doreen Soan (2.7, 2.9, 2.10, 2.12, 2.13, 2.14, 2.15, 2.17, 2.18, 2.19, 2.20, 2.21, 2.23, 2.24), Doris Martin (2.8, 2.11, 2.16, 2.22)
Construction Manager	Bill Waldron
Make-up	Basil Newall (2.1, 2.3, 2.4, 2.5, 2.6, 2.7, 2.9, 2.10, 2.12, 2.13, 2.14, 2.15, 2.16, 2.17, 2.18, 2.19, 2.20, 2.22, 2.23, 2.24), Eddie Knight (2.7), Connie Reeve (2.2, 2.3, 2.4, 2.5, 2.6, 2.8, 2.9, 2.10, 2.11, 2.13, 2.14, 2.15, 2.16, 2.17, 2.18, 2.19, 2.20, 2.21, 2.23, 2.24), Eileen Fletcher (2.8)
Hairdressers	Jan Dorman (2.2, 2.3, 2.4, 2.5, 2.6, 2.7, 2.9, 2.12, 2.13, 2.14, 2.15, 2.16, 2.17, 2.18, 2.19, 2.23), Jeanette Freeman (2.3, 2.4, 2.5, 2.6, 2.8, 2.9, 2.10, 2.11, 2.13, 2.14, 2.15, 2.16, 2.17, 2.18, 2.19, 2.20, 2.21, 2.23, 2.24), Michael Lockey (2.20, 2.22, 2.24), Patrick Grant (2.1), Masha Lewis (2.8)
Wardrobe	Masada Wilmot (2.1, 2.2, 2.3, 2.4, 2.5, 2.6, 2.8), Eve Faloon (2.7, 2.12, 2.16), Eileen Sullivan (2.9, 2.10, 2.11, 2.13, 2.14, 2.15, 2.17, 2.18, 2.19, 2.20, 2.21, 2.22, 2.23, 2.24), Barbara Gillett (2.8)
Assistant Art Director	Michael Ford
Special Effects	
Lighting Cameraman	Nick Allder
Camera Operator	David Litchfield
Electronic Effects	Michael S E Downing, Electronics Art Group
Processed by	Rank Film Laboratories

Space: 1999 Based on a Format by Gerry and Sylvia Anderson
Filmed at Pinewood and Bray Studios, England

UNCREDITED ON EPISODES

Miniatures	Martin Bower, Derek Freeborn, Terry Reed, Cyril Forster, Ron Burton, Space Models

Additional production crew as listed on a 'revised unit list' from the middle of Year Two (July 1976):

Film PA/Secretary	Margaret Nicholas
Secretary to Executive Producer	Kate Curry
Secretary to Producer	Diana Healy
Secretary to Associate Producer	Leigh Taylor
Script Co-ordinator	Debbie Spill
Second Assistant Director	John Downes
Third Assistant Director	Gerry Toomey

Follow Focus	Mike Tomlin
Clapper/Loader	Trevor Walker
Sound Mixer	Brian Marshall
Boom Operator	Peter Pardo
Sound Maintenance	Bob Taylor
Wardrobe Assistants	Elvira Angelinetta and Barbara Gillett
Casting Secretary	Susan Gillies
Draughtsman	Dennis Bosher
Art Department Assistants	Richard Holland and David Allday
Production Buyer	Sid Palmer
Production Accountant	Jeff Broom
Assistant Production Accountant	Margaret Woods
Electronics	ATT Group
Secretary to M Landau and B Bain	Lindsay Sterne
Publicity (thru ITC) and Stills	Pamela Godfrey, Davidson Dalling Associates Ltd.
Production Office Junior	Karen Saunders
Production Office Runner	Steve Homes
Unit Car Drivers	Steve Smith, Doug Weatherley
First Assistant Editors	Roy Helmrich, Peter Gray
Second Assistant Editor	Stephen Pickard
Assistant Dubbing Editor	Linda Pearce
Standby Carpenter	Denis Pack
Standby Stagehand	Len Bailey
Standby Grip	Mick Beauchamp
Standby Rigger	Ted Thomas
Standby Painter	Stan Hillis
Standby Plasterer	Jock Campbell
Chargehand Props	Chick McCarthy, Joe Swift
Standby Props	John Gillies
Supervising Electrician	Harry Woodley
Chargehand Electrician	Jack Thetford
Practical Electrician	Dick Reed
Electricians	Gordon Gowing, John Sullivan, George Walker, Frank Buck, Roy Saunders, Brian Pudney
Special Effects Unit	Bray Studios:
SFX Technician	David Watkins
Chief SFX Assistant	Terry Schubert
SFX Assistants	Alan Barnard, Andrew Kelly
General Assistant	Guy Hudson
Secretary	Sallie Beechinor
Main Unit Floor SFX Supervisor	Alan Bryce

2.1
THE METAMORPH

Screenplay by Johnny Byrne
Directed by Charles Crichton

Selected Broadcast Dates:

UK	LWT:	
	Date: 4 September 1976.	Time: 11.30 am
	Granada:	
	Sate: 15 April 1977.	Time: 7.30 pm
US	KRON (San Francisco):	
	Date: 21 August 1976.	Time: 10.00 pm

Credited Cast: Martin Landau (John Koenig), **Barbara Bain** (Helena Russell), **Catherine Schell** (Maya), **Tony Anholt** (Tony Verdeschi), **Nick Tate** (Alan Carter), **Zienia Merton** (Sandra Benes), **John Hug** (Bill Fraser), **Gerard Paquis** (Lew Picard), **Peter Porteous** (Petrov), **Nick Brimble** (Ray Torens), **Anton Phillips** (Bob Mathias)

Guest Stars: Brian Blessed (Mentor), **Anouska Hempel** (Annette Fraser)

Uncredited Cast: Sarah Bullen (Operative Kate), **Robert Reeves** (Operative Peter Reeves), **Pam Rose** (Operative P Rose), **Andy Cummings** (Command Centre Operative), **Jenny Cresswell** (Alpha Receptionist), **Chris Figg** (Alphan), **Nina Mitchen** (Alphan), **Reuben Martin** (Gorilla (Maya)), **George Lane Cooper** (Overseer), **Alf Joint** (Overseer #2), **John Dixon** (Small Alien), **Neil McCaul** (Zombie Alien), **Roy Stewart** (Coloured Alien), **Geoffrey Moon** (Short Alien)

Previously Titled: 'The Biological Soul' and 'The Biological Computer'

Plot: Alpha encounters the volcanic planet Psychon and its remaining inhabitants – the scientist Mentor and his daughter Maya. Mentor wants to use his biological computer – Psyche – to restore their world to its former beauty and asks for the help of the Alphans. While considering this request, Koenig discovers the evil secret that really lies behind Mentor's plan. When her world is destroyed, Maya escapes with the Alphans.

Quotes:
- **Helena:** 'Moonbase Alpha Status Report. Three hundred forty two days after leaving orbit. Dr Helena Russell recording. We have just survived our second encounter with a space warp. Central Computer states that we've been catapulted six light years from our previous position. We've had no casualties this time: our population remains stable at 297…'
- **Maya:** 'Would I make a good Alphan, father?'
- **Maya:** 'My father is an honourable man.'
- **Mentor:** 'True, you are clever, Maya. But one day we must find a better outlet for

your gifts.'

- **Helena:** 'They're all behaving in the same way. It must be some sort of brain damage.'
- **Koenig:** 'We live and hope.'
- **Maya:** 'Leave Psyche – Psyche made you do evil!'
- **Mentor:** 'No, Maya. Understand, please! I wanted to do good. I wanted to restore our planet. I didn't want to hurt anyone!'
- **Maya:** 'Everywhere but on Psychon I'll be an alien.'
- **Koenig:** 'We're all aliens, until we get to know one another.'

On-screen Date: 342 days since leaving Earth orbit.

Filming Dates: Monday 26 January – Monday 16 February 1976

Commentary:
Catherine Schell: 'There are not a lot of people who can say that on their first entrance into a programme they were a lioness. But I can!

'I do remember walking in to the Command Centre set, with all the televisions. It was new, it was unthought-of, but it also was easy to work in. Eventually, we felt very at home on that set. We were using it all the time.'

John Hug: 'When I first started, I didn't work at all the first day. I was put in a spacesuit. It was quilted and boiling hot. It was one of those wonderful occasional summers we get in England when it is actually hot. People were saying, "My God, isn't it hot?" Or, "Phew, what a scorcher." It was up in the 80s, but when you're in a studio all day wearing a quilted spacesuit, you start losing weight and melting. The first three days I was there I turned up at 7.30 in the morning, got into my outfit, and was cleared again at 4.30 in the afternoon. They would say, "All right, John, we won't get to you till tomorrow, but can you be back here in costume at 8.30?" So the next day the same thing happens: "Sorry John, we're not going to get to you today, but you'll be in the first shot tomorrow morning. Sorry about this." Next day I'm in costume and all ready to go again, and nothing happened. At 4.30 I finally get in front of the cameras with some epic line like, "Eagle One to Moonbase Alpha." Then they say, "Okay, John, that's you for the day. But be back tomorrow first thing in the morning." So at least I got started. But that's part of the humiliating process where they grind you down and get you ready for it. But they were all very nice. All the things I've heard about the first series versus the second series … Of course, I *loved* the second series! I was *in it*! Of course, Prentis would prefer the first series, for obvious reasons.

'Anouska Hempel played the part of Mrs Fraser in my very first episode. Unfortunately, that character was short-lived. Although Anouska was happy to do the one episode, I don't think she was particularly interested in being tied down to a series. Had she agreed to continue doing it, my character Bill Fraser would have had more to do. Originally, they called Anouska's character Antonia Fraser, but then it was pointed out to the producer, Freddy Freiberger, that there was a real woman named Lady Antonia Fraser. That meant they had to pick another name and they chose Annette. Obviously, I was a lousy husband and she left me. I probably spent too much time flying around space.

'Sarah Bullen, who played Operative Kate, came up and introduced herself to me that first day. I knew she had been in the first series of *Space: 1999*, but I had never seen it. It was a pleasure to meet her, and she has remained a good friend ever since.

'There was one scene where I had to rush in, say something to Brian Blessed and leave. I remember going in and saying something like, "The Commander's waiting," and then running away. He turned to me and asked, "What are you doing? Stay there and get your screen time. Don't rush off. You don't have much to do in this, so stay there after you say your line and I'll tell you when to go." So I came in, he grabbed my shoulder, and I said my line. He waited for a moment and then pushed me away. Afterwards he said to me, "Don't be afraid to stay there a second longer so that somebody sees you." I thought that was very kind of him.

'Charles Crichton … He just wanted as much fire as possible and things blowing up all over the place. [On] "The Metamorph" in the tunnel scenes and he just kept saying, "More flames. More flames! This is the last one I'm doing – I want more flames!" He was old then … He knew what he was doing. He'd done feature films.'

Johnny Byrne: '"The Biological Soul" was a very interesting concept. I suppose it harked back to this spiritual thing … Here the question was: what is the soul? And it was an attempt to offer some kind of explanation: that it is the kind of source of intelligence in human beings, the sort of thinking, reasoning areas of the brain. In the early script, Mentor was alone with his biological computer, which he calls Psyche. They would have conversations. It was a love affair between the two of them. It had a very different feel about it, but many of the same elements were there [as in the final version]: the attempt to lure Koenig down, and so on. It was the same story as "The Metamorph", but without Maya, who later arrived in Freddy's mental baggage. I never considered Mentor having the power to transform – nor, to my almost certain knowledge, did Freddy or anyone else.

'At the time, I had no idea it was going to be Catherine [playing the part], but I was opposed to the character in principle, at the earliest point. First because I was now the inheritor – the bearer of the torch – of Christopher Penfold (and some others, but particularly Chris, who had given everything he had in the formulation of the series; and George Bellack, who is the unspoken hero of the whole major concept). The reason why I objected to Maya was that on the face of it she was a façade solution to the kinds of problems we had been facing from ITC New York … What do we want? We want *Star Trek* – let's bring in our resident alien … That's fine; a resident alien is fine. But if you are bringing in an alien, and we had many aliens, it's a matter of perception. If those aliens came from outside we could deal with it in the universe that we had formulated and we understood, and which we were sharing – it was us against the great unknown. But when we bring an alien with shape-shifting powers among us, we are melding two very different forms of reality. The problems with the Maya character had nothing to do with the character *per se* – after all, I introduced her – but with the merging of two incompatible realities. I felt that was wrong. I felt it was going to take us in a direction we shouldn't go. Maya didn't belong in the universe of *Space: 1999* that we had created.

'So my first episode from being "The Biological Soul" became "The Biological Computer" and then "The Metamorph", which is when Maya first appeared. Writing the script for number one of the new series, I was definitely given no instructions to write any [of the non-returning] characters out. At one point it occurred to me that I couldn't simply ignore them, and I think I brought this to Gerry's or Freddy's attention.

I think I was asked to put in a line to [cover their absence]. The reason that I was not definitely instructed to write them out was that perhaps they were going to be brought back. You know, once [the actors] had seen sense and decided to take a huge pay cut, and all the other wonderfully sensible solutions that Gerry or whoever was putting into series two. Something did creep in [to my draft script], but that something crept out again, and [in the transmitted version of the] episode, "The Metamorph", it isn't there.'

Fred Freiberger: 'When the character [Maya] was introduced, she was supposed to be a cheetah, or a leopard – something female. Instead, we had a male lion. This was the situation she came into. Gerry told me that the trainer said it was impossible to control the animal. It was very dangerous; we had the whole stage and set wired in. Gerry said that if there was anything that happened with that lion, the law here [in England] would put the Producer in jail. I said, "Make anything you want – we don't want to go to jail!" So they wired the whole set in for safety.'

Bloopers: Strings are visible as Koenig's Eagle launches from Moonbase Alpha.

Observations: *Space: 1999* was always the champion of utilising glowing balls of light to represent alien forces and threats, and 'The Metamorph' is no exception. Here the balls of light are green and plentiful!

The Alphans seem to have spent the hiatus between seasons affixing overtly obvious labels around the base – is it really necessary to stick a label proclaiming 'WEAPONS RACK' above a rack of guns?

Review: Destined to be one of the finest episodes of the second season, 'The Metamorph' marks the return of Johnny Byrne who, along with Christopher Penfold, was more responsible than anybody else for the story direction and the heart and soul of Year One. His contributions to Year Two would unfortunately be lesser.

The immediate introduction of the altered, but engaging, Year Two cast and sets is generally successful. The change from Main Mission to Command Centre is very disappointing, but the new set is certainly functional, if unremarkable. The alterations to the Alphans' uniforms are effective, especially the incorporation of the identity badges and various jackets. Commander Koenig's vest, however, is a terrible addition. (Martin Landau later asserted that he gave it away to a fan visiting the set.)

Commander Koenig has survived the season transition with little discernible change, and Landau's performance is one of the strongest in the episode. The other anchor, Barbara Bain as Helena Russell, has been altered slightly to make her appear and act a little softer and more overtly warm. In fact, she will look marvellous throughout the second season. Her changes are subtle enough to be a natural progression and serve to make the character more easily likeable to casual viewers. Nick Tate continues as Alan Carter and remains one of the most appealing and dependable Alphans. Tony Anholt is well integrated into the cast as Tony Verdeschi, the new hot-headed Italian chief of Moonbase security and Koenig's new second in command. Verdeschi is essentially the replacement for Year One's Main Mission Controller Paul Morrow. Zienia Merton returns as Sandra (although her character will be re-named Sahn from the episode 'Catacombs of the Moon' onwards), and is given a very strong supporting role. Her presence is an undeniable asset to the series. Pilot Bill Fraser, played by John Hug, is a beneficial addition in a supporting role, with his new wife Annette, played by Anouska Hempel, adding additional depth to his character. Sadly, she will never be seen or mentioned again. However, as her only duty seems to be delivering coffee to Command Centre staff, her presence won't be greatly missed (except, one assumes, by her husband!).

Catherine Schell's first appearance as Maya is also one of her most wonderful in the role. She would have other notable opportunities to shine in later episodes, including 'The Rules of Luton' and 'The Dorcons', but Maya's introduction works perfectly, providing a rich background and a fascinating home world for the exotic alien. When Maya is introduced, she is lounging about in the form of a lion, immediately demonstrating her ability of molecular transformation. She changes back to herself and then plays with a partial metamorphosis into Commander Koenig. There is a brief and rare sequence that is normally edited out of the episode: after nearly becoming Koenig, Maya completes a transformation into an orange tree. This serves to give additional meaning to Mentor's next line, 'I teach you the priceless art of molecular transformation and see how you use it – childish games.' It's unfortunate that this orange tree transformation is almost always absent from prints of the episode. Maya is immediately appealing and fascinating, and emerges in this introductory episode as a fully realised three-dimensional character.

Brian Blessed is wonderfully theatrical in his second appearance in the series (the first having been as Dr Cabot Rowland in 'Death's Other Dominion'). Mentor is a classic mad scientist, complete with bubbling tubes of coloured liquid all around him and brain-draining glass helmets at his disposal. He has kept his innocent daughter sheltered from his heinous acts, and when she finally learns the truth about her beloved father, she is shocked and visibly saddened.

The father-daughter relationship between Mentor and Maya is truly the heart of the episode. Despite all the action, spaceships, brain drains and explosions, 'The Metamorph' is a very personal story.

Moonbase Alpha's new surface laser cannons are shown for the first time. Apparently Alpha has increased its weapons capabilities since the first season, and a new Weapons Section has been added to the base. All of this is in contrast to the initial intentions of the series, which posited the Alphans as Earthmen unprepared for their journey into deep space. They were meant to be vulnerable, and were purposely not heavily armed. It does, however, set up the atmosphere and style of Year Two. The laser cannons will be featured again in a number of upcoming episodes.

Another aspect that clearly differentiates the style of the seasons is Koenig's statement to Mentor, 'We'll determine our own destinies.' As mentioned previously, it is a strong statement in direct contrast with Year One's basic philosophical tenets, and is probably the single sentence that most clearly defines this new series of episodes.

Along with screenwriter Byrne, another major player on this episode who had already made a significant contribution in Year One (directing eight episodes) was Charles Crichton. While his work on the first series was always commendable, and often superior, he didn't do as well on the second series; 'The Metamorph' is probably the finest of the six episodes he helms, while a couple of his others rank among the series' worst.

Psychon is a once-wonderful world that has now become an 'environmental hell,' a world of erupting volcanoes. The special effects of the volcanoes have dated over the years, but still admirably depict a distinctly alien environment. The other 'hell' on Psychon is the steaming subterranean caverns that lie beneath Mentor's laboratory.

There he keeps enslaved the vegetative aliens whose minds he has stolen. These are among the many clear parallels with Brian Blessed's earlier episode, 'Death's other Dominion'. Mentor is one of the only Psychons to remain, along with Maya. It was Mentor's dream to transform his world back to the beauty it once possessed, and his dream blinded him. Obviously his dream was seen as futile by most of the rest of his people, as they left in spaceships to attempt to find new worlds on which to live. As viewers will later learn in the episode 'The Rules of Luton', Mentor would never leave Psychon because the grave of his wife was there and he couldn't bear to leave her. While he began his quest with undeniably good intentions, he became mentally warped by his ambitions, to the point of enslaving and draining the mental energies of other aliens in order to power his biological computer. Unfortunately, and ironically, Psyche's released energy is also what ends up ultimately destroying the planet.

Psyche itself – referred to in one working title as 'The Biological Computer' – is a veiled interpretation of *Frankenstein*: a creation (whether a computer or a monster) that ends up destroying its maker.

The culminating scenes are exciting and dramatic, finally ending with the destruction of Psychon and the introduction of Maya to Alpha's crew. The special effects are all impressive, especially the view of Psychon from above, with a remarkably believable display of clouds in the atmosphere. Set design excels with the Grove of Psyche and the striking orange colour scheme evident in the corridors and holding cell. The single aspect that serves to define most strongly the tone of 'The Metamorph' – and all of Year Two – is the enjoyable music of Derek Wadsworth, which conveys the new action-adventure orientation of the series.

The finest elements of the episode are those related to the characters, and the show ends on a touching note, with emotions conveyed with realism and validity. Maya begins as a naïve girl, and the most remarkable transformation in the episode is her journey to being a woman, spreading her wings and leaving the nest. Psychologically, as well, Maya alters her view of the world and her father, transitioning from her earlier sheltered naïveté to broad awareness as she moves on with her life in the alien, and undoubtedly scary, universe – the ultimate metaphor for life itself. These are the real metamorphoses with which 'The Metamorph' is concerned.

The weakest aspect of the episode is the lack of explanation for the changes between seasons, but the positive side of the missing characters not being killed off is that fans can still imagine that Professor Bergman, Paul Morrow and the others are still somewhere out there in the universe. But it would have been wonderful to see Bergman interact with Maya, not only because of the potential character combination, but also because Barry Morse and Catherine Schell were friends, having worked together on the series *The Adventurer*, and they had wonderful chemistry together.

Another quibble would concern the ability of one explosive-packed Eagle to destroy the entire planet Psychon, which clearly is in contradiction to the tenets of the first series. Finally, the date of this episode – 342 days since leaving Earth orbit – is too soon. Not only does this contradict the earlier dating of 'Dragon's Domain', it also artificially compresses all of Year One into far too short a time frame. With this, as with other aspects, the two seasons of *Space: 1999* seem to inhabit entirely different universes.

'The Metamorph' is an outstanding fast-paced introduction to the new series of *Space: 1999* and sets a high standard for future episodes to match.

Rating: 8.5/10

2.2
THE EXILES

Screenplay by Donald James
Directed by Ray Austin

Selected Broadcast Dates:

UK	LWT:	
	Date: 11 September 1976.	Time: 11.30 am
	Granada:	
	Date: 22 April 1977.	Time: 7.30 pm
US	KRON (San Francisco):	
	Date: 11 September 1976.	Time: 7.00 pm

Credited Cast: Martin Landau (John Koenig), **Barbara Bain** (Helena Russell), **Catherine Schell** (Maya), **Tony Anholt** (Tony Verdeschi), **Nick Tate** (Alan Carter), **Zienia Merton** (Sandra Benes), **Margaret Inglis** (Mirella), **Anthony Blackett** (Stal), **Peggy Ledger** (Old Lady (Maya)), **Anton Phillips** (Bob Mathias)

Guest Stars: Peter Duncan (Cantar), **Stacey Dorning** (Zova)

Uncredited Cast: Peter Porteous (Petrov), **Sarah Bullen** (Operative Kate), **Robert Reeves** (Operative Peter Reeves), **Pam Rose** (Operative P Rose), **Andy Cummings** (Command Centre Operative), **Quentin Pierre** (Security Guard Quinton), **Roy Everson** (Life Support Guard), **Ron Nichols** (Security Guard), **Vic Armstrong** (Rescue Operative), **Glenda Allen** (Technician), **Frank Maher** (Decontamination), **Charlie Price** (Doorman), **Bill Westley** (Doorman), **Jenny Cresswell, Tracey Hudson, Maryanne** (Nurses)

Plot: A fleet of missile-like objects enters orbit around the Moon, and when the first is retrieved they are found to be capsules containing alien beings. Two of these aliens – Cantar and Zova – conspire to use the resources of Moonbase Alpha to return to their home world, Golos.

Quotes:
- **Koenig:** 'Helena, they may have something. Something our sensors can't detect. My concern is with the survival of this base.'
- **Tony:** 'Look, you asked what sort of people they are. What sort of people are we?'
- **Helena:** 'I'm a doctor, John. I save life for the sake of saving life.'
- **Tony:** 'Is survival all-important? What sort of society is it that abandons 50 innocent beings?'
- **Helena:** 'There is once again a warm feeling of well-being on Moonbase Alpha.'

On-screen Date: 403 days since leaving Earth orbit.

247

Filming Dates: Tuesday 17 February – Monday 1 March 1976
Months later, on 7 June, director Kevin Connor filmed an additional scene for this episode, where Maya rescues Petrov by transforming into a gorilla.

Commentary:
Keith Wilson: 'The black panther was one of our most successful Maya transformations: when it leaps across the set in "The Exiles".'

Fred Freiberger: 'We did a black panther sequence on *Space: 1999* [in "The Exiles"] – Catherine Schell made a leap and transformed into this panther in mid-air. We spent the whole day and it cost us $5,000. In America it would have cost us $50,000!'

Review: 'The Exiles' was originally written in the autumn of 1975 for the Year One format, and was re-written to fit the new series by Donald James in early January of 1976. The script is well paced and the drama builds to a memorable climax.
 'The Exiles' is quite successful as a second episode. A suspenseful (and very well filmed) prologue generates interest in the presence of the alien capsules in orbit around the Moon and demonstrates admirable teamwork among the Command Centre staff. The space walk sequence with Koenig and Maya leaving the Eagle with jet packs is an example of fantastic production quality and effects. The Eagle 'arm' used to transport the alien pods to the base is an effective piece of novel technology that will feature again in the later episodes 'The Rules of Luton' and 'Space Warp'. Viewers are introduced to an impressive new remote research station, complete with launch pad, located at a safe distance from the bulk of the base. It is a logical addition – a distant lab where dangerous experiments can be undertaken or alien objects examined – and would have been very useful in Year One episodes such as 'The Last Sunset' and 'Space Brain'.
 The plot has similarities to that of Year One's 'End of Eternity', with the curious Alphans unwittingly releasing psychotic alien criminals from their eternal prisons. Helena identifies the dichotomy of this episode when she notices how young the aliens are, as a means of demonstrating their implied innocence. The implication is that youth and beauty equal innocence. Here youth and beauty are deceptive covers for the true history and evil purpose of Cantar and Zova.
 Anton Phillips has a sufficiently interesting role to play in this, his final episode of the series. The continuity of his presence will soon be greatly missed as a revolving door of doctors begin passing through Medical Centre.
 'The Exiles' features some effective and amusing banter and fun interplay between Helena and Maya, demonstrating their growing friendship. Helena's hobby as a sculptor is explored: she has created a bust of herself as a gift for John. It's a pleasant addition to her characterisation, and in general she seems to be more open with emotions that she would have restrained in the first season. For viewers unfamiliar with Maya, several demonstrations are given of her powers of molecular transformation. First is the harmless fun of her change into Helena. Second is her adoption of the form of a large gorilla creature (actually, another awful man-in-gorilla-suit) to save an Alphan trapped under a fallen metal beam. Third is her amazing mid-air shape-shift into a black panther – without doubt one of the finest transformations in the series. Sadly, the big cat doesn't seem to retain Maya's intelligence and quickly gets stunned.
 Keith Wilson recycles his Grove of Psyche set from 'The Metamorph' and converts

it into the control room on Golos, with quite impressive results. It's an indication that the budget had been decreased: In Year One, new sets were designed with virtually no re-use, and on a much larger scale. Now, they are scaled back in scope and this same set will return again, redressed, for episode three.

Golos seems to be an interestingly advanced world of high technology and compassionate criminal justice systems. The surface of Golos is similar to that of the planet from 'War Games', with tall buildings raised up over a surface quite green with trees and foliage. The scenes on Golos are excellent. Helena states her contempt for Cantar, who tells her she is crippled by her 'moral ideas of loyalty, gratitude and fair play.' Helena replies, 'And you and Zova are free spirits, I suppose. Free to hate, threaten and kill.' The name 'Golos' is actually derived from the Hebrew word 'Galuth', meaning 'exile'. Historically and specifically, this referred to the exile of the Jews from Palestine.

In a suitably alien manner, Cantar bleeds green blood when Helena scratches his face, piercing the protective membrane that preserves his youth. This culminating sequence is a dynamic combination of direction, action and pyrotechnics. Topping it all is the transformation of Cantar as his 300 years catch up with him in a matter of minutes. The ageing make-up is first-rate, as is Peter Duncan's performance as the dying and ancient Cantar; unfortunately Duncan's voice was dubbed (quite poorly) by someone who sounded more American, which is a shame, because the new voice is an eternal, though minor, distraction.

Frequent first season director Ray Austin makes his first of two stabs at helming segments of Year Two, and although his efforts here lack the visual flair he usually displayed in Year One, he is largely successful. Other memorable aspects of the production include the soundtrack by Derek Wadsworth and the impressive special effects by Brian Johnson and his team.

Thematically, there is a prominent argument over the ethical conflicts involved with survival, which is a worthy concept for the series, and was dealt with earlier in such episodes as 'Mission of the Darians'.

'The Exiles' is a very enjoyable second episode for Year Two.

Rating: 8/10

2.3
ONE MOMENT OF HUMANITY

Screenplay by Tony Barwick
Directed by Charles Crichton

Selected Broadcast Dates:
UK   LWT:
            Date: 25 September 1976.   Time: 11.00 am
            Granada:
            Date: 6 May 1977.   Time: 7.30 pm
US   KRON (San Francisco):
            Date: 29 January 1977.   Time: 7.00 pm

Credited Cast: Martin Landau (John Koenig), **Barbara Bain** (Helena Russell), **Catherine Schell** (Maya), **Tony Anholt** (Tony Verdeschi), **Nick Tate** (Alan Carter), **Zienia Merton** (Sandra Benes), **Geoffrey Bayldon** (Number Eight)

Guest Stars: Billie Whitelaw (Zamara), **Leigh Lawson** (Zarl)

Uncredited Cast: Sarah Bullen (Operative Kate), **Robert Reeves** (Operative Peter Reeves), **Pam Rose** (Operative P Rose), **Micky Clarke** (Number), **Glenda Allen** (Number), **Jurgen Anderson, Zena Clifton, Hilary Ding, Paul Hastings, Maggie Henderson, Laraine Humphrys, Jason Mitchell, Barry Rohde** (Vegans)

Movements Arranged by Lionel Blair
Assistant choreographer Hilary Ding

Previously Titled: 'One Second of Humanity'

Plot: Tony and Helena are kidnapped by the alien Zamara and taken to her planet, Vega. There they discover a dual society – one of androids pretending to be humans, and the other of humans pretending to be androids. The androids have taken over Vega and want to dispose of their human creators for good, but first they must learn how to kill.

Quotes:
- **Zamara to Helena:** 'You're a liar. It sticks in your mouth, you decrepit hag.'
- **Zarl to Tony:** 'You foul-mouthed lying cretin.'
- **Zamara:** 'You're beginning to sound human, Zarl. Be careful – you know the dangers.'
- **Zarl:** 'The way he looks at her. To feel something as strongly as jealousy … Can we be missing so much?'
- **Zamara:** 'Emotion is a weakness. We can use it, but we must never become ensnared.'

- **Zarl:** 'Chastened as an icicle, fashioned by the purest frost – I will melt thee.'
- **Zarl:** 'No, don't be sorry: it was worth it. One moment of humanity.'

On-screen Date: 515 days since leaving Earth orbit.

Filming Dates: Thursday 4 March – Wednesday 17 March 1976

Incidental Music: The seduction scene includes music composed by Canadian Gino Vanelli, titled 'Storm at Sunup'. Beethoven's 9th Symphony is also featured.

Commentary:
Barbara Bain: '"One Moment of Humanity" was sweet. I liked that one, too. Leigh Lawson, I thought, was an actor who would do very well here in the USA. He was in *Tess*, but he didn't kind of emerge out of it. I was surprised. He kind of didn't catch on with the American public.

'That dress [I wore] wasn't ready when we started shooting. We had to shoot it from a limited camera angle, because it wasn't stitched up yet. I had to walk around very carefully, because it was not closed up the back – it was maddening! I'm fairly easy to get along with, but when something isn't right, it's very disheartening. For some ungodly reason, it's your fault! Even though I wasn't making the dress: I was standing there. They kind of get really uptight with you. We kept stitching it the whole episode. By the time we got to the dance sequence it was still being stitched. I don't know what the problem was.'

Emma Porteous: 'We designed all these make-ups [for the aliens] with the dots, and bits and pieces in the hair. It was supposed to be a beautiful planet full of beautiful people, so it was as much exposure as you could get within certain limitations. The men were all well proportioned with bare chests, and the ladies' dresses were all totally transparent with body stockings underneath, so when they caught the light you could see their figures. The whole thing was very soft and beautiful. The set designer started that look off and we went with him. Everything was terribly diffused. It was very pretty, that one.'

Review: 'One Moment of Humanity' is one of the supreme productions of Year Two. Like everything else in this gem of an episode, all of the performances are carefully refined and highly polished. Leigh Lawson, in particular, is outstanding as Zarl – both throughout the episode and especially in the scenes as he achieves humanity. His is a performance resonating with strength and subtlety, and he succeeds in creating a truly memorable character. Billie Whitelaw is also excellent as the powerful Zamara. The talents of Lawson and Whitelaw certainly aid in elevating this episode above many others.

Barbara Bain excels in one of her most significant roles in the second season, especially during her highly emotional, tearful scenes on the duplicate Alpha (created by the androids in an attempt to trick Helena and Tony into believing that each is trying to kill the other), and during her seduction scene with Leigh Lawson's Zarl. While the seduction sequence depicts what is – essentially – the prologue to a rape, it is portrayed in a manner that makes it acceptable for a family audience. Koenig's anger at Helena's seduction is very appropriate in these circumstances.

The sequence on the deserted duplicate Alpha is played to the perfected hilt by both Bain and Tony Anholt, including the latter's humorous line, 'Bang, bang, you're dead,' and Bain's reaction. The opening sequence is also enjoyable as it portrays a simple scene of Helena and Maya interacting as close friends. It is to the credit of the performances of Bain and Catherine Schell that this scene rings true to the viewer and succeeds in the development of greater warmth and likeable interaction among the main characters.

Tony Barwick's script provides strong plotting, characterisation and dialogue, epitomising the Year Two emphasis on humanity and emotion, while Charles Crichton's direction delivers everything the viewer expects from his masterful eye. Visually, this is a beautiful episode. It is not heavy on special effects, and the view of the surface of Vega is actually a reuse of footage of Ultima Thule from Year One's 'Death's other Dominion'. Despite this, the limited number of new effects that do feature in this episode are all convincingly well executed. Of special notice are the set design and art direction evident on Vega, which fit perfectly with the elegant and beautiful Vegan androids. The sets of the grove, hallways and underground rock cavern are all borrowed and re-dressed from 'The Metamorph' (a consequence of the budgetary restrictions affecting every aspect of production, including the art department), though the revisions are extensive and lead to sets equally deserving of appreciation. The costume design on both the humans and androids is believable and adds to the pleasurable quality of this beautiful and sensual alien world.

'One Moment of Humanity' is an episode of great depth in characterisation, and of thoughtful warnings of the dangers of all-powerful technology: a theme *Space: 1999* has been professing since 'Breakaway'. The story revolves around the classic Man versus Machine conflict, heightened by the android Zarl's desire to be human. Furthermore, this is an episode of the second season that ends naturally and dramatically on an emotional note, rather than with a forced comedic sequence, as was often the case.

The series is all the richer for having provided 'One Moment of Humanity'.

Rating: 8.5/10

2.4
ALL THAT GLISTERS

Screenplay by Keith Miles
Directed by Ray Austin

Selected Broadcast Dates:
UK   LWT:
            Date: 30 October 1976.   Time: 11.55 am
            Granada:
            Date: 10 July 1977.
US   KRON (San Francisco):
            Date: 5 February 1977.   Time: 7.00 pm

Credited Cast: Martin Landau (John Koenig), **Barbara Bain** (Helena Russell), **Catherine Schell** (Maya), **Tony Anholt** (Tony Verdeschi), **Nick Tate** (Alan Carter)

Guest Cast: Patrick Mower (Dave Reilly)

Uncredited Cast: Barbara Kelly (Voice of Computer)

Plot: While searching for the mineral Milgonite on an alien planet, an Alphan reconnaissance party discovers a rock-like entity with tremendous powers of mind control. The rock is dying due to a terrible drought, and it sees the Alphans as a source of water.

Quotes:
- **Reilly:** 'The rocks understand me, Commander. Me wives never did, but the rocks do.'
- **Koenig:** 'You've got a one-track mind in a stone-age skull. Helena's trapped in that Eagle and all you can think about is that damned rock!'
- **Koenig:** 'That planet's going to be a piece of cake.'
- **Alan:** 'Fastest gun on Alpha.'
- **Tony:** 'For Milgonite, another time.'

On-screen Date: 565 days since leaving Earth orbit.

Filming Dates: Thursday 18 March – Wednesday 31 March 1976

Commentary:
Martin Landau: [Handwritten comments on his script] 'All the credibility we're building up is totally forsaken … The character of Koenig takes a terrible beating in this script – we're all shmucks!'

Tony Anholt: 'There was one big, big battle going on about the script "All That

Glisters". I got zapped pretty early on and spent my time walking around like a zombie carrying a piece of rock. Martin was desperately unhappy about the whole script; he thought it was absolute rubbish, as indeed we all did. Freddy, once he saw the opposition, just became utterly entrenched and would give nothing at all – [as he told it,] that was the greatest episode of the series, it was the most sci-fi type of story; it was going to stay, and he would prove his point. Short of walking off the set, completely screwing the whole series up, there was nothing we could do about it … I did say to Martin, who was quite upset about that particular episode, "Well, if you feel that strongly, why don't you just refuse to do it?" He said he found it very difficult to work like that. It would mean a whole unit standing around wondering what the hell was going to happen, the schedule would be put back, it would cost more money, ill feeling – so, for the sake of one episode, it really wasn't worth it.'

Catherine Schell: 'I had to be actually shouted at – very rudely – before I would stop laughing. It was like a cold shower. I don't know who wrote that script ["All That Glisters"]. There were things in it we had to say that were just so unbelievable for us. If you're really into the part and you're trying to say something with conviction, and then you realizes … there's this little monster on your shoulder telling you, "This is rubbish!" I just wept [with laughter] every time. It was actually worse than working with Peter Sellers, that particular episode. He was a great mate, actually, that director – Ray Austin. Ray actually shouted at me, "Catherine! Be professional!" … "I am! That's why I'm laughing!"

'It was a piece of rock that was changing in front of our eyes, and we would say, "It's doing this … It's going up … No, it's going down … Oh look, it's gone green … Now it's gone red." And when you knew what you were saying and knew what you were supposed to be looking at … it was just rubbish.

'If you ever see that episode, there are still creases around all of our mouths from laughing, and sometimes we're actually turning our heads away from the camera, because we didn't want the camera to see us laughing. We just became totally hysterical. Anyway, it was a good morning.'

Bloopers: Special effects sequences with the Eagle are inconsistent: a passenger module replaces the laboratory module as the ship takes off with Helena aboard.

As Catherine Schell mentions in her commentary below, she can be seen laughing and turning her head away from the camera while watching the rock-controlled Eagle go up and down.

Observations: One quirk of this episode is that not a single scene takes place on Moonbase Alpha. Another peculiarity is that this is one of two episodes of Year Two in which the Alpha computer speaks – and even here, it is through the Eagle. (The other is 'The Mark of Archanon'.)

Review: Following three strong opening episodes, 'All That Glisters' marks the first failure of Year Two, and remains little more than a parody of earlier quality. However, looked on as a piece of camp sci-fi, purely for laughs, it can still be enjoyed for what it is.

The title itself, 'All That Glisters', comes from Shakespeare's *The Merchant of Venice* where the Prince of Morocco states, 'All that glisters is not gold.' While being the closest this episode will come to literature, the title accurately reflects on the alien rocks, masquerading as the mineral Milgonite, required by Moonbase Alpha.

There had been a number of other science fiction episodes featuring living rocks, including *Star Trek*'s 'Devil in The Dark', *The Outer Limits*' 'Corpus Earthling', and *The Bionic Woman*'s 'The Vega Influence'. 'All That Glisters' was *Space: 1999*'s entry into this rather bizarre sub-genre. Keith Miles delivered his script in early March of 1976, and whether through fault of his own or through re-writing, it is certainly one of the worst in the series and contains numerous ghastly lines, including Koenig's pontificating 'Maybe they're like humans. When they're scared, they don't think too well.' While it could potentially be regarded as a tribute to *Star Trek*, Helena's line, 'I'm a doctor, John – not a miracle worker!' comes across as a shamefully derivative rip-off. One aspect of the script that is appreciated, though, as it was in 'The Metamorph', is the recognition of Alpha's occasional need for rare minerals to power such systems as Life Support.

Ray Austin provides direction that ploughs along with the pace of the script, though neither leads anywhere rewarding. Austin was reportedly – like the cast – very unhappy with the script, and following completion of this episode he opted to leave *Space: 1999* and join *The New Avengers*.

Patrick Mower delivers a genuine oddity of characterisation as the Irish cowboy Dave Reilly. His performance is admirable, despite his inconsistent accent and some occasionally overdone sequences where he comes across stiffly. To be fair, it would be difficult for any actor to turn in a stellar performance when faced with this script! What is completely unclear is why Dave Reilly had to be introduced at all. He does nothing that couldn't have been handled by a variety of other Alpha characters, including Alan Carter or Sandra Benes, and it would have been far more rewarding to have seen a regular in this large role. The main cast struggle through and uniformly give their best to maintain a sense of dignity in the face of this unchallenging and often idiotic material. Martin Landau plays Koenig with an edge – temperamental and easy to anger – which might be partly because Landau himself was extremely unhappy with the script.

The special effects are quite nice, and the depiction of the otherworldly alien planet – a collection of red skies, grey sand and bizarre twisted dead trees – is excellent. Not only is this planet a highlight of 'All That Glisters', it stands as one of the most memorable alien worlds visited throughout the series. The living rocks and their ability to emit different beams of coloured light are unbelievable in many regards, despite the appealing notion of life having evolved in so radically different a form than we are familiar with. Possibly the alien rocks are meant to be viewed as being akin to mood stones. Regardless, the exclamation 'Red is death!' marks one of the most ridiculous moments of the series.

. In concept, there is nothing wrong with an episode featuring living rocks – it was done with considerably greater success on *Star Trek*, *The Outer Limits* and *The Bionic Woman*. But 'All That Glisters' fails in both script and execution. A cloud of disappointment hangs over the resultant proceedings, although once forgiven its shortcomings, the episode does at least provide an exciting and enjoyably silly sci-fi hour, with a pleasant resolution.

Rating: 5.5/10

2.5
JOURNEY TO WHERE

Screenplay by Douglas James
Directed by Tom Clegg

Selected Broadcast Dates:

UK	LWT:	
	Date: 18 September 1976.	Time: 11.20 am
	Granada:	
	Date: 29 Apr. 1977.	Time: 7.30 pm
US	KRON (San Francisco):	
	Date: 18 Sept. 1976.	Time: 7.00 pm

Credited Cast: Martin Landau (John Koenig), **Barbara Bain** (Helena Russell), **Catherine Schell** (Maya), **Tony Anholt** (Tony Verdeschi), **Nick Tate** (Alan Carter), **Jeffery Kissoon** (Dr Ben Vincent), **Yasuko Nagazumi** (Yasko), **Roger Bizley** (MacDonald), **Laurence Harrington** (Jackson), **Norwich Duff** (First Operative Texas), **Peggy Paige (**The Old Crone)

Guest Stars: Freddie Jones (Dr Charles Logan), **Isla Blair** (Carla Cross)

Uncredited Cast: Sarah Bullen (Operative Kate), **Robert Reeves** (Operative Peter Reeves), **Jenny Cresswell** (Operative L Picard), **Robert Davies** (Mr Hyde (Maya)), **John Wood** (Second Operative), **Terry Walsh** (Highlander), **Peter Brayham, Eddie Stacey, Tim Condren, Terry Walsh, Doug Robinson** (Clansmen / Stunts)

Plot: Neutrino Transmissions from Texas City in the year 2120 reach Moonbase Alpha, promising that a return to Earth via new transportation technology is possible. A test package is successfully transmitted. This is followed by the attempted transfer of Koenig, Russell and Carter. An earthquake disrupts the procedure, and the trio awake in Scotland in 1339.

Quotes:
- **Maya:** 'You told me heroes were fools who had a talent for nothing else.'
- **Helena:** 'It's the Moon, John – it's the Moon!'
- **Alan:** 'Would you believe we lost our way?'
- **Helena:** 'With a history like that, who wants to go back to Earth, anyway?'

On-screen Date: None.

Filming Dates: Thursday 1 April – Wednesday 14 April 1976

Observations: The test device was previously utilised as one of the air canisters in 'The Last Sunset', while the costumes of the Scottish clansmen are re-used from the Roman

Polanski film of *Macbeth*.

Special effects footage of the domed Earth cities from 'Journey to Where' was borrowed by the *Wonder Woman* series for an episode titled 'Time Bomb'.

Review: 'Journey to Where' was written by Douglas James, who had already penned 'The Exiles' and would return again later in the series as author of 'The Seance Spectre'.

Upon the arrival of John, Helena and Alan on Earth, this episode hits its stride. The location shoot is beautiful and atmospheric, and the direction by Tom Clegg, which had been rather pedestrian in the Moonbase Alpha scenes, excels in the Earth ones. Martin Landau, Barbara Bain and Nick Tate all likewise deliver outstanding performances in these scenes, freed from the confines of the Alpha sets. Bain, in particular, gives her finest performance in Year Two. She is absolutely gripping as Helena succumbs to pneumonia, dropping her normally restrained demeanour and replacing it with a raw realism, demonstrating her courage as an actress. Helena, even in her illness, is a strong character: she is the one who identifies their Moon in the sky, and spots the fungus on the walls of the cell and directs the preparation of it into an antibiotic. The trio of Landau, Bain and Tate appear comfortable and at ease in their roles, and uniformly deliver three of the most natural and genuine performances in the series.

Catherine Schell imbues Maya with a sense of uncertainty and sadness at the thought of going with her fellow Alphans back to Earth – an alien world to her, where she would be even more alone; one amongst billions rather than one amongst approximately three hundred. She is left out and set apart from the rejoicing the others express in making contact with their home world.

The absence of Zienia Merton's character Sandra is profoundly felt: her replacement, Yasko, is portrayed by Yasuko Nagazumi, who gives a performance of remarkably limited talent and manages to stumble over every word in her apparently slim English vocabulary.

Isla Blair, in an entertainingly awful white wig, returns to the series, having previously played the Female Alien in 'War Games'. She and Freddie Jones have an interesting time with their American accents, yet do succeed in playing their parts with an earnestness that lends them credibility.

Director Tom Clegg delivers his first episode for the series, and would go on to helm a further four: 'The Bringers of Wonder' Parts 1 and 2, 'Devil's Planet' and 'The Dorcons'. While those others are all admirable episodes, this is his finest outing.

The Texas City miniatures are fun, with their pulsing disco lights. There are also similar lights on the Texas City laboratory set – an admirable bit of continuity between the special effects and set design departments. The effects of the earthquakes are quite engaging, especially for the period when they were produced. The shots of the devastated countryside of Earth, including foaming rivers and the carcass of a cow on a desert plain, provide suitably effective environmental warnings of the dangers of pollution.

'Journey to Where' is *Space: 1999*'s only time-travel story (in 'The Full Circle' the Alphans regress to a primitive state, but they do not actually travel back in time), and it is completely successful. It is a surprising and effective choice on the writer's part to send the Alphans to 1336 in Scotland at the time of the Black Plague. A far more interesting choice than to have put them, for example, on a back-lot Wild West town as other sci-fi programmes have done.

The script contains numerous allusions to the future, most notably in Alan Carter's singing (as in 'Death's other Dominion'). Prior to their journey into Earth's past, Carter sings, 'Fly me from the Moon at last; Let Alpha be my long-lost past.' He later sings, 'Fire, fire, burn so bold. Can't you see she's feeling cold?' This foretells of the fire that nearly burns them all, and also foreshadows Helena's realisation that she has her own worsening 'cold', which becomes pneumonia. Another notable instance is when Helena jokingly mentions the Black Plague, not realising that is exactly what the Scottish clansmen will accuse her of having.

Conceptually, the Alphans are allowed to connect with the Earth of the 22nd Century and see where mankind has wound up – 'Who needs nature?' is the brilliantly chilling summary of the state of humanity. Year One episodes, particularly those of Johnny Byrne, frequently contrasted the lives of technological and non-technological societies, seeming to suggest that the most desirable combination was a balance between the two elements of science and nature. The death of nature on future Earth leaves the humans – locked up in their futuristic cities – lacking a connection to the world that gave them life. Where Byrne often called for a return to and an embracing of the natural world, while eschewing a total abandonment of science, Donald James goes a step further. Helena personifies the disconnection between people living in an utterly technological environment and those in their former natural habitat. Demonstrating profoundly that the Alphans are now people of space, rather than of Earth, her return to the planet of her birth makes Helena deathly ill. While Byrne's scripts show a desire for a new Eden, James seems to say that the rift is too great, and that the Alphans – mankind itself? – are too far-gone to return to a natural state. Certainly, their future does not lie on Earth, as was also stated in Year One's 'Earthbound', when Professor Bergman said, 'Maybe I've had enough of Earth and its so-called civilisation.' Earth has become virtually as inhospitable to life as the Moon. Texas City and the other domed cities offer a life very similar to that on Moonbase Alpha. The question must be: does a return to Earth offer the Alphans anything more than they already have?

And speaking of those domed cities of future Earth, they do bear a notable resemblance to the domed city complexes of the novel *Logan's Run* – adapted as a movie in 1976 and as a spin-off TV series in 1977 – both physically and thematically, with the absence of nature in the lives of those within. Amplifying the parallel, the central characters even share the same name – Logan. Here D. Charles Logan is a slightly eccentric scientist who takes great risks with his largely untested equipment.

This is a strong story, well told, and heightened to a level of greatness by the performances of the three leads and the well-conveyed ecological concern of the script. No matter the weaknesses of Yasko, Isla Blair's wig or dicey accents, 'Journey to Where' holds even greater impact today than when it was filmed, and is absolutely one of the pre-eminent episodes of *Space: 1999*.

Rating: 9/10

2.6
THE TAYBOR

Screenplay by Thom Keyes
Directed by Bob Brooks

Selected Broadcast Dates:

UK	LWT:	
	Date: 6 November 1976.	Time: 10.55 am
	Granada:	
	Date: 17 July 1977.	
US	KRON (San Francisco):	
	Date: 25 September 1976.	Time: 7.00 pm

Credited Cast: Martin Landau (John Koenig), **Barbara Bain** (Helena Russell), **Catherine Schell** (Maya), **Tony Anholt** (Tony Verdeschi), **Jeffery Kissoon** (Ben Vincent), **John Hug** (Bill Fraser), **Yasuko Nagazumi** (Yasko), **Laraine Humphrys** (Karen), **Rita Webb** (Slatternly Woman (Maya)), **Mel Taylor** (Pilot Andrews)

Guest Star: Willoughby Goddard (Taybor the Trader)

Uncredited Cast: Sarah Bullen (Operative Kate), **Vicki Michelle** (Barbara), **Jenny Clare**, **Chai Lee**, **Penny Priestley** (Sunbathing Alphans), **Micky Clarke** (Medic), **Glenda Allen** (Technician)

Plot: An intergalactic trader named Taybor arrives at Alpha in his ship, the *SS Emporium*, and becomes infatuated with Maya. A robot duplicate of the Psychon is created to satisfy him, but the trader only collects originals. Taybor kidnaps Maya and takes her into hyperspace, but Koenig has devised a way to save her.

Quotes:
- **Taybor:** 'Taybor's the name, trading's my game.'
- **Taybor:** 'Just now? I've been trading my wares at the Three World's Fair on Azoth. Or do you mean where do I come from? My natal soil. Soil, did I say? Dust is more the truth of it, if you know Pinvith the Lesser … Sixty parsecs from the notorious Frontier Worlds of Shmagod, on the Inner Vesica Route. You may well wonder at my humble origins, and how a lad from Pinvith the Lesser has dragged himself two hundred thousand parsecs from the wrong side of a dusty world, on the wrong side of the wrong galaxy in the wrong universe. To haul himself up by the gravitron straps, so to speak. And to venture forth in search of beauty, beautiful things, beautiful people …'
- **Taybor:** 'Without beauty surrounding him, a man's soul corrodes into dust.'
- **Taybor:** 'It's a big universe; a lonely place to wander in.'
- **Taybor:** 'Nectar, Mr. Verdeschi – pure nectar. Best meal I've had since the Rainbow Room on the *Astra*, and that merited two starbursts in *The Gourmet's Guide to the*

Galaxy.'
- **Taybor:** 'I've darkened many a space port of call, Skipper, and while they all have their share of goods to offer, there's none that will suit you.'
- **Taybor:** 'My home – the old Emporium. Registered in Kantonrek for tax purposes.'

On-screen Date: None.

Filming Dates: Thursday 15 April – Monday 3 May 1976

Commentary:
Martin Landau: 'We have an episode called "The Taybor". He is kind of like a travelling medicine man from the Old West. He is a con man, a magician and a huckster of a certain kind with a lot of flamboyance, and that is a very interesting episode, all the while being terribly menacing.'

Review: A segment played for amusement, 'The Taybor' will be liked or loathed depending upon a viewer's response to its humour. While there are a number of very good scenes in this script by Thom Keyes, there are also a number that fall flat. The story lacks substance and seems obviously padded with filler material in order to extend it to fill the 52 minutes of screen time.

In a particularly notable example of 'borrowing' between science fiction shows, Taybor the Trader has some significant similarities to the character Harcourt Mudd from the original *Star Trek* episodes 'Mudd's Women' and 'I, Mudd'. Even more significant similarities can be seen between Taybor and the later intergalactic trader Kivas Fajo from the *Star Trek: The Next Generation* episode 'The Most Toys', where he encounters the Enterprise-D and kidnaps crewmember Data. While this book has generally avoided listing comparisons between the various incarnations of *Star Trek* and *Space: 1999*, simply to avoid becoming a litany of such examples, this cross-generational instance is one too obvious to ignore.

Physically, Taybor bears striking resemblance to the character Sir John Falstaff, who appeared in three plays by William Shakespeare. Falstaff – apart from being one of the great comic figures in drama – was a fat, vainglorious, lying coward and glutton, given to excessive consumption of alcohol – all of which characteristics will be familiar to viewers of 'The Taybor'.

Guest Willoughby Goddard, as Taybor, is mildly entertaining, however his role and performance are both rather over-the-top, and his significantly slurred speech is an annoying distraction. He doesn't so much speak his dialogue as chew it up before allowing it to fall out of his mouth. Goddard was best known for portraying Sir Toby Belch, another not dissimilar Shakespearean character, in productions of *Twelfth Night*.

Alphan characterisation and performances vary from merely acceptable to quite strong: Barbara Bain looks beautiful in her blue gown, and Catherine Schell is especially prominent, providing a depth of charm to Maya that reaches beyond the words of the script.

There are a number of aspects of the episode that don't fit into the series as a whole, including the *Star Trek*-style association of trading worlds – although in a vast universe, there are bound to be all kinds! But the most glaring is Helena's ability to create a walking, talking, robotic version of Maya that looks exactly like her. Sure, it's little more than a moving mannequin, but this is an instance of technology surely well beyond the realm of Moonbase Alpha.

Catherine Schell's appearance here as a robot version of herself oddly recalls her appearance as the Servant of the Guardian in 'The Guardian of Piri', and in both instances the robots she portrays end up with their faces blown apart.

Director Bob Brooks does a serviceable job with 'The Taybor', his debut episode for the series, but his style is mostly unremarkable. He would return to helm one additional episode: the vastly superior 'The Immunity Syndrome'.

Taybor's ship, the *SS Emporium*, is charming in internal and external design and was inspired by a NASA concept from 1970 for a Mars Excursion Vehicle. His home world also sports one of the most creative planet names in the series: Pinvith the Lesser. Some nice cinematography and special effects shine as highpoints of the episode.

Taybor's passion for beauty lies at the core of the story and is both his obsession and his downfall, though this is not achieved with any degree of subtlety: it is mentioned countless times throughout the episode. In trying so formidably to get its point across, 'The Taybor' only truly succeeds in hitting viewers over the head with something pretty.

'The Taybor' could be easily interpreted as commenting rather effectively on materialism and consumerism. The central dichotomy of the episode is that Taybor has lots of beautiful possessions, but he leads an empty existence. It is a valuable commentary on our economically orientated world. Taybor also bears parallels with Companion from 'The Infernal Machine' – a solitary being travelling space in a ship – and thus also recalls the themes of that earlier episode: isolation and loneliness. However, these more internal concepts were dealt with more effectively through the serious tone of 'The Infernal Machine', rather than the comedic approach found here.

There are a number of delightful lines in Taybor's dialogue where he refers to various travels he's had and planets he's visited. They are referenced so casually it's clearly just pure habit for him, but he succeeds in entertaining and dumbfounding the Alphans quite often.

'The Taybor' is charming fun, but – quite frankly – when a science fiction programme attempts to become a comedy, it has to be better than this. It has to be funny, like *The Hitchhiker's Guide to the Galaxy*, rather than slightly amusing. As something of an amusing romp, 'The Taybor' works reasonably well, but it commits the sin of ultimately being boring, and remains an unsatisfactory segment when compared to many other vastly better episodes of *Space: 1999*.

Sadly, 'The Taybor' is the first in a stretch of four of the worst episodes of Year Two.

Rating: 5/10

2.7
THE RULES OF LUTON

Screenplay by Charles Woodgrove (Fred Freiberger)
Directed by Val Guest

Selected Broadcast Dates:

UK	LWT:	
	Date: 23 October 1976.	Time: 11.00 am
	Granada:	
	Date: 3 July 1977.	
US	KRON (San Francisco):	
	Date: 16 October 1976.	Time: 7.00 pm

Credited Cast: Martin Landau (John Koenig), **Barbara Bain** (Helena Russell), **Catherine Schell** (Maya), **Tony Anholt** (Tony Verdeschi), **David Jackson** (Alien Strong), **Godfrey James** (Alien Transporter), **Roy Marsden** (Alien Invisible), **Yasuko Nagazumi** (Yasko)

Uncredited Cast: David Jackson (Voice of the Judges of Luton), **Annie Lambert** (Command Centre Operative), **Jenny Cresswell** (Operative L Picard)

Plot: While exploring the planet Luton, Koenig and Maya pick some flowers and eat some berries and find themselves accused of murder: the dominant species on Luton are plants, not animals! Koenig and Maya must fight to the death against alien beings accused of similar crimes; each endowed with a special power – invisibility, great strength and teleportation.

Quotes:
- **Koenig:** 'Obviously animals are a lower form of life on this planet. If we all kill each other, it's acceptable.'
- **Koenig:** 'All right, then I thank the bird for its keen eyesight and the lion for its terrible roar.'
- **Koenig:** 'She was like ... Helena.'
- **Koenig:** 'When I'm around, never pick a flower.'

On-screen Date: 892 days since leaving Earth orbit.

Filming Dates: Monday 3 May – Friday 14 May 1976

Commentary:
Martin Landau: 'We did one episode ["The Rules of Luton"] in which Catherine and I are alone on a planet which is very similar to Earth ... We shot that outside and we spent nine days out on location. It is virtually a chase picture.'

Catherine Schell: 'We were all so ill when we did ["The Rules of Luton"] – we were working with 104 degree fevers. England was suffering a drought and a heat wave, and that had hardly ever existed before. Working in the studios, the studios were obviously air conditioned, but going home or coming to work … The differences in temperature all the time [meant that] everybody came down with a terrible, terrible flu. Some of us had pneumonia, and we were working! So I remember that one, because we were having to work outside and we were sweating and everybody was terribly sick. But that's all I remember about it.'

Bloopers: Following Koenig's instructions to Maya for her to stay on hard ground in order not to leave footprints, watch Maya's jacket: it mysteriously disappears in one shot while she's running.

While Koenig and Maya swim across the lake, astute viewers will note the following on, or near, the far shore: a white post, several people walking, a park bench, and a man in a canoe!

After Maya and Koenig swim across that lake they are both completely dry.

Observations: Charles Woodgrove was a pen name used by Fred Freiberger to write three scripts for Year Two. Freiberger asserted that he was paid only expenses and wrote the scripts to help keep the second season's reduced budget in line.

Review: 'The Rules of Luton' is the ultimate mixed blessing. This is *Space: 1999*'s infamous 'talking plant' episode, but unlike its counterpart from *Lost In Space* – 'The Great Vegetable Rebellion' – this has not benefited from being elevated to the status of camp classic by the passage of time. This is also a 'double-up' episode, filmed on location while 'The Mark of Archanon' was shot on the studio sets.

Martin Landau and Catherine Schell deliver expressive and warm performances and are provided with a wealth of character-building material in the script. Koenig's speech about his wife and World War Three is striking (even if it is very difficult to reconcile with the timeline and history of Earth as evidenced in Year One episodes), as is Maya's recounting of Mentor's dream. Great depth is provided through the talents of Landau and Schell, and during these sequences the script shines: it is richly dramatic, emotional, character-driven material. Background detail on the civilisation of Psychon is fleshed out, portraying a very unified world with one class and one race, one religion and one government. As such there would be no conflicts or wars, no hatred or poverty. It's a wonderful utopian vision, even though the validity of Maya's comments can be questioned – after all, she was the naïve daughter of a mad scientist who drained the brains of passing aliens (which she didn't know about) and then used them as mine workers (which she also didn't know about). Whatever Maya's memories of her planet are, they are certainly framed by what Mentor told her and led her to believe, and cannot be taken as absolute fact. That Psychon could have been a utopian paradise is possible, but not certain.

The limitations of Maya's powers, as presented here, are debatable. The rule established in 'The Exiles' (and ignored in 'The Taybor') that Maya can hold a transformation for only one hour is repeated, but will be broken again later in the season in 'Seance Spectre'. Also anomalous here is the assertion that Maya is unable to transform directly from shape to shape without reverting to her own form in between, as she has been able to do in other episodes such as 'The Metamorph'. The inconsistencies are undoubtedly the result of writer Fred Freiberger using his artistic license to fit Maya's abilities into the confines of his own script.

Despite the stated pluses, the remainder of the script consists of nothing more than running to action music and a succession of tedious and predictable engagements with the alien trio, amounting to a laboriously dull viewing experience. The aliens themselves are merely grunting, one-dimensional caricatures, and their costumes are visibly cheap, especially in close-up shots. The talking trees (the 'Judges' of Luton) are an inexcusably stupid effort at presenting a plot based upon intelligent or purposeful plant life. It would have been far more intriguing if the plants on Luton had been portrayed as a more sinister, subtle or subversive threat, such as those in *The Day of the Triffids* or, from a later era, M Night Shyamalan's *The Happening*.

This episode belongs to Martin Landau and Catherine Schell, with the remaining characters in peripheral – and largely forgettable – roles. Helena is seen to be in command of Moonbase Alpha – sort of: she is never out of contact with Tony, and he seems to have the real authority.

The location shoot is welcome, as it was done so infrequently throughout the series. The locations are nicely dressed up with the odd tropical-looking plant, but the canyon setting for the final confrontation between plants and animals looks utterly unconvincing. It is actually the H F Warner Ltd landfill site in Knowl Hill, Berkshire, and looks entirely out of place on this world ruled by vegetation. Worthy of praise however are the dinosaur skeletons covered in vines, providing a striking visual impact.

It must be stated that this episode is little more than a combined duplication of the *Star Trek* episodes 'Arena' (itself based on the 1944 short story of the same name by Fredric Brown) and 'The Gamesters of Triskelion', along with elements of the previously mentioned 'The Great Vegetable Rebellion' from *Lost In Space*. The similarities are undeniable. The moral core of the episode can be found in the following exchange: Maya says, 'You mean people killed people just because they were different from each other? That's disgusting.' Koenig answers, 'The one virtue of that war, if war can have a virtue, is that prejudice was wiped out. People realised if they were going to survive they would have to work together, accept each other for what they were. So we began to create a brand new, wonderful civilisation.' The anti-prejudice theme is one always worth repeating, and the optimistic vision of all the peoples of the world coming together is an appealing notion.

'The Rules of Luton' is not to be recommended without a substantial warning of the radically different levels of quality between the superficial run-around plot and the pleasingly strong characterisation.

Rating: 4.5/10

2.8
THE MARK OF ARCHANON

Screenplay by Lew Schwarz
Directed by Charles Crichton

Selected Broadcast Dates:

UK	LWT:	
	Date: 16 October 1976.	Time: 11.30 am
	Granada:	
	Date: 26 June 1977.	Time: 2.35 pm
US	KRON (San Francisco):	
	Date: 9 October 1976.	Time: 7.00 pm

Credited Cast: Martin Landau (John Koenig), **Barbara Bain** (Helena Russell), **Catherine Schell** (Maya), **Tony Anholt** (Tony Verdeschi), **Nick Tate** (Alan Carter), **Veronica Lang** (Lyra / Maurna), **John Alkin** (Andy Johnson), **John Hug** (Bill Fraser), **Anthony Forrest** (Carson), **Raul Newney** (Dr Raul Nunez), **Yasuko Nagazumi** (Yasko)

Guest Stars: John Standing (Pasc), **Michael Gallagher** (Etrec)

Uncredited Cast: Quentin Pierre (Security Guard Pierce Quinton), **Annie Lambert** (Command Centre Operative), **Jenny Cresswell** (Operative L Picard), **Terry Walsh** (Rescue Eagle Pilot), **Barbara Kelly** (Voice of Computer)

Plot: In the lunar caverns, Alan Carter discovers two aliens – Pasc and Etrec – from Archanon, the planet of peace. But a strange 'killing sickness' infects these aliens, turning them into mass murderers.

Quotes:
- **Maya:** 'Archanon – it's the planet of peace … There are legends of the coming of the Peace Bringers; the conquest of evil by good.'
- **Lyra:** 'The terrible scourge we thought we had eradicated from our genes has returned.'
- **Pasc:** 'It's the last privilege of the killing sickness: to kill oneself.'
- **Helena:** 'As a doctor, I should have known. Besides, it's not a very satisfactory defence – ignorance.'

On-screen Date: 640 days since leaving Earth orbit.

Filming Dates: Tuesday 4 May – Tuesday 18 May 1976

Commentary:
Martin Landau: [Written on the front of his copy of this script] 'If the people on Alpha don't miss us – the audience won't!'

Barbara Bain: [On guest stars] 'Margaret Leighton [in "Collision Course"] was just wonderful and comes immediately to mind. Billie Whitelaw [in "One Moment of Humanity"] I had always admired. John Standing [in "The Mark of Archanon"] was great. There were a lot of good actors available because we were filming in London. As for directors, it was absolutely delicious to work with Charlie Crichton, who was a self-appointed oldest, meanest grouch in the whole world, but was actually a darling.'

Bloopers: A blooper in dialogue occurs as Tony orders Eagle One to launch: Eagle One is already launched, and away from the base – Koenig and Maya are in it!

Wires are visible pulling apart the rocks in front of the Archanon stasis chambers.

Observations: Alan Carter sings at the start of the show, as he has before on a couple of occasions. However, when he has sung before, his words have served to foreshadow future occurrences in the episode, while here it's utterly meaningless.

Review: *Space: 1999* continues a precipitous nose-dive in quality and manages the feat of producing the worst entry in its entire 48 episode run. There is little to redeem 'The Mark of Archanon'.

On the positive side, Barbara Bain has a highly prominent lead role, which she handles beautifully. The notion of the mining of minerals deep within the Moon is an admirable one, and stands as one of the strongest additions to the series' mythos initiated by the second season. The concept of ancient aliens buried beneath the lunar surface is also very intriguing, with possibilities that could undoubtedly have been explored in any number of more successful directions. If this had been Year One, the aliens might have been some of the original Arkadians who seeded life on Earth – but, as with most of Year Two, much of what came before has been forgotten. Like 'The Testament of Arkadia', this episode introduces elements of Erich von Däniken's *Chariots of the Gods* into the *Space: 1999* universe, with its premise of the Archanon's visits to early Earth and the presumed impact they might have had on any civilisations they encountered. Note the strong Babylonian influence in the Archanon costume design. While appealing, these notions fail to recall the past experience of the Alphans, and thus what could have been an enriching and elaborating addition to earlier concepts is simply a weak display of generic sci-fi.

The Archanon space cruiser is of appealing design and impressively filmed by the effects team. If only it was featured on screen for a little longer it could be appreciated more fully. Guest star John Standing's attempts to give some dignity to his preposterous part, horribly unconvincing beard, pointless make-up and cardboard costume are commendable but mostly in vain. Even worse for Standing is that Pasc fails to be a menacing threat and comes across as benign rather than as a killer. The closing sequence featuring Martin Landau and Barbara Bain is pleasant: their talents and charm provide a lift for the end of the show. But that's all there is.

On the negative side, shockingly terrible special effects see apparently tin-foil asteroids being hurled at Koenig's and Maya's Eagle. This is a sorry excuse for an asteroid field, utterly unworthy of appearing in any episode of *Space: 1999*. It also seems to be extremely localised – why don't Koenig and Maya simply fly around it; and, given the visibility of space and the aid of their instrumentation, why did they fly into it to begin with? Koenig and Maya make only token appearances so that the latter can deliver a couple of feed-lines back to the base. This is another 'double-up' episode, as Landau and Schell were off on location filming their marginally better segment, 'The Rules of Luton'.

The script is feeble and delivers nothing of substantive intellectual appeal or intrigue. Written by Lew Schwarz (whose name is misspelled in the credits as Schwartz), it contains countless nonsenses. Starting at the very beginning, why is Chief of Reconnaissance Alan Carter leading geologists through the catacombs of the Moon on a hunt for minerals? Perhaps it's a hobby, or a volunteer activity; but without an explanation, it's merely careless writing. In the same vein, why does Chief of Security Tony Verdeschi perform the scientific analysis of the Archanon equipment? Professor Bergman might be missing, but surely there are still scientists on Alpha! Again this displays utter disregard for audience intelligence and for the basic outlines of the main characters of the series. Why are the aliens repeatedly left alone and unguarded throughout the episode, so they can proceed to wander about Alpha on their own? Where are the security protocols, or any semblance of common sense? These Alphans are idiots who seem not only to have learned nothing from their previous encounters with aliens on the base (such as Dione, Balor or Cantar and Zova), but also to have lost any sense of caution they might have once possessed.

Unforgivably, this episode also completely forgets the single most important purpose – apart from basic survival – in the lives of the Alphans, which is finding a new world to live on. In Year One, the Alphans contemplated living on the frozen Ultima Thule, and later in Year Two they will give thought to the idea of colonising an asteroid field – clear illustrations of their occasional desperation and willingness not to rule out any possibilities. But here, with friendly aliens possessing an impressive spaceship and an unknown wealth of information about diverse worlds that might be able to support the denizens of Moonbase Alpha, not a single mention is made of their search. Not one thought is given to asking these compassionate aliens for help. It is inexcusable for the writers and producers to have abandoned the prime focus of the series simply because they found it expedient to do so.

The planet Crom II is mentioned, and apparently the Alphans have been there, but this has never been shown in any of the episodes. While not technically a blooper, since the Alphans could have had other adventures unseen on screen, this is another case of the scriptwriter resorting to an easy contrivance to provide the Alphans with knowledge they otherwise couldn't have. While some might consider this to be a welcome expansion of the scope of Alpha's past encounters, it can also easily be looked upon as lazy writing.

Watching Michael Gallagher portray Etrec is wearisome. Nearly every action he takes is agonisingly unconvincing, and his voice has been dubbed (badly) in much the same manner as that of Cantar in 'The Exiles'. And, unfortunately, he's not the only unconvincing actor in the episode. Never before, and never again, would Nick Tate be so wildly broad in his portrayal of Alan Carter, or be fed so much drivel by a script. This was an attempt, seemingly, to make Carter more likeable; but why? He *is* likeable. He has *always* been likeable. Here he is transformed into a stereotype of an Australian, tossing a football and throwing around words like 'cobber'. He becomes a caricature, rather than a character. His arbitrary and unconvincing friendship with Etrec and subsequent trips down the corridor for hamburgers should have been avoided at all costs. If anyone involved in the production had bothered to look back to Year One, they could have seen how comfortably and touchingly Carter had shown his paternal side and bonded with young Jackie Crawford in 'Alpha Child'. That was a well-portrayed relationship; this is embarrassing to all involved. Tate is an exceptional actor who certainly should have been used more effectively throughout the series. This was not the way to do it.

Actors John Alkin and Anthony Forrest, as Johnson and Carson, appear to be in a contest to see which one of them can produce the most stilted delivery of dialogue – it appears to be a draw. However, as English actor John Alkin has been dubbed in this part, it's difficult to judge him fairly. Actress Veronica Lang is the most impressive of the guest performers in her part as Lyra/Maurna. Watch for her dress to re-appear on Yesta (actress Kathryn Leigh Scott) in the later episode 'Dorzak' – perhaps both ladies purchased their gowns from the same intergalactic fashion designer?

The revolving door of secondary doctors on Alpha continues to spin. This time around it's Dr Raul Nunez, played quite capably by Raul Newney (who is wrongly credited as 'Raul Newey'). While it does begin to strain credibility to have so many doctors (Russell, Mathias, Vincent, Nunez and later Spencer) as well as countless nurses, all servicing a population that is now under three hundred, Alpha was undoubtedly serving as a medical research facility while still in orbit around Earth and many of these doctors might have been there conducting experiments rather than actively taking care of patients.

Director Charles Crichton faced an impossible task with this script, and failed through no fault of his own. To borrow a phrase from actor Barry Morse, it was almost as if he were being asked to construct the Taj Mahal out of chicken droppings.

The concept of an alien race of peace-bringers who can't kill, but are threatened by a 'killing sickness' that turns them into mass murderers, certainly has potential. Perhaps if it had been treated with the chilling approach of an episode like 'End of Eternity' it would have been more successful As it is, the jokes evoke winces, and moments like Pasc's strangling of Carter and Etrec's near-strangling of a dove (strangling the symbol of peace – no sign of subtlety in this episode!) shoot completely off the melodrama scale.

'The Mark of Archanon' is an absolute embarrassment to the series.

Rating: 3.5/10

2.9
BRIAN THE BRAIN

Screenplay by Jack Ronder
Directed by Kevin Connor

Selected Broadcast Dates:

UK	LWT:	
	Date: 2 October 1976.	Time: 11.00 am
	Granada:	
	Date: 13 May 1977.	Time: 7.30 pm
US	KRON (San Francisco):	
	Date: 23 October 1976.	Time: 7.00 pm

Credited Cast: Martin Landau (John Koenig), **Barbara Bain** (Helena Russell), **Catherine Schell** (Maya), **Tony Anholt** (Tony Verdeschi), **John Hug** (Bill Fraser), **Marc Zuber** (Security Guard), **Michael Sharvell-Martin** (Brian Robot), **Annie Lambert** (Command Centre Operative), **Yasuko Nagazumi** (Yasko)

Guest Star: Bernard Cribbins (Captain Michael / Voice of Brian)

Uncredited Cast: Quentin Pierre (Security Guard Pierce Quinton)

Plot: Brian the Brain is a robot found on board a Swift ship from Earth. It has survived an encounter on the nearby Planet D, which killed the crew of the Star Mission of 1996, consisting of four Swift craft and a mother ship. But its initial friendly appearance is deceiving: Brian kidnaps Koenig and Russell and takes them to Planet D.

Quotes:
- **Brian:** 'Don't step on my antenna! It gives me the heebie-jeebies, not to mention a headache.'
- **Fraser:** 'What is this Brain – some crazy, hijacking slot machine?'
- **Brian:** 'Wowee! It was simultaneous! You can have all your air back.'
- **Koenig:** 'That Brain is mad.'
- **Brian:** 'All I wanted was life, and friends. I'm so lonely – take it all. Take it all!'

On-screen Date: 1,150 days since leaving Earth orbit.

Filming Dates: Tuesday 18 May – Wednesday 2 June 1976

Commentary:

Martin Landau: 'One that is interesting is called "Brian the Brain", which [involves] a computer that talks like a human being and moves around. It sounds like a cross between Jerry Lewis and Mickey Rooney, but it turns out to be terribly dangerous. It starts out as a kind of charming object, and actually it is kind of a fun show.

'The English stuntmen are not as good as those in [the USA], and very often I would end up actually gaffing, or coordinating, the fight scenes, which really wasn't my job. Part of the reason for doing that was so I wouldn't get hurt. That was because I was in them! If you're not doing it right, you could get really hurt.'

Catherine Schell: 'I remember turning into a mouse. I had quite a good time turning into an ape. And I absolutely loved being the hawk. But the most fun I had was when I turned into Bernard Cribbins!'

Kevin Connor: 'It was great fun to shoot on those sets, because you can do anything you like. I mean, anything goes, because nobody knows really about that world. "Brian the Brain" was a tongue-in-cheek story, a humorous one. Bernard Cribbins was the voice, and he's a wonderful English comedian. We had a little dwarf inside. It was just great fun. It's a great genre to work in.'

Bloopers: Series continuity is broken when Brian the Brain mentions that the Moonbase computer doesn't talk – which is entirely contradictory to Year One, as well as the Year Two episodes 'The Mark of Archanon' and 'All That Glisters'.

Review: 'Brian the Brain', written by Jack Ronder, features an excellent and dramatic opening teaser. Sadly, this has nothing to do with the episode that follows, and before long a series of stunning stupidities are being hurled at the viewer: Maya calculates that the Swift spaceship (the size, more or less, of an Eagle) is a small planet. Tony vaguely states that the Alpha computer seems to have 'slowed up' (another rather pointless distraction from the lack of plot). An evacuation of Alpha is undertaken and immediately abandoned, while the mystery of what pulled the Moon off course is nearly completely forgotten. Ultimately, it turns out that Brian was fooling with the computer on Alpha and the Moon never was pulled off course in the first place – but it all makes one wonder what the point was, aside from stretching a threadbare concept into an hour-long episode.

On the plus side, the Swift is a very nice ship; a finely crafted miniature incorporating an enjoyably 1970s style and feel. As with the already established Eagle and Hawk ships, the name js taken from a bird, but it's also appealing that it implies a capacity for very high speed.

Series continuity is strained to breaking point by the disclosures about the Star Mission of 1996, involving a Mother ship and four Swift craft taking off on a major deep space exploration journey – which implies the ships were capable of faster-than-light travel. In the context of everything established in Year One, this level of technology was beyond the capacity of Earth technology at that time. Exploration in 1996 was on the scale of the Ultra Probe mission in 'Dragon's Domain', which involved just a single craft within Earth's own solar system. All the indications were that this – and potential other missions of its kind – was prohibitively expensive. The five-ship Star Mission posited by 'Brian the Brain' is totally out of scale for *Space: 1999*.

The Star Mission idea presents other problems. Following the unbroken chain of disastrous Earth space missions from Year One (the Meta Probe, the Astro 7, the Uranus Expedition, the Voyager ships and the Ultra Probe), it is becoming increasingly difficult to believe that there are yet more failed Earth missions out in space. Who funded them all? And where did the faster-than-light capability come from?

Planet D is a strikingly unique world of yellow lighting, low gravity, heavy mists, unbreathable atmosphere and dead trees covered in cobwebs. Its realisation is, in fact, excellent – thanks to Keith Wilson. Keith also got to play around with some nicely coloured Perspex while designing the interior set of the Swift, which certainly makes the episode more watchable … but when the colourful bits of Perspex are more interesting than the characters or plot, there is a clear problem.

What is annoying about Planet D is its name – had the production team run out of ideas for interesting names to give planets? Possibly it is meant to imply that it is the fourth planet in a star system, but it seems to be lazy scriptwriting when previous writers had come up with such marvellous planet names as Terra Nova, Zenno, Piri, Atheria, Ultima Thule, Ultra, Arkadia, Psychon, Golos, Vega and Pinvith the Lesser – just to cite some of the mostt memorable examples. In comparison, Planet D is insipid.

In flagrant disregard of their usual priorities, the Alphans ignore the fact that there are three Swift crafts and a Mother ship on Planet D (not to mention the fourth Swift that Brian is piloting), when they should be making every effort possible to salvage them and incorporate them into Alpha's fleet. The potential value of these ships is incalculable, and yet no one thinks to try to fly any of them back to the Moon.

Brian the Brain itself is embarrassing, irritating and manages to prove that a robot *can* overact. Of course, this was filmed prior to *Star Wars* and the introduction of C3PO and R2D2, but this big yellow box on wheels is just too primitive to be tolerated. This is another example of the show suffering from the reduced budget of Year Two: the resources were simply unavailable to create something more impressive.

While the psychological defeat of Brian is well done, it shows a blatant lack of originality. *Star Trek*'s Captain Kirk did essentially the same thing as Koenig does in this episode: talking computers to death was practically Kirk's trademark, and it should never have been Koenig's.

John Hug is likeable as Bill Fraser, while Catherine Schell and Tony Anholt try their best to play all of this drivel seriously. Martin Landau and Barbara Bain are excellent, as always, but they must have been questioning their fate, trapped acting opposite this annoying robot. They prove that great actors can do good work even when confronted with something as nonsensical as this script. Compliments, however, should go to the 'Love Test', which is a classic moment to fans of John and Helena, and is effectively menacing, albeit ultimately as pointless to the plot as everything else.

The story does eventually find a point of sorts on Planet D: Brian the Brain is insane! Brian's homicidal past is revealed and viewers learn that Brian's creator, Captain Michael, was working on a new and improved robot to take Brian's place as the new Brain. But other questions are raised. Why did the entire crew of the Swifts and the Mother ship go out onto the surface of the planet at the same time? Why did they go so far from their ships, into a poisonous alien atmosphere without environmental suits? The plan to defeat the robot successfully incorporates Maya's metamorphic abilities into the action, but astute viewers must question how Maya knows what Captain Michael sounded like. It's a trivial point, but a valid one. Once the Alphans finally succeed, they save Brian and decide to reprogram him with morality and the Ten Commandments – another instance of mindless writing. What good do the Ten Commandments do for a robot? 'Thou shalt not commit adultery'? It might sound acceptable to a passing ear, or an unthinking story editor, but once you scratch the surface, it is a pointless statement. What would have been far more intelligent, useful and respectable to a literary science fiction audience would have been to reference Isaac Asimov's famous Three Laws of Robotics.

Director Kevin Connor helms his first of two episodes (the second being the far superior 'Seed of Destruction'). Connor is a talented and accomplished director, but there is little evidence of his abilities here. Again, though, he isn't helped by Jack Ronder's script, which contains numerous lines that lead the viewer to wince, including Tony's painful comment to Maya, 'You know what your problem is? Your brain works like a computer, so you're jealous of that other computer.'

The excellent depiction of Planet D and the sound basic elements of *Space: 1999* – Moonbase Alpha, the Eagles and the main cast – are all that save this silly little hour from being a complete waste of time. It is somewhat cute, but this 'kidnapping power-mad machine that wants to live forever' story was told far better with Gwent in Year One's 'The Infernal Machine'. While the plots of the two episodes share certain surface similarities, there is no comparison at all in terms of execution. There is something to be said for the venerable theme of the danger of technology, which has provided some of the best plots in the series. Here, however, the potential of the theme is lost to the paucity of the script and realisation of the production.

The lightweight 'Brian the Brain' demonstrates how totally lost *Space: 1999* became in many of these mid-second season entries. This would have been more fittingly titled *Lost in Space: 1999*.

Rating: 4/10

2.10
NEW ADAM NEW EVE

Screenplay by Terence Feely
Directed by Charles Crichton

Selected Broadcast Dates:

UK   LWT:
            Date: 9 October 1976.   Time: 11.30 am
            Granada:
            Date: 20 May 1977.   Time: 7.30 pm
US   KRON (San Francisco):
            Date: 2 October 1976.   Time: 7.00 pm

Credited Cast: Martin Landau (John Koenig), **Barbara Bain** (Helena Russell), **Catherine Schell** (Maya), **Tony Anholt** (Tony Verdeschi), **Nick Tate** (Alan Carter), **Bernard Kay** (Humanoid), **Albin Pahernik** (Maya Creature), **Annie Lambert** (Command Centre Operative), **Barbara Wise** (Beautiful Girl), **Yasuko Nagazumi** (Yasko)

Guest Star: Guy Rolfe (Magus)

Uncredited Cast: Robert Reeves (Operative Peter Reeves), **Glenda Allen** (Technician), **Terry York** (Ape Man)

Fight Arranger: Romo Gorrara

Stunts: Frank Henson (for Bernard Kay), **Terry Walsh** (for Martin Landau), **Cliff Diggins** (for Martin Landau and Guy Rolfe)

Plot: An alien being appears in Command Centre proclaiming to be God, and offers the Alphans the opportunity to start again on a new world. Taking John, Helena, Maya and Tony to the new planet, Magus reveals his deception: he is an alien magician and mad scientist intent on creating a perfect race.

Quotes:
- **Koenig:** 'We're a bit low on sacrificial goats.'
- **Magus:** 'Sceptical, cynical, mean: maybe that's why I always had a soft spot for you. Some of my creatures are like tame rabbits.'
- **Magus:** 'Throughout its whole history, your species has been notable for two things: asking interminable questions and injuring itself.'
- **Magus:** 'You've been a great disappointment to me. All those wars; your wilful destruction of the natural resources of the planet I gave you; your pollution of it.'

On-screen Date: 1,095 days since leaving Earth orbit.

Filming Dates: Wednesday 2 June – Friday 18 June 1976

Incidental Music: The only instance of library music in Year Two is heard during the campfire scene: Robert Farnon's composition 'How Beautiful is Night'.

Bloopers: One of the most unforgivable bloopers in the entire series can be found here, but slow motion might be necessary to catch it. Towards the start of the episode, on New Earth, Magus uses Koenig's Stun Gun to prove his power by shooting himself. When Magus supposedly has the gun materialise in his hand, the gun does not materialise at all, but is *placed* into Magus's hand by an arm that reaches right across the entire screen from the lower right!

Maya transforms into an owl and is able to touch Tony, despite the magnetic force fields keeping them apart while she is in humanoid form.

Review: *Space: 1999* rebounds in quality with the excellent 'New Adam New Eve'. This was inspired by the 1896 H G Wells novel *The Island of Doctor Moreau*, in which the main characters are taken to an island and discover the inhabitants are the horrifying results of experimental vivisections perpetrated by Dr Moreau. These beings face a torturous existence full of suffering. The themes contained within the novel and this episode are the same: discussions of human nature, society, and the act of playing God, personified by one character; whether Dr Moreau or this episode's Magus.

In a far more chilling comparison, Magus could be equated with the notorious Nazi war criminal Josef Mengele, who performed experiments on prisoners in the Auschwitz concentration camp. His experiments were often focused on heredity and physical abnormalities, much like those of Magus in 'New Adam New Eve'. There are also undoubted similarities between this episode and the *Star Trek* segment 'Who Mourns for Adonais?'

Terence Feely's script cleverly drops clues to the Alphans – and the viewers – about the true nature of Magus, and combines with some unique direction from stalwart Charles Crichton to make this a very strong episode. The four leads contribute engrossing performances, and Guy Rolfe gives a standout turn as Magus, particularly during his verbal sparring sessions with Commander Koenig. An eerie and effective wind heralds Magus's arrival on Alpha, and Koenig quite appropriately tells Magus, 'We've learned to mistrust appearances,' which recalls any number of prior episodes. It is also entertaining to see Magus manipulating the Alphans into different relationships than they have chosen for themselves – Koenig with Maya and Helena with Tony.

The planet set is tremendous, and attentive viewers will recognise the birdsong from Year One's 'Matter of Life and Death'. Another borrowed sound effect – this one from 'The Taybor' – accompanies Magus's arrival, and the swirling visual effect overlaying his first appearance on Alpha comes from 'Dragon's Domain'. The new special effects are quite dynamic, culminating in the final explosions of New Earth. The use of real lizards filmed to look like giant monsters – in classic B-movie style – and the inclusion of the mutant (despite the obvious costume) add to the scope of the episode. There is some interesting character information given, including the revelation that Maya used to study Comparative Universal Theology, and that Tony comes from a long line of farmers. One of Maya's most striking transformations appears here, as she reverts to herself when Helena passes between her and the camera: it's an effortless but extremely effective visual trick.

Magus is an enigmatic false prophet who proclaims, 'I have been among you many times. I was Simon Magus, who offered to buy the Nazarene's powers from his apostles. I was Merlin. I was Nostradamus. I was the magician in ancient Egypt who contended in magic with Moses.' The most interesting of these claimed past appearances must be the first: Simon Magus was believed by the Gnostic sect of Simonianism to be God in human form. Simon was a magician said to have the power to levitate and fly. The etymology of the name 'Magus' is also quite fitting: the Magi (in singular, Magus) were a tribe from ancient Media who were responsible for religious practices. 'Magi' is also the root of the words magic and magician. Additionally, in ancient Greece, the word Magos referred to enchanters and wizards, particularly charlatans, which is clearly applicable to this episode.

Some of the religious concepts mentioned throughout the show are quite compelling and could lead viewers to further discussion or consideration. One interesting line has Magus discounting all of Earth's religions, 'But all these highly imaginative works of fiction that you call religion have clouded your minds; filled you with false gods.' Of course, he proclaims himself (falsely) to be the one true God, so everything he says is discountable. All this open and direct talk of God and religion is interesting, but it does again show the clear differences between Year One and Year Two. In the first season this would have been the vague 'cosmic intelligence' discussion from 'Black Sun'. It's an important distinction to note, regardless of which approach a viewer prefers.

Once again a Year Two episode ends on a dramatic note, rather than the all-too-frequent forced comedic moment; here it is Koenig's insightful comment on Magus, 'One chink of light as Earth broke up around him and Magus would still get away with it.' This final discussion also leaves open the possibility that Magus could return in another episode.

'New Adam New Eve' is strong science fiction television, featuring robust acting, appealing dialogue and music, and some attractive visuals. Overall, this is a highly recommended episode, and a virtual blessing following the season's previous four episodes.

Rating: 8/10

2.11
CATACOMBS OF THE MOON

Screenplay by Anthony Terpiloff
Directed by Robert Lynn

Selected Broadcast Dates:

UK	LWT:	
	Date: 27 November 1976.	Time: 10.55 am
	Granada:	
	Date: 6 November 1977.	Time: 1.15 pm
US	KRON (San Francisco):	
	Date: 13 November 1976.	Time: 7.00 pm

Credited Cast: Martin Landau (John Koenig), **Barbara Bain** (Helena Russell), **Catherine Schell** (Maya), **Tony Anholt** (Tony Verdeschi), **Zienia Merton** (Sandra Benes), **Jeffery Kissoon** (Ben Vincent), **Lloyd McGuire** (First Engineer), **Brendan Price** (Security Guard Morgan), **Alan Hunter** (Co-Pilot Bill), **Nova Llewellyn** (First Alphan Woman)

Guest Stars: James Laurenson (Patrick Osgood), **Pamela Stephenson** (Michelle Osgood)

Uncredited Cast: Quentin Pierre (Security Guard Pierce Quinton), **Harry Fielder** (Security Guard George), **Robert Reeves** (Operative Peter Reeves), **Pam Rose** (Operative P Rose), **Jenny Cresswell** (Operative L Picard), **Glenda Allen** (Operative G Allen), **Karen Ford** (Nurse), **Saul Reichlin** (Second Engineer), **Felicity York** (Second Alphan Woman)

Stunts: Cliff Diggins, Tracey Eddon

Plot: Patrick Osgood begins to have visions of the destruction of Moonbase Alpha in a vast cosmic firestorm. It seems Osgood's prophecy will be fulfilled as waves of heat begin to beat down on Alpha and Koenig discovers an incredible heat nebula heading for the Moon.

Quotes:
- **Co-Pilot:** 'Talk about Dante's Inferno.'
- **Osgode:** 'Oh, I have a different faith than yours – a more certain knowledge of what is to be and what is not to be.'
- **Tony:** 'Pat, is that what you came storming in here just now to tell me?'
- **Osgode:** 'Your medical science – your advanced quackery – is no substitute for the true faith. Only faith can out-face death.'
- **Helena:** 'I'm glad you have such tremendous faith in me.'

- **Osgood:** 'Be conquered by my faith. You weren't born to die. You are being and breath. What you are can never be destroyed.'

On-screen Date: 1,196 days since leaving Earth orbit.

Filming Dates: Monday 21 June – Tuesday 6 July 1976

Review: Another 'double-up' episode, filmed at the same time as 'The AB Chrysalis', 'Catacombs of the Moon' is edgy, moody and atmospheric. It is virtually a show right out of Year One, redesigned to fit the second season format. This must be due to writer Anthony Terpiloff, who previously wrote 'Collision Course' and, with his wife Elizabeth Barrows, 'Death's other Dominion' and 'The Infernal Machine' – all memorable episodes from the first series. His obvious prevailing themes are carried over into this episode, with the most clearly defined being that of faith.

Filled with surrealistic images of Michelle Osgood on a white-canopied bed surrounded by a circle of flames on the lunar surface, 'Catacombs of the Moon' is visually dynamic. These visions consume Patrick Osgood, along with his premonitions of a vast heat storm.

James Laurenson turns in an outstandingly strong performance as Patrick. Pamela Stephenson delivers a sweet and subdued turn as Michelle, a woman clearly in love with her husband, and it's enjoyable to see another couple on the Moon.

Alphan tempers flare as the temperature within the base rises. Zienia Merton shines in her strong supporting role, while Tony Anholt achieves a marvellous degree of subtlety and charm in such scenes as his talk with Patrick in the explosives storeroom. Barbara Bain conveys a tremendous strength in Helena Russell as she searches with determination for the answers to save her patient. To her optimism is contrasted Ben Vincent's pessimism. While always a capable actor, Jeffrey Kissoon rarely made an impact in his role as Dr Vincent, but here his character has some dimension and his cynical outlook provides for some character drama in the Medical Centre sequences. The joy is that everybody gets to sink their acting teeth into a script containing a wealth of edgy dialogue exchanges, and it's an opportunity the actors clearly took advantage of.

Martin Landau puts in a few brief appearances from an Eagle exploring the approaching heat storm, which adds his presence to the episode, unlike some other 'double-up' segments like 'Dorzak' in which he doesn't appear at all. Catherine Schell also has only two quite small scenes but, as with Landau, at least she's here. Her first scene, while she is off-duty, shows an exotic looking Maya walking in the base wearing a marbled green dress and elaborate hairstyle, adding dimension to her private off-duty life.

Unlike in a number of other Year Two segments, in 'Catacombs of the Moon' every bit part is performed by a capable actor who holds his or her own with the series regulars. Prime examples include Karen Ford as the Medical Centre Nurse, Alan Hunter as Koenig's co-pilot Bill and Brendan Price as Security Guard Morgan. To put this in perspective, contrast their fine work with the crimes against acting committed in 'The Mark of Archanon'.

There is much in this episode about altered states of consciousness. Patrick's apparently disturbed mind may not actually be disturbed at all, and he may be in some form of contact with whatever cosmic presence exists as, or within, the heat storm. Michelle in her state of declining health – near death – also seems to reach new levels of mental abilities. Both characters seem to communicate telepathically with each other. In Michelle's case, this is while she is asleep. Perhaps this is when her mind is most freed of the physical limitations of her body. Or is it all part of Patrick's psychosis?

The recurring vision sequences with Michelle in the bed on the lunar surface do have an interesting similarity to Koenig's Year One 'dream' sequences in 'Missing Link', where Victor Bergman is seen running towards the Commander but unable to reach him. Here it is Patrick who runs, arms outstretched, towards Michelle – but never reaches her.

It is also interesting to see the Alphan clothes getting more and more casual as the heat levels rise. Uniforms are replaced by an assortment of cooler casual wear, and this does add to the believability of life on Alpha – no-one would wear the exact same clothes all the time, every day, no matter how many different sets of uniforms they each have.

The Eagle is seen to be equipped with forward vision shields: when Koenig encounters the blinding light of the heat storm he calls for the 'glare shield' to be activated, and a screen descends, protecting forward vision ports from extreme glare. It's a logical feature for the Eagle to be equipped with, but has not been referenced before.

Adding to the drama of the episode, the heat waves pounding Alpha and the Moon cause tremors and quakes in the lunar crust, making the search for Patrick and Michelle more treacherous amid rock falls from the catacomb ceilings.

The show is well directed, well plotted and features excellent characterisation and an outstanding use of minor Moonbase personnel. There are some fairly impressive special effects, and some of the most cinematic visuals of the entire season – most especially those images of the nearly burning bed on the lunar surface and the smoking-hot exterior of Moonbase Alpha, lit in orange by the fire storm.

There are a couple of plotting issues: where does Maya go after the rockslide buries Patrick, and why doesn't she help Tony dig Osgood out? Osgood's life is clearly at stake, and while it is dramatic to have Tony struggle alone to dig his friend out from beneath a rock pile (and he is heroically successful), one wonders why Maya doesn't lend her abilities to the cause. Another lapse in series logic: although Anthony Terpiloff's script originally referred to the 'Dorfman' artificial heart as the 'Bergman' artificial heart, this was changed by Fred Freiberger prior to filming. The scripted reference to Bergman's heart would have leant a valuable degree of continuity between the seasons, and it's an absolute shame it was altered.

Nevertheless, Helena's transplant of an artificial heart into Michelle is successful – physically. But she cannot transplant faith, or the will to live. Michelle's recovery only really occurs when she is reunited with her husband.

As the characters speculate, who can say what the motivations of the heat storm were? How was it linked to Patrick Osgood in the condition he was in? And was it even real to begin with, or was it conjured from Osgood's own subconscious link with some cosmic intelligence? These are intriguing questions that are raised and left for viewers to consider on their own, while all the issues essential to the plot are resolved satisfactorily. Additionally, it's a delight to hear Helena state, 'We know so little about the universe.' It recalls the original spirit of *Space: 1999* and incorporates it into the less mystical second season, where the Alphans seem more accustomed to their journey, more able to cope and understand the universe around them.

'Catacombs of the Moon' is a very strong episode, made more appealing and unique within the realm of Year Two by these suggestions that a Mysterious Unknown Force may have been at work.

Rating: 8/10

2.12
THE AB CHRYSALIS

Screenplay by Tony Barwick
Directed by Val Guest

Selected Broadcast Dates:

UK   LWT:
            Date: 20 November 1976.   Time: 10.55 am
            Granada:
            Date: 31 July 1977.
US   KRON (San Francisco):
            Date: 6 November 1976.   Time: 7.00 pm

Credited Cast: Martin Landau (John Koenig), **Barbara Bain** (Helena Russell), **Catherine Schell** (Maya), **Nick Tate** (Alan Carter), **Robert Reitty** (Sphere Voice), **John Hug** (Bill Fraser), **David Sebastian Bach** (C – Guardian's Brother), **Sarah Bullen** (Operative Kate), **Albin Pahernik** (Kreno Animal (Maya)), **Yasuko Nagazumi** (Yasko)

Guest Stars: Ina Skriver (A), **Sarah Douglas** (B)

Uncredited Cast: Robert Reeves (Operative Peter Reeves), **Pam Rose** (Operative P Rose), **Quentin Pierre** (Security Guard Pierce Quinton), **Harry Fielder** (Alphan)

Previously Titled: 'The Chrysalis A B C '

Plot: Moonbase Alpha travels toward the source of huge, precisely timed explosions in space; the defence mechanism of an alien culture. Koenig must convince the aliens to stop the next explosion, or Alpha will be destroyed.

Quotes:
- **A:** 'You look well-featured, Commander Koenig.'
- **Koenig:** 'This is Commander Koenig. In less than a minute you will be hit by another energy wave. At this range, Moonbase Alpha may well be destroyed. At best you must assume severe damage and large numbers of casualties. Let the log show that I commend all personnel for their courage, fortitude and devotion to duty since we left Earth orbit. That is all.'
- **Koenig:** 'What happened is – we're coming home!'

On-screen Date: 1,288 days since leaving Earth orbit.

Filming Dates: Friday 18 June – Tuesday 6 July 1976

Commentary:

John Hug: 'Sarah Bullen, who's still a friend, had only one line of dialogue in the entire two series. There was always a possibility that she was going to have a line, or more lines, and when she finally got this line [in "The AB Chrysalis"], it was party time. "Yes! Sarah's got a line!" It was an incredible line – we still sort of rib her about it. More or less, there's an explosion in Moonbase Alpha, and she had this big thing on her desk that falls over. Koenig comes up and says, "Are you all right, Kate?" She says, "I'm fine, Commander, but I'm afraid my equipment's taken a bit of a battering." That was her line, and they never let her speak again. Which is very sad, really. I'd actually thought she was a bigger character, because the day I arrived, wandering around in my quilted space suit, she came up and introduced herself grandly, "Hello, I'm Sarah Bullen. I play Operative Kate." I didn't know who Operative Kate was. She showed me around the set, introduced me to people; she sort of took me under her wing. It was only later on I realised she didn't have any lines. But that didn't matter – she was wonderful. I think she should have been given whole speeches.'

Bloopers: Watch the pictures of Alan and Maya on their identity badges – the backdrop behind them both keeps changing from light to dark.

There are strings everywhere, blatantly obvious holding up the Eagles, as well as guiding the alien voice spheres.

Martin Landau partly lifts up his toupee in the early scene when he puts his hands to the sides of his head during 'blast procedure'.

Observations: This episode features use of the rare Yellow Alert (previously seen in 'Matter of Life and Death').

Review: 'The AB Chrysalis' is the 'double-up' parallel to 'Catacombs of the Moon' and is another of the best episodes of Year Two. Tony Barwick's script opens with mystery and frantic activity, bringing the viewer instantly into the crisis Alpha is facing and successfully demonstrating current Alpha base procedure, with nice shots of various sections and their urgent actions in emergency situations. Barwick's script is matched by sharp direction from Val Guest (far superior to his pedestrian efforts on 'The Rules of Luton').

The characters fare well in this script, although it is strange that Tony is absent for the entire episode. Perhaps he was injured in one of the blast waves? If so, it isn't mentioned. The notion of Helena commanding the base in John's absence is admirably portrayed, and is the only time she ever takes complete command of Moonbase Alpha. The often under-utilised Bill Fraser is well featured here, and Yasko comes across more successfully than usual. Catherine Schell conveys a desirable intensity, while Martin Landau is flawless, and Barbara Bain plays the part of 'Commander' Helena Russell with a subtle strength and humanity. Humour is well integrated into the story, such as when Koenig says, 'Isn't everybody after getting hit with three or four hundred volts?' Koenig's also afforded the opportunity to make a clear statement of his moral values: 'There are things more precious than safety. Loyalty is better than logic. Hope is better than despair. And creation is better than destruction. I just wanted to tell you that, you seekers of perfection.' This speech may be somewhat simplistic, but it has more of an effect than he realises: as the Alphans believe they are about to meet their likely demise, the aliens control their protective detonation and effectively save both the crew of the

Eagle and that of Moonbase Alpha. 'Creation is better than destruction,' remains a particularly poignant statement, which is easily applicable to the modern world.

Special effects are very good throughout, including the incredible shots of the first shockwave and of the base almost covered in places by lunar dust. There is some fascinating design work in the model shots of the globe-like towers on the alien moon. Direction, camera work and lighting all excel during the scenes on the heavily damaged base. Superior set designs on the alien moon include those of the red-orange rock walls and the floor detail, contrasted starkly against the white doorways. The alien probes are depicted as slow-motion bouncing balls in a well-conceived and executed idea that is suitably alien.

The intriguing science fiction twist to the story arises when the alien voice probe states, 'The intelligent life form of the planet – my masters – is not yet in existence. I am waiting for the first of them to be born.' Among the other admirable elements contained within 'The AB Chrysalis' are thoughts on democracy (the aliens voting to determine the fate of the Alphans), desperation (Koenig's pleading with the aliens in an effort to save Alpha) and the meaning of perfection. On the latter question, the alien A states: 'We seek perfection. We enter chrysalis fully grown adults. At the end of each cycle we are reborn … We emerge fully-grown adults on a higher level of intelligence, to mould our lives in any way we wish. We repeat that process continually in our search for perfection.') These lines show that thematically – as might be expected from the title – 'The AB Chrysalis' touches on the concepts of life, death and rebirth, which figure prominently in both religious and psychological realms.

There are several inconsistencies and contrived moments in the course of this episode, but they are forgivable. The worst of them is the unanswered question of how the alien computer identifies the Alphans as being from Earth when Koenig has provided so little information in his star chart drawing. However, more positively, in an admirable recognition of the language barriers between worlds (which virtually all science fiction programmes are guilty of ignoring for storytelling purposes), the alien voice sphere says, 'I am sorry for the delay. It took some time to align to your language.' Overall, the merits of the programme heavily outweigh any minor criticisms, and the happenings on the planet are intriguing and enjoyable. Later, facing death, the Alphans display a remarkable dignity and human spirit. Helena's reassuring yet resigned smile to Fraser is a prime example.

The climax is dramatic and effective, followed by well-conveyed elation. The light tone of the closing scene, with Maya explaining her mathematical ability to John, and with Helena quizzing John about the naked women on the planet, manages to hit all the right notes. 'The AB Chrysalis' is a very successful and enjoyable example of Year Two *Space: 1999* at its finest.

Rating: 8.5/10

2.13
SEED OF DESTRUCTION

Screenplay by John Goldsmith
Directed by Kevin Connor

Selected Broadcast Dates:

UK	LWT:	
	Date: 13 November 1976.	Time: 10.55 am
	Granada:	
	Date: 24 July 1977.	
US	KRON (San Francisco):	
	Date: 4 December 1976.	Time: 7.00 pm

Credited Cast: Martin Landau (John Koenig), **Barbara Bain** (Helena Russell), **Catherine Schell** (Maya), **Tony Anholt** (Tony Verdeschi), **Nick Tate** (Alan Carter), **Zienia Merton** (Sandra Benes), **Jeffery Kissoon** (Ben Vincent), **Martha Nairn** (Cranston), **Jack Klaff** (Security Guard), **James Leith** (Security Guard), **Albin Pahernik** (Maya Creature)

Uncredited Cast: Quentin Pierre (Security Guard Pierce Quinton), **Robert Reeves** (Operative Peter Reeves), **Pam Rose** (Operative P Rose), **Glenda Allen** (Operative G Allen), **Jenny Cresswell** (Medical Centre patient)

Plot: While exploring a strange jewel-like asteroid, Koenig becomes trapped by an alien force that sends a duplicate of him back to the base. This duplicate orders a beam of power to be fired at the asteroid, in order to destroy it. However, the power is actually re-charging the Heart of Kalthon, a seed containing an entire alien civilisation. The duplicate Koenig must be stopped before all of Alpha's power is drained away.

Quotes:
- **Helena:** 'Could something have invaded him – a virus, a life form, taken him over?'
- **Tony:** 'Discipline, discipline, discipline – a throwback to Captain Bligh!'
- **Helena:** 'Then it's conspiracy. That word may be too strong for me.'
- **Koenig:** 'Helena, you can tell us apart. The things we've shared, he can't know.'
- **Maya:** 'Instinct, training – you're hiding behind words!'
- **Helena:** 'Perhaps I have been upset. We've all been under a strain.'

On-screen Date: 1,608 days since leaving Earth orbit.

Filming Dates: Wednesday 7 July – Friday 23 July 1976

Commentary:
Kevin Connor: 'The challenge [in the hall of mirrors in "Seed of Destruction"] was in dealing with the reflections. But it wasn't only the reflections in themselves, but the fact

that everybody [had their image reversed] – they weren't what they appeared to be. It was a real nightmare. It all worked in the end: I don't know how, but it did. It was very difficult, because Martin doesn't like being photographed from his right-hand side. He would do anything to get his face the left side to the camera. So you had to plan your shots so you didn't end up on his right-hand side. When it came to the reflections and all that, he didn't mind the evil one (his duplicate) being shown from the right-hand side.'

John Goldsmith: '*Space: 1999* really got me back into writing for television. At the time, I had dropped out. I was living in the country and I couldn't think of anything to write. My basic problem was that I had peaked too early and I hadn't actually lived, so I had little to write about. I went away and lived a little and then I came back to London with nothing but a car. I flogged the car and bought an old banger and lived on the difference. Gerry Anderson had given me my start by hiring me to work on *The Protectors*, and I heard that he was starting a new series of *Space: 1999*. Initially I was told that the series was already fully commissioned, but I was invited to submit a story outline, which they bought, so I did the script for "Seed of Destruction". I sent the first draft in and went to see Freddy Freiberger and we spent about an hour going over it. He wanted a complete rewrite from page one to page 60, but I understood what he wanted, and it was much better.

'When you commission 24 episodes of a series it becomes like a machine. It's relentless and it's a very tight schedule with a very tight budget, and inevitably scripts get rewritten. Nobody has time to call the writer so there's a script editor to do it. Script editors tend to be good at their jobs. They're not in the business of making it worse; they're there to make it better. There was one thing that they put into my script, which was the trick of everything being reversed, a mirror image. The replica Koenig's hair is parted on the other side, and his badge is reversed. I hadn't thought of that, and it was an improvement.

'What it really boiled down to was pace. Whoever worked on Gerry's shows – which were pioneering, in that they aimed at an American market – had to write an American piece. You couldn't have scenes lasting 12 pages with a chap sitting around philosophising. It goes down great in Hampstead, but they fall asleep in Idaho. I think Gerry Anderson is one of the great producers, and he's very innovative. For various reasons he faded out for a few years and then came back, but all those early things he did are now huge again. Why? Because they're so good.'

Bloopers: Keep your eyes on Commander Koenig's Eagle. When first seen, it features a Laboratory pod, but this switches to a standard passenger module for subsequent scenes.

Observations: It is unfortunate that the duplicate Koenig uses a neck pinch to subdue the real Commander. While well presented, it does draw obvious comparisons with *Star Trek* and Mr Spock that *Space: 1999* could have done without.

Review: The crystalline asteroid featured in this episode is one of the most distinct alien environments Moonbase Alpha encounters in space. The interior hall of mirrors is striking both for the imagery it provides and for the way the icy blues in the crystalline forms are contrasted against the salmon pink of Koenig's jacket.

There is an effectively eerie atmosphere to both the sights and sounds as Koenig explores the asteroid cavern, leading to his imprisonment and replacement by his doppelganger. This episode is beautifully filmed, and the crystal cavern set is particularly impressive. The evil duplicate plot is a well-worn standard, but is given new life here through the focus on excellent character interaction.

The reactions of the Alphans (Helena, Maya, Tony, Alan and Sandra) to the duplicate Koenig's ranting and uncharacteristic behaviour are believable and well conveyed by all the performers. Alan's faith in Koenig is strained to the breaking point, and is probably over-stated by the script for the sake of dramatic conflict. Nick Tate's powerful performance effectively delineates Carter's inner conflict. As Tony says, 'How can you be such a dumb, blind kangaroo?' But the theme of the episode is one of loyalty and faith, and Carter's excessive loyalty to Koenig is potentially dangerous. (There are shades of Year One episodes like 'Collision Course' and 'Missing Link' in this aspect of the story.) The contrast between the characters of Alan and Tony is most clearly established here, as the two have opposing ideas about how to deal with their Commander. Some of the finest character moments in the episode occur as Tony, Maya and Helena consider Koenig's competence. Writer John Goldsmith clearly has a firm grasp on the fundamental aspects of the Alphan characters, and has successfully incorporated dramatic action with well-rounded characterisation. His script is complemented by the distinctive direction of Kevin Connor, which excels in the crystal cavern scenes. It is a pity this is the only script Goldsmith contributed to the series, and is the last of only two directorial turns by Connor.

The contrasts that Martin Landau portrays between John Koenig and his menacing evil duplicate hit the right balance, allowing the other characters justifiably to doubt the latter without being certain they are correct. Barbara Bain's performance is also particularly effective. Her reaction as she touches the icy cold skin of the evil Koenig is one of surprised confusion, but her look of total shock when her lover so formally and inappropriately calls her 'Dr Russell' is the key to her absolute conviction that he is not the man she loves, and it visibly frightens her.

The possibility that a duplicate Koenig could enter Alpha and take over, leading the base to its doom, is a chilling one. It brings into question the command structure of the base, and the potential for a dictatorship to become entrenched. This isn't a new concept – having been touched on in previous episodes such as 'Death's other Dominion' – and it will be returned to in the later episode 'The Seance Spectre'.

Zienia Merton's appearance is a welcome sight in 'Seed of Destruction', adding valuable dimension to the camaraderie amongst the command team. Her role provides a chance for some dramatic moments, and reminds viewers how much her presence means to the series, and how much she is missed when she is absent.

It is interesting to see Maya and Tony use their Commlocks as sonic weapons, which is an ingenious twist on a common piece of Alphan equipment. It is also noteworthy that reference is made to a 'black sun' being the cause of the destruction of the original Kalthon home world. That Year Two has continued referring to black 'suns' (rather than 'holes') – a distinctively *Space: 1999* term – is a valuable piece of series continuity.

The concept of the planet Kalthon being held in a form of stasis on a microscopic level is appealing, and could have withstood deeper consideration in the script. But, ultimately, the episode is not really about Kalthon, but about the Alphans themselves, and how they relate to each other with an imposter in their midst. This is a character-driven episode, with significant conflicts between the command staff, and that is where its greatest strength lies.

When Helena and Alan are finally about to take command away from the tyrannical double of Koenig, it's richly rewarding to see the real Koenig walk into Command Centre and calmly, quietly and quickly convince his friends that he is indeed the real Commander. The only disappointing element of the resolution is that it ends up being the parting in the duplicate Koenig's hair that finally convinces everyone he's an imposter, rather than the accumulation of the seriously out-of-character behaviour and paranoia he's previously displayed, or his endangering of Alpha. Besides, the hair parting should have been noticed earlier by others, and certainly by Helena. But that is an issue with the resolution of the episode, and not the story itself, which is very strong.

Notably, this is another Year Two episode that simply ends after the culmination of the dramatic events, rather than tacking on a feel-good closing scene. 'Seed of Destruction' remains a classic.

Rating: 8/10

2.14
THE BETA CLOUD

Screenplay by Charles Woodgrove (Fred Freiberger)
Directed by Robert Lynn

Selected Broadcast Dates:

UK	LWT:	
	Date: 18 December 1976.	Time: 10.55 am
	Granada:	
	Date: 13 November 1977.	Time: 1.15 pm
US	KRON (San Francisco):	
	Date: 22 January 1977.	Time: 7.00 pm

Credited Cast: Martin Landau (John Koenig), **Barbara Bain** (Helena Russell), **Catherine Schell** (Maya), **Tony Anholt** (Tony Verdeschi), **Nick Tate** (Alan Carter), **Zienia Merton** (Sandra Benes), **John Hug** (Bill Fraser), **Albin Pahernik** (Kreno Animal (Maya))

Guest Star: David Prowse (Cloud Creature)

Uncredited Cast: Robert Reeves (Operative Peter Reeves), **Roy Everson** (Les Johnson), **Harry Fielder** (Gerry), **Marc Smith** (Cloud Voice)

Plot: A strange illness sweeps over Alpha, and an Eagle returns with a huge creature aboard. Sent by the Beta Cloud, this monster attempts to steal Alpha's life-support system.

Quotes:
- **Cloud:** 'Sarcasm in your present circumstances is hardly a defence – accept your fate.'
- **Tony:** 'Open!' … 'Close!' [Verbal commands for opening and closing doors, which are repeated endlessly throughout the episode.]
- **Tony:** 'Psychon is my favourite planet.'
- **Alan:** 'Maybe I'll think better sitting down.'
- **Tony:** 'Maya, I love you.'
- **Maya:** 'It won't get up again.'

On-screen Date: 1,503 days since leaving Earth orbit.

Filming Dates: Monday 26 July – Friday 6 August 1976
Additional scenes filmed Tuesday 21 September – Wednesday 22 September 1976

Commentary:
Zienia Merton: 'Three months after I [initially] left the series, I got a call from lovely

Barbara. She said, "Zienia, darling, how are you?" I said, "Fine." She said, "What are you doing?" I said, "Not a lot." She said, "Would you consider coming back to *Space: 1999*?" I said, "Yeah, it wasn't a big walk-out." The point was that the parts had been getting smaller. I had been getting about half a day's work [on each episode. But at the same time], because I had already been on series one, and it's a small business, people thought I was under contract. So I then wouldn't get offered work elsewhere. So I'd walked, as they say. But Barbara was very sweet. She said, "Would you talk to Gerry?" I said, "Yeah, I'm not proud." So she said, "I'll get Gerry to call you." So Gerry called me and said, "Zienia, will you come have lunch with Freddy and me?" So I went and had lunch with them. Gerry, being Gerry, didn't say very much. Freddy spent the time saying, "I'm having to spend so much money on this series. I'm having to spend this ... and I'm having to spend so much money here, and ...' Money, money, money. I said, "What are you trying to tell me? That you're having to spend a lot of money, and there's a lot of inflation about? Because I understand it: I'm the number one cutback." I said, "Last time when I did *Space: 1999* I was under contract; I am not now. You pay me like casual labour. I know about cutbacks ... If you are that poor, I'll take *you* out to lunch!"

'Anyway, the reason they wanted me back was that Barbara and Martin had it in their contract that they would go on holiday. So one episode wouldn't feature them very much. [Remember that] they had got rid of Prentis and Barry, Clifton and Anton. They suddenly thought, "We're going to have an episode where we don't know anybody. Last year's audience won't know anybody, so we've got to have some old face back – any old face." So they bumped me into "The Beta Cloud", and that's why I went back. But they still didn't want to know about me. It was still; "We ring Zienia one day before we need her." Well, I was lucky and got a call from Norway to do a feature movie there. I left about three or four episodes before the end [of *Space: 1999*]. At the time, we weren't sure whether or not there would be a third series, and I decided to gamble.'

Catherine Schell: 'In ['Beta Cloud'] there was a scene [we planned], just a joke, between Tony Anholt and me. He's been injured and is in the sickbay, where I come and visit him. He's reading old Earth magazines, and in one of them is a picture of me as Catherine Schell, and he goes, "Oh wow, she's a good looking chick." I tell him what terrible taste he has, and then I metamorphose into Catherine Schell before I leave the sickbay. However, Barbara objected to the scene and it was eliminated. There was another thing – I'm not sure if it was in her contract, but I found it quite strange ... Each episode would end on a freeze frame, but it never, ever ended on a freeze frame of me. It happened to everyone else, but never to me, and I'm quite sure it had something to do with Barbara's contract. I suppose her way of thinking was that business was business. She was looking out for herself. I don't think that I would ever have thought about doing something like that in a contract for myself. However, she's American and she was brought up in the American schools, and that's how they think – they look out for their own careers.'

John Hug: 'A few years ago, I watched one I was in – "The Beta Cloud" – which was my favourite, for the selfish reason that [it gave me] probably my biggest part. I enjoyed that. It was great working with David Prowse ... He is a sort of gentle giant. He speaks with a West Country accent; he doesn't sound at all like a monster. He's about 6' 5" and he had polio as a kid. He compensated for that by doing workouts and became an incredibly strong man. It was in "Beta Cloud" that Tony Anholt and I had to fight this big monster that David played. They made him about 7 feet tall, but he had this scene where he had me tucked under one arm, and Tony – this 12 ½ stone person – jumped on his back. We were not exactly little, skinny people. You'd have thought he would have moved when this big guy jumped on his back, but he hardly moved at all.

'When we did the fight scene, there were cushions on the set [for us to fall on], but I had just dislocated my shoulder. I had my hand in a sling until we went to do the shooting. Dave said, "Don't you worry about it. Just you relax. Tuck your arm in and leave it to me. Just don't move your arm." So he picked me up, tucked me under his arm, chucked me onto a desk, got hold of my legs and flipped me over – [and] I landed on cushions and kept my arm tucked. I didn't do anything that was likely to get my shoulder injured. But it was really nice working with him – he knew exactly what he was doing. He was so gentle with us. Tony and I were chucked around a bit, but with clever editing it looks much more violent than it actually was. That certainly was my favourite episode.

'What was quite interesting in the second series [was that] Maya had been turning herself into all sorts of leopards and tigers, then in "Beta Cloud" she became a bee. Whether this was true or not [I don't know], but we put it down to budget restrictions. As we got further on, the budget constraints seemed to come in, so it was, "Ah, no, we can't afford the giraffe, so let's have her turn into a bee. Something cheaper."'

Dave Prowse: 'They asked me if I would do this episode of *Space: 1999*. I was playing this creature that was trying to steal the life-support from the Moonbase. Every stuntman in London versus me! They burnt me, they electrocuted me, they gassed me, they shot me, they did everything you could possibly think of to try to kill me during the episode. And eventually Maya turned herself into a bee, flew inside my ear and cross-circuited my circuitry, and that was the end of me.'

Bloopers: Maya transforms into the same Kreno monster she became in 'The AB Chrysalis' but, displaying an utter absence of continuity, while in the former episode the monster needed to breathe chlorine, here it breathes Alpha's atmosphere with no problem.

Tony Anholt holds his Commlock upside down while standing outside the Hydroponics Unit speaking to Carter.

Pay attention when Sandra Benes is watching the temperature monitor: in close-up the temperature is seen to drop from 20 to 15, but in the wide-shot the reading drops from 10 to 5.

Observations: The absence of Martin Landau and Barbara Bain from the bulk of the episode was due to them being on a scheduled holiday break.

Review: If you're looking for a satisfying plot, you're looking at the wrong episode. What 'The Beta Cloud' excels at is excitement: dynamic music, Maya transformations, bizarre alien creatures, and all of Alpha in peril. 'The Beta Cloud' is action-packed and fun, but undeniably juvenile.

The second of the 'Woodgrove trilogy', this is the weakest of the three scripts penned by Fred Freiberger. It lacks the character development at the heart of the earlier 'The Rules of Luton', and the accompanying powerful performances from Martin Landau and Catherine Schell, and similarly it lacks the superior performances of Barbara Bain and Nick Tate that will form the core of the subsequent 'Space Warp', a show that will also feature a memorable turn by Catherine Schell and a brilliant display of miniature special effects. While all three of Freiberger's scripts are hollow run-around exercises, this one has the least to recommend it.

It is oddly fascinating watching the Alphans fall, one by one; succumbing to some alien sickness and knowing no cure to save themselves. Then, with most of the base unable to fight, the threat of the monster from the Beta Cloud arrives – in fact, if this were a B-movie, it could very well be called *The Creature from the Beta Cloud*.

This is, in some senses, a lobotomised version of 'End of Eternity' from the first season. How do you stop an unstoppable alien? If you want to be fascinated by the possibilities of this idea, or the underlying motivations of the alien threat, watch 'End of Eternity'. If you prefer turning your brain off prior to watching television, tune in to 'The Beta Cloud'. What does work quite well here is the direction by Robert Lynn, in his second and final contribution to the series. He injects a stronger sense of pace into this episode than his counterpart Val Guest was able to bring to 'The Rules of Luton'.

There are impressive performances from Zienia Merton in an unaccustomed lead role that gives her more to do than most of the rest of Year Two, an out-of-action Nick Tate and Martin Landau (in a very small role). The story, though, is truly Maya's and Tony's. Freiberger creates what could have been a strong character-building scene where Tony professes his love for Maya'; but unfortunately he then undermines this by putting what amounts to a retraction into Tony's later dialogue, simply to create an amusing joke for the end of the show. There is also some astoundingly bad dialogue, including the following:

Maya: 'Give me a fix on its position.'
Beta Cloud: 'Our relative positions are of little consequence.'
Verdeschi: 'Who are you?'
Beta Cloud: 'Who we are is too complicated for your comprehension.'
Verdeschi: 'Try me.'
Beta Cloud: 'Time does not permit.'
Fraser: 'We've got time. A lot of it.'
Beta Cloud: 'You are in error. You have very little time.'
Tony: 'What do you want?'
Beta Cloud: 'Your life support system.'
Verdeschi: 'You mean we just give it to you?'
Beta Cloud: 'We have sent for it.'
Maya: 'We can't exist without it.'
Beta Cloud: 'Neither can we. So we must deprive you of yours.'

This lengthy exchange displays how lazy the script is – not one detail has been worked out in advance. What is the nature of the Beta Cloud? Where is it in relation to the Moon? What is the nature of the beings inside it? Why do they need Alpha's life support system? None of these questions – so obviously posed in this dialogue – is answered. All are diverted with weak comebacks that are supposed to sound mysterious or threatening.

Moonbase Alpha's giant surface laser cannons fire here for the first time, which is a positive on the effects side of the production, but unfortunately the realisation of the Beta Cloud itself is a massive disappointment.

The original script ran short and is obviously padded with endless repetition to bring it up to full length. It lacks any trace of substance and subtlety vital to quality *Space: 1999* episodes. Certainly, it features the fantastic music of Derek Wadsworth to great effect, but the problem is that without this pulsing score driving the pace, the episode would be completely tedious. The resolution, as well, is an absolute letdown. Once Maya realises the creature is a robot, she is able to fell the giant and end the crisis in a convenient matter of moments. But why does the Beta Cloud then disappear? Were the alien beings so close to death that they instantly perished when their robot was defeated? Did they not have a second robot they could send to Alpha? If they require a piece of Alpha's technology to survive, they must be a technological society, and if they can build a big hairy robot, they must be able to build spaceships of their own – right? What becomes obvious when one considers these aspects of the script is that the writer, Fred Freiberger, did *not* give them any consideration! And if the writer didn't care enough to provide a back-story, or any logical motivation at all for his monster, then why should an audience care for the filmed show?

As intelligent and challenging science fiction, this totally fails to make the grade. But as an empty piece of pure bug-eyed-monster sci-fi silliness, 'The Beta Cloud' has few challengers.

Rating: 4/10

2.15
SPACE WARP

Screenplay by Charles Woodgrove (Fred Freiberger)
Directed by Peter Medak

Selected Broadcast Dates:
UK   LWT:
            Date: 4 December 1976.   Time: 10.55 am
            Granada:
            Date: 14 August 1977.
US   KRON (San Francisco):
            Date: 8 January 1977.   Time: 7.00 pm

Credited Cast: Martin Landau (John Koenig), **Barbara Bain** (Helena Russell), **Catherine Schell** (Maya), **Tony Anholt** (Tony Verdeschi), **Nick Tate** (Alan Carter), **Zienia Merton** (Sandra Benes), **Jeffery Kissoon** (Ben Vincent), **Peter Porteous** (Petrov), **Tony Osoba** (First Security Guard), **John Judd** (Second Security Guard), **Trevor Thomas** (Refuel Eagle Pilot Gary), **Andrew Lodge** (Grasshopper / Captain Duro)

Uncredited Cast: Robert Reeves (Operative Peter Reeves), **Quentin Pierre** (Security Guard Pierce Quinton), **Jack Klaff** (Security Guard), **Nick Hobbs** (Security Guard – Medical), **Suzanne Heimer** (Nurse)

Plot: Alpha enters a space warp and is catapulted light years from its last position – but Koenig and Verdeschi have been left behind in an Eagle exploring a derelict spaceship. The duo must find the precise window into the space warp to return to Alpha, but the chances are a million to one. Meanwhile, Maya has developed a high fever and is beginning to lose molecular control.

Quotes:
- **Maya:** 'I'm beginning to lose molecular control – I don't know what will happen. You've got to put me in restraints!'
- **Koenig:** 'I guess there are going to be no miracles today.'
- **Helena:** 'Luck? In space? You think his chances are a million to one.'
- **Sandra:** 'You're the doctor, Helena, so forgive me for prescribing: but you need some rest.'
- **Tony:** 'Well, how about that! We've been beating our brains out trying to jump back through a space warp, and they've been doing nothing back on Alpha, except catching up on their sleep.'

On-screen Date: 1,807 days since leaving Earth orbit.

Filming Dates: Friday 6 August – Tuesday 24 August 1976

Commentary:

Nick Tate: 'In "Space Warp", Maya becomes a monster and they strap her down on the table in Medical, and I have to come in and talk to her. Whilst I'm talking to her, she metamorphoses back into the monster and she grabs me and throws me across the room ... They wanted to shoot [this scene] from the floor looking up, and we had a ceiling on the set. They don't usually have ceilings on sets, because that's where all the lights are. But it was a very low ceiling. Timmy, my stuntman, set up this little trampoline for me and told me to come into the shot, bounce on the trampoline and go up and over and land on the floor. Just doing a roll onto the floor I can do – even now. But I didn't want to bounce on a trampoline up into the air and then land on the floor. Then I said, "The more height I get, [the more risk there is that] I'm going to hit that roof." Then the director wanted to put the camera on the floor and have me come flying through the air and land smack right in front of the camera. This stunt was becoming one I didn't want to do. There was even more to it, and I didn't like the way it was going. So Timmy said, "I'll do it." I said, "You're going to land on the floor." He said, "We'll put a mattress down and the camera will be just above the mattress." So he wound up doing this stunt: he jumped on the trampoline, hit the ceiling, landed short of the mattress and snapped his two front teeth and broke his collarbone! So I'm glad I didn't do it. That was tough – it was very sad. There was one other time a stunt was done for me, when I fell off the top of the Main Mission balcony, but that wasn't Timmy. That was another guy who was an expert at falling; I don't like falling!'

Bloopers: As Alan and Helena, in a Moon Buggy, chase the Maya creature circling around a rock several times, the buggy is visibly ripping up the floor of the set.

Alan's space-suit helmet pops open while he is fighting the monster on the surface.

Another blooper occurs during the fight scene between the Maya creature and Alan, when his oxygen tank is damaged. As the Maya creature throws Alan, he is clearly seen landing on the flat ground, on his back. In the next shot, he is shown rolling off a large rock!

Observations: One of the Moonbase Alpha laser tanks from Year One is seen in the Eagle hanger segments of this episode. Obviously Alpha is still equipped with some of these tanks, and it would have been rewarding to see them featured again.

Also of note, an elevator is seen on Moonbase Alpha for the first time. It would appear again in 'The Seance Spectre'.

Review: 'Space Warp' is the third and final script penned by Fred Freiberger under the pseudonym Charles Woodgrove and is the 'double-up' pair to 'A Matter of Balance'. Here, two plotlines are combined into one episode. The half involving John and Tony out in space with the derelict ship is dull, poorly written and features lacklustre performances by Martin Landau and Tony Anholt, who both appear bored with the proceedings. While they're off being dreary in deep space, the more exciting and interesting half of the show features Maya ripping the base apart and Helena, Alan and the rest of the crew trying to stop her. The original premise of this is appealing: what would happen if Maya became ill? Unfortunately, the results are not as profound as they could have been.

The sudden shocking entrance into the space warp is successfully presented. There may be a bit too much camera spinning, but the blurring and twisting effects are highly dynamic and the sequence (and, indeed, the whole episode) is effectively accompanied by Derek Wadsworth's exciting music.

Most of the episode takes place in a dimly lit Alpha (due to power failures following the journey through the space warp), adding to the mood of the proceedings. This is certainly one of the most beautiful and cinematically-lit episodes of Year Two.

Catherine Schell is outstanding in the opening sequences, before Maya begins her wild string of transformations. Barbara Bain and Nick Tate are truly the stars of this episode, though, and they both deliver intense performances filled with conviction. Zienia Merton is also wonderful in significant scenes with both Tate and Bain. Although it amounts to little more than a string of contrived action sequences, it's entertaining to watch the Alphans, led by Alan and Helena, trying to deal with the various Maya creatures and her rampage through the base. Director Peter Medak has succeeded as well as possible, considering the limitations of the material he has to work with. While all three of his episodes are widely derided by fans of *Space: 1999*, Fred Freiberger's last script actually adds even less to the series in terms of character development than his previous efforts, 'The Rules of Luton' and 'The Beta Cloud'.

The climactic fiery effects sequence in the Eagle hangers – where Maya lifts off in an Eagle that's been brought down to the hanger bay – is an absolutely stunning display of miniatures and explosions. The Moon Buggy chase on the lunar surface is a lot of fun too, and marks another appearance of these iconic and appealing *Space: 1999* vehicles.

It is a thoughtful addition to the script that Koenig orders the derelict ship taken back to Alpha for further study and possible use. It may be a derelict, but the advanced technology could be greatly beneficial to the base, and it's rewarding to see the characters take advantage of that. What is more dubious is the simple manner in which Koenig and Verdeschi figure out the alien space warp locator and utilise it to get back to Alpha.

The plot of the episode is paper-thin, and the extended string of Maya's transformations merely highlights the inherent weaknesses of the concept. While there are no thought-provoking issues to be contemplated here, the near total focus on action remains entertaining, even while it highlights what might be considered the dichotomy of Year Two: that what appealed most to children watching in the 1970s is now what appeals least to an adult audience decades later.

Rating: 5.5/10

2.16
A MATTER OF BALANCE

Screenplay by Pip and Jane Baker
Directed by Charles Crichton

Selected Broadcast Dates:

UK	LWT:	
	Date: 11 December 1976.	Time: 10.55 am
	Granada:	
	Date: 7 August 1977.	
US	KRON (San Francisco):	
	Date: 15 January 1977.	Time: 7.00 pm

Credited Cast: Martin Landau (John Koenig), **Barbara Bain** (Helena Russell), **Catherine Schell** (Maya), **Tony Anholt** (Tony Verdeschi), **John Hug** (Bill Fraser), **Nicholas Campbell** (Eddie Collins), **Brian Osborne** (Chris Potter)

Guest Stars: Lynne Frederick (Shermeen Williams), **Stuart Wilson** (Vindrus)

Uncredited Cast: Robert Reeves (Operative Peter Reeves), **Jenny Cresswell** (Alphan), **Olive Greg** (Whispers)

Plot: On the planet Sunim, an anti-matter being called Vindrus lures Shermeen Williams into his plot to free his race from their imprisonment in an alternate universe. But for each of Vindrus's people who cross over into our universe, someone must be sent back in order to keep the balance between the matter and anti-matter universes.

Quotes:
- **Helena:** 'As Chief Medical Officer, I must retain my sanity.'
- **Maya:** 'Commander? You shuddered, but not from cold.'
- **Koenig:** 'It's almost as if a ghost had … I had a superstitious grandmother.'
- **Maya:** 'Well, if you want to knock on wood, there's plenty of that around.'
- **Tony:** 'The proper flow to the proper time to the proper place: that's the trick.'
- **Vindrus:** 'Because nature has to be kept in balance. For every one who crosses over into your world, one of you must cross into ours.'

On-screen Date: 1,702 days since leaving Earth orbit.

Filming Dates: Friday 6 August – Tuesday 24 August 1976

Commentary:
Martin Landau: [Landau was extremely unhappy with this episode. He wrote the following comments on his copy of the script – possibly as notes to himself in preparation for a confrontation with Fred Freiberger: note his use of 'you're'. He also

295

seems to be criticising the 'double-up' process, and his minimal appearance in some episodes.] 'I'm not going out on a limb for this show because I'm not in accord with what you're doing as a result … etc. I don't think I even want to do the promos – I don't want to push the show any more as I have in the past. It's not my idea of what the show should be. It's embarrassing to me if I am not the star of it and in the way I feel it should be. This year should be more important to it, not less important to it … I might as well work less hard in all of them.'

John Hug: 'We were talking about how the uniforms fit … Some of us had to wear jockstraps – they didn't want any big bulges. We were covered up with badges, trying to make the uniforms more interesting. They were not very comfortable. There were the big flares. I didn't mind them; you just didn't want bits of yourself hanging out.

'Stuart Wilson [Vindrus] was … slightly embarrassed by his costume. It was one of those things where you sort of bite your lip and think, "I'm getting paid for this. I'm doing three days on this and then I'm going to go away, to my pay cheque." The costume was rather unfortunate, wasn't it?'

Bloopers: When Vindrus first appears in Shermeen's room, the clapperboard is briefly visible in the lower right of the image. This blooper was edited out of the A&E DVD release, but still appears in other versions.

When Vindrus appears to Shermeen in Hydroponics, the first shot of him is actually from his earlier appearance in Shermeen's quarters.

Watch the Thaed monster: in one scene, the actor moves in such a way that the head-mask lifts up and separates from the body of the costume.

Observations: The name Sunim is 'minus' spelt backwards, and the monster that guards the temple on Sunim is called Thaed – which is (almost) 'death' spelt backwards.

Numerous props re-appear in this episode, including the 'stained glass' panels from Year One's 'Mission of the Darians' and an air capsule from 'The Last Sunset'. The obelisks around the temple on Sunim will later be used in both 'Devil's Planet' and 'The Dorcons'.

Review: 'A Matter of Balance' is another 'double-up' episode, which was filmed on location while the Alpha sets were being used for 'Space Warp'. It is also one of the cheapest-looking episodes of the series, and perhaps partly because of this, it is almost invariably given less credit than it actually deserves. Its shortcomings are probably attributable to the 'double-up' procedure having split the talented cast and crew in two directions and weakened the overall ensemble abilities of the team. Admittedly some of the 'double-up' episodes were successes (such as 'The AB Chrysalis'), but most were not.

Despite the unfortunate circumstances in which this show was filmed, the plot and ideas are somewhat thought-provoking. The treatment of anti-matter, although scientifically ridiculous, is interesting and plausibly presented.

The devious Sunim people, trapped in an anti-existence, devolving from their advanced form towards a more and more primitive future, are given sufficient detail as an alien race, and their motivations are understandable and believable. The writing is fine for the characters of Koenig, Maya and Verdeschi, although Tony Anholt's performance in the latter role is slightly stiff through part of the show. Bill Fraser is given a minor and rather bland part, while Helena's contribution is minimal, albeit well enacted by Barbara Bain. The guest roles are generally sub-par: Nicholas Campbell is weak as Eddie, Shermeen's neglected boyfriend; Stuart Wilson gives a dubious performance as Vindrus; and Lynne Frederick broadly over-acts as the immature Shermeen, to the point that her very presence is annoying. Shermeen is also problematic as a character, due to her young age. Actress Lynne Frederick was 22 during filming and this episode was dated almost five years after the Moon left Earth orbit, presumably making her character a 17-year-old student at the time of 'Breakaway'. Was she a particularly gifted young pupil sent to the base for some kind of study programme? This question is not addressed in the episode, and one comes away – rightly or wrongly – with the impression that neither the writers nor the producers gave it the consideration required. An additional problem with the character of Shermeen is the mention that she has been collecting plant samples from every planet Alpha has encountered – yet she's never been seen before!

The production values, as mentioned, generally look low. The Thaed monster is an especially sorry presentation of a man in a rubber monster mask, while the image of the fox in Maya's eye before her transformation is obviously a dead and stuffed example of the species. On the positive side, the temple is an excellent site, with an interesting-looking – although very dark – interior.

The direction of this episode is average, and is clearly one of Charles Crichton's lesser efforts. The script itself is fine – no more nor less than that – and the episode is sufficiently entertaining. There are some moments of grand stupidity, such as when Koenig says to Maya, 'That structure – obviously built by intelligent life.' Yes, obviously!

There appear to be no significant moral issues or themes to investigate in this episode, and the overall impression is hollow. However, if undemanding viewers go into this without expecting much more than some simplistic fun, 'A Matter of Balance' is a pleasing lightweight piece of '70s sci-fi.

Rating: 6/10

2.17
THE BRINGERS OF WONDER
Part One

Screenplay by Terence Feely
Directed by Tom Clegg

Selected Broadcast Dates:

UK	LWT:	
	Date: 15 October 1977.	Time: 11.00 am
	Granada:	
	Date: 18 September 1977.	Time: 1.15 pm
US	KRON (San Francisco):	
	Date: 19 February 1977.	Time: 7.00 pm

Credited Cast: Martin Landau (John Koenig), **Barbara Bain** (Helena Russell), **Catherine Schell** (Maya), **Tony Anholt** (Tony Verdeschi), **Nick Tate** (Alan Carter), **Zienia Merton** (Sandra Benes), **Jeffery Kissoon** (Ben Vincent), **Al Lampert** (Ken Burdett), **Billy J Mitchell** (Professor Hunter), **Earl Robinson** (Sandstrom), **Robert Sheedy** (Henry), **Nicholas Young** (Peter Rockwell), **Albin Pahernik** (Lizard Animal (Maya))

Guest Stars: Toby Robins (Diana Morris), **Stuart Damon** (Guido Verdeschi), **Jeremy Young** (Jack Bartlett), **Drewe Henley** (Joe Ehrlich), **Patrick Westwood** (Dr Shaw), **Cher Cameron** (Louisa)

Uncredited Cast: David Jackson (Bringer of Wonder Voice), **Nick Hobbs** (Clive Kander), **Sarah Bullen** (Operative Kate), **Robert Reeves** (Operative Peter Reeves), **Jenny Cresswell** (Operative L Picard), **Glenda Allen** (Operative G Allen), **Peter Brayham** (Security Guard), **Roy Scammel** (Records Lab Space Animal (Maya)), **Okimitsu Fujii** (Kendo Warrior (Maya))

Plot: The Bringers of Wonder arrive on Alpha, using their telepathic powers to convince the Alphans they are actually a rescue party of friends from Earth. John Koenig is the only one who sees through their deception – but can he convince anybody that he's not crazy, and that everyone else on Alpha is being deceived?

Quotes:
- **Koenig:** 'Hallelujah! There are angels everywhere!'
- **Helena:** 'Never underestimate the extent of human inventiveness.'
- **Helena:** 'Well, you know Diana Morris – she's like the fifth cavalry. Wherever she plants her flag is home.'
- **Koenig:** 'Would you believe we met at the jazz ballet group at MIT?'
- **Koenig:** 'Diana Morris … well, well. Now, Helena, please don't even joke

about that barracuda.'

On-screen Date: 1,912 days since leaving Earth orbit.

Filming Dates: Wednesday 25 August – Tuesday 28 September 1976

Bloopers: During Koenig's erratic flight in Eagle One he is not wearing the chest and backpack of his spacesuit, but when he is rescued both packs are miraculously on him.

Review: 'The Bringers of Wonder' Part One is visually dynamic, right from the opening sequence of Koenig's wild ride in Eagle One and the subsequent spectacle of him being rescued by a couple of silver-suited Alphans amid fire and explosions.

The reunion scenes between the Alphans and their apparent friends from Earth are nicely played. While the Alphans are immediately under the spell of the Bringers of Wonder, the viewer sees quite quickly that there is a mystery involved, and that things are not as they seem. The feeling of community and diverse friendships amongst the Alphans is strongly conveyed throughout the episode. Character interactions are very natural, and it's a guilty pleasure to watch the catty exchanges between Helena and Diana Morris, portrayed with particular aplomb by Toby Robins. The episode delivers a wealth of background information on various characters including John, Helena, Tony, Sandra and Ben, which is absolutely welcome. The main cast all appear to revel in the opportunities presented by this script, and each – Landau, Bain, Schell, Anholt, Tate, Merton and Kissoon – delivers a vividly memorable performance. Maya's alien nature is reinforced by her obvious discomfort at the prospect of returning to Earth, where she would be one alien amongst billions. This same nervousness on her part had already been expressed in 'Journey to Where', a stellar episode that was also directed – coincidentally – by Tom Clegg. Clegg's work stands out in several scenes here, displaying particular urgency when Dr Vincent is rushing to the rescue of Kander in the Records Lab. Kander's death by fire is surprisingly graphically portrayed, considering the younger portion of the audience *Space: 1999* was aiming for.

Screenwriter Terence Feely returns to the series (having previously contributed the witty 'New Adam New Eve') and delivers a well-crafted script with Koenig trying to convince his friends that they are being manipulated, while everybody else believes their Commander has cracked up. It's all a little high on the melodrama scale, but is earnestly played by the entire cast. It does, though, contain one of the most unfortunate lines of any episode when Tony states, 'He's gonna crash. Alan, get over there. Take a couple of nuclear physicists with you, just in case.' The nuclear physicists just happen to be standing around doing nothing in Command Centre, awaiting the line in the script. It's blatantly shoddy writing.

The sight of the aliens is effectively surprising as Koenig enters Command Centre and sees them as they truly are: grotesque mounds of glowing, pulsating plasma tentacles and green jelly, with exposed vessels pumping blood. The Bringers of Wonder are clearly the most impressive monster aliens introduced in Year Two: light years beyond the typical men in monster suits that were featured all too often. These protoplasmic jelly monsters rank with the dragon from 'Dragon's Domain' as the most thoroughly 'alien' of the physical species Alpha encounters, and hold up respectably to scrutiny decades later.

In 'The Bringers of Wonder', nuclear disposal areas are seen on the Moon for the first time since 'Breakaway'. The design is different, presumably because the areas featured in 'Breakaway' were destroyed and viewers are to assume that these are separate ones unaffected by the original explosions that hurled the Moon out of orbit, or perhaps entirely new ones developed for the Alphans to store their own nuclear waste.

Overall, this is an effective and engaging combination of Year Two bravado and extensive character development. The final cliffhanger is excellent, with the 'Dr Shaw' Bringer of Wonder attempting to smother Koenig in his Medical Centre bed. When the caption 'end of part one' appears, the viewer is definitely intrigued to tune in for Part Two.

Rating: 7.5/10

2.18
THE BRINGERS OF WONDER
Part Two

Screenplay by Terence Feely
Directed by Tom Clegg

Selected Broadcast Dates:

UK	LWT:	
	Date: 22 October 1977.	Time: 11.00 am
	Granada:	
	Date: 25 September 1977.	Time: 1.15 pm
US	KRON (San Francisco):	
	Date: 26 February 1977.	Time: 7.00 pm

Credited Cast: Martin Landau (John Koenig), **Barbara Bain** (Helena Russell), **Catherine Schell** (Maya), **Tony Anholt** (Tony Verdeschi), **Nick Tate** (Alan Carter), **Zienia Merton** (Sandra Benes), **Jeffery Kissoon** (Ben Vincent), **Al Lampert** (Ken Burdett), **Billy J Mitchell** (Professor Hunter), **Earl Robinson** (Sandstrom), **Robert Sheedy** (Henry), **Nicholas Young** (Peter Rockwell), **Albin Pahernik** (Lizard Animal (Maya))

Guest Stars: Toby Robins (Diana Morris), **Stuart Damon** (Guido Verdeschi), **Jeremy Young** (Jack Bartlett), **Drewe Henley** (Joe Ehrlich), **Patrick Westwood** (Dr Shaw), **Cher Cameron** (Louisa)

Uncredited Cast: David Jackson (Bringer of Wonder Voice), **Nick Hobbs** (Clive Kander), **Sarah Bullen** (Operative Kate), **Robert Reeves** (Operative Peter Reeves), **Quentin Pierre** (Security Guard Pierce Quinton), **Roy Everson** (Security Guard in corridor)

Plot: Maya is freed from the influence of the Bringers of Wonder and discovers their purpose is to deceive the Alphans into blowing up the Nuclear Waste Domes, providing the aliens with the radiation they need to live. But Moonbase Alpha will be destroyed in the resulting explosion!

Quotes:
- **Helena:** 'There may be no causal effect, but it is a tenable theory.'
- **Koenig:** 'Maya, when you look you see people from Earth. When I look, I see monsters from a different dimension.'
- **Maya:** 'They have the minds of geniuses and the instincts of vultures.'
- **Bringer of Wonder:** 'Isn't it better to live in a dream of happiness than to face a reality which you hate?'
- **Koenig:** 'So much for illusions.'

On-screen Date: 2,515 days since leaving Earth orbit.

Filming Dates: Wednesday 25 August – Tuesday 28 September 1976

Commentary:
Zienia Merton: 'I had another boyfriend in that show, "The Bringers of Wonder". In fact, I had quite a good sex life! But of course he turned into a jelly, and that seems to be the story of my life … [The Bringers] were rather nasty, because they had a lot of oozing liquid.

'I am well known as a screamer. Soundmen tremble! Those who've worked with me before when I've screamed actually get the ear plugs in, because I have such a high-pitched scream.'

Terence Feely: 'I remember *Space: 1999* for a wonderful character called Freddy Freiberger. I thought he was having me on when he introduced himself. He was Story Editor, and he was a great old Hollywood pro – there was nothing he hadn't seen, nothing he hadn't heard, no joke you could tell him that he couldn't give you the punch line to. I adored old Freddy and I got on with him like a house on fire.

'I had a very good experience with my first episode, "New Adam New Eve", and on the strength of it Gerry and Freddy asked me to do the two part "The Bringers of Wonder". I called it "The Globs", and they liked my script so much they decided to make it a feature-length story and asked me to double the length of it. I did it and they loved it. Then I went away on holiday for a month while it was being shot, and when I came back I said to Gerry, "How did it go?" It was a great script, and he thought it was, too. He said, "Terence, what can I tell you? A lot of very heavy editing went on, I'm afraid, while you were away." And I said, "Well, Gerry, you weren't away!" He said, "I know – I don't want to go into it all, but there was nothing I could do." We did lose a hell of a lot of good stuff out of that, and I do remember being very annoyed when I saw what they'd done with it.'

Incidental Music: Beethoven's 5th Symphony is featured.

Bloopers: There are numerous mistakes in this episode, apart from a number of inexplicable lapses in logic, which include Helena's absolute lack of reaction to Maya's transformation into a Bringer of Wonder.

The number '5' on Alan's and Erlich's Moon Buggy is backwards in a couple of the lunar surface scenes (owing to the fact that the footage was reversed).

When Koenig says, 'This is Eagle One to Alan Carter,' he is wearing a spacesuit with an 'Eagle 5' patch.

During the fight sequence on the Moon between Koenig, Alan and Erlich, support wires can be seen when the stunt men are thrown around. Also, at one point in this fight, Koenig's glove becomes unattached, exposing his right hand and wrist.

Observations: The entire epilogue was edited out of the later film compilation, *Destination Moonbase Alpha*. While this successfully served to create a far more serious and thoughtful ending, it was nevertheless regrettable because the epilogue is one of the most genuinely charming of Year Two's closing moments.

Review: Helena's opening Status Report re-caps the events of Part One, and brings viewers immediately back into the action with a sense of urgency. The purpose of the Bringers of Wonder is a mystery until Maya transforms into one of them and takes part in an unintentionally hysterical slow-motion chase scene through the halls of Alpha, accompanied of course by Derek Wadsworth's pulsing musical score. Maya provides a perfect description of the Bringers of Wonder when she states, 'They look like the plasma that forms on some organic matter when it begins to decompose.'

There is an incredible discrepancy between the dates of the two episodes: Part One is dated at 1,912 days since leaving Earth orbit, while Part Two is dated at 2,515. The surrounding episodes, 'Space Warp' and 'Dorzak', are respectively dated at 1,807 and 2,009 days since 'Breakaway'. Obviously, 'The Bringers of Wonder' Part Two is wildly out of sequence. The most likely explanation for this is simply that Barbara Bain got the date wrong when recording her voice-over; the script itself is dated just a couple of days after 'Part One', as would be expected. The events of this episode obviously do not take place over a span of 600 days. One way to rationalise this is to assume that, because Helena Russell is under the spell of the Bringers of Wonder at the start of Part Two, when she provides the 2,515 date in her status report, the creatures are deceiving the Alphans not only about where they are and who they are talking to, but also about the date itself. By altering the Alphan perception of time, they could increase their sense of distance from Earth and thus increase their feelings of loss. This would make the Alphans more susceptible to the suggestion that they are finally going home, and more eager to participate in the hallucinatory world the Bringers of Wonder are creating for them.

The hallucinatory sequences portraying Alan, Ehrlich and Bartlett as they believe they are – back on Earth – are entertaining, while the use of a harness to lower Koenig and Maya from their Eagle onto the lunar surface is a new and interesting piece of Alphan ingenuity.

Maya's transformation into a giant horned Cyclops creature presents another alien she is familiar with that is capable of surviving in the void of space. The other was in 'Space Warp'. She later identifies this Cyclops creature as a Larren, a natural inhabitant of a moon of Psychon, which had a very thin atmosphere (and was presumably destroyed when Psychon exploded in 'The Metamorph'). The creature has skin like a space suit and Maya says that it is 'very strong' as she picks Tony up by his jacket collar. Of course, the Bringers of Wonder themselves also survive for an extended period of time on the lunar surface, not requiring an atmosphere to breathe.

The last third of the episode is absolutely packed with action, and the final sequence with Koenig confronting the Bringers of Wonder, Alan and Bartlett at the waste domes is the absolute highpoint of the double show. The philosophies and ideas become clear and the lure of their spell is understood. The dream presented by the Bringers of Wonder is obviously tempting, and contains the rather profound statement, '"How long?" is a meaningless term, a pygmy's phrase. Time is relative. A butterfly lives a gloriously full life in a day … a single celled organism in a microsecond. So long as one is fulfilled, time is irrelevant.' It is a rewarding culmination and resolution, with another classic John Koenig Year Two moral declaration, 'It's better to live as your own man, than as a fool in someone else's dream.'

The most unfortunate aspect of 'The Bringers of Wonder' is the way the Alphans and the Bringers act based purely on the perception that the other race is ugly. The Bringers conclude that the Alphans are unworthy of living, while the Alphans' response seems to be that women should scream and weapons should be fired. That said, the audience is left with some tempting lines of thought to pursue in relation to the Bringers of Wonder. Were they really from a different dimension? With their limited kinetic energy and obvious ability to transport themselves, why did they need a spaceship, and how could they manage to operate it? Where did they go at the end of the episode? With his winning scripts for both 'New Adam New Eve' and now 'The Bringers of Wonder', it's a shame that Terence Feely didn't contribute further to the series. Director Tom Clegg meanwhile proves his adeptness with action sequences, and his work will be seen again on the upcoming episodes 'Devil's Planet' and 'The Dorcons'.

'The Bringers of Wonder' stands as a clear and pure Year Two vision in every way – style, feel, look and moral statements. It is also, due to the two-part length and well-known feature compilation *Destination Moonbase Alpha*, one of the most significant episodes of the season. But while it is undeniably highly entertaining, 'The Bringers of Wonder' ultimately remains a step below the best that the series had already produced, and that it would deliver again.

Rating: 7.5/10

2.19
THE LAMBDA FACTOR

Screenplay by Terrance Dicks
Directed by Charles Crichton

Selected Broadcast Dates:

UK   LWT:
              Date: 8 October 1977.   Time: 11.00 am
              Granada:
              Date: 20 November 1977.   Time: 1.15 pm
US   KRON (San Francisco):
              Date: 12 February 1977.   Time: 7.00 pm

Credited Cast: Martin Landau (John Koenig), **Barbara Bain** (Helena Russell), **Catherine Schell** (Maya), **Tony Anholt** (Tony Verdeschi), **Nick Tate** (Alan Carter), **Zienia Merton** (Sandra Benes), **Anthony Stamboulieh** (George Crato), **Michael Walker** (Carl Renton), **Gregory de Polnay** (Pete Garforth), **Lydia Lisle** (Sally Martin), **Lucinda Curtis** (Tessa), **Dallas Adams** (Sam)

Guest Stars: Deborah Fallender (Carolyn Powell), **Jess Conrad** (Mark Sanders)

Uncredited Cast: Robert Reeves (Operative Peter Reeves), **Shane Rimmer** (Maintenance Section Voice), **Glenda Allen** (Operative G Allen), **Harry Fielder** (Command Centre Operative), **Jenny Cresswell** (Alphan)

Plot: A strange space phenomenon increases the psychic abilities inherent in the Alphans. One woman, Carolyn Powell, is especially vulnerable and uses her new powers to take control of Alpha. The only person with the psychic ability to stop her is John Koenig, but he is in danger of losing his own mind due to the same phenomenon.

Quotes:
- **Sandra:** 'Minor bugs, Commander. False signals … ghosts.'
- **Maya:** 'I can only go by my instruments, Commander. I assume they are less fallible in their readouts than humans.'
- **Alan:** 'Maya – you sure play rough, honey.'
- **Koenig:** 'How do I command this base if I'm losing my mind?'
- **Carolyn:** 'Down on your knees, Mr Verdeschi. Now I command Alpha. Call me Commander!'
- **Helena:** 'Your ghosts hate you. Your ghosts are a creation of your own mind.'
- **Helena:** 'We were caught in a telepathic web.'

On-screen Date: 2,308 days since leaving Earth orbit.

Filming Dates: Sunday 19 September – Friday 15 October 1976

Commentary:
Zienia Merton: 'There was a scene with a chimp, where Maya transforms into a chimp in "The Lambda Factor". Well, I saw it coming, and I'm not a very brave person. Those chimps are quite strong. They weigh about six stone – they're not little monkeys. The director was Charles Crichton (all the best things always happened with Charlie, he really was a lovely man, absolutely smashing ... but so wicked) and he said to me, "Okay, Zienia, we'll have Catherine leaning here ..." I'm always very careful to position myself well away from special effects. This was a sequence where we all had to freeze, and this chimp was wonderful. It sat on my console, and three cameras were shooting this scene to get as much footage as possible. The chimp suddenly thought we were all very funny, because we had all frozen, so he sat there looking at me, and because I didn't move, he turned upside down, and of course I was dying to giggle, but I had to suppress myself. All those off set were killing themselves laughing and we, in front of the cameras, had to remain frozen. Then the chimp noticed a television screen, started twiddling the knobs, and I was still trying to keep a straight face. And then he suddenly got down and got hold of my leg and got very affectionate, and then finally he crossed the set, as he was supposed to do ...'

Tony Anholt: [Regarding animals used in the filming] 'One I recall was a black panther, and they had the whole of the set [made as] a giant cage with the trainer there and the cameraman looking very worried as the beast seemingly leapt at him. They had a chimp, too, in "The Lambda Factor". It had to climb over my face, and it slobbered all over me – fairly disgusting.'

Terrance Dicks: 'I wrote a very weird episode for *Space: 1999*, and the whole experience was very strange. Basically, I heard from my agent that they were making the show in England and were going to take a certain number of scripts from English writers. I went down to Pinewood, where they were making it, and had a very peculiar meeting with Fred Freiberger, who was the American producer and terribly high-powered. He said, "We're in the middle of discussing our storyline, aren't we?" I said, "No." Then he said, "But you've read all our material and seen the other films," and I said, "No."
'He told me briefly about the show and said that if I had any ideas to give him a call. Well, I went away thinking that it was never going to work, but after a while I got a nagging feeling that I really should give it a go. I worked out an idea that was basically about a combination of science fiction and the supernatural. The Moonbase and, in particular, the Martin Landau character were haunted. I phoned up Fred Freiberger and this voice at the other end said, "Okay, shoot." I told him the story and after a long silence he said, "We have a deal. I'll call your agent," and he put the phone down.
'A contract came through, and I wrote the script, sent it off and after a while the money came through, but I never heard anything more. I never got any feedback or an invitation to the shooting – nothing, not a word! The whole thing faded from my memory until an American *Doctor Who* fan told me he'd seen "The Lambda Factor", my *Space: 1999* episode. I didn't even know it had been made! I did eventually see it when it got relegated to 10 o'clock one morning on ITV. There had been minimal tinkering, but it was basically the show as I wrote it. I had one meeting and one phone call and that was it!'

Bloopers: Superimposing the images of Sam and Tessa into certain shots using half-silvered mirrors resulted in the reversal of their images – watch their badges!

Wires can be seen pulling objects around the Medical Stores in the opening sequence.

Observations: 'The Lambda Factor' provides an entertaining opportunity to watch the dramatic differences in lighting on Martin Landau and Barbara Bain, even when they are in the same shot standing next to each other. Virtually without fail he is dramatically cross-lit, while she is gently soft-lit. The lighting is successfully flattering on each of them, but it does look seriously incongruous.

Review: 'The Lambda Factor' features superb scripting by Terrance Dicks (a *Doctor Who* stalwart making his sole contribution to *Space: 1999*) and direction by Charles Crichton (in the last of his 14 episodes). The cinematography is excellent, especially during the death scenes of Sally and Mark. Sally's is preceded by a dynamic, dark, slow motion sequence. Prior to Mark's, there is a dramatic build-up of tension with the lights going out as he walks down an Alpha corridor (shades of Year One's 'Force of Life'), followed by the arrival of the winds and crushing psychic forces that kill him. The simple effects of objects moving, flying about the sets and crashing down, coupled with the lighting, direction, wind effects and noises, create a frightening and effective portrayal of powerful telekinetic abilities.

The main cast are mostly faultless, although Tony Anholt flagrantly overacts his way through the private interrogation scene with Carolyn Powell. Martin Landau is especially commendable for an acting triumph as John Koenig, confronting his ghosts. His is an Emmy-calibre performance and displays a depth and range of characterisation (as well as weakness in a lead character) rarely seen in science fiction television at the time. The addition of significant back-story on John Koenig, relating his past experiences on a Venus space mission and the epidemic that killed his friends Sam and Tessa – as previously mentioned in 'The Exiles' – is a wonderful example of inter-episode continuity, and adds greatly to his history.

Deborah Fallender excels when depicting the more sadistic moods of her character, and while her performance is somewhat over-the-top, she is playing an over-the-top character, so it does work quite well. Carolyn's psychic powers are effectively portrayed as a potent threat to the safety of Moonbase Alpha and to some of the most important characters in the series. Some of the minor supporting Alphan actors such as Anthony Stamboulieh and Gregory de Polnay give rather limited performances, but they are at least acceptable, and the characters are well-rounded human beings with appreciable emotions.

Watch for the incredible slow motion transformation of Maya into a tiger; Catherine Schell has the features of the animal perfected as she snarls and leaps into the air, and the sequence is reminiscent of her transformation into a black panther in 'The Exiles'. However, her ape shape-shift (utilised to rescue Alan, who is trapped in Engineering with an atomic motor about to blow up) leads to a sorry exhibition of a grunting man in an ape suit – at least it passes quickly.

Moonbase Alpha is expanded through the incorporation of the Recreation Area, with a nice glimpse of Alphan off-duty activities: playing games and relaxing. The Recreation Area is also one of the rare sets in Year Two to incorporate windows.

The effect of the lambda factor space phenomenon itself is the greatest weakness of the episode. It looks like the 'whirly-gig thing' it is referred to as, and this visual presentation does much to detract from the dramatic impact of the episode: it just looks silly. By contrast, one notably appealing, yet simple, visual effect is the on-screen blurring of the Engineering Section screen-saver while Alan has his dramatic encounter with the malfunctioning Eagle motor.

Helena provides a convincing explanation as to what the lambda variant is and how it was discovered, and the prominent exploration of ESP is intriguing. That a space phenomenon could be emitting waves with the ability to increase telepathic powers and cause mental disturbances is a very strong concept to base an episode around. In basic premise it does bear resemblance to the 1972 Russian film, and original novel by Stanislaw Lem, *Solaris* (remade in 2002).

The dramatic climax of the episode begins as Carolyn takes over Command Centre – sitting in the Commander's chair, freezing the personnel and forcing Tony to kneel and call her 'Commander.' Her psychotic madness and powers are then used to control Maya and make her transform into a chimpanzee[24] and then a caterpillar. In this memorable sequence, Carolyn first threatens to step on the Maya caterpillar, and then traps her under a clear Perspex box, ultimately deciding to discover how much air a caterpillar needs to survive and suggesting the others all 'pass the time by watching Maya die.' It's a very effective scene.

Koenig's final confrontation with Carolyn is an excellent climax, as he uses his own heightened ESP powers against hers. It is dramatic from both character and visual standpoints, and grips the viewer. What is most appealing about 'The Lambda Factor' is that it ultimately is not really concerned with the space phenomenon itself, but with the conflicts and interactions of the people affected by it. With a pleasing similarity to such episodes as Year One's 'Force of Life' and Year Two's 'Catacombs of the Moon', the alien phenomenon here remains utterly unexplainable. How did it come to exist, where did it come from, or go to, and what was its purpose? These are ambiguities that allow outer space to retain an appealing degree of mystery. There is also a prevalent theme stressing how power can corrupt and pervert, both psychically and politically. 'The Lambda Factor' is another highly recommended episode.

Rating: 8/10

---

[24] Carolyn actually orders Maya to change into 'a monkey'. As monkeys and chimps are not the same thing, one can only attribute this dichotomy to Maya's own interpretation of the term 'monkey'. This is not a completely satisfying explanation, however, as Maya previously transformed into a spider monkey in 'A Matter of Balance', so she obviously knows the differences in the primates.

2.20
THE SEANCE SPECTRE

Screenplay by Donald James
Directed by Peter Medak

Selected Broadcast Dates:

UK	LWT:	
	Date: 10 September 1977.	Time: 11.30 am
	Granada:	
	Date: 2 October 1977.	Time: 1.15 pm
US	KRON (San Francisco):	
	Date: 5 March 1977.	Time: 7.00 pm

Credited Cast: Martin Landau (John Koenig), **Barbara Bain** (Helena Russell), **Catherine Schell** (Maya), **Tony Anholt** (Tony Verdeschi), **Nick Tate** (Alan Carter), **Zienia Merton** (Sandra Benes), **Nigel Pegram** (Cernik), **James Snell** (Stevens), **Christopher Asante** (Security Guard)

Guest Stars: Ken Hutchison (Greg Sanderson), **Carolyn Seymour** (Eva)

Uncredited Cast: Robert Reeves (Operative Peter Reeves), **Jenny Cresswell** (Alphan), **Quentin Pierre** (Security Guard Pierce Quinton), **Harry Fielder** (Security Guard George), **Terry Walsh** (Security Guard / Stunt Arranger), **Paul Weston** (Security Guard / Stunts), **Christine White** (Maya Child), **Candy Wilson** (Maya Child), **Caroline Munroe** (Girl in Picture #1), **Venicia Day** (Bikini Girl – cut from final print)

Previously Titled: 'The Mutiny'

Plot: Moonbase Alpha is on a collision course with a planet in the earliest stages of development – a vast cloud of gas and dust in space that the Alphans have called Tora. A plan is devised to alter the course of the Moon by exploding the remaining nuclear waste dumps. But a few Alphans suffering from 'green sickness' believe Tora to be a habitable world, and will let nothing stop them from colonising it.

Quotes:
* **Koenig:** 'We'll be swallowed by a vast swamp of dust.'
* **Sanderson:** 'No! There is a habitable planet out there – the prediction said so.'
* **Koenig:** '1999: the way this whole thing started.'
* **Helena:** 'How long are we going to survive on a fleet of transporter Eagles? We'll be at each other's throats.'

On-screen Date: 2,012 days since leaving Earth orbit.

Filming Dates: Monday 18 October – Saturday 30 October 1976

Bloopers: During the fight sequence with Koenig, Sanderson's spacesuit visor is knocked open.

Review: 'The Seance Spectre' is a first-rate script by Donald James, filled with action and countless dramatic peaks. James previously scripted 'The Exiles' and 'Journey to Where', and once again he demonstrates himself to be one of the finest writers working on the series. For exciting and dramatic action in Year Two, 'The Seance Spectre' is certainly one of the very best episodes.

Many interesting possibilities are explored throughout, including the efforts to blow up the waste dumps in order to change the course of the Moon and avoid the collision with Tora. While by this point in the series it is getting to be a tired plot premise to place the Moon on a collision course with *anything*, it is certainly well handled here, and the concept of re-creating the 'Breakaway' explosion is effectively discussed. The aspect of blowing up the remaining nuclear waste dumps harks back to 'Collision Course', where the exact same proposal was put forth.

Another winning aspect of the script is the idea of the 'green sickness'. It makes sense that a group of people stranded on the Moon for such a long period of time (especially those surface workers who are sent out on extended tours of duty away from the relative comforts of Alpha) could develop an irrational, compulsive and potentially delusional need for an Earth-type planet, lending credibility to the mutiny seen here.

Director Peter Medak helms his second and last high-octane episode of the series, his first being 'Space Warp'. Medak seems a director ideally suited to the requirements of the season, and here he improves upon his first segment largely through the benefit of having a far superior script to work with.

Derek Wadsworth's score is again extremely effective and serves to help drive the sense of pace and urgency, as in many other episodes. His compositions suit the style of Year Two, just as Barry Gray's orchestral arrangements worked within the grand scope of Year One.

Martin Landau and Barbara Bain provide the most notable performances, particularly in the scenes where Koenig is dealing with the mutiny amongst his crew while Helena Russell is trying to treat the 'green sickness' the mutineers are suffering from. This is the last episode in which Zienia Merton appears, and as such it is an opportunity to bid a fond farewell to another member of the original *Space: 1999* ensemble. Happily, Sandra Benes has a respectable role to play in the proceedings. Catherine Schell's most memorable moment here occurs in the cute scene where Maya transforms into a young Psychon girl – perhaps herself as a child?

An over-the-top performance from Ken Hutchison (who is incorrectly billed as 'Ken Hutchinson' on-screen) detracts from his character's impact. Greg Sanderson is a madman and a tragic figure, similar in concept to that of Patrick Osgood in 'Catacombs of the Moon', and to some degree should be portrayed with obvious fanaticism, but Hutchison's lack of subtlety goes beyond this and creates a caricature. Perhaps if an actor possessing a more subtle menace (such as Peter Bowles from Year One's 'End of Eternity') had been cast in this role, the episode could have been even better. Carolyn Seymour shines in her role and successfully imparts a personality to Eva that extends beyond the words of the script.

The special effects are exemplary, including in the sequences of the space phenomenon Tora, and of the Eagle's crash, subsequent damage and flight back to Alpha. These are some of the finest effects produced for the series and remain visually astounding to this day. Brian Johnson and his team once more prove how advanced their effects were for 1976. Once again, viewers are presented with nuclear waste disposal areas on the Moon, and again they are different in design from those shown in previous episodes ('The Bringers of Wonder' and 'Breakaway', which itself featured two different waste dump designs – older and newer.)

When the Eagle carrying Koenig and Maya has less than enough oxygen for one passenger, the Psychon transforms into a huge amount of foliage in order to assist in oxygen production to help the Commander survive the flight. It's memorably the only instance where she becomes a plant. But she must have repeated the transformation three times, as the flight from Tora to Alpha is three hours long, and the maximum period of time for which she can hold a transformation is one hour. In a significant lapse of logic, Koenig and Maya fail to consider using the oxygen stored in the spacesuits on the Eagle.

The slow motion effects of Koenig and Sanderson duelling on the Moon's surface are first rate, with this scene probably constituting the finest lunar surface fight sequence of the series. While scenes of this type have certainly been prominent in prior episodes – 'The Bringers of Wonder' and 'Space Warp' specifically – this is an instance of practice making perfect.

The possibility of evacuating the base onto the fleet of transporter Eagles is investigated as well: it's something the Alphans certainly would not wish for, but a viable survival option that is explored effectively.

Conceptually, 'The Seance Spectre' is concerned with human conflict amongst the Alphans, and as such it bears similarities to other second season episodes such as 'Catacombs of the Moon' and 'The Lambda Factor'. Here the themes are betrayal and mutiny, and the original title of 'The Mutiny' was a more literal description of the episode than 'The Seance Spectre' – the seance itself actually bears little importance to the plot, and the episode might actually have been better off without it. The mutiny is the culmination of weaknesses in the Alphan command structure, which have been apparent in episodes of both seasons including notable examples in 'Missing Link', 'Collision Course', and 'Seed of Destruction', which all feature a crisis of command. Koenig himself is the reason for the mutiny, as his information lockdown serves to amplify mistrust that has already been simmering beneath the surface amongst Sanderson and his friends. Could this mutiny have been avoided? Certainly. But human nature being what it is, it was virtually inevitable that at some point Alpha would experience insurrection in the ranks. To make matters even more interesting, there is conflict within Sanderson's own group of supporters, who serve as a microcosm of Alpha itself.

The philosophical underpinnings of Year Two are again stated clearly by Helena: 'The John Koenig philosophy: if there are chips on the table, we're still in the game.' Koenig hammers the point by responding: 'Right on.' Not only consistent with other statements of the second season, this is also admirably in line with the ideas presented in Year One, where human resourcefulness and innovative thinking were often the keys to survival. It's worth pointing out again that Year One's Alphans remained Earth people lost in space, rather than the science fiction superheroes of Year Two (embodied by the powerful shape-shifting Maya). But while earlier Year Two statements like Koenig's 'We'll determine our own destiny,' would have been jarringly out of place in the first 24 episodes, this 'chips on the table' exchange would fit comfortably into such earlier episodes as 'War Games'.

For its successful melding of fast-paced action adventure with character-based drama, 'The Seance Spectre' is highly recommended as one of the finest episodes of the season, excelling in both concept and execution.

Rating: 8.5/10

2.21
DORZAK

Screenplay by Christopher Penfold
Directed by Val Guest

Selected Broadcast Dates:

UK   LWT:
                 Date: 5 November 1977.   Time: 11.00 am
                 Granada:
                 Date: 9 October 1977.   Time: 1.15 pm
US   KRON (San Francisco):
                 Date: 12 March 1977.   Time: 7.00 pm

Credited Cast: Martin Landau (John Koenig), **Barbara Bain** (Helena Russell), **Catherine Schell** (Maya), **Tony Anholt** (Tony Verdeschi), **Nick Tate** (Alan Carter), **Kathryn Leigh Scott** (Yesta), **Sam Dastor** (Dr Ed Spencer), **Seretta Wilson** (Clea), **Richard Le Parmentier** (Sam Malcolm), **Yasuko Nagazumi** (Yasko), **Paul Jerricho** (First Security Guard), **John Judd** (Second Security Guard)

Guest Stars: Lee Montague (Dorzak), **Jill Townsend** (Sahala)

Uncredited Cast: Quentin Pierre (Security Guard Pierce Quinton), **Jenny Cresswell** (Alphan)

Plot: A ship captained by the alien Sahala asks for help, but when it lands at Alpha it is discovered that there is a Psychon aboard called Dorzak. He is being held in stasis as a prisoner, accused of crimes on Sahala's planet Norvah, and is being sent to exile on Thesalena, the most distant planet in their Croton system. Maya doesn't believe Sahala: she remembers Dorzak as a kind man and a philosopher, and wants him to be set free.

Quotes:
- **Sahala:** 'Technologically, they were very advanced and we welcomed them on Norvah. But in time we realised the Psychons were a virus that would destroy our society.'
- **Alan:** 'Well, he sleeps easy for someone who perverts minds.'
- **Dorzak:** 'It may be dekons old, but your civilisation was based originally on military supremacy. Only when that was achieved could the luxury of culture grow.'
- **Dorzak:** 'But your civilisation is enfeebled by contentment. We Psychons are steeled by the struggle for survival.'

On-screen Date: 2,009 days since leaving Earth orbit.

Filming Dates: Tuesday 2 November – Tuesday 16 November 1976

Commentary:
Kathryn Leigh Scott: '[My episode of] *Space: 1999* I only just saw … I had no idea that I spent the entire show flat on my back! I still keep laughing that, aside from [delivering] one line and pointing that instrument [when] I was on my feet, otherwise I was flat on my back.

'I was obviously [supposed to be] comatose, but I take some pleasure in the fact that [despite] being the silent, comatose one I think I had the best costume. I must have been first in line when they handed out gowns. And I just loved those bracelets that I wore. I remember Jill Townsend being quite envious of those bracelets. Jill was wonderful – I just adored her. She was really quite a good actress.

'I should say that Martin Landau and Barbara Bain I did see quite a bit of. My husband and I had dinner with them, and I got to know Martin fairly well. By the way, I still see him frequently – not because we are friends, but he very often goes to the Playboy mansion. I wrote a book called *The Bunny Years* about the 25-year history of the Playboy clubs. I wrote it mainly because many of my fellow bunnies are still friends – Susan Sullivan you'll remember as an actress from *Falcon Crest*, Barbara Bosson from *Hill Street Blues*, Deborah Harry from Blondie and supermodel Lauren Hutton … So I wrote that book and I did a two-hour documentary for A&E. Because I wrote the book and because of my background, [Playboy boss Hugh Hefner] and I became very good friends, and so now my husband and I have become frequent guests up at the mansion, and who do I see there but Martin Landau! I don't know how long he's been a friend of Hef's but he's up there all the time! He's a lovely man, and I really got to know them well.

'Barbara Bain used to carry a mirror in her pocket, and when I was lying there on that gurney – for one of the earlier scenes that we shot – it was one of strangest things. They did all the lighting, make-up and everything and she would pull out the mirror and check how she looked, and how she was lit. I thought, "What in the world – I've never seen anything like this!' I have a feeling that she'd probably worked with one of the old Hollywood movie stars – the glamour queens of the '30s and '40s – and they really knew their lighting. I once worked with Lana Turner, and she had a mirror. So I have a feeling that it came from something like that, but it was quite bizarre. The only other person I've ever worked with who always works with a mirror is Donna Mills. Always. It sounds like I'm making fun of this, but I also think there's a professionalism involved, because they obviously really know their lighting, and they're women who are known for their beauty.'

Christopher Penfold: 'There were huge differences between the seasons. On the first series, the stories were initiated either by me or in the writing team that I had very closely around me, which was mostly Johnny Byrne. That's where the ideas were generated, and the scripts grew from there. I had no role as a story consultant on the second series and "Dorzak" was purely a commission by the producer of the second series, who I think was probably strong-armed into commissioning me by Gerry in some recognition of services rendered on the first series. I knew from the first meeting I had with Freddy Freiberger that I was dealing with a completely different animal. I attempted to adjust the writing of "Dorzak" to the requirements, as you do as a professional writer. By that stage I was not very interested in the way the second series was going. I wrote the script, I think I did a second draft, but there was a time lapse …

'I had offered the idea of "Dorzak", Fred Freiberger commissioned me, and I enjoyed writing the script. But as with many of the episodes in series one, which bear writing credits that don't bear any relation to the work that was actually filmed, this is true in my case on "Dorzak". I didn't enjoy when the script – which was about to go into production – was sent to me in a brown envelope dropped in my letterbox. About the only thing I recognised in it was my name on the front page. It had been completely re-written. Of course there came a point at which I had to decide whether or not I would allow my name to continue to be attached to it. In broad concept, the original idea does actually survive.

'As a result of fans having talked to me about *Space: 1999*, I feel there is a science fiction audience who look back with some longing for the kind of television that takes people out of the minutiae of everyday contemporary life. The BBC had *Doctor Who* for years without really understanding that there was an audience for it, and what the audience actually liked about it. Certainly the television executives were always rather bemused by it, even if they were delighted by its success. When I was working at the BBC a while ago, Jonathan Powell asked me what it was about science fiction that audiences liked, and asked me to go away and create a series. I gave it some thought, but quite soon after that the BBC got involved in *Star Cops*, which probably put a nail or two in the coffin of science fiction on television for a while. I certainly didn't enjoy that. Whatever else science fiction is, it isn't cops and robbers in space. I like science fiction that extrapolates from Earth situations in such a way that it allows us to understand our Earthly experience by looking back from outside. The driving force of my interest in the genre is that it enables us to ask questions about where we are going now.'

Bloopers: The Universal Plague Warning Signal is, as Helena says, 'the most terrifying sound in space.' But what has to be asked is, how can there be a *universal* plague warning signal? It's a minor weakness to the episode.

Observations: As in 'Seed of Destruction', it must be said that Dorzak's use of a Psychon nerve pinch on Sahala's shoulders draws unwanted comparison to *Star Trek*. Again, *Space: 1999* should have done everything possible to avoid this type of comparison, as it did in Year One. As this script was significantly re-written by Fred Freiberger, we can perhaps assume where some of these elements came from.

Dorzak is another in the line of exiles set free by the Alphans, including Balor ('End of Eternity'), and Cantar and Zova ('The Exiles').

Review: 'Dorzak' is a strong Year Two entry, told in flashback (like 'Dragon's Domain' and 'The Testament of Arkadia' from Year One). It showcases excellent performances by the four lead Alphans (Tony, Helena, Maya and Alan), all featured in equally important roles. Alan Carter also finds himself with a love interest in the alien Sahala, which was undoubtedly appreciated by Nick Tate.

The cast door revolves again as Sam Dastor makes an effective debut in the role of Dr Ed Spencer, the final supporting doctor in Medical Centre. The ever-changing supporting cast again proves to be one of the weakest aspects of the second series. While producer Fred Freiberger set out to humanise the characters and transform the Alphans into likeable people, the ever-changing roster of doctors – Bob Mathias, Ben Vincent, Raul Nunez and now Ed Spencer – fails to equal the consistent presence in

Year One of Bob Mathias. Yasuko Nagazumi appears again in her role of Yasko and is as unconvincing as ever – thankfully her part here is small. Lee Montague and Jill Townsend are excellent in their respective roles as Dorzak and Sahala, and Kathryn Leigh Scott is a pleasure to watch as Yesta. Sadly, Saretta Wilson is absolutely terrible as Clea, dragging down every scene she appears in.

It is interesting to hear Helena note that Koenig is away exploring a belt of asteroids which give 'some hope of colonisation' – explaining Martin Landau's absence as he was off filming this episode's 'double-up' counterpart, 'Devil's Planet'. It might be a questionable idea that a group of asteroids could provide any hope of colonisation – unless they are very, very large and have atmosphere, water and vegetation. Nevertheless, at least the Commander's absence is acknowledged and the ongoing Alphan search for a new home is briefly touched upon. While this is appreciated, it later makes no sense that the Alphans don't for a moment consider asking the Norvahns to transport them to one of the habitable planets they know of. As Sahala says, 'The Croton system is made up of many peoples and many planets, of which my planet Norvah was one. For thousands of dekons it has been cultivated into a peace-loving federation.' Surely there would be room in such a friendly federation for the 300 Alphans?

The Croton ship interior seems too large in scope and layout to be able to fit into the external form of the craft as demonstrated by Alpha's boarding tube and launch pad. That aside, however, the model of the Croton ship is a wonderful design, and the interiors are appealingly colourful, with pulsing disco lights and multi-coloured polka-dot decorations, which are similar to those seen in 'The Exiles'. The production design is quite fun. Unfortunately, Alphan furniture and shelving is used on the set of the Croton vessel, and regular viewers easily recognise such elements.

It's odd to see that Dorzak's powers are so different from Maya's. He has great abilities of telepathic control, which she doesn't. Yet he doesn't know how to perform molecular transformation, as she does. In one sense this gives wider scope to the Psychon capabilities, but in another it suggests a flagrant lack of continuity. Dorzak learns from Maya the ability to perform transformations, but she doesn't seem to learn any of his techniques for telepathy or mind control. It would have been preferable for Dorzak to be a metamorph from the beginning, in addition to having mind control ability, with the stasis field nullifying all his various talents.

Christopher Penfold's presence as scriptwriter is easily seen in the inspiration behind the name of the Croton system. Historically, Croton was founded in 710 BC and was an important and flourishing city in Magna Graecia. Its inhabitants were famed for their physical strength, and the city produced many champions in the Olympic Games. Pythagoras was the first man to call himself a philosopher, and whereas in our modern world science and religion are seen as separate realms, he held the two to be inextricably bound to each other. (Alpha's own philosopher scientist Victor Bergman in the 'Black Sun' episode stated, 'The line between science and mysticism is just a line. And sometimes it makes me feel quite old.') Pythagoras moved to Croton with 300 of his followers and there founded his religious, political and philosophical movement, the Pythagoreans, circa 530 BC. The Pythagoreans held significant influence over the ruling of the city until 510 BC, when an insurrection forced them from Croton and overthrew the supreme council governing the city, thereafter replacing it with a democracy. Thus, Dorzak can be seen as a futuristic counterpart to the ancient philosopher Pythagoras.

The dichotomy of good turned evil is at the heart of the episode, but it could have been explored more thoughtfully. For instance, why is the formerly peace-loving poet Dorzak now an evil killer? What motivations lie behind his actions? These are deep questions that are utterly ignored by the script. While 'Dorzak' is credited to Christopher Penfold (who had authored six previous episodes and performed substantial re-writes on other entries such as 'Black Sun' in his capacity as Year One story consultant), he is the first to state that this script was almost entirely re-written by Fred Freiberger. When one considers Penfold's predilection towards philosophical material – he himself commented about his work on the series, 'I was certainly interested in the idea of making popular the kind of science fiction that dealt unashamedly with metaphysical ideas' – the gap between the scriptwriter's ideals and the final episode becomes a chasm. It would be fascinating to read Penfold's original script!

The aspect that remains the closest to Penfold's prior thematic explorations is encapsulated in Dorzak's assertion, 'Philosophy doesn't win space for people to live. It's the struggle for survival that makes monsters of us all.' Is there some flaw in the Psychon nature that turns them all into monsters? First Mentor, and now Dorzak. The 'struggle for survival' theme could have withstood further examination, but it is instantly dismissed by Maya's response, 'But the Alphans aren't warped by their struggle.' The other appealing element, of course, is Penfold's insertion of a poet/philosopher (not unlike himself) in the centre of the story.

While it is not one of the finest episodes of the season, 'Dorzak' is certainly one of the most visually vibrant. The purity of the tints and the variety of the colour scheme are beautiful. Despite its flaws, 'Dorzak' remains a reasonably rewarding show. It advances the mythology of the Psychon race, while providing an entertaining and dramatic entry to the series.

Rating: 7/10

2.22
DEVIL'S PLANET

Screenplay by Michael Winder
Directed by Tom Clegg

Selected Broadcast Dates:

UK   LWT:
            Date: 24 September 1977.   Time: 11.30 am
            Granada:
            Date: 16 October 1977.   Time: 1.15 pm
US   KRON (San Francisco):
            Date: 26 March 1977.   Time: 7.00 pm

Credited Cast: Martin Landau (John Koenig), **Barbara Bain** (Helena Russell – in flashbacks), **Catherine Schell** (Maya – in flashbacks), **Tony Anholt** (Tony Verdeschi – in flashbacks), **Dora Reisser** (Interrogator), **Cassandra Harris** (Controller Sares), **Angus MacInnes** (Jelto), **Arthur White** (Kinano), **Michael Dickinson** (Blake Maine), **John Hug** (Bill Fraser), **Alibe Parsons** (Alibe), **Sam Dastor** (Ed Spencer)

Guest Stars: Hildegard Neil (Elizia), **Roy Marsden** (Crael)

Uncredited Cast: Robert Reeves (Operative Peter Reeves), **Jenny Cresswell** (Alphan), **Peter Brayham** (Garth), **Geoffrey Greenhill** (Phirly), **Del Baker** (Hunted Man), **Alan Harris** (Entra Prisoner), **Beulah Hughes**, **Rikki Howard**, **Vilna Riley**, **Vida Taylor**, **Katya Wyeth**, **Felicity York** (Guards)

Previously Titled: 'Devil's Moon'

Plot: On an exploratory flight to the planet Ellna, Koenig and Blake Maine discover a world filled with dead bodies. They fly to the planet's moon, Entra, where their Eagle malfunctions and crashes. There they are attacked by whip-wielding women and Koenig is captured. Elizia, the mistress of the Entran penal colony, is in charge of an elaborate deception, and she wants Koenig to stay with her forever.

Quotes:
- **Crael:** 'If you condemn the prisoner, then you condemn all life everywhere.'
- **Elizia:** 'Prisoners who try to think are dangerous.'
- **Elizia:** 'Stay with me and you will experience undreamed of pleasure. Well, until I tire of you.'
- **Koenig:** 'Doublethink – you're gaming with words. On my planet, we'd call it Doublethink.'
- **Elizia:** 'The failure of your race is your inability to see the positive in the negative.'

- **Elizia:** 'He must suffer more than an Entran. He's an alien who's shown contempt for our culture and our authority. After him, then: for the glory of Entra and rewards beyond your dreams.'

On-screen Date: 2,306 days since leaving Earth orbit.

Filming Dates: Monday 1 November – Thursday 18 November 1976

Commentary:
John Hug: 'There were a lot of stunt girls in ["Devil's Planet"] and they all seemed like Amazons, running around in these red devil-like costumes. Somebody, I remember, got incinerated, and I think Fraser thought it was Koenig, but it wasn't. It was just an enjoyable episode, and quite fun with all those girls in leotards charging about. It was also a pleasure to appear with Alibe Parsons, who was great to work with.'

Observations: Innovative aspects of 'Devil's Planet' include the use of a floor escape hatch in the Eagle, as well as the second appearance of the-top mounted laser on the craft, which debuted in 'The Seance Spectre'.

Review: 'Devil's Planet' is a fine script by Michael Winder, replete with character conflict and impressive sections of dialogue between Elizia and Crael, including thoughtful discussions about the rights of prisoners and of people everywhere. The consideration of prisoners (whether they be political prisoners, thieves or murderers) is seriously undertaken and rewarding. It bears contemplation as much today as ever, and calls into question how various societies on Earth deal with the same issue across the spectrum from humanitarian treatment to the death penalty.

'Devil's Planet' marks the introduction of Alibe, as portrayed by Alibe Parsons. As a replacement for the well-loved Sandra Benes, as well as the much-maligned Yasko, Parsons shows herself to be a strong and capable member of the team. It's a shame her introduction to the series came so late in the run of episodes, as she is an asset. Commander Koenig is the sole star of the show, leaving viewers to wonder why the rest of the regular Alphan characters are missing from this 'double-up' partner to 'Dorzak'. Incorporating at least a small appearance from another long-term series regular like Helena, Alan or Tony (other than just in the memories drawn from Koenig during the brain scan) would have significantly improved the scope of the episode. Bill Fraser remains an appealing supporting character in this episode, while Blake Maine comes across as rather generic.

Roy Marsden is outstanding as Crael, lending a subtlety to his character of a prisoner campaigning for rights, while Hildegard Neil is ingeniously compelling as Elizia, effectively portraying the disturbed aspects of her tyrannical leadership. The fine guest cast also includes Dora Reisser, delivering a cutting edge to her part as the Interrogator.

This episode contains some beautiful space effects of the Entra moon. As well, the Eagle crash is impressive, ripping the hull of the ship in both the command and passenger modules (though one does wonder why trees explode in showers of sparks when the Eagle hits them). The production design is also appealing, with visually dynamic set designs and excellent costumes for Elizia, the huntresses and Koenig.

The chase scene featuring the huntresses pursuing Koenig is a perfect Year Two action sequence, effectively driven (as always) by Derek Wadsworth's exciting score. The visual style is colourful, and the episode is notable for the occasion of Commander Koenig punching a woman (twice!); but at least she is a huntress and seemingly very strong.

There are a number of interesting issues raised by Koenig's line, 'Maybe I have some sort of immunity.' Well, clearly he does: not only is he immune to the bacteria or virus that has killed everyone on the planet Ellna, but he also has obvious political immunity while on the Entra moon (or the 'Devil's Moon', which was the original title of the episode, and shows clearly the inspiration derived from the infamous French penal colony known as Devil's Island.) In a circumstance parallel with his immunity to brainwashing in 'The Bringers of Wonder', here the Commander is unaffected by Elizia's brand of brainwashing. And just as in 'The Bringers of Wonder' he helps his fellow Alphans to see clearly, here he helps the prisoners of Entra come to their senses and realise Elizia's deceptions for what they really are. It's a marvellous resonance between these two Tom Clegg-directed episodes. With 'Devil's Planet', Clegg successfully balances both insightful character-driven drama and high-tempo action.

The banter between Koenig and Elizia is quite interesting. Elizia is a fully rounded character with a complex psychology. Hers is one of the most thoroughly well-realised and believable alien civilisations depicted in the series, with complicated political angles and criminal punishment systems.

'Devil's Planet' ends perfectly, too, with Koenig witnessing Elizia's death and then walking off towards the landing Eagle for his journey home. There is no need for any follow-up as Koenig's expression says it all. This episode is ideally suited for fans of Martin Landau, due to the overwhelming scope of his role and the strength of his performance.

But at the end of the episode, the question begs to be asked: why didn't the Alphans give any thought to initiating Operation Exodus and moving to the planet Ellna? It is an Earth-type planet obviously capable of supporting a large population (now deceased, of course). A colonisation attempt here would be eased by the pre-existing infrastructure, and all the Alphans would have to do is move in. They appear to have immunity to the pathogen that has killed the native population (although it could be speculated that their long-term immunity is unproven). The distasteful aspect remains that Ellna is covered in the dead bodies of its people, but that is a mess that could be dealt with. What about the moon Entra? It is habitable, and an arrangement could potentially have been worked out with those living there to forge a new society together. It could be argued in the case of either Ellna or Entra that the timeline for evacuating the Moon would be too short, but in other second season instances, Alpha manages to get everyone up in Eagles rather quickly (see 'Brian the Brain' and 'The Seance Spectre' for examples). Are they perhaps being more selective about a possible new home world? Or is this an aspect of *Space: 1999*'s storytelling that the writer has simply forgotten or ignored? Of course, in production terms, the Alphans couldn't be allowed to find a planet to move on to, as the series would then be over, but what is missing here is any depiction of them considering the obvious possibilities presented to them.

Despite this oversight and the absence of virtually the entire regular series cast, 'Devil's Planet' succeeds in combining a serious philosophical treatment of issues with the much-vaunted action orientation of Year Two, resulting in a well-rounded and rewarding episode of *Space: 1999.*

Rating: 7/10

2.23
THE IMMUNITY SYNDROME

Screenplay by Johnny Byrne
Directed by Bob Brooks

Selected Broadcast Dates:

UK	LWT:	
	Date: 29 October 1977.	Time: 11.00 am
	Granada:	
	Date: 23 October 1977.	Time: 1.15 pm
US	KRON (San Francisco):	
	Date: 19 March 1977.	Time: 7.00 pm

Credited Cast: Martin Landau (John Koenig), **Barbara Bain** (Helena Russell), **Catherine Schell** (Maya), **Tony Anholt** (Tony Verdeschi), **Nick Tate** (Alan Carter), **Sam Dastor** (Ed Spencer), **John Hug** (Bill Fraser), **Hal Galili** (Voice of I), **Alibe Parsons** (Alibe), **Walter McMonagle** (Les Johnson), **Roy Boyd** (Joe Lustig)

Guest Stars: Nadim Sawalha (Zoran), **Karl Held** (Jerry Travis)

Uncredited Cast: Robert Reeves (Operative Peter Reeves), **Jenny Cresswell** (Operative L Picard), **Quentin Pierre** (Security Guard Pierce Quinton), **Jack Klaff** (Security Guard), **Harry Fielder** (Survey Team Alphan)

Previously Titled: 'The Face of Eden'

Plot: The Alphans believe they have found the perfect world, until it starts to turn against them. The exploration team is stranded, and an alien entity has affected Tony, driving him mad and to the point of death. Helena and Maya must figure out a way to get help to the planet.

Quotes:
- **Helena:** 'Why should they have all the fun?'
- **Helena:** 'It's a big planet, Maya. A small error could put us hundreds of miles from base camp.'
- **Maya:** 'Then we'll discover the joys of walking, won't we?'
- **Zoran:** 'There is only one way out of this pitiless world – death.'
- **I:** 'There is none but I, and I am I.'
- **Koenig:** 'If we understand others, in time – I believe – we come to understand ourselves.'
- **I:** 'I cannot support this grief that I feel.'

On-screen Date: 2,310 days since leaving Earth orbit.

Filming Dates: Friday 19 November 19 – Monday 6 December 1976

Commentary:

Johnny Byrne: 'The scripts for Year Two were more or less commissioned on the concurrent scattergun principle. In Year One we wrote them pretty much consecutively. This was down to time. As I've said, our knowledge, as writers, of the great-out-there was growing at the same rate as Alpha's knowledge. It illustrates the major difference between Year One and Two. In Year One the Alphans were stumbling, unsure, fighting fear within as much as alien threats without. They were grappling not just with the great outer unknown of deep space, but also the uncharted regions within. They often failed to understand what was happening and why. Understanding how little they knew was a major revelation to them, and one of the philosophical constructs of the season. As I say, they were Earth people pretty much like us. In Year Two they were space folk, pretty knowing, with a can-do factor akin to *Star Trek*. Of course, by Year Three there would have been a progression, but not of the order established by Freddy. 'The Immunity Syndrome' perhaps reflects where I thought they would be in this respect.

'I think 'The Immunity Syndrome' is the saddest story of all, in the sense that it is all about communication and the lack of it, and an essentially benign, wonderful creature. I conceived it first of all, the planet, as a body that had been invaded by a foreign virus, which was the Alphans. And the immediate response would be, like in a body, to create antibodies and to repel it. That theme is still very much in it. The planet's a living organism, and as soon as they arrive it sets up its defence mechanisms, which turn the food poisonous and the water poisonous, and whatever. Also, [there was] the creature … hoping to [communicate] and [discover] that it is not alone. The *act* of trying to communicate destroys the creature. Getting no response, it sort of finishes off the process, as it were. That was the theme, and every time I see that sequence where the creature makes contact with Koenig, I feel that it's one that really belongs in the first series. It's not one that belongs in the second. It has that feeling of humanity, even though it's a truly alien creature; it desperately wants to communicate, and it's desperately sad, and it has also a slight sense of the ridiculous in the humour. When it is picking up on language it's repeating what Koenig is saying.

'It is a desperately lonely entity. All it has ever wanted throughout its ageless existence is the company of another sort of being or some kind of presence that it could communicate with, but the irony is that in the act of communicating with likely prospects that have appeared, it actually kills them, and then having killed them, it expels them. So all of these things are happening, and Koenig discovers all of this, and he has this remarkable encounter – which to me is one of the most touching things that I think I've written in the series – where he dons this protective covering, confronts this presence and starts talking to it. It reveals itself to be vulnerable, very human and very destructive, but unknowingly so.

'I found this deeply touching, and to me it expressed very much the essence of *Space: 1999* – that villains were not necessarily villains and that disasters were usually the result of cock-ups more than deliberate intent. This echoes all of the real things in life. Where we did bring in deliberate megalomaniacs and psychopaths, they tended to be less interesting stories. If you just compare episodes like "Force of Life" and "The Immunity Syndrome" with, say, "End of Eternity", I think you'll find that they're much better stories.

'I liked "The Immunity Syndrome" very much indeed, and I worked very hard on making it work as well as it did. If I was to point to something and say what I would have done with series two, it would have been to give it the kind of pace and immediacy of Freddy's image of it, and the heart of the first series. To me that's infinitely more interesting than forcing Koenig to have a gladiatorial duel with a creature on a planet … There was a certain kind of shallowness of purpose about some of the stories that you are forced to do in science fiction, where you concentrate so much on the science fiction that you forget about everything else.

'"The Immunity Syndrome" was the most difficult to get right, or suitable. It was a half hangover I'd considered doing for the first season. I had a hard time getting that right, because I was working closely with Freddy and he was a very demanding guy. It says a lot, you know, that I actually turned out something I could say was recognisably Johnny Byrne and hold onto it.'

Observations: The interior set of the alien structure on the planet is a revision of other Year Two sets, dating back to the start of the season.

This marks the second appearance of the functional Commlock screen in Year Two. (The colour screen was previously featured in 'The Rules of Luton'.)

Review: 'The Immunity Syndrome' is exciting, dramatic and insightful. It is one of the finest episodes of Year Two and is Johnny Byrne's richest contribution to the second season. The direction by Bob Brooks allows all of the best aspects of the series to shine through and is equally successful in conveying both dramatic characterisation and captivating action.

Perhaps the most interesting thing about the plot is the undeniable similarities it shares with 'Matter of Life and Death', Byrne's first script for *Space: 1999*. While that was the second episode of the series, this is the second-to-last, and in both cases a reconnaissance party discovers an alien world that initially appears perfect for the Alphans but quickly degenerates as the very nature and fabric of the planet turns against them. Instruments and equipment corrode, and Commlocks explode.

The cast are in top form, with Tony Anholt delivering his strongest performance of the series. Barbara Bain and Catherine Schell are both excellent, and it is a delight to see Helena and Maya working together and accomplishing what seems to be impossible. The most interesting feature of Maya's portrayal in this episode is that she doesn't make a single transformation throughout. The supporting characters – Alibe, Ed Spencer and Bill Fraser – are all used remarkably well by the script and are well portrayed by the actors. Fraser, in particular, seems especially likeable toward the end of the season.

The large-scale planetary exploration is well presented, with a significant number of Alphans actually seen on the surface. This is a very believable planetary set of an Earth-type world (as in 'Devil's Planet'), instead of a location shoot or the more otherworldly alien planet designs Keith Wilson often created for the series. Great attention is paid to detail throughout the episode, and the special effects are excellent. Especially notable are the Eagle crash and the sequence in which Helena's and Maya's glider – a sleek new non-powered plastic craft making its debut appearance – is struck by lightning.

Year One, particularly in the scripts of Christopher Penfold, occasionally depicted mankind as being little more than an invading organism or a virus in the universe. This perspective is explored in 'The Immunity Syndrome' as the arrival of the Alphans triggers the alien world's intrinsic defence mechanisms. The planet is linked with the alien that inhabits it, and its response to the presence of the Alphans is purely a biological and involuntary one. Maya states, "The planet … it's an ecological disaster. The computer registers a massive build-up in poisonous elements." The concern expressed over the ecology of the planet as it turns from life-supporting to hostile is certainly one of the more overt environmental statements made in *Space: 1999*.

The alien character, which calls itself 'I', is a marvellous creation: a being unaware of any other life apart from itself, and therefore oblivious to the deaths it has caused. It is a naïve being, and it's a tribute to Johnny Byrne's talent that this entity – even after it has inadvertently killed the entire previous alien expedition and nearly killed Tony – comes across as sad, sympathetic and lonely. Viewers are also left with questions to consider. Where did 'I' come from? How long has it been on the planet?

The only flaw with this script is the eventual arrival on the planet (or, in Alan's case, nearby in an Eagle) of every significant cast member, which leaves Moonbase Alpha without a command presence. The stated expectation of Helena and Maya is that they will probably not be able to return from their mission to the planet, so for the two of them to abandon those left on the base to a future without a strong leader seems highly self-centred. Certainly, their loved ones – John and Tony – are trapped and potentially about to die on the alien world, and naturally Helena and Maya would want to do all they could to help, but they also have a duty to everyone else on the base. Unless someone like Paul Morrow was brought back from his exile in the catacombs, who could possibly be in command? Yasko?

The final irony of the episode is almost tragic: having made contact and achieved a level of 'friendship' with the entity (which now knows it is not alone in the universe), the Alphans are left without the time to actually relocate to the planet (which is now once more as close to perfect as any world they've visited), and must leave the lonely being on its own again. Is 'I' destined to spend the rest of its existence alone, even though it is now aware that other life exists?

Once again, communication is the key to survival, and it seems fitting to recall Johnny Byrne's statement from 'The Metamorph': 'We're all aliens – until we get to know one another.'

Space: 1999's penultimate episode, 'The Immunity Syndrome' is filled with stellar moments and is one of the most sensitive and largest-scale productions undertaken by the series. Many of the latter episodes of Year Two are among its best, and this one goes a long way towards living up to its motto, 'Bigger, Better and More Exciting Than Ever!'

Rating: 9/10

2.24
THE DORCONS

Screenplay by Johnny Byrne
Directed by Tom Clegg

Selected Broadcast Dates:
UK   LWT:
           Date: 12 November 1977.   Time: 11.00 am
           Granada:
           Date: 30 October 1977.   Time: 1:15 pm
US   KRON (San Francisco):
           Date: 2 April 1977.   Time: 7.00 pm

Credited Cast: Martin Landau (John Koenig), **Barbara Bain** (Helena Russell), **Catherine Schell** (Maya), **Tony Anholt** (Tony Verdeschi), **Nick Tate** (Alan Carter), **Alibe Parsons** (Alibe), **Laurence Harrington** (Stewart), **Kevin Sheehan** (First Dorcon Operative), **Michael Halsey** (First Dorcon Soldier), **Hamish Patrick** (Command Centre Alphan), **Hazel McBride** (Female Dorcon Medical Officer)

Guest Stars: Patrick Troughton (Archon), **Ann Firbank** (Consul Varda), **Gerry Sundquist** (Malic)

Uncredited Cast: Jenny Cresswell (Maya transformation Alphan), **Quentin Pierre** (Security Guard Pierce Quinton), **John Clifford** (Security Guard), **Peter Brayham** (Security Guard / Stunt Arranger), **Frank Henson** (Security Guard / Stunts), **Cliff Diggins** (Alphan / Stunts), **Harry Fielder** (Medic), **Roy Scammell** (Maya Creature), **Del Baker** (Second Dorcon Soldier), **Les White** (Third Dorcon Soldier)

Previously Titled: 'The Return of the Dorcons'.

Plot: The Dorcons hunt Psychons to steal their brain stems, which once implanted make them immortal. Now the Dorcons have found Maya and want her brain stem to save their elderly Imperial leader, the Archon.

Quotes:
- **Maya:** 'Helena, kill me – please!'
- **Archon:** 'I dream an old man's dream of death, and find you here to arrange my immortality.'
- **Archon:** 'I know what is in your mind, Malic. Your advice is rejected.'
- **Malic:** 'Immortality is wasted on the old, isn't it?'
- **Varda:** 'Koenig, the security of an empire is at stake. An empire that controls thousands of inhabited worlds. What is the life of one Psychon compared with that?'
- **Tony:** 'Is there anything else in your Psychon past we ought to know about?'

On-screen Date: 2,409 days since leaving Earth orbit.

Filming Dates: Tuesday 7 December – Thursday 23 December 1976

Commentary:
Alibe Parsons: 'One of the reasons that I took the job was that if the series had gone to a third season then I would have been in it and my character would have been developed more. I was very sad when we were told that there wouldn't be a third series, first of all because I was enjoying it and I was just getting into knowing everybody and knowing the routine, but secondly because I think that the show was getting so much better and would have been even more so in a third series – and not just because I would have been in it! We finished the last episode, "The Dorcons", just before Christmas, which gave us the opportunity to have a great big Christmas party, but it was a bit bittersweet, because we all had a good time with Father Christmas, but it was a bit sad to think that it was also one of the last times that we were all going to see one another.'

Johnny Byrne: 'Because Freddy had rejected "Children of the Gods", to complete my assignment I wrote something called "Return of the Dorcons", which ended up as just "The Dorcons" … By that time I think I'd simply given up and wanted to finish my commitment precisely to the requirements of Freddy: that type of story. So I wrote "The Dorcons" as a kind of Freddy Freiberger-Johnny Byrne story. All the rest, it was me struggling to hold onto what I felt was good and what I felt could've been better about the second series. "The Dorcons" was on a par, I should imagine, with the rest of the stories of that season. It had no particular take on anything, no real psychological depth or spiritual dimension. It was just me trying to feed Freddy the kind of story that would get him off my back, so that I could go home and say goodbye to it all. I liked Freddy and I think that most people liked Freddy and found him wonderful – he was great company. I think he was an appalling disaster for *Space: 1999*, but that's just my opinion. So, it all ended in an anti-climax. Had we known then that it was going to be the end of the series … Well, we might have guessed it, given Freddy's past record.

'"The Dorcons" was a fairly easy one to write. The idea of using Maya was absolutely essential to this story. But it had to be done in such a way that she would be incommunicado – keeping in mind that this was the girl who could get out of everything. So it had to involve people who hunted Psychons and who, once having them, could sort of control them. The idea of taking the brain stem of the Psychon and putting it into an ageing guy, which would regenerate him, was a good science fiction story, but it didn't have anything awfully profound about it to say about the state of life or the state of the world, or anything.

'"The Dorcons" failed abysmally for me, because I felt the character of Maya was being pushed into a pale imitation of what a kind of shrinking female of the period was expected to do, which was to cower and shriek. The only one who had done it consistently and brilliantly was Zienia. No-one else could say, "The heat levels are rising," with quite such alarm and trepidation. I was really quite worried when the heat levels started rising!'

Observations: 'The Dorcons' marks the second appearance of transforming spaceships in Year Two. The first was in 'The Metamorph', in which Picard stated 'Molecular transformation. We've seen it in the spaceship and the balls of light. Here it is again.' Mentor's computer Psyche was capable of transforming matter in a similar manner to the Meson Converter in this episode. As Maya explains, 'It's a means of transforming matter into energy and reshaping it in whatever form they like.'

The Dorcons have been hunting Psychons a very long time. Maya states, 'For centuries they've pursued my people. Hunting us like animals.' It is easy to infer that a certain amount of technological cross-pollination has occurred over the years.

It's always a pleasure for *Space: 1999* fans to identify 'The Dorcons' as the source of the now-famous line, 'Resistance is futile,' even if it did become famed due to its later use by the Borg in *Star Trek: The Next Generation* ... Perhaps the Borg assimilated the Dorcons?

Review: 'The Dorcons' is Johnny Byrne's most strictly formatted script among all his contributions to *Space: 1999*. There is none of the brilliant mystery of his Year One work, and little of the humanity and discovery of his other Year Two stories. However, this is basically a well-written and well-plotted episode, and within the limitations of a strictly action-adventure format, it can be counted a success. It also seems fitting that the man who was responsible for more *Space: 1999* scripts than any other should be the one to have scripted its swansong.

In the Dorcons, Byrne created an outstanding enemy alien race with a wealth of background information on their society and qualities of personality and humanity underlying their outwardly aggressive nature. They are almost compassionate villains.

The enmity with the Dorcon race adds to the overall richness of the Psychon people, their planet and Maya's background. Maya remains a fascinating character, always played with charm by Catherine Schell. Johnny Byrne and Fred Freiberger are the two writers who did the most for the dimension and depth of Maya. Freiberger deserves credit for creating her in the first place, as well as for his Charles Woodgrove trilogy and extensive re-writing of Christopher Penfold's 'Dorzak'. Byrne made his major contributions to Maya's characterisation in 'The Metamorph' and here in 'The Dorcons'.

The performances of the regular cast, as well as the guests, are appealing. In particular, Martin Landau and Catherine Schell (pleading for her death, rather than letting the Dorcons take her brain stem) are outstanding. Barbara Bain imparts a fascinating conflict in Helena as she actually considers killing Maya in order to save her Psychon friend from the torture of the Dorcons.

All three of the primary Dorcon characters are believably written and portrayed. Malic, played by Gerry Sundquist, ends up becoming utterly delusional with his new-found and undeserved power – yelling at the mighty Meson Converter, which provides energy for the Dorcon ship, instructing it to "Obey!" The world-weary Archon, played by Patrick Troughton, is sad about, but resigned to, the fate that Maya must meet. Ann Firbank portrays Consul Varda as a powerful ally to the Archon, and while she is authoritative when necessary, she is also civilised and polite. As personified by Archon and Varda, the Dorcons are not an evil race, and their motivations are valid in the context they are presented in.

There are some intriguing parallels here with Year One's 'Mission of the Darians', inasmuch as both episodes explore the lengths to which societies are willing to go in the name of survival, and both question whether the end justifies the means. Koenig actually states to Varda, 'What are you doing – justifying your actions to me or to yourself?'

Less impressive are the sets, which are simplistic and fail to convince that they are anything more than false walls in a movie studio. Undoubtedly the production was even more limited by budgetary concerns as the season drew to a close. While the open ceiling sets of alien ships in Year One conveyed a vastness and a mystery (see both Arra's ship in 'Collision Course' and Gwent in 'The Infernal Machine'), here – lacking the atmosphere and mood of those earlier shows – it just seems cheap. In contrast to the sets, the special effects are top-notch, and the bombardment of Alpha is spectacular.

'The Dorcons' closes the series with a solid if unremarkable story packed with decent drama and adventure. It certainly isn't one of Johnny Byrne's finest scripts. It suffers from a jarringly inappropriate closing scene in which the sense of levity betrays the seriousness of the preceding events and deaths on the base, and the plot gets bogged down during Koenig's run-around on the Dorcon ship, but it is reasonably enjoyable science fiction television nevertheless.

Could there have been a superior last episode? Certainly. 'The Immunity Syndrome', for one, could have closed the series in a far more emotionally satisfying way, and with a slight rewrite could also have provided the Alphans with a new home. Johnny Byrne's un-produced script 'Children of the Gods' would also have been a marvellous note to end on. While 'The Dorcons' fails to draw the series to a close, the positive aspect remains that the adventures of *Space: 1999* effectively never ended. The Alphans were left out there, drifting through the universe on Moonbase Alpha …

'The Dorcons' also returned the series to the timeless topic of immortality, which resonates as the perfect theme for the final episode of *Space: 1999*. It can even be interpreted as a plea for the immortality of the series itself.

Rating: 8/10

YEAR TWO: OVERVIEW

Barbara Bain was quoted in 1976 as saying, 'Last season we got into blinding snowstorms. We got involved in interplanetary wars. You see, we have no control over the path we're travelling, so anything can happen. It would be very conceited of us to think we humans are the only form of life. There are so many possibilities. Who's to say there aren't other beings living in totally different environments?' Looking back on the comparison between the two seasons of Space: 1999, Bain said, 'You know, a good script is a good script. So if it's less this or more that, if it's a good one, you're happy. I couldn't evaluate it by season. I couldn't do that. I wouldn't know how to begin. You guys [the fans] could probably do it better than I could, because you're a little more on the outside looking in. I wouldn't know.'

Christopher Penfold relates his impressions of Year Two: 'I've heard Gerry express regret at the way the ITC influence affected the second series … What we wanted to do with the first series was to make it very believable in human terms – whatever the questionable physics of the whole premise … The series asked questions about the way we live now and where we're going in our lifetime, and it was bold enough to tackle the big philosophical questions, confident it could take the audience on the trip … I think the influence of Fred Freiberger was to really jack up the input of the monsters and to go much more for space fantasy. He may have attempted to make the second series funnier, too, but we had no sense in the first series that the situation was a funny one. I hope the individual episodes had an appropriate level of humour along the way, but we weren't making a comedy series. Looking back on the first series now, people refer to it as a kind of thinking person's science fiction. I'm very flattered by that. I wasn't interested in the monsters that came with the second series.'

Interviewed at a Space: 1999 convention in New York City in 2000, Penfold also said: 'Twenty-five years ago we had a lot of fun in a studio at Pinewood. The results came and went on British television. It felt like an interesting and thoroughly enjoyable episode in my life. Twenty-five years later I find here an appreciation of the work that we did that I've never come across before. What is to me so remarkable is the depth and quality of that appreciation.'

Anton Phillips commented: 'The first series had an epic sense about it, as well as size and scale. You felt that money was being spent on it. They wanted something that looked good and had a sense of class and style, which I think we achieved … With the second series, they cut costs, brought in American producers and so on, and the quality of the whole thing plummeted, I feel, considerably. It became a bit gimmicky; it was no longer about people whom you and I could identify with. We were talking about 1999, a year that was just down the road, and all of these people were our brothers, sisters, loved ones or whoever, who happened to be working out of town and one day got blown further out. By the time we got to the second series, that concept had been blurred somewhat and Space: 1999 lost that sense of identity. The production values had gone down, things looked cheaper and, in the end, the truth of the matter was that many people *didn't* like the second series as much as they did the first.

'The other thing that bothered me, of course, was the dropping of some of the cast. Dropping Barry was disastrous, along with Prentis and Clifton. It would be like *Star Trek* dropping Uhura and Chekov to cut costs. They had managed to build up a sense of family week after week. The audience had gotten to know these people and suddenly all of that was lost. What's the point of disrupting a formula that people had seen, accepted and tuned in to?

'When the second series started up, I think there was some question as to whether or not they were going to ask me back. And then they decided to ask me back … I had a clear idea of what [payment] people like Catherine Schell and Tony Anholt were getting, which was considerably more than I was. So we then went into negotiations. We had decided, my agent and I, what I would do it for. It took the two episodes I did do for them to agree to my terms. By that time, I had actually decided I didn't want to be in it. I had been on the set, and the atmosphere was so different. It had been a really warm, friendly atmosphere when we had done series one. There had been a genuine sense of camaraderie: a real ensemble thing, amongst cast and crew, everybody. There had been something really nice about it, and it wasn't there in series two. It just wasn't there … The whole feeling on the set just wasn't as good as it had been before. And half the people I knew weren't there. I just thought, "I don't really need this." So I decided I really didn't want to be in it. Also, by then, I had other offers, and I thought, "What the hell – I'll take the other offers." So I told my agent to tell them, "Thank you, but no thank you."

'What happened with the first series was it took over a year out of your life, and then in England they didn't show it for another six months or so. So I was out of the public eye, and I was out of the eye of casting directors. People thought I had died in that time. They thought I'd gone back to Jamaica, or gone to America, or gone to the Moon, for all they knew! It took me almost a year just to get back into show business. So I weighed the pros and cons and decided I wouldn't carry on with *Space: 1999*.'

Zienia Merton recalled: 'Anton was another [who left]. He got fed up, like me. They weren't writing for him, so he wanted to do other work … It's not actually to do with money – it's the respect people have for you, so they can pay you money. That is why I walked. If I'm not under contract, I'm not breaking anything. I said to Freddy, "Don't you understand? If you're not writing for me, there's no point my being here." I thought it was an easy concept to grasp.'

As Johnny Byrne pointed out, the Alphans of Year Two represented the antithesis of the concept that *Space: 1999* started out with: 'If there is a difference between what we were doing in series one and series two, it is that in series one we were Earth people, and in series two we were space people. [The Alphans] were there in series two to kick ass … In the first one they were there to understand what it was they were doing, why they were feeling as they did, and why everything was so strange and disturbing, and how to deal with it.'

Byrne also noted, however: 'Without Fred there wouldn't have been a series two. We must accept that, and we must acknowledge that. I have a vested interest, because my life had been involved in series one. So, if Fred had succeeded, at the end of it all there would have been a series three. Then maybe the dust would have settled and we could have forged something that was greater than the sum of those two individual parts. So I realised that the pull of these incompatibilities – the pull it was exerting in terms of stories, characters, situations and basic premise as I understood it – was taking me away from something that was very familiar to me and into something that was unfamiliar. And for me it wasn't sitting at all well with my perceptions of the series.

'This is not to say I was right, and it certainly was not a judgment that you could make at the time: "I'm right and Fred is wrong." You can make these judgments only retrospectively, and retrospectively there are two opinions about this. There are some very passionate fans who found enjoyment and found *Space: 1999* in the second series, with its less complex situations, more people friendly, the wonderful presence of Catherine – who is a fantastic actress and graced that part beautifully. But for me as a dramatist, quite apart from [my general feelings about] *Space: 1999*, that character presented far too many easy options. It seemed the more difficult the situation, the easier it was to resolve, because if [the Alphans] were not taking advantage of Maya's unique powers in the situation, then they were just being dumb.

'When Freddy came, it was apparent to me that there was no place for me in this new universe that was appearing. And anyway, trying to bend what I had written to the demands of this universe was simply not something that I was prepared to endure. That's what it would have meant – enduring something – whereas before one was really having fun. This wouldn't have been fun. It would have been stressful and confrontational, and indeed that was the case to a certain extent – purely in terms of story writing. I love Freddy, and I respect the work he has done, but he was not right for my *Space: 1999*, as I was not right for his *Space: 1999*. And there I would sort of draw the line.'

Nick Tate had a similar view: 'I like the second series, but I've always had a real soft spot for the first series. It was just like we were all growing together and we had this ongoing relationship. Year Two was very different. Fred Freiberger wanted to humanise the show. Great! He wanted to put some colour into it. He felt that Rudi Gernreich's costumes were boring. I didn't think they were boring at all – I thought they were great costumes. He was right that we should have had other things to wear, but a dress designer could have made that decision without being a producer. I might not like him, but he obviously knew a great deal about the industry and about making television. He did some good things. He wanted to put some comedy into the show – that was a good idea, as well. He wanted the peripheral characters to be not so peripheral anymore, but to have some real interaction in the show, and that was a very good idea and should always have been the case. They might have made a mistake in the first series – that they wanted to keep Martin and Barbara and Barry very strong in the show and they didn't want any of the other actors to really take major roles, so they didn't hire actors of any great standing. That's not to say they didn't hire actors of great talent – they did. But they didn't hire people who were already established stars, who would have demanded straight off the bat that they be used more. Prentis, Zienia, Clifton, me – none of us had any clout. We did what we were told to do. I got lucky – they liked my character and they started to write for me. Very lucky for me; it didn't happen so much for others. That was probably a mistake on their part that they didn't really go out and find some very exciting people.

'Those of us [supporting cast members] who went back [for Year Two] – Zienia and I – had no way of inducing this new producer to do what we knew would be right for the series. It would have made a more human series if we could have had more involvement. So they wrote in new people ... Tony Anholt was a very nice man and a really good actor, and so they were right [to cast him]; but maybe they should have hired him from the beginning [of Year One]. That would have helped, too. But they didn't. They went about some things in a very silly way.

'I think Gerry said to Fred, "Help me – I don't know what to do." Or, more than that, I think that after the first series was made and we all thought we were coming back in August and we didn't, ITC came to Gerry late and said, "Look – as you know, we're not going to go ahead with this series the way it was. But we've decided we will do a new version of this series – but we have to do it our way. We'll send out a man to you who will take over and show you what we want. And these are the things we want ..." And they told him and Gerry apparently accepted. I'm not sure what all of those things were, whether it meant that all of us went from day one or whether that was decided along the way. I don't know where that decision was made, or why. It was extraordinary.

'It's always been a mystery to me why they made the kind of changes they made. I can see how some of them were founded in good principles, but I think they made big mistakes. And we paid for it, because the series wasn't a success. At the time, I didn't think that *Space: 1999* had failed, and there was a tremendous amount of buzz and hope that it would go on. With all the fan mail and fan clubs, I can't deny that. If people want to stick with it and perpetuate it, I'm honoured.'

PRODUCTION

Fred Freiberger said: 'The writers, I thought, were horribly underpaid. I told the writers to go on strike! I didn't want it to come to that, but ... I couldn't understand the pay on *Space: 1999*. It just astounded me what we were paying our writers.'

Keith Wilson recalled: 'I would be working three scripts ahead. I would be planning sets and have people building them well ahead. I would have just ten days to strike what had been shot the day before or week before, and then to build those new sets. It was very highly organised. It was a small team of people – I think my whole department consisted of only about five people. Nowadays if you do something science fiction, you have hundreds of people. Then when it came to do monsters in the second series, I had to do monsters as well as the sets; there was just a make-up artist and me. If you do monsters now, you have hundreds of people doing wires and doing all that stuff. It was just me and one man, and he was doing other people's make-up as well, so it wasn't like he was there just to do monsters. I always felt the monsters were not very good, simply because we did it in ten days and there were only two people doing it. I'd design it; the make-up man would make it ... Wardrobe would help. That's all it was.'

Nick Tate said: 'Obviously I did not agree with the construction of the second series. I thought some of the premises, including trying to make the whole thing more integrated and not just a one-man show, were good. Fred Freiberger wanted to bring monsters into the show. But you can't say, "I want to bring monsters into the show," and then say, "But we're going to do it twice as fast and with half the budget." Monsters are hard to do ... It's easier today.'

Of the double-up episodes, Keith Wilson noted: 'It really threw me when we actually filmed two episodes together. The scripts would be written to accommodate my problems, and most of those second episodes we shot outside. That was the only time we started to use locations regularly. Up until that point, virtually all the exteriors were built on the stage. But to accommodate my problems, we started to shoot outside. You would get some of them set in a wood, or whatever. So that was a problem. But we got over it that way, by adjusting the scripts. It was all very carefully worked out weeks ahead. They were all locations very close to the studio: either on the studio grounds or in a forest, which we had right next to the studio. We never went anywhere extraordinary.'

Nick Tate has also been critical of the double-up procedure: 'The double-up episodes were a very unsatisfactory way to work. A lot of the time we had to sit and wait, because we would need Barbara or Martin and they were shooting on the other episode and we couldn't get them. It got very, very awkward. Eight episodes were [done in this way], with two being shot simultaneously [at any given time]. Martin was running from one soundstage to the other. Basically what they tried to do was separate the cast and put some of the minor cast solidly in four episodes and the others in the remaining four. Martin would be the main lead in one and they gave more to Barbara in the other. They would try to write the episodes in that way, so that Martin wasn't too taxed. Martin was singularly important in all the episodes and got all the action, and his character largely drove the shows. It was hard to do those eight episodes, because whilst he dominated four of them, he had to have less to do in the other four ... So they gave more to me, or to Tony Anholt, or to Catherine Schell, or to Barbara. And so it went ...'

John Hug also commented on the double-up episodes: 'I would have liked to be in more, with much more to do, of course. At one point, I can't remember which episodes they were, but we were shooting two episodes in different studios at the same time. And what tended to happen with the double ones was that someone who had a lot to do in one episode would have little to do in the other one, which was [a consequence of] the practicalities of using the two studios at the same time.'

Reflecting on his part as a spaceship pilot, Hug said: 'The Eagle's seats were there, it was a mock-up of the front. It was pretty much [as seen on screen]: there was a console, things to hold on to. It was pretty easy to feel that you were in an Eagle. It was quite nice to sit there. There were the usual things that didn't really work; you know, sticky numbers on a board. If they wanted close-ups of things they had to be functional, but usually you'd just press ... down there. You got used to your favourite buttons. You know, seven's a lucky number, so I'll have seven. It's like getting out of a car door – if it's your car and you've been driving it for five years, you suddenly don't fumble around and go, "Where the bloody hell's the handle?" You're on automatic pilot when you get in and out of your own car. So you need to know, if you're supposed to be an efficient Eagle pilot. You don't go, "Where's that button gone?" You just go for it. You've got to look as if you know what you're doing.'

Praising the special effects, Barbara Bain stated: 'What was really exciting was going over to Bray Studios ... It was very exciting over there. They were like a whole other genius group of people. I only wish they'd been closer, so we could have felt it more. But that was stunning stuff – really stunning stuff.'

ALPHANS AND OTHERS

Of his approach to playing John Koenig, Martin Landau said: 'I'm a lot of things – I think every person is. People are complicated, and you see a lot of sides of me that are in Koenig, obviously. But basically, I don't think I can play anything I'm not! I think it's a question of extending certain parts of yourself and subordinating other parts.'

Nick Tate recalled his time filming *Space: 1999*: 'I've done quite a few nice films since I did the *Space: 1999* series, but I don't think that I've done anything that was as constantly enjoyable, or that kept me as fully employed – I was there every day of my life for three years, basically. We built an extraordinary relationship between all of us;

we were very good friends and didn't have time for anybody else. You have to be on film sets very, very early in the morning. I'd get up about 5.30 in the morning, get ready at home, drive to the studio and get there by 6.30, go straight into makeup, hair and wardrobe, then be on the set at 7.00. You work until 5.20, with an hour break for lunch. Sometimes you might go through until 5.45. Then you go home, exhausted. Or, more often than not, many of us would go to the pub. It's a big tradition in England for actors to go to the pub. But we didn't drink during the working hours; we just drank at night-time. There was a lot of partying that went on.'

John Hug agreed: 'The bar at Pinewood was a pretty lively place when we got out of Moonbase Alpha, after shooting. People shouldn't have driven home. It was always trying to find someone who was sober enough to drive. That seemed to be the main criterion for Friday nights.'

Of his co-stars, Tate commented: 'Martin and Barbara were very private. Obviously, they were married and they had their kids. It was a working job to them; they did their work and then they'd go home. From time to time Martin would come out. He came over to my place a couple of times. Every Friday night there was a party at my house, and Martin and Barbara would come and they would sit there very politely while some people were falling all over themselves with beer. Barbara was very ladylike, incredibly well mannered and polite. She comes from a very good family, and is extraordinarily well read. We used to play and make up word games on the set – little crosswords – and we'd give each other clues and we'd have to guess the answers. Barbara was extraordinary at this – her knowledge of the English language is quite extraordinary. Martin was very clever, too. People don't get to be stars in this business and not be bright. It doesn't happen by accident. You might get one break – you might get one show – but most stars, I think, are very bright people.

'It was great. I loved working on the show. I loved Prentis and Zienia and Clifton and Anton. We were all great friends. It was lovely. I learned a great deal on that series. I'd done a lot of work before, but not on that kind of international level. I think I really learnt my craft, in terms of film, from working particularly with Martin. He is a superb technician, a very clever actor. I was lucky to have been in that series. I didn't think at the time how important it would be in my life; I didn't think it would mean so much to people after so many years.

'I loved all the people that I worked with. I genuinely liked Martin, and Martin genuinely liked me. It's like having a big brother, or an uncle or a father, or somebody you know who has got a particular thing that they just can't let go of. I knew Martin had this problem with me doing too much. But apart from that, he liked me and he loved working with me. He was just a little jealous, that's all. And I just had to cope with that. We had a lot of really good times together. He came to my house – I never went to his house. We did lunches and stuff together and he was a real pal. Some people are very generous with what they have – Martin is very giving of himself, constantly. He's a wonderful, *wonderful* raconteur; a very funny man, full of invention, and I think he's a fine actor. He deserves the Oscar that he finally got [for *Ed Wood* in 1995] – [two] years in a row being nominated [and not winning, in 1989 and 1990]; that's tough.'

Tony Anholt also spoke of Martin Landau and Barbara Bain: 'I think Martin and Barbara were very involved. They were the stars of the show, and if it was a disaster it would be that much more difficult for them to work as actor and actress subsequently. Whereas if the show became a big success and was acclaimed, then they'd go up in the ratings, and so their livelihoods and their careers would develop further. So it was very much in their personal self-interest to make the show work. Plus, they're very professional. They were always there, turned up on time, knew the lines and didn't muck about. One has worked with other people who, because they're the stars, think that nothing moves without them. But there was nothing of that with Martin and Barbara.'

Zienia Merton remembered: 'We were working with amazingly top-notch English directors. We had an extremely good crew. I would like everybody to remember one name – Frank Watts, our lighting man. He was terrific. It's thanks to Frank Watts that we had the quality on that show. Frank was on it both series; he was a delightful man. There was nothing he didn't know, and it was his meticulousness that made sure that all the sets and shots were set up … My God, the pressure on that! We were doing a television series like it was a movie. That shows – all these years later, the quality is terrific. It stands up. As well as the [model effects] boys at Bray, everyone should remember Frank Watts, because he did an awful lot and he's kind of been overlooked a bit.'

On the subject of the show's costumes, Merton said: 'We would break for lunch at 1.00. Because we were in our costumes, they were terrified that we would pour soup or ketchup or brown sauce over them. So, we had these hairdresser's little nylon slips. The boys had blue and the girls had pink. And we used to put them all on and then go off and have lunch, so we wouldn't make nasty messes on our frocks.

'All I can say is that I found the costumes ghastly. My tummy is not made for costumes like that. We always used to know the shots that were before or after lunch, because there were very pained expressions after lunch, while we were trying to look svelte. The poor wardrobe department had a terrible job trying to keep the uniforms clean and in shape, and with the top coming down over the hips, well, you just ended up "hippy". I always maintained that I didn't think that we should have been in uniform anyway, because it wasn't a military base. We used to make up little stories – like Sandra Benes volunteered for duty on Alpha to get away from all the kids in her terribly large family … things like that. At Cape Canaveral they don't dress in actual uniforms. They dress smartly, but casually. I mean, Main Mission and Alpha were still a job – it wasn't an army base. I felt they should have done what is practiced in some schools: you could wear what you liked, within reason, as long as it was navy blue and white, or something along those lines. The sleeves were useful, to identify the various sections, but I didn't like the skirts. Again, this was thrown in as a sort of "Let's see a bit of leg" sort of thing. I'm not a women's libber, but I resent it as being there just to titillate an audience.

'We had another problem, because the costumes were so fitting. There were lots of embarrassing shots of the guys. Not good in profile. I think that by the second day all guys had to wear jock straps. The women – no nipples – no protuberances: no protuberances on Alpha of any sort.'

Of her group of supporting characters, Merton states: 'I [christened them] in Year One "The Second Eleven", which is a cricketing term that means they are the inferior side – but if all else fails, bring them out! You know – Nick, Prentis, Clifton, Anton Phillips and me. Even Gerry Anderson – who's not actually known for his humour – called it the Second Eleven, and we used to post notices saying, "The Second Eleven invites the crew to drinks tonight." Things like that … But so much for the Second Eleven in Year Two – it was missing.'

Catherine Schell said: 'I don't go to see rushes. I go into a terrible depression and it's awful. When we started doing *Space: 1999*, Martin and Barbara went to rushes every night and they forced me – well, they didn't *force* me, [but they said] "Come on, Catherine, you've got to go. You've got to go." So I thought, "If this is really being professional, then I have to go and watch myself," and I walked out totally depressed. So I said, "Why do you do this? What are you learning from it?" Of course, Barbara was learning the best camera angles … Hands always above the elbows, which makes you look a bit like a puppet. And never move your neck, because you might get a wrinkle … I'm sorry, Barbara, but that's not what you should go to rushes for. You should try to be as natural as you can … It's a torture for me to watch myself; it's a waste of time. I think it actually harms. It isn't part of my job to watch myself. My job is to present myself and what has been written for me.

'Martin and I were great mates and we laughed a great deal together. It was a pleasure to work with him, and when we finished, we kept in contact. He used to come to London quite often and he always rang us, and we'd meet. And when I went to Los Angeles we'd meet up with him. So that contact remained. I haven't seen him now for about 12 years [as of 2000].'

Schell also recalled: 'Tony and I just had jokes together. There was almost never a scene where we actually embraced. The lovely thing about doing that series was that we all had a lot of laughs. Everybody laughed a lot … I don't remember any moments of conflict. Things might have been happening off the set, but certainly on the set we all greeted each other happily in the morning at make-up. I thought some of the fellows were far more vain than the women were. *My* make-up took less time than Tony's! And Tony and Nick made many comparisons with each other. You know, hair … "Should I put a bit of brown pencil on this balding spot here?" It is interesting to watch the vanity of men.'

John Hug noted: 'I never saw Freddy argue with Martin at all. It's a long time ago, but I didn't see any bickering. All I noticed were little slightly disgruntled vibrations from Zienia and Nick – just because people didn't know what was going on. I didn't know what was going on, either, but I didn't care. I was just very happy to have a job. I got on very well with everybody … Where are we going and what's on next? Nobody really understood what was happening. Was the third series being done? Are we going to be in it? There were always worries. Actors always wish about something.

'The screen test I originally did was actually for the part that Tony Anholt played. I was fiddling around with all sorts of strange beer-making equipment, which was one of the things Tony's character did – make his own beer. I just remember thinking what a *strange* thing it was to be doing: making beer on Moonbase Alpha. Obviously I did it well enough to get cast as somebody, but not well enough to get cast for Tony Anholt's role.

'First or second day, I was introduced to Martin, and he was explaining about the Commlock. There's this man with a bit of wood with numbers stuck on it, and I thought, "What sort of lunatic asylum have I walked into?" Martin was saying, "You press this when you want to go into the … and this operates those doors … and you press it and the doors open." Well, it was just a bit of wood with sticky numbers on it. No doors were opening – that was all happening later. I thought, "I've entered a lunatic asylum."'

Tony Anholt stated: 'One thing I think Freddy was right about is that he was trying to make the people more human, in the sense that everybody in the cast thought that if you're going to have a bunch of people stuck up on the Moon for God knows how long, whatever else they are, they are human beings. They would have relationships, recreation, be seen doing human things, and not just staring at a screen and launching into space and fighting the baddies, and coming back wondering whether or not they are ever going to return to Earth. I think that elements like Tony Verdeschi's beer-making were to try to give it a human face. I gather from what I'm told that fans fall into at least two camps – those who think that was rubbish, and those who think that it was right. As an actor, I think that the premise was right. I don't think it was ever realised anything like to the extent it could have been.'

Anholt admired Catherine Schell: 'She is sweet. One thing about that show is that you had a unit that, I suppose if you take into consideration everybody who worked on it from the highest to the lowest, numbered about 70. It's a lot of people, and there was very, very little upset or bitching or rowing going on. It was a very, very happy organisation, which worked together very well. What went on behind the scenes, and who called whom what, I don't know. But on the floor it was very smooth.'

Nick Tate said: 'I didn't have to dig too deep with Alan Carter. He was all the things I was as a young man: friendly, happy-go-lucky, someone who loved adventure and accepted a challenge. Although there were ten of us in the regular cast, the weight of the work fell on Martin, Barbara and Barry during the first series. I was, undoubtedly, the luckiest of the rest of the cast, as I ended up with some nice scenes. But it was not really until the second series that they started writing for the other characters. That's when they brought in Catherine Schell and Tony Anholt, and I shared that work with them.

'[Catherine Schell] was a very irreverent person. She wasn't like some polite little girl who came on the show and was shy. She was a very outspoken person; she could trade punches with the best of the guys. She was an all-around fun person to have on board … She was more bloke than most blokes I know. She was plenty of woman, too, I can tell you.'

Alibe Parsons remembered: 'Most of my work was with John Hug, who played Bill Fraser. He's a very good actor, and he was particularly easy to work with. I also did some scenes with Nick Tate and Tony Anholt, and they were very good to work with. Martin Landau was a lovely chap and liked to joke quite a bit and had time to have a bit of a laugh. Barbara Bain was okay, but she was a bit remote. Catherine Schell was quite different, she was very down to Earth and, God bless her, she had to be, because she had to be in before anyone else to put all that make-up on. I think she deserved a Brownie point for that – many Brownie points in fact! We all enjoyed each other's company very much and we had a lovely time.

'I had just done a film with Lynne Frederick in Spain the previous year, and when I was being costumed for the series, I looked inside my costume and there was Lynne's name. She had appeared in an earlier episode and her costume was being recycled for me, so I rang her up the next day and we had a great giggle about it. The series went on for a long time and had a lot of different people in it, so there was always somebody's costume that had somebody else's name inside it.'

Nick Tate reflected: 'I think *Space: 1999* would have run for years if certain people – not just Martin, but other people – had allowed there to be a much more symbiotic relationship [between the characters,] and other [cast members] had [been given] more things to do. It just centred way too much on certain figures and that was its downfall, ultimately, I think. Then they made all those changes for the second series … Catherine

Schell was a wonderful actress and a great asset for the show, but they made her do really stupid things. The whole premise of that character is so ridiculous – if she could turn into a gorilla or a monster she could save everybody! Suddenly she's not vulnerable anymore and nobody else is gong to be vulnerable, because she's always going to be there to protect them. She could become an ant and crawl under a door that couldn't be opened, and all those things. It was ridiculous, and it was all Fred Freiberger's idea.

'One of the reasons I feel *Space: 1999* eventually folded was that the second series didn't have the same sense of truth and honesty that the first did. I preferred the first season – [although] that's not to say that I didn't like doing the second series. Some of the episodes we did were very good, but overall I think our best shows were those first 24. We felt like we were making a successful series, and for it's time, it was.'

Johnny Byrne recalled: 'I had an exceptionally good relationship with the stars. I respect actors. They are not the kind of people I would like to spend all my spare time with, but professionally I respect them very much. Martin and Barbara were absolutely wonderful ... On the human level I had nothing but the nicest friendship with Martin and Barbara. They came to my wedding, and brought me a wedding present. At the end of shooting the first series, they gave every member of the cast a wonderful address book stamped "*Space: 1999*" and they gave a party. And at the end of the second season they gave everybody a little electronic clock stamped "From Martin and Barbara" and "*Space: 1999*". So ... they knew their stuff. They were professionals and they had come a long way. Nick Tate is still a good friend of mine. I didn't get to know Prentis Hancock awfully well. Catherine Schell I didn't know very well but that was essentially because I wasn't in the studio complex in the second series ... Barry was a very intelligent man with a wide range of interests. One became very friendly with the regulars who were there, and I made a lot of friends. Although I haven't worked with Gerry since then, we keep in touch. I have the greatest respect for him. The sad thing is that, [although he was] responsible for starting this kind of cycle of science fiction dramas, the whole thing should to a certain extent have gone by him, and that a man with such incredible science fiction know-how should not be employed all the time.'

MAYA AND MONSTERS

Catherine Schell recalled her role as Maya: 'Maya had met lots of aliens on her travels and they were usually pretty disgusting. They were usually pretty hideous. They were usually very big ogres ... I wish there had been more animals used, instead of monsters. I did give them some ideas, but they never used them. I said, "If I change into a dog, why does it have to be an Earth dog?" I suggested that they give it a rinse to change the colour of its coat, to make it look more alien. I also suggested putting a horn on a horse so that we could have a unicorn.

'There were some things I talked about with Freddy to make it just a little bit more imaginative. But I was thinking in different terms. Things of the future. Where people would never wear glasses – there would be something that [meant] we could all see much better than we do today. Ear implants – we would be able to hear much better. These things could be picked up eventually in the future. Having humans behave with instincts that animals have. We would have been born with these, since we are animals, but our science has actually stripped us of and stopped us

339

developing the instinctive things that we might have: the telepathy that we might have between us. And so we talked on those types of subjects. That people from another planet, maybe Maya, would still have these instincts, that they would not have been over-developed. By that I mean that they wouldn't have had something else placed over them. You know, we wear glasses; cows don't wear glasses; horses don't wear glasses; dogs don't wear glasses – they have other senses that take over when one sense begins to wane. We have stopped developing in that way, because it's easier to put glasses on. It's easier to wear hearing aids, so we haven't developed the senses the way we should have.

'I was very disappointed in all the monsters. I mean, why always monsters? All these great hairy apes, when there could have been far more interesting things. If you think that there is life on another planet, then it wouldn't be that much different from life here on Earth. I'm quite sure it would have all developed in the same way it has on Earth, so all these monsters you see from outer space – why? Okay, so the gorilla rules on another planet, but don't make it so different from what we know as life. Have the unicorn. On a planet there might be a unicorn … [Catherine puts on a deep, mocking voice] "Yes, Catherine, that sounds like a good idea – I think we'll forget about that."'

Johnny Byrne recalled: 'I had the same kind of problem with Maya as I had with the original notion of the Moon moving through space. One of the fundamentals of drama – television drama, anyway – is that you don't make things too easy for your people. It seemed to me that if you had a creature who could turn herself into a bug, a pigeon or an insect that could crawl under a force barrier, it was devaluing the elements of having humans getting out of difficult spots. It was a difficult thing, because virtually every plot was contrived around Maya. I think in the context of the second season, she worked. She was a good character, a good actress. And it gave a potential for a kind of love interest that I don't think was ever properly exploited.'

Keith Wilson related: 'We had to come up with an alien in two weeks. Therefore, I suppose, some of our monsters did look like somebody in a rubber suit, because we didn't have the time or the money to experiment. I mean, I think the aliens in *Star Wars* were brilliant, but they had all the time and all the money in the world to make it work. We didn't. Also you had to be thinking all the time, "Right, if I use that monster in this script, what can I do to it for the next one?" So you make pieces that attach to it and you design it in such a way that you know if you put another piece on it's going to look different. You had to be thinking ahead the whole time.'

Catherine Schell said: 'I played a prank on Keith Wilson. I laid monster footsteps down – they went all the way down from my dressing room, down the stairs, and all the way to his room. And I had all sorts of people helping me, cutting out these great black blotches. They went into his room, and I managed to get some blood, which make-up gave to me, to come out of his room. The door was closed; it was locked. But there was just this pool of blood in the morning when he arrived. We were great friends – we liked each other very much.'

Schell also recalled: 'A funny story about one of the monsters. Martin and I were working; it was one of those moments in between shots, in between scenes, and we were just sitting there thinking about nothing. There was somebody who had just played the monster, who was being unrobed. He had a great big head and a huge body. There were ladders going up to him and unzipping him, unzipping the outfit to get him out. So it was just one of those moments where you just look at something and watch it happening. Then they lifted this enormous head off this person, and underneath was someone who was just as monstrous as the monster! Martin and I just started laughing, and we understood why we were both laughing: "Why bother?"'

COMPARISONS AND DIFFICULTIES

Having produced seasons of both *Star Trek* and *Space: 1999*, Fred Freiberger said: 'I love all the best of science fiction. The thing that I loved about working on *Space: 1999* was the people in the crew, and the facilities were just wonderful. My wife fell in love with England … I liked *Space: 1999* better than I did *Star Trek*. One thing, though: the Moon going to other star systems – it could not really do that. In *Star Trek*, Roddenberry came up with the idea of having warp speed, which would be the rationale. So once you recognise that, you're not just doing something that might not be possible [– it is definitely impossible]. But you make adjustments with that … Somehow or other, I felt much more swinging on *Space: 1999* than I did on *Star Trek*. It was very formulaic on *Star Trek*, doing a morality play every week.

'I liked the Eagle, because we didn't have anything like that on *Star Trek*. We had this thing that Roddenberry came up with – the transporters.'

Martin Landau explained: 'I think we were given a bad rap at the time. We weren't in competition with *Star Trek*. *Space: 1999* was a different show. It had a different quality. We never intended to invade anybody's territory, as such. The fact that people started comparing them, well, I guess it's a logical comparison, but the texture of both shows was very different. So I never understood why that odd rivalry grew. I don't think anybody ever intended *Space: 1999* to be a rival, just an addition to the genre. There's something about *Space: 1999* that is lasting, interestingly. I think people admire it more now than they did then. Certainly, the kinds of special effects we had on a weekly TV show were virtually prohibitive [in cost] until then. I know, because when I was doing *Mission: Impossible*, *Star Trek* was on the next two soundstages at the same studio. The effects on *Star Trek* were quite primal, rather primitive, to say the least. But *Star Trek* wasn't about effects, where *Space: 1999* was.'

Asked if he felt *Star Wars* or other films were influenced by *Space: 1999*, Gerry Anderson said: 'I'm sure that they were. In retrospect, I think my problem was that my vision of the future was of everybody being spotlessly clean, wearing deodorants and nicely pressed clothes, with stainless steel and everything sanitised, and the show has that kind of look. But it was a show that combined people with special effects, and then of course came *Star Wars*, which had people of today, put in tomorrow's setting, and achieved a believability that triggered the whole thing. But I think that *Space: 1999* and *UFO* and those sort of shows certainly paved the way.'

Nick Tate also had a *Star Wars* story: 'When George Lucas came to Pinewood and he was going to shoot the first episode of *Star Wars* he asked to meet me … I was still doing *Space: 1999* – my agent said, "Go in and meet George Lucas." She said, "He'll only see you for about three or four minutes – he's seeing lots of people." I was with him for nearly an hour! I had a really great meeting with him, and I think he was really considering me for something in the movie. I don't know what. But I was still involved with *Space: 1999* – we were still shooting – so he might have thought I was too tied up. Life is cruel, but it goes on. But I excitedly went back to Gerry and I said, "I've just been

341

in a meeting with George Lucas and he's going to do this science fiction film!" I said, "Gerry, we're coming to the end of the series. You've got the sets – let's make a movie!" He said, "Nick, it only works for the small screen. It's not going to happen. I've tried." I said, "Well, we'll do it! Let's ride it – let's make a movie! Let's get this on the big screen." He said, "They've done the demographics, Nick – it's not going to work." He was absolutely adamant about this, and I really did try to talk him into it. I said, "I don't know who this guy is – he's made this little film *American Graffiti* – but people have got big hopes for this new *Star Wars*.' Gerry dismissed it and said, "We'll see … we'll see…" You know how it all turned out. It is amazing, though – nobody ever knows what's going to work.'

Barbara Bain said: 'I wasn't as happy with the second season. It wasn't as clear for me what the intent was, and the changes were cosmetic as opposed to philosophical. Some of the ideas were good, but some were not … I think the ratio of good to weaker scripts was higher on *Mission: Impossible* than on *Space: 1999*, but there were still some wonderful ones.'

There were difficulties and occasional confrontations between various members of the cast and crew during the filming of Year Two, as Martin Landau recalled: 'Very often I would say to Charlie Crichton, "Do I accommodate the script, or does the script accommodate me?" With Freddy I would always say, "I'm accommodating the script – Koenig wouldn't say that!" Fred would say, "Oh yeah? I wrote the script." You talk about a pre-emptive strike. I said, "The man never does that – he has his philosophies!" He said, "Oh, it'll work." And I said, "You can't. The entire script is based on that!" He said, "Well, it shouldn't be. That's where your job comes in." I said, "What you're asking me to do is the absolute antithesis of what I should be doing with this character!" He said, "Hey, you've had a lot of those." Freddy's not as quiet [as that]. [He uses] more short words … four letters.'

Catherine Schell said: 'Well, it's a civilised business in England – nobody takes guns to work, or anything. I think everybody behaved – certainly superficially – terribly well towards each other. I have to say I never had any problem with Gerry at all, as I didn't with Freddy, either. There was never a moment of argument. Things went more sour afterwards, but certainly not while we were working together, and I think he was very supportive.'

John Hug recalled his fellow cast members in positive terms: 'They were nice to work with – they were people who were quite happy. Technically, anyways, they were happy with the stuff. Even if people were not happy with some of the scripts.'

The broadcasting of the series in the UK remained a problem, as Keith Wilson recalled: 'I think it was an absolute disaster the way it was handled here in England – absolute disaster. It was being shown in London on Saturday morning at 11 o'clock. I never, ever understood it. I think it was the best quality science fiction show that had been made for television. You had *Star Trek* being shown year after year, and here we had a brand new show and it was being thrown away – why, I'll never know.'

SCIENCE AND SCRIPTS

Regarding scientific accuracy and a critical review of *Space: 1999* by Isaac Asimov, Gerry Anderson commented: 'I think that a show that is absolutely scientifically correct can be as dull as ditch-water. But I think the point he was making was that, if you are going deep into the universe, then you can say whatever you like and that's fine; but if you're dealing with subjects that we have up-to-date knowledge on, like the Moon, then you ought to be correct. I think that was a reasonable criticism. But I think the problem with scientific advisors is that if you had a scientific advisor in 1820 he would have told you that it was impossible to fly and to travel beyond the speed of sound. And today they're telling us that it's impossible to travel beyond the speed of light. I think, therefore, they are inhibiting to a production, and since the heading is science fiction – underline the word *fiction* – I don't really think there's any place for them.'

Martin Landau agreed: '*Space: 1999* tried to create a reality within what could possibly be a true Moonbase. The Eagle spaceships were framework machines, not something out of *Buck Rogers*. They were just a continuation and an extension of the technology at the time. Critics of the show used to question if there would be explosions out in space, or fireballs with the lack of oxygen, but there's nothing as dull as a "quiet" explosion. Obviously, licences had to be taken to create a cinematic element, so yes, there were licences taken. But by and large, much of what we did on *Space: 1999* was scientifically accurate, though other elements were not. It isn't that we were naïve. It was a question of creating a show that was interesting and watchable, because I think if you just followed astronauts around 24 hours a day in outer space, there would be a lack of drama, and at best it would be pretty mundane.'

Catherine Schell recalled: 'Most of the scripts had already been [written]. All the outlines of the scripts had already been [written]. [In that situation,] there's very little actors can do once they're playing the parts, to change it. If there's [going to be] another series, then you can have long discussions of how you want to change, how you conceive something developing, but it was too late by that point … It was a little bit too late to do more with the relationship. I'm not sure that it would have been good had Maya and Tony become lovers. I think it worked much better that they were sort of in love, but they were too frightened to do anything about it. You know that the two feel love for each other. I think that once you've taken the other step then it becomes something else – you're then writing a love story, instead of an adventure story.'

Tony Anholt had some reservations about the stories: 'I suppose one of the things … that disappoints me somewhat about science fiction is that if you're going to deal with that subject, the possibilities are so enormous, and all we seem to devise is more and more "goodies" versus "baddies". I mean, *Space: 1999* seemed to me to be a Western in a different set of costumes. Not just *Space: 1999*, most of what I've seen is just "goodies" versus "baddies" and instead of the six-shooter you've got a laser gun.'

Johnny Byrne stated: 'Freddy would say, "Above all, it's got to have humour." That's easily said. You put it in and what it boils down to is a kind of crass line that's been put in because now we've got to be humorous. So what you would try to do was finish a scene on a slightly intriguing sort of humorous thought. They didn't always come off, but we tried to do those in the first series as well. There were situations with Bergman, where the things he was doing in his confusion were funny … Simply to try to tell the story, that was the first requirement. Second was to try to deepen the characterisation. That was not always interesting. So what you had to do was to put people into interesting situations. We did find sufficient places, like during "Black Sun", when they're sitting around drinking, there's a certain amount of ironic humour in their situation. I can laugh at things that are not [overtly] funny … I don't like one-liners. They rarely work. You can put [one] in, but by the time it appears on the screen three months later, you wonder why you ever did it. Instead of sounding profound or interesting or amusing, [those types of lines] just sounded glib. And there was a lot of that kind of smart-alec glibness in the second series …

'And to see these characters – they looked as if they were suffering from food poisoning – having to respond to something that [met the requirement] "Above all, it has to be humorous" … That was a serious problem: it destroyed the credibility of the show.'

Fred Freiberger's had a different perspective: 'In the first season they were doing the show as an English show, where there was no story, [and] the people [were] standing around and talking. They had good concepts, they had wonderful characters, but they kept talking about the same thing and there was no plot development. *Space: 1999* opened extremely well in the United States and then went right down the tubes. In the first show I did, I stressed action as well as character development, along with strong story content, to prove that *Space: 1999* could stand up to the American concept of what an action-adventure show should be. Abe Mandell was pretty nervous, but we were well received by the reviewers. A few of them said, "Gee, this show is vastly improved, but it's too late to save it."'

Regarding the scripts, Fred Freiberger said: 'There were some [episodes] I was going to write, but I talked to Gerry about it and said, "I'm not going to be able to do that because I'm not able to use my name." It was the law – we had Barbara and Marty and me, and that was the limit of the number of Americans we could have. So Gerry said, "I have a pen name you can use – Charles Woodgrove." So I wrote [three] shows, for budget reasons … I took the job and was just paid expenses.

'At the beginning of the season you're very fussy about scripts, but as the year goes on and you reach 18 or 20 episodes, the stuff that looked terrible to you at the beginning starts to look like pure gold. I would explain to the English writers very carefully – because I was sensitive to their feelings – how the script should be written for the American viewer. They were very co-operative, very creative. There were several English plot structures I came across that I felt weren't right for us (mostly in terms of character), for an action-type series. As a television series producer, if you do 24 one-hour episodes, and end up with four clinkers, I think you've got one hell of an average.'

Nick Tate praised the work of Johnny Byrne: 'Johnny was a very dear man. He wrote for me in *Space: 1999*. He was one of the ones who recognised very early on the need and the desirability to write for a character like Alan Carter, and I loved him for that. Johnny was very much a champion of my character and helped Gerry and Sylvia Anderson see qualities in him that they hadn't initially conceived. We had a mutual respect for one another's abilities.

'Fred actually pretended all the time that I was working with him that he did like me … He always tried to befriend me and he always tried to be very friendly to me. But I kind of knew who he was from day one.'

John Hug recalled: 'Apart from saying, "Eagle One to Moonbase, come in please," or "Moonbase to Eagle One, come in please," or "I can't hold it, Commander," they would have these lines that one person could say, but it was rather interchangeable. Rather than have somebody new, or that nobody had seen, they would say, "Could John say this? We could have Bill Fraser say this line." But then it was, "No, what would he be doing there? We can't have him in the hospital area – he's not a doctor. Would it matter? Can we move it out of there? No? Okay, well we'd better get someone else to do it." So some of these things were negotiable.'

Catherine Schell noted: 'It was a job. I receive a script, I read it and I try to do it to the best of my abilities. The machinations that happen behind the scenes don't usually affect an actor unless they have a stake within it, so we can make comments about this – "That's a bit of a silly line," or "This is a terribly good script; wow, this is a bit deep" – but in the end our input is not, I think, what people imagine our input to be.

'Some of the scripts I thought were wonderful. Some were exciting, some were challenging, and some were awful. If you do 24 episodes you can't expect the same quality to remain. And if people are writing to a format anyway, it may tend to become repetitive. Even though ideas might be different, it always ends the same – happy ending.

'A lot of the dialogue that especially I had to say as the science officer on the Moon was complete gobbledygook. I didn't know what I was saying. I was just hoping that it came out okay. I just hoped that the rhythm was correct. I'm not scientifically endowed.'

Zienia Merton said: 'Remember that Moonbase Alpha is virtually Colditz. We can't get out … so what are we going to do? We'd all be mad on hobbies. We'd all have gone mad otherwise. There are bound to be cases of people not getting on … someone would be bound to be a kleptomaniac! But you did notice that as soon as you got a troublemaker, they died. It was always a guest star, but we would be reacting against each other as well. We tried very hard on series one – I would snap at Paul, and vice versa. You would understand that pressure; you wouldn't be nice and lovely all the time.'

Merton also observed: 'I always make a point, if I'm playing foreign, that I don't contract words. I don't use contractions. If you're speaking in a foreign language, you have to be really fluent to say "it's" and "you're". You would usually say "it is" and "you are". You have to be really comfortable to use contractions. And I always remembered with my dialogue in *Space: 1999*, I always tried to lengthen it – not to make my part longer, but just to give it that hesitancy that people struggling with a language have.'

Johnny Byrne offered his thoughts on where he would have taken the series in Year Two: 'I would have taken it where there would have been a greater concentration on making the storytelling more effective. Trying to enhance the unique qualities of *Space: 1999*, which were its epic dimension (that implies its philosophical and metaphysical sides) and its ability to surprise and intrigue and not to go for the easy options. To reflect on knowledge as it truly is – which is something that is never solvable, is never finite, but always infinite. Once you solve, that which you solve is simply a way of asking even more loaded, more important, more extraordinary questions. I think what that series represents is more applicable today and in the conditions that prevail today. We were ahead of our time in 1975. I think today we are with the time. We need to look beyond all these great fragmentations of small nations and coming-togethers in terms of new world orders; people are searching for a purpose over and beyond the idea of nation states and all of that, and it's only going to cause a lot of problems. If you look at Europe particularly, they are a group of nations in search of an identity. In the UK there's fragmentation – we're being told we have to think of ourselves as Europeans, but that is an anomalous, opaque thing. So, the *Space: 1999* that I'm talking about is something that I think could create that kind of thing in miniature: a sense of identity; something that people could identify with, provided the stories were good enough and all other things being equal. I think there is merit to that. I think there is no problem in resolving the anomalies between series one and series two because it happened and can be accommodated by some interesting and sympathetic writing.

'The point of my comments, really, is to say that there is no anomaly. That the arguments, such as they might be, between series one and series two are now redundant and sterile – they don't matter. You can discuss, we can all discuss, and have a point of view as to what we like. I like some of the things I did and I don't like some of the things I did. Same for Chris and everybody else connected with the show. That's democracy, that's having a point of view and the right and the will to express it, without people taking offence. There is nothing wrong in liking season two to the exclusion of series one. That is something one respects, but to say it's either *this* or *that* is perhaps incorrect, because it stops people thinking of what it might be. I look to the larger picture, the amalgamation of what was best. If anything, season two was a slight step aside, and a step back is easily arranged.'

THE TECHNICAL SIDE

Nick Tate has explained: '*Space: 1999*, because of its great innovation, and being such a technical show – as opposed to a fantasy show – inspired a lot of people and drew a lot of people to it that in later life went into technical careers. They went on to edit films and edit sound … I [sometimes] go to four or five studios a day, working, and I meet all kinds of technicians. Now I'm pretty well known, and it's not a discovery thing, but in the beginning I'd be going into recording studios and working with people – the producers and the writers – who generally didn't know me, or they would know me as Nick Tate the actor, *now*. But the technicians would come up to me afterward and say, "It's been driving me crazy – when I was a kid I used to watch a series called *Space: 1999*. Are you that Nick …" and I'd go, "Yeah." They'd get all excited and say, "Wow, man, I've got some things I've got to bring in next time – will you sign them?" So time and again that would happen – always from the technical side.

'I was wonderfully surprised at how well [the show] came together. I would be sitting there just looking at a black screen, in what was just a cutaway Eagle, with none of the rest of the stuff around me. I would look out and I could see all the crew. There were 60 people who worked on that crew. They would be playing cards or punching each other on the arm, or drinking coffee, or whatever. The only people who were really focused right at that given time were the director, the camera operator, the focus puller, the grip that would move the camera, some people that pulled the cables, and the soundman. All the rest of the people were doing other things – probably related to their work, but not necessarily concentrating on what I was doing. So I was having to look out there and see a monster, or see a star, or whatever. We really had to have an incredibly vivid imagination, and also have a great rapport with the director, who would help us understand that. It was later on, at Bray Studios, that they did all the models – I think for about the first four months of the first series none of us had ever seen the models! We didn't know what was going on. We didn't know what we were flying. We could just see drawings. So Zienia, Prentis, Clifton and I all went down to Bray and we looked at the models, and we all saw them. [There were] Eagles of various sizes, and they would fly them through the black studio. It was very interesting, but very slow and very painstaking. Then, when I would see it later on the screen, it was a blast for me – I loved that aspect of it.'

Tony Anholt recalled the difficulties involved with the two-way visual communication used throughout Moonbase Alpha: 'The one thing that used to take a little while was [scenes involving] those little monitor sets, where we'd press a button and be patched through to somewhere, and it would be a face on the screen. We'd be actually sitting up on some platform at the other side of the studio, and sometimes that went a little crazy and there was a bit of a delay.

'The thing we had clipped to our belts [ie the Commlock] was just a wooden thing, with a painted thing on it. It had no functional parts at all. You just sort of mimed that sort of thing that Martin used to do, slightly give it a shake, and make it look like you're switching something. When it came to the close-ups that you saw, then they wired you up with the wire up your arm. The same with the laser guns – they were plastic or wood, you just pointed them and they laid the laser beam on afterwards.'

Barbara Bain reflected on the spacesuits: 'We did have some interesting fittings with the spacesuits … [That was partly] in order to attach the Commlock and gloves to the wrist … They also had these things for the boots, around the ankles. They looked wonderful. They were big, square-edged, plastic objects that smacked the anklebone relentlessly! Their *work* was to hit the anklebone! Every step, you got a smack – there just wasn't any way to avoid it.'

Bain also recalled: 'I loved finding out that there was no point following certain scientific truths, like the fact there would be no sound on the explosions in space. We tried the effects without sounds, but it doesn't work – the audience is expecting a noise.'

Gerry Anderson has said: 'Whatever I did, my mental pictures cost a fortune to put onto film. It's a fault of mine: every show I make is desperately expensive.'

FILMING

Discussing the filming of the series, Martin Landau said: 'On any given day I might have six pages of dialogue, and another scene immediately after that where I have to run down the hall 40 times, followed by a hugely emotional scene where I have to break down and cry. *That* is a heavy day! At the end of the day, you have to go back and learn ten pages of dialogue. The following day they pick you up at 6.30 and you've got the lines in your head, or halfway in your head. While the guy is driving to the studio, you're sitting in the back – and it's so nice to sit in the back of a Rolls Royce. Well, if I were driving, I wouldn't have known anything! You're looking at the cows and sheep outside.'

John Hug stated: 'We did it until we got it right, or felt it to be right. Sometimes the actors messed up, sometimes the camera messed up, or something … and we had to go for several takes. By the time I got in there, most of the team that were filming were used to each other. They'd all been together and done a season, and most of them stayed on for the second season – the camera crews. There were several of them; different teams, but they all knew what they were doing. And everybody else, apart from me – well, virtually – had been in it before. They were quite happy with the set up. They knew where they were on Moonbase Alpha. Nobody worried about, "What's my motivation?" They got on with it. Martin, Barbara, Zienia, Nick – they all portrayed characters they were at home with.'

Nick Tate remembered: 'Strangely enough, while we were shooting *Space: 1999* in England, the English casting people and producers denied that *Space: 1999* had anything to do with the British industry – they really saw it as an American implant.

They didn't like it – it was not embraced by the British industry at all. I remember that my agent had tried to encourage some people (when I'd finished the series) to meet with me. I remember one casting director's response to my agent was, "Well, yes, I've seen him in that show, but can he act?" She said, "Well, what do you mean? You've seen him in the show." He said, "Yes, but he's just being himself." That's actually a backhanded compliment, because it is actually very hard to appear on screen just being yourself. It's hard to appear relaxed on television.'

Alibe Parsons said: 'It was a bit scary at first, coming on to *Space: 1999* … not only because everybody had been working as a team on the series for so long before I arrived, but also because nobody knew what was going to happen with the series. It was a bit daunting, but everybody made me very welcome, so it was easier than I had anticipated. I was really taking over Zienia Merton's role, because she was going off to make a film. So the role had already been established in the sense that there was a communications officer, but on a base that big it was obvious that they would have more than one communications officer, so I was just another one …

'The character didn't actually have a name in the scripts that had been written, because the part had been written for Zienia's character, but the producer said, "Oh, you've got a nice name that's unusual and sounds rather futuristic – do you mind if we use it?" I said, "Not at all!" But I'm not sure that it was the right decision, because it's sometimes difficult for people to divorce the character that you're playing from the real-life you, so using your own name – especially one as unusual as mine – probably wasn't a good idea.'

Explaining the part-time basis of his involvement, John Hug said: 'I wasn't in all of the episodes, but when I was employed, they employed me on a weekly basis – one week or two weeks, whenever they wanted me. When it got to the last episode, they specified the days that they wanted me. I suppose it was a budget thing – they wanted to cut back on the money that they were forking out. So they specified three days, whereas before they would book me for two weeks even if I didn't work every day. What happened was that all those three days that they booked me, they didn't use me. So then they had to employ me on other specified days. They finished up paying me more money for the specified days than they would have had to pay to me for two weeks! So it was cutting off their nose to spite their face.'

Of her departure from the series, Zienia Merton related: 'There were rumours, rumours, rumours about, "Is series three going to happen?" I don't drive, so I used to travel with Tony Anholt, who would ferry me in, and if we finished at the same time I'd get a lift back, or whatever. Everybody was gossiping. I was offered a lead role in a film that was going to shoot in Norway. I thought, "What should I do?" Then they eventually wrote a script where Sahn was let loose out of Command Centre and she went onto a planet! It was "Devil's Planet". I thought, "I don't believe it – I finally get three lines! I actually go down a travel tube! This is wondrous. This is amazing." But the dates clashed, didn't they. The Norwegian film that was offering me a lead role was very accommodating, but the *Space: 1999* dates changed and kept conflicting. I don't think they had that much imagination to be that mean, it was just in the planning that things changed.

'So I went to my agent, who said, "What are you going to do?" Poor Tony, giving me lifts in and out, would hear, "Oh Tony, what am I going to do?" Decision time came. I rang my agent and said, "Okay – go for the Norwegian job." I thought in regard to *Space: 1999* that they didn't really want me that much on the second series, so maybe by the third I could be really out in the cold. And the film was a lead. You have to take chances – that's what life's about …

'So on the next day of shooting in the afternoon Tony said to me, "Zienia, can you hang on? Are you in a hurry to get home? Because I've got to go see Gerry …" So I said, "Sure. Okay. I'll meet you in the bar." So I was waiting in the bar and finally Tony arrived and I remember he said, "Well, who's a clever girl then? There is no series three." And that is what I remember of it.'

Gerry Anderson acknowledged the difficulties the production faced regarding their filming and broadcast schedules: 'It is of course true that we, the production company, failed to maintain deliveries and keep pace with transmissions, but in fairness to myself, the decision to proceed with the second season was made so late that it was known both by ITC and me that a breakdown in deliveries was likely even before the cameras started to roll.'

SUMMARY

Christopher Penfold related: 'I didn't stay with the series. The series changed quite substantially in series two, and it wasn't repeated after that. So, in the scheme of things, I'm not sure that it is considered hugely successful. The fans consider it successful, and that's wonderful. I felt it was something that we could really have built on. I think *Space: 1999* – like *Star Trek* – could have gone on for four generations.'

Johnny Byrne said: 'If I had any regret it was that, due to the demands of the format, [we had to have our] main characters on screen for most of the time, [and that meant keeping] in the background a host of really fine actors and actresses, like Nick Tate and Zienia Merton, to whom we would otherwise have been able to give something a bit more profound. In one story we would have Sandra, in others Nick Tate, and of course Clifton Jones. It was very difficult because not only were these good actors – and like all actors and actresses they have egos – but also it was very demoralising week in, week out, for Sandra to have to say [lines like], "The heat levels are rising, Commander." You know, she wanted a bit more than that. I would like to have seen more of Zienia Merton, a very talented actress.

'The other regret is, looking back, I would have loved to have brought out a bit more acutely the sense of wonder that they were taking with them: to have made it an absolute point, and to have shown the degree of leadership needed to stop them reverting into any of one of ten thousand possibilities we never really examined. Occasionally, Alpha Moonbase was swept by great typhoons of unreason, mind control and things like that, but we never tackled the problem of people in such a desperate situation. Their morale would have crumbled but for having very strong leadership. We tried to show the strong leadership, and I think Martin did it well. He is a good actor, Martin. He is a very instinctive actor.

'I was very sorry when I had to move on. It was like having to pass on your favourite toy.'

Martin Landau has said: '*Space: 1999* fans are more die-hard than *Star Trek* fans. They are amazing. The show had an enormous following. It's very popular everywhere …. Barbara won the Bravo Award as most popular actress in Germany for *Space: 1999*. It was a much better show than most people realise. We hit some, we missed some, we tried things. I liked the first season better. It was truer. They changed it because a bunch of American minds got into the act, and they decided to do many things they felt were commercial. I think the show's beauty is that it wasn't commercial. It had it's own rhythm. I felt the episodes we started with in the first season were much more along the lines I wanted to go. To some extent, that was corrupted. I felt it would grow. Episodes like "Earthbound", "Black Sun" and "War Games" were ones with ideas and integrity. Fred Freiberger helped in some respects, but overall I don't think he helped the show. I think he brought a much more ordinary, mundane approach to the series. *Space: 1999* had a style of its own, a feel of its own, a look of its own that would have grown if it had been left alone. It needed time and wasn't given that time. They rushed the process. If the format hadn't been changed, I know it would have hit.

'I think *Space: 1999* is going to become a period piece. I enjoyed working on it. I liked the idea, as did Barbara, of a show set in the not-too-distant future. I liked the concept of a group of people being forced into a situation they weren't either emotionally or technologically prepared for. Had they wanted to, they couldn't have done it. They couldn't have gone into deep space with the technology they had and survived. So this accident caused them to face perils and the unknown and all kinds of things. And not being in control [of] their trajectory added a wonderful element. The characters in *Star Trek* were so far into the future that they were sort of in control of their destiny to a much greater degree than the denizens of Moonbase Alpha. And because *Space: 1999* was only 25 years into the future, it didn't remove us, or make us into beings that were too greatly advanced, beyond what is going on today … So I felt it was a great idea and an interesting show in terms of testing human capabilities and strengths and weaknesses, and coming into contact with many other kinds of species they were completely unprepared to encounter. Being on *Space: 1999* was an interesting time.'

Barbara Bain said: 'If one was philosophical about it, the show might be described as an allegory of the human will to survive … Most people thought of it purely as entertainment. And it was. Martin and I [had] a good time working on it.'

Nick Tate observed: 'There were a lot of damn good episodes that came out of the second year, and I got to do quite a few good shows. But, quite frankly, I preferred the majority of storylines from the first. In the first season there had been a sense of truth and humanity about the concepts. It was built around certain known concepts and wasn't just science fiction; it was more science fact. In the second season, they tried to be more fanciful, but they didn't spend the money and take the time that the show really needed … I'd had three years on *Space: 1999* – the first series started in November 1973 and we worked most of 1974 and finished in March 1975. So it was a 15-month production for those first 24 episodes. The second season was shot from about the end of January through to December 1976, all in 11 months … So if you notice any difference in quality in the shows [in the second year, remember that] they were made very fast.

'The show's original concept had been [formulated] by both Gerry and Sylvia Anderson. When they broke up, it really destroyed much of what had been established during its first series. It seemed as if Gerry was prepared to allow somebody else to come in and totally change the humanity Sylvia had brought to the programme. We moved further away from science fact and started moving deeper into stories that had a much weirder slant. In the second season we would up having, I think, some very silly characters. We weren't able to spend either the money or the time on the original concepts and, as a result, many of the creatures we encountered looked more like pantomime dragons.

'*Space: 1999* is loved by fans because it was about *real* people. It was the characters' humanity that I think made people love it so much. [It had] high production values, thoughtful storylines, strong acting, good directing and – in the end – staunch and loyal fans.

'It's like some distant dream, really. I've absolutely not lost contact with it, though, because I get invited to conventions and go to them whenever I can. I also have a fan club, the International Nick Tate Fan Club, and I get fan mail all the time. So it's never totally gone from my life. We all had a nice time working on *Space: 1999,* and we all felt that we were doing a show that could have longevity. Sure enough, here we are now, and people are still interested in it ... I'm proud of *Space: 1999.* The show was good. I've done lots of diverse work in theatre and film, and *Space: 1999* represents a section of my life that I feel good about. For me, it's a couple of years out of my life and they are proud years. I don't regret it in any way.

'*Space: 1999* finished in 1977. I've had to move on and have another life, and life's been really good to me and I've been very happy with my career. I can't keep on reliving what was in effect a disappointment to me. I thought *Space: 1999* would go on and grow, and I think it deserved to, but other factors caused its downfall. And that's disappointing, because the show itself wasn't disappointing. I loved working on it – I enjoyed the people immensely and I enjoyed what it did for me. But I can't keep reliving something that isn't going to come back. Unless it really does come back: and if it does, I'll be there, if they want me to be. But if anybody was to remake it, they'd have all young people [in the cast]. So I can't keep on going down that road.

'I think if a new *Space: 1999* were to come out now it would have to have brand new actors in it, and there might be one or two cameo appearances by some of us that are still around – Prentis and Zienia and Anton and Clifton. We would all love to do it, and we are all young enough to. And Martin or Barbara could be in it, and Catherine Schell, who is a wonderful actress. I was very sad to hear about Tony passing away – he was a lovely man, a good man, and a fine actor, too. He and I never had any problems working together – we were put into a situation where it was hard for us. As two guys, we got on well together. So there would be no objections from any of the actors who worked on the show to come back and do it again – I'm sure we'd love to – but just how it could all be put together, I don't know. It's a shame that nobody's ever done anything about reviving *Space: 1999,* because it was a great concept and had some really good characters.'

Zienia Merton asserted: 'I think Year Two was too simple. Everybody was doing silly jokes and stuff ... There were a lot of jokes in "Full Circle". There were a lot of nice moments in there. It's very difficult to try to get the right mix between a series about scientists – scientific stuff – and a soap. You know, it's very difficult. I know that we were told we were wooden in the first year, but it takes time ... I thought what was put in its place, what was thought to be warm and funny, was absolutely boring.

'*Space: 1999* is remembered because it was done with deep integrity, and the production values were brilliant ... If there had been a Year Three I certainly wouldn't have done it on the same terms as Year Two, which was absolutely ghastly for me. But I'm a very practical person and a very realistic person, and I [realised I] really wasn't wanted on Year Two. You win some; you lose some – that's life. The second year wasn't that memorable for me – if it was memorable at all, it was for all the wrong reasons. But I *loved* Year One. My affection for Year One is undiminished.'

Catherine Schell explained: '*Space: 1999* was my favourite, because we all got along so well. We had so much fun doing it, so many giggles and laughs, and it was really sad when that ended. I was really sad. It was wonderful. We laughed so much and had a terrific time. It was one of the best years of my life, doing that show. It was very hard work though. Sometimes we would be working until nine o'clock at night, and then had to get up again the following morning. But I never had a feeling of, "Oh, I have to go to work again." I always looked forward to it every day.

'If anything, *Space: 1999* had a detrimental effect on my career, as is often the case when one becomes closely associated with a particular part. I was very grateful for the "Bronze-Otto" awarded to me by the German magazine *Bravo* for my portrayal of Maya, but believe me – it isn't an Oscar! And I never received any work from Germany on the strength of the Otto.

'I still find *Space: 1999* a beautifully photographed show that deserves to be paid attention to … I still like my part as Maya, but I do not like to be identified with Maya all the time, because that has not been my only role. Martin Landau, Barbara Bain and the others were great colleagues. We were a great team and enjoyed each other's company a great deal. I also received quite a lot of fan mail, but hardly had the time to answer it. Sometimes my chauffer only showed me the photographs to sign. I did that, and he did the rest … It's always a risk to play a part like that: it would be very difficult to find another job afterwards for a long time, because people would see you identified with that part … I didn't work for well over a year after the series finished.'

Tony Anholt had a similar viewpoint: 'I would have had qualms about [doing another season], not because I thought the show or any of the people were not good enough. It wouldn't necessarily meet with my own particular aspirations as an actor, and having felt that *The Protectors* did me more damage, personally, than it helped, I would probably have had the same fears about *Space: 1999* … It seems to have done me more damage than good. I'd have probably fallen into the trap that actors tend to fall into: if there didn't seem to be anything better, if the money and the security were good, and if I thought the fact that there was a third series meant it was getting more successful, I might well have said yes.

'Following *Space: 1999* I had six months out of work; that is inevitable when you've been in work for quite a while. I had got rid of my agent, because I discovered he had no idea *Space: 1999* was being transmitted after seven episodes had gone out, and his interest in me seemed to be waning. I got another agent and said, "I want to get back to the theatre," because my own feeling was that … the casting people, directors, if they still knew I existed, had forgotten I was capable of doing a bit more than pointing a laser gun at some monster on a cloud.'

Schell summed up the series by saying: 'There was an awful lot of moving and running around in corridors, sudden head-turnings, meaningful looks. I don't know what they were about, but there was a lot of that … The scripts, on the whole, were fine; they were very good. But there were some really cheesy lines!'

John Hug said: 'Everyone who worked on *Space: 1999* was totally committed to it, and they made me feel completely at home. Nobody was standoffish, they were all very friendly, and it made for a pleasant working environment. I think we *all* thought *Space: 1999* was good. It looked polished, it was well made, the sets were good and it was fun to do. That's what I basically remember about it – it was an enjoyable summer.'

Emma Porteous recalled: 'The joy of being in the film business is that every new script is something different. There are always other nice things beckoning, and one has to move on. But I did enjoy *Space: 1999* very much.'

Fond of his time working on the series, Brian Johnson said: '*Space: 1999* was just the sort of show I'd always wanted to do, from the point of view of producing a lot of effects in a short time without an excessively large budget. And knowing we had to get all those shots in time made me try to think of new ways of doing things like Moon surfaces. For instance, I used a lot of photographic cut-outs. All those shots you see of Moonbase Alpha are photographs.'

Derek Wadsworth stated: 'I was extremely lucky. At the time I did the music, I imagined that it would go on air a week or two later and, with a little luck, might possibly enjoy a later repeat. There was no concept that it might still be showing actually in 1999! ... I am a science fiction fan. We are dreamers who sometimes get a bad press. Scientists are the ones who seek the answers; I like to think that sci-fi fans are amongst the ones who seek the questions. Thank God for imagination.'

Summing up his impression of the series, Fred Freiberger said: 'I thought it was a great show. I thought it was terrific, and the people I was working with – they were all just great. I loved them all. It was very, very pleasant – a happy set, as they say ... One of the things I loved about *Space: 1999* was that there was no interference from a network. If there was anything wrong, Gerry and I, as producers, had the responsibility. ITC may have spoken to Gerry about things, but I had no interference. When you're involved with a network, there's a lot of interference. There's somebody always on your back. But with *Space: 1999*, the greatest pleasure was there was no network to deal with. The mistakes you're making are your own – they're not forced on you. I don't expect the fans to make any allowances ... If anybody doesn't like the show, that's quite all right.'

Gerry Anderson said: 'This is only a gut reaction, but I would say that the more serious-minded science fiction fans preferred the first year. However, I think the higher proportion of letters I've received preferred the second. I think that if, as a producer, you do exactly what you want to do, it can be said that you're a strong personality and you know exactly where you're going. Equally, it can be said that you're pigheaded and are totally ignoring the advice of the people who know the market. I decided that, since I was not in America, I really should take the advice of the people who were there on a day-to-day basis. I don't think either the first year or the second year is necessarily the type of show I would like to make if I were left to my own devices.'

THE ABANDONED YEAR THREE

While Year Two of *Space: 1999* aired around the world, plans were underway for a potential third season, as was reported in the media: 'Now entrenched in its successful second season boom, ITC is looking forward to a third season with more fantastic events and additions, although mum's the word at the studio. They will only say that Maya and Miss Schell will be kept in and that the budget may be raised again. But that's all until final preparations and an official announcement are made.'[25]

It was rumoured that this third season would consist of 13 episodes, which was probably a proposed cost-cutting measure – reducing the number of episodes, yet maintaining the production values viewers had come to expect. These additional 13 episodes would have served the series very well in syndicated re-runs, increasing the total number of episodes from 48 to a far more marketable 61. Catherine Schell has talked about the potential third season: 'There were plans to do another series. There was even talk of a spin-off series … with – as I was told – Maya as the leading character. I don't remember Tony or Nick ever being mentioned, but I presume that they would have been featured in it … I would of course have gone on to make another series. Greed almost always wins over common sense, and I had been promised an American type contract, giving me residuals on all the foreign sales and repeats. It would have been an ideal form of a pension plan. As for Maya's character developing, that would have been entirely in the hands of the writers. I am sure I would have thought of something and made some suggestions, but this is now merely rhetorical … It wasn't only Freddy [who mentioned the thought that there might be a spin-off of the Maya character], it was also Gerry. [That] obviously would have been very interesting for me. The conversation was really about what would happen, what did I think, and would I want to do it? Yes, of course! And they were very sweet, because … I was with an agent at the time who was really a small-time agent. When I received the contract, even to sign, I had to send it back twice because I spotted mistakes [and payment issues] … I was sending the contract back [with queries], and they noticed that it was coming from me, not from my agent. My agent had actually said, "Catherine, don't make waves, for heaven's sake. These are important people and you want to work for them, so work for peanuts," or whatever. So they told me, "If we do another series, we advise you – as the 'enemy' – to find another agent. You have to go to a better agent." But, anyway, [the spin-off] never happened. It was in [just the early stages] of the planning system. There were no scripts involved. It was just a theory: there was some interest, and perhaps we could do this.' Martin Landau recalled the reason why Year Three never happened: 'We got sacrificed. Lew Grade was getting into the motion picture business and it turned out his advertising budget for his films, like *Raise The Titanic*, was our total budget for another season. It would have served them, from a syndication point of view, to have another season, but it came down to economic priorities. I think there was a very good chance of our going for another season if he hadn't gotten into movies and needed that money.'

Landau's recollection was confirmed by Johnny Byrne, who stated: 'The plug was

---

[25] Leider, R. Allen. *Circus* magazine: '*Space: 1999* Tries To Change Its Image', 28 February 1977, No. 130.

pulled by the *Titanic*. It was the *Titanic* that did in *Space: 1999*. The film *Raise The Titanic*. Lew Grade took all his money and followed this obsessive dream of raising the *Titanic*.' Catherine Schell has also related the same story, 'ITC used the money [instead] to publicise three films they feared would flop at the box office. The series wasn't made and the films [still] flopped.'

Plans for a possible Maya spin-off series aside, Year Three was estimated to begin filming in the summer of 1977, but the global response to Year Two was discouraging and, coupled with Lew Grade's ambitions for *Raise the Titanic*, Year Three was abandoned. Years later, Barbara Bain said, 'There must have been discussions about a possible series three, but I don't remember them. We were in England for four years. We stayed a little longer than the production lasted, and I was quite reluctant to leave, but it was time to move on to something else.'

Fred Freiberger stated: 'I wouldn't have made any changes if there had been a third series; if you have a show that's going well, why play around with fate? If [any changes had been proposed], then I would have gone to Gerry and seen what he felt about it. If we had gone into a third season, we would have probably had our budget extended, so there would have been more money. Things like that: the budget was always a problem ... I don't know if I'd make any changes [for a third series]. I think I injected a lot more humour, especially between Tony and Catherine. As for Martin and Barbara, I think I beat the bad relationships. I think if [the production] had had the budget for not only American guest stars but [also] high-class English actors, they would have had a hell of a lot better acting. But, in terms of changes, I think that American guest stars would be appealing for the American audience.'

Year One's Prentis Hancock said: 'If there was a series three, I think you could bring back everybody. If you were willing to look back, and look forward ... This series, like many other science fiction series, is really entirely imaginative. You use your imagination and look backward, look forward ... [The characters could] be on Moonbase Alpha #1, or Moonbase Alpha #2, or Moonbase Alpha #3 ...'

John Hug recalled: 'I don't really know why we didn't continue, because as far as I could work out, the series seemed to be successful. People were going around and talking about a third season, but eventually we heard it wasn't going to happen, so that was that. I was slightly surprised, because there are some things that seem to keep getting made again year after year for no real reason. While *Space: 1999* was particularly successful in America, they did do funny things with it in England, like showing it at 11.30, which is *not* peak viewing time. It had a certain following, and I think it could have gone on longer than it actually did.'

Fans of the series (aligned primarily in the US under an organisation known in the late 1970s as 'The National Save: 1999 Alliance') attempted to keep it afloat, and launched a letter-writing campaign. A report in *Starlog* magazine's fifth issue, dated May 1977, read: 'As we go to press, there is no word on the renewal of *Space: 1999* for a third season. According to ITC, the determining factor will be the number of renewal orders they receive from local stations. Whether, in issue No 6, we will be reporting the cancellation or the renewal of *1999* will largely be the result of letters that the stations receive (or don't receive) supporting the show. If you want *Space: 1999* renewed, write (and get everyone you know to write) to your local station. In addition, and this is very important, send a copy of your letter to ITC ... so they can gauge how much of an audience the programme has. This will be much more difficult than the famous *Star Trek* letter-writing campaign, because at least 100 stations need to be convinced ... not just one network.' Indeed, the task proved virtually impossible, and despite the valiant efforts of their campaign, the fans were unsuccessful. The possibility briefly arose that *Space: 1999* might be picked up by another production company or US network when reports surfaced in fan publications that a production executive at ABC was interested in purchasing the rights to the series[26], but this potential also failed to materialise.

Ironically, *Space: 1999* ended just as filmed science fiction experienced its biggest boom in history: *Star Wars* arrived on the scene in 1977, and spawned a new generation of science fiction television programmes in its wake (notable examples being *Battlestar Galactica* and *Buck Rogers in the 25th Century*). Had *Space: 1999* continued, it would have been well positioned to capitalise on the success of *Star Wars*, and could conceivably have continued for years to come as the established champion of televised science fiction.

---

[26] Cruthers, Michael. *Eagle 1*: 'Saving *Space*', September – October 1977, Vol 1, No 3.

THE *SPACE: 1999* MOVIES

The *Space: 1999* movies are compilations of episodes from the original series, released to television and home video markets. This practice was relatively common between the 1960s and 1980s, and other programmes with episodes constructed into compilation movies include *The Man from U.N.C.L.E.*, *The Saint*, *The Champions* and *Zorro*.

When discussing the *Space: 1999* movies, the initial Italian compilation, *Spazio 1999*, is not generally considered part of the package, due to its having been tailored specifically for the Italian market, as opposed to the worldwide market. Thus, although there technically were five films edited from *Space: 1999* episodes, fans generally refer to there being only four: *Destination Moonbase Alpha*, *Alien Attack*, *Journey Through the Black Sun* and *Cosmic Princess*.

These four *Space: 1999* movies are regarded with a certain degree of derision by aficionados of the series. This is due to a variety of factors. One is that the editing of the episodes was somewhat extreme on *Journey Through the Black Sun* and *Cosmic Princess*. Another is that the manner of the movies' release was in some cases rather embarrassing. Prime examples here were the US videotape releases of *Alien Attack* and *Journey Through the Black Sun* as part of the 'Sybil Danning's Adventure Video' range. These videotapes featured tasteless, sexually suggestive images on the packaging and introductions by actress Sybil Danning, and were eventually withdrawn from sale following reported legal action by Martin Landau and Barbara Bain. But fans were also troubled by the fact that the episodes contained in the films were removed from the syndication package of *Space: 1999* and thus, for many years, were unavailable in their complete and unedited episodic form. This procedure hurt the potential for *Space: 1999* to continue being syndicated in series form, because the episode package was reduced from 48 episodes to 40.

Although their very existence is of debatable merit, it is worth recording brief details of these *Space: 1999* movies.

SPAZIO 1999

This compilation of three episodes ('Breakaway', 'Ring Around the Moon', and 'Another Time, Another Place') served to launch the series on television in Italy in 1976, where it was also later released to home video. The episodes are heavily edited, with the resultant loss of approximately 60 minutes between the three shows.

Of particular note is a new musical score, composed for this film by famed Italian composer Ennio Morricone (who went on to be nominated for five Academy Awards, and was presented with an Honourary Academy Award in 2007).

Regarding this compilation, Keith Wilson said, 'The episodes always looked better on the big screen – they were made for the big screen. In fact, in Italy when they first came out, they put three of them together and the streets of Rome were empty because everyone was going to the cinema [to see this film compilation, *Spazio: 1999*].'

Length: 88 minutes.

DESTINATION MOONBASE ALPHA

ITC decided in 1978 that they could continue to market *Space: 1999* by creating a movie, and the most obvious and legitimate choice of episodes was the only two-part segment produced for the series, 'The Bringers of Wonder'. The film was edited (at Pinewood Studios) for ITC UK by David Withers and was subsequently released to television and home video markets. The opening narration is by Marc Smith, who had previously provided the voice of the Beta Cloud in the episode of the same name. Seemingly for the purpose of distinguishing this film from *Space: 1999* the series, the opening text announces that the year is 2100.

The only important scenes cut from 'The Bringers of Wonder' are the introduction to Part Two (which would have been redundant in the middle of a movie, as it was simply a summary of Part One), and the epilogue of Part Two. This latter cut is more significant as the missing scene is quite charming, but it permits the movie to end on a more dramatic note.

The end credits are accompanied by an entertainingly awful song composed by Italian musicians Guido and Maurizio de Angelis (with lyrics by Hilary Harvey). The de Angelis brothers together composed and sang music (frequently for film soundtracks) under the name Oliver Onions, which is how they are credited here.

Released in 1978, *Destination Moonbase Alpha* was first broadcast on American television in September 1979. There are anecdotal, but formally undocumented, accounts of some theatrical screenings, particularly in the US. In September 1980 it was released to the growing home video market in the UK. *Destination Moonbase Alpha* benefited from promotional material including a theatrical-style poster that became very well known and popular, painted by the British artist Chantrell.

Length: 96 minutes.

ALIEN ATTACK

Primarily comprised of the episodes 'Breakaway' and 'War Games', *Alien Attack* also featured some specially-filmed new material. Although shot at Pinewood Studios (by director Bill Lenny), this new footage, set on Earth, did not utilise any regular series sets or cast members. These additional scenes take place at the International Lunar Commission on Earth, and were written by Dennis Spooner (a long-time associate of Gerry Anderson). The additional cast members include: Patrick Allen (Lunar Commission Chairman), Weston Gavin (Lunar Commission Deputy Chairman), and Marc Smith (Commander Nardin / Narrator). These additional scenes are not generally regarded by fans to be part of series canon.

Alien Attack followed the lead of *Destination Moonbase Alpha* by re-setting the date of the film to the year 2100. Edits to 'Breakaway' are minor, while 'War Games' is uncut.

While there are no accounts of *Alien Attack* being screened in any theatres around the world, it was very successfully distributed to television markets, and again featured the artwork of Chantrell on its poster. *Alien Attack* was released in 1979.

Taglines: 'The ultimate space age disaster was just the beginning …' and 'The ultimate space-age disaster … and a desperate struggle for survival.'

Length: 105 minutes.

JOURNEY THROUGH THE BLACK SUN

While *Destination Moonbase Alpha* and *Alien Attack* were created by ITC in the UK, the last two *Space: 1999* films were compiled by ITC in New York. An independent company called Cinecontact Inc was hired to perform the editing, and the final product suffered in quality because the movies were edited from videotape copies of the episodes rather than from film, as the UK movies had been.

Journey Through the Black Sun is a heavily edited compilation of 'Collision Course' and 'Black Sun'. Unfortunately, many of the slower, character-building scenes have been excised, increasing the pace of the proceedings, but sacrificing the humanity of the characters and undermining the overall plot proceedings. A total of approximately 12 minutes is missing. Additional music has been added to the soundtrack of this film from such Anderson series as *UFO* and *Joe 90*, with questionable and intrusive results. Also added (without any seeming benefit) is Helena's Status Report from 'New Adam New Eve', which plays during the opening titles. The carelessness with which this movie was put together is further evidenced by the incorrect billing of Barry Morse as playing 'Dr Victor Bergman' rather than 'Professor Victor Bergman'.

Released in 1982 to television markets.

Tagline: 'There is no escape from its deadly pull.'

Length: 89 minutes.

COSMIC PRINCESS

Cosmic Princess is a heavily edited compilation of 'The Metamorph' and 'Space Warp', with each episode losing at least five minutes of footage. The cuts range from minor edits of many scenes, through to the complete removal of both episode epilogues. The music soundtrack has also been extensively tampered with, including with the addition of music from Year One, which sometimes overlaps the original score for these Year Two episodes. The results are jarring to anyone familiar with the series. Additionally, the dialogue of Captain Duro from 'Space Warp' is replaced by new dubbing, for no apparent reason.

Cosmic Princess holds the dubious distinction of having appeared as the tenth movie featured in the series *Mystery Science Theatre 3000* (aka *MST3K*), on 22 January 1989.

Released in 1982 to television markets.

Tagline: 'An alien beauty … hiding a beast within!'

Length: 91 minutes.

FAN-PRODUCED EPISODES

MESSAGE FROM MOONBASE ALPHA

Screenplay by Johnny Byrne
Directed by Tim Mallett

Premiere Screening: Los Angeles, California – Monday 13 September 1999, at 'Breakaway: The Convention'.

Cast: Zienia Merton (Sandra Benes)

Additional Cast (in flashbacks): **Martin Landau** (John Koenig), **Barbara Bain** (Helena Russell), **Barry Morse** (Victor Bergman), **Catherine Schell** (Maya), **Nick Tate** (Alan Carter), **Tony Anholt** (Tony Verdeschi), **Prentis Hancock** (Paul Morrow), **Suzanne Roquette** (Tanya Alexander), **Michael Gallagher** (Etrec), **Ina Skriver** (A), **Sarah Douglas** (B), **David Sebastian Bach** (Guardian's Brother), **Nicholas Young** (Peter Rockwell)

Credits:

Editor:	Tim Mallett
Director of Photography	Glenn Pearce
Sound Recordist	Andrew Frampton
Production Assistant	Martin Gainsford
Make-up	David McLaughlin
Construction Managers	Kit Bevan, David McLaughlin
Production Team	Maxine Cook, Nick Williams
Producer	Tim Mallett
Post Production	Kindred Productions

Clips courtesy of Carlton International Media
Original series production design by Keith Wilson
Original series costume design by Keith Wilson and Emma Porteous
Space: 1999 created by Gerry and Sylvia Anderson

Plot: A message emerges from static featuring Sandra Benes, who explains that this is the last transmission from Moonbase Alpha to Earth, being sent 20 years after contact was lost. Alpha's life support systems are failing, and a much-disputed decision has been taken to initiate Operation Exodus and move to a nearby habitable planet that the Alphans have named Terra Alpha. Their time in range of the planet is only six days, which Sandra says is insufficient for a thorough analysis. Sandra is the last to remain on the base, and her message will be encoded by Alpha's Computer, using a new technology created by Maya, which will allow the message to navigate both time and space to reach Earth. When Sandra completes her recording, it is encoded and transmitted, and a visual of the coded message shows it to be the Meta Signal.

Quotes:

- **Sandra**: 'However, one thing is certain … Moonbase Alpha is no more.'
- **Sandra**: 'Though deserted and silent now, Alpha was our refuge. We can never forget our life here … The memory of what we shared here will forever remain part of the very fabric of this place, our home, Alpha.'
- **Sandra**: 'We want you all to know that we, the people of Moonbase Alpha, did exist. Our presence – the knowledge of Earth and her people, their strengths and weaknesses, pride and arrogance, genius and insignificance – has an imprint on this vast universe that we share with so many races and beings.'
- **Sandra**: 'And to Alpha, wherever you go on your onward journey, our hearts go with you, and hope of reunion in the future will never fade …'
- **Sandra**: 'And finally, to you the people of planet Earth, we say goodbye and ask but one thing: remember us. Remember us.'

Filming Dates: Saturday 28 August – Sunday 29 August 1999

Commentary:

Zienia Merton: 'I thought "Message from Moonbase Alpha" was brilliant. It was a kind of closure. I loved it, I really loved doing it, and I was amazed at how it took off. We were all amazed – I think we felt it would be shown once and then be forgotten, to be honest. I treasure that.

'On 17 August, Tim came round and we looked at the script. I nearly died, because that was a lot of pages for Sandra. She's also 25 years older and a lot of brain cells have died. So we just ironed things out. Tim did say he thought my accent was a bit heavier than it used to be, and I said, "Yeah, well, you've never heard me speak this long before." The costume was actually my second year costume and I managed to get into that. And that's it – we went for it. It was in August. The sets were wonderful. Obviously, I knew Tim and Glenn, and I knew Nick, and Johnny. But I met for the first time Kit Bevan and David McLaughlin, who did the set. And David, being a make-up artist in his own right, helped me out. We decided I couldn't go back to the old make-up, because I'd look like some kind of warp freak. It had to be a bit less, because when you get older less is better. And we went for it. It was at Andrew's house, outside London, and we had to worry about dogs barking and planes taking off and kids splashing in pools, but we managed.

'I'm not a very intellectual actress. When I see the words I have to make them work. I have to think of the pacing, but I think that comes from within oneself. I had the luxury that the words were already there. I had the luxury that I was working with people I trusted, so I was not under pressure. The only pressure I was under was whether or not my brain could cope. I see it there and I give it, hopefully, 120% – that's all I can do.

'I'm very grateful for everyone's reaction. It deserved it, in the sense that it was done from the heart, and it was done for the most simple of reasons. There was no huge gain. It was Tim's idea. It was a gift: a present to the fans at the Breakaway convention. The fact that it took off and got a life of its own is due to Johnny and Tim. I'm so pleased that everybody enjoyed it, because that's what this business is about – for people to believe and to enjoy. If they can forget all the nastiness that's going on in the rest of their lives, I think we've done our job.'

Tim Mallett: 'It was a hell of a lot of responsibility. Fortunately, I'd got to know Zienia and Johnny a little bit through doing documentaries. They are very charming people, easy to get on with, and they immediately put me at my ease. But when I actually thought of doing a little "Message from Moonbase Alpha" for the Breakaway Convention, it was intended to be a closure for *Space: 1999*. Since then it's turned into something that perhaps has opened up a few possibilities. I approached it tentatively. Johnny's obviously a very busy writer. Zienia's a busy actress. They've got their reputations to think of: why should they trust me to produce a Space: 1999 film? The other thing was, the production values of Space: 1999 were extremely high. They had millions of pounds to play with, and [following on from] that was quite a lot of responsibility. One thing I would like to say is that, as Zienia [has pointed out], she had a lot of lines to say in comparison to what she had to say in the series, and with very few cutaways. Previously to that, she was doing a very complex and technical commercial film, so she couldn't even look at the script until probably about two or three days beforehand. So, her efforts, talent and ability were even more [admirable]. She was absolutely stunning.

'And Johnny's script was absolutely fantastic to work with. You don't get these opportunities very often, and I had a great time doing it. It was all very quick: we shot it in about six hours, which is an incredibly short time. It is extremely flattering that people have said we've created the forty-ninth episode of *Space: 1999*. I was stunned at the reaction to it, and I was very emotional at the time. But we kind of had a little bit of a preview when we were making the film. Zienia's first take, the very emotional part at the end, left the whole crew in tears. So we sort of thought, "I think she's got it right." That was a good indication … It turned out fantastically.'

Johnny Byrne: 'The idea came from Tim to do something. I was asked if I would be prepared to write it and I said, "Of course." I think I did say to Tim, because time was of the essence, that he should just pass along all the ideas that were circulating around in his mind. And I took those and fashioned them into a short little film.'This strange show, *Space: 1999* … You only have to dip your fingers into this quirky, magical pool before all sorts of other chemical things start happening. There was no intention at the very beginning, or even after I'd started writing it, to make it into a kind of philosophical loop – a storytelling loop – with anything that had gone before. I did want to present it as an idea that while maybe one or two doors had closed, a thousand were flying open in terms of where this series could go. Whether we stepped back a bit and then shot forward, or whether we took the purely linear step of moving on from the end of season two. Those were little challenges that were ever-present in my mind as I was writing it.

'The joy for me, personally, came at the very end of the process – it suddenly occurred to me what was happening in this little piece. And what was happening, in keeping with so many elements of the series – certainly the episodes or the attributes of it that had obviously excited me – was that it was closing that loop, in terms of the Meta Signal. A lot of questions had been raised about it in people's minds. What was Meta? Was it a planet? Was it a signal? It was featured in episode one and I don't think it was mentioned thereafter, largely because there wasn't a second script [at the time], and I was brought in to write a second script. So, in the rush of events, it was left by the side. It occurred to me that the Meta Signal was in fact a signal that Sandra was transmitting at that stage, and that the signal that we encountered in episode one was, in fact, the Alphans in the future trying to make contact with themselves in the past. It seemed to me a fairly mind-blowing *Space: 1999* theme.

'I loved the whole theme. It was one of those things that made it worthwhile for me. It opened up a few dodgy areas I didn't want to pursue in the context of a seven-minute film – in the event it went into nine minutes – big budget stuff. But, who were these Alphans who were receiving this message? We saw them in episode one. Were they the Alphans that subsequently were left behind in "Another Time, Another Place"? And was the place that we were sending this message from actually Terra Alpha, or Terra Nova, or wherever? This is an area of that little film that is worthy of development into another little film, and if a series was going – into another very big film. But those are for the future ... In terms of this short, seven-minute film, it was a joy for me to do. And how beautifully it was captured – every nuance – by Zienia. I was thrilled when I saw it and saw how wonderfully [it was done]. It was as if the curtain of time had been brushed aside and there we were, locked in this little state of being on Moonbase Alpha ... after 25 years.

'Tim liked it, fortunately – I don't know what he was expecting, but I think he liked it. I have to say that without Tim, this would not have been done. And I had no idea what I was letting myself in for, in terms of pure enjoyment, when I said, yes, I would do it ... Yes, I wanted to close it. But more so, I wanted to open it. I firmly believe that no door closes without several opening. It's that kind of world we live in. I wanted to find out where those doors were, as far as Space: 1999 was concerned. For me it was a question of putting the whole thing into a pot, and letting the very best rise to the surface. Demolishing any kind of distinction – creatively, aesthetically or however – between season one and season two, which is a sterile argument.

'The whole question of any kind of revival has to be one that incorporates every aspect of Space: 1999. So for that reason I was determined to include references to season two, although obviously I'd been more associated with season one. But I was looking in a micro way at the whole thing. By saying, "Goodbye," as Tim wanted, I was also saying, "Hello – here's something Space: 1999." And suddenly I wanted to write the next episode, which is a two-hour thing. Even without any retrospective fine-tuning of "Message from Moonbase Alpha", it was all there. The little conundrums we'd left sort of hanging, like the time dilation, the Moon coming back, the people and how they have they aged. Indeed, who were these people that Sandra represented – were they the Alphans that we took to be our Alphans, or some other Alphans?

'The presence of the Maya character in any revival would all depend on whether or not Catherine was available. If she was not available, then Maya would rest in repose in the most beautiful mausoleum on this planet called Terra Alpha. Her offspring would now be minus her metamorphic powers, but would still be alien. There would be either a male or female offspring – if Catherine was unavailable, or maybe even if she was available – and you would have a very interesting, complex character, not quite knowing who he or she was, where his or her place was, what his or her basic nature was, and still trying to come to terms with this insider/outsider syndrome. The same would apply to other characters. Someone has even suggested that we might find Barry Morse somewhere in the catacombs of the Moon, in suspended animation, or reciting Dickens ...

'One thing that should happen in any revival is to bring back that whole universal feel of how many Alphas there are. Somehow, we have to bring that line and make it converge in a way that makes sense of their experiences out in space. For me, it's very simple. The Moon comes back; they have to leave Terra Alpha; they go to the Moon. The Moon is uninhabitable for various reasons, and they have to make it habitable. Whether it's occupied or not is another matter – occupied by something that is not Alphan – but they have to survive the problems of how they reconstruct Moonbase Alpha after 25 years. What is it that needs doing? What are the dangers that are out there, implicit in the fact that nobody has been on the Moon for 25 years? What has gone seriously wrong?

'That whole journey thereafter is one fraught with not just threats from the external universe, but also from the internal universe. And also from the complicated make-up of the people themselves, many of whom will have lived a completely different existence. And so all of this is a very rich dramatic mix, and it's fantastic grist to the mill. I don't see that as a problem. I see it as something so useable and makeable and doable.'

Review: Regarded by many fans as the forty-ninth episode of *Space: 1999*, and series canon, 'Message from Moonbase Alpha' brings the programme full-circle from the premiere of 'Breakaway'. In that first episode, one of the main plots involved the Meta Signal being received by Earth and Moonbase Alpha, seemingly transmitted from the approaching planet Meta. As is revealed here, the Meta Signal is actually a message from Moonbase Alpha, transmitted back in time and space, and being received at Earth in 1999, just before the Moon breaks out of orbit. This is a superb piece of symmetry from writer Johnny Byrne, bringing the series both to an end and a new beginning.

Byrne's script is perfectly matched by the screen presence of Zienia Merton. Always a great favourite of fans, Merton was the perfect choice to star in this film. Her performance depicts a slightly older Sandra with subtle edges to her, adding layers beyond those obvious in the dialogue. Merton poignantly conveys the emotions not only of Sandra Benes, but also of all the Alphans.

With this script, Byrne succeeds in summing up and drawing to a close the journey of Moonbase Alpha. He maintains the integrity of the series, while also adding to its mythology. He gives the Alphans, finally, that new world they were searching for. However, it is a world that will hold many challenges, and the stage is set for future stories …

Byrne championed 'Message from Moonbase Alpha' as a launching off point for a new series. He envisaged that this would pick up 25 years after the colonisation of Terra Alpha, when the gravitational slingshot effect would return the Moon to the same point in space. Life is difficult on the planet and the Terra Alphans are divided over whether to stay there or return to the Moonbase. Koenig remains to lead those who stay behind, because Helena has passed away and he won't leave her grave. Many others however – both old characters and a new generation – do decide to return to the Moonbase, embarking once again on a journey through the galaxy on Earth's runaway Moon, encountering whatever lies ahead. Byrne speculates in the commentary below that those who returned to the Moonbase would face threats both external and internal as they worked to repair and update the base, and would discover that it was now also inhabited by something 'not Alphan.'The story possibilities inherent in this proposed revival of *Space: 1999* appear even greater than in the original. Unfortunately, *Space: 1999* lost its greatest advocate when Byrne passed away in 2008, and it is doubtful that these concepts will ever result in the new television film and subsequent series he envisioned.

Regardless of whether *Space: 1999* returns in a new form or not, 'Message from Moonbase Alpha' will remain a lasting achievement due to the care and talent with which it was produced. This short film was a labour of love on the part of all involved, and Tim Mallett is to be commended for having instigated, produced and directed it. The contributions of Kit Bevan and David McLaughlin in constructing the remarkably accurate reproduction of a Moonbase Alpha set must also be specifically noted and highly praised.

'Message from Moonbase Alpha' is most powerful because it is a character piece, driven by a challenging script, a gripping performance, and thoughts, ideas and human emotions. While it runs for only seven minutes, it packs a massive emotional impact, carries unlimited promise for the future, and is a fitting finale for *Space: 1999*.

Rating: 9/10

THE RETURN OF VICTOR BERGMAN

Screenplay by Robert E Wood and Barry Morse
Directed by Robert E Wood

Scheduled Premiere Screening: Austin, Texas – Friday 16 July 2010 (at the Journey to Where Con).

Cast: **Barry Morse** (Professor Victor Bergman)

Additional Cast (in flashbacks): **Martin Landau** (John Koenig), **Barbara Bain** (Helena Russell), **Prentis Hancock** (Paul Morrow), **Zienia Merton** (Sandra Benes), **Nick Tate** (Alan Carter), **Anton Phillips** (Bob Mathias)

Credits:

Producer	Anthony Wynn
Editor	Eric Bernard
Camera Operator	James Ommert
Story Consultant	Anthony Wynn
Sound Recordist	James Ommert
Digital Transfer	Aaron Carlson
Lighting	Anthony Wynn
Commlock prop	Mark Shaw
Video Storage	Aaron Carlson

Produced by Planet Productions Ltd for Fan Distribution
Filmed at Vulkon, Cleveland, Ohio, USA
Space: 1999 created by Gerry and Sylvia Anderson

Plot: A Moonbase Alpha Status Report, recorded by Professor Victor Bergman in the year 2030.

Details: This fan-produced short film features actor Barry Morse reprising his role of Victor Bergman in order to provide fans with a resolution explaining the disappearance of the Professor following Year One. The footage was filmed in Cleveland, Ohio in 2002, following a performance of Morse's one-man stage play *Merely Players*.

Filming Date: Saturday 27 April 2002.

JUDGEMENT

If longevity is valued as a sign of success, then *Space: 1999* remains triumphant indeed. Now, decades after the show's original run ended in 1977, fans continue to gather at conventions around the world to celebrate it. Many people continue to hold Space: 1999 in high regard as the most spectacular space science fiction series ever produced for television. Very few programmes can lay claim to the unyielding endurance of Space: 1999, or the stalwart passion of its fans.

In the opening of this book, both positive and negative critical responses to the series during its original run were presented. Well, the passing of decades hasn't changed things in this regard, and in this new millennium the show continues to elicit fresh reviews as passionately conflicted as those of the 1970s. Negative views include:

'Uniquely for a television show, *Space: 1999* always managed to be less than the sum of its title sequences. They were, without exception, pulse-troublingly fab… And each week we would dupe ourselves that yes, this time it would be the funky, sexy experience it promised to be and not the tedious old tommyrot it always was.'[27]

'Unfortunately, the science is often insane, and the stories range from intriguing to dumb.'[28]

'It's hard to develop much empathy with a crew who seem as distant as their surroundings … Everything depicted in this show is very flat. Perhaps that was a creative decision to reflect the bleakness of space. While there's a certain logic to that, from a dramatic standpoint, it doesn't work. It does look marvellous, though.'[29]

'While the first season offered talkative and methodically paced stories, the second season tried to capture the quickly-fading attention span of American viewers with more action and humour – not necessarily a good thing for a serious sci-fi show.'[30]

'From the stiff acting to rip-offs of *Star Trek* plotlines to the I-can-see-the-strings special effects, this is painful stuff … *Space: 1999* isn't so much science fiction as it is science mysticism, with weird things just randomly happening to the Moonbase … If you liked the tone of the last few seasons of *The X-Files*, in which nothing really made sense but everything seemed important, you may appreciate *Space: 1999's* mystical tendencies… If you're nostalgic for the days when you could hang an

---

[27] Setchfield, Nick. *SFX*, number 77. Spring 2001.
[28] Rovin, Jeff. *Science Fiction Chronicle*. May 2001.
[29] Soyka, David. *Sci-Fi Weekly*: 'Earth's moon goes out of orbit in a lavishly produced, slick adventure series that spins out of control itself.' 5 March 2001.
[30] Szadkowski, Joseph. *The Washington Times*: '*Space: 1999* crew faces nuclear threat in space.' 28 July 2007.

entire episode around a single space warp, go ahead and revisit *Space: 1999.'* [31]

While those critics continue to be harshly judgmental of the series, there are also many who come up with favourable reviews:

'*Space: 1999* approached the genre differently, placing its characters in a far less controlled, bleaker situation than ever before. The question for the Alphans, certainly when the series was at its best, was never "What do we find out now?" but rather "How do we survive long enough to find it out?" The first season plays this card particularly strongly, and enters some surprisingly dark territory as a result. The series would move away from this theme but at its best, *Space: 1999* remains a combination of sheer pulp energy and some genuinely surprising, very human stories.'[32]

'*Space: 1999* was less science fiction than a trippy journey through the Me Decade, with plots that focused inordinately on mind control, demonic possession, the quest for nirvana, would-be messiahs and other hallmarks of an era of expanding consciousness. The whole notion of the Moon cut loose reflected a Watergate-era mentality of unprecedented chaos ... Commander John Koenig and Dr Helena Russell were, in effect, parent figures, looking for a new Eden where their charges could be fruitful and multiply.'[33]

'*Space: 1999* is as good-looking and lush as any series of the 1970s ... At the very least, the show must be given its due for visual splendour and general ambition. Its contemporaneous fans included the peerless rocket scientist Wernher von Braun; a notable naysayer was SF writer Isaac Asimov, who unnecessarily picked the show apart on scientific grounds in a 1975 piece for the New York Times. Asimov was nitpicking. Braun, conversely, remarked that the show "characterises mankind's exploration of space." We tend to the latter view.'[34]

'The DVD release will electrify the legions of cultists in this country and abroad who have grabbed on to the show as if it were Star Trek ... "They wanted the TV successor to *2001: A Space Odyssey,*" said Scott Bosco, a writer and consultant on DVD projects ... "They wanted grand sets and costumes and special effects not even seen in films, an action series but cerebral and driven through theory and mysticism, raising questions of life and the creation of the universe ..." Today the show looks remarkably good, a testament to the expense of each episode ... [And]

---

[31] Dillon, Jeff. *Signonsandiego.com*: 'Whimper from the Past: *Space: 1999.'* 24 May 2004.

[32] Stuart, Alasdair. *Sci-Fi Now*: '*Space: 1999* – Classic Seventies heroism on a runaway moon.' Issue 10. 2007.

[33] Vinciguerra, Thomas. *The New York Times*: 'The Future: Bright. The Fashion: Blinding.' 12 August 2007.

[34] Hogan, David J. *FilmFax Plus*: 'New & Unusual DVDs Under Scrutiny.' October/December 2007.

for the first year, *Space: 1999* tackled big issues. Lead characters performed nobly.'[35]

'The first batch offers eight or nine of the greatest pieces of TV science fiction ever put on film. The superb effects are obvious, as is the starkly impressive design of Main Mission, but it's easy to overlook the arc-plot embracing the first season. It's understated and entirely dependent on seeing certain episodes in the correct order.'[36]

'*Space: 1999* was without doubt the most lavish television series made up to that point. Its tremendously high production values, including absolutely first-rate model work and special effects, stand up particularly well … The original concepts and storylines were a first in TV terms and its thinking person's approach to sci-fi is easily the nearest any television series has come to the science-fiction of the literary world.'[37]

While the critics will undoubtedly continue to be divided over its merits – as they always have been – the fact is that these 48 episodes from the 1970s (through all their highs and lows) continue to generate fervent discussion, rather than fading into history. So long as this discourse continues, the series will remain as vital and as stimulating as when it began, and so long as there is an audience enjoying it, *Space: 1999* can be judged a triumph and the odyssey of Moonbase Alpha will continue.

---

[35] Nichols, Peter M. *The New York Times*: 'The Noble Two-Season Mission of *Space: 1999*.' 4 February 2001.
[36] Brown, Anthony. *SFX*, Number 39, June 1998.
[37] Richardson, Michael. *Action TV*: 'Back To The Future.' Spring, 2002.

HINDSIGHT: 1999

Alpha: 2012 was a *Space: 1999* convention held in Burbank, California in September of that year, with guests including series stars Martin Landau, Barbara Bain, Nick Tate, Prentis Hancock, and Anton Phillips, as well as script editor and writer Christopher Penfold. This event included discussion sessions with the guests, which provided a wonderful sense of hindsight and numerous entertaining anecdotes. All of the quotes in this section are specifically drawn from that event.

Barbara Bain's recollections included memories of her daughters, prior to moving to England: 'There were a couple questions the kids asked. My older daughter wanted to know if she had to wear a uniform at school, and if she was, she wasn't going. I said, "No, you don't have to wear a uniform at school," and she said, "Okay, then I'm going." That ruled that out. My younger daughter I went in and said (which is a feeble thing a parent does – you learn), "Would you like to go to England?" And she said, "Do I have a choice?" We made it an adventure; it was an adventure for them. And they learned to keep touch with their friends [in the US] by writing letters. So they actually rediscovered the art of letter writing … Everything about it [moving to England] was fine. You know, if you're an actor, what does it matter changing where you live? You're already half a gypsy; or even a whole gypsy, I don't know. But the point is you're used to going where the work is. That's what you do … 'There were some questions when we went to England, because we were going to be so 'seen'. [Our daughters] came to us and said, "We want a meeting… Will we not go to school at first," so they could make friends, and then their friends wouldn't say, "Oh, your parents are on television," or whatever they would say. They wanted to find their way. They also wanted to not be driven in that Rolls; they thought that was really disgusting. So I said, "Here's your choice, you can walk (it's about 18 blocks, but you can walk – you're young; you're strong), or you can take the bus. You have to think of it as a piece of transportation: you get in, you get out, and you get to the place you're going. And if that doesn't do it for you, check the Daimler's that are out in front of the school." So the Rolls was like *nothing* at that school. But we came to a compromise: they got driven almost to the school. They did not want to get out of a Rolls Royce and go to school, and I didn't blame them.'

Martin Landau also recalled: 'It was very good for my family. My kids got out of a school in Beverly Hills; they went to school with a lot of people from all over the world; from oil and embassy to even CIA kids, which I didn't know about at the time. The experience was a joyful one, and Barbara and I were still together …'

As the actors were coming on board to star in the series, the writers were working behind-the-scenes, as Christopher Penfold remembered: 'It's probably not widely appreciated how much the show was shaped by the first script, which was initially written by George Bellack, and the insistence upon a powerful role for a woman at the head of the show was hugely emphasized by George, as indeed was the whole ethnic diversity of the cast. That is one of the great things I remember George Bellack for… In the script department we had that amazingly free hand. The trio of George Bellack (initially), and Johnny and I, were able to set the tone of the series, which did have literary and philosophical aspirations, which [the fans] seem to appreciate, which is very nice.

'We didn't sit down and write together. We had story meetings between ourselves. After George's departure, mainly it was between Johnny and me. We would talk the story through and then disappear into our separate rooms and write... I've spent my life either as a writer or as a script editor, and I've tried always to separate them out, and of course it wasn't very easy to do that on *Space: 1999* series one, but the way in which we tried to do it was that Johnny would edit me and I would edit Johnny.'

Penfold also recalled, 'What was so exciting about *Space: 1999* from the beginning – as you know, it grew out of *UFO*, and when the decision was taken to move it away from earth and into space, and it became *Space: 1999* I think we all – Brian Johnson, Keith Wilson, myself – all the people on the original creative team, were very excited about that prospect. What was so great about Gerry and Sylvia was that they also had a real sense of how that was going to present them with a completely original opportunity. And so we went to work on the scripts with a sense that we were doing a kind of science fiction for television that perhaps hadn't been done before. I think of it as the thinking man's science fiction.'

Prentis Hancock said of his first day filming: 'I think the day we walked on to the set and the guy sitting next to me said, "We could be here in five years," and I said, "We could be doing this in wheelchairs," I meant that we could be doing it for a long time. It was sad that we didn't. It could have gone on for a long time.'

The impression the sets made on the actors remain to this day, as Martin Landau recalled: 'I think in the first year we did some more interesting work, and I felt the set – even though it was vast and big and took more time to shoot because it was harder to light, and then we condensed it – but I did think that first set, with the opening [from the Commander's Office to Main Mission] and the desk ... there was something very theatrical about the set itself. It didn't look like anything else. The next Main Mission, as such [Command Centre], became much more conventional, I felt. Although we did do some interesting shows; [One Moment of Humanity] with Billie Whitelaw that Charlie directed [for example].'

Nick Tate also spoke on the subject of the sets: 'In Main Mission it felt big, the room was all there, the ceiling was in, and all the furniture was around you so you had a sense of being in the place. But in the Eagles we were at a console and the whole thing was open, with the whole studio floor out there with sixty film crew walking around eating their sandwiches from the commissary, and the camera here, and guys waving around and stuff... and you're supposed to believe you're in space with nothing out there whatsoever ... except 60 crew ... And you know, they weren't always being very professional. I saw one guy – I'm in the middle of a serious scene and another guy comes up, and he grabs hold of this guys pants and pulled them down. He pantsed a guy. And I'm saying, "Commander, there's a ..." Charlie Crichton goes, "Cut, cut! What are you doing? Why did you stop there?" "Uh ... I uh, I just had a funny moment Charlie, that's it." You couldn't tell on the guy, they would have fired him. Then I had to go to the guy and say, "Don't pants somebody when I'm out in space!"'

Nick Tate also remembered occasional challenges with the space suit costumes: 'There was an episode in which Martin and Barbara and I were all in the space suits together during the time that it was the hottest summer in history in England, in 1976, and the air conditioning broke down on Stage L that we were working on. And everybody was walking around wearing shorts and t-shirts, but Martin, Barbara and I had to wear these bloody suits, which were like being in Swiss sleeping bags; in fact I think they made them out of Swiss sleeping bags. They were full suits, like jump suits.

You had to put the whole things on, and yet we were only being shot half the time from [chest] up. So what we did was we took [the pants] off and just had the tops on. We were sitting there in our bare legs, and I had little more than underpants on, and there we were sitting in the Eagle.'

Of his character, Anton Phillips said: 'I thought about him [Bob Mathias] as being a very efficient guy, and someone who was on top of his game, who could be relied on. He wasn't thrown by anything, in spite of the weird things that were thrown at him … I've played other doctors in various television things where you have to deal with a broken arm or something, which is quite different. Here you're looking at dials and reading things off screens and so on, which we hadn't quite got to that stage yet. 1999 must have seemed far enough away for all this fantastic stuff to be happening. But here we are in 2012 and we haven't even got a man on the moon, so perhaps it should have been set 100 years ahead, and even then I'm not sure we'd have that kind of space station and facilities to be self-sustaining … So we're a long way away from a *Space: 1999*. I read a lot of science fiction and some of them are set in the far distant future where all sorts of strange things are happening… We're only just catching up with George Orwell's *1984*, and circling Britain certain aspects of it are becoming more and more real in as much as the population is under more and more observation, which certainly suggests what Orwell said in *1984* where everyone is watched all the time. If you walk through the streets of London they estimate you are photographed something like 300 times during your walk from one side of London to the other. So we are coming on well with that police state aspect of Orwell's book.'

Of the scripts, Prentis Hancock said: 'We had a script read every fortnight. Martin and Barbara, I suspect, already had looked at the script with the writers. We [the supporting cast] were included, but not included. It was difficult because we had an enormous amount of people working on the show: three stars, then you had me – I led the second line billing, if you like. Which in America would have been billed, but of course we didn't do things in the American style completely in those days. They didn't take billing very seriously. But in the rear-end crawl, I'm always top of the list. Those people on the rear-end crawl were invited to the script reading, but in fact the comment from us was quite a way down the line. It would be Barbara first and then Martin … We did [have input], but not hugely. Not enough to disturb the pond.'

Contractual issues were a problem that Nick Tate recalled: 'We [the supporting cast] did have a network contract. Martin and Barbara had some other deal with America, but we were signed to the British Equity contract, which was a network contract only. And it was pretty tough for us because we therefore weren't involved in the syndication. It made it even tougher when Abe Mandell made it very clear and boasted that they had the largest syndication deal ever in the history of television for *Space: 1999*. And the British actors didn't have that contract.'

Martin Landau recalled some of the technical aspects of filming *Space: 1999*: 'We were the only show in Britain at the time shooting film, at that moment in time. Everything else was on tape. Everything. And this gave a lot of work to not only actors, but technicians, camera people… this is why they actually let Barbara and me do the show, because the British do protect their actors. Even Broadway shows that go there from the States can only play a limited time there before the British company takes over. We don't do that here. In fact, there are probably more British and Australian actors on television [in the US] than there are American. But think of that – we were the only show in our first season shooting film on a weekly television show. Everything else was on tape. And 35 mm; it wasn't 16.'

Nick Tate agreed: 'Going on to that show was like being in the Moon program. It was the most high-tech thing I'd ever seen in my life. We were using full 35 mm Panasonic feature film cameras with feature film crews. Every episode was like shooting a mini feature film.'

Christopher Penfold explained how the majority of his episodes came to be directed by Charlie Crichton: 'There's a certain amount of maneuvering that you can do as the story consultant, and I think most of the episodes that I wrote were actually directed by Charlie Crichton. I had a wonderful relationship with Charlie, and I suppose I ought to confess that when I had an episode coming I would slot it into the schedule when I knew Charlie would be on the job.'

Barbara Bain recalled a day when: 'We had a flat tire in Mayfair, in that Rolls, so Ray the driver said, "It's a bit awkward, madam." What's a bit awkward? So we got out of the car. Martin was always complaining about the car, "Why am I driving around in this fancy car, I don't like it, etc …" So we got out and we're walking around Mayfair while Ray is fixing the car, and I said to Martin, "Don't tell me this isn't the best flat tire you ever had." He never complained again …

'There was another thing I thought was pretty funny … We had a fire next door at Burnham Beeches. It was on fire. Our lot was right next to it, and the wall was right next to where it was burning. We were coming back from lunch, and the cars were all parked there. So, someone told me when I was in about fourth grade that you can't have cars and fire; it's going to blow up, right? So we walked in, and we ran into Reggie and I said, "Has anybody called the fire department?" He said, "Oh, someone will come along." I said, "You know something, I want an American hysteric here right now." I didn't want an Englishman telling me, "Oh, it will be alright," with the flames burning about ten feet high! "Someone will come along," he said. I said, "An American hysteric," that's what I asked him for. I didn't get one, but they did come along and put the fire out.'

Of their producers, Christopher Penfold recalled: 'Of course the person who has most reason to be proud of what we achieved in *Space: 1999* is not here, and that's Gerry Anderson himself. What was really quite unusual in my experience in television – and I've had a lot of it – was the way in which Gerry Anderson was so open as an Executive Producer (and Sylvia, too) to the kinds of ideas and storylines which we came up with. And Gerry and Sylvia came up with some of them themselves, which made the series so distinctive, and it was a privilege to work under those circumstances, and it's not one that you often get in this business.'

Barbara Bain also reflected on the Andersons: 'Sylvia had a marvelously ebullient personality, and she had that kind of 'Up' thing. You can't argue about that with anybody, actually. She did have that. She had a kind of fun and light feeling. Gerry was very serious. Very serious. At least in my estimation. That's what I saw.'

Prentis Hancock recalled an unproduced concept for an episode: 'There was an interesting idea that Gerry ran past Nick and I, and we thought we were going to do at one time. There had been a camera attachment to a helicopter, which allowed it to be a steady-cam for a 9-minute [film] magazine. And he wanted to have a planet surface which was all water. And there's one area – I think above Swansea – where you can find spots on the horizon where there are no ships in the range of the camera shooting all the way around. So Nick and I would be in a rubber dinghy in the middle of this area, and the helicopter would come in and we could play a 9-minute scene using the whole magazine of the camera. And this would save them building a planet surface of water on L stage, which would be rather difficult. You'd have to build a bloody big tank to put it in. It never came to fruition, but he was considering it. It would have used the latest technology, which was available for aerial shots, and our incredible acting abilities, against the water.'

The second season of *Space: 1999* continued – as always – to be a point of contention, as when Martin Landau said: 'I was never happy about Freddy's changing that idea [getting rid of Barry Morse] … Though Catherine was a wonderful girl, but you know – a metamorph and all that – some of that was not my favorite stuff. I think the second year was not as good as the first year, for a lot of reasons: Prentis not being there, Nick being there less … All of that. I felt the family was breaking up, for no decent reason, and I think it hurt the show. I always felt if we had kept that first year going, in the way it was going, we would have had a third year. It was being tampered with for the wrong reasons. Too many cooks, and not enough palatable food.'

Nick Tate agreed: 'I sensed this was going to be huge. I just thought the thing was going to be bigger than *Star Trek*. And as you know, it hasn't been. But personal triumphs within it, yes, it was wonderful. And there are many people around the world who still love the show … It was science faction; it wasn't science fiction. That whole premise. That's what went wrong with the second year when they tried to make it into all the fanciful crap. Freddy Freiberger was the worst thing that ever happened to the series, quite frankly. But there wouldn't have been a second series without him. Well, there might have been, and it would have been a much better second series. But he was commissioned to do the hatchet job that he did. He axed all the original players, and he was wrong: totally wrong. I think the series would have gone on and been an equal to *Star Trek* if we'd stuck with the original premise that it was science faction. That's what people loved about it, and I think it's what drew most people to it originally … The first season was just so wonderful and exciting, and we all felt a huge responsibility in a sense that we were bringing this new form of science fiction … This was the first big series that – they said – was going to rival the popularity of *Star Trek*, and that was very exciting for all of us. And we knew that we were doing it more in terms of fact than fiction; scientific principles that we understood that could happen, and that there wouldn't be any pantomime characters appearing, which is what went wrong with the second series.'

When asked about fan mail, Anton Phillips said: 'I only get fan mail from *Space: 1999*, and it always comes as a bit of a surprise when it does come; a pleasant surprise, by the way. It's funny because there are a whole load of people – friends of mine – who don't know that I was in *Space: 1999*. I remember the gym that I go to – there was one guy there who was a real fan of *Space: 1999*. He worked in the building; he wasn't working out. And he was retiring and he had one of the *Space: 1999* books and he brought it in for me to sign, and I was signing it and someone else came by and said, 'What are you doing?' I said, 'I'm just autographing his book for him.' He said, 'Why?' I said, 'Well, because I was in the series.' He said, 'What, you were in *Space: 1999*?' I said, 'Yes.' He said, 'I never knew that!' And this is someone who had been a friend of mine for six or seven years, and knew the series. But that was when I had the [big] hair and the moustache, and the … slim [waist]. The surprise is when people do recognize me, which occasionally happens.'

Martin Landau also talked about the enduring legacy of the show's viewership: 'Buzz Aldrin – the second man on the Moon – is a friend of mine, and he mentions the fact that a lot of people he knows, kids and so on, were addicted to *Space: 1999*. And he watched it. John Glenn watched it. I learned this years later. It's kind of flattering, really. These are the real guys. And Neil Armstrong watched it. We had an interesting audience out there … It was before *Star Wars*, and after *Star Trek*, and both of those things were taken pretty well. We wanted to go on network; we never did. We were syndicated. In fact, Norman Lear picked up our thread and put *Mary Hartman, Mary Hartman* into syndication when the networks turned that down, and we inspired him to do what we did; what Lew Grade did. Which was to not allow the rejection by the networks to stop our show from going on the air, which is exactly what happened. So we started our own network, in a sense, which was groundbreaking.'

In summing up his recollections of *Space: 1999*, Christopher Penfold said: 'What I really have liked about looking back [at *Space: 1999*] is to see how brave and original many of the ideas were.'

Perhaps the final summary should go to Martin Landau, *Space: 1999*'s Commander, who said: 'In doing a science fiction show – or anything that demands effects and post production – you often work with lots of things that aren't there. That's what's good about these actors and their imaginations. It's like a child playing Cowboys & Indians or Cops & Robbers, when their mother calls that child and says, "It's time to …" that interruption is enormous. A lot of these actors believed in a crazy, wonderful way that we were out in space. When you walked onto that set and put that suit on you really felt you were hurtling through space, in an odd and strange and wonderful way … I'm asked to sign a lot of things from *Space: 1999*, and I'm always amazed at how zealous the *Space: 1999* fans are. They seem to have more energy than fans of other things I've done. I love this show, and we had a good time doing it.'

A RETURN TO MOONBASE ALPHA?

News reports broke in late May 2009 that legendary Hollywood producer Robert Evans (*Chinatown*, *Marathon Man*) was revamping *Space: 1999*'s immediate predecessor, *UFO*, as a new major motion picture. Evans was quoted as saying, 'We know the importance of the *UFO* series brand to ITV Global, and we will work closely with them to build this into a franchise.'[38] Unfortunately, despite the passing of five years since that announcement, there has been no further news about the *UFO* movie and it is widely considered to be dead in the water.

A similar announcement in February 2012 saw ITV Studios America and HDFilms announce *Space: 2099*, intended as a reboot of *Space: 1999*. Although few details were divulged publicly it quickly became clear this project would be a radical departure from the original series premise, as when Executive Producer Jace Hall said: 'Will the Moon play the same role that it did in *Space: 1999*, the answer is that it will not. It will be present, and it has a purpose, but it will not play the exact same role that it did in *Space: 1999*.' A large proportion of fans were turned off by this and other tidbits of information, resulting in Hall meeting a significantly negative reception when he made a public appearance at the Alpha: 2012 convention. On 23 January 2014 a new statement was released by Jace Hall updating fans with news that considerable background and script development had taken place, along with visual effects tests, and that ITV had 'initiated discussions with various networks / distributors / destinations in regard to what will be the right home for this tremendous series.' Included in Hall's statement were the comments: 'To be clear, *Space: 2099* is not *Space: 1999*. It is not a continuation of *Space: 1999* in any way … *Space: 2099* is much more serialized in story than *Space: 1999*. Character progression and story telling can now have meaningful long arcs and significant impact.' Hall also indicated that fan input has had an impact on the development of the series: 'We have gained some insight by reading and listening to the *Space: 1999* community in terms of some thoughts, concerns, fears, and assumptions that can and will be made as the *Space: 2099* story is digested. Knowing some of this has helped us craft an even more compelling story and universe, putting in twists and turns that specifically will tap into some of these fan assumptions and then suddenly shatter them with a completely unexpected turn of events. It's exciting stuff.' Fan response to Hall's new statement was once again largely negative, with concerns remaining focused on the perception that *Space: 2099* will have only tangential connections to its predecessor. It remains to be seen if this perception is accurate, or if Jace Hall and ITV have listened to the concerns of *Space: 1999* fans.

But another hope remains for a return to Moonbase Alpha. The first project known as *Space: 2099* was begun by Eric Bernard as a remastering of the original *Space: 1999* series, incorporating new and augmented special effects and select edits with an eye towards improved pacing. This project evolved to a second phase: the development of a sequel series known as *Moonbase Alpha: Legacy*, picking up the story of the Alphans approximately 40 years later. While extensive details have not been made public (as the project is not yet authorised by ITV), a huge amount of work has been completed,

---

[38] Falconer, Robert. *CinemaSpy.com*: 'Gerry Anderson's *UFO* Headed for Big Screen.' 25 May 2009.

including a feature-length pilot script, first season story outlines, a detailed series bible, and pre-production design artwork. Test special effects footage of Eagles and Moonbase Alpha, created by Wes Sargent (the *Stargate* franchise), have met with enthusiastic response from fans. In addition, fans are pleased to know that the *Moonbase Alpha: Legacy* team includes original series story editor Christopher Penfold, and model maker Martin Bower, who has designed and built his first ship in the *Space: 1999* universe since the original series ended; a one-off craft called the Vulture. Along with Christopher Penfold, the writing team includes Steve Warnek (*Star Trek: Deep Space Nine*), Gregory L Norris and Laura A Van Vleet (*Star Trek: Voyager*), as well as the author of this book, who guarantees fans that everything being done for *Moonbase Alpha: Legacy* is respectful and inclusive of the original series, while also bringing it forward in a very modern and exciting way.

Artist and designer Eric Chu (*Battlestar Galactica*) made the following tantalising comment: 'Cearly the various titles in the Gerry Anderson catalogue are prime candidates for making a comeback as well as being a designer's wet dream. Hopefully, you'll see a little more of that.'[39]

Only time will tell if audiences and fans may yet make a return trip to Moonbase Alpha …

---

[39] Falconer, Robert. (Illustrations by Eric Chu). *CinemaSpy.com*: 'Drawing on Imagination: *UFO – The Movie* Concept Art.' 10 June 2009.

AFTERWORD
Barry Morse

Not many television shows have accumulated and kept such a loyal body of supporters, for so long, as our old *Space: 1999* has. When I mention that I am about to attend another gathering of *Space: 1999* fans in the United States or England or France, or wherever, sceptical people in our trade will often say to me, 'That old *Space: 1999*? It wasn't much good, was it? What is it that keeps all these people enthused?'

The fans are drawn together by a supposition of the human race confronting an impossible situation – and that, in a curious way, is what kept inspiring us while we were doing it. The philosophical impact of *Space: 1999* has resulted in such a remarkable union of human beings. I'm always greatly touched and moved at the conventions I'm able to get to, to realise that this has been brought about by the philosophical commercial, as you might call it, engendered by such people as Johnny Byrne and Chris Penfold. They, first and foremost and pre-eminently, are the ones who delivered the philosophy of *Space: 1999*. And George Bellak, of course, in his original treatment of 'Breakaway', tried to assemble a kind of humanist philosophy, which should permeate the whole of the series, and to a very large extent did.

I like to think – and I believe – that one of the ingredients that welds us all together and compels those dear young people to gather together at conventions around the world to this day is the awareness of how human beings can be drawn together and can – forgetting all their personal differences or temporary problems – work positively, hopefully and constructively towards a common end for good. And, please God, I hope it's catching, because our planet needs it.

This species of ours is not notable for great successes in many areas. The last time I looked, there were 32 wars going on around this planet; almost all of them in the name of so-called religions. That's why when I'm asked about my religious faith I always say, 'I'm a born-again agnostic.' Your friend and mine, George Bernard Shaw, used to say the greatest accomplishment of the human species was destruction. And when one looks at the planet as we presently deal with it, one is inclined to think that he was rightBut the fans of *Space: 1999* have obviously sensed and felt in our old series, that there is something Above and Beyond, and Better than those infuriating, meaningless squabbles. That means a great deal to me, and gives me hope for the future of our world.

Finally, I would like to put forth these thoughts from 'Black Sun': 'To everything that might have been … To everything that was,' and add, 'To everything that might yet be!'

Barry Morse

APPENDIX
SPACE: 1999 BOOKS AND MERCHANDISE

NOVELS AND NOVELISATIONS (1970s)

Numerous novels and novelisations have been published based on *Space: 1999*. The first of these even appeared on bookstore shelves prior to the premiere of the series in 1975.

The novels based on Year One are as follows:

1. *Breakaway* by E C Tubb. Published in 1975. (The UK Orbit edition was released in February 1975 – months ahead of *Space: 1999*'s worldwide television debut, while the US Pocket Books edition was released in September 1975 – the same month the series premiered.) Featuring adaptations of the episodes 'Breakaway', 'Matter of Life and Death', 'Ring Around the Moon' and 'Black Sun'.

2. *Moon Odyssey* by John Rankine. Published in 1975. (February 1975 by Orbit in the UK; September 1975 by Pocket Books in the US.) Adaptations of 'Alpha Child', 'The Last Sunset', 'Voyager's Return' and 'Another Time, Another Place'

3. *The Space Guardians* by Brian Ball. Published in 1975. (Its August 1975 release by Orbit in the UK made it the last book published prior to the premiere of the series on television. Pocket Books didn't release the novelisation in the US until November 1975.) Adaptations of 'Missing Link', 'Force of Life' and 'Guardian of Piri'.

4. *Collision Course* by E C Tubb. Published in October 1975 (Orbit, UK) and February 1976 (Pocket Books, US). Adaptations of 'Collision Course', 'The Full Circle', 'End of Eternity' and 'Death's Other Dominion'.

5. *Lunar Attack* by John Rankine. Published in November 1975 (Orbit, UK) and March 1976 (Pocket Books, US). Adaptations of 'War Games', 'The Troubled Spirit', 'The Last Enemy' and 'Space Brain'.

6. *Astral Quest* by John Rankine. Published in December 1975 (Orbit, UK) and April 1976 (Pocket Books, US). Adaptations of 'The Infernal Machine', 'Mission of the Darians', 'Dragon's Domain' and 'The Testament of Arkadia'

7. *Alien Seed* by E C Tubb. Published in June 1976 (Pocket Books, US) and August 1976 (Orbit, UK). This is an original novel. Back-cover plot synopsis: 'The fantastic intergalactic odyssey of the courageous men and women of Moonbase Alpha comes to a terrifying climax when the space wanderers confront the ultimate alien world. A silent planet of never-ending night, its smooth, mysterious surface is thick with

an ancient space dust. And buried under the cloak of darkness are innocent-looking pods. Are they the seeds of new hope for Alpha, or of an incredible nightmare no one has ever before dared to imagine?'

8. *Android Planet* by John Rankine. Published in August 1976 (Orbit, UK) and September 1976 (Pocket Books, US). This is an original novel. Back-cover plot synopsis: 'The mysterious planet Pelorus stares out of Main Mission Control's star-scanning screen like a monstrous orange unblinking eye. Is it daring Alpha to make the first move? Or is Pelorus – millions of light years from Mother Earth – their long-awaited new home? The Alphans make their fateful choice, and they are thrust into the heart of an android world where superhuman beings wield bizarre weapons. Their only chance of rescue is to trust a humanoid tribe whose friendly smiles hide a secret of devastating impact!'

9. *Rogue Planet* by E C Tubb. Published in August 1976 (Orbit, UK) and September 1976 (Pocket Books, US). This is an original novel. Back-cover plot synopsis (under the heading 'Turn back, for death awaits you!'): 'The chill warning echoes from the depths of the unknown, shattering the icy silence of space. But the bold Alphans must spin faster and faster toward an electrifying confrontation with their unknown enemy. Ageless against the stars stands Omphalos. A giant green "brain", this galactic monster spins a web of deadly horrors, trapping Alpha in a ghastly psychic war!'

10. *Phoenix of Megaron* by John Rankine. This is an original novel, and was published only in the USA by Pocket Books (November 1976). Back-cover plot synopsis: 'A lush, green planet beckons from Main Mission Control's star-scanning screen … and to the homeless Alphans, it looks like Earth. But descent reveals a wasteland of towering, silent cities, mute testimony to an atomic holocaust! Two pockets of civilisation survive: the drug-controlled inhabitants of Caster, and the freedom-loving people of Hyria. Soon the Alphans find themselves caught in the treacherous quicksands of civil war, their only allies a beautiful Hyrian with golden-brown eyes and an ancient man, the last custodian of the old wisdom.'

11. *Earthfall* by E C Tubb. This is an original novel, and was published only in the UK (Orbit, March 1977). The plot is a re-imagining of the entire series, encompassing the multi-generational journey of Moonbase Alpha from 'Breakaway' through to an eventual return to Earth. It was billed as 'The epic story of Moonbase Alpha.'

The Year Two novelisations are:

1. *Planets of Peril* by Michael Butterworth. Published in 1977. Adaptations of 'The Metamorph', 'The AB Chrysalis', 'The Rules of Luton' and 'New Adam New Eve'.

2. *Mind-Breaks of Space* by Michael Butterworth. Published in 1977. Adaptations of 'Brian the Brain', 'The Mark of Archanon', 'Catacombs of the Moon' and 'One Moment of Humanity'.

3. *The Space-Jackers* by Michael Butterworth. Published in 1977. Adaptations of 'Seed of Destruction', 'A Matter of Balance', 'The Exiles' and 'The Beta Cloud'.

4. *The Psychomorph* by Michael Butterworth. Published in 1977. Adaptations of 'The Lambda Factor' and 'The Bringers of Wonder' Parts One and Two.

5. *The Time Fighters* by Michael Butterworth. Published in 1977. Adaptations of 'Space Warp', 'Dorzak', 'Devil's Planet' and 'Seance Spectre'.

6. *The Edge of the Infinite* by Michael Butterworth. Published in 1977. Adaptations of 'All That Glisters', 'Journey to Where', 'The Dorcons' and 'The Immunity Syndrome'.

The Year Two novelisations were based on early drafts of the scripts and consequently many details such as character names differ considerably between the books and the televised episodes. 'The Taybor' was the only Year Two episode not adapted into a novelisation.

These *Space: 1999* novels were also published as translations into other languages, including Japanese, Italian and German. The German series is of particular note as it was continued on beyond the Michael Butterworth novelisations of Year Two (with Butterworth's ending for *The Edge of the Infinite* altered to accommodate this), with an additional six original novels that have never been translated or published in any other country or language. These original German novels are:

1. *Das Andromeda-Ratsel* (*The Andromeda Mystery*) by H W Springer. Published in 1978.

2. *Das Erbe der Roboter* (*The Robot Inheritance*) by H W Springer. Published in 1978.

3. *Die Ewigen von Luna* (*The Immortals of the Moon*) by H W Springer. Published in 1978.

4. *Invasion der Esper* (*Invasion of the Telepaths*) by H W Springer. Published in 1978.

5. *Aktion Exodus* (*Operation Exodus*) by Kurt Brand. Published in 1978.

6. *Der Stahlplanet* (*The Steel Planet*) by M F Thomas. Published in 1978.

NOVELS AND NOVELISATIONS (2000s)

The arrival of the new millennium saw the return of *Space: 1999* to the professional publishing world, with books released by several different publishers.

Eagle One Media Inc published a reprint of E C Tubb's original novel *Alien Seed* in January 2002. The book featured a new introduction by the author.

Fanderson (the Official Gerry Anderson Appreciation Society) then released two

Space: 1999 novelisations under their Century 21 Books imprint. These are:

1. *Earthfall* by E C Tubb. Published in November 2002. A re-publishing of Tubb's original 1977 novel.

2. *Earthbound* by E C Tubb. Published in August 2003. Featuring new adaptations of 'Earthbound', 'The Exiles' and 'Face of Eden'. ('Earthbound' had not been adapted in the original run of novelisations, while the latter two stories are based upon early scripts drawn up in the Year One format.) As Chris Bentley wrote in his Afterword to the book, 'The original Year One versions of the stories offered a fascinating opportunity to explore an alternative *Space: 1999* universe … in which Professor Bergman, Paul Morrow and David Kano don't mysteriously disappear after the events of "The Testament of Arkadia", in which the Alphans never meet the metamorph Maya, control of the base remains in Main Mission … and the parameters of the first season's credible fictional reality are maintained. In short, a continuation of *Space: 1999*'s first season which imagines that Year Two never happened.'

Powys Media have also published a series of books based on the series, beginning in 2002. Their titles include:

1. *Resurrection* by William Latham. Published in May 2002. Featuring an introduction by Johnny Byrne.

2. *The Foresaken* by John Kenneth Muir. Published in January 2003. Featuring an introduction by Prentis Hancock.

3. *Survival* by Brian Ball. Published in March 2005. Featuring an introduction by Barry Morse.

4. *Eternity Unbound* by William Latham. Published in March 2005. This title includes three sections: *Eternity Unleashed*, which chronicles the origin of Balor, *End of Eternity*, in a new adaptation, and an expanded version of Latham's earlier title *Resurrection*.

5. *Year Two* by Michael Butterworth. Published in April 2006. This volume contains revised adaptations of all 24 episodes of Year Two (including 'The Taybor', which had not previously been adapted to novel form), as well as a foreword by the author.

6. *Shepherd Moon* (anthology by various authors including Brian Ball and E C Tubb) Published in January 2010.

7. *Born for Adversity* by David A McIntee. Published in February 2010. Featuring an introduction by Catherine Schell.

8. *Omega* by William Latham. Published in February 2010. Featuring an introduction by Christopher Penfold.

9. *Alpha* by William Latham. Published in February 2010. Featuring an afterword by Christopher Penfold.

10. *Chasing the Cyclops: The Making of the Powysverse Mythology* by William Latham. (Nonfiction) Published in December 2010.

11. *The Powysverse Compendium: The Authorized Companion to the Powys Media Space: 1999 Universe* by Patricia T Sokol. (Nonfiction) Featuring an introduction by Zienia Merton, and an afterword by Martin Willey. Published in February 2012.

12. *Johnny Byrne's Children of the Gods* by William Latham (based upon the lost Johnny Byrne script). Published in January 2013. Featuring an introduction by Sandy Byrne.

In May 2010 Powys also released an audio book version of *Resurrection*, recorded by Barry Morse in 2004. At the time of writing (early 2014), Powys Media has a number of additional *Space: 1999* novels in development, including *Year One* (omnibus edition featuring revised episode adaptations by original novel authors Brian Ball, E C Tubb and John Rankine), *The Whispering Sea* (by John Kenneth Muir), *Black Doves* (by Elena Cambio, with a foreword by Nick Tate), *The Final Revolution* (by William Latham), *Odysseus Wept* (by William Latham), and *The Prodigal Moon* (anthology by various authors).

MERCHANDISE

It would take a complete specialised book to detail fully all of the *Space: 1999* merchandise that has been produced globally over the decades. The intent of this section is to focus on merchandise that is commercially or readily available at the time of publication (2014). These details are subject to change as items sell out, are discontinued or are superseded by new products (which seems to be happening at a rate unseen since the mid-1970s!)

The greatest difficulty encountered by companies wanting to release new *Space: 1999* merchandise has been the unwillingness of Martin Landau and Barbara Bain to agree to license use of their likenesses for anything other than DVDs. This has meant that recent action figure releases have gone forward without Commander Koenig or Dr Russell figures, and that other projects such as CDs and books have either had to proceed without use of their images, or be shelved altogether. However, even faced with this challenge, merchandising for *Space: 1999* does continue. Here is a sample:

PROP REPLICAS

STUN GUNS AND COMMLOCKS

Commercially released props of both the Stun Gun and Commlock were issued as a collector's set by Iconic Replicas in 2007. This limited edition of 1,000 sets quickly sold out, although the props were not completely accurate. Fully constructed prop replicas of both the Stun Gun and Commlock are available (at the time of printing) from CY Productions in the US. (CY's Commlock is cast from a replica made by UK fan Mark Shaw, who is renowned for the accuracy of his Commlocks.)

EAGLES, MOONBASE ALPHA AND OTHER SPACECRAFT

Since the 1970s, the Eagle has been the most frequently and widely marketed item of *Space: 1999* merchandise. The 12" MPC Eagle model kit has been re-issued by Round 2, with each box containing a photo card of Alan Carter (100 of which are hand-signed by actor Nick Tate.) Round 2 has also re-issued the vintage MPC moon buggy kit (an original design not based on anything seen in *Space: 1999* called 'The Alien'), including a photo card featuring Maya, with 100 of these cards signed by actress Catherine Schell. The Moonbase Alpha model kit has also been accuratized to feature five landing pads (previous releases only had 3), along with other pieces to accurately portray the layout of the base. New in-scale Eagle Transporters are also included in this 2014 release from Round 2.

The UK company Robert Harrop released a ceramic resin figurine in September 2013 depicting an Eagle blasting up from the lunar surface, in a limited edition of 250.

Various Eagle models in 12" and 23" sizes were produced by Product Enterprise/Sixteen 12, and although they are no longer in production, can be easily found on the secondary market (although at significantly higher prices than during their original release).

Custom-commissioned builds of various *Space: 1999* models can also be ordered from original series model-maker Martin Bower through his website (www.martinbowersmodelworld.com).

ACTION FIGURES

An extensive series of 8" action figures are currently available from the Figures Toy Company (www.classictvtoys.com), featuring such regular characters as Professor Bergman (in two different versions, including the aged Bergman from 'Black Sun'), Maya, Alan Carter, Paul Morrow, Sandra Benes, Tony Verdeschi and David Kano. Guest characters have also been well-represented by this series, including Balor, Raan, Companion, Female Alien (from 'War Games'), Mentor, Number 8 and Dan Mateo. The Figures Toy Company has also re-issued a four-character set based on the original 1970s Palitoy action figures. These 8" figures include the characters Paul Morrow, Alan Carter, Mysterious Alien (from 'War Games') and Captain Zantor. (The original Commander Koenig figure was not reissued because of the aforementioned refusal of Martin Landau to authorise use of his likeness for merchandising.)

SOUNDTRACKS

Commercially available at the time of this printing are Year One and Year Two soundtracks released by Silva Screen Records. Year One and Year Two soundtracks were previously released via Fanderson, as double CD sets, but those are sold out. Derek Wadsworth also produced a CD of his compositions from Year Two, but this was a limited release produced for the promotional purposes of the composer only (although a certain number of copies did find their way onto the commercial market). The Derek Wadsworth and Fanderson CDs are highly sought-after and command substantial values when they can be found on such sites as eBay, which is very rarely.

DVDs & BLU-RAYs

Various DVD releases of *Space: 1999* are readily available around the world, in countries such as the UK, US, Canada, Australia, France, Germany, Italy, Japan, Portugal and Spain.

But even more impressive than the DVDs are the Blu-Ray releases of Year One, which have been released by Network in the UK and A&E in North America. The high definition images are absolutely stunning, and fans are now eagerly awaiting the Blu-Ray release of Year Two as well.

The *Space: 1999* movies (*Alien Attack, Destination Moonbase Alpha, Journey Through the Black Sun* and *Cosmic Princess*) have also found their way to DVD. They were released as a box set in Portugal in 2004 and in Italy in 2007. Two of the movies (*Destination Moonbase Alpha* and *Cosmic Princess*) were released as a set in the Netherlands in 2006. Similarly, two (*Alien Attack* and *Cosmic Princess*) came out as a box set in France in 2007.

GRAPHIC NOVELS

Blam! Ventures has released two major *Space: 1999* graphic novels, as well as an extensive range of comics. The first graphic novel is *Aftershock and Awe*, which expands on the "Breakaway" origin story and expands it to show what happens to Earth after the Moon is blown out of orbit. The second is *To Everything That Was*, which compiles selected remastered works from the original 1970s *Space: 1999* comics. These titles are available via Amazon and more information can be found online at the Blam! website: www.blamventures.com .

OTHER MERCHANDISE

Other diverse merchandise is currently available for avid fans, including high-quality metal lapel pins of the Eagle, the Mark IX Hawk, the series logo, and the Alpha Moonbase crest; patches; posters; blueprints; door-mats; T-shirts; stickers; accessories for your home fleet of 12″ Eagles (as well as stands and display cases); and more … Most of these items can be obtained online through sources such as eBay or specialist retailers like FABGearUSA.

It is certainly a good time to be a merchandise-loving fan of *Space: 1999*!

APPENDIX
PHOTOGRAPHS

The following pages contain a selection of photographs from the private collections of several fans and professionals. We are grateful to them for allowing us permission to reproduce their work.

Nick Tate holding the new Eagle model © Paul Stankevitch.

CG Eagle © Wes Sargent.

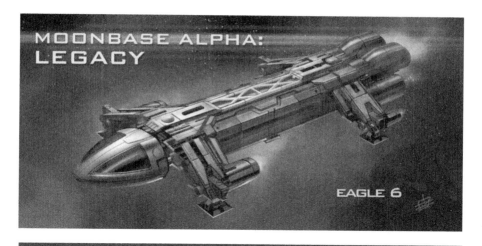

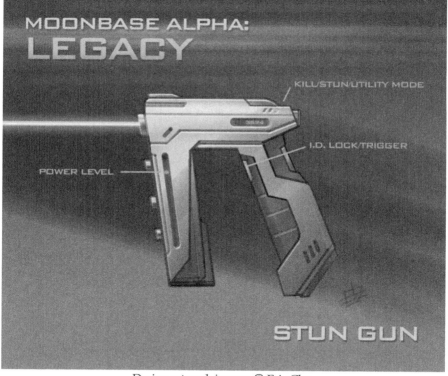

Design artwork images © Eric Chu.

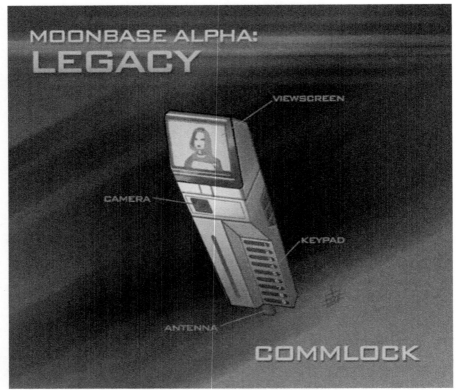

Design artwork image © Eric Chu.

Design artwork image © Eric Chu.

CG image of Moonbase Alpha © Wes Sargent.

CG Eagle © Wes Sargent.

CG images of Moonbase Alpha © Wes Sargent.

All photographs on this and following pages © Martin Bower.

Alpha buildings with the Eagle - (A staged effects shot not seen on-screen).

The *SS Daria* – 'Mission of the Darians'.

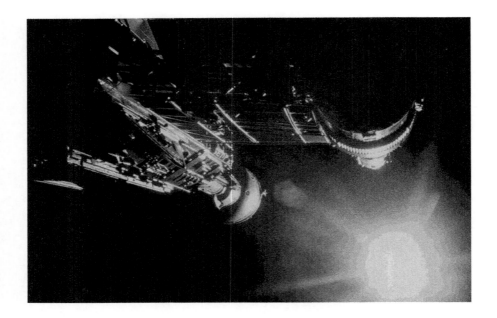

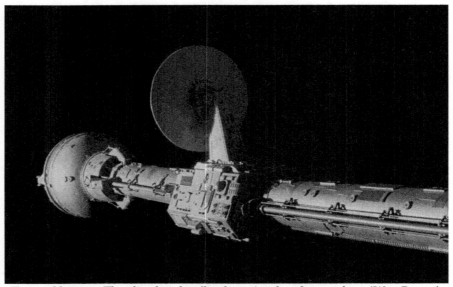

Top and bottom: The alien bomber/battle cruiser best known from 'War Games', and also seen in 'Alpha Child', 'Dragon's Domain', 'The Last Enemy' (revamped), and 'The Metamorph' (nose piece only).

The *SS Daria* – 'Mission of the Darians'.

The Dragon Ship during construction – 'Dragon's Domain'.

Moonbase Alpha laser tanks, which were prominently featured in 'The Infernal Machine'.

Moonbase Alpha laser tanks, which were prominently featured in 'The Infernal Machine'.

Moonbase Alpha laser tanks, which were prominently featured in 'The Infernal Machine'.

Martin Bower with the alien ship from 'Alpha Child'.

Martin Bower with the Swift model - 'Brian the Brain'.

The completed Phoenix model - 'Death's other Dominion'.

Sidon Ship model footage - 'Voyager's Return'.

Superswift model - 'The Bringers of Wonder parts 1 and 2'.

Swift model – 'Brian the Brain' (note the lack of the large fuel tanks as seen on-screen, and in the photo with Martin Bower).

Taybor's gun - 'The Taybor'.

The Ultra Probe in space - 'Dragon's Domain'.

Mark IX Hawk, from 'War Games'.

Ultra Probe command module, from 'Dragon's Domain'.

INDEX OF TITLES

INDEX OF NAMES

Printed in Great
Britain
by Amazon